The Happy Warrior

James Thomas Byford McCudden VC

> … A young squire,
> Of twenty year he was of age I guess.
> And he had been sometime in chivalry,
> In Flanders, in Artois, and in Picardy.
>
> Chaucer

Alex Revell

The Happy Warrior: James Thomas Byford McCudden, VC, DSO + MC + MM, *Croix de Guerre*

The Happy Warrior

James Thomas Byford McCudden VC

Alex Revell

This book is dedicated to all those who served in the Royal Flying Corps
and Royal Air Force during the Great War, 1914–1918

Interested in WWI aviation? Join The League of WWI Aviation Historians (**www.overthefront.com**) and
Cross & Cockade International (**www.crossandcockade.com**)

© 2015 Aeronaut Books, all rights reserved
Text © 2015 Alex Revell
Design and layout: Jack Herris
Cover design: Jack Herris
Color Profiles: Bob Pearson
Digital photo editing: Aaron Weaver & Jack Herris

Aeronaut Books

www.aeronautbooks.com

Publisher's Cataloging-in-Publication data

Revell, Alex, 1929–
   The Happy Warrior: James Thomas Byford McCudden VC /
by Alex Revell.
   p. cm.
   ISBN 978-1-935881-34-6
1. McCudden, James T.B. 1890–1918. 2. World War,
1914–1918 --Aerial operations, Great Britain. 3. Fighter pilots
-- Great Britain. 4. Aeronautics, Military --Great Britain --
History. II. Title.

ND237 .S6322 2011
759.13 --dc22   2011904920

Table of Contents

Acknowledgements	6
Foreword	7
Introduction	7
Chapter 1. Family & Childhood	8
Chapter 2. The New Recruit	12
Chapter 3. War	23
Chapter 4. France	24
Chapter 5. First War Flights	34
Chapter 6. Fledgling Instructor & NCO Pilot	52
Chapter 7. Scout Pilot	60
Chapter 8. Fighting Instructor	80
Chapter 9. France Again	98
Chapter 10. 56 Squadron	107
Chapter 11. Autumn Above the Salient	118
Chapter 12. Gains and Losses	139
Chapter 13. Cambrai: A Change of Scene	149
Chapter 14. A Remarkable December	159
Chapter 15. 1918: For Valour	172
Chapter 16. Ayr & Turnberry: Teaching the Young Idea	194
Chapter 17. The Last Flight	218
Postscript	223
In Memoriam	228
Appendices	
I. The Fatal Crash	232
II. James McCudden. The Leading Airman of the War	236
III. Publicity for Leading British Pilots	237
IV. Aerial Victories: An Evaluation	238
V. The Aerial Victories of James McCudden	240
VI. McCudden in the Eyes of His Contemporaries	244
VII. McCudden on Airfighting	249
VIII. Greentail	253
Endnotes	254
Glossary	288
Select Bibliography	289
Index	290

Acknowledgements

This book has been over 60 years in the making. In the early 1960s my interest in the air warfare of World War One was reawakened by the discovery of an American society dedicated to the subject: *Cross and Cockade:* The Society of World War One Aero Historians. I joined the society and it was clear from the quarterly journals that a considerable number of people were interested in those early years of aerial conflict and that some were serious researchers in the subject. I had never forgotten my boyhood admiration of James McCudden – I would re-read *Flying Fury* nearly every year – and I decided that I would like to repay the pleasure the book had given me over the years by writing a biography of McCudden, which I felt was long overdue.

As a first step I traced McCudden's youngest sister, Kathleen. I visited her at the McCudden family home in Kingston, but she told me that someone was already working on a biography and had been for some months. This was Christopher Cole, then unknown to me. I decided there was no point in carrying on with my own attempt and, although disappointed, abandoned the idea. Only a month later I received a letter from a complete stranger, an American Cross and Cockade Society member, asking if I would interested in researching and writing a squadron history of 56 Squadron. As this was the squadron in which McCudden had scored his greatest successes, it seemed the next best thing to a biography and I agreed to undertake the research work on this side of the Atlantic. During the research of the next 15 years I met many people who had served with McCudden in 56 Squadron, and others who had known him at other times in his life. Chief amongst the latter was his elder sister, Mary Cobley, who became a good friend, always ready to talk about Jimmie, her beloved younger brother.

Chris Cole's fine biography of McCudden was published in 1968, but in the following years – both from the specialist research into the history of 56 Squadron and the on-going research into the air war of 1914–18 in general, which constantly uncovers new knowledge and aspects – I found a great deal of new information on McCudden's life which was not available to Chris Cole. Consequently, the idea of a new biography of James McCudden was born.

Many people, many now, alas, no longer alive, contributed to this book, either directly or indirectly. I would first like to record my admiration and gratitude for the work which Chris Cole undertook for his 1968 biography. I am particularly indebted to him for his research into the ancestry of the McCudden family, and I have unashamedly drawn on his findings in this respect. Pride of place must next go, of course, to Mary Cobley. I shall never forget the first time we met. To find myself suddenly staring into Jimmie McCudden's eyes, so often looked at in his portraits, was a slightly shattering experience.

I am also indebted to the many ex-RFC/RAF people I met during my researches, both general and into the history of 56 Squadron, who shared their memories of McCudden with me. Sadly, all are now no longer with us:
Group Captain G. H. Bowman. Squadron Leader C.M. Crowe. Colonel E.D.G. Galley. Wing Commander William M. Fry. L. Baker. H.N. Charles. J. Cooper, E.R. Macdonald. C. Parry. E.L.L. Turnbull.

My thanks are also due to people who gave a great deal of their time to answer my many questions:
Sue Adams, Lynne Cowley, Russ Gannon, Barry Gray, John Grech, Roger Harris, Peter Hart, Ian Hatton, Trevor Henshaw, Jelle Hieminengen, Phil Jarrett, Knut Erik Hagen, Geoffrey Morris, Diana Neal, Graeme Neale, Colin Pengelly, Jonathon Saunders, Bob Sellwood, Andrew Smith. Dr. J. Sugden, Alan Taylor. W Vandersteen, K Wood. In Germany, the late Dr. G. Bock was also of immense help with his knowledge of German records.

Of these I must single out for my special thanks: Trevor Henshaw, whose magnificent book *The Sky Their Battlefield* is never more than three feet from my computer. Russ Gannon, a friend of over twenty years, whose tireless, painstaking and never-ending work of many years into the detailing and tabulating of the daily air fighting over the Western Front is incalculable. His help and advice was of immense value. Jonathon Saunders for his perseverance in tracing Diana Neal, the niece of Teddie O'Neal, and to Diana Neal for her memories of her aunt – elusive for so many years – and for the superb photographs of her.

My thanks also to those of my fellow members of Cross and Cockade International, The First World War Aviation Historical Society, who have done so much over the years in compiling an incredible record of all aspects of aviation during the Great War.

I must also thank the members of the Kenthistory.com website and Neil Clark and David Hughes of Kentfallen.com. for their personal photographs and kind permission to use them.

I am indebted to the Imperial War Museum, London, for the text of McCudden's letters to 'Addie.' Last, but far from least, my thanks to my wife, Linda, for her patience and eagle-eyed proofreading skills. Any remaining errors are purely my own.

Photograph credits: Unless otherwise credited, all photographs are from the author's collection, the majority of which are from James McCudden via Mrs Mary Cobley (Sis).

Foreward

My interest in James McCudden began when I was a schoolboy during the Second World War. A proportion of my weekly pocket money was spent on a loan fee to the local subscription library for a rather battered copy of *Flying Fury*, the 1930s Hamilton edition of McCudden's autobiography, *Five Years In The Royal Flying Corps*. After some months the owner of the library suggested that I might like to buy the book. As he put it: 'You renew it every week, no-one else can take it out, so you might as well buy it'. I still have it in my collection, with a dust cover added, and an inscription inside. 'Sold by Ruggs Library. 27/8/43.' It has been a treasured possession now for 70 years.

Introduction

This book is the story of a young man's remarkable courage and total dedication to his chosen profession. In these days of perhaps greater political and social awareness it is fashionable to decry the unquestioning patriotism and sense of duty which took the young men of 1914–1918 to war; to scorn the values which sustained them – and their families – through those tragic and terrible four years. These views have a certain validity, for no-one would deny the senselessness, horror, and ultimately the waste and futility of war; of a generation of young men killing and maiming each other for no other reason than that they have been persuaded by an older generation that it is right to do so. But neither time nor fashion can detract from the gallantry, courage and selflessness of those young men who fought in what we now know as The Great War. James Thomas Byford McCudden was a man of his time; his values were direct, uncomplicated. It was enough that his country called him in its hour of need; he did not question that need. As did millions of other young men, McCudden answered the call: for King and Country; for the Emperor and the Fatherland. If they died, as Wilfred Owen so rightly put it, for 'The Old Lie: *Dulce et decorum est pro patria mori*', then the loss is ours, not theirs.

Ch.1: Family and Childhood

James Thomas Byford McCudden was born into a military family: but it had not always been so. In 1861, when his grandfather, James McCudden, threw up his 'respectable' job as a clerk to enlist as a private soldier in the 86th Foot Regiment – later the Royal Irish Rifles – his father, Henry, from Newry, County Down, a studious man with literary tastes, was utterly disgusted. Like many people of the time he considered that the common soldier was recruited from the dregs of society. James, however, found army life to his liking: by 1864 he had been promoted to corporal, married a girl from Carlow, Honora Dolland, and in 1865 they had their first son, William.[1]

William was eager to follow in his father's footsteps. In 1879, as soon as he was fourteen years of age, he enlisted in the Royal Engineers and was posted to Bermuda as a bugler. In November 1880, he was on duty at Hamilton harbour, helping to load the baggage of a draft returning to England onto the troopship *Crocodile*. The troopers and their families were being ferried out to the troopship in a number of small gunboats and in the excited hustle and bustle of the embarkation a small boy fell into the sea from one of them, HMS *Viper*. William immediately dived in and swam to the boy, keeping him afloat until a boat arrived. For his prompt action and bravery he was awarded the Royal Humane Society's Bronze Medal.[2]

In September 1881 a nationalist movement in Egypt, led by Colonel Ahmed Orabi, rose against Tewfik Pasha, the Khedive of Egypt and the Sudan, forcing him to appoint a nationalist ministry in the following February. In June 1882, despite earlier French and British diplomatic moves to avert the crisis, anti-foreign riots in Alexandria killed fifty Europeans and Britain decided to act to re-establish the Khedive's rule. The Royal Navy shelled Alexandria in July, and in August a large British force under Sir Garnet Wolseley embarked for Egypt from Southampton to re-establish the authority of the Khedive.

William McCudden, now serving in No.24 Field Company, Royal Engineers, landed at Port Said and went into action against the rebels at the battle of Tel-el-Kebir, lower Egypt, on

Three generations of the McCuddens. Gillingham. 1905. Left to right, standing: William Thomas James (bugler); Corporal J.V. McCudden; Sergeant Major William T. Henry McCudden; Lance Corporal C.J. McCudden. Left to right, seated: Anthony; Mary Ann McCudden; Kathleen Annie; Honora (Anne) McCudden; Maurice Vincent; Amelia Emma. Front row seated on ground: John Anthony; Mary Amelia (Cis); James Thomas Byford.

12 September. The rebels were defeated and two days later the British forces occupied Cairo. Ahmed Orabi surrendered and was banished to Ceylon.

The eighteen-year old William McCudden had distinguished himself during the battle of Tel-el-Kebir, tending a wounded British officer while under fire with complete disregard for his own personal safety. A recommendation for a gallantry award was put forward, but withdrawn when it emerged that he had been acting against orders. Nevertheless, news of his gallantry had reached England. When he returned to Chatham with his regiment in October 1882, William and another young comrade were carried shoulder high through the streets by a cheering crowd. Amongst the crowd was a young girl – still at school – and family tradition has it that William noticed her in the throng and gave her a cheeky wink, never expecting to see her again.

William remained at the Royal Engineers Chatham depôt. With his small, dapper figure – he was only five foot five, which earned him the nickname in Chatham of 'Little Mac' – resplendent in his smart walking-out uniform of pill-box hat and scarlet tunic, his campaign and gallantry ribbons on his right breast and the fashionable large walrus moustache he had cultivated, he was soon a well known figure in the town. Like all soldiers he liked his beer and his favourite public house was the Shipwright's Arms in Richard Street. The landlord, Thomas Byford, was a widower, son of a veteran of Waterloo, an ex-drum major in the Royal Marines, a local councillor and a person of some standing in Chatham. Thomas kept an immaculate establishment, testimony to both his service career and the housekeeping abilities of his daughter Amelia. A strong-minded young girl, Amelia had left home to be a teacher, but on the death of her mother had returned to run her father's household. The Shipwright's was renowned for the excellence of its porter, but an added attraction for William was Amelia Emma.[3] Amelia was the pretty young schoolgirl that William had cheekily winked at on his return from Egypt, now grown into an extremely attractive young lady. The attraction was mutual.

In the summer of 1890, Corporal William McCudden and Amelia Emma Byford were married at St.Michael's Church, Chatham. Their marriage brought together two military families: the Byfords were of Scottish descent – members of the family had served in the Royal Marines since the Eighteenth Century – and Amelia's grandfather had run away from home in 1813 at the age of ten to join the Marines.

It was a happy marriage and their first child, born on 3 April 1891, was a boy, named William, after his father. William junior was followed by Mary Amelia (23 January 1893), James Thomas Byford (born in the Female Hospital at Brompton on 28 March 1895), John Anthony (14 June 1897), Kathleen Annie (1 December 1899), and Maurice Vincent (31 October 1901).

In 1902, William, promoted to sergeant major, was appointed as an instructor in Survey and Astronomy at the School of Military Engineering in Gillingham and the family

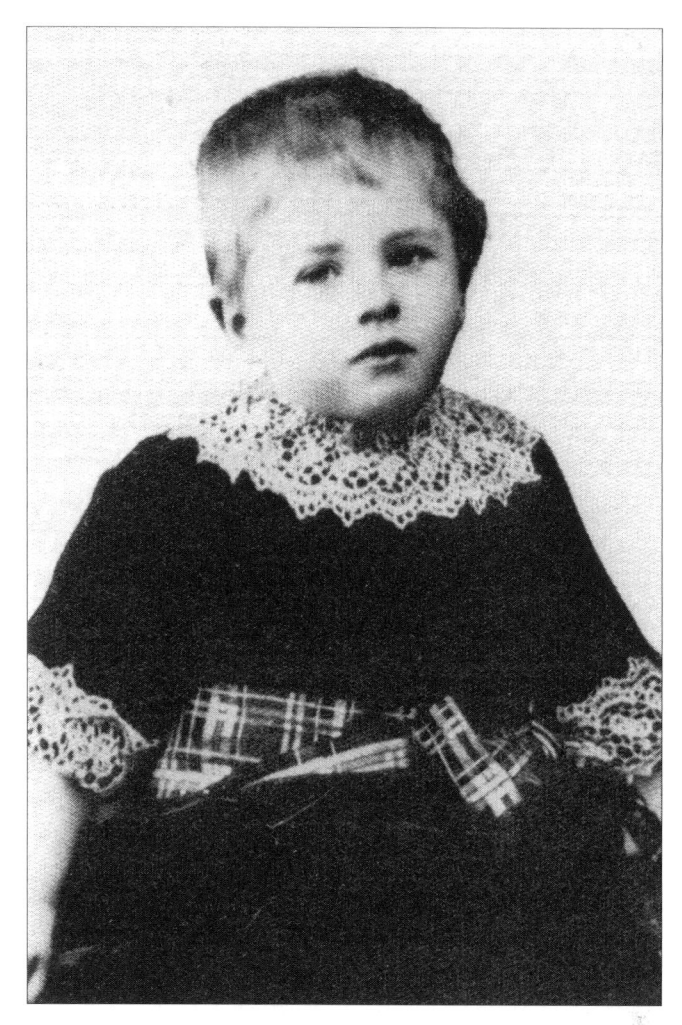

The infant James McCudden.

moved from 22 Belmont Road Gillingham to Brompton Barracks in the town, the married quarters of the School.

The McCuddens were a close, happy and united family. William, now approaching middle age, was inclined to be easy going, especially towards the activities of his two eldest sons, William junior and James – Jimmy or Jim to the family. Both were high-spirited and mischievous boys and like all boys of spirit became involved in various escapades. One, which Mary recalled with some relish, was their digging for gold in the family garden. Their strenuous excavations broke a sewer pipe, causing 'a dreadful smell'. For this episode they were punished by their father, but the strongly dominating member of the family was their mother, Amelia. With her teaching background, she was determined that her sons should have the best possible primary education the family could afford and rather than attend the local state school she sent them to a small private school run by a Miss Cooper.

Amelia was in indifferent health at this time and Mary, the eldest girl – 'Cis', as she was known to the family – took over many of her mother's household duties and looked after the younger children of the family. As with all families with a number of children, alliances were formed between those

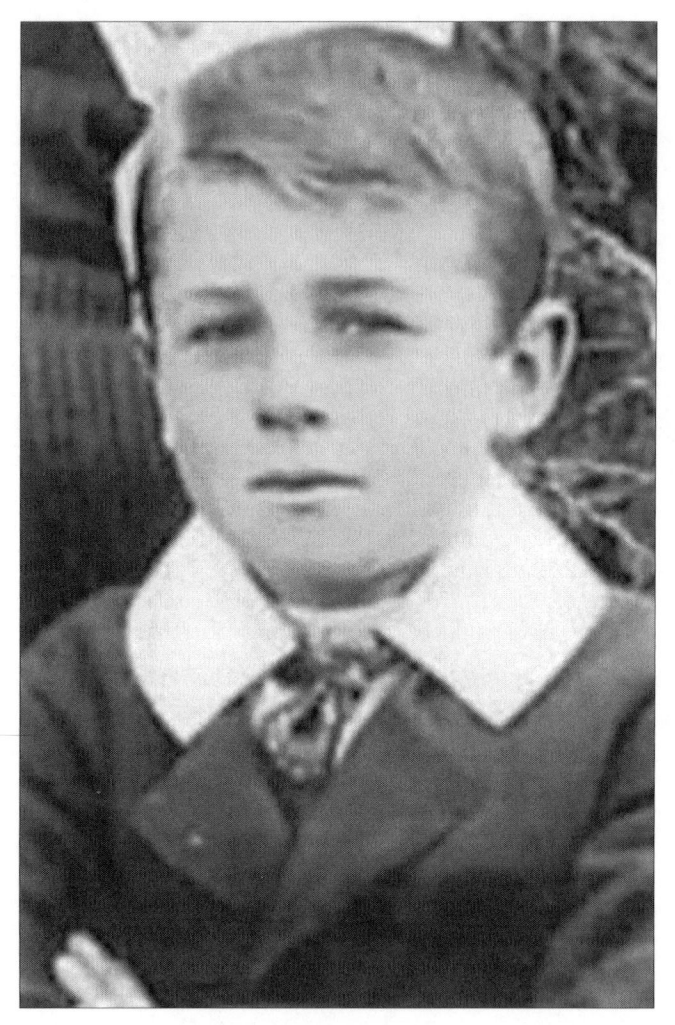

James McCudden at ten years of age.

Gibraltar 1911. Boy James McCudden. No. 20083 Royal Engineers. Bugler.

McCudden siblings of similar temperament. Mary and James, alike in many ways, especially in both having a particular passion for order and neatness, became especially close. James was a rather tearful, moody boy, with a quick temper that could occasionally flare up, especially when teased by other boys about his third Christian name, Byford, which they considered odd.[4]

His initial schooling over, William – Bill or Willie to the family – entered the garrison school at Brompton barracks and became a 'Barrack Rat' – the nickname for all those sons of regular soldiers who attended the army garrison schools. The school was run on military lines: the headmaster was a senior warrant officer, 1st Class Army Schoolmaster, D W D Kimm, and the teachers all members of the Corps of Army Schoolmasters.

Four years later, William was joined by James, aged nine, but the brothers were not reunited in school for long: in July 1905, a few months after his fourteenth birthday, William followed in his father's footsteps and joined the Royal Engineers as a Boy Bugler. Mary recalled:

'I have quite a good remembrance of Willie, especially his joining the Royal Engineers at the age of fourteen. We were then living in the barracks so of course he came home almost daily and recounted events, some happy, others not so happy. As you know, there is always some awkward character lying in wait to " bait " those young lads. Willie was the happiest brother, always joking and keeping us all in fits of laughing with his mimicry, but some days he would come home almost in tears, so something had gone wrong. Jimmy, on the other hand, was always on the serious side and as a very young boy mostly tearful. Jimmy had a peculiar cry, almost a moan, and Willie would tease him and call him "Bull". At that time there was a Bovril advertisement on the local hoarding of two cows in conversation: "Alas, my poor brother. I hear he wants more Bovril". Willie would tease Jimmy with this and of course he didn't take it quietly. But this apart, they had a deep admiration for each other, which was proved in the years that followed.'[5]

The school at the Brompton Barracks was to mould the character of James McCudden. Although the emphasis was on physical training and fitness, with the addition of rifle drill and shooting, the three 'Rs' were not neglected. The teaching was of a higher standard than many of the state schools of the time and most of the boys who attended the various barrack schools were later commissioned in the 1914–1918 war.[6] James did well. He was small, wiry, full of energy, and gained good results both in his academic schoolwork and athletics. He was also a useful boxer, but was particularly outstanding on the shooting range, a portent of things to come. Like many successful people, James was single minded and thorough in everything he attempted, aspects of his character which would later become even more marked.

William senior retired from the army in 1907 and the family moved house to nearby Chatham. Their stay was brief: in 1909 William obtained a civilian clerical post with the Army Service Corps at Albemarle Fort and moved his family again, to Sheerness. This move meant a change of school for James, to the Sheerness Garrison school.

With William's pay as a sergeant major, plus the various entitlements due to an army family, the family had enjoyed a comfortable living standard, but it was now on a considerably reduced income. The official leaving age of the garrison school was fifteen, when its pupils would be of an age to enlist in the regular army, but James, conscious of the family's financial position, left school at fourteen, taking a job as a telegram boy at Sheerness Post Office until he was old enough to enlist.

It was while the family was at Sheerness that Bill and James' interest in flying was initially inspired. Both boys were mechanically minded – Bill, now graduated from bugler to despatch rider, was notorious for his high speed motorcycle exploits – and they were fascinated by flying, regarded in those days as an the exciting new sport. In 1909, one of Britain's aviation pioneers, Griffith Brewer, had been searching for a suitable flying field near London.[7] In comparison with the open spaces enjoyed by the pioneer French aviators, the fields of the Home Counties of England were both small and hedged, but Brewer, widening his search, had found a suitable site at Leysdown on the Isle of Sheppy. Within a year, in the climate of the rapid development of flying in England, a larger field was opened at nearby Eastchurch, only a few miles from Sheerness, and it was here that the two McCudden boys spent all their spare time, fascinated by the flying machines and dreaming that one day they could also become pilots, an ambition that must have seemed unobtainable, the expense involved in learning to fly being well beyond their modest means. But the spark was there, and James, still a messenger boy, spent what small part of his wages he kept for himself on the new aviation magazines. On 26 April 1910, James Thomas Byford McCudden enlisted in the Royal Engineers as Boy Bugler McCudden No.20083. It was the beginning of a remarkable career.

Ch.2: The New Recruit

James was desperately unhappy during his first few weeks in the Army. The time to which he had looked forward to for so long was marred by the attentions of a bullying junior NCO who singled out the small, rather shy boy for his exclusive attention. McCudden senior heard of this treatment from a former colleague and took action. Mary recalled that her father 'had a few words' with the offending NCO. Whether or not this was effective, the problem was soon solved. Although retired, McCudden senior was not without friends and influence in the army and he arranged for James to be transferred. On 24 February 1911, Boy Bugler 20083 McCudden was en-route to Gibraltar.

James spent eighteen months in Gibraltar, where he served under a regular army NCO, mindful of the care of his young charges. His maxim was 'what's worth doing at all is worth doing well,' which precisely fitted young James's own philosophy and he brought to his duties the same sense of responsibility as his teacher, being careful and conscientious in everything he did. James had always shown great promise as a marksman and while on the Rock he developed this skill to such an extent that in one contest he equaled his captain's score – no small feat for a boy of his age. He could hardly have envisaged the effect this would have on his future.[1] While in Gibraltar, James kept abreast of the developments in flying, studying the theory of flight, aero engines, and the construction of aeroplanes. One of his treasured possessions while on the Rock was the 1910 Flight manual, a well-thumbed copy, which he later passed on to his younger brother Anthony.[2]

On his return from Gibraltar in September 1912, James was just a few months short of his eighteenth birthday and as soon as it was reached, and he had entered into the men's service, he

'I assure you that you would not know me in civilian clothes.' A rare photo of the young James in 'mufti'.

The new recruit. James in 1913.

Caudron 311 at Farnborough. This was the adventurous Caudron, powered by a 45hp Anzane engine, which almost prematurely ended the career of James in the RFC. *Credit F. Cheesman.*

A Maurice Farman S.7. This was possibly the Maurice Farman that attempted to foil the escape of Cauldron 311 on the afternoon of 6 May 1913. *Credit F. Cheesman.*

applied for transfer to the Royal Flying Corps.

While James had been serving in Gibraltar his elder brother Bill had taken the first steps of realising the dream of both boys of becoming pilots. In December 1910, just before his younger sibling had left for Gibraltar, Bill McCudden, now a sapper, had been posted to the Royal Engineers Balloon School at Farnborough. On 1 April 1911 the school was amalgamated into the Air Battalion, Royal Engineers. Number 1 (Airship) Company worked with balloons, airships etc., while No.2 (Aeroplane) Company concentrated on work with aeroplanes.

Baron James.

Bill McCudden, serving as a motor transport fitter, was transferred to No.2 Company and easily adjusted his skills with the internal combustion engine to the early aero engines of the day, his study of the Flight manuals no doubt standing him in good stead.

The Royal Flying Corps was formed on 13 April 1912 and a month later, on 13 May, absorbed the Air Battalion of the Royal Engineers. No.1 Company RE. became 1 Squadron RFC; and No. 2 Company RE., 2 Squadron RFC. A detachment from No. 2 Company, then stationed at Larkhill, became 3 Squadron RFC under the command of Major H R M Brooke-Popham.[3] Three Squadron had six aeroplanes on its strength: four monoplanes, a configuration not yet out of favour with the authorities, and two biplanes. Bill McCudden, serving with the detachment, was now Air Mechanic W T J McCudden. RFC No.61.

The earliest plans for the Military Wing of the RFC

Just a face in the ranks; James marching to parade.

envisaged a total of seven squadrons with a complement of 364 pilots, half of whom would be non-commissioned officers. The decision to employ NCOs as pilots was not taken from any democratic ideal, indeed many people were opposed to the idea that officers should be employed on the same general duties as some NCOs. The class system in England was still very much in evidence in 1912 and it was thought that only those men of suitable education and ability would make the best pilots; in addition, as a general rule the NCOs then serving were mainly older, married men, thought less liable to succeed in the hazardous business of flying. However, those in favour of the proposal pointed out that the role of a pilot in the two-seater aeroplanes of the day was merely that of a driver, freeing the officer observer to carry out the important

James on his Moto-Rêve CF 76. 'There was more Rêve about it than motor, for though it had two cylinders it would never go on more than one at a time.'

duties of observation, duties that his training as an officer made him ideally suited.[4] Before an official decision on the matter had been taken, Brooke-Popham informed the squadron's air mechanics and NCOs that those amongst them who were selected would be given the opportunity to learn to fly. Three mechanics successfully completed the pilot's course in June 1912. The first two were Frank Ridd, a corporal rigger,[5] and Staff Sergeant Wilson.[6] The third was air mechanic Victor Strugnell,[7] a great friend of Bill McCudden. Both Strugnell and McCudden had vied for the third brevet, but although Bill made the first completion flight, flying a Bristol Boxkite, he was unsuccessful, failing to land within the prescribed circle. Strugnell won the race by a few short weeks, gaining his Royal Aero Club brevet No.253 on 24 July 1912, with Bill McCudden finally being awarded his brevet, No.269, on 13 August 1912.

In contrast with his younger brother James, Bill McCudden was a complete extrovert. Always in the thick of things, a practical joker; a talented mimic, musical, with a good singing voice, Bill was extremely popular with all ranks. He was also a first class rugby player – a skill that stood him in good stead in his relations with his officers. In the popular parlance of the day he was a 'card'. He was also something of a ladies' man, at one time successfully courting the daughter of a local gentry, in direct competition with one of his officers. He was also a young man obsessed with speed, his skill in riding a motor cycle earning him the nickname of 'Mad McCudden'. However, in January 1913 he fell foul of the local Salisbury constabulary. He was seen driving an official car at speeds estimated to be between 17 and 18 miles per hour. Although this speed, even for 1913, was relatively innocuous and only maintained for 150 yards, there was one small problem: Bill was driving the car in reverse. He was fined two shillings and sixpence (12.5p) with costs.

James was meanwhile serving with No.6 Company RE at Weymouth. He had been regarded as a sapper on 26 April 1913, but two days later his application for transfer to the Royal Flying Corps was approved and he was given the rank of Air Mechanic 2nd Class. No.892. It was exactly a month after his eighteenth birthday. He later wrote: 'I think that I have never done a more sensible thing in my life'. On Friday 9 May 1913, King George V, accompanied by the Queen and the Princesses Mary and Victoria, visited his newly formed corps at Farnborough, inspecting officers and men and enjoying a fly past by its aeroplanes. Air Mechanic 2nd Class McCudden also arrived at Farnborough that day. He had left his barracks at Weymouth and pedaled his motorcycle – he ruefully admitted that it would only go by pedaling – to the train station and boarded the Farnborough train. He arrived at Farnborough at 6pm: 'just in time to see a 70hp Bleriot (flown by Captain

> **James was used as a despatch rider on many occasions during his first months with 3 Squadron, riding various makes of motorcycles.**

James on N1424. A Rex Speed King model. In its time, this motor cycle was very powerful and appealed to those interested in speed. It had no clutch or gears and was a 'jump, ride machine – a real handful.'

Fox[8]) go overhead at a few hundred feet, followed by a most weird collection of aeroplanes at about half minute intervals. I think there were 23 machines altogether, including Henri and Maurice Farmans, Bréguets, and BE2s, and the above mentioned Bleriot'. This was an impressive sight in 1913, as rarely more than three or four machines were seen in the air at the same time.

James reported to the Orderly Room and was assigned to a room in barracks, where he found a dozen fellow transfers, mainly from the Royal Engineers and Artillery. The NCO in charge of the room was an ex-Royal Engineer, so James soon felt at home. 'They were most amusing lads… there was no end of wit and chaff, which is an irreplaceable asset in barrack rooms.' The next day, James was sent to Jersey Brow, on the northern side of Farnborough Common, where he reported to Sergeant J Starling[9] to be interviewed and assigned his duties. The interview went well: Starling soon realised that this new recruit had a better than average knowledge of engines and sent him over to Sergeant C J Brockbank[10] who was in charge of the maintenance of the aeroplanes at the Flying Depot.

Brockbank took James to the sheds, stood him in front of

James on a Douglas, with fellow Air Mechanic Robert Ware, during the RFC 1913 manoeuvres.

James' elder brother William also ran his Sabella cycle car while at Farnborough. James McCudden is in the front seat; the driver is possibly William. The Sabella was a French cycle car, costing nearly £100 in 1913.

Maurice Farman No.223, powered by a 70hp Renault engine – the first aeroplane engine James had ever seen – and informed him that, not only was this particular aeroplane's engine his responsibility, but that he would also be required to swing the Farman's propeller – 'a most formidable looking guillotine'. Realising that this recruit had never swung an aeroplane propeller in his young life, Brockbank took him to a corner of the shed to 'a most inoffensive looking little aeroplane'. This was a Caudron, powered by a 45hp Anzani engine. Showing James how to swing the propeller, and assuring the rather nervous new recruit that the engine of the Caudron had not been run for some months, Brockbank told him to practise swinging the propeller on the Caudron for the rest of the morning.

James practised his propeller swinging conscientiously and with some success until the mid-day lunch break. After lunch, he was given various other small tasks in the aeroplane sheds, including rubbing the rust from the multitudinous rigging wires of the Farman. Having finished this task by the early afternoon, James went back to the shed containing the Caudron, keen to resume practising his propeller swinging skill. In his ignorance he did not check the ignition switch on the Caudron's engine, and since the morning an unknown hand had been tampering with the engine controls. On the first hearty swing the engine of the Caudron burst into life. Now, this Caudron 'badly wanted to fly, even without a pilot' and started for the entrance to the shed and freedom. Unfortunately, its path was blocked by another aeroplane, the Maurice Farman. 'The Caudron was very annoyed at this and determined to make a fight for it.' With its propeller running at its full 1,400 revs per minute, the Caudron made short work of the offending Farman, chopping up its twin tail booms and demolishing most of one wing. James, who had had the presence of mind to throw himself flat under the Caudron's

Eric Lewis Conran.

wing as it made its bid for freedom, managed to scramble into its cockpit and switch off the engine. By this time the interior of the shed was full of blue castor oil smoke, with mechanics running from all directions carrying fire extinguishers and

Conran's Gnome-engined Blériot XI, No.219.

These two Blériot XI are at Wantage, en-route for Port Meadow, Oxford, during the RFC manoeuvres in September 1913. During November 1913, James did a great deal of flying with Conran in Blériot 292, the machine in which he had hoped to fly to France in August 1914.

ladders. All was suddenly calm as Major Raleigh[11] entered the shed and began to question the culprit. He listened to the stammered explanations in silence. Then: 'Sergeant-Major! fall in two men!' Sergeant-Major Hudson,[12] the first recruiting Sergeant of the RFC, marched the culprit off to the guardroom. Over fifty years later, Tom Hudson, then a retired Squadron Leader, commented. 'I've never, before or since, seen a lad so crestfallen, almost in tears.'

James served his detention in the guard room of Blenheim Barracks. The guard room was opposite the officers' mess and outside the mess each evening the band of the Grenadier Guards played the popular hits of the day: *The Mysterious Rag* and *Oh! You Beautiful Doll*. Young James's feelings can be imagined. His start in the corps was little short of disastrous: he would probably be sent back to his regiment, an end to all his dreams of becoming a pilot.

After five days in detention James was released under open arrest while awaiting his trial. It was a fine afternoon so he went down to the aerodrome. By lucky chance, Lieutenant Baron James[13] had that evening been ordered to fly tests in a BE2a

The Officers and NCOs of the RFC at Farnborough in 1913. William McCudden is seated on the far right.

that had been fitted with the first wireless experimental set. Five days in the guardroom and his experience with the Caudron had not tempered James's desire to fly. As Lieutenant James walked out to the silver doped BE, James diffidently asked if he would take him up: 'with his usual good nature he said he would, and so I had my first flight'. After landing from this first flight – during which he decided that flying was not as easy as he had imagined – James was ordered to report to the Commanding Officer of the Military Wing of the RFC, Major F H Sykes.[14] To a lowly recruit, Sykes was an awe inspiring figure, but for all his formidable appearance he was a kindly man and saw at once how contrite this young recruit was. After a stern lecture, impressing upon the youngster how serious a crime he had committed – however unwittingly – and stressing how such carelessness around aeroplanes could be a matter of life or death, he sentenced Air Mechanic Second Class No. 892, James Thomas Byford McCudden, to seven days detention and the loss of fourteen days pay. It was a decision Sykes was never to regret.

On his release from the Detention Barracks at Aldershot, from which he emerged 'a much wiser man – or boy,' James returned to the Flying Depot at Farnborough and took up his duties, consisting mainly of being cook's mate and scraping the carbon from the exhaust valves of Gnôme engines.

James had his second flight in an aeroplane at the end of May, when Lt. T.O. 'B Hubbard[15] took him up in a Maurice Farman. James later wrote that this flight further modified his views on flying, although he omitted to say in what way. While at Farnborough he was impressed by the flying of two pilots in particular: Geoffrey de Havilland and Ronald Kemp.[16] Also

William McCudden (enlarged from above photo).

flying trials at Farnborough was the airship *Astra-Torres*, which on its first flight buckled badly at 2,000 feet and was got down safely only by the behaviour of the naval ratings under the direction of a 'very cool naval officer'.

On 15 June 1913, James was posted to 3 Squadron, stationed at Larkhill on Salisbury Plain. The next day the

Officers of Nos. 4 and 3 Squadrons at Netheravon, 1913. Back row standing are the officers of 4 Squadron: From the left: Joubert de la Férte is first; G.H. Raleigh is 6th; H.R.N Brooke-Popham is 7th. Front row, sitting, are the officers of 3 Squadron: From the left: 3rd is E.L.Conran; 4th V.H.M Wadham; 5th R.Cholmondeley; 8th is A.G.Fox.

squadron moved the few miles to Netheravon, a large new aerodrome, where the mechanics were billeted under canvas, just behind the aerodrome sheds. The weather was good and everyone had 'a most pleasant time'. James was posted to C Flight and put in charge of Lt. Conran's Bleriot.[17] In common with the other squadrons of the RFC, 3 Squadron was equipped with a varied assortment of aeroplane types: Avros, 50hp Bleriots, Henry Farmans, BE4s, and a sole 70hp Bleriot, 'considered at the time the latest thing in aeroplanes'.

While at Netheravon James obtained a Moto-Rêve motorcycle.[18] Its engine was a two-stroke, but despite his knowledge of engines James never managed to get both to run together. During his free time on Sunday afternoons, his efforts to rectify the dud cylinder, running the engine for a few seconds at a time, did little to endear him to his fellow mechanics who were trying to sleep during their rest period. In desperation for some peace they finally took several parts from the engine and hid them.

At Netheravon, the mechanics of 3 Squadron had ample opportunities to fly, and James had his third flight with Lieutenant Reginald Cholmondeley[19] in a Henry Farman. They flew over Bulford and several of the local villages, and on their return to Netheravon, Cholmondeley landed from a series of spirals, modifying still further James' views on flying. James was now taking full advantage of every chance to fly: in one flight he was amazed to see that the aeroplane was flying at 70mph, although he did admit that this fantastic speed was achieved nose down.

While at Netheravon, James shared a tent with two others:

a mechanic named Pyne[20] – described as a 'veteran' – and a well travelled youngster, Cuth Barlow.[21] If anything, Barlow was even keener on flying than James and the two became close friends. Barlow helped James get his Moto Rêve into running order, enabling James to make the run into Salisbury, a distance of fifty-five miles, in the record time of two hours fifteen minutes, breaking the previous record held by Sergeant Major John Ramsey.[22]

During the summer of 1913 the RFC carried out several mobility exercises. On 13 August both A and C Flights of 3 Squadron, three aeroplanes and thirty NCOs and mechanics, under the command of Captain Allen,[23] were sent to Worcestershire in the Vale of Evesham. The object of the exercise was to ascertain under what conditions the care and maintenance of the Squadron's aeroplanes could be carried out in the event of mobilisation. Some of the NCOs and men travelled in two light tenders – a Mercedes and a Daimler – but James travelled in a lorry, possibly a Leyland. The final stretch of the road, from the village of Broadway to Evesham, was a one-in-ten mile long gradient, in those early days of motoring a potentially hazardous road. The driver of the lorry in which James was travelling was AM. Thomas Hinds,[24] renowned for his reckless driving. 'I don't know what happened, but we turned every corner on two wheels, sparks flew from the brakes, and I was very pleased indeed when we slowed down. Hinds laconically remarked that he wanted to put the draught up us. I admit that he certainly achieved his purpose as far as I was concerned.'[25] Even peacetime soldiering was not without its dangers.

'Addie.' Miss Adelaide Meakin.

On arrival at Evesham, the ground party were informed that the three aeroplanes had landed at Ford, some seven miles to the south, in the neighbouring county of Gloucestershire, on the estate of Lord Wemyss - possibly an acquaintance of Capt. Allen. The ground crew retraced their steps to Ford, and James and Cuth Barlow were billeted in the Plough Inn, where they were made very welcome. Aeroplanes were a novelty in those days; the local people took a great deal of interest in the machines and were very hospitable to the 3 Squadron mechanics and men. After three days of perfect weather, the detachment returned to Netheravon. James described it as 'a most enjoyable time', an idyllic interlude in the peaceful English countryside before four years of war.

Three Squadron was now receiving regular replacements in the shape of 80hp Bleriot Type 11bis. Although these were arriving only at the rate of one per month, even more flying was now possible. The 1913 manoeuvres were now drawing near and preparations were in hand to mobilise the RFC. James travelled throughout southern England for three weeks on these preparations, returning to Netheravon in time to motorcycle to Brooklands in order to see the great French pioneer aviator Adolphe Pégoud fly a loop, the first performed in Britain.

During the remainder of 1913, James flew a great deal, even in the extremely adverse wind conditions of autumn over Salisbury Plain. In one flight, with Lt. Wadham[26] in a Bleriot, the wind was gusting at over 55mph. During November, James flew as a passenger with Lt. Conran on Bleriot No.292 and in December alone he flew thirty hours, in very cold weather.

At the end of the year Bill McCudden was posted back to 3 Squadron from Farnborough. He now had the reputation of being one of the finest pilots in the RFC and during the early months of 1914 he gave his younger brother several – very unofficial – flying lessons on the Farman trainers.

At the end of April 1914, Captain J M Salmond[27] took command of 3 squadron from Brooke-Popham, and began to make the squadron ready for the Concentration Camp to be held in June, when all seven squadrons of the RFC were to amalgamate at Netheravon for four weeks of demonstrations of aeroplanes, competitive trials, tactical exercises, lectures, and discussions. Important visitors were expected, among them Lord Roberts, and the military attachés of many countries, including the German and Austrian Military Attachés – James later wrote these last showed 'a particularly lively interest in the proceedings'.

At the time of the Concentration Camp, the RFC numbered roughly eight hundred NCOs and men plus about forty pilots. It was now a highly disciplined and efficient corps of the British Army. All the original NCOs had been seconded from the Guards and the mechanics and tradesmen of the corps were nearly all ex-Royal Engineers: men highly skilled in their various duties, far more so than the average private soldier in the regular army. The adjutant of the RFC was Lt. B.H. Barrington-Kennett,[28] an ex-Grenadier guardsman whose brief for the new corps was that it should combine the efficiency of the Royal Engineers with the smartness of the Guards.

At the end of June, at the conclusion of the Concentration Camp, the squadrons returned to their various aerodromes, and with the extra duties of the camp behind him James found time to write to a Miss Adelaide Meakin of Plumstead, London. It appears that they had met as teenagers, while James was in Gibraltar in 1911; that Adelaide was there, possibly with her family, her father also serving on the base. The letter is quite formal, signed with his rank and full name, with the tentative hint that he often passes through her home borough on the way to his home in Sheerness, suggesting that they could perhaps meet.

3rd Squadron
Royal Flying Corps
Netheravon
12-7-14

Dear Adelaide,
You will no doubt be surprised to hear from me, as I expect you still think I am in the RE. I came home from Gib. in September 1912 and then went to the 6th Company Weymouth. I was there until March 1913, when I was promoted sapper. I then transferred into the RFC as my brother was a sergeant in it & I thought that I should like to take up flying. I went to Farnborough in the RFC and was then transferred to my present squadron, here at Netheravon.

I am very glad that I transferred as I like the life and do a great deal of passenger flying.

My brother has been a Flying Pilot for over two years now being one of the first NCOs to get the certificate. I shall have the chance to get mine in about six months time and of course I want to get it very much.

My work is all connected with aeroplanes as I am the mechanic in charge of an 80 Bleriot monoplane and do (words on crease, indecipherable.A) passenger flying with my officer (Lt. Conran) every day. My officer is a very nice chap & thinks the world of me as a very lot depends on me. He often flies to Brighton from here to some friends for the weekend, and I always accompany him. My people live at Sheerness and I'm going home on ten days leave this Friday. I often pass through Plumstead on the way down.

Trusting you will reply, I remain.
1st Class Air Mechanic. J.McCudden.

James wrote again on July 27. This time to 'Addie' and signing himself 'Jim', a less formal letter which suggests that they had now met. James was on ten days leave, staying at Alma Road, Sheerness-on-Sea, and after thanking her for her last letter, continues:

'I am down here on ten days leave & am having quite a good time. Of course I have got a couple of good civilian suits which enable me to get about more freely than if I wore uniform. I assure you that you would not know me in civilian clothes.'

After telling Addie of his latest acquisition, 'a powerful motorcycle' on which he can obtain speeds of 70miles an hour, and on which he gives his sister Mary and her friends joyrides, 'I tell you they all like it immensely', he signed off with 'trusting to hear from you soon. I remain yours sincerely Jim. SWAK. PS. What college of music are you going in for as I am very fond of music. Jim.
PPS. My sister has got quite a lot of certificates for music and theory.'

At Netheravon, 3 Squadron began to prepare for the August holidays. Few had seen the reports in the newspapers of the assassination on June 28 of Archduke Franz Ferdinand of Austria-Hungary at a little known town, Sarajevo in Bosnia. Even those who had could not have foreseen that the bullet fired by the assassin, a nineteen year old Serb-Croat student named Gavrilo Princip, would plunge the World into a long and bloody four years of war.

Ch.3: War

On the morning of 4 August 1914, hearing that war had been declared, James borrowed Bill's motorcycle and rode to Amesbury to buy a newspaper with the momentous news, covering the six miles from Netheravon to Amesbury in eight minutes. 'Speed limits? What nonsense when we had just declared war on Germany.'[1,2]

As with all the squadrons of the RFC, 3 Squadron was put on an immediate war footing. All the officers of the squadron who were in the Special Reserve were ordered to report for duty; NCOs and men were instructed to give details of their next of kin and were issued with field pay books; armed guards slept in the aeroplane sheds and all personnel were issued ammunition. During the day, the squadron's aeroplanes were made ready to fly to war, James being fully occupied with Conran's machine, Bleriot XI No.389, fitting a rack for a rifle, ammunition bags and a map case.

The situation was intense; spy scares were the order of the day. On the evening of 7 August the guard was turned out to search the surrounding countryside after a report that suspicious characters had been seen loitering with intent to blow up the sheds. Not surprisingly, none were found.

By 10 August, the squadron's stores and equipment had been loaded onto the waiting lorries and tenders. All was ready. Orders were received that the aeroplanes were to fly to Dover on 12 August.

On Wednesday, 12 August 1914, the squadron was up before dawn, the aeroplanes rolled out onto the tarmac in front of the sheds. Last minute adjustments were made to engines, rigging and equipment; engines were started up; the throbbing roar of the rotaries filling the air with sound and the smell of castor oil. Men ran to and fro, carrying out last minute shouted orders or requests. There was an air of ordered chaos; a sense of tension, the realisation that the momentous event of leaving for war had finally arrived. Dawn broke at 4.30PM: the sun rose on a beautiful, clear summer sky.

It had been intended that James would fly to France with Conran in 389, but two days before Conran had flown to Farnborough to collect a Parasol Blériot, a single seater machine.[3] Conran was to fly this machine to France and a severely disappointed James had to be content to travel with the transport.

The Blériots and BE4s of A Flight were first to take off, followed by the Henry Farmans of B Flight. C Flight was the last off. Captain Philip Joubert de la Ferté,[4] with Air Mechanic Gardiner[5] in the rear seat, was first in the air, followed by Conran in the single seater Blériot – watched by a still disappointed and envious James – then Lt. G F Pretyman,[6] with Corporal Arthur Robins.[7] Last to go was 2Lt. R.R. Skene,[8] and Cuth Barlow. Just before take off, Barlow had been standing in the rear cockpit of the Blériot, saying goodbye to James and Corporal Reginald Macrostie.[9] 'I shall never forget it. Barlow knew the machine was slow and unhandy.'

James swung the prop of the Blériot, the engine started, and Skene ran the engine all out, calling for the chocks to be taken away. The heavily laden Blériot staggered into the air, flying tail low, at eighty feet, before disappearing behind the C Flight shed. James and Macrostie then heard the engine stop, followed by 'that awful crash, which once heard is never forgotten'.

James ran for half a mile and found the wrecked Blériot in a small, fenced copse of fir trees. He climbed over the fence and pulled the wreckage away from Skene and Barlow. Both were dead. 'I shall never forget that morning at about half past six, kneeling by poor Keith Barlow and looking at the rising sun and then again at poor Barlow, who had no superficial injury and was killed purely by concussion and wondering if war was going to be like this always.'[10]

Major Salmond arrived at the scene of the crash soon afterwards. He asked a few questions then turned away 'apparently unperturbed', but James heard what he said in an undertone to himself and was left in no doubt that Salmond's feelings were identical to his own.

As with nearly all the squadrons of the RFC, 3 Squadron had more pilots than aeroplanes and although reputedly one of the finest pilots in the RFC, Bill McCudden had been put in charge of the squadron's transport, which had left for Southhampton at first light. After breakfast, no doubt still shaken by the death of Cuth Barlow, James and three other AMs left for Southampton with Lt. G L Cruickshank in a Sunbeam touring car.[11]

Arriving at Southampton at noon, James found the port full of activity, with guns infantry and cavalry arriving 'by the thousands'. That evening the brothers were reunited and Bill sent a postcard home.

Southampton Docks Wednesday.

Dear Mother, Just a line to say goodbye from Jim and myself. We leave for somewhere in France, probably tonight. I have made arrangements for Jim and myself to send you a couple of guineas weekly as long as the war lasts. I trust you will look out for the doing of our squadron at the Front. Give our love to Father and all at home, and we must express our sorrow at not being able to come home to say goodbye.

From your loving sons
Willie and Jim

James and Bill McCudden left Southampton at 6PM that evening, Bill with the main party and James on the *Dee*, 'a very small tramp steamer'. The French coast was sighted at 1PM. James commented 'I know there were many silent thoughts of what lay in store for us over there. However, it was generally expected that we should all be home by Christmas.'

Ch.4: France

2Lt. E.W.C. Perry and his observer, A.M.H. Parfitt, were both killed in this BE8 No.625 on 16 August 1914. *Credit L. Rogers.*

The *Dee* docked at 3PM. James met up with Bill, who had already made friends with Maurice, 3 Squadron's French interpreter. Maurice was a useful man to know as neither of the McCudden brothers spoke a word of French. The French population were enthusiastic, welcoming the disembarking troops with shouts of '*Vive l'Angleterre*', which to James's unaccustomed ear sounded like 'live long and tear'. The port was extremely busy embarking troops, guns and equipment of all kinds, but the organisation was efficient and the Squadron's transport had been unloaded by 9PM.

The McCudden brothers spent their first night in France sleeping on the pavé of the quay, but were up by 4AM to breakfast on biscuit and bacon before leaving for Amiens, where the aeroplanes of the squadrons had landed the day before. James travelled with Lieutenant Cruickshank and three other AMs in a Daimler tender, driven by a man named Chapman. It seemed that James was fated to be driven by drivers of a reckless disposition: Chapman was another Hinds, who had scared him so thoroughly on the pre-war trip to Evesham. Just outside of Boulogne there was a steep hill, at the bottom of which was an unguarded railway crossing. Chapman was negotiating the hill at forty miles an hour, uncaring that a train was almost at the crossing or that the Daimler's brakes were ineffective on the level, let alone on a hill travelling downhill at speed. It became a race as to which reached the crossing first, the Daimler or the train. James estimated that the Daimler won by a foot.[1] Arriving at Amiens, James's first thought was for his machine.

He found Conran, shirt sleeves rolled up, sitting under the Blériot, sheltering from the blistering heat, and with a rigger named Abraham.[2] James began to fit the small wooden racks which had been designed to carry hand grenades and *flêchettes*.[3]

That night, James decided to sleep under the Blériot's wing, being concerned that the machine could be tampered with by any enemy spy. He was unlucky: at about midnight a tremendous thunderstorm broke, the heavy rain continuing for some hours, but after covering the open cockpit of the Blériot he kept reasonably dry under the wing.

On 16 August all four squadrons flew from Amiens to their aerodrome at Maubeuge, south of Mons, ten miles behind the line designated to be held by the BEF.[4] Taking off from Amiens, 3 Squadron suffered its second casualties of the war: BE8 No.625 flown by 2Lt. Perry crashed on the aerodrome and burst into flames, killing Perry and his passenger, AM H.E. Parfitt.[5] James travelled to Maubeuge via Villers-Bretonneux, St. Quentin, Le Cateau and Berlaimont, in a Sunbeam.[6] This time the driver was presumably more cautious as James described the journey as 'splendid', remarking on the warm welcome they were given everywhere by the French population. Outside the village of Estreé-en-Chaussée some apples trees were seen; the car was stopped and James climbed a tree, shaking a bough to bring down some fruit. One of the falling apples hit the goggles he was wearing and broke the lens, knocking a small piece of glass into his eye. Luckily, they were travelling with an ambulance, and a RAMC Corporal, with the

Philip Joubert de la Ferté.

aid of cocaine, removed the offending glass, much to James's relief.

The Sunbeam arrived at Maubeuge at 9PM. James immediately found Conran's Blériot, only to be told by Conran that one of the exhaust valves had broken during the flight, with such a bang that he thought one of the grenades had exploded. Despite being both tired and dirty from the journey, James renewed the exhaust valve. It was this conscientiousness that made him so valued by the pilots of 3 Squadron. After changing the valve, a flight hangar was erected, two machines put into it, and James and Abraham spent the night under cover.

*

At 2.30PM on the afternoon of 22 August the first hostile aeroplane to be seen by the RFC flew over Maubeuge aerodrome at 4,000ft. Two BEs and a Henry Farman took off in an effort to intercept the intruder, the pilot of one of the BEs intending to drop hand grenades on the enemy machine, but before the BE could climb to his height the German pilot turned east and escaped. The Henry Farman carried a Lewis gun, but the added weight so impaired its performance that half an hour after the German machine had gone it was still laboriously climbing, having reached only a 1,000ft.

During the day, twelve reconnaissance flights had revealed large bodies of enemy troops moving towards the British held positions at Mons. The second machine to return from these flights contained the RFC's first casualty by enemy action, Sergeant-Major D S Jillings of 2 Squadron, flying as an observer.[7] Jillings had been hit in the leg by a rifle bullet, the first British soldier to be wounded in an aeroplane, and James saw him being assisted from his machine. It suddenly seemed that the war was much nearer.

At Maubeuge that evening the sound of heavy gunfire was heard for the first time – an ominous sound – and in the evening the sky to the northeast of the aerodrome was illuminated by the flash of heavy guns and the fires of burning villages. The next day British troops were in action against an enemy force vastly superior in numbers. It was clear that the situation was rapidly worsening and the squadrons of the RFC received orders that they were to evacuate Maubeuge the following day, 24 August. For some reason, 3 Squadron had already made ready and on the morning of 23 August began the move to La Câteau.[8] James was the last of the squadron to leave, in a Bleriot piloted by Philip Joubert, and his final view of the RFC's first aerodrome in France was a Henry Farman, which had refused to start because of engine trouble, burning on the ground. Away to the north east he could see the smoke from burning villages and streams of refugees, with all their worldly goods behind them in every description of transport: carts, prams, bicycles, donkeys, horses, oxen and dogs, a slowly moving mass, blocking the roads in all directions.

Soon after leaving Maubeuge the Blériot developed engine trouble and Joubert was forced to land. James inspected the engine but could find nothing wrong, other than that the engine was boiling hot. They had been flying at under 3,000ft and he suspected that the intense heat – unkind to the air-cooled rotary – was the cause of the trouble. They took off again and flew to Berlaimont, where they found the rest of the squadron's machines. The squadron stayed at Berlaimont for only a few hours before moving on to Le Câteau, James again flying with Joubert. After a flight of some thirty-five minutes, the landing field at Le Câteau came in sight and they landed just as the light was almost gone. The squadron's transport had not yet arrived and James and a mechanic named Webb[9] were the only ground crew available to look after the four machines of their Flight. They filled the machines with oil and petrol and at 11PM began grinding in the exhaust valves of Joubert's Blériot, finishing the job at 3AM. The transport then arrived, but stopped only a few hours before setting off again for St. Quentin.

The next morning, James and Webb having no rations, they had breakfast with the officers of C Flight, who shared their food with them. At 11.00AM a German machine, a 'Rumpler *Taube* monoplane', flew over the airfield. James's expert ear for

Lionel Evelyn Oswald Charlton.

engines discerned that it was powered by a four-cylinder, 90hp Mercedes engine. Everyone had a shot at the enemy machine – James standing on a petrol tin in an attempt to increase the trajectory of his Webley Mark IV revolver – and several BE2as and an Avro took off to intercept the intruder. Lt. Harvey-Kelly and Sgt-Major E.J. Street, in one of 2 Squadron's BEs, forced the enemy machine to land, landed beside it and chased the pilot and observer into a wood, where they made good their escape.[10,11]

At midday the squadron left for St. Quentin, James flying this time with Captain L.E.O. Charlton[12] in a Blériot. Before taking off, James noticed that Charlton was sitting in the Blériot 'looking grave' so asked him if the BEF were retreating. Charlton assured him that they were merely drawing the Germans on until they could encircle them and capture the entire German army. James did not believe this explanation, but understood the reason it was given. 'Of course it was necessary for our officers to keep our spirits up as much as possible as it was obvious that we were not exactly winning.'[13] James and Charlton arrived at St. Quentin aerodrome, just south of the town, a little before 4.00PM.

After staying a day at St. Quentin – a welcome rest – the squadrons moved again on 26 August, due south to La Fère. Weather conditions were atrocious, with driving mist and rain, and only two pilots managed to land at the designated airfield. James travelled to La Fère by road in one of the squadron's tenders, driven by an old acquaintance, G.S. Chapman. On arrival he found Conran and his Blériot in a very muddy, ploughed field. James filled the machine up with petrol and oil, checked it over, then tied it down for the night. It was raining hard and sleeping under the wing again, in the mud, was out of the question, so James slept in the pilot's cockpit covered by a waterproof sheet.

The squadrons stayed at La Fère until 28 August, a respite from the daily moves and a chance to relax a little. The road that ran past the aerodrome was covered with blackberry bushes laden with unpicked fruit, the French considering them as poison, and food during the retreat being always a problem, full opportunity was taken to have a feast of blackberries. James considered they were the best he'd ever tasted. One mechanic, more ambitious, raiding a nearby apple orchard, was brought before Joubert by an officious NCO on a charge of looting. Joubert dismissed the charge out of hand, asking the NCO if he had never scrumped apples as a boy.

Despite being always in the open, day and night, subjected to the hot sun during the day and the wet mists at night, the squadron's Bleriots were standing up well under the difficult conditions of the retreat, due in no small part to the sheer hard work of the ground crews, and all took off for the French aerodrome at Compiègne after two days at La Fère, James again travelling with Chapman, in a Daimler tender. It was a dusty and very thirsty journey in the heat, but on arrival at 3PM all the mechanics went straight to their machines to carry out the usual servicing and checks.

That afternoon a German machine flew over the aerodrome and dropped three bombs, one of which fell near the latrines. A welcome comic diversion from the tensions of the last few days was the sight of a certain unpopular sergeant – perhaps he of scrumping fame – sprinting from his ablutions partially undressed. An even more welcome event was the arrival of the first post from England.

While at Compiègne, the full effect of the retreat was seen as a few lost British Tommies staggered into the camp dead beat, bootless, hatless, with no equipment save for their rifles and bandoliers. Distressed as they were, in the best tradition of the British Army, they had retained their weapons

On Sunday 30 August, James flew again with Captain Charlton, to Chantilly near Senlis. The weather was very hot, the Blériot was badly rigged, and Charlton had his work cut out controlling it in the bad 'heat bumps' in the air On arrival at Chantilly, the Blériot not being needed for the day's operations, James took out the inlet valves, cleaned and reground them, then replaced them. To his satisfaction, the engine responded by giving an additional twenty revolutions per minute.

The next move, on 31 August, was to Juilly, where the personnel of 3 Squadron enjoyed the luxury of their first bath

At the outbreak of war in 1914, many civilian commercial vehicles were impressed into service with the BEF. This bright red Thorneycroft van, belonging to H P sauce, was used in 1914–1915 by 3 Squadron as an ammunition carrier.

since leaving England. Near the landing field was a deserted convent with an ornamental lake and James and several of his fellow mechanics went down to bathe. 'We spent a very pleasant afternoon there and we also found some very nice apples in the grounds.' Food was still short, but augmented by apples scrumped from the convent and wayside orchards plus the ubiquitous blackberries, with officers and men sharing their improvised provisions

The weather being fine, James slept under the wing of the Blériot, only to be awakened during the night by the hysterical shouting of some French sentries who were convinced they had seen a spy prowling round the machines. However, later there was a disquieting rumour that there were no British troops between the aerodrome and the advancing German army and it was feared that the field would be overrun by the enemy during the night. A sunken road ran from east to west past the landing field and all the available mechanics who had been left behind with the light transport and machines – the squadron's heavy transport had left earlier in the afternoon – were armed with rifles. Under the command of Captain Charlton they were ordered to hold the road until first light, when the machines could be flown away. A squadron of the Royal Irish Horse relieved the situation before dawn and on 2 September the machines were got safely away to Serris, south east of Paris.

The retreat was now coming to an end and 3 Squadron's next move was to Pézarches.[14] Despite the dedication of the squadron's mechanics, the constant moves during the eight days of the retreat now begun to take their toll on the serviceably of the machines. Joubert forced landed soon after leaving Serris and the breakdown party had to dismantle his Blériot and take it to Pézarches by road. Replacement machines at this stage in the war were hard to come by – new Blériots, for example, would have to be fetched from Paris – and on arrival at Pézarches, James and Abraham worked all night servicing Conran's Blériot No.616.

The weather was now very hot and dry. The squadron stayed at Pézarches for two days before moving to the French aerodrome at Melun, a large town south of Paris. The retreat from Mons was finally at an end.

*

The location of the new aerodromes during the retreat had presented no undue problems. As early as 1911 Captain Frederick Sykes, later to become commanding officer of the Military Wing of the RFC on its formation in 1912, had cycled the countryside of northern France to select possible landing grounds, but the strain, so early imposed on the transport and servicing facilities of the RFC, the youngest corps in the British Army, was a severe test. That the RFC came through with flying colours, even learnt valuable lessons from the retreat, is testimony to the improvisational skills of both officers and

Eric Conran with a Blériot of 3 Squadron.

men. Billets were found in farmhouses, private houses, barns, and haystacks; even, when the weather was kind, under the wings of their aeroplanes. A great deal of credit should be given for the dedication of the NCOs and men of the squadrons. James commented. '…the NCOs and men worked day and night on the retreat. As long as we got something to eat everyone was very cheery and did not mind a bit.'

Daily operations had still been flown during the retreat and visits from German aeroplanes were common, taking place at nearly every aerodrome occupied by the RFC throughout the withdrawal. The accuracy of the RFC reports to Sir John French, commanding the BEF, had dispelled any previous reservations as to their value. The daily reconnaissance reports from all squadrons had warned him of the heavy concentration of German troops on his front at Mons, and, importantly, the various attempted enveloping movements on his flank by von Kluck's First Army. The German advance had been extremely rapid. On 31 August, while the squadrons were on Senlis racecourse, two officers motored to Paris for aeroplane spares.

Returning that evening, driving up to the cottages that had been the headquarters of the RFC that morning, they found them occupied by the enemy, Luckily, in the dusk they were mistaken for Germans and succeeded in making good their escape.

Any lingering doubts of the value of the aeroplane in war were finally ended by a reconnaissance report from Juilly on 1 September, warning French that German cavalry were in a thickly wooded area to the north, only two miles from his HQ with no British troops between. HQ hastily decamped.

The RFC had also harassed the advancing German troops – small and crude as these attempts were – by dropping hand grenades and petrol bombs on them during daily dawn reconnaissance flights.

The German forces were finally halted at the Battle of the Marne, and it was after the successful conclusion of the battle that Sir John French, in his despatch of 7 September, made the first official mention of fighting in the air.

'I wish particularly to bring to your Lordships' notice the admirable work done by the Royal Flying Corps under Sir David Henderson. Their skill, energy and perseverance have been beyond all praise. They have furnished me with complete and accurate information, which has been of incalculable value in the conduct of operations. Fired at constantly both by friend and foe, and not hesitating to fly in every kind of weather, they have remained undaunted throughout. Further, by actually fighting in the air, they have succeeded in destroying five of the enemy's machines.'

General Joffre, the French Commander in Chief of the battle, also paid tribute to the RFC and his appreciation of its reconnaissance work He wrote: 'Please express most particularly to Marshal French my thanks for the services rendered to us every day by the English Flying Corps. The precision, exactitude, and regularity of the news brought in by them are evidence of their perfect organisation and also of the perfect training of pilots and observers.'

The RFC had weathered its baptism of fire on the Western Front.

*

At the successful conclusion of the Battle of the Marne, 3 Squadron received orders to return to their previous landing field at Pezarches. It was on the way there that James for the first time saw first-hand the evidence of war: dead horses, shell craters, and numerous small pits – which the infantry had dug while fighting in open and extended order – surrounded by empty shell cases. It was the obscene detritus of war.

The squadron arrived at Pezarches, to find that Lt. Lindop was missing from a reconnaissance.[15] Lieutenants Conran and Joubert made reconnaissance flights from Pezarches, but landed back at an advanced landing field close to Coulommiers with the news that the enemy was still retreating. Conran's Parasol was badly shot about during this reconnaissance, and the propeller and tailplane had to be replaced. Although Conran's Parasol was powered by an 80hp Gnome, its tailplane and elevator were of the type fitted to the 50hp Blériot. Spares were

At the end of the retreat from Mons in 1914, RFC HQ and the RFC squadrons occupied the French aerodrome at Melun aerodrome, where this photograph was taken. This group of 3 Squadron NCOs enjoying afternoon tea and Crawford's Biscuits includes Flight Sergeant Bill McCudden (in braces) and Sergeants A. Kidd, H. Robbins, E. McEvoy and Corporal G.H. White.

still in short supply and the only tailplane and elevator available were those for the 80hp Blériot, which were a good deal larger. However, these were fitted and James commented that the Parasol still 'behaved quite well'. His machine being badly shot about does not seem to have affected Conran unduly. During lunch at the advanced field – bully beef fried in an open petrol can – it was found that they had tea, but no milk. Conran rose to the occasion by milking a cow in a nearby field.

After lunch, the detachment moved to the landing field at Coulommiers, James flying with Joubert. During the short flight, from a height of 2,000ft, the smoke of the battle to the north-east was clearly visible, and long convoys were moving up in clouds of dust. Gliding in to land at Coulommiers, James and Joubert had a narrow escape, almost colliding with Conran, who was landing at the same time.

On 9 September, the four squadrons moved to Coulommiers, where close by the landing field a party from 3 Squadron found the burnt out remains of Lindop's BE8. While at Coulommiers, several machines flew to an advanced landing ground at Nanteuil, just south of the Marne, to observe the retreat of the German forces. James was one of the advance party, commenting that the village of Naneuil had been thoroughly sacked by the retreating enemy, but that some villagers had remained, including a young French girl who presented them all – officers and men – with a large basket of peaches.[16]

While at Nanteuil, Conran flew a reconnaissance, landing near Montreuil, just behind the British infantry. James went up by road with petrol and oil for the Blériot and passing through the village saw his first prisoners of war, mostly cavalry, and a horse battery of guns that had been captured complete. James found the Blériot and filled it with petrol and oil. He was then detailed as a guard for Lt. Dermott Allen,[17] who was carrying an important reconnaissance report to the HQ of General Smith-Dorrien, some eight miles north of the river Marne. James and Allen set off in Major Salmond's car, James with a loaded rifle across his knees because of the close proximity of the German army rearguard, still at large in the various woods and copses on the way. Having successfully delivered the report, James and Allen returned to Coulommiers. After 'replenishing the inner man' James worked all night on Conran's Parasol, cleaning and grinding in the inlet valves and fitting new inlet valve springs.

The squadron stayed at Coulommiers for four days before moving to Fère-en-Tardenois, James travelling by road with the transport. Passing through the town, full of hundreds of

German prisoners captured in the advance, the transport found the landing ground, just west of the village. No sooner had the machines been attended to and staked down for the night, than it began to rain heavily. No tents had been erected and James, covered with a waterproof sheet, settled down for the night under the wing of the Blériot, listening to the sound of heavy gunfire. James was not asleep for long. A gale sprung up. At 1AM he was woken by shouting, opening his eyes in time to see Captain Charlton's Blériot, picketed close to Conran's Parasol, stand vertically on its tail, then poise there for a second before falling over onto its back with a resounding crash. A Henry Farman soon followed, but by then everyone was awake and they managed to save the remainder of the machines. After the gale had blown itself out, two mechanics utilised the nacelle of the wrecked Farman as a shelter for the remainder of the night. James recalled that one bright spot of the episode was that the Technical Sergeant Major, reporting to Charlton on the state of his completely demolished Blériot, informed him that he had 'covered up the magneto, sir!' Due to prompt action, 3 Squadron had suffered lightly, but 5 Squadron had four Henry Farmans completely wrecked.

The four squadrons were now to remain at Fère until October, their main duties being liaison with the artillery, with 3 Squadron often flying from an advanced landing ground near the village of Serches, near Soissons. With the settled conditions, the workload of the ground crews, exacerbated by the continual moves and difficult conditions during the retreat from Mons, was more manageable. Operating at Serches, however, which was only some 4,000 yards from the German front-line trenches, all ranks of 3 Squadron were nearer the war, and one morning a German two-seater came over the aerodrome at 2,000ft. James recalled: 'We had some fine fun shooting at it with incendiary bullets from Martini carbines, but no luck.'

Working over the front lines, the machines of the squadron were now coming under increasing amounts of anti-aircraft fire and the term 'Archie' for the enemy fire came into common use: 'because they always missed our machines, the pilots used to sing the refrain of "Archibald! Certainly not!" a popular music hall song of the day.'

While at Serches, James called Conran's attention to an enemy balloon, the first they had seen. Taking Abraham as his observer/gunner, Conran took off. The intention was that Abraham should throw a bomb at the balloon: not surprisingly the attack failed.

On 28 September, 3 Squadron received a Bristol Scout B, flown in by Lt. R. Cholmondeley.[18] The fast little Bristol, No.648, was armed with two fixed rifles, one on each side of the fuselage, fitted to fire forwards at an angle to miss the propeller.

The personnel of the squadron was now slowly changing. While the squadron was at Serches, 2nd Lieutenant V.H. Wadham and Captain Charlton had crashed, Charlton's injuries being sufficiently serious for him to be invalided back to England, and Phillip Joubert had been transferred to Home Establishment, Conran taking over command of C Flight.

On 5 October the squadron moved to Amiens, James travelling by road – 'a long and pleasant run'. All the squadron's aeroplanes had arrived safely and James and his fellow mechanics carried out the usual overhauling procedures.

On 8 October the squadron moved again, to Abbeville, James flying to the new aerodrome with 2Lt. A.L. Bryan.[19] While at Abbeville, Sergeant F. Dunn[20] joined the squadron, to fly the squadron's Blériots. On 9 October the squadron moved yet again, to Moyenneville. Although the squadron was now a long way behind the front lines, the usual German aeroplane visited them, James estimating its height as at least 10,000ft, an unusual operational height in those early days, certainly far higher than then flown by the machines of the RFC.

Three days later the squadron moved to St.Omer, where it was to stay until the last week in November. All the tents and hangers were erected at St.Omer, until in James's words, 'the place assumed the aspect of a travelling circus'.

The personnel of the squadron now had time to relax and have a little spare time. James took the opportunity to have his second bath in seven weeks and change his underclothes for the first time in nine. He also found time to write to Addie, his first letter in four months.

11/11/14
Dear Addie,

I received your welcome letter last week, for which I thank you, but have been unable to answer before this. I am in the best of health at present and hope to remain so. The weather is getting very cold now, but having plenty of warm clothes we do not mind. I often have a passenger flight with my officer and as the weather is getting colder the conditions for flying are better than if it was hot as a machine climbs much better in cold weather.

We often get a German aeroplane over our camp. As soon as it is seen about 4 of our fast machines chase after it with rifles, revolvers, bombs, grappling hooks and all sort of machine-destroying devices, and we have succeeded in bringing down several German machines in this way.

Do not trouble to send me out any cigarettes as I rarely smoke, and then only a certain brand.

I expect the war to last several months yet. I think it will finish up sometime next summer, mind you I am not a pessimist, but I am only thinking of the preparations that Germany has been making and so it means life or death to them. Therefore they will make a big effort to win. But we will whack them in the end.

As for the Zeppelin yarns that are going about in England, do not take any notice of them, as it is all piffle, and they have not got half a dozen in all Germany.

I must now conclude, hoping you keep well.

I remain yours faithfully
Jim

This Maurice Farman No.352 was destroyed in the storm of 12 September 1914.

While at St.Omer, another gale, which lasted for three days, blew down nearly all the hangers, and a Henry Farman, which had been securely tied down with fourteen ropes, was seen to be flying, with all its wheels off the ground, straining to the full extent of the restraining ropes. The weather in general was now very cold, especially at night, but the ground crews were still sleeping under the wings of their machines.

At about the middle of the squadron's stay at St.Omer, C Flight was detached to Hinges, near Bethune. James flew down with Conran, and soon after they arrived at the landing field it began to rain heavily. The Flight worked all night erecting a hanger, the officers working as hard as the men. While at Hinges, a further detachment of Sergeant R.H. Carr[21] and his observer, Captain Evans,[22] was based at a landing ground between Gorre and Festubert, flying for six or seven hours each day, ranging for the artillery, and James went every morning for a week with petrol and oil for their machine. The advanced landing field at Gorre was close to the front line, in advance of the British heavy artillery; each time the Blériot returned, the German 4.2 cm artillery attempted to find it and the field was often under heavy shell fire.

After a week at Hinges and the advanced landing field at Gorre, C Flight rejoined the rest of the squadron at St.Omer.

On 27 September, the squadron was issued with an SE2 scout, which was fitted with two rifles in a similar fashion to that of the Bristol Scout. Although fitted with the same 80hp Gnome engine as the Bristol, and faster, it did not climb as well.[23] James, always interested in technicalities, remarked that it was the first British machine on active service to be fitted with the RAF streamline wires. About this time the squadron also received several 80hp Avros to replace the Henry Farmans of B Flight, but rumour in the squadron was that it was soon to be re-equipped entirely with Moranes.

While at St.Omer, James flew his first wartime operational flight. Armed with a rifle, he flew with Conran from St.Omer to Calais and back, 'looking for German machines.' They saw none, no doubt to James's disappointment.

On 20 November, James was promoted to Corporal, wryly admitting that he 'celebrated' by doing a week's Orderly Sergeant. Although James was keen on all the technical aspects of his duties, he was less keen on the disciplinary side of service life.

About this time, Conran's Blériot Parosol was returned to the Aircraft Park to be fitted with wireless equipment and he took over one of the squadron's two-seater Blériots, which gave James more opportunities for flying.

On 24 November, 3 Squadron moved to Gonneham, only to find that the proposed landing ground was a beet field. Luckily, some nearby Indian cavalry had a roller and with the aid of this, plus every available man marching up and down the field for the entire afternoon, they managed to compact the beet enough until, although still soft, it was firm enough.

The weather in France that winter was very wet with frequent gales. As soon as hangers and tents were erected, a gale

An SE2 of this type was issued to 3 Squadron on 27 September 1914.

would spring up and blow them down. The almost constant rain poured down in torrents, the wind 'howling like mad', with all the blown down hangers, 'flapping like mad around the machines'. Deep drainage pools were dug around the hangers to catch the water, but many a mechanic fell into these, with the accompaniment of curses and oaths, which at least supplied some light entertainment. There were not enough hangers to house all the squadron's aeroplanes and those that could not be housed under cover had to be tied down, day and night. This had the added operational hazard that a 80hp powered Blériot, that had been tied down all night and was subsequently sodden with water, carrying pilot and observer plus a full war load, had difficulty taking off from the still soft beet field. Cinders were needed to further compact the field and twelve tons were spread and compressed on the field every day.

On 2 December, 3 Squadron received its first Morane-Saulnier Type L Parasol, delivered direct from Paris. This machine, No.1829, was the first of the type to be delivered to the RFC, but it lasted only a week; on 9 December, Captain Cholmondeley side-slipped into the ground, completely wrecking the Morane, fortunately with only slight injury to himself. Replacements were not long in arriving: No.1843 arrived from Paris on 24 December and No. 1845 on 26 December, Boxing Day.[24]

James had written twice to Addie during the month. In his first, dated the 6th, he stuck to his previous forecast that the war would only last twelve months in all, but conceded that it could possibly last longer. He also gave her the news that he was a now a corporal. As Christmas was approaching, he asked if she remembered the Christmas of 1911 in Gibraltar, and did she still dance, adding that he had been a keen dancer himself in 1913, then rather ironically observing: ' but have no opportunity as yet, this year'. Addie had obviously previously written to say that she had had some social problems, and in almost a big brother mode he warned her: 'There are snobs everywhere of both sexes, so your best plan is to entirely ignore them as those sort of people are not worth troubling about.' He also requested a photograph of her.

It seems that he did not receive the usual prompt reply to his letters and sent her a Field Service Postcard on the 18th, with the line 'I have not had a letter lately.' This brought a response and he wrote again on the 29th, thanking her for her latest letter. He thought her photograph 'excellent' and promised to take good care of it. Christmas had made no difference to them, he said, as they had 'worked as usual', but admitted that: 'there was terrific slaughter of poultry as 20 of us had 30 geese and two chickens between us and had them cooked at a farm where we are billeted at present.' He had had 'lots' of Christmas presents, including 'lots' of puddings 'which I severely dealt with'. Addie had obviously been dancing over the holiday, but he agreed with her that 'outside' dances could not compare with a military one.

The weather was bad and the squadron had not done much flying, but he had 'taken over a new machine for my

France 1914. No.3 Squadron. Major John Salmond receiving a report from Sergeant Hayward. The officer on the left is Geoffrey Salmond, John Salmond's brother.

officer, which does 83 mph.' and which he thought would be useful for chasing enemy machines, although they seldom saw these anymore. He told her he would like to chase a German machine and bring it down with a rifle. 'But do not think me blood thirsty, will you, as it is only my duty if I get the chance.'

In late December 1914, the Germans had begun daylight bombing operations against England, and on the third raid, on 25th December, a lone Friedrichshafen seaplane was fired on by the anti-aircraft batteries at Sheerness. James asked Addie what she thought of this, then gave her a graphic account of the anti-aircraft on the Western Front.

You should see some of our machine being shelled by the German 'Archibalds'. As many as 40 or 50 puffs of smoke can be seen around one machine, each puff denoting a shell burst. The composition of the shells is shrapnel, which is timed to burst just above the machine if possible, some of them are very close as we often find holes in the wings and body of the machine where shrapnel bullets have passed through. The machine is often hit by rifle shot. It is, however, extremely difficult to take aim accurately with a rifle on a machine in the air, as you have to allow a lot for the speed of the machine, also you can only judge the height of it approximately, so as to adjust your sight. The majority of rifle bullets we get through our machines are, I think, more by luck than judgement.

After telling her that his brother Bill is in the squadron – 'you know, that demon who used to ride the motor cycle through St. Mary's' – he told her how he had recently met his some of his old Royal Engineers Company, but saw only a few he knew: 'as I have left the 15th now over 2 years and a lot of the company were reservists and transfers. I also met Sgt. Collins, who was on the butcher's shop at Gib. He was a corporal then. Lottie was his nickname. Your father would remember him well.'

As with several of his letters to Addie, James then veered completely away from the war, asking her if she had seen in the papers that George Edwards, the London theatre impresario, was producing a new musical comedy called *Betty* at the Gaiety Theatre, with music by Paul Ruebens, 'who usually produces music for George Edwards, songs such as *The Sunshine Girl* and *The Girl on the Train*'.

He then asked if she spoke much French, as 'I am getting quite fluent with mine' before ending by wishing her a bright and prosperous New Year, signing off, still rather formally, as 'I remain, yours faithfully, Jim,' but adding a PS. 'Please write.'

*

The squadron was now operating with artillery batteries north and south of the La Bassée canal, C Flight operating each day from an advanced landing field. Each dawn, if the weather was possible for operational flying, a tender was loaded with petrol, oil, tools, a landing 'T' and a day's rations, and driven the five miles to the advanced landing ground at Annequin, on the Béthune to La Bassée road. This field was only 4,000 yards behind the British front line and as soon as the Moranes had landed, the German artillery would search for them. In addition, an enemy aeroplane would often fly over the field, possibly to range the enemy guns. The squadron personnel would stay at this location until dusk, then pack everything up and return to Gonneham. This duty went on day after day, and as corporal in charge of engines James was fully occupied with servicing and running the engines of every machine before dawn.

By the end of 1914 the duties of the RFC had taken on their definitive form of reconnaissance and artillery work. The New Year was to see further development in the air war.

Ch.5: First War Flights

By the January of 1915 the accommodation at Gonneham had improved, much to the relief of the squadron's men and NCOs who were now billeted in a large barn which was both comfortable and warm, a welcome change to sleeping under the wings of the machines.

James wrote to Addie, on 10 January. The letter is headed: Bonjour ma Cherie, Comment çe va, çe va Bien.[1]

'The weather here is beyond words, nothing but rain and mud. *Il fait, ici main tenant*', adding rather unkindly, 'If you do not understand my written French, you will have to get a dictionary. I wish this confounded war would hurry up. I am getting fed up with it. The weather alone is enough to drive one mad. I've got so used to getting wet, that I am absolutely indifferent now to being wet or dry. We keep on grumbling, but our heads are above the water and mud so you can see the simile. I see by the papers that home is just the same, everywhere being flooded.'

After touching briefly on the sinking of HMS *Formidable*[2] – 'Rather hard lines about the *Formidable*, but still it is all in the game', in the next sentence he informs Addie, 'We get some nice cheese out here, it is so like soap that very often after dark chaps start washing with lumps of it.'

After telling her that Bill is on leave and not due back until the 14th, he tells her that he is hoping to be home in two months himself, 'but I shall not build on it'.

'Well Addie, I am afraid that I have not got much news this week, other than my work, which I do not think would interest you, so I shall now close, trusting you are well as it leave me at present.

I remain *Votre petit garcon, ma cherie*
Jim
PS. Write soon.'

Above: John Maitland Salmond.
Left: Flight Sergeant William Thomas James (Bill) McCudden. Bill was posted home from 3 Squadron in France early in 1915.

Reginald Cholmondeley.

Hubert Dunsterville Harvey-Kelly.

Additional thought was now being given to arming the machines. The squadron began to receive one or two Lewis guns and most of the mechanics were given instructions in their firing, mechanism and maintenance.

With the arrival of the first two Moranes, with more being expected, a party of three mechanics, James, Webb and Bowyer,[3] under the command of Sergeant F.G. Dunn[4] were sent to the Le Rhône engine works in Paris for instruction on the 80hp Le Rhône 9C engine. The party went by rail to Paris and were billeted in a small hotel in the Boulevard Kellerman, close by the Le Rhône works. Dunn, who was staying near the Odéon, knew Paris fairly well and was able to take his charges on a tour of the city's many places of amusement. As the result of one evening's adventures, Webb and Bowyer became lost – at least that was their story – and only found their way to the Rhône works the following morning, guided by the daily roar of the engines being tested. James recorded that they were both in a 'dilapidated' state but had thoroughly enjoyed themselves. Dunn, being also in Paris to collect a new Morane and fly it back to the squadron, James, Webb and Bowyer returned to the Gonneham by road in a Crossley tender – in Paris to collect spares – a considerably quicker journey, if colder, than by train.

It was about this time that James was detailed to fly a reconnaissance with Lieutenant Cholmondeley. Keen as he was on flying at every opportunity, James had no faith at all in Cholmondeley's abilities as a Morane pilot – he had witnessed Cholmondeley's sideslip which had written off the first of the squadron's Moranes – and he employed the old soldier's trick of avoiding an unpleasant duty by going sick. James mentioned in a letter to his mother that he was in hospital, but confided the real reason in a letter to his brother Bill, now in England, who in his next letter home told the family the truth, remarking: 'It was rather amusing to hear about Jim being in hospital. He was only there for two days. Jim never has anything wrong with him.'

James had no such qualms about flying with Conran. One morning he took off with Conran, flying as his gunner. They left the aerodrome at 10AM to 'look for Germans'. James considered the wing-warping Morane had a very fine climb for those days, recording that they reached their height of 6,000ft over Bethune in twelve minutes. Conran crossed the front lines just south of La Bassée Canal and turned north-east. James saw three little specks over La Bassée, which Conran assured him were enemy aeroplanes, but they were far higher than the Morane. Going north over Violanes, James had his first experience of anti-aircraft fire. 'I heard a c-r-r-r-ump, then

James. The newly promoted sergeant, complete with walking cane. April 1915.

Henry Robert Moore Brooke-Popham.

another and another, and looking above me saw several balls of white smoke floating away.'[5] Conran took evasive action, but although he described it as a 'bad experience' James felt little more than a curiosity as to where the next shell would burst. Although Conran took the Morane up to 9,000ft the enemy aeroplanes were still above them and after keeping an eye on them for a while they returned to Gonneham. This experience confirmed James's opinion that at this period of the war the German aircraft flew much higher than the British, an opinion strengthened by a large German two-seater which one Sunday morning flew over Gonneham at 7,000ft on its way to bomb the railway at Lillers. A Morane from 3 squadron took off to intercept the two-seater on its way back, accompanied by a French REP monoplane from the nearby French aerodrome on the outskirts of Bethune. Both allied machines got within range of the bomber and the listeners on the aerodrome distinctly heard machine gun fire and single shots from a rifle, but the intruder got away.

Under the command of 1st Wing, No.3 Squadron was now a fully-fledged reconnaissance and artillery squadron, covering the area from Armentières to Lens, responsible for both tactical and strategic reconnaissance and ranging for the artillery. As well as these duties a great deal of photographic reconnaissance was also undertaken in preparation for the coming battle of Neuve Chapelle. Despite the technical difficulties of early aerial photography, 2 and 3 Squadrons photographed a mosaic of the entire German trench system to a depth of 700 to 1500 yards.

James wrote to Addie on the 23rd, expressing both his and the RFC's annoyance at what was seen as the undue publicity being given in the English papers to the exploits of the RNAS force operating on the Belgian coast under Commander C R Samson.

The Naval raid was rather a good stunt, but it got too much publicity. As our pilots do splendid work, that never gets known. All you can see in the papers is the dare-devil Sampson

'Little Mac' framed by his two sons: Anthony (left) and James. July 1915. *Credit Sue Adams via Jonathan Saunders.*

(sic). Some of our pilots do more flying in some days than he does in a week.

I had a flight over the German lines recently and 3 of their archies shelled us just to show there are no ill feeling. But my word, they do put the wind up you. The German 'Archie' have not brought down any of our machines yet, but our own 'Archie' have had better luck in bringing down the German machines.

Well, six months of the war is over and I am game for another 6, although a few days leave would not be amiss. But still, the next 6 months will go quicker than the last.

My elder sister has just got married. If I get a few days leave, I would be sure to visit you.

Must close now with best of love & good wishes.

I remain faithfully yours,
Jim

*

At the opening of the battle of Neuve Chapelle on 10 March, three machines from 3 Squadron set out at 6AM to bomb the German Headquarters at Fournes, attacking at three-minute intervals. Captain Conran, with Major Salmond as observer, dropped their bombs in three passes at 100ft followed by Lieutenants W.C.K. Birch[6] and D.R. Hanlon,[7] flying without observers. Several direct hits left the buildings in flames. All three machines returned safely, although Conran's Morane was badly shot about, one bullet having passed between Conran and Salmond, at right angles to the line of flight.

James had also taken off in the morning, as an observer for Lieutenant Corbett-Wilson,[8] but dense smoke obscured the battlefield and it was difficult to see the progress of the ground fighting.

At 5PM in the evening of 12 March, James had just seen Conran and Lt. Pinney take off in a Morane and was walking back to C Flight's sheds. Passing the A Flight sheds he saw Captain Cholmondeley's Morane being loaded with six Mélinite bombs. James had just reached his own sheds when there were two explosions in quick succession and he distinctly felt the displacement of air from the blast. Turning round, James saw Cholmondeley's Morane was on fire, from wing tip to wing tip. James immediately ran to the scene. Over a dozen men were lying around the Morane, all badly mutilated. Men began running to the scene from all directions. Although the flames of the Morane had died down, it was quickly realised that unexploded bombs were still in the wreckage and that it was essential to get those men still living away from the immediate area. James, with Lieutenants Pretyman, Blackburn,[9] Cleaver[10] and Sgt. Burns[11] carried four seriously wounded men away. Major Salmond now arrived. Realising

August 1915. James, wearing proudly his wing as a newly-qualified observer.

at once that the unexploded bombs were still in the Morane, he ordered everyone to clear the area immediately, with strict orders that no-one should go anywhere near the remains for the rest of the day. The following morning, it was found that most of the wreckage had been cleared away and with the remaining unexploded bombs taken out and buried overnight by Salmond and Sergeant John Angell.[12]

This was a severe blow to 3 Squadron. Cholmondeley and eleven men had been killed, with an additional four seriously wounded.[13] The accident had a generally depressing effect for days on the officers and men and of the squadron, particularly on the men, as fatal casualties were relatively rare amongst those serving as ground crew. However, as James later wrote: '…the squadron settled down to its work again, but we who had seen the accident can never forget it; at least I never can.'[14,15]

Cholmondeley's Morane was being bombed up for a raid on the railway station at Don. The next morning, Pretyman flew the mission, his bombs blowing up the central carriage of a train standing in the station.

James wrote to Addie on 21 March.

There will be some big fighting soon now. I think the war may possibly finish up in about August, but very likely later. Still, I am not particular how long it lasts as I am quite contented with my lot, although, of course, the longer the war the more suffering there must be. But I believe we have got the Germans well in hand. Roll on the time when I can go and see a good musical comedy at one of the London theatres, that is if I get a furlough, if I get back. I think that this May, June or July, we shall see some very tough fighting.

I shall get another motor cycle & sidecar when I get back, as motor cycling is a jolly good sport.

Don't you think that our Navy is doing splendid work, if our Navy had been smashed up at the start we should have been helpless. I'm sure we owe a lot to our Navy & sailors.

We are doing a good deal of flying now that the weather is set in for the better.

Well, dear Addie, I have no more news at present than hoping this letter finds you well, as it does me at present.

I remain, yours faithfully
Jim

On 26 March, Captain Conran and Lieutenant Woodiwiss bombed Langhin-au-Werppes. As they came into land, James noticed that some flying wires were hanging loose and a stream of petrol was pouring from the machine. He quickly ran to the Morane and found that Conran had been badly wounded in the arm by shrapnel. One ball had embedded itself into Conran's right arm and another had gone into his right side, with an exit wound very near his spine. Woodiwiss was miraculously unharmed, although the Morane (1872) was riddled with shrapnel. Conran was taken to a Casualty Clearing Station and was later invalided home to England. Captain Harvey-Kelly was posted in to take command of C Flight.[16]

On 30 March, James wrote to Addie, hoping that she had had a good Easter holiday, but pointing out that Easter made not the slightest difference to the troops in France. That said, the time brought back happy memories of the Easter of 1913, spent in England.

Myself and a couple of chums, all on motor bikes, went down to Canterbury rink, with three fair passengers on our carriers. Well, on the rink, one of my chums was not what you might call an expert. On end of the rink was a buffet, which he found himself making a bee-line for. Unable to stop, he sat down with a bump and shot right through the panelling of the buffet counter with an awful crash. When we went to his rescue, we saw a heap of cakes, buns, steaming coffee, and a lot of arms and legs. My word! I shall never forget it.

Proper march weather here at present with a lot of Easterly winds. I think we should be on the move now.

Let me have a photo as soon as you get one of you please.

No more news at present, so will close trusting this little epistle will find you as it leaves me at present.

I remain, yours faithfully
Jim

On 1 April, four days after his twentieth birthday, James was promoted to Sergeant and placed in charge of all the engines in C Flight. James had earned his promotion on sheer merit, but his rapid rise caused some ill feeling amongst some of the older, non-technical NCOs in the squadron, whose knowledge of engines and airframes was far inferior to his.

By the first week of May, the Morane in which Conran had been wounded had been repaired and was ready for use. James went up with Corbett-Wilson on its first test and reported that the climb was now extraordinary. However, on 10 May, Corbett-Wilson, with Woodiwiss as observer, failed to return from a reconnaissance. A German machine later dropped a note confirming that Corbett-Wilson and Woodiwiss had been shot down by an anti-aircraft battery at Fournes, and that both were dead. This battery was well known and respected by the pilots and observers of 3 Squadron: they had nicknamed the gunner 'the ninety-year-old-gunner' as he was such a good shot.

On 2 May, James was ordered to report to the adjutant of the squadron who mutely handed him a telegram. It was the devastating news that his brother Bill had been killed in a flying accident while instructing at Gosport.[17] Hardly taking in the news, James stumbled out of the orderly room, made his way to the rear of the hangers and read the telegram again. One of the pilots found him there a little later, crying inconsolably and offered what comfort he could.[18]

James later wrote to Addie. 'I could not get leave to go to my brother's funeral… I am sure he would have preferred to go the way he did to any other as he lived for flying.'

At the end of May, the squadron's much respected and loved commanding officer, Major John Salmond, relinquished command to Major D S Lewis.[19]

On 1 June, 3 Squadron moved to Lozinghem, near Auchel. The squadron were sorry to move as they had settled in well at Gonneham: the people of the village were very hospitable, especially the owners of the comfortable farm where C Flight was billeted. After seeing the machines safely off, James travelled to the new aerodrome by road. Motoring along the Lillers road, James realised that he had no idea as to the exact whereabouts of the aerodrome at Lozinghem and pulled up to have a look round. On his left, to the south, about four miles away, he could see the tail of a Morane standing vertically, silhouetted against the sky like a signpost. Keeping the Morane in sight they finally arrived at their destination. Their signpost was a machine that had overshot the landing ground and had ended, tail up, on top of a bank.

The aerodrome – that James called Auchel but was officially Lozinghem – was in the mining area of France, the 'black country' above Souchez and Lens. A long straight road ran alongside the landing field, bordered by rows of miners' cottages, some unoccupied, potential billets both for the

Max Immelmann.

officers and men and the various offices of the squadron. By nightfall the hangers and tents and all been erected. It had been a hot, summer's day and James was glad to turn into his tent, only to find it was infested with earwigs. Ever resourceful, he chased them out with the aid of a syringe filled with petrol. However, he soon found a new billet, in a cottage used by the wireless section of the squadron where the other occupants soon became accustomed to his early morning rising routine: singing an accompaniment to a favourite record played on his portable gramophone.

The view from the aerodrome was superb. Being on high ground, it gave a clear view of the surrounding countryside. On clear evenings the La Bassée canal could be seen, and the movements of British machines easily followed by the German anti-aircraft bursts.

At Lozinghem James began to fly regularly on operations as an observer, and towards the end of June both he and Webb were recommended for a course of flying instruction. Webb was accepted and went off to Le Crotoy in early July but James was not so lucky, being considered too valuable to spare because of his skill with engines. James was extremely disappointed but as always he philosophically accepted the decision, taking comfort from the work and responsibility of his daily work. He had some consolation at the end of July, when he was officially tested for his suitability as an observer. Given a map and taking off with Harvey-Kelly, he was directed to fly a roughly circular course: Béthune, Lillers, Aire, Hazebrouck, Cassel, Armentières, Merville, Béthune and home. With his exceptional eyesight, map reading skills and his location awareness – later to become a byword in the RFC – James had no difficulty in passing the test and was qualified to train as an observer, in addition to his daily work on engines. Surprisingly, despite these distractions, James was frustrated by the monotony of the daily work, writing to his youngest sister, Kitty: 'It is very monotonous being out here – the same thing day after day. Please remember me to any fair maidens I know.'

James had now been eleven months in France, and in the middle of July he was given ten days welcome and well deserved leave. In all his time in France, in common with the other men and NCOs of the squadron, he had not had one day off from duty 'not even on a Sunday' and the daily workload had given little opportunity for even spare time.

Returning to Lozinghem after his leave, James flew his first operational flight as an official observer on 1 August, taking off in a Morane with Lieutenant R.A. Saunders[20] to look for a German machine which was directing its artillery onto the British trenches north of the Bois de Biez.

As they reached their height and approached the front lines, James began to wonder just what aerial combat would be like: what would happen if he or Saunders were shot; what would happen to the enemy if they shot him first. However, he put these thoughts out of his head and concentrated on the job in hand, attending to his Lewis gun and making sure the extra two drums of ammunition were to hand.

Arriving at the lines the enemy aeroplane was seen as a speck in the distant sky, at about the same height, flying a reciprocal course from east to west on its spotting duties. When the Morane had closed the distance to within half a mile, the enemy pilot saw them and turned east. As they set off in pursuit, James could distinctly see the large black crosses on the top wings of the enemy machine, but it was obviously faster than the Morane, and after a while Saunders turned back. However, during the chase they had flown a considerable distance east of the trenches; they were now well over German held territory and were beginning to be a target for Archie, which was making good shooting at them. As Saunders turned west, James ascertained where the most troublesome battery was and opened up with his Lewis from 5,000ft. The German gunners seemed not to mind this at all and continued firing, 'much to our discomfort'. Regaining the safety of the British side of the lines, and avoiding any further fire from Archie, Saunders and James patrolled for a while in case the German pilot resumed his duties, but as he declined to do so they returned to Lozinghem. After they had landed they were told that the enemy pilot had returned, and was now again working over the lines. 'This was most annoying of course, but the incident will just illustrate to the uninitiated one little thing that we were up against in trying to stop the German from directing his artillery.'[21]

At the end of August a Sergeant Pilot Watts[22] was posted to 3 Squadron and allotted to C Flight. James soon discovered that Watts was a superb pilot of the unstable Moranes and had many flights with him, during which Watts allowed him to take control. In this way, James gained some invaluable experience in piloting, especially because the Morane, being extremely sensitive fore and aft, enabled him to early develop a firm but light touch on the controls.

*

In July 1915, 11 Squadron, equipped with the Vickers FB5, had arrived in France. The Vickers was a two-seater pusher aeroplane, a configuration with an uninterrupted view forwards, which allowed a Lewis gun to be fired from the nacelle. The arrival of the Vickers – colloquially known as the Gunbus – gave the RFC virtual control of the air. By September, aerial fighting had became more common, and the pilots and observer/gunners of the Vickers constantly engaged the German two-seater aeroplanes, with some success.

The whole concept of fighting in the air was now to take on an entirely different aspect, which would fundamentally change the whole concept of aerial warfare and air power. With the war now static, with the trenches stretching from the Belgian coast to the Swiss border, the role of the reconnaissance aircraft was now of prime importance and it became necessary for each of the combatants to destroy them – to deny the enemy his eyes in the sky. It naturally followed that the task would fall to fast, well-armed aeroplanes, in essence, fighters. Each side would therefore have to protect its reconnaissance aircraft from fighter attack by attacking and destroying the enemy's fighters with its own. It logically followed that the fighter aeroplane had three main tasks: to destroy the enemy's observation machines; to protect its own by attacking and destroying the enemy fighters; and to escort its own observation machines to protect them from attacks by enemy fighters that had evaded its standing patrols. By the summer of 1915, the age of the fighter aeroplane had arrived.

In February 1915, Lieutenant-Colonel Brooke-Popham,[23] realising the importance of destroying the enemy observation machines, had issued a set of notes and recommendations for fighting in the air, pointing out that the moral effect of a fast machine, however skillfully handled, was very small if no effective weapon of offence were carried. Brooke-Popham recognised that a gun was the most effective way of attacking the enemy, but that only a revolver should be carried by the pilot of a single-seater and a rifle by the observer in a two-seater, arguing that the weight of a machine gun would adversely affect the performance of the aircraft then in use. Despite Brooke-Popham's reservations, Lewis guns began to be mounted on some machines, with various makeshift and experimental mountings, and an expert in the use of the gun was detailed to tour all the squadrons of the RFC to instruct the pilots and observers in the art of deflection shooting and other skills.

Immelmann stands by the remains of his seventh victory, Morane Parasol Type LA. No.5087 of 3 Squadron, shot down on 15 December 1915, after it had been taken to Valenciennes.

The early attempts at destroying the enemy's aeroplanes were frustrated by the difficulty of aiming accurately. A Lewis gun mounted on the Bristol scouts was angled outwards at an angle to miss hitting the propeller, which called for considerable skill – and luck – on the part of the pilot, both in flying ability and marksmanship.[24] The obvious solution was to be able to fire a machine gun through the propeller, aiming the entire aeroplane as a gun, in line with the pilot's line of sight, but no successful means to do this had yet been devised.

On 1 April 1915, Lt. Roland Garros, a pilot serving with the French *Escadrille de chasse* NS12, flying a Morane-Saulnier Type L Parasol, shot down a German Albatros two-seater. The Morane's propeller was protected by steel deflector plates, designed by Jules Hue, Garros's mechanic. Exploiting this initial success, Garros shot down three enemy aeroplanes in eighteen days, but on 18 April the Morane was hit by anti-aircraft fire and Garros was forced to land behind enemy lines. Examining the Morane – Garros had unsuccessfully attempted to set it on fire – the Germans at once realised the reason he had been so successful, and were quick to realise the potential of a fighter aeroplane which could fire along its line of flight. Their first attempt to emulate the method of deflector plates was unsuccessful – it was both a makeshift and dangerous solution to the problem – and a Parabellum LMG14 machine gun was issued to Antony Fokker, a Dutch aeroplane designer and manufacturer who was working for Germany, with instructions to design an efficient interrupter gear which would enable a fixed gun to fire through the propeller.

In 1913, a Swiss-born engineer, Franz Schneider, technical director and chief designer of the German LVG aeroplane company, had patented a device for an interrupter gear, his conception being that the firing of the gun should be interrupted if the blade of the propeller was in the line of fire.

Details of Schneider's design had been published in the German aviation magazine *Flugsport*. Fokker's engineers, Luebbe and Heber, were familiar with Schneider's design and within a week Antony Fokker was demonstrating to the German *Feldflugchef* a gun synchronisation gear fitted to a Fokker M5K, a single-seat tractor monoplane of his own design, hoping to sell both the aeroplane and the gun interrupter gear. Fokker was successful in this and the *Feldflugchef* placed an immediate order for fifty Fokker monoplanes armed with the synchronisation gear. By July 1915, eleven especially selected pilots from the two-seater units, Feldflieger Abteilungen, were flying the new fighters.

On 15 July 1915, *Leutnant* Kurt Wintgens[25] of *Flieger Abteilung* 48, flying one of the new Fokker fighters, shot down a French Morane, the first in a long series of victories by the emerging German fighter pilots flying the Fokker E.III. The RFC suffered its first loss at the hands of the Fokker pilots on 1 August. *Leutnant* Max Immelmann[26] of *Flieger Abteilung* 62, scored his first aerial victory, forcing down a BE2c from 2 Squadron.

On 13 September, James wrote to Addie, now living in Portsmouth, a short, almost perfunctory letter.

'I am pleased to hear you are having a great time. I wish I was with you. The weather is simply topping. I envy you your sea dips. I very much enjoy a sea bathe.

'There has been a good deal of fighting here lately. I am afraid the war will last a long time yet. Sorry to say I have not much news this week.'

He followed this with a longer letter on the 21st.

Many thanks for your letter of the 16th inst. Am pleased to know that you are having a good time.

We are getting topping weather at present.

I hope to go away to obtain my certificate soon. If I do I

The crew of Morane No.5087, both killed. Left: A.V. Hobbs (pilot) Right: C.E.G Tudor-Jones (Obs).

shall probably spend this winter in England. I wish the war would hurry up and finish. Things will seem tame after the war though. Some people who survive the war will be paying others to shoot at them just to relieve the monotony. Also aviators will go up and allow their own 'Archie' to shell them for the sake of giving the gunners practice. The German anti-aircraft gunners are hot stuff, and usually get our machines' height in the first few shots, the higher we fly the more accurate does their shooting seem. You see, so many of our machines are constantly over the lines, that the Hun gunners are always getting practice. Our gunners do not seem to have much success at Zep strafing. I suppose it is because they do not get much practice in the daytime.

We had a machine hit not long ago at 11,500ft, nearly two miles high or over rather. Still, 'Archies' might only be pea-shooters for all the notice most of our pilots take of them.

No more news at present so must conclude, trusting you will write soon.

Yrs very sincerely
Jim

*

On 25 September the British First Army attacked between Lens and La Bassée on the first day of the Battle of Loos. As a component of 1st Wing, 3 Squadron was fully engaged with reconnaissance work and ranging for the artillery. The day was fine and sunny at first, but towards the evening, rain set in and the machines became 'rather wet'. On the second day of the battle, Sergeant Burns was fatally wounded by shrapnel while signaling from a shell hole to a machine of the squadron flying above the battle. James commented: '…and so died another of the gallant little band of the original 3 Squadron.'[27]

On 10 October, 2nd Lieutenant Johnson[28] and his observer Corporal Roberts,[29] were flying a photo reconnaissance when they were attacked by a Fokker E.III. Roberts was hit in the thigh, but they evaded the Fokker and returned to Lozinghem. James was on the aerodrome when they landed, helped Roberts from the Morane, and took him hospital.

The squadron's next casualties were Sergeant Francis Courtney,[30] an NCO pilot, and his observer, Sergeant George Thornton.[31] On 21 October, without the sanction of their Flight Commander, they set off, armed with a Lewis gun, hand grenades, *flêchettes*, plus, for good measure, a Very Light pistol, to attack an enemy balloon over Salomé. During their attack, they were attacked by a Fokker E.III. Thornton was hit in the hand, his face was grazed by a bullet, and while getting out his rifle, he was hit in the other hand. Courtney dived for the lines but was hit in the leg, with another bullet stopping the engine. Luckily, a BE2c arrived, joined in the fight, and the Fokker pilot broke off the action.

James wrote to Addie on the 27th telling her that the squadron was not doing much flying due to the bad weather. He was now more pessimistic regards the progress of the war: 'The whole war seems a complete mix up.' He seems to have been equally downhearted about his personal prospects. 'If I am lucky I may get some leave before Xmas, that is, of course, assuming that I do not get a course of flying before.'

The Moranes of 3 Squadron were now coming under frequent attacks from enemy two-seaters and the occasional Fokker monoplane, but they had one Morane Type N (5067) single-seat fighter on charge and were also carrying the fight to the enemy. On 28 November, Lieutenant Henderson,[32] flying the Morane, attacked an Albatros two-seater at 8,000ft over Vendin-Le-Vieil and drove it down to 1,500ft. However, the observer in the two-seater, armed with a rifle, hit Henderson in the eye, forcing him to break off the action. Despite being almost blinded by blood from his wounded eye, he managed to return to Lozinghem and made a good landing.

On 15 December, detailed to fly a long reconnaissance to the railway centre at Valenciennes, which passed close to the German aerodrome at Douai, home of the Fokker pilots, 2nd Lieutenant A.V. Hobbs[33] and his observer 2nd Lieutenant C.E.G. Tudor-Jones[34] were shot down and killed by Max Immelmann for his seventh victory.

James was now making regular flights over the lines as an observer, accumulating valuable experience. At the end of November he began to record these flights in a red-covered Hatchett school exercise book. The first entry detailed a two-hour forty-minute flight with Major Ludlow-Hewitt[35] on 27 November, directing artillery, repeated the following day with the additional excitement of chasing a two-seater Albatros for fifteen minutes. In the first two weeks of December, James flew eight patrols, directing artillery fire and patrolling, sometimes twice a day, with various pilots of the squadron. Ludlow-Hewitt, who had taken over command of the squadron on 2 November, was so impressed by the keenness and reliability of James – the youngest of his observer NCOs – that whenever possible he chose James to fly with him.

Flying so often, it was now only a matter of time before James experienced his first combat in the air. When he did, on 19 December, it was with the redoubtable Immelmann.

Wing still needed information of the movement of the railway traffic at Valenciennes. It was essential that the unsuccessful long reconnaissance, on which Hobbs and Trevor-Jones had been shot down by Immelmann on 15 December, was attempted again, and Wing ordered that it was to be flown as soon as possible. Conscious of the threat of the Fokkers, Ludlow-Hewitt decided that three machines should undertake the long flight, flying together for mutual protection, the first time the pilots of 3 Squadron had flown in formation.

On three consecutive days the weather was so bad that there was no flying and the strain of waiting began to play on the nerves of the pilots and observers. James, detailed to fly in the reconnaissance, had faith in the ability of his pilot, Lieutenant Saunders, and he knew he could shoot better than most, but his chief concern was the possibility of being forced to land behind the enemy lines by engine failure. Determined to have a good shot at repairing the engine if it failed and they had to land, he utilised the waiting time to thoroughly check the engine and gun mounting of the Morane, and packed his tools, plus some spare spark plugs and ignition wire.

On the morning of 19 December the weather had

Edgar Ramsey Ludlow-Hewitt.

improved: the morning was clear, bright with frost. At 9.30AM, three Moranes took off, led by Ludlow-Hewitt, the Morane of Saunders and James the last machine in the formation. The formation reached its height over Bethune, crossed the lines over Bois de Biez at 7,000ft, and immediately came under heavy and accurate anti-aircraft fire. Being the last machine, Saunders and James bore the brunt of the shells, one exploding under the fuselage of the Morane, severely 'bumping' it.

About five miles east of the front lines, Saunders pointed to his left: James saw 'a long brown form, simply streaking across the sky'. The German machine, a Fokker monoplane, climbed above and behind the middle machine of the formation, flown by Lieutenant Mealing,[36] and opened fire. Mealing quickly turned away, evading the attack, but not before his Morane had been hit in several places. The Fokker pilot now turned his attention to Saunders and James, coming at their Morane nose on and from slightly above. James stood up, put his Lewis gun to his shoulder and fired at the Fokker as it flashed by the right wing. The Fokker flew on and was lost from view.

The Morane formation was now over the enemy aerodrome at Douai. Looking down, James could see several machines taking off. While he was watching these he saw the Fokker

Two views of an attacking Fokker E.III as it must have been seen by James in his first aerial combat.

again, climbing up under the tail of the Morane. James told Saunders to turn and fired half a drum at the Fokker from three hundred yards. The Fokker pilot, surprised by having been seen, first turned away, then climbed to 300ft above the Morane and dived to attack again. James had been waiting: before the Fokker pilot opened fire, James again put the Lewis to his shoulder and fired a short burst. The German pilot quickly pulled out of his dive, abandoning his attack, and circled five hundred yards away, waiting for another opportunity, but each time he made as if to attack again, James gave him a short burst from his Lewis, keeping him at a distance. As the Moranes flew on to Valenciennes, this cat and mouse situation went on for twenty-five minutes, James firing short bursts of four or five shots every time the Fokker pilot seemed about to attack.

The Moranes finally reached Valenciennes and circled to ascertain the amount of railway rolling stock in the station. The formation then turned west for home. The Fokker was still keeping what James described as a 'respectable distance' doing vertical turns, but as the Moranes turned westwards it followed them '…just like a vulture, no doubt waiting for one of us to fall out with engine trouble'. As the Moranes reached Douai on the way back, the German pilot left them and landed on his aerodrome. James surmised that he was out of petrol. Passing over the enemy aerodrome, James saw numerous enemy two-seaters, flying at 8,000ft, unable to reach the height of the Moranes, and he gave two of them a drum each of Lewis 'for a present, but I'm sorry to say I had no luck'.

The Moranes all landed safely at 11.50AM – on inspection James machine was found to have over thirty shrapnel holes in it – and the pilots and observers climbed stiffly down and made for the squadron's office to make out their reports and discuss the morning's reconnaissance. In his report – the first of many he would make – James gave a remarkably accurate description of the Fokker and its estimated speed and also reported having seen a British Morane on the aerodrome at Douai.[37]

James, brimming with pride and confidence after his success in driving off the Fokker pilot and keeping him at his distance, had no qualms when Ludlow-Hewitt told him after lunch that he was to fly with him that afternoon.

Leaving the ground at 2.30PM, Ludlow-Hewitt made for the Auchy and La Bassée area. Although the morning had been fine, a leaden sky now threatened rain. Ludlow-Hewitt had almost finished his observations and James was busy sketching a new German trench he had seen, just north of La Bassée, when something made him look up from his sketch. A Fokker E.III was above them, just about to attack. James snatched up his Lewis gun, put it to his shoulder and fired, just as the Fokker was about to begin its dive. Ludlow-Hewitt, sensing by James's movements behind him that something was amiss, turned the Morane as James opened fire. The German pilot broke off his attack, then continually turned, twisting first one way then another, in an attempt to gain a position on the tail of the Morane, but Ludlow-Hewitt turned quicker and the German pilot finally gave up and flew east. As he left James could see that he was sitting very high in his machine and was wearing a black flying suit.

On 20 December 1915, still excited by the events of the day before and elated by his successful tactics against the dreaded Immelmann, James wrote to his mother.

20.12.1915
B.E.F
Dear Mother,

Just a line as a kind of thanksgiving. Yesterday, Lt Saunders and myself as observer, and two other machines, had to do a long reconnaissance a good distance behind the German lines. We left our aerodrome at 8.0AM(sic) and crossed the lines at about 8.30, ours being the last machine of the three. Well, the Hun ' Archies ' gave us a very warm time. Each of our machines had two machine guns, one for the pilot and one for the observer, and 400 rounds of ammunition each. Well, we had barely crossed the line when my pilot pointed out a very fast monoplane streaking after our second machine, which was about half a mile in front of us. The monoplane turned out to be a German 'Fokker' piloted by the dreaded Lt. 'Immelmann'. As soon as he got within 100 yards of our middle machine, he dived just like a hawk at them, firing as he dived. However, he found them ready for him, so he turned round and came over us like a flash, with the black crosses on his fuselage as plain as daylight. I managed to get half a dozen rounds at him as he passed. He then turned and followed us at a distance of about 300 yards, and little higher. I had him like that for about 25

Rupert Henry Steinbach Mealing.

minutes, and kept him off with bursts of 4 or 5 shots every time he attempted to come nearer. Mind you, all this time we were over hostile territory and up at 8,000 feet. However, we reached our objective, got the required information, and turned homewards, still with the Fokker following us up. When we had nearly got to our lines the Fokker turned away, but two large 'Albatroses' joined in the chase, but having the speed of them we soon left them after firing about 50 rounds at them (Reads like a fairy tale, don't it?)

We then reached the lines and ' Archie ' gave us another warm time, and all three machines landed safely again on our aerodrome at 10.15AM, having spent about 2hrs 15mins in the air, and fully an hour and a half over hostile country. We then examined our machines and found that the machine the Fokker had dived on had been struck by about twenty bullets all round the pilot's and passenger's seats, although the Hun had only fired a burst of 30 rounds, which shows what a marvelous shot he must be. The machine I went in had 36 holes in it from shrapnel from 'Archie'. One beast burst right under our tail and nearly blew me out of my seat.

The Major was very pleased we got back safely, as we did the same reconnaissance that Lt. Hobbs and Jones were on when they were brought down by 'Immelmann'. At 2PM I had to go up with the Major, and was sketching in some new trenches at about 3.30, and previous to this I had not seen a machine

Tone Paul Hippolyte Bayetto with a Morane-Saulnier Type N. Bayetto was a popular officer in the RFC, not least because his father, head chef at one of London's leading hotels, was always happy to give any of his son's RFC comrades a superb meal, free of charge.

of any description as the weather was dull, and I happened to glance around and saw that beast 'Immelmann' in his beastly 'Fokker' about a hundred yards behind us, and a little higher, preparing to dive. I do not believe I ever moved so quickly in all my life. I dropped my maps on the floorboard, and grabbed hold of my machine gun and fired at him from my shoulder, as the machine guns we use are very light and we use them in the machines just like rifles, and also the position I was in I could not use the gun in its proper mounting. Directly the Major heard me firing he turned to the left, and put a steep bank on and started spinning like a top, so as to put 'Immelmann' off his aim. By this time 'Immelmann' was firing as well, and about a hundred feet above us. In one position he passed over us and I was able to get some good shots in at him, and we then had the satisfaction of seeing a large piece of paper or map fall from the 'Fokker'. After that he turned away and made for his own aerodrome. We then finished our work and arrived back at the aerodrome at 4.25.

I am very pleased with my work yesterday – 4 hrs 40mins in the air and two fights with the famous 'Immelmann'. I do not think he will catch me napping again, because I now know what quarter to expect him from (the back). One cannot help admiring the man because his handling of his machine, which does about 100mph, is simply superb.

Well, I think I have given you enough thrills for the present. I think I am being excused all duty and work to enable me to devote all my attention on observing. I might add that the sergeants here are most of them as jealous of me as anything, just because I am getting on well. Anyway, I don't give two pins for any one of them. The fact that I have done about 16 hours in air with this new Major does not half stick in their gills, so they try to say sarcastic things, which ends in me hitting one of them on the nose and telling him to hold that while I fetch a policeman (please laugh).

A new Sergeant pilot has arrived here named Bayetto[38] who knew Will at Gosport. He is chummy with me and is very musical, having his MA for both violin and piano. He is splendid on piano.

We have got up a concert for Boxing Night and have got 25 turns up to the present. We are alright for Xmas in our Mess and going to have a good time.

Sergeant Bayetto is shortly getting his commission I believe. He is a good pilot, and took his brevet as far back as April 1912.

I hope and trust Cis and her son are well. I shall let you know as soon as I receive the parcels.

Lt. Saunders was up in his machine this afternoon over the aerodrome at about 2,000ft when the bus caught fire. He

A Morane-Saulnier Type BB.

brought her down safely and just singed his nose a little! The machine burnt a lot after reaching the ground and we are condemning it.

I must now conclude, hoping all at home will have as happy an Xmas as circumstances will admit, and trusting this finds all well as it leaves me at present.

Your loving son,
Jim

PS. You will often see 'Immelmann' mentioned in the German official news in the Daily Mail – Jim.

7.15AM. 21st Dec.
PS. Enclosed are some stamps that may be of use to you. I had a dozen sent to me as balance of some cigarettes I sent for. I kept the letter about a week, and then tore up all the letters I had accumulated for about a week, and also tore up the one up with the stamps in, forgetting they were there.

Also please send me out two pairs of cycling stockings for use with my flying boots. Please send the sort with nice fancy edges, but not too loud. Any colour will do. There will be no flying today as it is raining cats and dogs. Please send out soon, as I am flying on every good day, and it is jolly cold I may mention.

Goodbye for the present
Jim[39]

Writing many years after the events of 19 December 1915, Air Chief Marshal Ludlow-Hewitt wrote:

"I was wholly engaged in ranging a battery of heavy howitzers on something or other when McCudden suddenly broke in by excitedly directing my attention to a little monoplane, with a little black head and shoulders sticking out of it. We both knew what that was.

"The encounter was quite an undramatic affair except in relation to McCudden's future career. The Fokker was away up on our right, travelling at an impressive speed. The best plan for the rabbit in such circumstances was to try to baffle the fighter by waiting for the dive, and then go into the tightest possible turn and stay there, and that is what I did.

"But I was soon made to understand that this manoeuvre was not at all pleasing to my gunner, who was banging on the fuselage and urgently signaling to me to flatten out, to give him a better chance of shooting at the other chap, but a manoeuvre that could favour the fighter. However, it was no time for argument and so I reluctantly straightened out and McCudden let fly with his Lewis gun. Whether it was his good shooting, or whether the German concluded we were too wide awake to be easy meat, I do not know, but anyway he sheered off eastward and went away at high speed, very much to my relief and to McCudden's disgust.

A Morane-Saulnier Type LA in 3 Squadron. The man on the left is James.

"Many of our casualties at this time were said to be due to the crew failing to detect the approach of the enemy fighter, but McCudden was not to be caught out in this way.

"And so McCudden, soon to become a famous fighter ace himself, won his first air fight and that against the most noted of all the German aces. After that there was no holding him, and he never left me in peace.

"My squadron was an army co-operation unit and it was understood that when ranging a battery you kept at it until the job was done. The army gunners rightly resented the airman going off on his own devices in the middle of a shoot, leaving him high and dry. But my air gunner had quite different views: to him every 'Hun' that he spotted was by divine providence only there to be hunted by him. Occasionally when it was possible, I let him have his way, but it was always a waste of time, for all the German aircraft that came over the lines were a good bit faster than our Moranes. The frustration must have been hard for him.

"Although McCudden was a quiet, unassuming, essentially modest person, he was nonetheless one of those people who are not easily forgotten. He was far from being the glamorous, fire-eating hero of fiction, and yet there was about him an elusive distinction which somehow arose out of his naturally self-assured and serene disposition. He was a gentleman in the true and real meaning of the word. High principled, tolerant and very generous in his judgements of others, he had a natural modesty which I am sure remained untouched by his subsequent fame and success."

An indication of Ludlow-Hewitt's confidence in James and his judgement was his willingness to respond to James' request – order even – to come out of his turns in order to give James a chance of a shot at the Fokker. James was now fully confident in the air, with an acute sense of situational awareness, a skill that took many pilots some time to acquire. The two fights on 19 December mark an important step in his career, a precursor of things to come.

On Christmas Day 1915, there was no rest for the pilots and observers of the RFC. In the afternoon, Ludlow-Hewitt and James spent two hours over the Hohenzollern Redoubt and Fosse.

In the evening, following the army custom, all the sergeants of the squadron waited on the men at dinner. The sergeants then retired to their own Mess and had their own dinner, followed by the inevitable, light-hearted speech-making, then by recitations and jokes. Chief turn for these was James's particular friend, 'Fonso' Ellison,[40] whose rendering of his own version of the Rudyard Kipling's popular poem, Gunga Din, brought the house down with screams of laughter. James later recalled: 'Altogether, that Xmas of 1915 at Auchel was, I think, one of the very best I have ever spent.'[41]

On Boxing Day it was a return to the business of war. Ludlow-Hewitt and James spent three hours, flying at 1,500ft in a snowstorm, ranging for the 10th Siege Battery. The next day they repeated the duty for another two hours. James had now flown a great deal with Major Ludlow-Hewitt and intensely disliked being flown by any other pilot, his faith in Ludlow-Hewitt being such that: 'if he had said "Come to Berlin" I should have gone like a shot'.[42]

During the first month of 1916, James flew over fourteen patrols with various pilots. On 2 January he flew with Ludlow-

This Morane-Saulnier of 3 Squadron has 'Certainly Not' painted around its cowling, an admonishment to the German anti aircraft batteries: 'Archibald, certainly not!'

William Spurrett Fielding-Johnson.

Hewitt for two hours, ranging artillery near La Bassée, having the satisfaction of seeing enemy batteries at Salomé blown 'quite off the map, for a 9.2 high explosive shell is not to be despised at all when it gets going'.[43]

On the 5 January, two Moranes of the squadron – James flying with Bayetto – flew an escort for fifteen BE2cs of 2 Squadron to bomb the German aerodrome at Douai. After the raid, the formation was attacked by four Fokker E.IIIs. Seeing one of the enemy machines on the tail of a BE2c – the pilot was flying straight, seemingly unaware of any danger – James drove it off with a burst of Lewis from 300 yards. The enemy pilot then broke off the action and dived away. For once, James was quite content to see him go as the engine of the Morane had developed a nasty knock, later found to be a broken ball bearing.

On 11 January, James flew a patrol with Lieutenant R.J. Lillywhite[44] in a Morane Type BB Biplane. Powered by a 110hp Le Rhône, this was the first Morane BB type to be issued to the squadron: it had a higher performance than the squadron's Morane Parasols, was fast and had a very good rate of climb. Lillywhite and James patrolled for two hours between La Bassée and Lens, looking for enemy aircraft, but the very rough weather forced them to return. James commented on the new Morane in his diary: 'Very fast and good climber, but very bad in rough weather.'

On 12 January, James was to experience his first crash. Returning after a patrol with Ludlow-Hewitt, the undercarriage of the Morane BB collapsed on landing and it overturned. Neither James nor Ludlow-Hewitt were hurt, but the Morane was wrecked.

January 19 started badly, a pattern of events which was to repeat itself during the day. Detailed to fly as escort for a reconnaissance flight to Lille later in the day, Lieutenant H.R. Johnson flew his Morane in a thirty minute local flight test to Bapaume. On returning to Lozinghem, unhappy with the result of the test, Johnson flew another test of fifteen minutes, during which the engine seized.

The first decoration. James receiving his *Croix de Guerre* from *General* Joffre. 21 January 1916, Lillers, France.

At 10.30AM, five Moranes left the ground to fly a reconnaissance from Don to Lille, Johnson flying a replacement Morane with James in the rear seat. The formation crossed the front lines to the west of La Bassée at 6,000ft, flew to Don, then turned north. A little south of Haubourdin, James saw an enemy Albatros coming up behind the Moranes. He was surprised that the enemy machine was rapidly overhauling the formation, as the Moranes were thought to be as fast as any enemy aeroplane – with the exception of the Fokker monoplanes. To discourage the enemy pilot, James took some long-range shots with his rifle at the Albatros, reserving his Lewis gun for later. Undeterred, the German pilot came on. At two hundred yards James opened fire with his Lewis, but after firing only two shots the Lewis seized with a severe jam. The Albatros came to within fifty yards, flew in front of the Morane, then turned to fly abreast, the observer in the rear cockpit opening fire. James, his Lewis now inoperative, got off several fifteen rounds rapid with his rifle. This soon expended his rifle ammunition and he was forced to take cartridges, one by one, from his Lewis gun. The German pilot repeated this tactic three times, giving his gunner ample opportunity to fire at the Morane, hitting it in the wings several times. Johnson had flown straight during the attacks, taking no evasive action, but as they came over Quesnoy, nearer to the British front lines, the enemy pilot broke off his attack and turned away, much to the relief of James. However, their troubles were not yet over. Gliding in to land at Lozinghem, Johnson found that his controls were jammed – some empty cartridge cases had got under the rocking lever of the control column – but fortunately these were quickly cleared away and they landed safely.

However, the day was finally to end in tragedy for Johnson. Taking off in the afternoon to fly an artillery patrol, the Morane stalled at a hundred feet and crashed, only five yards from where James was standing watching the takeoff. The unconscious observer, Captain W.S. Fielding-Johnson,[45] was extricated from the wreckage, with only minor injuries, but Harold Johnson was found to be dead.

On the morning of 21 January, James was told that he had been awarded the French Croix de Guerre. That afternoon he travelled to Lillers to receive the medal from the French commander in chief, General Joffre. Paraded in a bleak field, on a bitterly cold day, with a biting easterly wind, six British NCOs and men waited three hours for Joffre to arrive and present the awards.

James flew only two more patrols in 3 Squadron. On 22 January, a flight was cut short after only five minutes in the air by the machine 'behaving badly'. The last patrol James was to fly as a member of 3 Squadron was a shoot, ranging for artillery north of La Bassée. Flying with Lieutenant Mealing, James saw a German observation machine, west of the British trenches,

On Leave, February 1916. Now a Flight Sergeant, James on his Rex. The pillion passenger is his sister Mary (Cis).

but at 9,000ft well above the Morane. Mealing, no doubt urged on by James, gave chase, but the enemy machine easily outclimbed the Morane and they last saw it gliding east. Mealing then flew north and patrolled the area of Givenchy, La Bassée and Violanes. There were a number of enemy machines in the air – James particularly remembered two brown ones sitting over La Bassée the whole afternoon – but Mealing, having finished their shoot, returned, landing in time 'for a nice big tea'.

On January 24, boyhood dreams were at last realised: orders came through for Sergeant James Thomas Byford McCudden to leave for Home Establishment for training as a pilot. James left 3 Squadron on the last day of the month, was promoted to Flight Sergeant the following day, and left for England for a well-deserved fortnight's leave. His delight in leaving for home to train as a pilot was tempered by sadness at leaving 3 Squadron. He later wrote: 'I often look back and think what a splendid squadron No.3 was. We had a magnificent set of officers, and the NCOs and men were as one family.'

Outside the family home in Kingston-upon-Thames: James solo on his Rex.

Ch.6: Fledgling Instructor & NCO Pilot

A Henry Farman F.20. James took his first flying instruction on this type in February 1916.

On 20 February 1916, after a fortnight's leave, which James 'enjoyed immensely,' he reported to the Royal Aircraft Park at Farnborough. The Park held many memories, some happy, some less so. It was here that Lt. Baron James had taken the young recruit for his first flight, but also where James had spent five anxious days in the guard room after his adventure with the unruly Caudron, fearful that he would be sent back to his regiment.

In the early days of flying instruction, the pupil, seated behind the pilot, was expected to watch and note the effect of the various controls as they were operated by his instructor, then progressing to placing his hands over those of the instructor to get the 'feel' of the aeroplane. By 1916, flying instruction methods had improved considerably: dual controls were now in use, although there were still no means of communication between the instructor and his pupil other than by hand signals and shouting.

James began his training on the morning of 22 February with a twenty minute flight in Henry Farman No.294.[1] It was a cold day with disconcerting gusts of wind making for a very bumpy flight, but his instructor, Sergeant-Major W.B. Power,[2] soon realised that this particular new pupil was out of the ordinary run of would-be pilots, thoroughly at home in the air and both apt and responsive to the feel of the Farman. This was hardly surprising. James had now flown over a hundred hours as a passenger – with twenty-five different pilots – including forty-six hours as an observer. In addition, his unofficial instruction by Sergeant Watts on the extremely sensitive Moranes of 3 Squadron had already given him that essential 'feel'. With his vast amount of knowledge gained as a mechanic – plus no doubt that 1911 Flight manual, studied on the Rock – James was also exceptionally well versed in the theory of flight.

That first flight covered the basics of control and two days later Power gave James a forty-five minute lesson, carrying out straights and six landings. Unfortunately that same afternoon the Farman – the only instructional Farman at Farnborough – was written off in a crash by another pupil, but even at this early stage of his instruction Power was confident enough in James's progress and abilities to carry on with his instruction the next day on a 80hp Gnome-powered Avro 504A.[3] The Avro was considerably faster and more powerful than the sedate Farman but the lesson passed without incident, with a further six landings and straights. At this point, James' luck ran out. Another pupil completely wrecked the Avro, putting it in the repair shops for a month. Unlike the CFS and other flying schools, where officer students were trained, Farnborough was not a regular training aerodrome, but was used for the training of those NCOs who been picked as suitable for pilot training. The loss of both the Avro and Farman meant that there were no other aeroplanes available for instruction and James was forced to curb his impatience until they were repaired. James wrote to Addie on 27 February,

> I am now at Farnboro (sic) learning to fly. I expect to go out to France again in about three months time, as an aeroplane pilot. I am learning to fly on a 80 horse-power Avro biplane. It does about 80 miles per hour and is a splendid machine.

We have several captured German machines here which we are using.⁽⁴⁾

In the event, it was the Avro which was serviceable first. On 28 February, his twenty-first birthday, James recommenced his instruction, again with Power, flying straights and landings for twenty minutes. These were repeated the following day, this time for forty-five minutes. On 30 March, during James's sixth lesson, Power varied the routine with circuits and landings. Landing at the end of the lesson, Power climbed down and nonchalantly told James to take off again, on his own.

James got off the ground safely, but later had no recollection of what happened once he was airborne. He had only a vague recollection that he had sat quite still, flying automatically, until he landed, a landing that was spectacular in itself. James had seen too many accidents caused by pilots' stalling on either take off or landing – and no doubt had his brother's accident in mind. He was determined that he would not stall on his first solo and flew the Avro onto the ground, tail up, at 70mph, well above it's normal landing speed.⁽⁵⁾

Power seemed 'quite pleased' and James was both relieved and delighted: 'Oh that feeling when one has done one's first solo. One imagines oneself so frightfully important.'⁽⁶⁾

This was James's last flight at Farnborough. Later that same day he was posted to No.1 Reserve Squadron. On 9 April, he was posted again: to 41 Squadron, which was working up to strength at Fort Grange, Gosport, travelling there with Walter Webb who had served with him in 3 Squadron's C Flight.

On 11 April, James resumed instruction under Sergeant Maurice W. Piercey.⁽⁷⁾ Piercey was a pre-war regular soldier, who had gone to France in August 1914. Known in the sergeants' Mess as 'Tich' he was a short, red-headed, cheerful character, popular with all. A short flight of ten minutes in Maurice Farman Shorthorn No.7361 was enough to show Piercey that James was ready to take his Royal Aero Club certificate, but for some unexplained reason Piercey then seems to have completely forgotten him and it was not until five days later, on 16 April, that Piercey suddenly announced that James was to fly the test for his RAeC certificate that day.

After a short local flight of ten minutes in Maurice Farman Longhorn No.6700 to allow James to get the feel of the Longhorn – a type he had not flown before – followed by another five minutes of circuits and landings, James took off on his first official solo flight of fifteen minutes. Landing from this, James then successfully flew the RAeC test: two figures of eight, followed by shutting down his engine and gliding down from twelve hundred feet, then completing two further figures of eight before landing within forty yards of the assigned mark. His total time under instruction had been four hours, plus forty minutes of solo.⁽⁸⁾

After obtaining his certificate, James made a further twenty two flights in the various Farmans at the school – climbing to 7,000ft in one – until 28 April, when he was posted to the Central Flying School at Netheravon, flying there on 3 May in Maurice Farman Shorthorn No.480, which he found 'sloppy'.

William Boyle Power.

Later in the day, flying the same Farman, he successfully flew the CFS test for a Pilot Second Class, his certificate No.107, dated 7 May 1916.

The original purpose for the posting to the CFS had been for training as a scout pilot – as fighter pilots were then known – but James's arrival there coincided with complaints from General Trenchard, General Officer Commanding of the RFC in France, that replacement pilots being received by the squadrons in France were both insufficiently trained and experienced. An expansion and lengthening of the training programme meant that more instructors were needed and many of the more promising pupils, James among them, were assigned the duty despite their own small number of flying hours.

On 3 May, having a solo flying time of exactly nine hours five minutes, James took up his first pupil, a Lt. Sloane,⁽⁹⁾ for a forty-five minute instructional flight in Maurice Farman No.4019. The following day he gave four more instructional flights. On 5 May one of his four pupils during the day was a young officer seconded from the Royal Warwickshire regiment, Lieutenant Geoffrey Hilton Bowman,⁽¹⁰⁾ who was later to serve with James in 29 Squadron and as a fellow Flight Commander in 56 Squadron.

An Avro 504A.

Over the following months, until 3 August, the sheer slog of instructional flying went relentlessly on, day after day, the routine only broken by the occasional drama, as on 17 May, when one of the Longhorn's tyres burst on taxying, sending it into a stack of asbestos sheeting, twisting an undercarriage skid and breaking two of its many struts. Neither James nor his pupil, a Lieutenant Glew, were hurt.

On 18 May, James flew a DH.1[11] for the first time, with a pupil named Ellis in the passenger seat. At 4,000ft, James was demonstrating a left-hand turn to Ellis, when the de Havilland suddenly began to behave in a strange way, and 'felt no more like a flying machine than a red brick. I knew we were going round and round one way, but did not know why.' It was James's first spin. More by instinct than knowledge, James jammed on opposite rudder and the DH came out of the spin. The gyrations had been seen from the aerodrome, the emergency vehicles started and preparations made for a serious crash, but by the time James had landed he had regained his *sang-froid*, leaping lightly from the nacelle and laughingly asking the astonished ground crew: 'How's that for a stunt?' The effect on Ellis was not recorded. At this time the spin was a relatively unknown phenomenon and few pilots knew how to recover from it. This early experience was later to stand James in good stead.

On 24 May, James flew the DH.1 again, this time with a Captain Riddel in the passenger seat. James had now flown nearly sixty hours, well over the official time of fifteen hours required by RFC HQ of a squadron pilot, and this was the first part of the test for his *Brevêt* as a First Class Pilot. James easily completed the test, climbing to 6,000ft and flying for thirty-five minutes. On 27 May he undertook the second part of the test, a two-hour flight at 4,000ft, via Salisbury, Southampton, and Basingstoke, landing back at Netheravon with an engine-off touch down within a fifty-yard diameter circle. His *Brevêt* was awarded on 30 May.

James would remain at Netheravon until he was posted to France in July. During his period at Netheravon, from 3 May to 5 July, he had given 169 instruction flights to no less than fifty-two student pilots, and had amassed a personal flying time of 115 hours 50 minutes. This was far in excess of the early service pilots, and would prove to be of inestimable value in the months that followed.

*

The war in the air had changed considerably in the seven months that James had been in England. In the late spring and early summer of 1915, with the Vickers FB5 – the Gunbus – dominating the Arras front, the RFC had enjoyed air superiority, but by October 1915 it had began to suffer heavy casualties at the hands of the Fokker pilots. At the beginning of 1916 these had reached such an unacceptable level that on 14 January RFC HQ issued an order that until a machine capable of combating the Fokker was available, any machine proceeding on a reconnaissance should be escorted by at least three fighting machines, all flying in close formation. Further, in the advent of any one of the fighting escort machines being detached the reconnaissance machine should abort the mission. This order had the effect of seriously depleting the operational strength of the RFC. However, the decline of the Fokker monoplane had already begun. On 23 January 1916, 20 Squadron, equipped with the FE2b, arrived in France, and three weeks later, on 7 February, 24 Squadron, the RFC's first true single-seater fighter squadron, landed its little DH2 pushers at St.Omer.

*

On 5 July, James was posted to France with orders to collect a brand new BE2d[12] (No.5802) from Farnborough for delivery to St.Omer. Apart from his two hours on the tractor Avro at the beginning of his flying instruction, all James's subsequent experience had been on the Farman pushers. The BE2 was a tractor, plus being the first of the type he had flown, but he successfully flew it to Folkestone – with an air mechanic in the back seat – stayed the night and set out for St.Omer the next morning. There was an anxious ten minutes over the Channel, when a cylinder head cracked, but James successfully nursed the engine and staggered on to St.Omer, landing safely with a hundred feet to spare. James then reported to the Pilots' Pool, where he learnt that he had been listed as a pusher pilot. On 8 July, while waiting in the Pool to be posted to a squadron, James took the opportunity to fly a DH2[13] (No.7860): two flights of twenty minutes each, on the second taking the little scout up to 8,000ft. Whether or not James reported anything amiss with DH2 7860 is not known, he certainly makes no mention of anything, either in his logbook or his autobiography, but later in the day, it was the subject of a report by the officer in charge of the School at St. Omer to the Officer Commanding No.1 Aircraft Depot.

On examining the nacelle of the School de Havilland Scout No. 7860 on July 8th, it was found that there was a bolt missing which holds the left-hand bracing strut in its bracket. There was a piece of broken file in the hole for the bolt and a piece of fabric was doped as if to hide it.

The implications of this report are staggering. Potentially, James' flying career could have ended prematurely on July 8th 1816.

Given his record at the CFS, James was hoping that he would be posted as a scout pilot to one of those squadrons flying the DH2 in France, but his hopes were dashed on 8 July when he was posted to 20 Squadron at Clairmarais. The squadron's duties were mainly reconnaissance and it was equipped with the two-seat FE2d,[14] a large, powerful, but somewhat cumbersome pusher; a far cry from the nimble little DH2 that James had been hoping to fly. However, he was a professional soldier, orders are orders, and although severely disappointed he accepted the posting with his usual good grace.

James arrived at Clairmarais in the evening, just as the FE2ds were returning from a patrol. On reporting he was met by Sergeant-Major Goodard,[15] an old acquaintance from 5 Squadron, who immediately made him feel at home. James then reported to the commanding officer of the squadron, Major G.J. Malcolm.[16] Answering a few questions as to his general experience, James admitted that he not yet flown an FE and the major ordered that he should fly a practice flight the following morning.

The next day James took off alone in FE2d A6 – presumably observer/gunners were too valuable to risk until this new pilot's flying abilities had been assessed – climbed to 3,000ft and flew around the area of the aerodrome for forty minutes. Although a large aeroplane, the FE was an easy and comfortable machine to fly and James was very pleased with A6, feeling that he flew it well: 'with great vigour' as he put it. Major Malcolm seemed equally pleased, but that same evening he was killed in a flying accident when taking off from St.Omer.

On 10 July 1916, James flew his first war flight as a pilot: a patrol at 13,000ft from Ypres to the Bois de Biez with Lieutenant E.H. Lascelles[17] as his gunner. Their duty was to prevent any enemy machines from crossing the British lines, but none were seen and they returned to Clairmarais after two hours forty-five minutes, landing at 8.30AM. This patrol was

Maurice Walter Piercey.

repeated the following day, but again, no hostile aeroplanes were seen.

On 18 July, James was one of five FE2ds that flew a reconnaissance of the Dixmude-Thielt-Roulers area, flying FE2d A7, with Corporal J. Stringer[18] as his gunner. Although two Fokkers were seen getting their height they did not attack, no doubt reluctant to tackle such a large formation.

The next morning the FEs flew a reconnaissance to Menin, Roubaix, Tourcoing, and Lille. The FEs were at 12,000ft, but other than being severely archied they had the whole sky to themselves. At this time, most of the enemy air activity was farther south, engaged in the Battle of the Somme, that had been raging since the first of the month, and the FEs saw only the occasional Fokker, which usually dived on the rearmost machine in the formation, made a half-hearted, unsuccessful attack, then dived away.

On 27 July, the monotony was broken – tragically. The day dawned bright and clear and five FEs, led by Captain R.S. Maxwell,[19] took off early on an offensive patrol. Orders were to form up over Clairmarais at 10,000ft, but as James was climbing he noticed a heavy ground mist blowing in from the north-west – a not uncommon occurrence during the summer months in France – and by the time he had reached his height

A typical example of the Maurice Farman Série 7 'Longhorn.' James soloed on Maurice Farman No.6700 on 16 April 1916, qualifying for his RAeC Certificate. *Credit L Rogers.*

A Maurice Farman Série 11 'Shorthorn.' James took his CFS Pilot 2nd Class certificate on this type (No.480) on 7 May 1916. *Credit F Cheesman.*

and joined the formation, the ground could no longer be seen. The patrol flew east for twenty minutes, then turned east-south-east. By now, James reckoned that they should be over the vicinity of Lille but the ground was completely obscured and no landmarks could be seen. After flying for another twenty minutes on the same course, the formation turned west. Occasionally the mist cleared, giving a brief view of the ground and several unrecognised villages: it was obvious that the FEs were over unfamiliar territory. Maxwell signaled for the patrol to be abandoned and the FEs began to independently make their way back to Clairmarais.

James flew west for some time, he and his observer, Lieutenant G.H. Exley,[20] catching brief glimpses of the ground. Through one of the intermittent gaps in the mist, James saw a town, which he mistook for Bailleul. Thinking that he now knew his whereabouts, James decided to go down, get under the thick mist into clearer air – hopefully lower down – and follow the main road to Clairmarais.

James took the FE down to 2,000ft, but realised that the mist was lower still. He cautiously lost more height and finally ran into the murk at 600ft. This was decidedly dangerous, but James had no option but to drop lower still, engine off, with the FE gliding just above stalling speed. Suddenly, Exley, standing in the front of the nacelle, shouted a warning. Looming up out of the mist in front of them was a line of trees, bordering a road. James switched on the engine, which thankfully caught immediately, and hauled the FE up over the trees, trusting to luck that the field behind them would

James in the front seat of a Maurice Farman Série II 'Shorthorn.' at the Central Flying School at Upavon in 1916. He wrote home. 'I've done a lot of instructing on this machine. Jim.'

be clear. Miraculously, it was. James put the FE down. It ran on for some yards, smashing though a small fence, before stopping in the back garden of a farmhouse. After placating the understandably agitated farmer who had run out of his house, James and Exley inspected the FE, found that it was undamaged, and walked to the nearest village, where the mayor told them they were only a few kilometres from St.Pol, about forty miles south of Clairmarais, and invited his two unexpected guests to breakfast, which they gratefully accepted. While they were eating, they heard the deep characteristic organ-like note of a Rolls-Royce engine; an FE was circling overhead, the pilot looking for a gap in the still thick mist, trying desperately to find a place to land. All they could do was to wish him the same good luck they had enjoyed.

At midday the mist had cleared. James and Exley were about to make their way back to the FE when a gendarme arrived and told them that a machine had crashed about a mile away and that both the pilot and observer had been killed.[21] Knowing there was nothing they could do, James and Exley walked back to their FE. James took off and they flew back to Clairmarais, a short flight of thirty-five minutes. As they landed they could see that half the squadron's personnel were congregated by the sheds. Climbing out of the FE, James and Exley were anxiously questioned. Only two of the five machines that had left that morning had returned – Captain Maxwell and James – the remaining three had all crashed. It had been a disastrous day for the squadron.

The loss of six men and three machines was not allowed to interfere with the squadron's daily work. The next day, two FEs took off: James, with a Lieutenant C.C. Statt[22] as his observer and Capt. Maxwell with Lieutenant H.J. Hamilton.[23] Their duty was a line patrol from Bois de Biez to Ypres. Climbing for their height over Robecq, the FEs saw British anti-aircraft bursts over Béthune, pointing out an enemy machine. The FEs gave chase but the enemy was too high – and too fast – and easily evaded them, flying east before gliding down to its aerodrome.

Turning north, the two FEs next sighted a German two-seater Albatros over Quesnoy. They managed to close the distance to within four hundred yards and James opened fire with his fixed Lewis. The enemy pilot immediately dived to 6,000ft, easily outstripping A6 – reputedly the slowest FE in the squadron – but followed by Maxwell in his faster machine.[24] Maxwell and Hamilton fired five drums of Lewis into the fleeing Albatros, the last from seventy to sixty yards, and it went down, trailing smoke, and was lost to view in the clouds at 2,000ft. Regaining their height, the FEs turned south. Half an hour later, two more enemy machines were seen, just south of Freuge, but these were too distant, and by the time the British formation had reached the area the enemy machines were well east of the lines. James resisted the urge to follow them, suspecting they were attempting to lure him into a trap: 'caution has ever been my watchword whilst fighting the wily Hun'.[25]

Instructing at the CFS Netheravon. James in the rear seat of a DH1. May 1916.

James and Maxwell then returned to Clairmarais for breakfast, feeling pleased with themselves, having seen several enemy aircraft during the patrol, an unusual occurrence, and with Maxwell convinced that he had seriously damaged the Albatros.

It was five days before James flew again: a photo reconnaissance from Ypres to Comines, again with Lieutenant Exley as his observer. The weather was 'very clear' and the resulting photographs were excellent.[26]

The squadron at this time was flying the FE2d, powered either by a Mark I or Mark III 250hp Rolls Royce engine, and James commented what a wonderful aeroplane it was: pleasant to fly, despite its size, and very stable. This last led to some flying liberties being taken by the pilots, who would climb about in the roomy nacelle while airborne, leaving the machine to fly itself. James took full advantage of this stability and confessed that he often, while on patrol, stood on his seat and looked back over the tail, a procedure not viewed kindly by his observer, especially on one near disastrous occasion: one of James' gloves blew off into the propeller, which shed one of its blades and nearly wrecked the engine before James managed to regain his seat and throttle down the Rolls.

On the last day of July, the BE2cs of 5 and 6 Squadrons bombed the wharf, barges, and ammunition dump at Wervicq. James, flying with Lascelles in A6, escorted by five additional FEs, was detailed to photograph the results of the raid. The photographs were taken from 6,000ft, an uncomfortable height as it was below the bombers, 'who were shying bombs all around us' plus being severely heavily archied. However, Lascelles managed to take some very good photographs, one showing five different bomb bursts on the target.

During 1916, the Zeppelin raids on London and other cities were causing some dismay and loss of morale amongst the general public in England. On 2 August, taking off at 10.50AM, six BE2cs of 5, 6 and 7 Squadrons, escorted by three Moranes of 1 Squadron, set off to bomb the Zeppelin sheds at Brussels, the BEs flying without observers in order to carry a larger bomb load. On the way to the target, a BE of 5 Squadron was shot down by anti-aircraft fire over Ledeghem, but the remainder carried on. Reaching the target, the BEs went down to 1,000ft to make their bombing runs, but despite this failed to score any direct hits on the sheds.

This was a very long flight of over five hours, beyond the endurance of the Moranes, and six FEs of 20 Squadron were detailed to meet the bombers on their way back, between Audenarde and Courtrai. James flew on this escort with Lieutenant Hamilton, but the only enemy machine seen was 'the old solitary Fokker who got his height over Courtrai, came and had a look at us, and then went off home'. All the FEs returned safely, much to the relief of James. Although the BEs had met with the FEs within five minutes of the appointed time, those five minutes meant that the FEs had had to circle while waiting and by this time James had 'a very wholesome respect for the German anti-aircraft gunners'.

On 6 August James flew his last operational flight in 20 Squadron: a reconnaissance of Ypres, Roulers and Dadizeele, again with Exley as his observer.

On the morning of 7 August, James took up his mechanic

FE2d A6516. This presentation aeroplane, *The Colony of Mauritius No.13*, was flown by 20 Squadron in the summer of 1916.

Corporal George Farmer[27] for a ten-minute flight in A6. Landing from this, James then took Hughes,[28] his other mechanic, for a further flight of ten minutes in A6. These flights were officially tests, but in reality were joyrides for his mechanics, to show his appreciation for their hard work on his machine. James understood the daily grind of their work – who better, having so recently carried out the same duties himself – and no doubt was on more familiar terms with his mechanics than were the officers of the squadron with theirs.

On landing from the last of these flights, James was summoned to the CO's office. He was apprehensive that he was going to be reprimanded for the joyrides, but someone at RFC HQ had finally sorted out his record at the CFS and noted the recommendation that he should be a scout pilot. To his delight – and relief – the CO, Major W. Mansfield,[29] informed him that he had posted to 29 Squadron to fly DH2s.

James packed his kit, said goodbye to his comrades, and took a tender to 29 Squadron's aerodrome at Abeele, a short drive of sixteen miles.

Although James had now realised his ambition to fly single-seater scouts in France, it was tempered by his sorrow at having to leave 20 Squadron. He had made many friends of 'all the jolly good people who were in it' and had come to appreciate the many qualities of his 'cumbersome old FE' which in his view had earned the respect of the German pilots.

'We stood to fight.' The extremely precarious position taken up by the observer/gunner of an FE2d in order to fire at an enemy machine attacking from the rear. The pilot's forward-firing gun was also very near his leg.

Ch.7: Scout Pilot

A DH2.

Number 29 Squadron was the second squadron equipped with the DH2 to arrive in France. The squadron had been formed at Fort Grange, Gosport, in the November of 1915, and by the following February began to receive its DH2s. Although the squadron's transport and ground crews left for France on the 14 and 16 March 1916, its aeroplanes were not ready to leave until the twenty-fourth of the month. The first DH2 squadron, 24 Squadron, had flown its entire complement of DH2s to France in February 1916, with the loss of only three aeroplanes on the way – the high winds in the month causing takeoff and landing crashes – but 29 Squadron failed to match this success. At Gosport, on the morning of 24 March, three DH2s refused to start owing to engine trouble and only nine left for Dover, the first stage of their journey, engine failure causing the loss of another on the way. During the flight the bad weather deteriorated further into a snowstorm, forcing four more pilots to land en-route, and only four DH2s managed to land at Dover. Only three of these left for St. Omer later in the day and one crashed on landing. Because of these accidents and forced landings, the majority of the squadron's pilots had no aeroplanes to fly to France and there was a two-week delay before replacement aeroplanes were delivered. Before the entire squadron was safely in France on 14 April it had lost another two DH2s – one ditched in the English Channel and another crashed due to engine failure flying from St. Omer to the squadron's aerodrome at Abeele. A later enquiry into this disastrous debut concluded that in bringing the squadron up to its full operational strength of twelve DH2s, a total of 26 or 27 DH2s had been 'consumed'. It was an inauspicious start.

At Abeele, 29 Squadron were under the orders of 11th Wing, II Brigade, flying over the front of Second Army, covering the Salient at Ypres, a relatively quiet sector of the front, the offensives being fought further south. Geoffrey Bowman, who joined the squadron on 7 July 1916, recalled: 'Nothing much happened in 29 Squadron during 1916. We were in the Ypres Salient and all the Huns had gone down to the Somme.'[1]

*

On arriving at Abeele James reported to the squadron to find that his new CO was Major Conran, who was delighted to see his old mechanic from their days in 3 Squadron together. After only a few minutes of conversation, talking over old times in 3 Squadron, Conran quickly realised that James had lost none of his enthusiasm for flying and that with his impressive number of hours of flying time – James had now accumulated a hundred and fifty hours – he would be a valuable addition to the squadron. In 1916, NCO sergeant pilots flying scouts were rare in the RFC, but Conran already had one in his squadron, and with the arrival of James, now had two. Conran was an experienced and understanding officer, sensitive to the incongruous situation that, as NCOs, they could not Mess with his commissioned officers, even though they shared the same dangers in combat. They were also denied the opportunity to talk over the day's fights, discuss tactics, or even to form that sustaining bond of comradeship forged by daily facing the dangers of fighting in the air. Conran's other NCO pilot was in C Flight, and conscious of the situation he assigned James to the same Flight.

After his interview James wandered down to the Sergeants' Mess, where he found Conran's other NCO pilot: Sergeant Pilot Jack Noakes,[2] another old acquaintance. Noakes was a exceptional pilot, full of confidence in his ability: in 29 Squadron he threw his DH2 about in the sky in a manner which had earned him many reprimands from his horrified Flight Commander, Captain Latch.[3] After Noakes had introduced James to the other members of the Sergeants' Mess, he took him down to the C Flight hangers and found the machine that had been allotted to him – DH2 No.5985. As a type, the DH2 was not universally popular with pilots – among its other vices they thought it had a tendency to spin – but Noakes assured James that the supposed deficiencies of the little pusher were unfounded, more imagined than real. DH2 5985 had already flown eighty-nine hours, in the hands of various pilots, and had just been overhauled after a landing accident the week before. With his mechanic's eye, James thoroughly inspected his new machine, checking rigging and flying wires, before climbing into the nacelle to check the movement of the controls and look over the flying instruments – few as they were. James found everything in order. A mechanic lifted the tail of the DH2, ducked under the twin booms and swung the propeller. The 100hp Gnome Monosoupape burst into life, and with a hurried look at the windsock James took off for a twenty minutes flight, climbing to 1900ft before making several circuits of the aerodrome. He was delighted with his new mount, finding it 'very nice and light to fly after flying the heavy FE.'

After James had landed from this practise flight, Captain Latch asked if he felt confident enough to join him in an early morning patrol the next day. With the experience he had gained with his month of operational flying with 20 Squadron, James was confident in his ability to fly the little DH2 well enough to get into – or out of – any trouble that might arise, and he needed no encouragement to get on with the war.

Soon after dawn the next morning, 8 August 1916, James took off with Captain Latch on his first patrol as a scout pilot, the first of many. Climbing towards the front lines, they reached their height of 12,000ft over Boesinghe, the starting point of their designated patrol, then turned south to fly to Saint Eloi, passing over the Ypres Salient. Reaching Saint Eloi they turned north again, back to the Salient, where they spotted a German two-seater just crossing the British lines. They flew to attack this machine, but the German pilot saw them in time and dived for the safety of his own lines, easily outdistancing them. After a patrol lasting two hours they returned to Abeele, to a welcome breakfast. During the patrol, Latch had taken them up to 14,000ft and for the first time James learned what a cold little aeroplane the DH2 could be. Unlike the FE2d, where the pilot sat almost directly in front of the engine, in the DH2 he sat in the very front of the nacelle, with the engine – an air-cooled rotary – a long way behind him, providing no warmth at all.

In the afternoon, at 3.30PM, C Flight took off to escort a formation of BE2cs of 6 Squadron which were to bomb enemy positions in Houthulst Forest. Number 6 Squadron was also based at Abeele and the DH2s formed up with the BE2cs over the aerodrome. The raid passed without incident and no enemy machines were seen. James very much liked flying on escort duty, with a number of machines 'all trying to dodge Archie as best they could'. Another source of amusement was the sight of a BE2c, heavily laden with two 112lb bombs, 'staggering' through the air.

Jack Noakes.

Over the next month James flew fifteen routine patrols, all in the venerable 5985, adding over twenty-six hours to his total flying time. His logbook comments are full of entries such as: HA Patrol. No Huns seen. Special Patrol. Patrol washed out. The routine of the daily patrols was broken only when the weather was unfit for flying – three days towards the end of the month – and by the occasional high flying German machine flying over the aerodrome: on one occasion, at dawn, dropping some bombs that exploded on the outskirts of the field, doing no damage at all. When not flying a patrol during the day, James would often fly to his old aerodrome at Clairmarais, ostensibly to carry out some shooting practice on the pond there, but really to see his old comrades in 20 Squadron. On one occasion, Noakes went with him and flying back to Abeele they ran into a heavy storm over Cassel. The DH2s eventually emerged from the storm clouds over Steenvoorde, with James and Jack Noakes soaked to the skin. On landing at Abeele they found the varnish on the propeller blades of their DH2s had been completely stripped off by the heavy rain.

Although the German Army Air Service was relatively inactive over the Ypres sector of the Front during this time, the German anti-aircraft batteries were remarkably accurate. At 12,000ft the DH2s were very slow and were heavily and

A DH2 being readied for a patrol. *Credit B. Gray.*

accurately shelled every time they crossed the front lines. James developed a healthy respect for several of the enemy gunners, notably one at Bixschoote, others at Passchendaele and Houthem and one near Fromelles. James greatly admired the enemy AA defences in the Ypres sector during the summer of 1916, considering that they helped the German Army Air Service to concentrate its main forces over the fighting further south where they were more urgently needed.

On 6 September, James was on patrol at 14,000ft between Armentières and Ypres, when he saw an all white Albatros two-seater approaching the British Lines over Messines. James dived to intercept it, but the enemy pilot put his nose down and dived east. James followed, but could get no closer than four hundred yards. Realising that he was only just matching the speed of the enemy machine, anxious that it should not escape, James opened fire with a full drum of Lewis. The enemy pilot continued in his dive. James changed drums and fired another full drum. There was no reply from the enemy gunner, but the Albatros pilot steepened his dive. James put on a third drum of Lewis and expended it all. The Albatros, still going steeply down, but apparently still under control, went into the clouds over Gheluve at 2,000ft. James turned away. He was now well east of the lines, over enemy territory at only 4,000ft, and conscious of the ever-present danger from Archie. In his combat report of the action, James made no claim for the Albatros, considering that when he had seen it last it was still under control, but the RFC weekly communiqués – known irreverently throughout the RFC as 'Comic Cuts' – later reported: 'Flt. Sgt. McCudden, of 29 Squadron, on a De (sic) Havilland Scout, engaged a hostile machine over Houthem. The 1st Anzac Corps report that this machine crashed.' The Anzac report was later confirmed by an agent, who reported that the white Albatros had crashed on the road from Menin to Gheluve.

Because the enemy gunner had not fired a single shot during the fight, James considered that the Albatros crew were new, flying without a gun, and were out merely learning the country. 'In any case, this was a very easy German to get for one's first,

and it bucked me up a lot.' In his diary, he recorded: 'This machine was officially acknowledged as having been shot down by me.'

On 7 September, the BE squadrons of II Brigade bombed enemy aerodromes and positions in the area of Lille. Several DH2s of 29 Squadron escorted one such raid, to the east of Lille. An offensive patrol of FE2ds was also in the general area: these joined in and the whole formation crossed the lines south of Armentières. James, flying with the contingent from 29 Squadron, observed that all the bombers then became separated and 'were wandering all over Hunland'. Most of the allied machines then returned, but there were still one or two FE2ds east of Lille, 'wondering what to do with their bombs'. By this time the escort for the bombers had dwindled to James and an FE, so they collected the last of the stragglers and saw them safely back across the lines.[4]

On 4 September, Major W.A. Grattan-Bellew[5] had replaced Eric Conran as CO of 29 Squadron and the change of command seems to have brought James a change in luck in finding and engaging enemy aircraft. Only two days after shooting down the white Albatros, James was in action again. After lunch on 8 September, he took off on an Offensive Patrol with Capt. Latch and Lt. Readman.[6] The DH2s crossed the front lines at 12,000ft over Boesinghe and flew east to Passchèndaele, where they received their usual 'hate' from Archie. Reaching Ploegsteerte, the southern limit of their patrol line, the DH2s turned north east. As they approached Gheluvelt, James saw a machine approaching the formation from the direction of Ypres. As it got closer he recognised it as an old friend: the solitary Fokker monoplane which he had so often seen while flying with 20 Squadron. Flying a DH2, James had no fear of the Fokker and dived to attack it. 'I went at him and we both opened fire together nose on. After two shots my gun stopped.'[7] While James was rectifying the stoppage the Fokker pilot turned quickly and got behind him. 'I now did a silly thing. Instead of revving round and waiting for the other two DHs to help me, I put my engine off and dived, but not straight.'[8] As James spiraled down in a series of S-turns, the

May 1916. DH2s of 29 Squadron on Abeele aerodrome.

Fokker pilot followed, shooting at every opportunity, and James distinctly heard the bullets, 'coming far too close to be healthy', and at one time glanced up and saw the Fokker pilot just above him, duplicating his S-turns. At 8,000ft – the combat had started at 14,000ft – James managed to clear his stoppage. He put his engine on and zoomed. The Fokker pilot also zoomed, but came out just ahead and a little higher than the DH2. This was an ideal opportunity for James. He pulled down his Lewis and opened fire. After four shots the gun stopped again. The Fokker dived away, with James following – feeling 'very brave' – while attempting to rectify the stoppage, but by the time he got the gun working again the Fokker pilot was 2,000ft below him, still diving. Knowing the diving capacity of the Fokker, James knew that he had no hope of catching it and he last saw it re-starting its engine in a cloud of blue smoke over the German aerodrome at Coucou, west of Menin. On landing back at Abeele, James inspected 5985 and found that the Fokker pilot had put a bullet into a wing spar and another into one of the tail booms. James also tested the Lewis gun, which of course now worked perfectly.[9]

In his usual pragmatic fashion, James learnt valuable lessons from this fight with the Fokker. He reasoned that if the German pilot had been only a little more skilful he would probably have been shot down. 'But still, this was all very good experience for me and if one gets out of such tight corners it increases one's confidence enormously.'[10]

By 10 September, DH2 5985 had been repaired in the squadron's workshops and James test flew it twice during the day. Four days later it had been fitted with a new engine and after a ten minutes test James pronounced it 'OK'.

On September 15, James flew twice during the day. On the first of these, a routine patrol to the St.Eloi area, a brown coloured two-seater was seen over Messines, flying west. James gave chase, but although the German machine was only 400 yards away, he could not catch it. The enemy gunner was firing back at the DH2 and James replied with two drums of Lewis, but the enemy pilot dived steeply, with his engine full on and left the DH2 far behind – with a speed estimated by James to be 100mph – still diving steeply but apparently under control and he last saw it at 2,000ft over Quesnoy. James had to be content that he had forced it to abandon its reconnaissance.[11&12]

At 5.30PM six DH2s left Abeele on escort duty to BE2s that were to bomb Quesnoy. Forming up with the bombers at 10,000ft, the formation crossed the trenches over Messines and flew southwards to Quesnoy. Arriving over the target, the BEs dropped their bombs, while the DH2s hovered above them: 'simply longing for some Huns to arrive looking for trouble'. No enemy aircraft having put in an appearance, the DH2s escorted the BEs back to the trenches. Having seen the bombers safely on their way home, James and Lt. Brearly[13] turned away and flew to the north-east: 'to look for Germans'. Brearley sighted a low flying enemy machine, but as he and James dived they lost sight of it. As their petrol was now running low, they returned to Abeele. James later commented: 'I simply loved these shows in the summer evenings, and asked for nothing better than to be in a scout squadron with a good lot of fellows doing this sort of work daily.'

In the fine mornings, a number of enemy observation

While presenting no difficulties to the slightly built James, the snugness of the cockpit of a DH2 is evident in this view from above. *Credit B. Gray.*

balloons could be clearly seen from the aerodrome at Abeele. Observations from these were causing a great deal of trouble to the British trenches around Ypres, and it was decided to deal with them. A balloon strafe was organised.

On 16 September, James took off at 1PM to attack the balloon over Poelcapelle. As he approached the Front Line he could see that the balloon's crew had already seen him: it was being hauled down and was now down to 2,500ft. James lost height and crossed the trenches at 2,000ft. The only British machine over the trenches, the DH2 came under heavy fire from the ground, both Archie and small arms fire. Flying through the black smoke surrounding him, James got to within half a mile of the balloon before the ground fire became so intense and accurate that at seven hundred yards, after firing a whole drum at it, with no effect, he was forced to turn away and make for the safety of the British lines behind the Ypres Salient. Crossing the front line trenches at a thousand feet over Bellewarde Lake, he flew back to Abeele, deciding that any pilot who brought down a German balloon was a hero.

In the evening, despite his reservations, James decided to have another crack at a balloon: this time one that was aloft just east of Polygon Wood. He left the ground at 6PM and flew east to Ypres, where he noted the height of the balloon and took a compass bearing. There were thick clouds at 4,000ft and he decided to take advantage of these, approaching the balloon from above the clouds before making his attack. He climbed above the overcast and flew on a compass bearing for six minutes, estimating that he would then be close to the balloon, but when he came down through the clouds it was still half a mile ahead of him. The enemy anti-aircraft batteries then saw him, but managed to fire only two or three bursts before James climbed back into the safety of the cloud cover. After again flying east for half a minute, James came down through the cloud again: 'for a peep'. As he came out of the cloud – this time just above the balloon – an Albatros was coming towards him, nose on, about two hundred yards away. James forgot the balloon, opened fire at the Albatros, and saw his tracers hitting its wings before it turned sharply to his right and dived away. James did not follow it down. He was at 3,000ft, four miles behind the enemy lines, and Archie had now seen him and was finding his height. James turned for the nearest part of the Front Line, which was Ploegsteert Wood. The German gunners put up a tremendous barrage in front of the fleeing DH2, forcing James to keep turning at right angles to throw them off their aim – he once had to turn 180 degrees and fly east to momentarily escape their attentions. His Monosoupape Gnôme was now giving a good 1,300 revs, the pitot tube showing 100mph. As James got closer to the front line trenches he decided to make a dive for it, finally, with a sigh of relief, crossing them at 1,000ft. Looking back, he saw the balloon being hauled down.

The DH2 had been badly hit, the base of one shell having gone through a spar in its right hand bottom wing which was 'wobbling about like a jelly'. James cautiously flew back to Abeele at 65mph so as not to put too severe a strain on the damaged wing. He was glad to get safely down, after an hour's 'concentrated excitement'. He decided that he positively did not like German balloons and resolved to leave them well alone in the future.

On the morning of 17 September the squadron received a report that a Zeppelin was flying at 12,000ft between Calais and Bruges. Captain Honnet[14] and James were despatched to deal with it, each loaded with four drums of incendiary ammunition for their Lewis gun.[15] They climbed north towards the coast, which they reached over Dunkirk at 11,000ft. There was no sign of the Zeppelin, so they flew out

The first victory. An Albatros C.III. *Credit A. Imrie.*

to sea. Seeing nothing, they then turned east towards Nieuport. As they crossed into enemy-held Belgium they came under some fire from Archie, so Honnet turned out to sea for eight miles, out of range of the batteries. The DH2s passed Ostend, Blankerberghe and then Zeebrugge – James could plainly see its curved mole – and finally arrived over the Scheldt estuary. They were now at 13,000ft, but there was still no sign of the elusive Zeppelin. Much to the relief of James, Honnet then turned west and retraced their flight along the coast, this time nearer the shoreline, and they again came under heavy and accurate fire from the Archie batteries at both Blankenberghe and those at Ostend, where James noted three guns firing together, the shells bursting half a minute later at the height of the DH2s, but thankfully just a little behind them. This was too close and Honnet led him out over the sea again.

The only aircraft seen during this long flight, searching for the Zeppelin, were as the DH2s were passing Ostend. James felt rather uneasy on sighting these machines – they had the height of the DH2s and he thought they looked decidedly 'Hunnish' – but he felt 'very much more brave' when they turned out to be RNAS Nieuports.

New Opponents

In the late summer of 1916, the Germans had begun to reorganise their experimental *Kampfeinsitzer Kommandos* – in which a few single–seater fighters were grouped together – into self-contained fighter squadrons, each of which was equipped, in theory, with twelve aeroplanes. These squadrons were designated as *Jagdstaffeln* (literally: hunting echelons) and the first seven *Jagdstaffeln* were in existence by the autumn of 1916, with another thirty being planned for the spring of 1917. In the early autumn of 1916, the RFC squadrons operating on the Somme were reporting an increase in the strength of the German Army Air Service, plus the appearance of several new types of fast, well-armed, single-seat scouts. These were the series of German D-Type fighters: the Halberstadt D.II and III; the Fokker D.III; and the Albatros D.I and D.II, all of which were operative with the first of the *Jagdstaffeln*.

The pendulum of air superiority that the RFC had enjoyed with the introduction of the DH2, the FE8 and the FE2d, which had ended the dominance of the Fokker monoplane, was to swing again, in favour of the German Army Air Service. The DH2, FE8 and FE2d were now to be outclassed by the new German D-Type fighters, which were faster, in some cases more manoeuvrable, and better armed.[16]

James had his first experience in fighting the new German fighters on 22 September. He had taken off at 11AM with Lieutenants Curlewis[17] and Payn[18] to patrol from Menin to Gheluve. At midday, an enemy machine was seen, at 1,000ft below the DH2s. For some reason – they were in an advantageous position with the benefit of height – the patrol decided not to attack this machine until it had got higher. This was a mistake in tactics that could have had serious consequences. When the Flight reached the end of their patrol line at Menin, and turned north, the enemy machine was now above them: they had seriously underestimated its rate of climb. The enemy pilot, seemingly undeterred by the odds, dived to attack Payn, opening fire from long range. Payn easily out-manoeuvred the enemy pilot, got on his tail and opened fire. The enemy machine at once went down in a vertical dive, from 13,000 to 6,000ft, before, to the astonishment of the British pilots, it flattened out and flew away. They had never seen a machine, under control, dive so steeply and for so long, and had felt sure that Payn had shot it down. This was the first of the new Halberstadt D-Types encountered by the squadron.

That afternoon, the deficiencies of the DH2 were again demonstrated when James took off to intercept an enemy reconnaissance machine over the British lines at 15,000ft. By

William Arthur Grattan-Bellew.

James relaxing outside his tent at Abeele.

the time the DH2 had climbed for nearly an hour, reaching only 14,000ft, the German pilot and observer were back on their aerodrome, as James surmised: 'having a good lunch'. In the coming weeks, in a foretaste of things to come, James often went up alone, climbing to 14,000ft and waiting over the lines in the hope of catching one of these enemy observation machines, but without any luck.

During the day Captain S.E. Cowan[19] was posted in as the new C Flight commander. A valuable addition to the squadron, Cowan was a vastly experienced DH2 pilot who had flown to France in February 1916 as a member of 24 Squadron. He had won a Military Cross in May 1916 and a Bar in late September.

On an evening patrol with Ian Curlewis on 23 September, the engine of 5985 suddenly spluttered to a stop, possibly with some fault in the petrol supply – as an experienced pilot James would have been unlikely to have unexpectedly run out of petrol. At 13,000ft over Menin, James had plenty of height in hand and turned west. Visibility was extremely bad, the glare of the setting sun exacerbated by a heavy ground mist. However, as he got down to 7,000ft, James could see Ypres, and by the time he was over the town he had some 2,000ft to spare: time enough to chose a site for a forced landing. Picking out a field of cut corn near Vlamertinghe James put the DH2 safely down, missing a large shell hole by a matter of inches. An artillery battery was nearby and James walked over to telephone the squadron, to let them know his location, and ask for petrol and oil. The battery commander, newly arrived from England, was not happy at the location of the DH2, which was close by his guns. He was worried that the German artillery ranging on the DH2 would shell him out of his position. However, his fears were not realised and the squadron tender and mechanics arrived soon after dark. At 11PM, James went to bed under the wing of his DH2 – shades of the retreat from Mons in 1914 – and was soon asleep, only to be woken after three hours by the stentorian voice of the battery's sergeant who was directing the battery fire onto enemy positions. Star shells were flaring up into the night sky, accompanied by the staccato fire of machine guns in the trenches, 3,000yards away. It was not a restful night and James was glad to be up at first light to help the mechanics fill the DH2 with petrol and oil. Having run up

A 29 Squadron casualty. Kenneth Kestell Turner was shot down in DH2 5994 on 25 August 1916 and made prisoner of war. *Credit A. Imrie.*

the engine, he took off and made for Abeele, the main planes of the DH2 streaming with water as the night's mist ran off them. The morning was extremely misty and he had some difficulty in finding the aerodrome, finally taking some trees, which he knew to be at the north end of the field, as a guide. He touched down safely in the thick mist, narrowly missing some cows that had strayed onto the field.

For the rest of September, James flew another eleven patrols, all uneventful. On 1 October, he was told that he been awarded the Military Medal, the citation reading, in part: 'for conspicuous gallantry, courage and dash, during September 1916, in attacking and destroying an enemy machine and forcing two others to land. He also twice crossed the enemy lines at a very low altitude in attacks on a hostile balloon under very heavy fire.'

At this time, enemy aeroplanes that had been forced to land were often credited to a pilot as a victory, but James had made no such claims, considering the 'two others' of the citation as being under control when he had last seen them, and they were not included in his later, official total of aerial victories.

James flew three uneventful patrols in the first three days of October until leaving on the 6th for a welcome seven days leave.

James 'enjoyed a most interesting week's leave, which, of course, as usual, went all too soon.'

Returning to France from leave, many pilots, anxious to avoid a hazardous and possibly choppy channel crossing, followed by a long, tedious train journey through France, with its inevitable delays, often opted to fly a replacement aeroplane to the Depot at St.Omer. James was one such, and even though it meant relinquishing a day of his leave, he reported to Farnborough on 13 October and collected BE2e 7153 for delivery to France. It was an inauspicious date: not only was it a Friday and the 13th of the month, but the day was dull, with low cloud at 1,500ft. However, James got away at 2.30PM with a mechanic named Robinson in the rear seat.[20] At Redhill, the clouds were considerably lower and the BE was hemmed in, with hills on either side. James, wondering about the luck of the day, flew at 200ft along the railway line to Ashford until he came to the village of Marden. The weather was closing in; it was obviously both dangerous and foolish to carry on, so James, unable to turn back because of the hills, had no alternative other than to land. He makes no mention how he and Robinson spent the night – possibly sleeping in the BE – but next morning, the weather having cleared, he flew it on to Folkestone, a short flight of twenty-five minutes. After a brief stop for breakfast, James took off again and made the forty-minute flight to St.Omer. Despite this adventurous flight he pronounced the BE a 'nice machine'.

Back at Abeele, James first concern was if anyone had flown 5985 while he had been on leave. He had lavished a great deal of care on the engine and rigging of his DH2, had everything to his liking and despite its age considered it one of the best machines in the squadron. To his great relief, he found that it had not been flown in his absence.

The week's leave had been very refreshing: James felt 'very bloodthirsty', anxious to get back in the war, and quickly slipped back into the routine of daily patrols. These were uneventful until 21 October when James took off on an Offensive Patrol led by Geoffrey Bowman, one of his erstwhile pupils at the CFS. The three DH2s crossed the front lines east of Armentières at 13,000ft and flew east, climbing hard. By the time they were over the Lille area they were at 14,500ft. They then flew west, flying an erratic course to throw Archie off its aim. The only hostile machines they had seen were one or two, well over their own back areas, beyond Lille, too far east to chase. As they again approached the front lines, by this time at 16,000ft – the highest James had yet flown – he saw a white-coloured enemy machine 5,000ft below him, crossing the front lines over Armentières. James dived and got behind the enemy

Geoffrey Bowman in the cockpit of a DH2, in this instance during training with 10 Reserve Squadron.

machine, but the enemy pilot saw him coming in time, turned away and dived towards his own lines. James chased after him, closed the range to 300ft and fired a complete drum of Lewis. This had no apparent effect. James changed his drum, noticing that the enemy machine, although clearly a two-seater, had no gunner.[21] James closed the range and fired another drum, but again his fire had no visible effect. By now the enemy pilot was well behind his own lines and, ever cautious, James left him, realising that his petrol was now running low.

Just as James had landed back at Abeele, a British observation balloon over Armentières went up in flames, the British anti-aircraft batteries later reporting that the same machine that James had engaged had later returned, crossed the lines, and destroyed the balloon. James conceded that the enemy pilot 'must have been a fairly stout fellow'. In his dairy, recounting the fight, James concluded. 'Had I sighted in front of him instead of at him, I think I would have got him. Experience teaches.'

James took off the next morning at 9AM with the intention of gaining a height advantage over the lines, where he would then quietly sit in wait for a German two-seater that habitually flew over St.Omer every Sunday morning at about 11AM. James got his height of 15,000ft and patrolled for three and a quarter hours between Ypres and La Bassée, but the enemy machine failed to appear. He later learnt that the enemy crew had flown their reconnaissance the previous day, when the weather was better. James commented that he came down from this high altitude flight a sad but wiser man, but it was a portent of a tactic that he was to use so successfully later in his career.

During this time, several pilots of the squadron were carrying out 'balloon strafes'. Bowman flew one with Noakes on 21 September and another with Geoffrey Hill,[22] who brought one down in flames. On 27 September, an enemy balloon was reported to have broken loose and was being driven over the British lines by the south-westerly wind. Drifting over Kemmel Hill, the balloon could easily be seen from Abeele, and Bowman and Noakes set off to bring it down. What happened next is succinctly described in Bowman's logbook entry.

'Whilst at 12,000ft saw Hun balloon at 14,000ft over Hun lines. One plug cut out so could not climb. Came back to get new machine. Set balloon on fire over Kemmel Hill. Engine cut out so had to land. Hit telegraph pole and crashed completely in same field as balloon. Captured Hun officer in balloon.'

This incident caused a great deal of merriment in the squadron, Bowman was teased unmercifully about it, but it was not to be the last of Bowman's balloon adventures.

The Opposition

The Albatros D.I. Powered by a 160 hp Mercedes D.III engine, it was armed with two synchronized, forward-firing guns. *Credit A Imrie.*

The Albatros D.II was a development of the D.I. The wing was lowered to improve the pilot's view. *Credit A.Imrie.*

Bowman's early service with 29 Squadron was full of unusual incident. Only a few days before the balloon escapade he had had a narrow escape while escorting BEs on a bomb raid. He recorded in his logbook.

'Went on a bomb raid and saw a 2c being attacked by a Fokker. Dived on Fokker, who left 2c. I was then attacked by a Roland scout and while flying nose on to each other, I shot him. Being out of control the HA came straight on and took off his R.top plane on my R.wing. My lateral control was Na Poo. HA went down over Linselles. I came back to lines at 2,000ft.'[23]

A Change of Scene

On 23 October, 29 Squadron moved south to an aerodrome at Izel-le Hameau, ten miles west of Arras: the DH2s being flown, the transport, stores and ground crews making the day's journey by road. The squadron now came under the orders of III Brigade, to patrol the front of 3rd Army between north of Arras to Gommecourt.

The aerodrome at Izel was large – the landing field measured 1,300 yards by 500 yards – and housed two RFC camps. At the eastern end of the aerodrome, Filescamp farm was set in amongst orchards; at the western end was the village of Izel-le-Hameau. Both ends of the field contained hangers, huts, workshops and various squadron offices, and both Filescamp Farm and Izel-le-Hameau were names used to identify the aerodrome. At various times during the war, the field housed two squadrons flying two-seater aeroplanes (Corps squadrons) and two squadrons flying single-seater aeroplanes (Army squadrons) but at the time of 29 Squadron's arrival only 11

The second patrol flown by 29 Squadron on 9 November resulted in four casualties. In combat with the Albatros D.IIs of the *Jagdstaffeln*, three pilots were shot down and taken POW and one returned, wounded. One of those taken POW was Ivan Curlewis in DH2 A2543. *Ltn*. Hans von Keudell of *Jasta* 1 claimed two DH2 pilots taken POW from this combat: Curlewis and H.A. Hallam. *Credit L. Rogers.*

Squadron, flying FE2bs, but with some single-seater scouts on its strength – Vickers FB5; Bristol C types and Nieuports – were in residence, also based at the Izel-le-Hameau end of the aerodrome.

On arrival at Izel, James and Noakes, being old soldiers, quickly found themselves a comfortable billet in a little wooden hut. They spent their evenings either in their own Mess, visiting the sergeants' Mess in 11 Squadron, or walking, accompanied by a small mongrel terrier they had adopted.

Although sorry to leave their comfortable quarters at Abeele in Flanders, the squadron was pleased to be now on the Somme front with its increased activity in the air. However, they realised that they were not going to have such an easy time as they had experienced in the relatively intermittent fighting over the Ypres Salient.

The first few days at the new aerodrome were spent in practice flights for the pilots to learn the surrounding country and familiarise themselves with the front line positions. On 26 October, the pilots of C Flight flew a patrol from Thiepval to Arras to mark the landmarks and the position of the trenches. By the time they had flown twice over the patrol area, the increase of enemy activity in the air to that of the Ypres Salient was obvious. Several formations of enemy machines were seen, patrolling east of the lines, and in one instance, near Gommécourt, 'a very high, fat old two-seater' flew over the DH2s, 4,000ft above them, too high to catch and engage. The patrol lasted two hours, during which James was forced to modify his opinion that the best of the enemy anti-aircraft batteries were all in the Ypres area. On the left of the formation, while flying south, he was the nearest DH2 to one particular battery on the edge of large wood, which paid persistent attention to him.

As the only two Flight Sergeant Pilots in 29 Squadron, James and Noakes were in an ambiguous position in respect of their relationships with some of the other NCOs, most of whom were older men, and who resented their success. Both had done remarkably well, were conscious of their own undoubted abilities and were full of the confidence of youth, confidence which was seen as arrogance and conceit by some of the other NCOs. The piloting skills of both were equal to those of the officers they flew with daily – in some cases, far better. In particular, James also had a vast amount of knowledge, of engines and airframes, far superior to that of any of his officers, normally disinterested in such technical matters. However, once their flying duties for the day were over, both James and Noakes were back in the circumscribed world of Officers, NCOs and Men. Relegated to the Sergeant's Mess, where they had little in common regarding the events of the day with the other NCOs, they were denied both the camaraderie and invaluable shop talk of the officers' Mess. As Regular soldiers, both James and Noakes accepted that in peacetime, promotion through the ranks was a gradual, sometimes long, drawn-out process. But this was not peacetime: in the heady days of war NCOs could quickly become officers. James and Noakes discussed the matter at length and on 1 November 1916 they both applied for commissions.

The Halberstadt D.III, powered by the 120 hp Argus As.II engine. This was almost certainly the Halberstadt variant met by the 29 Squadron patrol on the morning of 16 November. Easy to fly, fast, stable, and robust, with no vices, the Halberstadt was popular with the pilots of the *Jagdstaffeln* in the winter of 1916. *Credit A. Imrie.*

The morning of 9 November dawned bright, with good visibility. Knowing that C Flight was down for the early morning patrol, James and Noakes were up early. Dressing in their hut, James remarked that the enemy were no doubt also dressing in preparation for a morning's strafe on the *Verfluchter Englander*.

The patrol, six DH2s, left the ground at 7.30AM. The plan was that they would fly first to Albert to get their height, then fly to Bapaume, before going north to Arras. This would take them well east of the front lines, ideally positioned to cut off and intercept any enemy aeroplanes returning to their aerodromes. However, by the time the Flight had reached Bapaume, their number had been reduced to three by various technical troubles, leaving Lt. O.F.G. Ball,[24] Noakes and James. Noakes, as the most experienced pilot of the three, took command and led the depleted force towards Arras. As they were passing over Achiet-le-Grand James saw six small specks to the east. He drew Noakes' attention to these and Noakes altered course a little to the west, considering that the patrol was too far east into enemy territory. But the enemy machines were coming up fast: as the DH2s reached Adinfer Wood, they were in range. The DH2 pilots turned to fight.

One of the enemy machines attacked James, nose on, but then turned away. As it did so, James got a good look at it. It was a type he had never seen before, one of the new Albatros D.I scouts. By now the DH2s were in the thick of the enemy formation, a long way east of the lines, and they knew that they would have to fight hard to survive.

James saw one Albatros on the tail of Ball's DH2, firing its twin guns from ten yards range, 'absolutely filling him with lead'. Ball was flying straight, apparently changing a Lewis gun drum. James was busy fighting two of the Albatros, who were 'fairly screaming for my blood' and was unable to go to Ball's assistance, but Ball had somehow survived the hail of bullets, half-rolled and put in a burst of a full drum of Lewis into the Albatros as it overshot. Although James thought that three of the enemy pilots were half-hearted, they were all co-operating extremely well, their tactics being for one of them to dive at a DH2 from the front, then turn away, inviting it to follow, which allowed one of their *Jasta* companions to dive and attack it from behind. James fell for this tactic, following the first attacking Albatros three times. On the last he heard 'a terrific clack, bang, crash, rip behind me'. An Albatros was ten yards behind him, firing continuously. James did a half roll and as the Albatros passed over him he saw that it was the enemy formation's leader, flying black and white streamers from his interplane struts.

Noakes was duelling with another of the enemy pilots, both turning tightly in an attempt to bring their guns to bear. The light little DH2 was more manoeuvrable than the heavier Albatros. Noakes turned inside it, got on its tail, and fired two drums, closing to within a hundred feet.

James, having expended five drums of Lewis, was out of ammunition, but he stayed in the fight, mock-attacking any of the enemy machines that were fighting with Ball and Noakes, causing them to break off their attacks.

The fight went on for twenty-five minutes, the DH pilots sticking together, gradually fighting their way back towards the British lines, realising that their only hope of survival lay in the manoeuvrability of their DH2s. When they finally reached the front line trenches, the Albatros pilots broke off the action and dived away to the east.

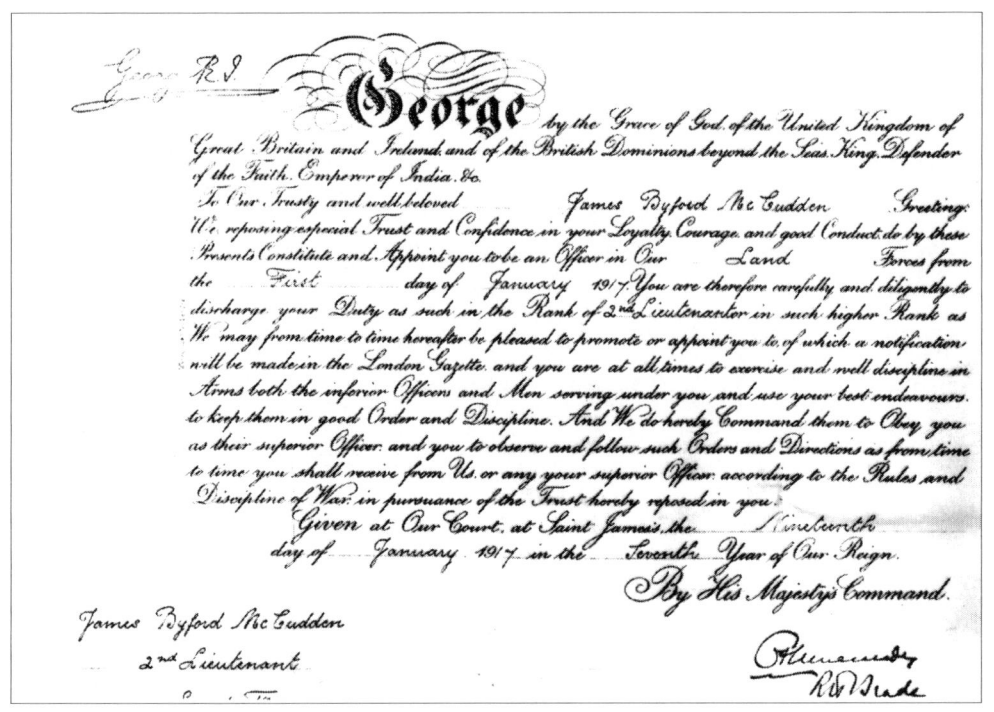

James' commission as a 2nd Lieutenant, dated 1 January 1917.

As the three DH2s made their way back to Izel, James had time to look over his machine and assess the damage: the tailplane was a mass of torn fabric – mute evidence of the accuracy of the marksmanship of the Albatros pilot who had been on his tail during the fight – various wires were hanging, cut by gunfire, and his controls felt sloppy.

All the DH2s landed safely. As James, Noakes and Ball climbed stiffly from their battered machines they were met by Grattan-Bellew, full of congratulations. The latter part of the fight had been witnessed by British anti-aircraft batteries and they had telephoned the squadron to say that it was the best they had seen for a long time. James later carried out a more thorough inspection of 5985. The enemy pilots had scored twenty-four hits – one severing a rudder control wire – the greatest number he was ever to have. James did not believe in having his aeroplane shot about, maintaining that it could be avoided by good flying, but 5985 carried a gruesome reminder of the closeness of the morning's fight; the front of its nacelle was splattered with blood.

The DH2 pilots owed their survival to both the manoeuvrability of their aeroplanes and their own piloting skills – Noakes and James in particular were superb pilots – and the outcome of the fight raised the morale of the squadron. Reports had already circulated, telling of the superiority of the new German fighters, but it was now realised that by using the right tactics they could still be successfully fought, even by the obsolescent DH2.

Unfortunately, this boost to morale was not to last. Later that morning the squadron flew an escort for sixteen BE2s of 12 and 13 Squadrons on a bombing raid of the German ammunition dump at Vaulx-Vraucourt, four miles north east of Bapaume. In addition to the six DH2s of 29 Squadron, ten FE2bs of 11 Squadron and twelve Nieuports of 60 Squadron, made up a formidable escort.

Over the target area the British formation was attacked by a large force of enemy fighters, estimated to be between twenty-five and thirty. In the ensuing heavy fighting, two BE2cs were shot down and their pilots taken prisoner – the BEs were flying with no observer in order to carry a heavier bomb load – and one pilot returned wounded. Number 11 Squadron suffered a pilot and observer wounded, and a pilot killed, but all the Nieuports of 60 Squadron returned safely. Number 29 Squadron suffered the heaviest casualties of the escorting aeroplanes, losing three pilots wounded, shot down and taken prisoner. These overall losses were relatively light, given the number of enemy fighters involved, testimony to the effectiveness of the fighter escort.

In the afternoon, James took off in DH2 A 2552, his confidence unshaken by the morning's fight. He attacked a two-seater over Gommécourt, firing all his ammunition into it, but it dived away, apparently unharmed. James landed at the nearest aerodrome, rearmed and took off again. Getting to 4,000ft and feeling pleased with life, he decided to try a loop. He dived the DH2 until the speed had built up to 90mph, took a deep breath, then pulled back the stick. Half way up into the loop, he made a near fatal error: he changed his mind, pushing the stick forward, transferring all the considerable load from his flying to his landing wires. The upward pressure was so great that all the ammunition drums shot out of the nacelle, back over the top wing and into the blades of the propeller, three of which disappeared in a mass of splinters, setting up a terrific vibration, the engine running at 1600 rpm on only one blade. James immediately switched off his engine, removed the Lewis gun from his knees, where it had fallen after being wrenched from its mounting, and found that he now needed full right rudder keep the DH2 on a straight course. Looking round, he saw even worse damage, potentially fatal: the lower right hand tail boom had been cut cleanly in two by one of the disintegrating propeller blades. The tail of the DH2 was now held on only by a diagonal, 10cwt tail-boom bracing wire.

As the engine was still revolving slowly, the DH2 was very unstable – 'wobbling badly' as James described it – but he pulled himself together, picked out a landing field and put the DH down. As it finally came to a halt, the DH2 tilted over onto one wing. With the centre section bracing wires broken, there was nothing to hold the wings in their correct position with the nacelle. James climbed out of the wreckage and 'thanked God for my salvation', although with the aeroplane in such a damaged condition it was only his superb piloting that had enabled him to land it at all.

James was still standing by the remains of the DH2, no doubt still somewhat shaken by his lucky escape, when an officer from 3 Squadron arrived on horseback. He had seen various pieces of aeroplane dropping from the sky and had come to inspect the largest remaining piece. The officer rode back to 3 Squadron for a tender and James stayed by the wreckage until it arrived. Leaving a guard on what remained of DH2 A2552, James rode back in the tender to 3 Squadron, where he telephoned the squadron, who promised to send a car for him as soon as possible, and a breakdown party next morning to salvage what they could from the remains of the DH2.

In 3 Squadron, James was back among many old friends. That evening the NCOs were giving a celebration party for one of their sergeants named Leach,[25] who had recently been commissioned. James spent a very cheery evening and had 'some real fun'.

The tender from the squadron arriving at midnight put an end to the party for James and he set off on the three hour, thirty mile drive back to La Hameau. The next morning he reported to Grattan-Bellew, fully expecting that he would be asked to explain his reasons for destroying one of the King's aeroplanes, but Grattan-Bellew was delighted to see him as there had been a rumour that he had last been seen going down in flames near Gommécourt.[26] Since Grattan-Bellew had taken command of the squadron on 4 September, only one pilot had been lost to enemy action, on the squadron's penultimate day on the Ypres front. Grattan-Bellew felt keenly the loss of the two pilots on the Vraucourt raid, Bolton[27] and Curlewis, and two additional pilots, 2Lts. Brearley and Hallam[28] had been lost the same day during an Offensive Patrol at 11.30. The reality of war on the Arras front was harsh.

After lunch on 10 November, James and Noakes took off alone. Over Miraumont they spotted an Albatros C-Type ranging for artillery. The Albatros was at 4,000ft, slightly below the DH2s, the black crosses on its top wings, painted on a white background, vividly clear. James dived to attack it, closing to 200 feet before firing a whole drum of Lewis. But his aim was faulty, he could see his tracers too far ahead of the Albatros that by now was diving steeply away to the east.

A patrol of eight DH2s on a morning patrol on 16 November were to receive a salutary lesson in combat flying from a German pilot of consummate skill. The patrol had just driven away an Albatros two-seater spotting for artillery over Blainville, when British anti-aircraft bursts pointed out to them an enemy machine over Humbercamp. The patrol turned south, to cut off the enemy's line of escape eastwards. With the expense of losing some height, James was first to reach the enemy scout, arriving underneath it, the pilot slowly circling: 'apparently enjoying the scenery'. By now the remainder of the patrol came up, completely surrounding the enemy machine, a single-seat Halberstadt. James flew east and slightly higher, reasoning that if the enemy pilot succeeded in evading the attacks of the other DH2s he would have to pass him to reach the safety of his own lines. But the German pilot seemed undeterred by the odds and fought the seven British scouts for five minutes: twisting, turning, diving and zooming to escape their fire. All the British pilots fired bursts at the elusive Halberstadt – they later estimated that they had expended over 600 rounds – but none hit any vital spot, and eventually the German pilot put down his nose and dived away. This was the chance James had been waiting for. He quickly got on the tail of the Halberstadt and opened fire at a hundred yards. The enemy pilot turned quickly, easily evading his fire. Another DH2 then attacked, but turned away, having had no more luck than James, who renewed his attack, again diving onto the tail of the Halberstadt. 'For fully five minutes I was on his tail firing four drums at ranges varying from 30 to 200 yards.' At one point the Halberstadt was only twenty yards away, flying across the nose of the DH2: James could clearly see the enemy pilot's face and goggles; was sure that he was actually grinning. James was now alone, the rest of the DH2s having been left behind, but as the enemy pilot reached his own lines he zoomed, easily outdistancing the slower DH2 – 'just as though he had previously only been using half throttle while he was fighting us' – then spun down to 2,000ft before flattening out and diving across his lines. James, having used all his ammunition, turned for home.

Back at Le Hameau, the pilots made out their combat reports, all agreeing that the German pilot had put up a remarkable fight. James later commented. '…he was a very cool and experienced hand, for I must admit that he made us all look fools, although it must be borne in mind that he was flying a machine which was then superior to ours… Anyhow, I give that Hun full marks.'[29 & 30]

It may seem incredible that none of the patrol, in a fight which lasted over five minutes, had managed to hit the Halberstadt, but gun sights were still crude and although the concept of deflection shooting was well known and understood – many pilots were of the social class that regularly hunted – firing from a fast moving aeroplane at another, that was also flying at speed, and at different and varying angles, was still a skill that was being learnt the hard way, by practical experience. James was no mean shot, his rifle and Lewis gun marksmanship in 3 Squadron are amble proof, but he had yet to master aerial gunnery. A memorandum of the time, circulated by RFC

A Fokker D.III, this one flown by Oswald Boelcke. Power was a double-row 160 hp Oberursel U.III rotary. Credit A.Imrie.

HQ, attempted to formulate the tactics for fighting in single-seat scouts. Some of the points in the memorandum were self evident and were dismissed by many pilots – some with over six months experience in combat flying – as so much headquarters hot air, but James studied the reports carefully and much of his later success was due to following its precepts.

Grattan-Bellew also took notice of the memorandum, particularly the passage that read: Pilots must give constant attention to increasing their skill, not only as pilots, but also as machine gunners, and to keeping their machines in fighting trim. Important as are self-control and courage in action, an attack to be successful must be thoroughly carried out. The chief characteristic, however, of a fighting pilot is a fixed determination to bring down the greatest possible number of adversaries.

Grattan-Bellew also stepped up training in firing practise and formation flying, placing it on a more regular and formal basis than the rather ad hoc system it had previously been.

The weather was now remarkably fine for November and the squadron flew regular patrols throughout the rest of the month. On 17 November, the squadron lost another two pilots when the C Flight Commander, Captain S.E. Cowan, and 2nd Lieutenant W.S.F. Saundby,[31] were both killed in a mid-air collision while attacking an enemy scout.

Patrolling the Gommécourt area on 23 November, James had a long fight with an enemy two-seater over Miraumont, but was forced to break off the action when the steel breach bolt of his Lewis broke owing to the extreme cold. This two-seater, flying red, white and black streamers from its struts, was a type he had not seen before – he learnt later that it was known to the local British AA batteries as the 'Slug'.

During the rest of November, James flew three uneventful patrols, with an additional three in December – all his logbook entries detailing: 'Chasing HA. 2 LVGs seen high. No Huns seen' – until 20 December, when he had his next combat.

An afternoon patrol of six DH2s had been depleted by various troubles, leaving only James and his Flight Commander, Captain Payn. Enemy aircraft were particularly numerous and active, and at 12,000ft, flying south over Mercatel with Payn, James was attacked by an Albatros, which having finished its reconnaissance was flying east from the British lines. James returned fire at 200 yards, turning after the Albatros as it passed him, but by the time he had completed his turn the Albatros was 300 yards away. James fired the remainder of his drum at it, with no apparent effect. Payn then dived 'almost vertically' at the Albatros, firing a full drum, but again, this had no effect and it dived away.[32]

During the day, A Flight had been in combat with Jasta 2, during which the Flight Commander, Captain A.G. Knight[33] had been shot down and killed by Manfred von Richthofen[34] for his thirteenth victory. Two other DH2s were badly shot about in the fight and crash-landed, but both pilots were unhurt.

The weather was now bitterly cold. Flying at 12 to 13,000ft, the unfortunate pilot of a DH2, seated in the nacelle, gaining no warmth from the rear-mounted rotary engine, was utterly frozen. On one patrol James was so intensely cold and miserable that he did not trouble to even look round to see if any enemy aircraft were about to attack him: 'in fact, I did not care whether I was shot down or not. I was so utterly frozen.'

Patrols were flown on the morning of Christmas Eve, but the weather later deteriorated, patrols were cancelled, and the squadron settled down to its Christmas celebrations: dinner, followed by an evening concert. The weather was still bad on Christmas Day, there was no flying, and the pilots enjoyed a day's well-earned rest. 'Christmas 1916 came and went very quietly on the whole, and in a few days was completely forgotten.[35]

In the afternoon of 27 December, six DH2s of the squadron and six Nieuports of 60 Squadron flew a patrol from Arras to Monchy: the Canadian ground forces were undertaking a large raid in the area and it was essential that no enemy machines were allowed to interfere with the operation. The DH2s left the ground at 2PM and crossed the front lines at 10,000ft near Arras, the Nieuports of 60 Squadron being further east and higher. Three of the patrol returned to Le Hameau with technical troubles, leaving only Captain Payn, the leader, with Alexander Jennings[36] and James. After an hour patrolling a mile east of the lines, several German Albatros scouts from *Jasta* 2 came up from their aerodrome at Pronville.[37] Getting up to the height of the DH2s, the German pilots flew a parallel course with the British scouts, gradually edging nearer, until one of the enemy pilots flew close enough for Payn to attack him. This was a *Jasta* tactic: as soon as Payn attacked, another Albatros pilot dived onto his tail. Jennings saw this and immediately dived to Payn's aid. Two more Albatros pilots then dived on Jennings, forcing him to take drastic avoiding action. Seeing this, James dived, attacking the Albatros nearest to Jennings. The German pilot turned quickly and came at James nose on, firing as he came. As the Albatros and DH2 closed the distance, James also opened fire, but his gun stopped after twenty rounds with a cross feed. Defenceless in the middle of five enemy machines, James half rolled away out of trouble and spun vertically for a few hundred feet before leveling out. As he did so he heard machine gun fire again. A hasty glance over his shoulder showed that the Albatros pilot had followed him down, was now just behind him. James half rolled and spun again but the enemy pilot was insistent and had stayed with him, still firing at every opportunity. James continued to half roll, each time spinning away, edging towards the British lines until he was over the trenches and down to 2,000ft. But the Albatros pilot was still behind him and drove him down to 800ft over Basseux, a mile west of the front lines. The enemy pilot, now coming under heavy anti-aircraft fire, finally left James and climbed away to the east. James cleared his gun jam and returned to the trenches, climbing in pursuit of the Albatros, which easily out-climbed him, rejoined its companions and flew away to the east.[38]

Jennings now appeared and joined up with James. Seeing some FE2s fighting near-by they hurried to join in the action, but by the time they arrived at the scene the German machines had broken off and dived away eastwards. James and Jennings were now coming to the end of their petrol and they turned for home.

Landing at Le Hameau, James reported to Captain Geoffrey T.R. Hill, his new Flight Commander. Hill was astonished to see him back – 'looked at me as at a ghost'. Payn, who had landed earlier, having left the fight with the German scouts due to engine trouble, had reported that he had last seen James going down 'out of control over Hunland, with a fat Hun in attendance' and it had been assumed that James had been shot down and had crashed on the other side.

Later, looking over 7985, James was gratified to find his evasive flying had been so effective; it had not been hit once by the German pilot, despite the length of the fight and the number of rounds he had fired. Jennings, on the other hand, who had only been fired at for a few seconds, found his machine riddled with bullet damage.

Even against the vastly superior Albatros – which by virtue of its speed could break off any action when out-manoeuvred by the DH2 – James enjoyed these fights: 'so long as I came out of them, but it was no fun fighting an enemy who was 15 miles an hour faster and had almost twice the climb'.

The next day, James was notified that his commission had been granted, to take effect from 1 January. Four days later, he left on two weeks leave.

*

While at home, James took the opportunity to purchase his new uniform, discarding the universal wrap-over maternity jacket[39] which he had proudly worn since his earliest days in the Corps, in favour of an officer's regimental tunic. As usual he thoroughly enjoyed his leave, being one of those people who can compartmentalise their various activities. On duty, James was the professional soldier, fully committed and focused on the job in hand, but at home he switched off, enjoying the social life of his family and seeing all the latest musical and revue shows in London – the last almost obligatory for officers on leave.

On 19 January, James returned to France, taking the leave boat to Calais. The journey was not without incident. His train from Calais to Amiens not leaving until the next morning, James had lunch at a hotel, where he met a captain in the Yorkshire Regiment who was catching a train that evening to Béthune. James decided that this would be a far better way to travel back to Le Hameau: train to Béthune, then try to get a lift in a car going towards Le Hameau. James and the captain had dinner together at the hotel and caught the train to Béthune at 6PM. All the windows in their second-class carriage were broken and it was intensely cold. By midnight, James and his companion were so thoroughly frozen that in desperation they lit some paper on the floor of the compartment. This warmed them a little, although they were choked by the smoke, the lesser of two evils. After a miserable eight hours, the train finally arrived at Béthune, where James stayed the remainder of the night at the Station Hotel. Next morning, having no luck in finding a car going towards Le Hameau, James caught another train, this time to St.Pol. Here he was more fortunate and managed to get a lift to Le Hameau, arriving at the squadron in time to just miss Jack Noakes, who had left for England that morning after flying on active service in France for thirteen months.

At breakfast – for the first time in the officer's Mess – his now fellow officers were welcoming and friendly, but there was a certain constraint in the air. At first, James put this down to a slight awkwardness at having a newly-commissioned NCO in the Mess, but when he enquired if anyone had flown his 5985 in his absence, Lieutenant N A Birks,[40] somewhat shamefaced, confessed that ten days ago, during a firing practice, he had crashed it, damaging it beyond any repair possible in the squadron's workshops. If James was a little peeved about this – he had lavished a great deal of personal care on 5985 – he nevertheless joined in the general laughter.[41]

After breakfast and unpacking his kit, James went down to the hangars, found his replacement machine, DH2 7858, and took off for a ten-minute test flight. Finding the DH2 satisfactory, he flew it that afternoon in a twenty-five minute solo patrol from Arras to Monchy, his logbook entry: 'chasing HA' recording the usual frustration at being unable to catch the fast German two-seaters.

Snow storms stopped all flying the next day, but on 23 January, four inches of snow having been cleared from the aerodrome, a patrol led by Captain Hill took off at 8.30AM. After patrolling for an hour and a half, Hill dived on a two-seater, 3,000ft below them over Monchy-le-Preux. Suspecting that the two-seater could be a decoy, Hill wisely signaled for the remainder of the patrol to stay at 6,000ft in order to deal with any enemy scouts that might be in the vicinity. This was wise decision: six enemy scouts came out of the sun, diving through the higher DH2 formation to attack Hill. The three DH2s followed them down and a general mêlée began, the British pilots fully aware that being a considerable distance east of the trenches it would be a hard fight.

James attacked one Albatros and fired half a drum. The Albatros pilot shut off his engine and went down, his dive becoming increasingly steeper. James followed, sure he had seriously damaged the Albatros, but a burst of fire made him look back: the blunt nose of a rotary-engined Fokker D.III was behind him. James turned sharply and the Fokker pilot overshot in his attack, passing in front and slightly above the DH2. James pulled down his Lewis gun,[42] but after only a few shots the DH2 began to vibrate alarmingly – several spent cartridge cases had fallen back into the propeller, breaking it.[43] James immediately switched off his engine and dived westwards, followed by the Fokker. James was now in an extremely precarious position. Any attempt to steepen his dive to gain speed immediately caused the engine to increase its revolutions, setting up the vibration again. At 2,000ft the Fokker pilot turned away. James, not knowing why the enemy pilot had left him, but thankful that he had, hurriedly looked for a place to land. Picking out a field just behind Arras, he put the DH2 down, close by a field battery. James walked over to the guns and telephoned for the squadron to send a mechanic with a new propeller. While he waited, the officers at the battery gave him breakfast and kept him amused until the tender arrived from the squadron with Curteis, his engine mechanic, and a replacement propeller. Curteis and James fitted the propeller, started the Monosoupape, and James took off, successfully dodging the numerous shell holes in the field.

Arriving back at Le Hameau, James found that he had his CO to thank for his escape from the Fokker. Grattan-Bellew had arrived at the scene of the fight, had seen that James was in trouble and had driven off the enemy scout.

One of the pilots on this patrol was Cecil de Burgh Rogers[44] who failed to return from the fight. It was feared that he had been shot down, but later in the day he turned up. He had been chased back as far west as St.Pol by two of the Albatros pilots, who had finally hit his petrol tank, forcing him to land. St.Pol was over twenty miles behind the British lines and as it was extremely unusual for German pilots to venture so far over, James surmised that the enemy pilots must have been so infuriated at taking so long to bring Rogers down that they had thrown their customary caution to the wind.

With Lieutenant A. Norman Benge[45] leading, James flew another OP in the afternoon. South of Arras, over Ficheux, the patrol spotted an Aviatik two-seater spotting for German artillery at 7,000ft, well below the DH2s. Benge attacked first, but turned away with a gun stoppage. James then dived steeply in a series of S-turns, got into position on the Aviatik's right rear, five hundred feet above it, and opened fire. There was no return fire from the enemy gunner. Closing to within two hundred feet James quickly switched to the Aviatik's left rear, finishing the rest of his Lewis gun drum at fifty yards, watching his tracers traverse from its left to right wing tip. As James turned away to put on a new drum he saw the enemy gunner, standing up in his cockpit, his gun pointing away from the DH2, evidently struggling to rectify a stoppage. By the time James had loaded a new drum, the Aviatik, diving steeply, was well behind Adinfer Wood, too far east to re-engage. James later confided in his dairy that his aim 'was too hasty, otherwise I think I would have got him'. Later, giving some thought to the fight, James was furious with himself, arguing that if he had had sufficient courage to get to within such close range of the enemy machine – all his fellow pilots remarked on how close he had been – then he should surely have had enough to sight carefully and deliberately.[46]

That night, James wrote to his father:
23-1-17
Dear Dad,
Just a line hoping you are well. I am now settled down here

again. A Hun airman lost his way a few days ago and landed in the middle of our aerodrome. He blew up his machine before we could get to him. I had a few Huns in the air today and had two scraps. I sent one down in a very steep dive but did not see him hit the ground because I was attacked by another Hun behind me, and he attracted all my attention.

It is intensely cold the wind being N.E. We have four inches of snow down.

The evenings are drawing out again now thank goodness.

Well, Dad, I have a lot of letters to write so must close trusting this finds

You well as it leaves me at present.

Your Affec 'te Son
Jim

PS. Cis's birthday today although I have not written my thoughts are with her.

The next day, James flew two patrols, both of which were unsatisfactory. The first, led by Hill, saw another frustrating encounter with an enemy two-seater, pointed out to the patrol by British anti-aircraft fire over Humbercamp. This intruder, carrying out a high reconnaissance, was flying at well over 14,000ft, three thousand feet higher than the DH2s, whose effective ceiling was 14,000ft. James coaxed the DH2 to within 500 feet of the enemy machine, elevated his gun and opened fire, but with no result.

The second patrol of the day was equally unproductive. James recorded in his logbook: '2 HA seen too far off to engage'.

The morning of 26 January brought far better luck. A patchy but heavy ground mist caused the first patrol at 8AM to be washed out after only fifteen minutes, but an hour later the weather had improved, the faint sun having burned off the mist, and the patrol – Geoffrey Hill, Norman Benge and James – took off again at 9.20AM. Forty-five minutes after takeoff, an enemy two-seater was seen flying north over Ficheux at 4,000ft. Hill and Benge both went down to attack, but had no success. James then dived and opened fire from two hundred yards, closing the distance, firing all the time, and finishing his drum at a hundred yards. The enemy machine rolled over onto its right wing, then side-slipped for five hundred feet before going down in a vertical dive, a sure sign that the pilot had been hit, before disappearing into the ground mist at three hundred feet. This machine was credited to James as out of control, but it had not recovered before plunging into the mist and he was confident that it must have crashed. This C-Type enemy two-seater was James' second official victory.

On 1 February James' logbook entry shows only: 'OP 6 Huns seen' but a patrol the next day had a more positive result, with James claiming his third victory.

C Flight, with James leading, took off after lunch. Going south over Monchy-au Bois at 2.45PM, they sighted an enemy two-seater crossing the British lines just to the south of Monchy. James led his patrol – consisting of two new pilots – down to attack the intruder. Lieutenant A.J. Pearson[47] attacked

James wrote to his a father after returning to 29 Squadron as a newly-commissioned officer.

first, but was forced to pull away with a gun stoppage. James closed to within two hundred yards of the enemy machine and fired half a drum, but as he closed the range to a hundred yards he almost collided with another DH2 coming in from his left, also firing at the two-seater. James was forced to turn away to avoid a collision, cursing the pilot of the DH2 whom he assumed was one of the new pilots. Meanwhile, the two-seater had gone down, but was later confirmed by an anti-aircraft battery to have crashed.

On landing James found that the pilot of the other DH2 was none other than Grattan-Bellew. He had taken off on a lone sortie, forty-five minutes after the patrol, had seen the action and had decided to join in. James was convinced that Grattan-Bellew had got the two-seater, being the last to fire, but Grattan-Bellew insisted that it should be a shared victory between himself and James.

Since James had returned from leave on 20 January, the weather had been settled: every day being intensely cold, with heavy frost, but with good to fair visibility, and C Flight was averaging two patrols a day. At 7AM each morning, James consulted the thermometer on the outside of his hut. It regularly registered between twenty four to twenty six degrees of frost, but he observed that, remarkably, the atmosphere at 10,000ft seemed warmer than on the ground. The freezing weather, however, had its positive side, at least for the pilots of 11 Squadron. They had not flown for a week. Every morning, as they poured boiling water into the radiators of their FE2ds, and started their engines, the water immediately froze solid.

On 5 February, C Flight took off at 3PM to escort bombers on their way back from bombing Douai. James was a little apprehensive about this duty. Close by the town was a large German aerodrome: 'it was there that crowds of Albatroses and Halberstadters made their home.'

The DH2s crossed the front lines at 9,000ft over Rollincourt and flew eastwards, following the Sensée river. Over Vitry, a large formation of British aircraft was seen coming from the north-east, under heavy fire from Archie. The DH2s formed up with the formation – FE2bs, FE8s, BE2ds – and James felt again 'that pleasant thrill that I always felt when about thirty of our machines were all together over the German lines, all turning and intertwining to miss the numerous Archie bursts.'

Below the British machines, a considerable number of German scouts had left their aerodrome, but made no move to attack such a large formation. As soon as the bombers had been seen safely over the British lines, James turned the Flight back towards Douai, only to find that 'the Huns had all gone home to tea', so he fired the washout signal and the DH2s returned to Izel, James and his good friend Pearson having a final, high-spirited practise fight over the aerodrome before landing.

A patrol in the early morning of 6 February saw several enemy machines, but these were too far off to engage. After lunch, James took off alone: 'looking for Huns'. He had not long to wait. As he approached the front lines, British anti-aircraft bursts pointed out an Albatros C.III flying east over Berles-au-Bois, two miles behind the British front line, evidently returning from photographing the British back areas. James intercepted the Albatros just to the west of Monchy-au-Bois and opened fire at two hundred yards range. The enemy gunner returned fire: 'we both blazed away at one another'. The Albatros then went into a steep dive. For a moment James thought that he had brought it down in the allied lines – every pilot's ambition – but the enemy pilot flattened out and flew off to the east. James put a fresh drum on his Lewis gun and attacked again. This time the Albatros made an 'unmistakeable plunge' and the pilot finally put it down in the north-eastern corner of Adinfer Wood, where it turned over onto its back in the snow and was later destroyed by British artillery. James then returned to Izel to claim his fourth victory.[48] He had been in the air for only thirty-five minutes.

At this time, James, ever the tactician, had realised that although the DH2 was at a severe disadvantage when fighting the new German scouts, the German two-seaters could still be successfully attacked if the right tactics were employed. He was now flying at every opportunity, studying the habitual flight patterns of the enemy two-seaters, their methods of working and the different types used.[49] They were generally faster than the DH2, and could escape any attack by diving away, but given the advantage of height, this evasive tactic could be negated. Accordingly, after his usual Flight patrols, he began to fly daily solo missions, gaining his optimum height and waiting for any enemy two-seater to appear.

During the next three days James flew several such solo patrols, and another with the Flight, all without incident, but on 10 February C Flight were in a large scale action with enemy scouts.

The Flight had taken off on the morning patrol and was flying in two groups, one slightly lower than the other. Over Mercatel the lower group was attacked from behind by six Albatros scouts that dived on them from out of the early morning sun. None of the DH2s were damaged in this first attack and the German pilots zoomed, turned, and again dived on the DH2s. The higher group then dived into the fight and a typical free-for-all began. For once the British pilots had a slight advantage in numbers – the Albatros pilots had evidently not seen the higher group before attacking the lower – and the fight went on for some time, just west of the front lines, until the enemy pilots took advantage of their superior speed to break off the action and clear east.

Birks had attacked and fired at two of the Albatros scouts, until his gun jammed, forcing him to turn away out of the fight. James had got onto the tail of one of the enemy scouts, but after firing only eight shots his gun had also stopped with a double feed.

The Flight reformed and continued to patrol, flying south. Forty minutes later they saw three DH2s of 32 Squadron in trouble with six Albatros over Gommecourt. The DH2s were obviously getting the worst of the fight and the Flight dived to their aid. James and Leslie Essell[50] drove two Albatros off the tail of one of the 32 Squadron DH2s, the rest of the patrol also picking their targets, but with the odds now against them the enemy pilots again used their superior speed to break off the action.

On the morning of 15 February, James led 2nd Lieutenants R.J.S. Lund[51] and L.L. Carter[52] in an Offensive Patrol over the Arras area. Flying north over Adinfer Wood at 11,000ft, a pair of two-seaters were seen, an Albatros C-Type escorted by a Roland C.II, also flying north. James dived on the Albatros, closed the range to two hundred feet and fired a whole drum of Lewis into it. Turning away to change his drum, he was attacked from behind by the Roland. James turned quickly, reversed the positions and fired half a drum at his new attacker, which dived away to the east, as usual easily outdistancing the DH2.

Later in the patrol, going north over Blainville, James again saw the Roland approaching the British lines. He dived to 1,500ft over the trenches and got within fifty feet of the enemy machine before it turned away. James followed and the DH2 and Roland circled, each manoeuvring for an advantageous attacking position. The enemy pilot suddenly steepened his turn, causing his gunner to hold onto the fuselage with one hand, while erratically pointing his gun at the DH2 with the other. James saw this and realised it was his opportunity. He tightened his turn to inside the Roland, 'banged' on a fresh drum and expended it all from twenty feet. The Roland went down in a steep dive, pouring black smoke, made an attempt to land, but wiped off its undercarriage and stood up on its nose before falling back. Turning away to change his drum,

The fifth victory: An L.F.G. Roland C.II (this mid-production aircraft shown at the front). Unofficially known as the *Walfisch* (Whale), the Roland C.II began to equip the *Flieger Abteilung* units of the German Air Service at the beginning of 1916. All production C.II aircraft after the first production batch had a synchronized gun for the pilot. Credit A.Imrie.

James was down to three hundred feet, a little to the west of Adinfer Wood, but his engine was missing badly and he turned west, crossing the front line trenches at a hundred feet, luckily attracting less ground fire than he had anticipated.

Landing at Izel, James made his report, claiming the Roland that had crashed east of Monchy. He had pressed home his attacks on the Roland with determination, and was 'very bucked indeed' when Grattan-Bellew called him 'a young tiger'. Lund and Carter both confirmed that the Roland had crashed. It was James' fifth victory, his last in 29 Squadron.

After lunch, Grattan-Bellew took six pilots in formation to Monchy. Diving from 1,000ft, they each took turns in firing three drums into the wreck of the Roland for practice.

The next day, James led his patrol over the trenches at Arras. The clouds were low, at 5,000ft, and James had too much respect for the enemy anti-aircraft gunners to venture too far east. Flying over Monchy – where the wreck of the Roland still lay on the ground – James saw a BE2 fighting two enemy scouts over Gommécourt. He led the Flight to assist the BE, but as they hurried to the scene one of the enemy scouts went over onto its back, then into a vertical dive, finally going through the roof of a house in Hébuterne, 'with an awful whack and a lot of flying debris'. The remaining enemy scout, not wishing to share a similar fate, made off. 'By Jove!' James thought. 'That's the stuff to give the Hun.'

Later in the patrol, eight Albatros D.I were seen, two miles east of the German trenches. Six of the Albatros went up into the cloud cover, leaving two below as decoys. These edged nearer to the DH2s, hoping to entice them into a fight, but James now had enough tactical expertise not to fall into the obvious trap.

On landing back at Izel, James was met by Grattan-Bellew with two pieces of news – one gratifying, one less so. The first was that Brigade HQ had endorsed Grattan-Bellew's recommendation for a Military Cross, submitted after the victory over the Roland. The second, less welcome, was that he had flown his last patrol with 29 Squadron: he was posted to Home Establishment, taking effect on 23 February.

James was extremely disappointed at this last. He felt that he had at last hit his stride as a fighter pilot, plus the current rumour that the squadron's aging and obsolete DH2s were shortly to be replaced by Nieuports, an aeroplane perhaps more capable of fighting the enemy Albatros and Halberstadt scouts on equal terms.

James travelled to Home Establishment with Captain Henry 'Duke' Meintjes,[53] Captain John Quested,[54] and another pilot, named Thomson.[55] The quartet left Izel-le-Hameau early on the morning of 23 February, had breakfast in Hesdin and completed their journey to Boulogne by car. That evening, James was home again in England.

Ch.8: Fighting Instructor

Edward 'Mick' Mannock while training at Joyce Green in March 1917.

Albert Ball. Photographed at London Colney in Hertfordshire about the time James met him in London.

At home, reflecting on his progress in his chosen profession, James must have felt a great deal of satisfaction and justifiable pride. At the outbreak of war in August 1914 he had left for France as an air mechanic. In thirty-one months he had risen steadily through the ranks: from corporal, to sergeant, to flight sergeant pilot, and finally to commissioned rank as a 2nd Lieutenant. As a mechanic in 3 Squadron he had won the respect of all, not only for his technical expertise with engines but for his enthusiasm, his willingness to tackle any task he was given, and for unswerving devotion to his duties. Later in the squadron he had also served as an unofficial observer and gunner, his courage and coolness in combat earning further respect from his commanding officer, flight commander and other pilots with whom he flew. In his eight months as a service pilot flying a total of 214 hours, including 28 Offensive Patrols, he had destroyed three enemy aircraft, sent another two down out of control, no doubt damaged several others, and had driven off many more, preventing them from carrying out their duties. He had also been awarded a Military Medal, a Military Cross, and the French *Croix de Guerre*.

In the extremely structured and class-conscious times of the early Twentieth Century, when autocracy rather than meritocracy was the general rule, James' rapid rise through the ranks, even given the heady atmosphere of war with its enhanced opportunities for promotion, is an indication of what a remarkable young man he was – he was not yet twenty-two years of age. He was not alone, of course. To replace the many young men from the public schools and universities, the traditional officer class, who had been killed or wounded in the slaughter of the trenches, men from a wider section of society had to be commissioned. This resulted in the commission of many able and talented men, either from the ranks or newly recruited. As an indication of the still prevalent class conscious attitude, these were ironically known as 'temporary gentlemen'.

Unlike many of his contemporaries, who regarded fighting in the air as a glorified form of sport – often describing it in sporting terms – James had given a great deal of thought to the whole subject. His tactics in attacking enemy machines, and his shooting skills, had both been refined and steadily improved during his time with 29 Squadron and he had gained at great deal of combat 'savvy'. He knew exactly when or when not to fight, freely admitting that at times of tactical disadvantage, 'discretion is the better part of valour'. His avowed intention was the destruction of as many of the King's enemies as possible with the least loss to himself or his Flight. As his friend 'Duke' Meintjes put it: 'To wage war with much cunning'.

However, James was far from complacent. He knew that he still had much to learn. His diary entries are full of self criticism, both of his tactics and gunnery. He was also aware that given the casualties suffered by 29 Squadron during his time with the squadron – twelve pilots, two thirds of the squadron's strength, had been killed, wounded or taken prisoner of war – that he had survived his first eight months of active service flying due to a certain amount of luck, luck which had seen him through several dangerous situations.

*

While waiting for his next posting, James spent his ten day's leave at his parents' new home in Burton Road, Kingston-on-Thames. His father was not living at home. He had taken up the position of chief clerk at the A.S.C. depôt in Sheerness, and was living in lodgings near the depôt. For James, this was probably a mixed blessing. William senior smoked a powerful plug tobacco, which he sprinkled with lavender oil to improve the aroma, and was in the habit of eating raw onions with his tea, maintaining that they were good for his health. Although very close to his father, James, who both drank and smoked in moderation, no doubt found this rather trying. His mother Amelia, and sisters, Kathleen and Mary, were overjoyed to have James home. It seems that Amelia had by now come to terms with the loss of Bill, her eldest son, and was extremely proud of all her remaining boys in uniform. James was now a decorated, commissioned flying officer; Anthony – Jack to the family – had started his ground training in preparation for becoming a pilot; and Maurice, at fourteen years old the baby of the family, had just become an apprentice in the RFC. Following Bill's death, Amelia had no illusions in respect of the risks of flying, but James was now home for the immediate future: safe from the war for the time being.

During his leave, the London Gazette carried the notification of James' Military Cross. Brushing aside the requests from his sisters and various girlfriends, Amelia took upon herself the task of sewing on the blue and white ribbon beneath his wings. On his previous leave, with excusable logic, she had placed the ribbon of the French Croix de Guerre, James' first decoration, first on his tunic, not knowing that the ribbon of the British MM took precedence. This time she made

Miss 'Teddie' O'Neill.

no mistake. As she sewed on the ribbons, now three, beneath the pilot's wings, she no doubt remembered that Bill had once told her: 'Mother, you will see Jim covered in medals one day.'

It was during this leave that an incident occurred which became an in joke among the family. While James was out one day, Amelia brought his Military Cross down into the kitchen to show her friends. After they had gone, having been duly impressed, Amelia put the medal in the knife drawer of the kitchen dresser, meaning to return it to James' room later. She forgot. James came home. Not finding the medal in his room he asked where it was and Amelia had to explain. James was justifiably proud of his Military Cross and his other decorations, seeing them not so much as bravery awards but as official recognition of his success in his chosen profession, and was furious with his mother. He told her off in no uncertain terms, angrily explaining that it was a decoration awarded by the King himself, not a medal from the Band of Hope.[1] James was very close to his mother and later, having calmed down, was extremely contrite and apologised profusely to her. The episode became known to the family as The Medal in the Knife Drawer.

Vickers FB9 No.A8601 in which James instructed Mannock at Joyce Green.

James spent his leave in a way typical of many young officers home from the war. He spent the mornings and afternoons in the RFC club in Bruton Street, no doubt talking shop with both old and new friends, occasionally breaking the routine to take his sister Mary, working at the War Office, to lunch. James also delighted in taking Mary to the theatre. On one occasion he took her to the Lyceum in the Strand, to a matinee performance of *Romance* starring Doris Keane. Leaving the theatre, he said. 'Sis, I think we'll go to see *Tonight's the Night* at the Gaiety, now.' Mary thought this very extravagant, two shows in one day, and said so, but James just laughed and said that it was alright, she was not to worry about it. To kill time before the start of the show, they walked along the Strand to Piccadilly. Mary was unfamiliar with London's West End, with its maze of streets and squares, and after walking for some time James stopped and asked her if she knew where she was. She admitted she didn't. 'Well,' he said, laughing, 'You're exactly where you were five minutes ago.'

James thoroughly enjoyed the theatre, and in the evenings took one or other of his girl friends to a West End show, usually a musical: *Maid of the Mountains*, staring Billie Carleton; *The Bing Boys Are There*, at the Alhambra, with the ever-popular George Robey and Violet Lorraine, and *Chu Chin Chow* at His Majesty's Theatre, were all favourites – *Chu Chin Chow* ran for five years, a staggering 2,238 performances. These shows, and others, extremely popular with servicemen, were a great morale booster and attracted huge audiences.

James was also fond of the popular songs of the musicals and revues – *If You Were the Only Girl in the World* was the current favourite – and he would buy the sheet music, bringing it home to Kingston for Mary to play them on the family piano, sometimes as late as midnight, patiently explaining to her the subtleties of the phrasing of the melody – he had an excellent musical ear and sense of time – not apparent in the written score. Many years later, Mary vividly recalled one occasion when she failed to pause before a particular note. James stopped her. 'No, Sis,' he remonstrated, 'That won't do.' He explained that at that point the dancer made a high kick and that she, Mary, must give the dancer time to complete it.

As a good looking, beribboned young pilot, James was not short of female company – Mary remembered that he was not averse to playing the field a little – but in early 1917 he met an exceptionally beautiful young girl: 'Teddie' O'Neill, a Gaiety Girl starring as Venus in *Samples*, a review playing at the Vaudeville Theatre, and the relationship quickly became serious.[2]

While on leave James met Captain Albert Ball,[3] at that time the RFC's leading pilot with thirty-one aerial victories. James was very impressed by Ball: 'this keen-eyed pilot with his determined jaw'. Ball also wore three medal ribbons below his wings, his MC, the DSO and Bar, and the recently awarded Russian Order of St.George. Noting the three worn by James, Ball remarked that he would like to add the ribbon of the French *Croix de Guerre*. 'By Jove' James thought, 'that man is wonderful'. The example set by Ball was unparalleled and James was convinced that when Ball returned to active duty in France he would be sure to win a Victoria Cross.

Reporting for duty at the completion of his leave, James

A Martinsyde G.102 from the same production batch of A6250–A6300 as A2652, the machine in which James reached 18,500ft on 24 April 1917.

again met up with Meintjes and Thomson and the trio went to Hythe in Kent to give a series of lectures on fighting techniques and the performance of the latest German machines. After staying at Hythe for a few days, they travelled up to Ayr on the west coast of Scotland, the home of the No.1 School of Aerial Fighting. On 14 March, as a short break from his lecturing duties, James took up a Maurice Farman Shorthorn – his first opportunity to fly for nearly a month – his logbook recording a ten-minute flight. James and his companions were billeted in the large hotel at Ayr, and as the early spring weather was exceptionally fine they played a great deal of golf on the hotel's famous links. On the serious side of the war, they were shown the workings of the new Constantinesco interrupter gear, which James thought both ingenious and effective.

After two days at Ayr, James, Meintjes and Thomson travelled south to Orfordness in Suffolk, and it was here that James first flew a single-seat tractor scout, a Bristol Scout D. James had seen an earlier version of the Bristol in late September 1914, when a type B had been allocated to 3 Squadron, but he was then still a mechanic. Like many pilots, James thought the little Bristol a delight to fly, so much so that on his first flight he plucked up enough courage to attempt six loops, no doubt careful not to repeat his last ill-fated attempt at the manoeuvre in the DH2.

While at Orfordness, James was shocked and saddened to hear of the death in France of Major Grattan-Bellew. On 21 March, his squadron now fully re-equipped with Nieuports, Grattan-Bellew had taken off in the squadron's last DH2 to return it to the No.2 Aircraft Depot at Candas. Taking off, the DH2 was seen to suddenly side-slip, crashing on the far edge of the airfield. Grattan-Bellew was seriously injured and died of his injuries three days later.[4]

*

At the beginning of 1917, the ever-growing demand for new pilots to replace the casualties suffered by the squadrons in France – especially heavy after the fighting in April – led to an unprecedented expansion of the Royal Flying Corps. These new pilots had to be trained, not only to fly but in the rapidly evolving tactics of air fighting. Pilots with combat experience who were being rested after their tour of duty in the front line squadrons were utilised in this role, and James' next posting was as a fighting instructor to the 6th Wing at Maidstone, Kent. He was based a short distance from Maidstone, at Joyce Green, an aerodrome near Dartford. Joyce Green lay below the level of the nearby River Thames, on land formerly known as Frank's Farm, and pilots were often startled to see ships travelling up river, seemingly above their heads.

At Joyce Green, James' duties were to lecture and teach combat techniques to the advanced pupils of Nos.10 and 63 Reserve Squadrons. He was to do this by flying in mock

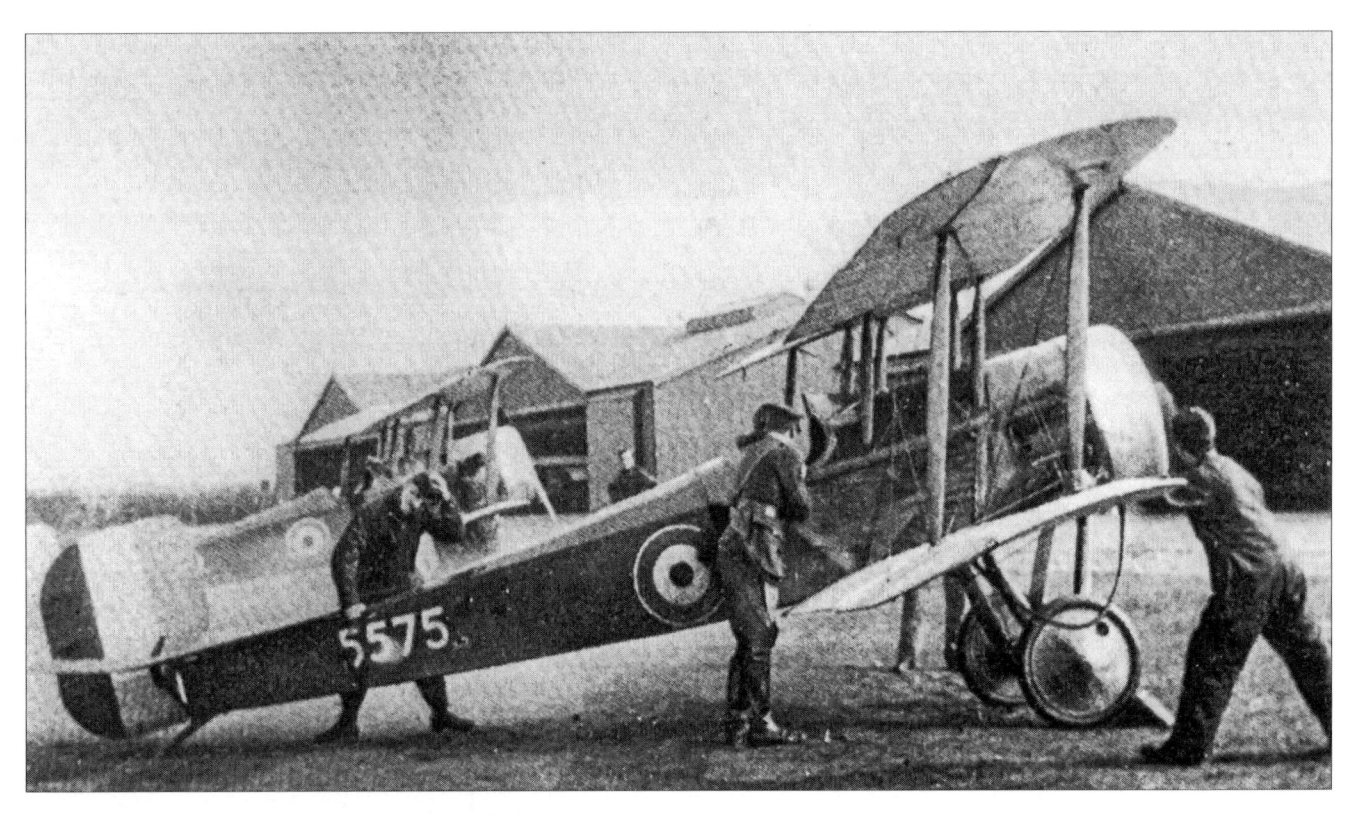

Bristol Scout D.5575 at Joyce Green, April 1917.

combat with them, giving solo flying demonstrations to be studied from the ground, and dual instruction. This last was initially given in a Vickers FB9, development of the earlier FB5, the Gunbus. The FB9 had been intended to replace the earlier version, but by late July 1916 various troubles had caused the type to be withdrawn from active service with the squadrons in France. James had been allocated a Bristol Scout for his solo demonstration duties, but it was not yet ready and on the morning of 23 March he flew a DH2 (A4798) in a ten-minute demonstration flight for the pupils, following this the next day with another in DH2 7867.

The serious business of dual instruction began on 24 March. On arrival at the field James was faced with a list of twelve officer pupils, all to be given a five or ten minute instruction flight: over two hours of demanding, intensive instruction. As the morning progressed he crossed them off, one by one: Captains Bush and Holman, then Lieutenants Reed, Lethbridge, Martin, Cadford, Tattersall and Hughes. After Hughes, with only four more pupils to go, James decided to take a break for lunch. After lunch, his first pupil was a Lieutenant Edward Mannock.[5] As they walked out to the Vickers, James thought that Mannock seemed rather old for a pupil so decided to give him an extra five minutes of instruction. Carman, Hunt and Skeffingham completed the instructing duties for the day.

These instructional flights consisted of James taking each pupil up in a dual control Vickers FB9. Before leaving the ground James would detail what he was about to show them, explaining that he wanted them to closely observe how he put the Vickers into the various positions used in combat. After demonstrating these in the air, in order for the pupil to understand the controls and to become used to the feel of the machine, he would hand over control to the pupil, who would then attempt to duplicate the manoeuvres. If the pupil did these to his satisfaction, James would then take off in another machine and mock-fight the pupil. After landing, he would point out their faults. This routine was followed until each pupil was considered proficient enough to progress to further instruction, flying the school's more advanced aeroplanes, the DH2s or FE8s.

Over the course of the next week, James flew a further fifteen demonstration and instructional flights, adding an additional four pupils to his list. In the first three days of April, he flew another series of instructional flights, with two new pupils. On 4 April, his mundane logbook entries of demonstration, instructing and joyride flights are broken by notation of a flight of fifteen minutes at 2,500ft in Vickers 8601. In the 'Passenger' column: 'Miss T. O'Neill'. The aerodrome at Joyce Green was also used by the Vickers company and James probably smuggled Teddie in through the company gate, although security at many of the RFC aerodromes in England was hardly stringent.

Early in April, James received a letter from an old friend, Sergeant Major Raymond Longman[6] stationed at Cramlington, Newcastle-upon-Tyne with 63 Squadron. Longman and James had both been at the Central Flying School in July 1916 and Longman wrote asking for news of other NCOs who had been there. James replied on 6 April, thanking Longman for his 'welcome letter'. After telling him of his whereabouts and details of his work at Joyce Green, he continued:

Yes, of the four who left the CFS last July, Mottershead,[7] Pateman[8] & Haxton,[9] I am the survivor (touch wood). I was in 20 on Rolls FEs from 7th July to 7th August. I then went to 29 and stayed with them until Feb 24th. During the last four months which we had on the Somme we lost twenty pilots, and I am very lucky to say that I dodged it… I saw Beere[10] in 41, they relieved us at Abeele when we went on the Somme.

I am afraid we are in for some heavy casualties in the RFC during the next few weeks, before we get our best machines out there. I am flying one of the De Havs' here and they think I am an awful nut because I spin it and turn it upside down. My machine I tour the sqdns on is a "Rhone" Bristol and a topping little bus.

I want to go out soon again and fancy the Sopwith camel (sic) which does 140 and climbs 10,000ft in 6 mins.

My heartiest congrats on your well earned promotion.

Well, old thing, no more news at present, so Cheerio and drop me a line any time.

Yours V Sincerely
Mac

Although the DH2 was no longer a front-line aeroplane, to the pupils at Joyce Green it was a fast scout that they had yet to master, plus it still had a reputation of being an aeroplane prone to spin. In early 1917, the spin was still not fully understood and the method of recovery had yet not been formalised or taught. James knew of the pupils' concern, and as he relates in his letter, often took up a DH2 and deliberately put it into a spin, only correcting and flattening out at low height to show them that it was perfectly safe if handled correctly. Mannock was extremely impressed by James' piloting abilities and after one such demonstration asked James how he had recovered from the spin. The advice James gave him was simple: to put all the controls central and to then offer up a quick prayer. Over the aerodrome the next morning, a DH2 was seen at 3,000ft, coming down in a spin. The pilot successfully pulled out at 200ft, but the DH2 was not over the landing field and disappeared from view behind the dyke. The watchers waited, expecting to hear a crash, but heard nothing. Later that day, Mannock buttonholed James to tell him that his advice on how to recover from a spin had that morning saved his life. James was impressed by Mannock, and they later became firm friends. Both were from military backgrounds – although James' home life was vastly different from that of Mannock – and were of the same political persuasion, Mannock in particular being an ardent socialist.

James enjoyed his time at Joyce Green, despite the gruelling teaching schedule. His fellow instructors were all pilots who had previously flown the DH2 in France – Captains: H.S. Long,[11] H.J. Payn,[12] von Poellnitz[13] and Martin[14] – and with the delights of London only a forty minutes run away: 'this little band of fellows made life very cheery, I can assure you'.

James with Bristol Scout D.5575.

Another source of interest was that the Vickers Company had their experimental testing field at Joyce Green and many different types of machines were being test flown there. James became friendly with Harold Barnwell, Vickers chief test pilot, and they had many technical discussions. James gained a great deal of aeronautical knowledge from Barnwell and flew with him in several of the Vickers machines he was testing.[15]

After three weeks at Joyce Green, James was posted to Dover. During his time at Joyce Green he had flown 57 demonstration and instructional flights, instructing 35 pupils.

The aerodrome at Dover was large, housing training squadrons of both the RFC and the Royal Naval Air Service, their sheds and hangers half a mile apart. In James' opinion, Dover was far from being the ideal aerodrome at which to instruct new and inexperienced pilots. Weather conditions were variable and could be extremely dangerous: there was usually a high wind and frequent sea mists would blow in, enveloping the landing field in minutes. It was not uncommon for one lot of sheds on the field to be in brilliant sunshine, while the others, half a mile away, were covered by a thick blanket of sea mist, and it was not unusual for the entire aerodrome to be

D.5575 with 'Teddie' now painted between the interplane struts.

bathed in sunshine one moment, but as dark as night the next under a blanket of sea fog.

James had been allocated a Bristol Scout D for his instructional duties at Dover, but the Bristol was not yet ready and he was given a Martinsyde G.100, which he flew for the first time on 16 April. The Martinsyde was a large, rather heavy machine, that had earned the nickname of 'Elephant', but James found it comfortable and warm, ideal for cross-county flights, and liked it immensely.[16] Later in the day he flew another type new to him, an RE8 (A3444) a machine from the third production batch. In the evening the Bristol (5575) was pronounced ready and James immediately took it up for a 15-minute test flight, finishing with four loops. James was delighted with his new mount and not a little proud, as it was the only one at Dover. All the pupils at the station looked with longing at the little Bristol, wondering if they would ever be expert enough to fly it, but in fact it was a delightfully easy aeroplane to fly: of all the aeroplanes produced during the war, the pilots of the era considered it, along with the Sopwith Pup, as the most enjoyable aeroplane to fly. It is perhaps no coincidence that both were developed from pre-war sporting aeroplanes.[17]

The only reservation James had about the Bristol was its engine, an 80hp Le Rhône. These engines were usually very reliable, but James commented that the Bristol's engine was a 'dud'. It gave only 1,050 revs per minute, whether climbing, flying level, or even diving with the engine full on, and it would take the Bristol no higher than 10,000ft. 'However, it was just powerful enough to get me off the ground, and that was the main thing.' Despite this fault, the Bristol was the first machine in which James was able to experience for himself the pure joy of flying for its own sake, unsullied by the possible presence of enemy aeroplanes, or with a pupil in the rear seat. 'Dud' engine or not, James evidently enjoyed the responsiveness of 5575. Over the next four days he flew it in seven demonstration flights, looping no fewer than 15 times. After his demonstrating duties on 20 April, James flew another type he had not flown before, a BE12a (565) an aeroplane that had been an abortive attempt in developing the two-seat BE2c into a fighter.[18]

After landing from his 'joyride' in the BE12, James took off in the Bristol to accompany Major Henderson,[19] the commanding officer at Dover, on a cross country flight to Croydon, via Ashford and Maidstone, with the major flying the Martinsyde. After staying the night at Croydon, they set off in the morning for the return flight to Dover. Conditions were very bad, with a heavy mist and clouds at 300ft, and James had to fly within fifty yards of Henderson to keep the Martinsyde in sight. He did not know the country at all well but Henderson evidently did, for they arrived back at Dover at 150ft and in good time.

There were several new and interesting types of aeroplanes at Dover, and James made full use of the opportunities to fly them, but the machine he liked most was the Martinsyde. After his return from Croydon, the weather evidently having improved, James flew Martinsyde G.102 (3949) on a cross-country flight to the Isle of Sheppey, via Deal and Herne Bay, then returning to Dover.

On 22 April, an old friend, William Mays Fry, called in for lunch with James. They had first met in 1915 and had met again while Fry was serving in 60 Squadron, based at Izel-le-Hameau and James was a sergeant pilot with 29 Squadron, flying from the same aerodrome. Fry, known as 'Willie', and James were similar in many ways and became firm friends over the years, meeting often at the RFC Club when their periods of leave coincided. Fry was on his way to France for his second tour of duty with 60 Squadron and after lunch caught the afternoon Folkestone boat.

Over the next few days, interspersed with his instructing duties – flying various marks of BE2s – James flew several cross country flights on one or the other of the school's Martinsydes. Being used only for training, the Martinsydes at Dover were lightly loaded, with no war load, and on 23 April James took off in Martinsyde A3996 to see just how high it would go. He managed to coax it up to 17,000ft, a thousand feet above its official ceiling, but on landing one of his fellow pilots told him that another Martinsyde, A6252, had a better performance, possibly because it was a true G.102, powered by a 160hp Beardmore engine. The next evening, after a morning flight in a Monosoupape-powered Avro 504 (A5905) – another type flown for the first time – James took off in A6252.[20]

It was a beautiful evening. James climbed steadily towards the Goodwin Sands, then turned north, still climbing, reaching 10,000ft over Canterbury twenty minutes later. After an hour, James was over Joyce Green at 18,000ft, still attempting to coax the Martinsyde higher, but over the south-eastern suburbs of London, at 18,500ft – 2,500ft over its official ceiling – the Martinsyde would go no higher. Visibility was exceptional and the view from this height was magnificent, the whole of the Kent coastline, from the mouth of the Thames estuary to Dungeness. However, James had taken off wearing only his British Warm, flying cap and goggles, and at this height, the highest he had ever been, he was feeling the intense cold. He throttled back the Martinsyde's engine, put its nose down, and began the long, slow descent back to Dover. During the twenty-minute return flight, James conjectured on the likelihood of meeting one of the German raiders which occasionally came over to bomb Sheerness or Chatham, idly speculating on the possibility, the Martinsyde being unarmed, of damaging the enemy's rudder with his undercarriage. Fortunately, he saw no enemy aeroplanes and landed safely at Dover to endure a splitting headache for the rest of the day, a

James, in less formal mood, with Bristol Scout D.5575.

legacy of his flight of two hours fifteen minutes at height.

Even at the training schools in England, the harsh realities of the war across the Channel could still intrude. There were several NCOs at Dover, recently returned from active service, who had been with 3 Squadron both before the war and in France. They had the latest news from the Front and James was saddened to learn that his old friend in the squadron, Sergeant Webb,[21] had been killed in January while flying a reconnaissance over Menin. James reflected that of the members of C Flight who had gone to France with 3 Squadron in August 1914, only half were still alive.

On 26 April James made three flights in his Bristol, performing no less than thirty loops, no doubt to relieve the tedium of the daily routine of demonstration and instruction, although this was broken on 29 April when he crashed BE2d 7345. The BE was due for an air test and James took it up, accompanied by his rigger, Corporal Skinner,[22] who came along for a joyride. Things did not go to plan. As they left the ground, one of the wheels of the BE came off. Unaware of this, James climbed to 2,000ft. It was a fine day and both he and Skinner were thoroughly enjoying themselves, blissfully

BE2d 7345 after the crash-landing on one wheel on 29 April 1917.

unaware of the missing wheel. After twenty minutes, James returned to the aerodrome. On his approach, the ground crew, having seen the wheel detach itself on takeoff, fired off a series of red Very lights to attract his attention, one of their number running out into the middle of the field, holding aloft the culprit wheel and pointing at the BE. James, realising what had happened, ascertained which wheel was missing, then brought the BE down as slowly as possible, landing gently on one wheel. The BE lurched along the ground until the axle dug into the grass, putting it up onto its nose. The BE was not seriously damaged and both James and Skinner were unhurt, although Skinner no doubt later reflected on the exact meaning of the term 'joyride'.

On the last day of April, James flew a DH5 for the first time, although he had added another de Havilland aeroplane, a DH4 (2164) to his logbook several days previously.[23&24]

On 2 May, James flew BE2e A1277 to Lympne, to lecture at nearby Hythe. For the moment, this was an end to his duties at Dover – he had instructed a further twenty-three pupils while there – and on 7 May he was assigned to lecture the various squadrons of 7th Wing in East Anglia. James suggested to Wing that a more up to date aeroplane than the Bristol Scout would be more suitable for this assignment. Wing agreed, and on 7 May he flew to Hounslow to collect Sopwith Pup A7311,[25] flying it the same afternoon to 65 Reserve Squadron's aerodrome at Wyton, Huntingdonshire, to begin his lecture tour, throwing in six loops on his arrival over the aerodrome. The next morning he took up the Pup for a height test, climbing to 10,000ft in thirteen minutes. The Pup had a far superior rate of climb than the Bristol Scout, and at this height, although powered by the same engine as the Bristol – an 80hp Le Rhône – and heavier, the Pup was 16mph faster.

While at Wyton, James gave a demonstration on a Bristol Scout – including the usual number of loops – and took the opportunity to add another new type flown into his logbook: a Nieuport 12 A5198.[26]

The following day, James flew four demonstration flights; one in Bristol Scout 5326 and three in the Pup, performing twenty loops in the last.

On 10 May, another new type was added to his logbook: a Grahame-White XV trainer, No.1689, from the first and only production batch for the RFC. Later in the day, after two more demonstration flights, he flew the Pup to 64 Squadron at Sedgeford, Norfolk, close by the Wash. The squadron was equipped with the FE2b and James, with some experience of the type, gave them what advice he could on how to counter attacks by German scouts. On his second day at Sedgeford, flying during the day was curtailed by the extremely hot weather and James, armed with a .303 rifle, spent the time in helping to cull the hares that were overrunning the surrounding countryside. Arriving back at the aerodrome with his bag of four hares and a partridge, James was dismayed to be given a dressing down by the commanding officer: not only was game out of season, but he had been poaching. The last two days at Sedgeford were spent in lecturing and demonstration flights, before flying on to 9 Reserve Squadron at King's Lynn. On his second demonstration flight at King's Lynn, James performed thirty loops, but in his next flight there, in an FE2b (7688) coming in to land too slowly, he lost speed and landed heavily, smashing a wheel. He admitted that this was sheer carelessness on his part, his only excuse being that he had become accustomed to bringing the Pup down at 40mph in a series of S-turns. The Pup being such a pleasure to fly, with no vices, and so controllable over a wide variation of speeds, pilots became

Sopwith Pup A7311. James was first allocated this Pup in May for his lecture tours of the training squadrons of 7th Wing in East Anglia.

so used to it that they sometimes forgot that the art of flying was not as easy as the Pup would have them believe. Flying other machines they tended to forget this, and James was of the opinion that the forgiving little Sopwith could very well be the cause of some of the flying accidents on other machines.

The next day, three more demonstration flights and lectures brought his brief tour of the East Anglian reserve squadrons to an end and he set off to fly back to Joyce Green. On the way, he landed at the RFC's testing aerodrome at Martlesham Heath to visit an old friend, Captain Reginald Carr.[27] After tea with Carr, James had a look at some of the experimental machines being tested at Martlesham before flying on to Joyce Green.

James was now thoroughly at home in the Pup. During his East Anglian tour he had flown it for over fifteen hours, thoroughly mastered the art of looping and had added the roll to his aerobatic skills. After lunch on 15 May, now fully confident in his ability to put on a flying display in the Pup, he succumbed to the temptation, known to all pilots of the time, to give his home town a flying display.

He arrived over Gillingham at 2,000ft and treated the town to a dazzling display of aerobatics, including over twenty loops. He then flew on to Sheerness, where his father was working, and repeated the performance, throwing in more loops to bring the total during the two displays to fifty. Although an aeroplane was now a fairly common sight in the skies above England, such displays were not and they caused a sensation in both towns. Rumour soon spread that the pilot was young James McCudden, and the editor of the local newspaper, the Sheerness Guardian, making the connection between Gillingham and Sheerness, put two and two together and sent a reporter to interview James' father. McCudden senior, however, knowing that the RFC did not look favourably on such displays – in fact they discouraged any publicity of its pilots or their achievements – guessed rightly that it would cause trouble for his son, declined to confirm that it was James and persuaded the reporter to drop the story.[28]

One of the pupils now at Joyce Green with No.10 Reserve Squadron, was James' younger brother Anthony,[29] and after returning to Joyce Green from the displays, James took him for an instructional flight in the dual-controlled Vickers FB9 (8601). James acknowledged that Anthony was 'keen' but thought him inclined to be over-confident, 'which always spells trouble for the fledgling' and cautioned him. After his morning activities, this advice of James is somewhat ironic, never having been short of confidence himself.

During the next six days, James checked out another seven pupils. On 21 May, he flew to the Central Flying School at Upavon to attend a Fighting Instructor's course. Over the next nine days, in addition to the lectures, James flew thirteen demonstration flights, adding another 63 loops to his logbook entries. The course was attended by many old friends, all of whom had served in France, and it had the added benefit of the exchange of experiences, plus the inevitable shop talk.

*

At 5PM on the evening of 25 May – the Friday of the Whitsun weekend – a force of twenty-one twin-engined Gothas of *Kagohl* 3 crossed the Essex coast. The target was London, but the low cloud cover was thickening, obscuring the ground, and the leader, *Hauptmann* Ernst Brandenburg, aborted the attack on the capital. The German bombers turned south, flew

On 8 May, while at Wyton, during his lecture tour of the training squadrons in 7th Wing, James flew this Nieuport 12 A5198. '1st trip on Nieuport.'

along the Kent coast, and dropped most of their bombs on the town of Folkestone and the nearby army camp at Shorncliffe. No warning had been sounded and 95 people were killed with another 195 injured. The bombers had flown over England for over ninety minutes but although more than 77 defence sorties were flown, only one bomber was shot down. Lack of communications to give warning of the raid, or the course flown by the bombers, plus the wholly inadequate performance of the available fighter aircraft, exposed the failure of the Home Defence forces. Only two pilots had engaged the Gothas, but these were ferry pilots, waiting to deliver machines to France, and not from a Home Defence squadron. It was not until the Gothas were approaching the coast of Belgium that they were successfully attacked: by nine Sopwith Pups from 4 and 9 RNAS squadrons, based at Dunkirk. One was shot down into the sea and another went down, apparently out of control. It was obvious that this raid would be repeated, and James began to give some thought to the arming of A7311.

At this time, the Vickers Company was test flying two of its new scout (fighter) designs at Joyce Green. One of these was a development of the Vickers FB12, the FB26 Vampire, a pusher design, powered with an air-cooled 200hp Hispano engine. James had renewed his acquaintance with Harold Barnwell, and after its first flight on 31 May, Barnwell allowed James to fly a ten-minute test flight in the new scout.[30] The other scout being tested was a tractor design, the FB16d, but James did not have the opportunity to fly this machine until later.

James was now dividing his time equally between Joyce Green and Dover, but was also making frequent lecture and demonstration visits to the reserve squadrons in 6 Wing. This nomadic existence entailed living out of a suitcase – that he strapped to the side of his Pup – taking advantage of the hospitality of the various squadrons' Officers' Mess. During these visits, James' professional and serious approach to his instructional duties earned him the reputation of being somewhat aloof and terse in manner with the pupils, many of whom had an exaggerated sense of self importance in respect of their new status as RFC pilots and were inclined to take his teaching less seriously than he wished. Knowing full well from his own experience the dangers they would soon be facing – perhaps in only a few short weeks – when flying operationally in France, he had no patience with this happy-go-lucky, laissez-faire attitude. In general his lectures were relaxed, informal affairs: he would sit on the edge of a table, smoking the occasional cigarette, illustrating his points with quick sketches on a blackboard, but despite this, for some pupils the underlying seriousness of his lecturing style seemed to be that of a professional instructing a group of amateurs, which was, of course, precisely what it was.

At the beginning of June, Sopwith Pup A7331 went into the squadron's workshops for an overhaul, and James travelled to Lympne to collect a Bristol Scout (A1767) and ferry it back to Joyce Green. Approaching Gravesend, engine failure forced him to land in a field just outside the town. Whatever the problem, it was soon resolved and a flight of fifteen minutes at 500ft saw him back at Joyce Green. Next day, 2 June, he took off, again in A1767, to visit 6 Wing HQ at Maidstone. After a short flight of only fifteen minutes, with no warning whatsoever, the engine of the Bristol cut dead over the village of Barming. At only 1,000ft, James was too low to reach the nearby aerodrome at West Malling and he quickly looked for a suitable place to put the Bristol down. Being Kent, most of the fields below were covered in hop poles, but he saw what he thought was a possible landing site: a meadow of uncut grass being grown for hay. However, this meant landing downwind, giving him two choices: to land downwind in the meadow, or upwind

The Bristol Scout and Sopwith Pup at Dover.

into the hop poles. He chose the meadow. Coming in at just above stalling speed, and seeing for the first time the height of the grass, he attempted to 'pancake' the Bristol, but hit the ground hard, wiping off the undercarriage, the impact pushing the engine up through the petrol tank. The Bristol slid on its bottom longerons through the grass for twenty yards before coming to a stop. James was unhurt and stepped quickly out to the Bristol, conscious of the possibility of fire. He was fully aware that this crash was entirely his own fault for flying so low over terrain that had little or no suitable landing grounds in the event of having to make a forced landing. Only the previous day he had been gazetted a Flight Commander, with the temporary rank of Captain, and he was conscious that the crash was not exactly an auspicious start to his new rank.[31]

Arriving back at Joyce Green, James found that his Pup was now ready and he immediately took off again for Maidstone. Arriving over the aerodrome, perhaps to convince himself that his nerve had not been affected by the morning's crash, he descended in a series of twenty loops, landing straight off the twentieth, completed at low level, just above the ground.

*

After what was seen as the success of the previous raid, The *Kommandeur* of *Kagohl* 3, *Hauptmann* Brandenburg, was under mounting pressure from the German High Command to bomb London. Fully aware that the capital was at the extreme range of his aircraft, Brandenburg knew that there was no margin of error, that he needed ideal weather conditions, with good visibility, to find the target quickly. On 5 June the weather was good but there was a strong easterly wind, which would considerably slow the Gothas on their flight home, so he chose Sheerness and Shoeburyness as alternative targets to London.

The Gothas crossed the English coast over Foulness Point at five minutes past six in the evening, turned south and began to drop their bombs twenty minutes later. Casualties were light, some bombs failing to explode, with others falling into the sea. Only three pilots of the Home Defence squadrons managed to find and attack the intruders and it was not until the bombers were approaching the Belgian coast that they were again attacked by the Pups and Sopwith Triplanes of the naval squadrons based at Dunkirk. The RNAS pilots claimed two of the Gothas as destroyed with another four sent down out of control, but the only loss admitted by the Germans was a Gotha that had been hit by the anti-aircraft guns at Sheerness and Shoeburyness, that fell into the sea. In this raid 13 people had been killed and 34 injured, less than the previous attack, but the next sortie by the Gothas of *Kagohl* 3 was to be more successful.

James had realised that his Pup was one of the few fighters with a performance capable of catching the enemy raiders, and on 3 June he flew to 49 Squadron at Dover to discuss with Corporal H. Parker[32] how it could best be armed. Parker improvised a mounting on the top wing of the Pup to carry a Lewis gun, with the provision of being able to elevate the gun and fire upwards, in a similar manner to that used previously by Albert Ball on a Nieuport. James had insisted on this, realising that any bomber he could catch and engage would almost certainly have the advantage of height. A rough aiming sight of wire, rings and beads was made and the little Pup was ready, as James later put it, 'to wage war with great skill'.

Next day, back at Joyce Green, he patrolled at 15,500ft over Dover, Deal and Ramsgate, the first of several standing patrols in the hope of intercepting any German raiders. On 5 June, although unaware that a raid was in progress, he flew another patrol, but was too far south of the Gothas, over Sheerness and Shoeburyness, and missed them entirely. He flew another patrol on 7 June, this time taking the precaution of patrolling further north, as far as the Thames estuary, but there was no raid that day. Landing back at Joyce Green, he ended the day

A group of pilots at Joyce Green in the early summer of 1917. James is on the extreme left. The officer on his left is possibly L.P. Aizlewood MC. The remainder are unidentified.

with a ten-minute flight in a Vickers, described in his logbook as a 'Sociable' commenting that it was 'a nice old bus.'[33]

During June, in connection with his lecturing duties, James was visiting several squadrons, and one frequently visited was 40 Reserve Squadron at Dover. On 13 June, scheduled to give a lecture there, he arrived in the Pup in the early morning. Taxying to the hangers, he realised that everyone was in a state of some excitement. As James got out of the Pup the commanding officer of the squadron came running up with news that a formation of Gothas had crossed the coast and was making for London. Cursing the fact that the Pup's Lewis gun and ammunition had been left behind at Joyce Green, James immediately took off again. He wasted no time in climbing, and flying at a 1,000ft he made the flight back to Joyce Green in just under 15 minutes, an average speed of 105mph. As he landed and taxied to the hangers he noticed a group of German prisoners, working on the aerodrome, gazing up at the sky with a great deal of satisfaction. James jumped from the Pup, yelling for his mechanics to fetch the Lewis gun and ammunition. While they were fixing the gun in position and loading the ammunition drums into his cockpit, James – no doubt fretting with impatience – was looking towards Woolwich, where he could both see and hear the bursts of the anti-aircraft guns of the capital. There were irregular layers of cloud at 5,000ft cutting off any sight of the Gothas, but as they passed overhead at Joyce Green the roar of their engines could be plainly heard. James estimated that there must be well over a dozen.

As soon as the Pup was ready, James took off, climbing up through the cloud layer until he came into clear air at 10,000ft. Through a small gap in the clouds below he saw that he was just over Chatham, so he turned east, still climbing, and finally arrived over Sheerness at 13,000ft. Intending to attack the Gothas as they left their target, James was unsure which route the bombers would take in returning to their base at St.Denis Westrem, in Belgium, but he reasoned that they would fly directly south-east, leaving British airspace over either the Essex or Kent coasts, so he climbed for additional height, reaching 15,000ft over Sheppey. Suddenly, he caught the flash of a gun fired at Southend and saw the characteristic black and white bursts of British anti-aircraft shells over Shoeburyness. James increased his speed and flew towards the bursts. After a few minutes he saw a large formation of machines, flying towards the south-east. James sacrificed a little height in order to gain speed and finally caught the enemy formation as it crossed the Essex coast. The loss of height to gain the necessary speed to catch the bombers meant that he was now 1,000ft lower than the rearmost Gotha in the formation, and by the time he had got to within 500ft feet of the enemy machine he realised to his dismay that the Pup was rapidly losing ground to the faster Gotha. They were now some twenty miles out to sea. James had visions of a long swim home if the Pup was hit in any vital part, so he made up his mind to fire all his ammunition before leaving the bombers. He fired his first drum, which seemed to have no effect – 'the Hun did not take the slightest notice'.

James in the cockpit of a Bristol Scout.

Another Pup now appeared at the scene of the action, close behind the Gotha, but it turned away as if the pilot were having some trouble with his gun.[34] James fired another drum of Lewis. This time, the Gotha seemed to swerve slightly, and one of its gunners opened fire at the Pup. He made good shooting; James could smell the incendiary bullets as they passed, but he put on his last drum of Lewis and emptied it into the Gotha, which flew serenely on, again taking not the slightest notice. Having expended all his ammunition, James turned west and flew back towards the Kent coast, because of the poor visibility an indistinct blur in the distance. Arriving over the coast, getting his bearings and setting a course for Joyce Green, James was furious that the Gothas were able to fly over England, bomb London, and then escape so easily.[35]

From the German point of view, the raid on 13 June had been highly successful. Included among the 162 civilians killed were 43 children, and an additional 432 people had been injured. Material damage was estimated at £129,498. In Germany, Brandenburg became a national hero and was awarded the *Pour le Mérite*, Germany's highest award for gallantry. In England, there was considerable public outrage at the ineffectual response of the home defences. The War Cabinet met during the afternoon of the raid to discuss the reports as they came in and to decide what action should be taken. The long term plan, decided upon the next day, was the expansion of the RFC and RNAS – to literally double their strength – but in the short term it was decided to bring over from France a 'crack' fighter squadron to give the next raiders 'one or two sharp lessons'. Field Marshal Sir Douglas Haig, commanding the British forces in France, was due in London on 17 June to attend a meeting of the War Cabinet and he was advised on June 15 that the question of detaching a fighter squadron, or squadrons, from France to address the question of the Gotha raids would be on the agenda for discussion. At the cabinet meeting on 17 June, it was decided that fighter patrols should be flown on both sides of the Straits of Dover. Both Haig and Trenchard were reluctant to spare even one squadron from the fighting in France but, much against their wishes, 66 Squadron was moved to Calais and 56 Squadron to Bekesbourne in Kent.

*

The morning after his unsuccessful attack on the Gothas, James flew to 50 Squadron, based at Bekesbourne. Four of the squadron's pilots had also attempted to tackle the bombers the previous day and James was anxious to compare notes with them. One pilot of the squadron, flying a lone Vickers ES1, the others in the obsolete FE8, had not the slightest chance of

A curious crowd of RFC personnel and civilians collects around Bristol Scout D. A1767. After an engine failure, James force landed this Bristol on 2 June 1917 near the village of Barming in Kent.

catching the higher performance Gothas, even if they had seen them, and were as frustrated as James at their lack of success.[36]

From his logbook entries over the next few days, James seems to have abandoned his standing patrols in the Pup. He still took the opportunity to fly any of the Vickers machines that Barnwell was testing and on 18 June he flew Vickers FB12 A7352, a machine of the second production batch that had been re-engined with a 100hp Anzani engine. James recorded that it was 'a nice bus.'[37]

On 22 June, James flew another new Vickers type, A8963, the second prototype FB16a, with minor modifications to the airframe and re-engined with a 200hp Hispano-Suiza, transforming it into a FB16d. James was impressed with the new scout: 'a fine little machine and tremendously fast'. He climbed to 10,000ft in eight minutes, recording that its speed was 136 mph, at least thirty miles per hour faster than any machine he had yet flown. 'Whilst flying this machine I got some idea of the speed of future machines.' Wearing his pilot's analytical cap, he thought the FB16 was hard to fly, but that it had some excellent points as well as one or two bad ones.[38]

*

On 21 June, in accordance with Haig's orders, 56 Squadron had flown into the aerodrome at Bekesbourne, in Kent. The squadron had flown to France in April 1917, the first squadron to be equipped with the latest product of the Royal Aircraft Factory, the SE5. The SE5 was a fast, strong aeroplane, with an excellent performance, the first of the RFC's single-seat fighters to be armed with two guns, and the first, along with its contemporary, the Sopwith Camel, to be able to fight the Albatros scouts of the German *Jagdstaffeln* on equal terms. Great things had been expected of the new squadron, but on the evening of 7 May, only two weeks after beginning operational flying, in its first clash with the experienced German fighter pilots, it had suffered four casualties: two pilots killed and two wounded. Two of the pilots lost were experienced Flight Commanders, one of whom was Albert Ball. It was an inauspicious start, but under the inspired leadership of its remaining Flight Commander, Captain C M Crowe,[39] the squadron had since recovered, and the service grapevine was full of stories of its continued success. One of the original Flight Commanders wounded on 7 May was Henry 'Duke' Meintjes, an old acquaintance of James, and his replacement had been Geoffrey Bowman, James' pupil at the CFS in 1916, and later a comrade in arms in 29 Squadron. James knew that he would soon be due to return to operational duty in France and was keen to do so flying an SE5. With these personal links to 56 Squadron in mind, he flew to Bekesbourne on 25 June to sound out the possibility of being posted to the squadron for his next tour of duty. Bowman introduced him to Major Richard Blomfield,[40] commanding officer of the

During its overhaul the under surfaces of A7311 had been painted a light whitish blue, extending along the side of the fuselage, the cowling, wheel covers and rudder. 'The mechanics had made a splendid job of it.' *Credit T Henshaw.*

squadron, who was immediately taken by this young officer's commonsense and keenness. In turn, James was impressed with the squadron. 'There was a wonderful spirit in this squadron which was entirely different from any squadron with which I had yet come in contact, and everyone in the squadron was as keen as anything to get at and strafe the Huns.'

On 27 June, enemy aircraft were reported to be approaching the coast. James took off in A7311, and patrolled from Joyce Green to Southend, but it was a false alarm. On 1 July he flew A7311 to Dover, where it was due for overhaul in the ARS workshops, but making a detour on the way to visit 56 Squadron at Bekesbourne, probably to again press his case with Blomfield for a posting to the squadron.

*

Possibly because of the inclement weather conditions there had been a lull in the activities of the Gothas, but on 4 July they resumed operations with a raid on the Naval installations at Harwich and the RNAS station at Felixstowe. The defences were again disastrously slow to give the Home Defence squadrons any warning of the raiders: telephoning patrol orders to the squadrons far too late, and forgetting completely the Pups of 66 Squadron at Calais, ideally placed to intercept the bombers on their way back to their base. Pilots from thirteen RFC squadrons took off to intercept the raiders, including 56 Squadron, but only one made contact with the intruders. With ample warning of the raid, the RNAS squadrons at Dunkirk again attacked the bombers as they returned. Five Sopwith Camels of 4 Squadron RNAS attacked the Gothas thirty miles north west of Ostend, claiming two damaged.

For some time, Trenchard had been pressing the War Cabinet for the return of 56 Squadron to France – recommending 46 Squadron[41] as its replacement in England – and on the afternoon of 5 July, 56 Squadron flew back to France. On 7 July, the Gothas of *Kagohl* 3 returned to bomb London.

At 9.15 in the morning of Saturday 7 July, RFC Headquarters was advised that a large formation of Gothas, estimated at twenty-two machines, was approaching the Essex coast.[42] James was at Dover, collecting the overhauled A7311, when the warning reached the station at 9.50. He had just test flown the Pup and mechanics were attending to a minor technical fault. James fumed with impatience at the delay, resisting the urge to push them aside and do the job himself, and it was ten minutes before the Pup was ready. James took off, climbing hard towards the Thames estuary. Over Bekesbourne he saw a signal laid out on the aerodrome, indicating that the enemy bombers were in the London area. James altered course slightly, towards Southend on the Essex coast, still gaining height.

In his previous meeting with the Gothas, their superior

'I now had nothing else to do but except fly alongside the Huns and make faces at them.' An evocative depiction by renowned aviation artist Leonard Bridgman of the fight with the Gothas on 7 July 1917.

James in the Spring of 1917, possibly at Joyce Green.

speed over that of his Pup had hampered his attacks, necessitating that they had been carried out in too hurried a fashion. James had decided that the best way to successfully attack the Gothas was from above, with the advantage of height compensating for his lack of speed, and to this end he had had the under surfaces of the Pup painted a whitish blue to blend with the sky when above the bombers: 'so that I could hover above the Gothas unseen and pounce down on them in the approved Immelmann fashion'.

James arrived over Southend at 16,000ft. Seeing British anti-aircraft shells bursting over Tilbury, he flew westwards along the bank of the Thames. He had ample time to decide on his attack tactics, and plenty of height in hand. As he approached Tilbury he could see the Gothas flying towards him, 500ft below. James waited until the enemy bombers had almost passed him, then dived at right angles to attack the last machine in the formation, firing a whole drum of Lewis into it from close range. In his eagerness, he came too close to the top wing of the Gotha. To avoid a collision he pulled out so abruptly that the downward pressure of his weight broke the Pup's seat bearers. At the top of his zoom, thankful that it wasn't his wings that had broken, James decided that his next attack should be from a different quarter. Putting a new drum on his Lewis, he dived to attack the Gotha from its right rear. Closing to within 300ft, he suddenly swerved, switching to its left rear, hoping the enemy gunner would not have had time to swing his gun back to meet the new angle of attack, and fired a whole drum of Lewis before zooming away. The Gotha flew on, apparently undamaged. James put on the last of his three drums, determined that this time he would press home his attack and destroy the bomber. Diving from above the Gotha's top right wing, he passed over the bomber, turned quickly to the right, and fired a full drum from fifty yards range.[43] He could see his tracers hitting the Gotha's fuselage and wings, but other than the pilot putting its nose down a little, his fire seemed to have had no effect on the bomber. The Gothas were now flying over Southend, with James still above them, in an ideal position from which to attack again, but he was now out of ammunition. Annoyed that he had been 'silly' enough not to carry more drums than three, when he could have carried at least a dozen without affecting the performance of the Pup,

James running up Bristol Scout D.5575.

James now had nothing else to do but to 'fly alongside the Huns and make faces at them'. He flew alongside the Gotha he had attacked, keeping within 200yards, but making sure that the Pup was shielded from any fire from the enemy gunners by the wings and struts of their machine. At this range, James could see that the nearest Gotha was marked on its fuselage with the large letters 'K.A.' with another marked 'S'.

Despite his lack of ammunition, James still shadowed the Gotha formation, reasoning that he could possibly distract the attention of the enemy gunners away from other British machines that were now arriving, but these pilots seemed not to understand his stratagem, failing to press home any close attacks on the bombers.

James continued to fly alongside the Gothas for another twenty-five minutes, only relaxing his vigilance for one brief moment, that allowed an alert enemy gunner in 'K.A.' to get in a good burst at the Pup, putting one bullet through its windscreen. Deciding that the gunner was 'a very nasty man' James kept a little further away from the Gothas, still hoping that his diversionary tactics would allow other British pilots to attack. In fact, two were already doing so, 'firing for all they were worth', but at a range that James estimated to be at least half a mile. As the two attackers came closer he could distinctly hear their bullets and he wondered if, owing to the Pup being painted blue and flying alongside the Gothas without attacking them, he had been mistaken for an escorting German scout.[44]

The formation was now forty miles out to sea and James decided that he could do no more. Turning away from the enemy machines, he put the Pup into a short spin 'for the amusement of the *Boches*' that resulted in a later report that one of the Gothas had been seen to spin down: 'but in reality it was only me, fooling around'.

On his way back to the coast, James passed any amount of 'comic machines' ranging at heights from 15,000ft downwards: Sopwith Triplanes and Camels; more Pups; Armstrong Whitworth FK8s; RE8s; Martinsydes; Bristol Fighters; DH4s, and numerous marks of BEs.

On landing back at Joyce Green at midday, James found that a pilot named Salmon had been killed, his Pup crashing just outside the aerodrome.[45]

After lunch, James was told that he had been selected with two other instructors to fly a three-week refresher course with a squadron in France. This course was to enable the instructors to experience for themselves the latest advances in fighting tactics and techniques in order to pass them on to their pupils training in England.

On the following Monday morning, James flew to 6th Wing HQ to find that he had been posted to 66 Squadron, based at Estrée Blanche.

Ch.9: France Again

John Bowley Quested.

On the morning of 12 July, James and the two other selected instructors, Captains John B Quested and Philip Le Gallais,[1] caught the leave boat from Dover, disembarking at Boulogne in the evening. They were met by an RFC tender and within two hours James arrived at Estrée Blanche.

The aerodrome was large, home to four fighter squadrons: the Spads of 19 Squadron, the SE5s of 56 Squadron, the Sopwith Camels of 70 squadron and the Sopwith Pups of 66 Squadron. The aerodrome itself was a large field directly above the village of Estrée Blanche, on the eastern side of the road that runs steeply down into the village and as steeply out again to continue on to Arras, thirty-six miles away to the south east.

James was met by Major George Henderson, his erstwhile CO at Dover, now commanding 66 squadron. Henderson was fully aware that James was a pilot of considerable experience, but he stressed that his duties while with the squadron would be that of an ordinary flying officer.[2] He would be allocated no particular Pup for his exclusive use and although he could fly any solo patrols he might wish, for the day by day patrols he would be flying under the command of the flight commanders in the squadron.

The next day, Major Henderson and James took off to patrol the Lens to Arras area to look for enemy two-seaters. After an hour they attacked one just west of Lens, but the enemy pilot put his nose down and dived east, easily outdistancing the Pups. Another patrol in the evening, led by Captain John Andrews,[3] crossed the front lines over Lens and flew towards Douai. No enemy aeroplanes were seen, but the Pups met up with a patrol of SE5s from 56 Squadron, all painted in various colours, with one striped like a zebra.[4]

Towards the end of their patrol time the Pups saw six Albatros scouts over Bullécourt, but before they could attack them the enemy scouts, faster than the Pups, dived east. Andrews turned the patrol away, but as they did so the Albatros pilots turned back, opening fire at long range: 'and fairly spoilt the lovely summer sky with their beastly white tracer smoke'. The Pups returned to Estrée Blanche, landing just before dusk.

On 14 July the squadron flew an escort for the Martinsydes of 27 Squadron that were bombing Cortemarck, north of Roulers. The Pups formed up with the bombers at 11,000ft over Dunkirk and the formation crossed the front lines over Dixmude before turning east towards their target. Visibility was poor, with large cloud formations from 2,000 to 10,000ft. However, these conditions suited the Martinsyde pilots, who were adept at using such cloud cover to approach their target unseen by any marauding enemy scouts. Over Cortemarck, the Martinsyde leader fired a red light. It was the signal to unload their bombs. As soon as they had done so, the Martinsydes turned west for the British lines. Without their bomb load they were faster than the Pups and soon left them behind. As the Pups approached the front lines a heavy thunderstorm broke, with vivid lightning, and the lightly loaded Pups were violently thrown about by the turbulence on their way back to Estrée Blanche.

That evening James was invited to dinner at 56 Squadron's Mess. After preliminary cocktails, dinner was served to the accompaniment of the squadron's fifteen piece orchestra: a morale-boosting innovation of 'Dickie' Blomfield. After dinner, James decided that he simply must get a posting to the squadron, under any pretence whatever, and approached Blomfield. To his delight, Bomfield agreed, saying that he would immediately apply for him to be posted, suggesting that in the meantime he might like to fly a patrol with the squadron in one of its SE5s. It was the perfect ending to a perfect evening. James later wrote: 'We had a wonderful time that night and I thoroughly enjoyed it.'

James flew a patrol the next morning, that passed without incident, and in the afternoon flew to La Lovie to visit Philp Le Gallais who was undertaking his refresher course there with 23 Squadron, flying Spads. Close by La Lovie was Poperinghe aerodrome, home to 29 Squadron, now flying Nieuports, and James took the opportunity to visit old friends in the squadron.

On 16 July, an evening patrol of six Pups ran into a formation of Albatros scouts at 13,000ft east of Ypres. Pup pilots in France had found that the best altitude at which to fight the Albatros was at 16,000 to 17000ft: at this height, the light wing loading of the Pup gave it superb manoeuvrability while the heavier German scouts were near their ceiling, their performance adversely affected. However, these Albatros pilots stayed to fight and the Pup pilots were soon fully engaged, each with an individual opponent. One of the German pilots had not joined in the mêlée, staying a little above the fight, and no sooner had James made up his mind to watch him, than he dived onto the tail of one of the Pups below. James immediately went to the aid of the Pup pilot, getting onto the tail of the Albatros, but the enemy pilot had also been keeping a close eye on James. As soon as James got within range he half-rolled and dived away from his fire. Most of the other Albatros pilots had also broken off the action, diving away east, and after one or two indeterminate skirmishes with the remainder the Pups returned to Estrée Blanche. James made no claim for the Albatros he had attacked, but entered it in his logbook as driven down.

This short but intense fight was typical of air fighting above the Ypres Salient in the long summer evenings of 1917. In addition to the two-seater aeroplanes of the Corps squadrons, the British Army (fighter) squadrons usually had at least eight patrols in the skies above the Salient. James would later write: 'The evenings were simply wonderful, as the fighting was usually very fierce and well-contested.' The 'fun' as he called it, usually began at about 7PM, just east of Polygon Wood, and the 'death flirting' usually went on until dusk, sometimes even later.

*

The war in the air over the Western Front had changed considerably since James had last fought there in February 1917. In the autumn and winter of 1916, the RFC had suffered a devastating number of casualties: nearly 400 between the months of September and November, when the new Albatros and Halberstadt scouts equipping the *Jagdstaffeln* – thirty-two were operational by December 1916 – had begun to outclass and outnumber the best aeroplanes that the RFC could put into the air. In January 1917, Haig had warned the British War Cabinet that the RFC would have insufficient aeroplanes and men to support any offensive in the coming spring and by February the RFC was under strength by at least seven squadrons.

During late March and early April 1917, the improved version of the German Albatros D.II, the D.III, began to make its appearance at the Front. With a redesigned wing layout – giving it the V-strut configuration which was to become so familiar to the pilots of the RFC and earn it the colloquial name of the 'V-Strutter' – the new fighter, in the hands of the emerging fighter pilots of the Jagdstaffeln had a devastating effect on the slow reconnaissance and observation aeroplanes of the Corps squadrons of the RFC. In late 1916 and the early

John Oliver Andrews.

months of 1917, of the fighter aeroplanes flown by the Army (fighter) squadrons of the RFC, only the excellent Sopwith Pup and Sopwith Triplane – the last used exclusively by the squadrons of the Royal Naval Air Service – the Nieuport and Spad could meet the new German fighters on anything approaching equal terms. Although these aeroplanes were in the main more manoeuvrable than the German Albatros, the British fighter pilots still fought at a serious disadvantage. Their armament of a single Vickers or Lewis gun, against the twin Spandau guns carried by the German scouts, plus the superior speed of the Albatros, enabled the German pilots to avoid, initiate, or break off combat at will.

Trenchard's insistence that the RFC should always be used offensively cost the Corps dearly in the first days of the Battle of Arras, which began on 9 April 1917. In the first days of the battle, personnel casualties were 19 killed and 13 wounded, with an additional 73 missing in action. The matériel cost was also high: 75 aeroplanes lost in combat and a further 56 lost in flying accidents – these last being mainly due to the pilots replacing the heavy casualties suffered in the previous six months being poorly trained. Worse was to come. By the end of April, the total casualties for the month were 316 aircrew killed or missing, and in the region of 245 aeroplanes destroyed as a direct result of enemy action, casualties that earned the

The 56 Squadron Band. Key to band. 1. G.H. Rolls. 2. H.T. Walters. 3. J.D. Thomas. 4. Corp P.P. Rossini. 5. Flt Sgt H. Smith. 6. Unknown. 7. F.H. Pitt. 8. Sgt P.E. Gayer. Leader. 9. W. Milton. 10. Davies. 11. W.W.A. Mason. 12. T. Taylor. 13. E. Cunningham. 14. S.R. Pegg. 15. Unknown. All air mechanics except where noted.

month the sobriquet of ' Bloody April. '

In late April 1917, the majority of RFC fighter squadrons were still fighting on with the Sopwiths, Nieuports and Spads – 41 Squadron was still flying the long-obsolescent FE8 in July. However, with the introduction of the SE5 and Sopwith Camel – both able to meet the German Albatros on equal terms in both performance and armament – the pendulum of air superiority would begin to once again swing in favour of the RFC as more squadrons began to be re-equipped with the new fighters.

*

On 17 July, James having no patrols to fly, he and Major Henderson flew to Leffrinckhoucke, near Dunkirk, to visit 54 Squadron, also flying Pups. One of the most successful pilots in the squadron, with six victories, was William 'Struggy' Strugnell,[5] an old friend who had been at school with James and his elder brother William. By this time, Strugnell had flown a great deal on active service and was about to go home for a well-deserved rest.

While flying with 29 Squadron in 1916, James had realised that important as the destruction of enemy fighters was for the protection of the British reconnaissance machines, the destruction of the corresponding observation machines of the German Air Service was potentially even more so: of more value strategically than fighter downing fighter on a one-for-one basis. While with 66 Squadron, James often flew lone patrols at considerable height with this tactic in mind. Although he had no success at the time, he stored up invaluable experience: a portent of things to come.

On the morning of 20 July, James took off alone on one such mission, climbing to 14,000 and patrolling the Arras,

Lens, Ypres area. He saw several enemy machines, but they were too far east to chase. After lunch he again visited 29 Squadron at Poperinghe. Back at Estrée Blanche, he flew another lone patrol in the evening, but again with no success.

The next day, Major Blomfield asked James if he would like to fly as a member of A Flight on its evening patrol. James was only too pleased to accept and at 6.30PM he took off from Estrée Blanche in SE5a A8946. His companions were Captain Phillip Prothero,[6] leading Lieutenants Maxwell[7] and Rhys Davids.[8]

Prothero first took the Flight to its patrol area of Nieuport to Dixmude but finding no activity there, led them south. Arriving over Houthulst Forest, Prothero saw a formation of Albatros scouts and went down after them. James, unused to the speed of the SE5a in a dive – far faster than that of the Sopwith Pup – was left far behind.

Prothero and Maxwell attacked three of the Albatros, leaving Rhys Davids to tackle two others that were flying slightly above. Prothero's opponent dived away east to escape his attack. Maxwell also drove an Albatros down, but was then attacked by a pair of black and white two-seaters. He zoomed above these, but oil began to pour from his engine from a cracked oil pipe. With his pressure gauge showing zero, he broke off the action and returned to Estrée Blanche.

Rhys Davids, attacking the two higher enemy scouts, came under attack from an additional seven he had not seen. A confident and skilled air fighter, even Rhys Davids baulked at fighting nine V-Strutters single-handed. He summed up his reaction in two words: 'I fled'. Arriving over the Ypres area, he joined up with Lieutenants Barlow[9] and Cronyn[10] of B Flight, which had taken off from Estrée Blanche in the last patrol of the evening.

A large number of enemy aeroplanes, scouts and two-seaters, were in the area, but the fighting did not begin until Cronyn dived to attack one of the two-seaters, sending it down in a series of side slips. This brought the Albatros pilots into the action. Rhys Davids send one down out of control, but both his guns then jammed – his Lewis with a double feed and his Vickers with a stoppage. Clearing his Vickers, Rhys Davids stalled his SE5a and fired at an Albatros above him. At this juncture, James finally arrived at the scene of the fighting. Rhys Davids left the Albatros above him and dived to attack another, 8,000ft below, but as he went down another Albatros flew over him. James attacked this machine, closing to within 100 yards before opening fire. The Albatros, painted a silvery-grey, 'turned east and wobbled laterally'. After flying east for half minute the Albatros stalled and went down in a very steep, right hand slow spiral, its starboard wing right down. James watched it fall, from 15,000 to 6,000ft, until he lost sight of it in the gathering darkness.

Looking around for Rhys Davids, James was startled to hear machine gun fire, the tracer smoke passing close by him. He could see no enemy machines near him, and failed to locate his attacker until he banked slightly and looked down: an enemy two-seater was below him, the gunner still firing. James

Richard Graham Blomfield.

immediately dived, secured an advantageous position at 100 yards behind the enemy machine and got in a good burst with his Vickers gun – only to have it stop. James turned away, forgetting that the SE also carried a Lewis gun on its top plane: 'there again, I missed a Hun through sheer carelessness'.

James then flew back to Estrée Blanche. It was nearly dark and he was the last pilot to land. He did not claim the silver-grey Albatros, in his opinion it was still under control when he last saw it, but the rest of the squadron had done well. Prothero had sent down a black and white Albatros out of control over Langemarke; Rhys Davids was credited with another of the black and white scouts; and the large green two-seater shot down by Cronyn was the squadron's hundredth victory.

That night, James stayed to dinner in the 56 Squadron Mess: a double celebration dinner for the award of a Bar to Rhys Davids' MC and the squadron's hundredth victory. 'We again had a very cheery evening and in my dreams that night I was flying a 200hp SE5.'

The Opposition in 1917/1918

Above: The Albatros D.III, a development of the successful D.I and D.II types using the same 160 hp Mercedes D.III engine and armament, began to equip the *Jagdstaffeln* in 1917. Thirteen were in service with the *Jagdstaffeln* in January, 137 in March, and 327 by May, with production continuing alongside the next development, the D.V and D.Va until the early months of 1918. By November 1917, 446 were in service at the Front. The Albatros D.III was the first of the Albatros scouts with the sesquiplane layout, so successful in the French Nieuport, and noted by Robert Thelen, the Albatros designer. The D.III was soon dubbed the 'V-Strutter' by the pilots of the RFC.

Below: The Albatros D.V. The next development of the D.III, again using the same 160 hp Mercedes D.III engine and armament, the D.V began to arrive at the front in July 1917, followed by a further development, the D.Va, with 170 hp Mercedes D.IIIa engine, in November. The Albatros scouts were the mainstay of the *Jagdstaffeln* until the introduction of the Fokker D.VII in the Spring of 1918, and there were large numbers still in service at the time of the Armistice.

On the evening of 22 July, James took off alone in Pup B1746, a machine he had not flown before, to look for enemy two-seaters. At 4.10, flying north at 10,000ft over Armentières, he saw three, registering their artillery on the British trenches just south of the town. James climbed for a little extra height before diving on the lowest enemy machine, closing to 200 yards before opening fire with a burst of forty rounds. The enemy pilot immediately shut off his engine and began to glide east. James attempted to follow, but both the other two-seaters attacked him, forcing him west, until he turned and tackled the nearest. This was 500ft above the Pup and although James closed to within 300 yards he was unable to fire with any accuracy. The two-seater turned away and flew east. James followed both these machines until just over the front lines, where he saw the two-seater he had first attacked still going down, now very low over Quesnoy. James had now been out for three hours, his petrol was low, and deciding he had successfully prevented the enemy machines from carrying out their artillery ranging mission, he returned to Estrée Blanche. However, the evening was fine, and knowing there were large numbers of enemy machines still operating over the Armentières area, James took off again, this time in Pup B1762. He climbed to 14,000ft and patrolled the Armentières, Ypres and Warneton area for an hour and thirty five minutes, but the enemy machines he saw were too far east to engage.

The next day, James flew two more solo patrols but had no combats. Weather on 24 July was generally fine, but with a thick ground mist. Escorted by the Pups of 66 Squadron, the Martinsydes of 27 Squadron again bombed the railway siding at Cortemarcke. No enemy scouts attempted to interfere with the raiders and all the British machines returned safely. James thought that the whole mission was uninteresting, reflecting that some days in France were full of interest and incidents, while others were just the opposite.

There were low clouds and mist in the early morning of 26 July and no patrols were flown until the evening. James took off, patrolling from Auchel to Bruay, but conditions were very cloudy and he returned after forty minutes. Conditions were a little better later, and James and Major Henderson took off to patrol over the Ypres Salient, crossing the front lines at 14,000ft over Bixschoote. There were a number of enemy machines working over the lines, and Henderson and James climbed for more height, intending to fight at 16 or 17,000ft, where the Pup was at its most manoeuvrable. They flew east, almost to Menin, reaching 17,000ft. Looking west, they could see a very large fight in progress, involving a large number of machines, and they flew towards the action.[11]

Over Gheluwe, a lone Albatros scout attacked the Pups from slightly above. Attempting to get behind James, the enemy pilot lost height and got below him. James did two very quick half turns – 'such as the Pup can do' – and dived on the dark green enemy scout, firing a burst of thirty Vickers into it from a range of eighty feet, watching his tracers pushing into its wings and fuselage until his Vickers gun stopped with a separated cartridge case. The Albatros dived steeply away to the east.

William Victor 'Struggy' Strugnell.

James, with an inoperative gun, and with numerous enemy machines between him and the front lines, was forced to let it go.[12]

Henderson then signalled that he also had a gun stoppage and the Pups flew west. On their way back to the front line, thanks to the manoeuvrability of their Pups, they had no problem in avoiding the unwelcome attentions of any of the numerous enemy scouts, and as they crossed the trenches at 15,000ft James cut his engine and glided further west while attempting to rectify his gun stoppage. He knew that a separated cartridge case was practically impossible to clear in the air, but he was anxious to get back into the fighting. Holding the control stick between his knees, he began to work on the stoppage. Down to 5,000ft, he finally lost patience with the Vickers and decided to restart his engine. He turned on his petrol, but nothing happened. Thinking that the plugs had probably oiled up during the glide, he turned the petrol on full. The Le Rhône gave one kick, but still stubbornly refused to fire. James then realised that his legs felt warm. Looking over the side of his cockpit he was horrified to see flames licking around the Pup's cowling. He hurriedly switched off. Looking down

Philip Bernard Prothero.

for a suitable landing area he saw that he was in luck, Bailleul aerodrome was almost immediately below him. Fortunately, the flames seemed to have subsided but as he got down to 500ft, still glancing round to see if his tail was alight, he saw that he was short of the aerodrome. He quickly picked out a cornfield just outside the airfield, and made his approach, but when only twenty feet off the ground he saw some telegraph wires, bordering the field and just in front of him. Hastily pushing down the Pup's nose he just scraped under the wires, holding off the Pup for as long as he could and finally dropping into the corn at thirty miles an hour. The little Pup immediately turned upside down, breaking the propeller and damaging the top wing. James was unhurt.

The next day, 28 July, James had a narrow escape from being shot down. He was alone over the lines at 15,000ft in the vicinity of Lens. The ground was obscured by heavy cloud and there was a strong north-westerly wind. A patrol of six Albatros D.IIIs were coming from the direction of Annay and James flew towards them with the intention of quickly attacking one, then diving away. The Albatros were painted in a variety of garish colours, but James singled out the leader, who was flying slightly higher than the others, closed the distance and opened fire. The enemy pilot immediately dived away. James followed him down, but realised that he was now below the rest of the V-Strutters, obviously the enemy leader's intention. The five Albatros all dived at him and opened fire. James experienced 'that strange feeling that one does on those occasions' and remonstrated with himself: 'Now Jimmy, pull yourself together or you'll be for the sports.' Looking down, through a gap in the clouds, he saw that he was a long way east of the lines, with a strong headwind to fly against. He quickly made up his mind that his only choice was to run for the nearest cloud cover, just east of Lens, and he flew a zigzag course towards it, engine full on. Although the Albatros D.III was considerably faster than the Pup, for some reason he managed to outstrip all but two of his pursuers and he turned on these, performing rolls, loops, and spins to outmanoeuvre them, finally getting into the cloud cover at 6,000ft, just west of Lens. He knew that he had been lucky to get out of a extremely hazardous situation, that he had allowed his eagerness for a fight to outweigh his better judgement, but reasoned that these 'little scrapes' were both good experience and confidence boosting. On landing at Estrée Blanche he found that the Pup had been hit in only two places.

On 31 July, his refresher course now coming to an end, James flew his last two patrols with 66 Squadron. The weather was dull, very cloudy, and the first patrol passed without incident, with no sign of any enemy machines, but in the afternoon it was reported that they were very active over the lines and James took off at 1.30PM, directly after lunch.

At 4,000ft he climbed out of the low cloud and flew towards the front lines. Seeing through a gap in the clouds that he was over Polygon Wood, he circled, waiting. After a while his patience was rewarded by a lone Albatros scout coming from the direction of Menin. James dived and had a shot at the enemy scout, that took no notice of him whatsoever. James, keeping an eye on the Albatros, climbed to 6,000ft for a little extra height. The Albatros pilot climbed to 13,000ft and turned west. When he was vertically above James, he cut off his engine and glided west into the British lines, losing height. James, puzzled, kept east of the Albatros and watched. The enemy pilot leveled out just below James, glided even further west, then suddenly restarted his engine. James then realised that the Albatros pilot had been going down to attack a British balloon, but in taking a last look round he had seen the Pup, had restarted his engine and was climbing to get above him. As the distance closed the Albatros pilot turned quickly to get on the tail of the Pup, but James had already banked steeply, easily out-turning the enemy scout, and was now close behind it. Realising his danger, the enemy pilot dived vertically, disappearing into a large cloud over Mont Kemmel. James followed it through the cloud, fully expecting to see the enemy pilot contour-chasing home at ground level, but there was no sign of the Albatros. Realising that it must still be in the cloud, James climbed to the eastern end, just in time to see the Albatros emerge from the northern end. Although only 300 yards away, at 2,000ft the Albatros was much faster than the Pup and rapidly outpaced James, who had no alternative but to let it go, cursing himself for having missed an ideal opportunity to bring down the Albatros in the British lines.[13]

Climbing to regain his height, James saw a patrol of four

Gerald Joseph Constable Maxwell.

Arthur Percival Foley Rhys Davids.

Albatros scouts over Houthem. He was now so confident that the Pup could out manoeuvre any Albatros, however good the pilot, that he flew underneath the enemy scouts, hoping to tempt one to come down and attack him. The enemy pilots, probably suspecting he was a decoy, refused the invitation and flew east.

Leonard Monteagle Barlow.

Verschoyle Phillip Cronyn.

Four days later, James left Estrée Blanche, met up with Le Gallais and Quested, who had also finished their course, and all three embarked for Dover on the Victoria, a boat they had used many times. That evening they had a quiet dinner at London's Savoy hotel, no doubt talking shop, discussing their recent experiences and comparing the relative virtues of the Sopwith Pup, which James and Quested had been flying, with that of the Spad flown by Le Gallais.

*

After a short leave of two days, James resumed his instructional duties at Joyce Green. He was delighted to find that his favourite Pup A7311 was still at Croydon, had not been crashed or damaged in his absence, and on 9 August he flew an Avro 504 to Croydon collect it. Taking it up that evening, testing its performance with a stop watch, he found that it climbed to 10,000ft in twelve minutes with a level flying speed of 85 mph at that height, whereas the Pups he had been flying with 66 Squadron rarely obtained that height in under fourteen minutes. He realised of course that the Pups in France had carried a Vickers gun, heavier than the Lewis carried by A7311, but it had now done over a hundred hours of flying and was getting old.[14]

On 12 August, James was riding his motor-cycle through Rochester when he saw a policeman with a placard warning people to take cover. He rode to Joyce Green as fast as he could, reaching the aerodrome in twenty minutes. A7311, always kept in a state of readiness, had been wheeled out onto the tarmac for an immediate takeoff. James climbed in the cockpit, waved away the chocks, and took off at full throttle. The Pup's tail came up within five yards, but in his haste James had not seen a BE2e coming in to land, no more than twenty yards directly in front of the Pup. James did the only thing he could. Offering up a quick prayer, he pulled the stick right back. 'The dear old Pup took it like a bird and sailed over the top of the 2e at 30mph, with the support of the 30mph wind I was taking off against. I don't suppose on that occasion my wheels ran more than twenty yards.'

James climbed towards Herne Bay on the Kent coast, arriving at 17,000ft. Dozens of British machines were 'flying around' but there was no sign of any bombers, and there was an 'All Clear' sign out on a nearby naval aerodrome. James was thirty minutes too late. The Gothas had already attacked Southend, most of their bombs falling into the sea, with only a few hitting the aerodrome at Rochford, and were on their way back to their base. On James' way back to Joyce Green an inlet pipe on the Le Rhône broke in two, the banging and vibration giving him some anxious moments until he had landed.

After dinner that evening, James was told that he was to go back to France as a Flight Commander in an SE5 squadron. He was extremely pleased, knowing that it could only be 56 Squadron.

Ch.10: 56 Squadron

Having said goodbye to family and friends, James reported to Mason's Yard early on the morning of 14 August. Receiving his orders, he travelled from Victoria to Folkestone, arriving in time to catch the midday sailing of the good ship Victoria to Boulogne. His arrival in France to report to his new squadron could not have been more different to when he had returned to rejoin 29 Squadron. He was now a Flight Commander, a person of some importance: there would be no tedious journey by rail through France. A telephone call to the adjutant of 56 Squadron, 'Grandpa' Marson,[1] resulted in a tender being sent. By 7.30 that evening, James arrived at Estrée Blanche and reported to Major Blomfield, his new commanding officer.[2]

That evening at dinner, with the squadron orchestra playing quietly in the background, Blomfield sat at the head of the table, with James on his left, Captain Geoffrey 'Beery' Bowman, the C Flight Commander on his right, with Captain Gerald Maxwell, the A Flight Commander, on Bowman's right. The remainder of the dinner company included such redoubtable air fighters as Leonard Barlow, Richard Maybery,[3] Robert Sloley,[4] Eric Turnbull,[5] Keith Muspratt,[6] Reginald Hoidge,[7] and Verschoyle Cronyn. James commented: 'I don't think I have often experienced such pleasure as when I was able to call myself a Flight-Commander in 56 Squadron.'

As B Flight Commander, James was the replacement for Ian Henderson.[8] Henderson had been posted to Home Establishment, effective from 10 August, but had not yet left the squadron and he introduced James to the pilots he was to command: Lieutenants Barlow, Muspratt, Cronyn and Coote,[9] 'as splendid a lot of fellows as ever set foot in France'. Another member of the Flight, Arthur Rhys Davids, was still on leave.

Next morning James inspected the NCOs and men of his Flight. He then turned his attention to the SE5a that had been allocated to him. This was B519, built by the Vickers Company, which had been flown from 1AD to the squadron two days previously. James soon saw what he perceived as a fault: an aileron control cable was the coarse four-strand type, instead of the standard type, that had seven strands. James immediately had this changed and a report was sent to Wing, pointing out this apparent manufacturing fault.[10] James then had B519 set up on trestles at the squadron's excellent firing range, that had been built by German prisoners of war, and spent the entire morning aligning and sighting its guns to his satisfaction. One of the B Flight mechanics, Ernest Etherington,[11] recalled: 'he must have fired the best part of a thousand rounds from each gun before he was satisfied'. Etherington is no doubt guilty of some exaggeration as to the number of rounds fired, but when James went into the Mess for lunch there was a certain amount of booing from his fellow officers, some of whom considered his morning's activity as showing off.[12]

To the other pilots in the squadron, James was just another of the RFC's promising flight commanders – no more, no less. For him to have been appointed as a flight commander they would have known that he had already flown in France, although it is doubtful if any – apart from Geoffrey Bowman – were aware of his vast amount of flying hours in all types of aeroplanes, but the pilots in his Flight were all much more experienced in fighting in the SE5a: Rhys Davids had been credited with eleven victories, Barlow with eight, Muspratt with four, against their new flight commander's five, all gained flying the now laughably antiquated DH2 in 1916, a lifetime ago in the fast changing and developing art of air fighting. However, unlike them, James was a professional soldier; he knew just what he wanted and how he meant to achieve it. His aim was simple: a well trained and disciplined Flight that would fight as a unit, and by the use of tactics, carefully thought out and applied, would shoot down the king's enemies without loss to itself. It was inevitable that his thoroughly professional attitude led to a great deal of misunderstanding of his character in the mostly happy-go-lucky atmosphere of the RFC Messes, but it is significant that those of his contemporaries whose regard and admiration of him were unqualified, were themselves professional soldiers.[13]

In addition, James' previous experience as a mechanic, allied with his interest in the technical aspects of aircraft and flying, extended to the mechanical aspects of his machine: of engine, guns and airframe, aspects of which many of his fellow pilots had no knowledge, or indeed interest. In his first days with 56 Squadron he quickly gained a reputation with the NCOs and men as a somewhat strict disciplinarian. He expected high standards of attention to duty, standards that he himself had always followed during his days as a mechanic in 3 Squadron. One of the squadron's air mechanics, Alex J Gray,[14] recalled:

"When McCudden came to 56 he certainly kept us all on our toes to begin with. In the first few weeks he tried out just about every fitter in the flight and none of them seemed to please him. Finally Corporal Tom Rogers[15] and myself were detailed as his fitters, with Corporal Bert Card[16] as his rigger, and from that day on we formed a great friendship with him. Tom Rogers, who was in charge, was a first class engineer and could always hold his own with McCudden. We were the only two Scots in the flight and Tom, who came from Dundee, took great delight in talking his broadest Scots and sometimes I don't think Mac understood more than half of what he said. It was always amusing to hear Tom and Mac argue as to how they would do a job – but Tom always seemed to come out on top. If McCudden came to us as a strict disciplinarian, he left a hero and liked by every man in the squadron."

One example of James' attention to detail was the method of firing both guns of the SE5a, a clumsy, cycle-type brake handle arrangement on the control column. In James' view this led to

Estrée Blanche (Liettres) aerodrome.

a slight jerking of the control column to fire the guns and was detrimental to accurate shooting. The squadron's engineering officer, Hubert Charles[17] remembered: 'McCudden wanted touch buttons of not more than three ounces of pressure to fire the guns. A joystick top from a Sopwith Camel was obtained and by skillful modifications and adjustments, Mac was given his three ounce pressure triggers. The spade grip with the twin triggers was later made standard on the SE5a.'

In the evening of 16 August, James led his new command off the ground to patrol from Zonnebecke to Menin. On the way to the Lines, both Cronyn and Muspratt had trouble with their engines and were forced to return to Estrée Blanche. The remainder of the Flight, James, Leonard Barlow and Herbert Johnston,[18] carried on, crossing the Lines at twenty minutes to seven and patrolling from Gheluve to Dadizele. An enemy two-seater was pointed out to them by British anti-aircraft bursts, but at 18,000ft it was too high for them to reach. The area north of Wytschaete and Roulers now being under heavy cloud James led the Flight to Menin, but seeing no enemy aircraft they returned. James later flew a short flight of ten minutes to test his guns.

The next afternoon, James was sent out alone to look for an enemy machine that had been reported being over St. Omer, but he saw nothing and returned after just over an hour. That evening, James and Barlow took off at 6.40PM, patrolling from Wervicq to Zandvoorde. After crossing the Lines it appears that they split up in the evening sky, James flying to the area of Wervicq and Zandvoorde, Barlow slightly further north to Roulers and Menin. Although his logbook has the notation 'Several EA engaged' James saw no decisive action, nor did he

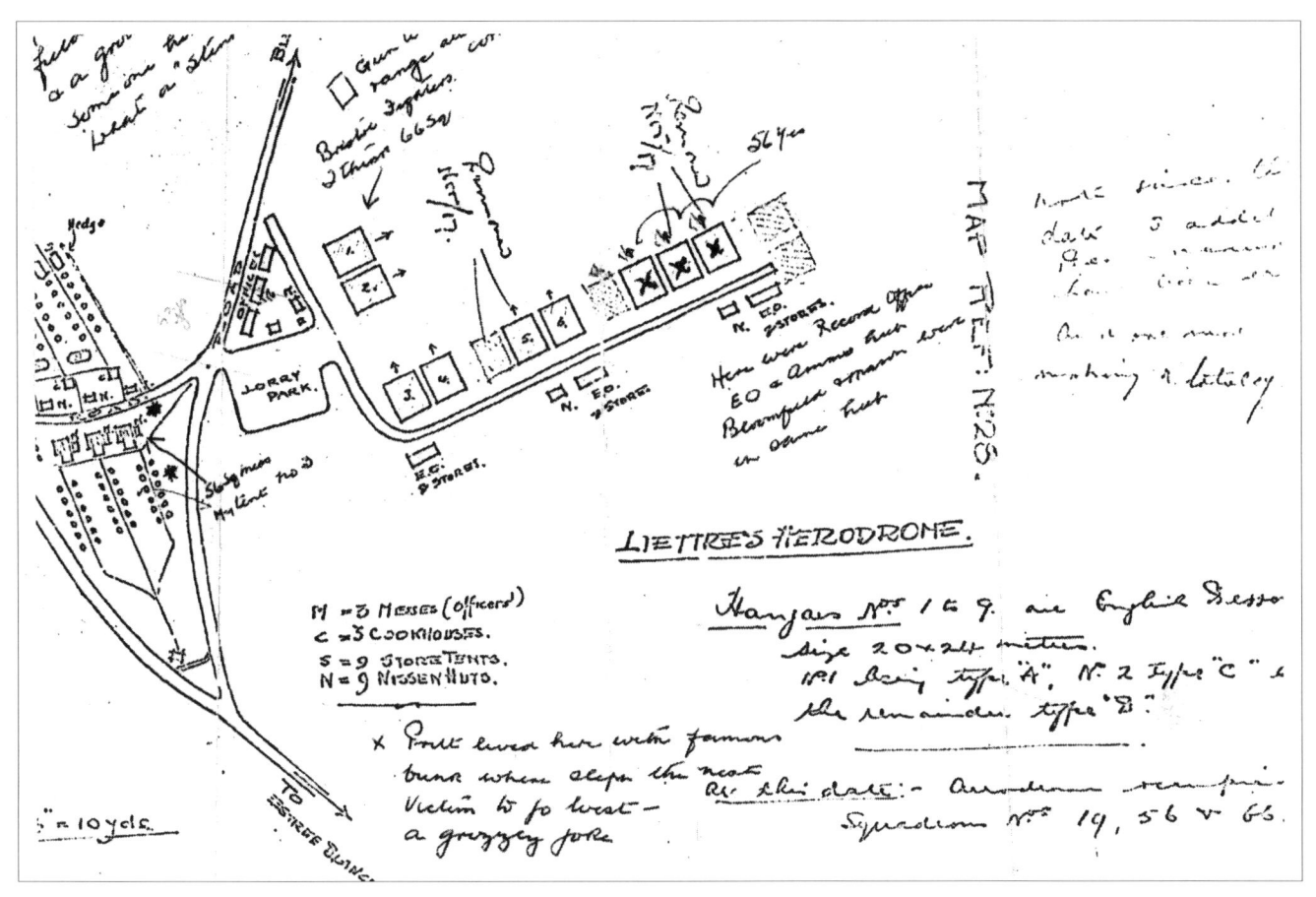

In this contemporary plan of Estrée Blanche aerodrome the 56 Squadron hangars are marked with an 'x'. The squadron's Mess and tented accommodation were in the triangular section on the left, marked with a *. At this time the aerodrome was occupied by 56, 66 and 19 Squadrons.

submit a combat report, but Barlow shot down two Albatros scouts in the Roulers/Menin area: the first went down in a 'series of tumbles' obviously out of control; the second in flames, crashing just east of the road to Moorslede.

Weather conditions on 18 August – the last day of the battle of Langemarck – were changeable: generally fine, but cloudy, with high winds. At 6.00AM, two patrols left Estrée Blanche: Gerald Maxwell, leading A Flight; James leading B Flight: Barlow, Muspratt, Johnston, Coote and Cronyn.

James led his Flight across the Lines at 14,000ft over Ploegsteert and four hostile two-seaters were seen west of Menin, flying south. These two-seaters had just been in combat with Maxwell's Flight and James led B Flight down to attack them. He secured a position behind one, closed to thirty yards and fired both guns – which immediately jammed: the Vickers with a faulty cartridge chute; the Lewis with a misplaced round. These were serious faults, not repairable in the air, and James broke off the action and returned, landing at 1 Squadron's aerodrome at Bailleul. The stoppages remedied, James took off again, recrossed the Lines at 8,000ft over Zonnebecke and met up with Barlow. Barlow had also suffered gun stoppages in the initial attacks on the two-seaters, and had then had combats with a number of others, all indecisive due to continual trouble with his guns. After the last of these fights he had returned to the Lines, where he joined up with James.[19] James and Barlow first attacked an enemy two-seater directing its artillery over Polygon Wood, and drove it east. They then flew east towards Houthem, where they saw six Albatros scouts and a pair of two-seaters at 2,000ft, just east of the town. From a height advantage of a thousand feet, they attacked this formation. One Albatros, attacked by Barlow, dived away from his fire and came towards James, head on. James opened fire at a hundred yards, closing to within fifty yards, firing both guns. Just when a collision seemed inevitable, the nose of the Albatros went down and it passed under James, continuing down in a very steep, vertical spiral, until James lost sight of it, still falling, at 6,000ft. James and Barlow were now outnumbered, several more enemy scouts having joined the fight, and they both flew west, using their superior speed to outdistance the pursuit. Barlow's petrol was now very low and he landed at Bailleul.

Over breakfast in the Mess, the morning's combats were discussed. Maxwell had sent a black and white Albatros down out of control – possibly *Leutnant* Albrecht Weinschenk of *Jasta* 18, who was wounded – and also wounded an enemy observer in one of the two-seaters. Johnston and Sloley had also killed an observer. On the debit side, Lieutenant Harold

Thomas Marson (left) fooling around with 'Billy' Crowe.

Geoffrey Hilton Bowman.

Rushworth[20] had been shot down and taken prisoner. James was congratulated on his victory over the Albatros scout, his first in the squadron, the general wish being expressed that it would be the first of fifty. Commenting on this patrol and its conclusion, James, reflected: 'It was very fine to be on a machine that was faster than the Huns, and I may say that it increased one's confidence enormously to know that one could run away just as soon as things became too hot for one.'[21]

At this time the 56 Squadron pilots were experiencing a great deal of technical troubles with engines, plus the new radiators fitted to the SE5as were all found to be leaking badly. But their guns were the worst problem, both Vickers and Lewis were almost constantly jamming, for a variety of reasons. With his technical expertise, no doubt ably assisted by Tom Rogers, James took personal care and attention of his engine, and consequently had little trouble in that respect, but he also devoted a great deal of time in both testing and aligning his guns, holding the view that the alignment of the guns was of paramount importance: that it was far easier to get into a good attacking position of an enemy machine than to then fire with accuracy. However, despite his precautions James was also to experience the frustration of his guns jamming at the crucial moment in combat. James was also a self-confessed 'stickler' for detail in every respect, reasoning that in aerial combat it is the detailed preparation that counted more than the actual fighting; that even such a mundane detail as having dirty goggles could make all the difference between getting or not getting a victory.

On 19 August, James led an afternoon patrol, taking off at 3.30PM with a mixed bag of pilots from various Flights, including Gerald Maxwell, the A Flight Commander. Soon after crossing the Lines east of Zonnebeck the Flight was attacked by five Albatros scouts, which dived on them from a height advantage of 3,000ft. During the general manoeuvring for position and desultory attacks, Maxwell succeeded in driving one of the enemy scouts down through the clouds before the remainder dived east, breaking off the action. The SEs then reformed, with the exception of Cronyn whose engine had been hit in the fight, forcing him to return and land at Bailleul.

Later, flying over Langemarcke, James saw a Sopwith Triplane from one of the Naval squadrons diving west from Poelcapelle, closely pursued by two Albatross V-Strutters. James

Richard Maybery.

Eric Turnbull.

led the Flight to the naval pilot's aid, driving one of the enemy scouts off with a burst of thirty rounds from each gun. After this brief action, Maxwell returned with carburettor trouble.

The Flight was now dispersed, with James and Eric Turnbull flying alone. A formation of Albatros scouts was seen coming north over Gheluvelt. James got above the enemy scouts and attacked one painted red, with bands of yellow stripes round its fuselage. He fired a good burst from both guns into the Albatros, sending it down out of control. James had now expended all his Lewis gun ammunition and the trigger bar of his Vickers had broken, so he extricated himself from the remaining V-Strutters, and he and Turnbull returned to Estrée Blanche.

The following evening, James took out a large formation of ten SE5s, again a mixed bag of pilots from A and B Flights. Soon after crossing the Lines the formation split into two groups: James leading Barlow, Johnston, Muspratt and Coote; with Maybery leading Turnbull, Potts,[22] Jeffs,[23] Sloley, and Geoffrey Wilkinson.[24] The Flights kept fairly close to each other, James patrolling the Houthulst Forest and Poelcapelle area, with Maybery's formation a little to the south east, patrolling from Polygon Wood to Menin. At 6.50PM, James saw a formation of V-Strutters coming north from Zandvoorde. It was obvious that the enemy pilots had not seen the SEs, and James led them to the east of the enemy scouts, cutting off their retreat, finally attacking them from the south.

James selected the leader and opened fire with his Vickers at 150 yards range, closing to within thirty yards before opening fire with both guns. A trickle of flame came out of the fuselage of the Albatros and it went down in a vertical dive. Fanned by the rush of air, the flames increased until the whole of the tailplane and fuselage of the enemy scout were burning fiercely. The stricken Albatros finally crashed in a small copse south east of Polygon Wood, starting a blaze that was still burning when the Flight flew home an hour later.[25]

While this action was taking place, another formation of Albatros scouts had appeared. These were above B Flight, but were frustrated in any attempt to dive and attack them by the timely arrival of Maybery and A Flight. The B Flight pilots climbed into the fight. James went for two of the V-Strutters that were attacking an SE. He drove one off with a burst from both guns at 200 yards range, then closed with the

Reginald 'Georgie' Hoidge in an SE5 at London Colney.

second, firing a burst from both guns from thirty yards. The enemy pilot dived, then zoomed, attempting get above the SE, but James also zoomed, catching the Albatros at the top of its zoom. James opened fire with both guns at thirty yards, continuing to fire until he nearly collided with the tailplane of the enemy machine. 'By Jove, it was close.' The Albatros turned upside down, fell for two hundred feet, righted itself momentarily, came out into a vertical dive, then stalled, finally going down in a series of sideslips. Owing to the close proximity of other enemy scouts, James could watch it no longer, but it was seen to continue down, still out of control, by Herbert Johnston.

Back at Estrée Blanche, combat reports were made out. The Albatros James had sent down in flames was awarded to James as his tenth victory. The second Albatros was credited as his eleventh. Barlow was credited with an Albatros as destroyed and another as out of control, and Sloley was also credited with another as out of control. The overall tally for the two Flights was two enemy scouts destroyed and three out of control. All the pilots concerned were pleased with the result, with the exception of James, who was both sickened and haunted by the sight of the flaming Albatros, the first of his victories to fall in flames.

The next morning, B Flight was the first to leave the ground, taking off at 6.00AM.[26] Cronyn failed to get off owing to a faulty carburettor, but the remainder, James, Barlow, Johnston, Muspratt and Coote, climbed for height, crossed the Lines at 13,000ft and flew to Roulers. Over the town they were attacked by twelve Albatros V-Strutters of the same *Jagdstaffeln* fought the previous day. Anxious to avenge their comrades the enemy pilots pressed home their attacks with some spirit, and being heavily outnumbered James turned the Flight for the safety of the British front Lines, knowing that the enemy pilots would not press home their attacks once they were reached. A running fight developed, during which Muspratt succeeded in driving down one of the attackers. True to form, the Albatros pilots left them at the Lines, and James reformed the Flight and led them to the area of Houthulst Forest. Just south east of the forest, the Albatros formation was now fighting with a patrol of Sopwith Camels of 70 Squadron. The fight was well above the height of the SEs, but two of the enemy scouts were driven down to their level by the Camel pilots and were driven off to the east.

The SE formation was now split up and James, Muspratt and Coote patrolled towards Gheluve. At 7.45 they attacked a formation of enemy scouts, one of which James sent down in a vertical dive. The SEs were now very low, both Cootes's guns were out of action with stoppages, and they returned. The scout James had sent down in a vertical dive was credited to him in the squadron's victory lists as 'driven down'. It was to be his last victory for over three weeks.

On 22 August, B Flight was detailed to escort the DH4s of 55 Squadron that were to bomb the enemy aerodrome at Ascq and the railway station at Bavay, and James led the Flight off the ground at 6.00PM. The SEs met up with the bombers at 10,000ft over Aire, climbed hard for an hour and a half and finally crossed the Lines over Armentières, the SEs at 17,000ft, the limit of their ceiling, the bombers slightly lower. After the DH4s had dropped their bombs and turned for home, a number of Albatros scouts climbed to their height and made a series of half-hearted attacks. The SEs immediately dived to

Estrée Blanche. August 1917. Three Flight Commanders: James McCudden, Ian Henderson and Gerald Constable Maxwell. James was taking over command of B Flight from Henderson.

Maxwell Coote.

attack the enemy scouts. James got on the tail of one, but his guns refused to fire – the Vickers with a No.4 stoppage and the Lewis with a misfire. The enemy pilot dived away. The rest of his Flight having driven the remaining Albatros east, James reformed the Flight and they escorted the DH4s safely across the Lines. Having cleared his guns' jams, James then led the Flight north to Zonnebecke, but over Ypres they saw a formation of FE2ds fighting a number of V-Strutters. James' reaction was immediate: 'Now then chaps. The Squadron to the rescue.'

James attacked a purple and black Albatros, a machine he had seen before, closed the range and opened fire. The enemy pilot dived away, then zoomed. James followed, still firing, seeing his tracers passing to the right of the fuselage of the Albatros. The enemy pilot half-rolled and dived away. James did the same, coming out a few feet above the Albatros. Looking down, he could see the enemy pilot – 'he seemed only a boy' – looking upwards at him, although he seemed completely unperturbed. James realised that here was a very good, experienced pilot, who would be extremely difficult to bring down, and turned away. Not a moment too soon: four of the Albatros were coming down on him. James evaded these and being now low on petrol broke off the action and returned to Estrée Blanche.

That evening, James again took out his Flight, crossing the Lines just to the south of Ypres. A few miles to the north, over the edge of Houthulst Forest they saw C Flight – Bowman, Maybery and Hoidge – fighting three Albatros scouts. Knowing full well that the German pilots would have their hands full fighting such opponents – plus Turnbull and Sloley, who joined up with them – James led his Flight further east. He had seen three DFWs, going west over Zanvoorde, and he meant to cut off their retreat. The three enemy two-seaters crossed the Lines near Ypres and James led the Flight down to attack them, each of the Flight picking a target.

After a long burst from James' guns, his opponent went down in an erratic dive, badly damaged. Muspratt attacked another of the trio and sent it down in a flat spin, increasing in speed until it finally crashed west of the Lines, near the St Julien to Ypres road. James, with scant sympathy, commented: 'I have never seen anything so funny as that old Hun going round and round for over two minutes. I bet the pilot and observer had a sick headache after that.'[27] Cronyn also shot down one of the DFWs, which went down 'turning over and over like leaf', but its gunner had put a bullet into his radiator and he forced landed at 1 Squadron's aerodrome at Bailleul.

During the remainder of the patrol time, James had two brief, inconclusive skirmishes with Albatros scouts before

Above: Arthur Rhys Davids took this photograph of James, his Flight Commander, flanked by Keith Muspratt on the left and Maxwell Coote on the right.

Left: James took over the camera for this photograph, with Arthur Rhys Davids taking over the central position between Muspratt and Coote. This triumvirate of Rhys Davids, Muspratt and Coote were known to the squadron as 'The Children.'

Keith Knox Muspratt.

The cockpit of an SE5a showing the spade grip with the triggers requested by James.

returning to base, landing at 8.30PM.

The weather, that had been fine and sometimes extremely hot – Muspratt had written home on the 18th: 'the heat is appalling, but flying and washing give great relief' – now gave way to a period of eleven days of winds and rain. The squadron flew no patrols for the next two days and only one patrol was flown on 25 August, a day of strong winds and low cloud. Hoidge, leading the patrol, forced an Albatros to land, under control, east of the Roulers to Menin road, and Jeffs sent another down in a steep dive over Roulers.

James took the opportunity during the lull in operations to write to an old friend, Tryggve Gran,[28] a Norwegian, serving in the RFC.

No.56 Squadron, 9th Wing
BEF France 25/8/1917
Dear old Boy,

I hope you are well. I have just heard from a fellow who knew you at 10T.S. I have a flight in this Squadron (200hp S.E.) and if you would like to come out again, I should very much like to get you, so let me know and if you want to come, I will apply for you at once.

These are damn fine machines. I came out on the 15th and up to the 21st got 4 Huns, including one in flames.

Buck up and make up your mind soon old chap. This is a topping Squadron. Good C.O. good everything.

Cheerio and write soon
Yours very sincerely,
J B McCudden

*

Deteriorating weather conditions now effectively stopped all war flying by the squadrons of 9th Wing for the next five days and it was not until the evening of the last day of the month that the squadron were able to resume patrols, Gerald Maxwell and James leading their Flights off the ground at 6.00PM.

Maxwell and his Flight attacked a group of Albatros scouts over Moorslede. Attacking one of the enemy scouts, Maxwell had stoppages in both guns and was severely handled by a 'very good red-nosed EA' which chased him back to the Lines. Wilkinson saw his flight commander's predicament and shot the Albatros off Maxwell's tail, sending it down out of control. This was confirmed by a pilot of 66 Squadron.[29]

Just previous to the A Flight action, James and his Flight had a brief, indecisive combat with several enemy scouts, before flying south towards Langemarcke. At 7.10PM, they saw two French Spads fighting a formation of black and white Albatros scouts north east of Bixschoote. The Flight dived to assist the French pilots and in the fighting Coote sent one scout down with blue-black smoke pouring from it. After a great deal of skirmishing and manoeuvring for position, the enemy scouts finally dived away east towards Armentières. It was now nearly 7.30PM, darkness was falling and all the SEs returned to Estrée Blanche, landing at 8.00PM.

The latter half of August 1917 had been reasonably productive for James: the squadron's victory lists credit him with three enemy aircraft out of control, another destroyed and one driven down. He would improve on this in the coming month.

*

The continuing rain during the last weeks of August 1917 and

The Headquarters Flight of 56 Squadron 1917. Hubert Charles, the squadron's brilliant engineering officer, is 4th from the left in the middle row.

the first two days of September turned the ground in the Ypres area into a morass, bringing the fighting on the ground to almost a standstill. Those ground attacks that were carried out were of a purely local nature, but plans were being made for a resumption of the offensive as soon as the ground had dried sufficiently and an intensive programme was being prepared for the RFC squadrons of II and III Brigades, and 9th Wing. September was to see a great deal of fiercely-contested fighting in the air.

Trygvve Gran. Gran, a Norwegian, served in the RFC as a Canadian, under the pseudonym of Teddy Grant.

German prisoners of war working on Estrée Blanche aerodrome.

Herbert Arnold Johnston.

Ch.11: Autumn Above The Salient

Arthur Percival Foley Rhys Davids. Killed in action 27 October 1917.

By the beginning of September 1917, 56 Squadron was a formidable fighting unit. In James McCudden and Geoffrey Bowman the squadron had two of the finest flight commanders in the RFC – James was to later emerge as perhaps the finest of the war – and Gerald Maxwell, with no previous experience before joining the squadron, had developed into an able flight commander and an aggressive fighter. Other pilots in the squadron were no less successful: the raw beginners of a few short months ago were now resolute and experienced fighter pilots. Barlow, Maxwell and Rhys Davids, all talent-spotted by either Ball or Foot,[1] were to give ample evidence of their worth in the coming month.

In Arthur Rhys Davids the squadron considered that it had another Albert Ball. Since his first operational flight on 3 May, Rhys Davids had been credited with thirteen victories. Maurice Baring, aide to General Trenchard, later wrote of him: 'He was passionately fond of books and poetry, and his mixture of scholarship, enthusiasm, fun, courage and airmanship made me feel that if these were the sort of pilots we had, whatever else might happen, we should never be beaten in the air.'[2]

Leonard Barlow was another pilot who had more than fulfilled his early promise. He had been credited with his first victory on 24 April, the day the squadron had flown its first operational patrols, and by the beginning of September had added another eleven enemy machines to his total.

Geoffrey Bowman had joined the squadron on 11 May as the replacement flight commander of C Flight after the loss of Captain Meintjes on the evening of 7 May. He had been credited with a balloon and an enemy scout while flying with 29 Squadron in 1916, and by September 1917 had added another thirteen enemy aircraft to his personal score.

Another successful pilot was Richard Maybery. One of the stalwarts of C Flight, Maybery was a professional soldier who had served on the Indian frontier with his regiment, the 21st Lancers, and had been badly wounded at the battle of Shabkdar in May 1915. Maybery had joined the squadron on 17 June, and by the beginning of September had been credited with nine victories. Modest to a fault, Maybery was an expert marksman and would become one of the squadron's top scorers.

A Canadian, Reginald Hoidge, nicknamed Georgie, was another member of C Flight. One of the squadron's original pilots, he had scored his first victory on 5 May, adding another seventeen by the end of August 1917.

There were of course other promising pilots in the squadron: Robert Sloley, Keith Muspratt, Charles Jeffs, Verschoyle Cronyn and Eric Turnbull, but these four men, along with the three flight commanders, were the heart of the squadron.

*

September started quietly. Wind, rain and low cloud kept the squadron on the ground for the first two days and patrols were not flown until the morning of 3 September, Rhys Davids and Maybery taking off at 10.50AM on a Special Offensive Patrol. Their orders were to patrol the front lines from Ypres to Armentières and prevent any enemy air activity along this line, but they saw no action and returned at 12.50PM.

Maxwell and Hoidge, leading A and C Flights off the ground at 5.30PM, had a successful evening. Eric Turnbull claimed an Albatros scout as out of control and William Potts sent another down with its propeller stationary. C Flight, patrolling a little to the south of A Flight, attacked eight Albatros V-Strutters over the Ypres-Comines Canal. Rhys Davids, who had taken off at 6.30PM with James, saw this action and hurried to join in. Aided by Maybery, he attacked one of the enemy scouts and shot it down to crash close by the village of Houthem.

James had left Rhys Davids soon after taking off and had flown to the Ypres Salient 'to look for stray Huns'. He met up with Potts and Jeffs, who had become separated from A Flight

Charles Hugh Jeffs. Shot down and taken POW on 5 October 1917.

William Janson Potts. Killed in action 21 September 1917.

during the fighting, and the trio saw three V-Strutters going north over Poelcapelle. They went down to attack these, but James' engine 'choked' and he passed below an Albatros, whose pilot he could see looking down at him. The next thing James saw were tracers going into the enemy scout, that immediately burst into flames. James had no time in which to avoid the blazing Albatros as it went down, distinctly hearing the roar of its engine as it passed by him, barely fifty feet away.[3]

James now got his engine going again and attacked another Albatros. He admitted that he 'could not shoot this fellow', its pilot being extremely skilled in manoeuvring defensively, but the enemy pilot, no doubt unnerved by the fate of his companion, broke off the action, diving away to the east.

At this time, Major Blomfield was on leave and James was temporarily in command of the squadron, but on 4 September, escaping from these onerous duties, he led B Flight off the ground after lunch with orders to escort the DH4s of 55 Squadron that were returning from bombing Audenarde.

The rendezvous point was over Cambrai at 2.10PM. Punctual to the minute, the bombers appeared amid a flurry of black anti-aircraft fire. While escorting the DH4s back to the lines James saw a number of Albatros[4] scouts gaining their height over Lille, and after seeing bombers safely on their way home he turned the Flight back to look for them, finally locating them over Lille at 16,000ft. However, the enemy scouts were flying east and James knew they would be far too deep into enemy territory before the SEs could catch them. He was not prepared to fight at such a tactical disadvantage, ignoring Arthur Rhys Davids who consistently called his attention to the Albatros formation, being all too eager to chase them.

A little later, James' patience was rewarded when the Albatri turned back and attacked the SEs over Becelaere. During the fighting, James got on the tail of one enemy scout, but the pilot immediately went down in a steep evasive spiral. James chased him down to 8,000ft – the fighting had begun at 17,500ft – firing an excessive amount of ammunition, before finally turning away, realising 'it is the most difficult thing imaginable to shoot an opponent who is spiralling'. James then

DH4s of 55 Squadron.

reformed the Flight, saw that it was time to return, and fired the 'washout' signal.

The next day, B Flight attempted to fly the first offensive patrol, taking off at 6.40AM, but James washed out the patrol because of the heavy mist and they returned after ten minutes. The mist having cleared, the Flight took off again at 8.45, crossed the lines at 15,000ft east of Bixschoote and immediately spotted a pair of DFW two-seaters coming west. James tackled one DFW, but after firing only five rounds the lock spring of his Vickers gun broke and he was forced to turn away. Muspratt attacked the other DFW, which spiraled down, coming out still facing west. Muspratt dived and resumed his attack, but the enemy observer put some shots into his SE, severing two flying wires and hitting two main spars, before dropping his gun and falling back into his cockpit.

James then reformed the Flight and they began to return to Estrée Blanche. However, visibility was now excellent, and James thought that there was a distinct possibility that he might catch any enemy two-seaters that were making for home, so he decided to conserve his height. Sure enough, as he crossed the Lines at 16,000ft he saw a two-seater, flying east, five hundred feet above him. James pulled down his Lewis gun – his Vickers was still inoperative – and fired a whole drum, but the enemy pilot put his nose down and continued east. James let it go: he had spotted a DFW coming towards him in a much more favourable position for an attack.

James had been giving a considerable amount of thought on the best way in which to attack enemy two-seaters, in order to give them no chance to reply, and he took up his favoured position – at two hundred yards, behind and slightly below – and fired a complete drum of Lewis into the DFW. The DFW flew on, apparently unharmed. James, while putting a fresh drum on his Lewis gun, slipped out of position for a moment and the enemy gunner got in an accurate burst of fire, which James distinctly felt hit the SE. 'Never mind' he thought and closed again, firing his only remaining drum of Lewis. This caused the DFW to 'wobble and pitch like anything' and the enemy gunner disappeared down into his cockpit, evidently hit. The enemy pilot dived away, under control, in the direction of Quesnoy. James was now out of ammunition and let it go.[5]

Back at Estrée Blanche, James found that the enemy gunner had put an incendiary bullet into one of the SE's longerons, just at his feet, plus there was additional slight damage from other hits.

The casualty report on the SE5a B519 states that 'the machine can be flown with care' and Robert Sloley flew it to No.1 AD for repair, returning with a replacement aeroplane: SE5a B4863. This aeroplane was to give James and his mechanics a great deal of trouble before they got it going really well.

There was a considerable amount of enemy air activity in the autumn evenings and the squadron had found it advantageous to send out patrols at full strength. On the evening of 5 September a large force of eleven SE5as went out, although

Star turns of C Flight; Summer 1917. 'Georgie' Hoidge; 'Beery' Bowman and 'Dickie' Maybery. Maybery seems amused at the bandage of Bowman's leg, a result of the accident with a hot exhaust pipe.

gun and engine troubles soon reduced this to nine. Hoidge, Rhys Davids and Sloley reached the lines together and were attacked by twelve black and white Albatri. These odds were a little too much and they broke off the action. In a later combat, Rhys Davids attacked an Albatros scout with a red fuselage circled by a black band. The Albatros went down steeply, its right wing detached from the fuselage, floating down in small pieces. Rhys Davids was then attacked by an Albatros with a dull green fuselage, again circled with a band, this time yellow. The enemy pilot manoeuvred well and put some shots into the SE, but Rhys Davids finally succeeded in getting above him. However, the Albatros pilot was an old hand: he half rolled and dived away. Rhys Davids followed, firing continuous bursts from both guns. The green Albatros went down in a steepening dive and finally crashed in a small copse a mile north east of Poelcapelle.[6] This was the third Albatros that Rhys Davids had sent down, but his engine had been giving trouble for some time and he returned.

It had been a successful evening for the squadron: three enemy scouts had been sent down out of control, two others destroyed and Sloley was awarded a two-seater out of control.

Low clouds, mist and rain in the early morning of 6 September curtailed flying and the squadron flew only one patrol: James leading Johnston and Coote, plus two members of A Flight – Jeffs and Sloley – off the ground at 6.05AM.

The SEs crossed the Lines at 11,000ft over Bixschoote and at 6.30 attacked a formation of enemy scouts over Houthulst Forest. The formation included two types that were new to the pilots of the squadron: one of these was a Pfalz D.III (later described by the pilots as a new-type Fokker biplane) and two Fokker Triplanes. As far as is known, only two Fokker Triplanes were at the Front at this date: the pre-production triplanes for evaluation at the Front, still carrying their original specification of F.I 102/17 and F.I 103/17. These had been allocated to *Jagdgeschwader Nr*.I on 21 August 1917, with F.I 102/17 being taken by Manfred von Richthofen,[7] the *Geschwader Kommandeur*, with F.I 103/17 by *Leutnant* Werner Voss,[8] the *Staffelführer* of *Jasta* 10, a component of *Jagdgeschwader Nr*.I. It seems more than probable that the formation attacked by McCudden and his Flight was a patrol from *Jasta* 10, led by Voss flying F.I 103/17 and a member of *Jasta* 11 flying F.I 102/17 – possibly Manfred von Richthofen, taking the

SE5as of C Flight at Estrée Blanche sometime between 15 August and 25 September 1917. The squadron marking of a small dumbbell can just be seen behind the identification letter on SE5a R. In C Flight this was in red.

opportunity of a flight in his new Triplane before going on leave later in the day – or Oskar von Boenigk, a pilot in *Jasta 4*.[9]

The SE's lack of height, and the position of the early morning sun, made an attack difficult, but Sloley attacked the Pfalz, firing a drum of Lewis at it. The enemy pilot turned to the east and dived under the cover of his companions. As Sloley turned away, one of the triplanes dived at him and fired a burst from long range. Sloley's report that this triplane pilot 'showed little determination in spite of a very favourable position' makes it very unlikely that this was Voss, a brave and aggressive fighter pilot. After a little further, indecisive skirmishing, the enemy scouts cleared east.

James had been unable to participate in any positive manner during the fighting, his Vickers gun being inoperative owing to a defect in the Constantinesco gear, and he reformed the Flight and led them west, later attacking two Albatri going north over Poelcapelle. James got on the tail of one, but his Lewis only fired a single shot before stopping and the enemy scout spun away. Jeffs attacked the other Albatros, a burst from his Vickers sending it down to crash just east of Poelcapelle railway station.

After a short brush with four enemy two-seaters - one of which Sloley sent down in a slow right hand spiral – the patrol returned to Estrée Blanche, landing at 8.15. After breakfast both James and Robert Sloley wrote descriptions of the new German scouts. Apart from James' impression that the triplanes had a stationary engine – understandable given the fact that the engine of the Fokker Triplane was almost completely cowled – the descriptions were reasonably accurate. James made no mention of the colour of the enemy machines, but Sloley described the Pfalz as being grey and the triplane that had attacked him as being yellow and brown.[10&11]

James spent the remainder of the morning working on the guns of A4863. Taking a short break, James wandered up to speak with Bowman, who had just landed from a patrol. Getting out of his machine and listening to James, Bowman inadvertently put the back of his leg, just above his knee, on the still red-hot exhaust pipe of his SE. As he was wearing shorts ending above the knee, the painful result was that Bowman's bare flesh made contact with extremely hot metal and he leapt 'about four foot into the air shouting most angry profanity.' James beat a hasty retreat: as he told Bowman later, 'the smell of roast pork was most appetizing'.

James was to spend two whole days with his armourers, attempting to rectify his guns, coming in for a great deal of teasing by the other pilots and 'Grandpa' Marson, who suggested that the reason his guns would not work satisfactorily in the air was because he had worn them out on the ground. But James was determined that his guns would work perfectly, and did not give up until they did so.

On 7 September, James wrote again to Tryggve Gran.
56 Squadron 9th Wing, France. 7/9/17
Dear old sport,

Many thanks for your welcome letter dated the 1st instant. Sorry to hear you have a gammy leg still, but trust it will soon be O.K. I am very sorry you cannot come out at present, but I shall certainly claim you as soon as you are allowed to come out.

I have had no Huns down lately as I have had a rotten spell of gun trouble, but it is alright now. Yesterday I caught a two-seater a long way our side at 18,000. Got behind him, Vickers jambed, and only had one drum of Lewis, so pumped that into him at close range but did not get him, so as he was still our side and I was heaps faster, I shot all my Verey's lights at him,

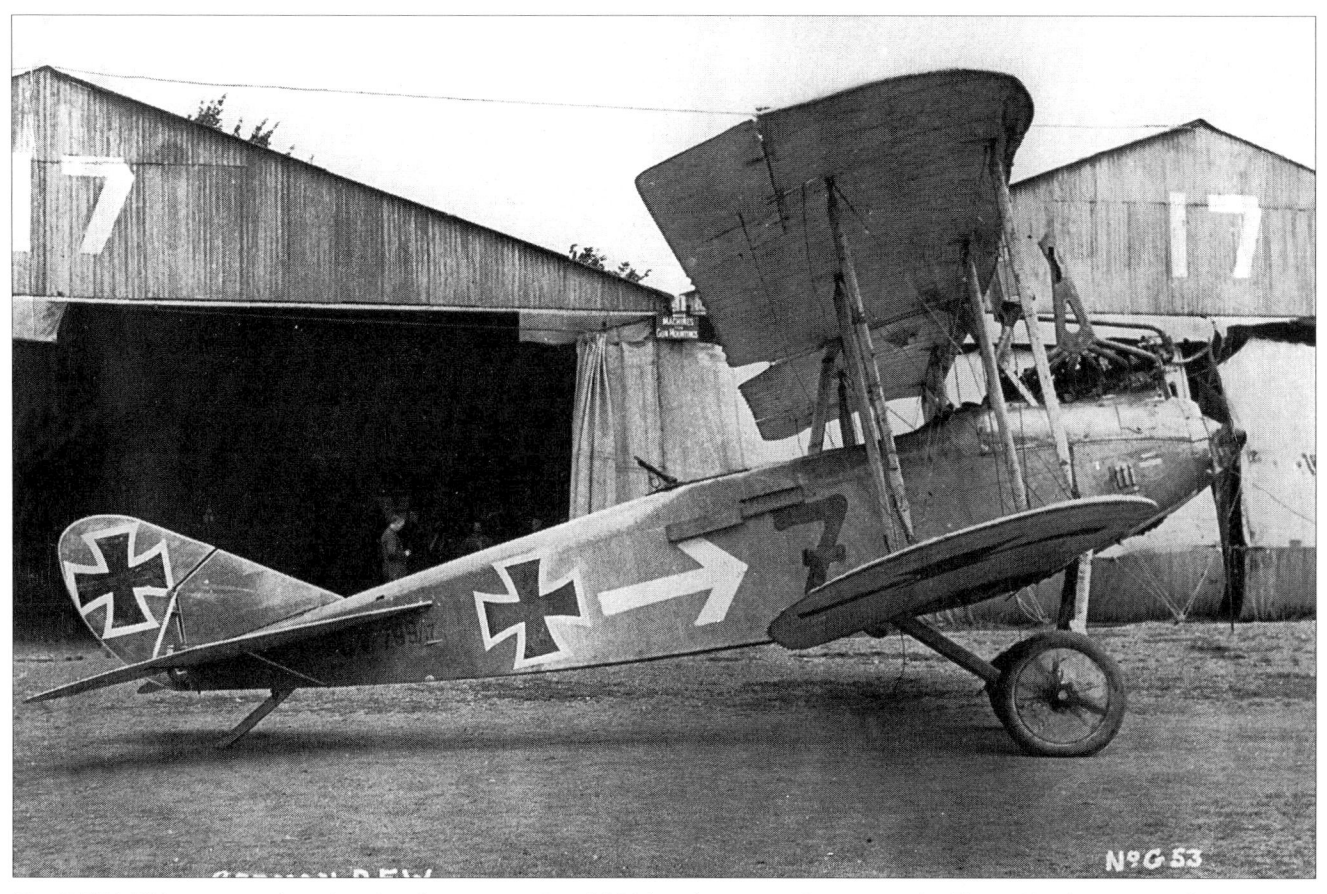

The DFW. C.V. was introduced in the closing months of 1916 and continued to equip the *Flieger Abteilung* units of the *Luftstreitkräfte* until the end of the war. James shot down nine of the type and damaged several others. This particular DFW C.V, No. 799/17, was shot down and captured intact by Keith Muspratt and Arthur Rhys Davids on 12 July 1917. It was given the captured aircraft reference number G53.

and he got the awful wind up, but got over the lines O.K.

During the Verey's light stunt he put an explosive bullet in one of my engine bearers and wrote the grid off, so now I have a new tub which is a topper.

29 are doing well but have a lot of casualties.

Yesterday morning, we ran into two new types of Hun. A Triplane and a new Fokker biplane. The triplane is an awfully comic old thing, and I am awfully keen to see one out of control. I reckon it will be like a venetian blind with a stone tied to it; it is very fast though and has a good climb.

Collet is here on this aerodrome with Camels and is doing well.

The other evening Richthofen, who is flying a new type V-Strutter Albatros Scout, drove Collet down to 1,000ft from 10,000 and riddled Collet with bullets, so as you know how Collet can fly, you can guess what sort of a star turn 'R' is.

Well cheerio old bean, hope this finds you well, and drop me a line soon.

Sincerely yours,
Mac

*

The weather now clamped down again, with rain, low clouds and ground mist, and there was no war flying for the next two days. The pilots of the squadron amused themselves in various ways. Tenders were available for trips to the trenches, or more popular, into St Omer to visit 'the fair maids of France'. James, rather diplomatically, wrote: 'Most fellows had an attraction of some sort in St.Omer, and the teashops, where there was usually to be had wonderful French pastry, were always full. In the mess we had many games, ping-pong being easily the most popular. Then we had the inevitable cards, gramophone and piano, which several fellows could play quite nicely.'

Another game, played outdoors when the weather was fine, was Bumble-Puppy: a ball was suspended by a length of cord from the top of a pole and two players, on opposite sides of the pole, each armed with a tennis racket, hit the ball in opposing directions, the winner being the player who first succeeded in winding the ball up to the fullest extent of the cord. James commented: 'This does not sound very exciting, but it is when two good players get going.'[(12)]

On fine days bathing was possible in a little stream a few miles from the aerodrome, until the day a contingent of Portuguese soldiers were found in possession. James commented, rather unkindly: 'Needless to say, the water never recovered its pristine clearness or odour.'

On one occasion, when the day was dud and there was

SE5a A4863 outside the B Flight hangars at Estrée Blanche.

James in SE5a A4863.

no possibility of flying, James and Leonard Barlow set off in a tender to visit Vimy Ridge, calling on the way to visit James' brother Anthony, flying DH4s with 25 Squadron at Lozinghem. Resuming their journey, they visited a cousin of Barlow at an artillery group headquarters before driving through the valley of Notre Dame de Lorette, Carency and Souchez, scene of heavy fighting by French forces in early 1915. Carency and Souchez were in ruins – 'merely a pile of rubbish' – but the formidable natural fortress of Vimy Ridge towered over the landscape, and James was amazed that it had fallen to a direct frontal attack by Canadian troops in April 1917 after being held by the Germans since 1914. They sheltered the tender on the eastern slope of the ridge and walked to a nearby observation post. From here, using binoculars, they could see the face of the clock on the church tower of Haines, a small village some way behind the German

Fokker Triplane F.I 103/17. Werner Voss is in conversation with Anthony Fokker (back to the camera). *Credit Alex Imrie.*

lines, and Wingles Tower, the enemy's massive, steel observation post. They then visited the battlefield of Vimy itself, finding the ground extensively littered with war matériel of every description: rifles, grenades, trench mortars and shells of all calibres. They had room for only a few souvenirs, but James found a German rifle in good condition. After having 'some fun' pulling the strings of German bombs – known by the Tommies as potato mashers – and throwing them to explode into one of the numerous craters, they spent some time in examining the graves of fallen German soldiers. They then returned to their tender, thankful that they were not called upon to do their own fighting in such appalling conditions.

On their way back from Vimy, James and Barlow passed through Bèthune. During 1915, James had been a frequent visitor of a little patisserie just outside the town, on the road to Lillers, and he and Barlow stopped there for tea. To his delight, James found that the same 'dainty little Madeline' who had so often served him tea when he was a corporal in 3 Squadron was still serving there. Her fiancé, a lieutenant in the French infantry, had been killed at Verdun, and James, in his admittedly none too perfect French, attempted to express his sympathy. Madeline merely shrugged: '*Ah, M'sieu! C'est la Guerre!*'

After tea, they went back into Béthune to shop for a few essentials. Although the town square had initially been extensively damaged, the town had subsequently suffered little from shelling since James had last seen it and he found it almost unchanged. Passing one shop, James was delighted to see that it had a large stock of a brand of brilliantine that he particularly liked. He had last bought a stock in Avensnes-le-Compte in 1916, but had recently finished his last bottle and had never been able to find any more. He went into the shop and bought up the shopkeeper's entire stock at a cost of thirty francs.

James and Barlow then made their way back to Estrée Blanche, arriving just in time for dinner. During the day, some of their fellow pilots had been to Calais, some to Ypres, others to St.Omer, and dinner was a lively affair of travel anecdotes.

Heavy mist and low clouds on 9 September again curtailed war flying. There was considerable enemy activity on the front of Third Army and some squadrons were dispatched to deal with it, but 56 Squadron flew only one patrol during the morning, led by Hoidge. Although there were some clear areas, there was heavy cloud at 5,000ft and the Flight returned having seen no aeroplanes other than a patrol of Sopwith Triplanes.

The weather improved considerably during the day and by the evening conditions were good enough for two patrols to take off at 5.00PM: A and B Flights led by Gerald Maxwell and James. This was a strong force of eleven SEs, but engine troubles forced both James and Barlow to turn back – James landing at 29 Squadron's aerodrome at Poperinghe, returning to Estrée Blanche at 8.00PM – and Gerald Maxwell returned with a badly vibrating engine. The force was further depleted by a collision between Turnbull and Potts of A Flight, but

Pfalz D.III. The Pfalz D.III entered service with the *Jadgstaffeln* in August 1917.

luckily both were able to return uninjured. The remainder of the patrol saw a good deal of fighting during the evening, the squadron lists crediting Rhys Davids with an Albatros scout destroyed and another driven down.

After flying a forty-five minute morning test flight in B4863, James left the ground alone at 5.45PM on the evening of 10 September, a flight detailed in the Squadron Record Book as a Special Mission. He returned after thirty-five minutes, but he submitted no combat report so presumably saw nothing of interest.

The fighting on 11 September resulted in a great deal of frustration for James. He took his flight off the ground at 6.15AM and they crossed the Lines at 13,000ft over Bixschoote before turning east towards Roulers. Seeing no enemy activity there, James led them south to Menin before turning north-west again. A formation of Albatri was then seen going south over Becelaere. James led the Flight west, circled to the east, then attacked the enemy scouts from out of the eye of the early morning sun.

The fighting began at 15,000ft over Houthulst Forest. James secured a favourable position on the tail of one of the Albatri, closed to within thirty yards and pulled both triggers. Neither gun fired a single shot: the Constantinesco gear of the Vickers malfunctioned and the Lewis had stopped with a double feed. The Albatros pilot dived away. James followed, working on his Vickers, which he managed to rectify, and chased the Albatros down to 9,000ft, where it evaded his fire and cleared east. This Albatros pilot was lucky to get away: '(he) was very lucky, for he was very dud. My word! You cannot realise what it is to get on a Hun's tail time after time, and then have your guns let you down.'[13]

Additional enemy scouts now arrived at the scene, but the increased odds against the SEs were offset by a formation of Sopwith Triplanes from the RNAS. James and Rhys Davids saw an SE in trouble, being driven down by a skillful Albatros pilot, and dived to assist it. Rhys Davids initially drove away, then left the persistent enemy pilot, but James then attacked him, driving him down to 2,000ft, getting in good bursts with his Lewis gun, his Vickers CC gear again being inoperative. However, with a series of S-turns, the enemy pilot managed to evade James and dived still lower towards Passchèndaele. James, ever cautious, realised that he was now east of Zonnebeck, very low, and he climbed west. He was certain that his shots had hit the enemy scout, but later reported that it was still under control when he left it.[14]

James rejoined his patrol. They later attacked several two-seaters north of Comines, but before they could get within effective range the enemy machines dived away over their own lines. All the Flight had now been out for two and a half hours, and were low on petrol. James fired the washout signal and they returned.

In the evening, James took off with C Flight. Bowman fell out with carburetor trouble and 'Georgie' Hoidge took over leadership of the Flight. An hour after taking off, the Flight attacked six Albatri north-east of Houthulst. Hoidge sent one down completely out of control, but James was again frustrated by jambs in both guns and his opponent dived away. During the fighting the SEs became separated, but fifteen minutes later Hoidge met up with James and they attacked a pair of two-seaters at 7,000ft over Houthulst.

James fired both guns into one of the enemy machines, but although his Lewis worked well his Vickers stopped after only a few shots and he was forced to zoom away to avoid a collision. At the top of his zoom, James saw six Albatri, at about his height, just to the west. He attacked one of these but failed to gain a decisive result.

The two-seater attacked by Hoidge had a red fuselage and the enemy gunner made good shooting at the SE, using

Manfred von Richthofen.

Werner Voss.

explosive bullets, but Hoidge silenced him with a drum of Lewis and he disappeared inside his cockpit – either wounded or dead. The two-seater went down, white smoke pouring from its engine, but Hoidge did not follow, having to change his Lewis gun drum.

James and Hoidge were now running low on petrol, and after successfully eluding several indecisive attacks by enemy scouts they returned: Hoidge to Estrée Blanche; James to Bailleul, where he landed for petrol before returning to Estrée Blanche at 8.30.

That evening James wrote to his father, venting his frustrations of the day.
My Dear Dad,

Your very welcome letter to hand this morning. For which many thanks. Jack is not posted to a squadron yet but I expect he will be during the next few days. He is quite near me.

I am entitled to another ribbon now (the Mons Medal) so I hope to put it up soon.

Splendid weather at present, and a lot of flying. I have had a lot of trouble with my guns jambing of late and have lost a lot of Huns over it. Anyway, I think my armourers have got to the base of the trouble now.

This morning I got twenty yards behind a Hun, and took sight on the back of his neck and pulled the triggers, and neither gun fired a single shot. And while I was rectifying the stoppages the Hun got away.

Well Dad old chap, I must now close as I am up to strafe the Hun at 3PM.

Your affec t Son
Jim

PS. Hope you are well.

Weather conditions were bad on 12 September, with low clouds and poor visibility. Maxwell took out A Flight at 11.30AM, but returned after two hours having seen no enemy activity. James and Bowman took out their flights at 5.15PM, the SEs crossing the lines at 13,000ft over Ypres and patrolling the Menin-Roulers area. Silhouetted against the low clouds, the SEs were an excellent target for the German anti-aircraft batteries, and both James and Bowman reported that their fire was continuous and accurate. Their aerodromes being covered by thick clouds, no enemy machines were seen until 6.55PM.

John Anthony 'Jack' McCudden. Killed in action 18 March 1918.

Julius Schmidt. On 14 September, while serving with *Jasta* 3, Schmidt out-fought Rhys Davids, hitting his SE5a in the petrol tank. Rhys Davids was forced to land away from base at Bailleul.

Bowman and his Flight chased nine enemy machines east of Staden, but the Flight had been out for nearly two hours and Bowman turned back over Roulers.

James led his Flight down to attack some V-Strutters at 13,000ft, a little to the east of Houthulst Forest, one of the Albatri spinning away from James' fire. He then engaged another, which also spun away. James reformed the Flight and after patrolling for some time, they returned.

There was no war flying on 13 September, the weather being extremely bad, with low clouds, strong winds and rain, but the next day there was a great deal of intense, hotly contested air fighting.

Bowman took C Flight out at 8.05AM. Over Zandvoorde they attacked eight Albatri, Bowman sending one down to crash in a field a mile north east of Menin. Sloley sent another of the Albatri down out of control, the pilot either wounded or killed, and Jeffs and Horrell[15] each claimed two others as out of control. On the debit side, Hoidge had been shot down. One of the enemy pilots had put an accurate burst into the engine of his SE and he force landed just north of Zillebeke Lake.

James took out a patrol in the evening and had 'some fine sport'. Over Roulers, James led the SEs down in an attack on seven Albatri of *Jasta* 10. At 75 yards range, James' fire hit *Oberleutnant* Ernst Weigand's Albatros in the engine. The Albatros began to vibrate alarmingly.[16] Weigand, slightly wounded, shut off his engine and went down in a flat spiral, but he managed to land the damaged fighter. Rhys Davids had attacked another of the Albatri, opening fire at sixty yards. The enemy scout went down in a steep spiral, smoke pouring from its engine.

James and his Flight now joined up with Maxwell's A Flight and the combined force of eleven SEs patrolled towards Menin. Arriving over the town at 14,000ft, a formation of twelve or fourteen red-nosed Albatros V-Strutters came in from the east. James and Rhys Davids flew under the enemy formation, continually turning, tempting the enemy pilots down to attack them. Eventually, the leader of the formation dived on Rhys Davids and they fought for some time. Rhys Davids noted that the Albatros was immaculately finished, with a green fuselage and tail (although James reported that its tail was silver). The enemy pilot[17] flew brilliantly, out-manoeuvred Rhys Davids completely, and hit his SE5 in the petrol tank. Petrol poured over Rhys Davids feet, and he zoomed west and shut off his engine. The pilot of the Albatros made no attempt to follow him and Rhys Davids glided down to 6,000ft over Comines, switched over to his gravity-fed fuel tank and force landed at Bailleul aerodrome.

James had seen Rhys Davids glide away out of the fight, saw that the Albatros pilot had not followed, and went to the aid of Wilkinson, who was under attack from another of the Albatri. After driving this enemy scout away from Wilkinson, James flew down through the cloud cover, coming out into clear air at 9,000ft. Another bank of cloud was slightly lower; coming out of it was a solitary Albatros. 'By Jove!' James thought. 'Here's a sitter', and went down to attack it. He was just about to open fire when he heard gunfire. There was an old RFC adage that if you could actually hear a gun firing it was being aimed at *you*. James looked back, just in time to see 'three red noses coming for me'. He dived into the cloud cover, saw through a gap that he was well east of Menin, and flew west, shaking off his pursuers in the clouds and recrossing the front lines over Frelinghien. On landing back at Estrée Blanche, he learnt that Rhys Davids and Crow had not returned. Rhys Davids later telephoned from Bailleul, to say that he was down safely, but Norman Crow had been shot down, the Germans later dropping a note to say that he was dead.[18]

James flew twice during the morning of 15 September. At 8.15AM he flew A4863 for 65 minutes, entered into the Squadron Record Book as a 'Test Flight' but his logbook entry reveals that he flew to the Auchy-La Bassée area and shot up some trenches. Later, at 11.15, he travelled to 1AD at St.Omer to bring a new SE5a, A4861, back to the squadron, a short flight of five minutes.

There were high winds during the day and no regular patrols were possible until the evening, when a force of twelve SE5as left the ground at 5.00PM: Maxwell taking out A Flight and Bowman C Flight. James tagged along with C Flight, returning at 7.25PM. He submitted no combat report, so presumably saw no action.

Neither Maxwell nor Bowman's Flights saw any decisive action. An Albatros, from a formation of eleven, was seen to dive on the last man in a patrol of Sopwith Camels and Maybery dived to attack it, but the enemy pilot sheered off and flew east. Bowman did not attack the hostile formation as there was a strong, adverse wind blowing. Bowman flew slowly back to the Front Lines, hoping to lure the enemy formation west, but commented: 'EA would not follow'.

Conditions had improved considerably the next morning, and A Flight, plus a formation of Bristol Fighters, escorted a

Norman Howard Crow. Killed in action 14 September 1917.

formation of Martinsydes of 27 Squadron to bomb the fortified village of Hooglede. The British bombers were attacked over the target area by a pair of enemy two-seaters. Maxwell attacked one of these, silencing its gunner and sending it down in a slow spin. Sloley had seen four enemy scouts coming up from Roulers with the obvious intention of attacking the Martinsydes. He attacked these, sending one spinning down for 5,000ft, turning over and over, before disappearing into the cloud bank lower down.

The second patrols of the day took off at 5.00PM, a combined force of eight SEs of B and C Flights led by James and Bowman. C Flight were soon in action with a number of Albatri south east of Houthulst Forest. Bowman attacked one of these, which dived away from his fire – straight under James and B Flight, who had arrived at the scene. James saw one of the enemy scouts attacking Richard Maybery, so he dived to Maybery's assistance. The enemy pilot promptly executed 'some very weird manoeuvres' and James lost sight of him. James turned to the left, but still could not locate his opponent. Twisting in his seat, he looked round: just behind him, yards away, was the nose of the Albatros. However, much to James' relief, the enemy pilot was just as disorientated, looking back over his shoulder, no doubt wondering where the SE had got to. This rather comic situation was resolved by the German

A Rumpler C.VII. Introduced in early 1917, the Rumpler C.IV had an impressive performance at height, was fast, and was well liked by the German crews. A development of the C.IV, the C.VII, was a long-distance reconnaissance aeroplane, powered by a high-compression 240hp Maybach engine. Stripped of all extraneous equipment and armament, a version of the C.VII, known as the *Rubild*, was fitted with a specialised camera for use at extremely high altitudes. Operating at 20,000 to 24,000 feet – higher than any contemporary British fighter could reach – with a speed at this height in the region of 100mph, these Rumplers were almost impossible to intercept. With his specially tuned SE5a, James was possibly the only British fighter pilot capable of reaching the heights usually flown by the *Rubild* Rumplers, but although he shot down a total of 15 Rumplers, a study of his combat reports makes it very unlikely that any were the *Rubild* version, being attacked at heights considerably lower than the 20,000ft at which these aeroplanes habitually operated. The *Rubild* Rumplers gave sterling service with the *Luftstreitkräfte*, bringing back excellent and much-needed photographs of the Allied back areas. *Credit Alex Imrie.*

pilot diving away to the east.[19] James reformed the Flight and led them to Houthem, where he had seen a formation of SEs from 60 Squadron fighting with another formation of Albatri. James attacked one, but choked his engine at the last moment. Restarting his engine, James was just in time to witness Leonard Barlow dispatch one of the enemy scouts in 'great style', the Albatros going down in a very fast spin to crash near Wervicq.[20]

The next day the weather had deteriorated again and no flying was possible for the next two days. On the 19th, bored with the inactivity, James took off alone 'to look for two-seaters.' He climbed to 18,00ft and flew north from Lens. There was a strong westerly wind, with clouds lower down. As James was passing over the Bois de Biez, watching a two-seater a little east of him, he looked down and saw another passing under him – a DFW, only 400ft below, flying west. James closed his throttle and went down, getting under the DFW's tail and firing a short burst from both guns. The enemy pilot

dived away, so violently that a small black box fell out of his aeroplane and what James thought was a shower of signal light cartridges, or photographic plates. James drove the DFW down to 10,000ft, finally leaving it over Quesnoy, without gaining a positive decision.

James then returned to the Lines, climbing to regain his height. Thirty-five minutes later he saw a Rumpler crossing the lines south of Armentières at 14,000ft. James flew to get the sun behind him, waited until the enemy pilot had flown well to the west, then attacked over Estaires, getting behind and under the tailplane of the enemy machine. His Lewis gun having previously stopped with a double feed while attacking the DFW, James fired a burst of thirty rounds from his Vickers gun: the propeller of the Rumpler jerked almost to a stop and it began to glide down, blue smoke coming from its engine. James' Vickers now stopped with a No.3 stoppage, but he quickly rectified this and pressed home his attack, firing another ten rounds. The Rumpler continued to go down 'very

The LVG C.V. The LVG C.V entered service with the *Flieger Abteilungen* in mid 1917, a later version, the C.VI, in mid 1918. The LVG was employed on reconnaissance and artillery spotting duties. James shot down 11 LVG C.Vs.

erratically', smoke still pouring from its engine. At 4,000ft, passing over it, James saw that the enemy gunner was slumped on the floor of his cockpit, leaving his gun unattended. James drove the Rumpler down to 1800ft, just east of the lines, until it glided into the ground, downwind, crashing a mile behind the German front lines near Radinghem.[21] James was a little disappointed, as he had been determined to crash the Rumpler on the British side of the lines, the fight having started over Estaires, well over the British back areas, but the strong westerly wind had driven the fight eastwards. Nevertheless, he was pleased with a definite, final result, not having been able to claim a positive victory since 21 August.

While making out his combat report, James was joined by Gerald Maxwell and Robert Sloley. They had also driven down a pair of two-seaters after wounding or killing the observers.

The battle of the Menin Ridge Road opened the next morning. Weather conditions were bad: low clouds at fifty feet, strong winds and rain, with a low mist covering the battlefield, that failed to clear until nearly 8.00AM. The fighting on the ground went well, with the infantry aided by the valuable work of the Corps squadrons, whose timely reports gave ample warnings of German counter attacks building up, at least eight such attacks being reported and successfully broken up by artillery fire. Because of the weather conditions the original orders for the air offensive could not be carried out, but the Camel, Nieuport and RNAS squadrons carried out dozens of attacks on ground targets, dropping sixty seven 25lb Cooper bombs and expending over 28,000 rounds of ammunition.

Verschoyle Cronyn took out the first patrol from 56 Squadron. Only a few enemy aircraft were seen and these 'declined combat', diving away to the east. The patrol was plagued by various technical troubles and four were forced to land away from Estrée Blanche. Bowman took out the second Offensive Patrol of the day, a mixed bag of C and B Flight pilots, but was forced to return after only thirty minutes with a leaking oil pipe, and Barlow took command. The Flight saw a great deal of fighting, with four separate formations of enemy scouts, but gained no decisive results.

Maxwell and Sloley left the ground at 10.50AM on 'Special Missions'. They flew above the thick cloud to Armentières, and over Wervicq attacked a two-seater escorted by a scout. In their initial attack, the scout pilot made off, leaving his charge, and they sent the two-seater down with smoke pouring from its engine, Maxwell estimating that it would crash just east of Ypres.

In the evening, Bowman, the oil pipe leak having been rectified, took out a patrol at 5.00PM. Again, this was an assortment of pilots from all Flights, including James. The SEs crossed the lines over Ypres at 10,000ft and spotted nine enemy aircraft well east of the Roulers-Menin road. Although the enemy formation was above the SEs, and flew towards them, they did not come down and dived away to the east. The SEs climbed to 17,000ft in an attempt to get above the enemy scouts, that still refused to come down, again clearing to the east. Frustrated, the patrol then came down to 10,000ft and attacked four Albatri below them, but these dived steeply away into the cloud cover.

On the morning of 21 September, James took off alone at 6.20AM on a Special Mission to look for two-seaters, but he returned at 8.40, having seen no enemy aeroplanes. A later flight had slightly better results. James and Leonard Barlow took off at 12.20, to seek out several enemy two-seaters that

Harold Alan Hamersley. Hamersley was credited with 11 victories in WWI.

had been reported as operating over the Ypres Salient. Before leaving the ground, Barlow had laughingly asserted that his SE was faster than B4863, being flown by James, and on their way to the Lines, they had a race to see whose machine was the fastest. Such a youthful challenge serves to remind us that for all their seriousness in undertaking their daily work, these were still young men, with all the youthful enthusiasm of their age. The innocent pastime of a race, on their way to kill, or be killed by, their fellow human beings, seems to have struck no incongruous note in their minds. James' SE was the faster.

Thirty-five minutes after taking off they attacked a two-seater coming west over Houthem at 9,000ft. James closed to within fifty yards and fired a burst of twenty rounds from both guns, that for once worked splendidly, his tracers pushing into the two-seater's fuselage. The enemy machine dived steeply away and the gunner stopped returning his fire. James followed it down and fired a second burst. The two-seater continued to glide down and James last saw it within 500ft of the ground over Gheluwe. James felt sure that he had badly damaged this two-seater, and it was credited to him as driven down damaged.

Half an hour later, James saw three two-seaters coming west at 14,000ft over Warneton. He climbed to their height and attacked one of these from fifty yards range, but his fire seemed to have no effect and all three enemy machines dived away to the east.

Barlow had been having trouble with his engine – possibly due to over revving it during the race – and was forced to land at Morbecque, where a new engine was fitted. Sometime during this busy day, James found the time for a joyride in a 'Sopwith' most probably a Sopwith Pup, borrowed from 66 Squadron, also based at Estrée Blanche and equipped with Pups. Unusually for James, he makes no comment in his logbook entry as to its merits, presumably because of his long familiarity with the type.[22]

James flew again in the evening, leading his Flight off the ground at 4.45PM, accompanied by Bowman leading C Flight – a strong force of ten SEs. Both Flights saw a great deal of fighting.

James led his Flight across the Lines at 13,000ft over Bixschoote. No enemy aircraft were seen for thirty minutes, when a large formation was seen east of the Menin to Roulers road. Cronyn, a member of B Flight, commented in a letter home: 'I had never seen so many Huns before: there must have been about sixty altogether, and only about ten were two-seaters. They were all very much afraid to attack us and as the wind was very strong we didn't wish to go far over to attack them.'[23]

Seeing a pair of two-seaters over Comines, James led the Flight into an advantageous position and dived to attack them. Although he engaged one at close range he failed to gain a decisive result. Half an hour later, several Albatros V-Strutters approached the lines between Zonnebeke and Poelcapelle. James tackled one of these, just to the east of Langemarck, but the enemy pilot dived away and 'would not fight'.

Arthur Rhys Davids had been more successful in the attack on the pair of two-seaters, sending one down with smoke pouring from its engine, but the other members of the Flight had no luck.

C Flight saw a great deal of fighting, but nearly all of it indecisive skirmishing, and only 'Georgie' Hoidge claimed any decisive result: Hoidge saw an Albatros fighting with an SE5, got very close to avoid hitting the SE and fired a whole drum of Lewis into the Albatros, which went down for 2,500ft before finally breaking into pieces over Gheluwe. Hoidge was then attacked by what he described as a "double V-Strutter", and having expended his Lewis gun ammunition, and with a No.3 stoppage in his Vickers, he retreated to the British lines.[24]

It had been a day of mixed fortunes for the squadron. Although Maxwell and G.M. Wilkinson in an early patrol had claimed two victories: a two-seater destroyed by Maxwell and an enemy scout out of control by Wilkinson, plus the Albatros destroyed by Hoidge, A Flight had lost William Potts, who had last been seen with both wings of his SE broken off.[25]

No patrols were flown by 56 Squadron on 22 September. Barlow returned from Morbecque and two new SE5as were collected from the depot, otherwise there was no flying. People amused themselves in various ways: Bumble Puppy, bridge, chess, the ever-popular table tennis, and a rugby match was played in the evening.

Weather conditions on 23 September were cloudy, with a heavy ground mist, and no patrols were flown until the evening, James and Bowman leading their Flights off the ground at 5.00PM. James led the Flight across the front lines at 8,000ft over Bixschoote, unable to go any higher because of a wall of thick cloud at 9,000ft that extended for a thousand feet, effectively putting a ceiling over the entire Front. James noticed that there was a great deal of enemy activity – abnormally so – and that all the aeroplanes, both British and German, were concentrated under the main cloud bank.

The SEs patrolled between Houthulst and Becelaere, flying at 7,000ft. Silhouetted against the cloud they were an ideal target for Archie and came under heavy and accurate fire. All the enemy machines that could be seen were well east of the Lines, but as the Flight were passing over Gheluvelt James spotted a DFW, just south of Houthem, coming north and three thousand feet below them. James led the Flight down and attacked the enemy machine from above and behind, closing the range to twenty yards, and firing a short burst from both guns before being forced to turn away in a steep climbing turn to avoid a collision. The DFW went down vertically, water pouring from its centre section, and crashed just north east of Houthem.[26]

The Flight then turned north, climbing to regain their height. Under the dark cloud, from ground level to 9,000ft, visibility was good. Far to the east were clusters of aircraft – at this distance, 'little black specks' – moving swiftly, first one way then another. To the north were masses of British machines: Sopwith Pups, Camels, SE5s, Spads and Bristol Fighters, all protecting the RE8s of the Corps squadrons working at lower levels.

James had seen a patrol of six Albatros scouts and was about to attack these when he saw an SE5 under attack from a hostile triplane over Poelcapelle. 'The SE certainly looked very unhappy, so we changed our minds about attacking the V-Strutters and went to the rescue of the unfortunate SE.'

The 'unfortunate SE' was Captain H.A. Hamersley[27] of 60 Squadron. Led by Captain Keith 'Grid' Caldwell,[28] two Flights from the squadron were returning from a patrol, with Hamersley and Captain Robert Chidlaw-Roberts[29] bringing up the rear. Hamersley had been keeping a wary eye on a large formation of enemy scouts, when he saw what he thought was a Nieuport being attacked by an Albatros. Hamersley left the formation to attack the 'Albatros', but the 'Nieuport' turned towards him and he saw that it was an enemy triplane. The pilot easily out-manoeuvred Hamersley, severely damaging his SE5 with an extremely accurate burst of fire. Hamersley put his SE into a spin, but the enemy pilot followed him down and Hamersley had to resort to an inverted dive in order to escape. Chidlaw-Roberts, seeing Hamersley was in trouble, dived to attack the triplane in an attempt to draw it away from Hamersley, but the enemy pilot hardly paused in his pursuit: 'in seconds he was on my tail and had shot my rudder bar about. I retired from the fray and that is all I saw of it.'[30] Caldwell had seen Hamersley going down with the triplane in hot pursuit but James and his Flight had now arrived and had engaged the triplane, taking it off Hamersley's tail. 'It was really 56's affair and we felt that six to one was pretty good odds. We

Keith Logan 'Grid' Caldwell. A New Zealander, Caldwell flew with 8 and 60 Squadrons before being given command of 74 Squadron in 1918. A highly successful and popular pilot, Caldwell was credited with 25 victories. He died in November 1980.

were more or less spectators, in my opinion, as there was little room to join in.'[31]

James had attacked the triplane from the right, Rhys Davids from its left, both getting behind it together, but the enemy pilot had seen the threat and turned 'in a most disconcertingly quick manner, not a climbing or Immelmann turn, but a sort of flat half spin'. The triplane was now in the middle of the SEs, but none could get in an effective burst of fire: 'its handling was wonderful to behold. The pilot seemed to be firing at us all simultaneously, and although I got behind him a second time, I could hardly stay there for a second. His movements were so quick and uncertain that none of us could hold him in sight at all for any decisive time.'[32]

At one point, the triplane was flying towards James, nose on, from slightly beneath, and the enemy pilot had obviously not seen him. This was a good opportunity. James dropped the nose of his SE and opened fire with both guns. Immediately,

Robert Leslie Chidlaw-Roberts. Chidlaw-Roberts flew with 20, 18, 60 and 40 Squadrons. He was credited with 10 victories.

the nose of the triplane came up: James saw the red and yellow flashes from the enemy pilot's twin Spandau guns, heard the noise of the bullets as they passed close by, and as the triplane swept past him he could plainly see that the enemy pilot was bareheaded. C Flight, Bowman, Maybery, and Hoidge, had now arrived at the scene of the action, Hoidge in time to fire at the triplane as it passed by James.

The pilot of the triplane seemed undeterred by the added odds: he made no attempt to escape from the SEs, attacking Cronyn and damaging his machine so severely that it sent Cronyn down out of the action. A red-nosed Albatros now joined in the fight, its pilot co-operating magnificently with the pilot of the triplane. Maybery fired a burst at the triplane but the Albatros fastened onto his tail and he was forced to turn away before turning and diving again at the triplane, firing both guns until his Lewis stopped. Both enemy pilots then turned on him and Maybery was saved only by the intervention of two other SEs.

The fight continued: the triplane now in the middle of the British scouts, all firing at it as an opportunity presented itself. James later wrote: '(it) was in the apex of a cone of tracer bullets from at least five machines simultaneously'. Maybery remarked that it seemed 'invulnerable'. Maybery saw Rhys Davids under attack from the red-nosed Albatros and went to his aid, getting in a burst from his Vickers before overshooting. This was the last time the Albatros was seen, although none of the British pilots later claimed to have sent it down.

The triplane pilot was now once again alone, still fighting McCudden, Rhys Davids, Bowman, Maybery, Muspratt, and Hoidge, avoiding the circling SEs by virtue of the manoeuvrability of his machine allied with his superb piloting skills.

James was not the only pilot to note the enemy pilot's amazing ability. Bowman later recalled that the combatants were now at 2,000ft, a little behind the German Front Line, and that the triplane pilot was now alone, still fighting six SEs, 'which did not appear to deter him in the slightest. At that altitude he had a much better rate of climb, or rather zoom, than we had and frequently he was the highest machine of the seven and could have turned east and got away had he wished to, but he was not that type and always came down on us again. His machine was exceptionally manoeuvrable and he appeared to be able to take flying liberties with impunity.'[33]

The triplane pilot fought on. Keith Muspratt was the next to be put out of the fight: his machine was hit in the radiator, sump and oil pipe, and he was forced to return, landing at Bailleul.

Bowman reported: 'I, myself, had only one crack at him: he was about to pass broadside on across my bows and slightly lower. I put my nose down to give him a burst and opened fire, perhaps too soon; to my amazement he kicked on full rudder, without bank, pulled his nose up slightly, gave me a burst while he was skidding sideways, then kicked on opposite rudder before the result of this amazing stunt appeared to have any effect on the manoeuvrability of his machine.'[34]

Distracted by Bowman, the enemy pilot was now flying straight for a brief moment and Rhys Davids was behind him with, as Bowman observed, 'his prop boss almost on the tail of the triplane, flying nose down and straight for the first time in the entire fight'. Rhys Davids had earlier got in several good bursts at the triplane, twice having to replace his Lewis gun drum, and he now fired a whole drum of Lewis into it, plus an equal number rounds from his Vickers before zooming away to avoid a collision, the triplane missing his right wing 'by inches'. Looking down, Rhys Davids saw the enemy scout was now gliding west, its engine apparently off. He dived to attack it again, but his Vickers stopped after a single shot. Rectifying the stoppage, Rhys Davids dived again and fired a long burst into the triplane, which did a slight right hand turn, still going down. The combatants were at 1,000ft and Rhys Davids overshot, zoomed, and never saw the triplane again.

From above, James had seen Rhys Davids make his last attack on the triplane, observing that its movements were now very erratic. He watched it go down in a steep dive, hit the ground and 'disappear into a thousand fragments, for it seemed to me that it went to powder'.

The time was now between 6.35 and 6.40; the SEs reformed and returned to Estrée Blanche.

At dinner that night in the 56 Squadron Mess, the fight with the enemy triplane was the entire topic of conversation. Rhys Davids was showered with congratulations, but his only reply was: 'Oh, if only I could have brought him down alive.' All the pilots who had taken part in the fight shared his regret. Bowman recalled: 'Our elation was not nearly as great as you might have imagined. Rhys Davids, I think, was genuinely upset.'[35] There was a great deal of speculation as to who might have been flying the enemy triplane. It had obviously been one of the very best German pilots and opinions differed as to whether it had been Wolff, Voss, or even von Richthofen. Speculation was also rife in the 60 Squadron Mess at Ste-Marie-Cappel, but from precious experience 'Grid' Caldwell had little doubt that it had been Werner Voss. 'I, for one, felt it could be Voss as I had experienced him before. He was a terrific chap, and rated easily No.1, including von Richthofen.'[36]

Later that evening, news came from Wing HQ that it had been Werner Voss. His Fokker Triplane, F.I 103/17, had crashed at the site of Plum Farm (map ref. 28C.24.C.8.3) just north of Frezenberg. The crash was very near the Front Line and Voss had been buried where he fell by a Lieutenant Kiegan: 'without a coffin and without military honours, in exactly the same manner as all soldiers are buried in battle'.[37]

The next morning, General Trenchard, who had seen the report of the fight, sent his aide Maurice Baring to the squadron for details. All the pilots who had fought Voss were generous in their praise of his flying skills and his courage, but it was perhaps James who paid the finest tribute to the twenty-year-old Voss: 'As long as I live I shall never forget my admiration for that German pilot who single handed fought seven of us for ten minutes, and who put some bullets through all our machines. His flying was wonderful, his courage magnificent, and in my opinion he is the bravest German airman whom it has been my privilege to see fight.'[38]

The morning of 24 September was misty and no patrols were flown until the afternoon. James led the third patrol of the day, but was forced to return after only five minutes due to a broken oil pipe. Leonard Barlow took command of the Flight and during the evening's fighting he and Rhys Davids destroyed a pair of two-seaters: Rhys Davids' in flames; Barlow's crashing just south of Houthulst Forest.

In the afternoon, James flew SE5a, B17 to report to V Brigade HQ. The reason for this visit is not known. The following day, having returned to Estrée Blanche, he flew a short test flight in B4863, but its engine was still giving trouble and in the afternoon he flew twice in another SE5a, B4861. Both these flights were entered in the Squadron Record Book as being test flights. The first flight, one of ten minutes, obviously was, but the second, taking off forty-five minutes after the completion of the first, lasted ninety minutes, and James'

logbook entry details a flight at 18,000ft from Arras, Lens and La Bassée, and under Remarks, states: 'Stalking. 1 EA driven down'.[39]

The day had been fine and bright, although there had been a heavy ground mist in the morning. In the afternoon ten SEs took off at 4.30: Barlow, in the absence of James, leading B Flight, with Bowman leading C Flight. Over Houthulst Forest, British Archie pointed out an enemy two-seater below them. Bowman and Barlow both went to attack it, but it evaded them and dived away. Bowman was then joined by Maybery, who had driven off an enemy scout that was about to attack Bowman. Bowman and Maybery then witnessed a remarkable display by Leonard Barlow who had gone down to attack four enemy scouts – two V-Strutters and two Pfalz D.III – at 15,000ft over Houthulst Forest. Barlow first despatched one of the 'V' Strutters, which went down in pieces under his fire, before bursting into flames. Zooming away, Barlow turned at the top of his zoom and attacked one of the Pfalz, which went down in a steep spiral, pouring smoke, to finally crash at Stampkot. Barlow then turned his attention to the remaining Albatros, that was making off to the east. Barlow had time for only one short burst before zooming away – he had seen additional enemy scouts diving to attack him – but his aim was good: the Pfalz continued down and Bowman confirmed that it crashed half a mile from the north-west corner of Houthulst Forest. These three enemy scouts had been shot down by Barlow in as many minutes.[40] The next day he received a telegram from Trenchard: 'Congratulate you on doing the hat trick yesterday. It was splendid work.'

The weather deteriorated on 26 September: there were bright intervals but a great deal of cloud and ground mist. In a morning patrol, Gerald Maxwell and his Flight attacked a large formation of twin and single-engined machines that they described as 'Gothas.' They forced the bombers to jettison their bombs, and retreat to the east, but gained no victories.[41]

On 27 September the weather deteriorated still further, with low mist and cloud. Ten SEs from A and C Flights took off in the afternoon but although they saw a little action, there were no positive results. After lunch, James took off alone in B4863, ostensibly to test a new engine that had just been installed, but he climbed to 13,000ft and while over Ypres saw a Rumpler over Houthulst Forest, ranging for its artillery. As James was manoeuvring into a favourable position to attack this Rumpler, a Spad suddenly appeared and dived to attack it. However, the enemy crew were alert and the gunner made good shooting at the Spad, which went down out of control. The Rumpler crew then flew a little to the east, but no doubt pleased with having shot down the Spad turned west again and resumed their duties.

The Rumpler was now below James, who dived, got into his 'two-seater position' of just behind and under its tail, and fired a long burst from both guns, turning sharply away at the last moment to avoid a collision. The enemy gunner, however, was an old hand: as James turned away he held his gun in a central position to the rear, waiting to see which way the SE

A pensive Werner Voss with Fokker Triplane F.I 103/17. Voss was shot down and killed in this triplane.

would go. James went to the right. As he passed the Rumpler, twenty yards away, the enemy gunner fired four shots, two of which James distinctly felt hit his SE. James half rolled away to get clear of the gunner's fire, but as he looked down he saw that his long burst had hit home: the Rumpler was going down in flames, passing the vertical and going over onto its back, the enemy gunner falling out – or jumping – from his blazing machine at 12,000ft.[42] The remains of the Rumpler and its pilot ultimately hit the ground behind the British lines, just north of the Ypres to Poelcapelle road, 1,500 yards south east of Langemarke, but the courageous gunner fell in his own lines. This Rumpler was the first of James' victories to fall in the British Lines and as he flew back to Estrée Blanche he was 'very pleased, for it is the wish of most pilots to bring Germans down in our lines, so as to get souvenirs from the machine'.

The next morning, James took his Flight off the ground at 7.45AM. As the SEs approached the front lines, James saw a formation of Albatri going south over Houthulst Forest. James went down to attack these at a tremendous speed – although he thought he was diving 'fairly slowly' the other members of the patrol later reported that they were diving at over 180mph in order to keep up with him. James selected an Albatros flying on the left of the enemy formation and opened fire at 200 yards, holding down his triggers until the range closed to fifty yards. The left wings of the Albatros broke away and it went down, breaking into smaller pieces at 9,000ft, the enemy pilot falling out and going down quicker than the remains of his machine.[43]

James flew on and attacked the leader of the enemy formation, but the pilot, seemingly unshaken by the loss of his comrade, turned before James had got within range. The usual circling for a favourable position then began, both James and the enemy pilot attempting to turn tighter in order to bring their guns to bear. The fight, that had begun at 8,000ft, gradually drifted down to 4,000ft, the combatants still circling, trying to get behind their opponent. Suddenly, James saw that the Albatros, passing by on the opposite side of the circle, was slightly below him. He stall turned to get on its tail, but lost a great deal of height. The Albatros, now above him, got behind James and opened fire. James was now in an extremely hazardous position: he had been out-manoeuvred by the Albatros pilot, was very low, at 2,000ft, and a mile behind the German lines. He made a series of violent manoeuvres to throw the enemy pilot off his aim but these cost him more height, height he could ill afford, and at 1,000ft he dived with his engine full on, intending to contour chase back to the safety of the British lines. Snatching a hasty glance over his shoulder, James was both amazed and relieved to see that the pilot of the Albatros had turned away and was flying east. It is possible that the German pilot thought that James, in his dive, was out of control – certainly no Albatros pilot, conscious of the weakness of his wings in a prolonged high-speed dive, would have dared to attempt such a desperate manoeuvre. If so, this mistake by the enemy pilot was to cost the *Luftstreitkräfte* dear during the coming months. Such are the fortunes of war.[44]

James regained his height, re-crossed the Lines and flew to the previously agreed rendezvous to reform his Flight. Failing to find them he climbed to 10,000ft and flew to Menin, where he found Barlow leading the Flight 'miles east of the Lines, with dozens of Huns west of them'. These were faulty tactics: James fired a recall signal, that was ignored, and it was only after firing another that the Flight reformed around him, minus Rhys Davids.[45]

Their patrol time over, the Flight flew back to Estrée Blanche for a well-earned breakfast. Comparing notes, Rhys Davids and Barlow – who had both sent an Albatros down out of control in the first fight – were in high spirits over their victories. Dickie Maybery, also at breakfast, being told of the fight, dryly remarked that James was becoming quite expert at turning Huns out of their aeroplanes. After breakfast the serious business of the day was undertaken: James played Maybery for the ping-pong championship of the squadron. Maybery won. James later wrote: 'I believe there was a keener competition in the Squadron to be ping-pong champion than to be the star turn Hun-strafer. Maxwell and Maybery were our ping-pong experts and put up a wonderful game every time.'

The successes of the day were not yet over. In a morning patrol, Bowman sent an Albatros down in a vertical dive, and although it was not credited to him in the squadron's lists, he was sure the pilot could not have recovered before he hit the ground. An afternoon patrol saw a more positive result.

James, a keen photographer, took this evocative shot of Gerald Constable Maxwell taxying out at Estrée Blanche. The Bristol Fighters of 22 Squadron can be seen in the background.

Bowman and Hoidge were flying just above the clouds when a pair of V-Strutters cautiously poked their noses into the clear sky. Bowman's opponent went down in a vertical dive; Hoidge's in a spiral, before falling into a wood, a mile west of Westroosebeke. Bowman's logbook has the cryptic entry. 'Got one V-Strutter. Broke up in mid-air after 4,000ft. First EA of mine to seen break up. Splendid.'[46]

It had been a good day for the squadron and with the news received during the day that both Hoidge and Bowman had each been awarded a Bar to their MC, dinner was a celebratory affair.

Only two patrols were flown on 29 September: Maxwell, Johnston, and Jeffs each being credited with an Albatros during the morning patrol – Maxwell's seen to break up in midair, the two others out of control. These victories were confirmed by pilots of 22 Squadron. A patrol by C Flight had no success, gun stoppages robbing them of several potential victories.

At dinner that night there was a lively discussion as to which Flight should fly the first patrol the next morning. The number of enemy machines brought down by the squadron since commencing operations in April now stood at 198 and everybody was keen that their Flight should have the distinction of bringing down the squadron's 200th enemy machine. In fact, it was B Flight's turn of duty to fly the first patrol, not having flown on the previous day, and James, despite a certain amount of resentment from others, stuck firmly to his Flight's claim.

However, on the morning of 30 September the ground over German held territory was almost totally obscured by a thick mist and James and B Flight saw no positive action. Many of the squadron's pilots took off alone during the morning in an attempt to gain the elusive two victories but with no result, and it was not until the usual patrols of the afternoon were flown that the victories were finally gained: Maybery, scoring the 199th victory and Maxwell, half an hour later, scoring the 200th.

Celebrations began with a firework display of the squadron's entire stock of Very lights being fired into the evening sky – forty red, green and white lights lit up the countryside for a considerable distance around. Dinner was a gala affair. The food was excellent, the squadron band played magnificently, and there was 'much speech-making'. After a great deal of high-spirited horseplay in the ante-room, all went to bed, elated and proud of the squadron's record. The next day, a congratulatory letter was received, direct from General Hugh Trenchard.

23-9-17. At 6-5 pm on patrol dived followed by my formation on a 2-seater coming N. of Houthem at 3000. I opened fire with both guns at 150 yds and fired until I was within 20 yds, when I did a climbing turn to avoid running into EA. Looked down and saw him hit the ground in a vertical dive N.E. of Houthem. A 2nd was seen to crash by rest of patrol. At 6-25 saw an SE being driven down and pooped by an E.A. triplane (Voss). R.D. and I dived on this E.A. who left the other SE and engaged us. A Red nosed Albatros now arrived and appeared to be looking after the triplanes tail. The 2 E.A. fought my formation (5 SE5s) for nearly 10 mins, and then the triplane which was very low crashed in a steep glide in our lines after having been finally engaged by R.D. at 1000 ft. The red-nosed Albatros was also put out of control. The triplane fought magnificently and pit pulled through all of my formation before he was brought down. Bravest and most skilful Hun I have ever seen.

Confidential
Officer Commanding
No.56 squadron RFC.

I congratulate the whole Squadron on the magnificent work of having brought down and driven down out of control two hundred German machines during the last six months.

The work of this Squadron has been really wonderful and it reflects the greatest credit on you as Squadron Commander, the Flight Commanders, Pilots, NCOs and men, and it has no doubt helped largely towards reducing the enemy to a proper frame of mind in the air.

I hope it will encourage all the pilots now in the Squadron, not that they want it, but all the new pilots coming to the Squadron, to keep up this splendid reputation and by persevering to the utmost of everybody's ability to help make their weight felt in the victorious final efforts of the Flying Corps in the Field in this war.

I am taking an early opportunity of bringing forward the remarkable work of this Squadron to the notice of the Commander-in-Chief, and I should be glad to have complete statistics of what your Squadron has done to give to the Commander-in-Chief as early as possible.

I am sending this letter direct to you as it is such a special case, and I hope shortly to be able to come and see the whole Squadron together. It is only the pressure of work that has prevented me from visiting you today as the war has still to be won.

H Trenchard. Major General
Commanding Royal Flying Corps.
In the field.
Adv. HQ. RFC.
30th September 1917

The entry in James' diary relating to the fight with Werner Voss on 23 September 1917.

Ch.12: Gains and Losses

September 1917 was in many ways the swansong of the original 56 squadron. Despite the seasonal October weather that was to render twelve days totally unfit for any war flying, the squadron was to suffer eight casualties during the month, the highest casualties for any month since it had arrived in France. Six pilots were to be killed in action, another fatally wounded, and one taken prisoner. Included in the casualties were some of the squadron's best and most promising pilots. In addition to these casualties, several of the original members of the squadron were coming to the end of their tours and would be posted out to Home Establishment. Major Blomfield was also due for promotion and would be relieved of command towards the end of the month. By the end of October, of the original pilots who had flown to France in April, only Hoidge would remain. However, at the beginning of October, the squadron was still at its zenith, both in numbers and morale.

The first day of the month was bright and cloudless. James took off alone after lunch on a Special Mission to look for an enemy two-seater reported to be working over the Lines. At 2.00PM, thirty minutes after leaving Estrée Blanche, he saw the enemy machine – a Rumpler – over Bethune. The Rumpler was at 20,000ft, 8,000ft above James. He knew he could not to climb to the height of the enemy machine in time to make an attack but he shadowed it, flying underneath it as it passed over Bethune, Estaires, Caëstre, Hazebrouck, Aire, St Omer, Liettres, then back to Bethune.

Over St.Omer, James had been joined by a Nieuport from 40 Squadron flown by Captain A.W. Keen,[1] but the Rumpler pilot climbed even higher, contemptuously adding another 2,000ft to his height, still 3,000ft higher than James, and recrossed the Lines over Bois de Biez. James had now followed this Rumpler for nearly an hour and realising that further pursuit was useless, he gave it best and turned to the north-west. Almost immediately he saw another Rumpler, over Melville, at 18,000ft, a thousand feet below him. James dived, got under the tail of the enemy machine, and opened fire from both guns, silencing the enemy gunner, who slid down onto the floor of his cockpit. The Rumpler pilot pushed his nose down, turned to the east and dived for the safety of his own lines. James followed. His Vickers had stopped with a No.3 stoppage, impossible to rectify in the air, so he put on a fresh drum on his Lewis gun before getting into position and again opening fire. A great deal of black smoke came out of the Rumpler and for a moment James thought it was in flames, but the enemy pilot merely steepened his dive. James put the last drum on his Lewis and attacked again, but the Rumpler pilot, although making no attempt to avoid James' fire, continued down in a flat dive towards Herlies, his propeller now stationary, and smoke pouring from his aeroplane.[2] Having fired over four hundred rounds into the Rumpler from an average range of seventy-five yards, James was now out of ammunition and turned away.

Robert Hugh Sloley. Killed in action 1 October 1917.

He knew that he had most probably killed the enemy gunner, but had not succeeded in seriously damaging the machine. He had sighted his guns before taking off and during his attacks it became apparent that he had made a slight error while doing so. James landed back at Estrée Blanche at 3.00PM, not only disheartened by his failure to destroy the Rumpler, but with a splitting headache, the legacy of an hour spent at high altitude without oxygen in his futile pursuit of the first Rumpler.

His headache presumably having cleared, James led his Flight on an Offensive Patrol in the afternoon, taking off at 4.30PM. Over Becelaere the Flight attacked a trio of enemy two-seaters, but the enemy crews were experienced, co-operated well, and successfully evaded their attacks, diving into the mist at lower level. The Flight was now split up, but James and Arthur Rhys Davids had stayed together and climbed back to 11,000ft. West of Moorslede they saw a formation of Albatri

Charles Jeffs after capture with his victor *Oblt.* Bruno Loerzer, *Staffelführer* of *Jasta* 26. Both Jeffs and Loerzer are wearing English leather flying coats, much prized by the German pilots. Any Allied pilots who were taken POW were immediately relieved of them.

led by a black and white Pfalz and flew under it in an attempt to lure the enemy pilots nearer the lines and under Maxwell's A Flight, which was due in the area. Two of the enemy pilots took the bait and the Pfalz and one of the Albatri dived to attack them. Maxwell and A Flight had now arrived and a furious dogfight developed: the SEs reinforced by a formation of Bristol Fighters; the Albatri by more of their type, bringing their number to around twenty.

Looking round, James saw an SE circling in the midst of four of the Albatri. In a frozen moment of time he saw one of the Albatri turn inside the SE and shoot off its left wings from a range of twenty-five feet. The SE went down in a spin. 'It was poor Sloley, who was, as usual, where the Huns were thickest.'[3] James then saw another SE pilot who was in also trouble, fighting four black and white coloured Albatri. He had no doubt as to the identity of this pilot: 'This SE was fighting magnificently, and simply could be none other than Rhys Davids, for if one was ever over the Salient in the autumn of 1917 and saw an SE fighting like hell amidst a heap of Huns,

one would find nine times out of ten that the SE was flown by Rhys Davids.' Maxwell had also seen the unequal contest and joined James as he dived to the aid of Rhys Davids – '…for the next few minutes we fought like anything, but the Huns were all very good, and had not Maxwell and I gone to Rhys Davids' assistance when we did, I think the boy would have had a rather thin time.'

The odds having been evened, the Albatros pilots flew off, 'having other fish to fry' and James and Rhys Davids flew south. As they reached the Zonnebeke area, British anti-aircraft fire drew their attention to a pair of enemy two-seaters flying at only a 1,000ft, east of the village. James and Rhys Davids each attacked these machines, but their attacks were unsuccessful and the enemy pilots flew east. James and Rhys Davids then flew west and attacked another two-seater, this one flying at 200ft over Polygon Wood. James got in a good burst, but the enemy pilot flew on, apparently unperturbed. James then pulled away and watched as Rhys Davids attacked. James could see Rhys Davids' tracers hitting home, but the enemy pilot flew on, taking no notice, and James was convinced that the enemy machine was armoured.[4] Rhys Davids lost sight of the low flying two-seater against the chequered background of the terrain and climbed away. He had used up all his remaining ammunition in this attack, without result, and when he was attacked by four Albatri he used the superior speed of his SE to evade these and return to Estrée Blanche.

James was forced by engine trouble to land at 100 Squadron's aerodrome at Treizennes, where he stayed the night, returning to Estrée Blanche the next afternoon.

Two Albatros scouts were claimed as out of control from the large dogfight: one to Rhys Davids, the other to B Flight as a whole, but the squadron could ill afford the loss of Robert Sloley, a extremely popular and highly promising pilot who had been awarded eight victories since joining the squadron on 21 July.

The first patrols on the morning of 2 October were flown by C and A Flights, ten SEs leaving Estrée Blanche at 10.00AM. Both Flights saw a great deal of action, Maxwell summing it up in his diary entry for the day: 'plenty of scrapping'. Other than the observer of a two-seater that Maxwell had attacked, who was seen to be laying over the side of his fuselage, obviously dead or wounded, the morning's fighting yielded no positive results for his Flight, but a little to the north of A Flight, C Flight saw a great deal of fighting with formations of the same black and white Albatros scouts fought the previous day.

The first of these actions took place over Moorslede at 12,000ft. The Albatros pilots had lost formation: two were flying below the SEs, one at their level. Maybery attacked one of the lower Albatri, getting onto its tail and firing a long burst from both guns before zooming away. Bowman saw the Albatros go down to crash half a mile west of St. Pieter.[5]

After this brief action, the SEs chased a pair of two-seaters – which evaded them by flying under the protection of their anti-aircraft batteries – before again attacking the black and white Albatri, now ten in number, over Zonnebeke. During the fighting, Bowman sent one of the enemy scouts down in a steep spiral, but the inexperienced members of his Flight, Stanley Gardiner[6] and John Gilbert,[7] were both severely handled by the Albatri pilots. Gardiner's SE was badly shot about, forcing him to land near Borre, and Gilbert, who was seen to be spiralling down, was escorted back to the lines by Hoidge, finally force landing in a field near Poperinghe.

In the absence of James, still not returned from Treizennes, Barlow commanded B Flight in the afternoon patrol, accompanied by Bowman leading C Flight in its second patrol of the day. Bowman's Flight was in a bad tactical position from the onset of the patrol. The enemy scouts seen had the advantage of height, made dive and zoom attacks, but refused to stay down at the level of the SEs. These tactics were advantageous until the arrival of Barlow and B Flight, which were at the same height as the enemy scouts, and a general engagement began.

Muspratt attacked one of the Albatri that initially dived west, but it was seen to flatten out at 14,000ft and clear east. Muspratt was then attacked by three enemy scouts, one of which was a Fokker Triplane, but he was joined by Rhys Davids and together they succeeded in driving the enemy scouts away.[8]

All the pilots returned safely from the afternoon's fighting with the exception of David Reason, who crash landed on his return to Estrée Blanche. His SE5a (A8906) was extensively damaged and Reason, badly shaken, was taken to hospital .[9]

Weather conditions were bad on 3 October, with low clouds, wind and rain, and there was no war flying. During the morning a telegram was received from Wing advising that Rhys Davids had been awarded a DSO; Leonard Barlow a second bar to his MC and James a Bar to his MC. It was decided to hold a special, celebratory dinner that evening, to mark the occasion with some style, and at 8.30PM the officers marched into the Mess to the strains of 'Old Comrades' by the squadron's orchestra. After dinner came toasts and speeches. Rhys Davids began by saying how honoured and pleased he felt to be awarded a DSO, but then caused some consternation by proposing a toast to the bravery of the enemy pilots, fought on a daily basis, who almost invariably displayed such fine examples of courage. He then went even further, taking the unprecedented step of proposing a toast to Manfred von Richthofen, 'our most worthy enemy'. All the pilots rose to their feet, with the exception of one non-flying officer who refused to drink to 'the health of that devil.'

On the wall behind Major Blomfield's head was the Squadron's Honours Board: at its head, in letters of black and gold, was the name of Albert Ball VC. All felt that in Arthur Rhys Davids the squadron had another Ball. Both were utterly fearless and had set a splendid example to their fellow pilots, that had enabled the squadron to do so well at a time when collectively the morale of the German *Luftstreitkräfte* was at its highest. After more speeches – including those from Leonard Barlow and James – everyone adjoined to the ante-room, where the evening ended with the now almost traditional RFC Mess games, accompanied by the orchestra playing all the old

Maurice Baring.

favourites: *Somebody has to Darn His Socks*, *Hello, My Dearie*, *Dixieland*, and a particular favourite of the squadron, *I'll go back to the Shack where the Black-Eyed Susans Grow*. James fancied himself as something of a drummer, and 2AM Sidney Pegg, an A Flight fitter, the regular drummer in the band, remembered him taking over his snare drum on this and similar occasions.

On 4 October the weather was still too bad for any operational flying. Major Blomfield, mindful of the effect of inactivity on morale, insisted that all the officers should leave the aerodrome for the day for a change of scene. James decided that this would be a good opportunity to see if he could locate the remains of the Rumpler he had shot down in the Allied lines on 27 September, so he borrowed a motorcycle from the squadron's transport and set off, riding through Aire and Hazebrouck, then on to Poperinghe, making for St. Juliaan, the site of the crash. By the time he had arrived at Poperinghe it was time for lunch, so he decided to call on 29 Squadron, his old squadron, that was based nearby. Many of the people from his time in the squadron were still there; they made him welcome, gave him lunch and he afterwards caught up with

This Rumpler No.C8431, brought down on 21 October 1917, was James' eighteenth victory. These three views of the crash vividly illustrate the total destruction of a machine brought down from 18,000ft.

all the squadron news with an old friend, Sergeant-Major Harrison.(10)

Setting off again, James rode towards Ypres, but he made slow progress here owing to the roads being blocked by all manner of traffic, heavy fighting still taking place in the Salient. He managed to negotiate his way through the town and carried on through St.Jean and Weiltje, finally arriving at St.Juliaan. There were a number of derelict tanks here making it impossible to go any further on the motorcycle, so he left it propped against the side of one of the tanks and began to walk the half mile to von Tirpitz Farm, the site of the crashed Rumpler. Long before he reached the site he began to wonder if it was worth going on. German guns were heavily shelling the ridge on which the farm lay, and although he could see the tail of the Rumpler sticking up – 'which greatly bucked me up' – he gave up the idea of getting to it as shells were falling all round it.

James retraced his steps to St.Juliaan, the tank and his motorcycle, arriving just as it began to rain heavily. The time was now 4.00PM and James decided that it was high time he began to make his way back to Estrée Blanche. To his annoyance the motorcycle was reluctant to start, and when he finally succeeded in getting it going he found that after riding a hundred yards or so it was impossible to ride it any further: the thick, sticky mud had jammed between the mudguards and the wheels, locking them solid.

James was now covered in mud, wet through and 'very fed up'. The back wheel still locked, he began pushing the cycle through the glutinous mud, but wearing only a pair of thin shoes he was slipping at every step, and it was such exhausting work that he was forced to stop for a rest after only fifty yards. Carrying on, still slipping and sliding, he managed to at last reach a small side road, free of traffic, that led uphill to Weiltje. All he fervently wished for now was a cart or transport of any description to come along, so that he could load the bike and himself onto it until they reached some pavé, where he could clear the clogged wheels. But nothing appeared and he was forced to push the bike still further. Stopping for a brief rest, he was nearly deafened by a battery of guns, each side of the road, that began 'banging away to their heart's content'. Sitting there, utterly exhausted, soaking wet, covered in mud, he thought longingly 'of my clean SE and the gentlemanly way in which we fought aloft' and began fully to appreciate once again the dreadful conditions in which the ground troops had to daily live and fight, amazed that they could still carry on so cheerfully.

Presently, he came to Weiltje, where he thankfully put the motorcycle on a General Service wagon that was passing. His relief was short lived. After only a few hundred yards the driver curtly informed him that he was going no further. James reluctantly got down, retrieved the motorcycle, and again began to push it. The road seemed endless, but after another mile he at last came to some pavé, where he cleared the wheels of mud. With the aid of a push from two Tommies, James managed to start the now thoroughly cold engine. Riding through St.Juliaan and then Ypres, he passed a long column of German prisoners being marched to the back areas, an officer at their head. He was a large, fine-looking man, and as James passed he was struck by the expression on his face: 'well, never mind; I've done my share, and I'm proud I'm German'.

James rode on, through muddy puddles, splashed head to foot from water from the wheels of an endless chain of passing lorries. By the time he reached Hazebrouck, with still a long way to go, it was dark. He lit the headlamp of the bike, but after ten miles, just as he reached Aire, the lamp generator fell off and he failed to find it in the dark. Luckily, a tender was just leaving the town and James followed a few yards behind it, guided by the glare of its headlights until he finally arrived back at Estrée Blanche: wet through, cold, extremely tired, and very fed up. He vowed that it would be a damned long time before he rode another motorcycle up to the trenches again.[11]

The next morning the weather had brightened a little and two patrols were flown. Maxwell led the first, taking off at 7.00AM. The patrol saw a great deal of action in two separate fights with large formations of Albatri. Reginald Preston-Cobb's SE5a was so badly damaged by fire from one of the enemy pilots that he was forced to crash land at Caestre. Preston-Cobb was unhurt but the SE was returned to 1AD for repair. The patrol also lost Charles Jeffs, who was shot down by *Oblt*. Bruno Loerzer of *Jasta* 26 and taken prisoner.[12]

James led B Flight in the second patrol of the day, leaving Estrée Blanche at 9.45AM. Over Zandvoorde, a formation of enemy scouts was seen, above the SEs. James led the Flight below the Albatri, hoping to lure them down into a fight, but the enemy pilots refused to come down and cleared to the east. The patrol saw no other enemy machines and returned after patrolling for an hour and a quarter.

The weather now clamped down again and there was no war flying for the next five days. The days and nights were now becoming very cold and in preparation for the coming winter with its promise of more leisure time, it was decided to enlarge the squadron's Mess to make it more comfortable. Hoidge, an architect in civilian life, designed a magnificent fireplace for the room. Centrally placed, it had a cone-shaped hood that could be raised or lowered, and seating was built around it. Thought had also been given to the question of firewood for the new fireplace, and a circular saw had been designed and constructed for cutting up logs. On the day it was decided that the new saw should be officially opened, Maurice Baring and the artist William Orpen were visiting the squadron for lunch.

It was agreed that all officers and men were to attend (no flying was possible that day) and that Maurice should make a speech, after which he was to cut the end of a cigar with the saw, then a box was made with a glass front in which the cigar was to be placed after the ADC (Baring) had smoked a little of it, and the box was to be hung in the Mess of the squadron. It was all a great success. Maurice made a splendid speech. We all cheered, and then the cigar was cut (to bits nearly). Maurice smoked a little and it was put safely in its box. Then Maurice was given the first log to cut. This was done, but Maurice was now worked up, so he took his cap off and cut this in halves. He was then proceeding to take off his tunic for the same purpose, but was carried away from the scene by a cheering crowd. It was a great day.[13]

During the period of inactivity James took the opportunity to write again to Tryggve Gran.

56 Squadron. France. 9/10/17
Dear Old Bean,

Very many thanks for your cheery letter dated 30th ult. Awfully glad to hear you have hitched onto a 'fairy' with some boodle.

I lunched with 29 recently and saw Jones-Williams[14] and De Crespigny.[15] The C.O., named Chapman[16] has just been killed by a bomb from a Hun.

I brought a Rumpler down in flames on our side a few days ago and am getting some souvenirs from it. The observer jumped out at 12,000. The same evening I shot a V-Strutter's wings off and the Hun fell out of that too, at about 8,000ft.

These are damn fine grids. You can hardly fail to get Huns on them.

I have just got a bar to my MC. I don't know what for; I think it is because I saluted the Colonel smartly the last time I passed him.

When do you expect to have a board? You might let me know, as perhaps the C.O. here can hurry it up. How much longer do you expect to stay in Blighty?

Yes, I know Dean from 70. 70 have had an awful time, have had 20 casualties in September. This Squadron brought down their 200th Hun last week, after being out six months.

This beats the record of Pursuit Flight No.11, commanded by Richthofen, who downed 200 of ours in 7½ months.

You will be pleased to hear that I was leading the patrol who got Voss. He put up a damned stout show and scrapped 5 SEs for 10 minutes, after which Rhys Davids downed him. Voss put some bullets into three of us, and wrote off 2 more SEs in this scrap. It was Rhys Davids who got Schafer,[17] another Hun star turn. He has just got a D.S.O.

Well, cheerio old bean, drop me a line very soon and let me know what fun you have with the heiress.

Best of Luck
Yours ever
Mac

PS. Counting bars, have 8 M.C.s in my flight and a D.S.O and 16 M.Cs in the Squadron

M.

On 10 October, although the weather was still very wet, the grim business of war was resumed: two patrols – C and A Flights – left the ground at 3.40PM. On the way to the lines Bowman's engine temperature climbed to 100 degrees and water began pouring from his top tank. Being the only experienced pilot in the Flight, Bowman attempted to find Maxwell's Flight, to hand over his command to Maxwell, but failing to find him, brought them home.

Maxwell and his Flight attacked twelve Albatri east of Ypres. During the fighting, Geoffrey Wilkinson was shot down and killed by *Ltn.* Dannhuber of *Jasta* 26. Gerald Maxwell entered in his diary: 'Saw Wilkinson go down in pieces with a Hun on his tail'. No victories were claimed by the members of A Flight from the fight, although Maxwell sent one Albatros down in a steep dive.[18]

There were low clouds and rain in the morning of 11 October, but nine SEs took off at 6.15AM, James leading B Flight, which was well up to strength with only one inexperienced pilot. Bowman was less fortunate: for some reason, Hoidge was not flying, Maybery had left on leave two days previously, and Bowman was leading three inexperienced pilots. However, the SEs stayed together and a ratio of six to three still constituted a reasonably effective force.

James led the combined Flights across the lines at 14,000ft over Bixschoote. It was intensely cold, so cold in fact that he had difficulty in keeping the water in his radiator warm enough. Soon after crossing the Lines, James saw a formation of twelve Pfalz D.IIIs over Westroosebeke. The Pfalz D.III scout was a new type to the pilots of the squadron, only a few had been fought and they were an unknown quantity, but these were a little below the Flight, and as soon as they were near enough James led the SEs down to attack them.

James secured a good position behind one of the Pfalz, but owing to the intense cold both his guns refused to fire. James could get neither gun to work, so chasing after the Pfalz, passing only a few feet above it, he fired his Very pistol at it 'in the hope of making him panic, which he apparently did'. However, he had not allowed enough deflection and the blazing flare fell short of the enemy machine.

Additional Albatri now arrived at the scene of the action, diving into the fight from out of the eye of the morning sun. Rhys Davids got on the tail of one of these new arrivals and fired both guns: the Albatros went down to the south west in a steep dive, smoke pouring from it. Muspratt attacked another of the Pfalz, 'silver, like a Nieuport', but in his eagerness he nearly collided with the enemy scout.

Looking round, James saw that James Cunningham, a new pilot, was in trouble, an Albatros on his tail 'shooting like anything'. Muspratt had also seen Cunningham's predicament, and joined James in attacking the Albatros. The enemy pilot rolled twice, then spun, built up speed in a dive, then zoomed, coming out at almost the same level as the SEs. James commented: 'he was certainly a good Hun, that fellow'. But the damage had been done. Cunningham had been severely wounded and although he managed to return, crash landing at Pont-de-Nieppe, and was taken to hospital, he died of his wounds on 18 October.[19] All the Flight landed back at Estrée Blanche, thoroughly perished, for it had been bitterly cold at height, and they were all glad to be down again. The squadron had as yet no news of Cunningham, but Reginald Preston-Cobb, a C Flight pilot, had also failed to return.[20]

James keenly felt the loss of James Cunningham, only the second member of his Flight to have been lost in action since he had taken command in August. The safety of the pilots under his command was of paramount importance to James. Gerald Maxwell recalled one occasion when he saw James in the Mess looking 'very down in the mouth'. Asked what was wrong, James replied that during a patrol that morning one of his pilots, a new boy, had been hit in the tail-plane by fire from an enemy scout. Maxwell told James that he was hardly responsible for such minor damage, but James refused to be conciliated. In his view, even for the enemy pilot to have had the chance of a shot meant that his tactics in leading the patrol had been at fault.

On the morning of 12 October, James took his Flight out at 10.25AM augmented by Eric Turnbull and Stanley Gardiner from A and C Flights. The formation crossed the Lines over Bixschoote and patrolled between Cortemarck and Menin. It was nearly an hour after taking off before they saw a formation of nine enemy machines over Roulers. These attempted to lure the Flight further to the east, but their tactics were all too obvious. At 13,000ft the wind was very strong – James estimated that it was quite 40mph[21] – and the clouds were building, getting lower. James was too old a hand to make such a tactical error. He turned the Flight to the west and after an indecisive attack on an enemy two-seater south-west of Becelaere, he brought the Flight home. The high wind had taken its toll. Three of the Flight were forced to land at Bailleul for petrol before returning to Estrée Blanche.

There was no flying on 13 October, the weather again bad, but although it was still raining the next morning, with a low cloud base, six SEs, led by James and Bowman, took off on an escort duty for the Martinsydes of 27 Squadron that were to bomb Ledeghem. Having seen the bombers safely back to the Lines, James took the Flight towards Roulers, where a formation of seven Albatri were seen flying south. These retired to the east at the approach of the SE formation, but ten minutes later James led the Flight down to attack six V-Strutters over Wervicq.

The Albatros selected by James spun away from his fire so he turned his attentions to the enemy Flight Commander, but stoppages in both guns forced him to break away to rectify them. He then attacked the Albatros again but the pilot was highly skilled and evaded his attacks easily, finally diving away to the east to rejoin his companions.

The Flight had been broken up during the fighting, and James, with only John Gilbert, an inexperienced pilot, was then attacked by a pair of Albatri over Zonnebecke. One enemy pilot broke off the action and dived away, but the other stayed and fought James and Gilbert for some time, manoeuvring 'very well', but while he was engaged with Gilbert, James finally succeeded in getting onto his tail and drove him down to 7,000ft, where the enemy pilot made his escape by diving into the cloud cover.

There was no flying for the next two days, the weather

Clive Franklyn Collett in Albatros D.V. D1162/17. Collett was accidentally killed in this Albatros on 23 December 1917.

having again deteriorated, but on 17 October a large force of eleven SEs – B and C Flights – took off at 10.25AM. Conditions were still bright, but hazy. Bowman led the Flight to the area of Ypres, and seeing an enemy two-seater over Wytschaete, he attacked it from below, pulling down his Lewis gun and firing a whole drum into the enemy machine, although having to recock the gun after every five shots because of the intense cold. The two-seater dived east towards Menin. After this disappointment, Bowman attacked another two-seater, which he chased as far as Hoogelede before British anti-aircraft fire pointed out another over Poperinghe. Bowman sent this machine down with a long stream of smoke pouring from it, 'but unfortunately the smoke did not change to flame'.[22]

James and B Flight had more positive luck, attacking a pair of enemy two-seaters over Bailleul. One flew off, chased by Muspratt and the remainder of the Flight, but the other, its pilot thinking that he could out-climb an SE5a, stayed to fight, flew west, and was attacked by James, who got into a good position and fired a long burst from his Vickers gun. The centre section of the enemy machine – an LVG – burst into flames and the enemy pilot turned to the left, his observer standing up in 'an attitude of abject dejection'. James turned away but saw that the flames had now subsided – apparently having exhausted the petrol in the tank – although not before having burnt off all the fabric from the rudder of the LVG. This left the enemy pilot no means of turning and he glided northwards. James followed, knowing that the LVG must now come down in Allied territory. However, both Barlow and Muspratt now arrived. Seeing that the fire had gone out, they both attacked the LVG, which steepened its glide into a dive. Both wings of the enemy machine finally broke off and it crashed just south of Vlamertinghe.[23]

James landed alongside the crash 'on some good stubble', and pushed his way through a crowd of Australian troops who had gathered around the body of the enemy observer who had fallen out of his machine at 5,000ft. Seeing that he was dead, James went over to another group of men, about a hundred yards away, who were crowded around the remains of the LVG and its pilot.

James, with his military and disciplined mind, was horrified by the behaviour of these troops, who in a very short time had stripped the LVG and the dead pilot of anything of value. Seeing he could do no more, he met up with a Sapper officer who took him back to his headquarters for lunch. Returning to his SE after lunch, James restarted his engine and returned to Estrée Blanche. He had managed to salvage several items from the wreckage of the LVG – a new type, with all the controls 'balanced' and powered by a 200hp Benz engine.[24]

Back at Estrée Blanche, James found that everyone was pleased that the LVG had fallen behind the British Lines, an unusual occurrence, the fighting being almost invariably far over the German side of the front lines, but James was still so disgusted at the unedifying way in which the Australian troops had looted the LVG and its pilot, that Blomfield submitted an official report, pointing out that the troops had gone so far as to strip the dead observer of his clothing.

James flew only a short 'test' flight in SE5a B4863 the next day. A 'test' lasting an hour and that took him to Bailleul, Ypres and Houthulst at 10,000ft, 'stalking EA'.

During the day's patrols Hoidge had shot down a two-seater over Comines, but in a fight with some Albatros scouts, John Gilbert – James' companion of five days before – had been shot down and killed.[25] Geoffrey Shone had also been shot down, crashing in flames behind the British lines near St.Juliaan.[26]

On the morning of 20 October, James took a formation of seven SEs to escort home the Martinsydes of 27 Squadron that had been bombing Cortemarck railway station. James failed to find the returning bombers, so took his force to patrol between Cortemarck and Menin. Visibility was very poor and after seriously frightening the crew of an enemy two-seater over Houthem – all the Flight took shots at it from various angles – they returned, landing at 12.45PM. During the afternoon, James flew to Ste-Marie-Cappel to visit 60 Squadron. No reason is known for this visit, or for a similar flight to 40 Squadron two days later, but possibly he was giving a talk on his methods to the pilots of the two squadrons.

The next day, Wing HQ telephoned just before mid-day to order the squadron to intercept a trio of enemy two-seaters that were coming south from Calais. After saying goodbye to Gerald Maxwell and Leonard Barlow who were just about to leave for Home Establishment, James, Keith Muspratt and Arthur Rhys Davids took off to look for these intruders. Arriving in the area in which the enemy machines had been reported, only a British DH4 was seen, that James took a brief look at before turning away. James then climbed for some extra height, but Muspratt and Rhys Davids returned to Estrée Blanche where they laughingly told 'Grandpa' Marson that they had left their Flight Commander carefully stalking a friendly DH4.

James meanwhile, had climbed to 16,000ft and flown to the south-east. Arriving over Bethune, he saw a Rumpler, slightly higher than himself, coming west, passing over Givenchy. James flew towards the enemy machine, but the pilot saw him coming and turned off towards the south-east. James knew that he did not have the speed to catch this Rumpler and watched it disappear, well behind its own lines. However, he knew that the Rumpler crews were both skilled and determined in carrying out their photographic duties, and knowing they carried at least four hours of petrol he reasoned that they would return to carry out their photo reconnaissance if he made himself scarce. So he flew off, north towards Armentières, and although his engine was not going well, carefully hoarding his height. Arriving over the town he searched the sky to the south-east, just catching sight of a very small speck against the herring-bone sky. He was sure this was the Rumpler, as it was over Don, some miles east of where he had first seen it. He flew east, towards Haubourdin, arriving over the town at 17,500ft, then turned south, still keeping his eye on the speck, that continued to fly west. James had now arrived over Don, well to the east of the Rumpler, cutting off its retreat into its own lines, and he continued to follow it until he was passing over La Bassée, with the Rumpler a little further west, along the canal towards Bethune, where James finally succeeded in getting very close to it.

Having approached them from over Don, far to the east of their own lines, the Rumpler crew had assumed that James was one of their own scouts, but they now realised their mistake and the pilot turned and dived towards Lens, hoping to outdistance the SE, but James soon caught up, got into position and fired a long burst from both guns. From 18,000ft, the Rumpler went down in a right-hand spin, pouring clouds of steam. James followed – at 6,000ft, the SE was doing nearly 200mph – thinking the enemy pilot was merely taking evasive action, but the Rumpler hit the ground near Mazingarbe.[27]

No doubt remembering the unedifying episode of five days previously, James landed nearby and ran over to the wreck of the Rumpler. British troops and a number of French civilians had already gathered around the crash. The enemy observer was dead, but although he was badly injured the pilot was still alive. James quickly ordered the Tommies to find a stretcher in order to take the pilot to the nearest casualty clearing station, but the pilot died before it arrived. For the second time in five days, seeing again at first-hand the results of his work, James was brought up with a jolt, feeling a deep sorrow for the enemy pilot and observer. However, seeing there was nothing further he could do, and having put a guard put on the wreckage of the Rumpler, he flew back to Estrée Blanche. Making out his combat report with 'Grandpa' Marson, he had the last laugh when he was told that Rhys Davids and Muspratt had been convinced that when they had last seen him he had been stalking a DH4.

James was particularly pleased with the result of this action. He had patiently stalked the Rumpler for nearly an hour before finally attacking it exactly where he had planned – over the British lines. It was the first example of his art of stalking the high-flying German reconnaissance two-seaters, an art that he would hone to perfection over the coming months.

After a hurried lunch, James and Blomfield drove to wreckage of the Rumpler, a short drive of under an hour. James knew Creeth, the officer of the guard over the wreck, and he presented James with a beautiful silk cap that had belonged to the enemy pilot, who by papers found on his body had recently been on leave in Berlin. James was much taken by the cap, which fitted him perfectly, and he later had it copied in khaki.

Blomfield and James stayed at the site for some time, James taking photographs with his small folding Kodak camera –

Albatros D.V 1162/17 over-painted with British insignia, but still carrying the spiral marking of *Vzfw*. Ernst Clausnitzer of *Jasta* 4. Clausnitzer had been forced down by Spads of 23 Squadron and taken prisoner on 16 July 1917 after a balloon attack.

strictly against official orders, that stated that no personal cameras were allowed, an order that applied to all ranks. Viewing the remains of the Rumpler, knowing the fate of its crew, Blomfield remarked on the pity of war; of not being able to bring down enemy machines without killing the occupants. James agreed, but silently reasoned that he could not afford to become sentimental over his work.

Having collected what they wanted from the Rumpler, James and Blomfield came away as it was now getting late. As they were leaving, an enemy shell burst only a hundred yards from them. James considered this was just an accident, but the Germans had an artillery observation post at Wingles Tower, under three miles away, from which they had a clear view of the crash.

James and Blomfield arrived back at Estrée Blanche in time for tea. James ate his with an 'immense appetite', very pleased that in the last ten days he had brought down three enemy two-seaters in the British lines, an exception to the general rule. For the last fortnight both his SE and his guns had been going well, and he could see no need for any improvement in either. Life was very good, full of promise, and he was due for leave in two days time.

James made only one more war flight before going on leave: a lone patrol on 22 October: 'stalking' at 17,100ft, from Lens, Arras and Ypres, but he saw no enemy machines and returned after an hour and forty-five minutes.

James left Estrée Blanche on the morning of 23 October for a well-earned fortnight's leave. He spent the first week with his family, but lunched at the RFC club nearly every day in order to catch up on all the latest news. In the evenings he saw nearly every one of the current West End shows, no doubt taking Teddie to supper after she had finished her performance in her current revue. On one of his visits to the RFC club in Bruton Street, he met an officer of the squadron who told him that Rhys Davids was missing.[28] James was shocked; it seemed only hours since he had last seen him, leaving him in charge of his Flight, and he knew that Rhys Davids was due to come home, having completed nearly eight months with the squadron in France.

One evening, leaving the Shaftsbury Theatre after enjoying comedian Stanley Lane in the musical comedy 'Arlette', James met an officer who had just returned from France, who gave him the unwelcome news that his SE5a B4863 had been completely wrecked by another pilot and struck off strength. James asked his informant if he was sure that it was his SE. 'Yes', was the reply: 'because I heard one of the 56 fellows say, "won't McCudden be mad when he comes off leave to find his pet machine crashed."' Until he finally had it to his satisfaction, James had lavished a great deal of care and work on B4863 and he confessed to being 'very fed up' at hearing it had been wrecked.[29]

On 5 November, James travelled to Joyce Green to visit old friends. The Vickers company still had their hangars there and James flew a joyride in a Vickers 'Bullet' (possibly a Vickers

Ltn. Karl Gallwitz of *Jasta* Boelcke. Arthur Rhys Davids was his fourth victory of an eventual ten. Gallwitz was injured in a crash in late April 1918 and was made an *Inspecteur de Flieger*, ending his operational flying.

E.S.1) that he described as 'a nice machine.' Two days later, having met an old friend in the RFC Club, Clive Collett,[30] they went to Hendon aerodrome to fly a captured Albatros scout.[31] James had what he described as 'a nice ride' in this example of the enemy machines he had been fighting, but found it not at all easy to handle and was mystified by how the enemy pilots manoeuvred them so well.

In the afternoon he flew to Martlesham Heath as a passenger with Collett in a DH4. Never one to let pass an opportunity to learn, James spent the entire flight ascertaining how, as a gunner, he could best frustrate any attacks by an enemy scout, an experiment he could put to good use when next tackling enemy two-seaters. Landing at Martlesham Heath he was reunited with Verschoyle Cronyn, who had flown in his Flight during the summer, and his old friend, Reggie Carr. After tea, James and Collett returned by train to London, talking over tactics and air fighting in general. Collett's approach to the subject was the antithesis of that favoured by James. Collett, in James words, 'was always for downing the Hun, whenever and wherever he could find him' and invariably came back from patrols with his Camel shot to ribbons. James held the view that one should endeavour to shoot down the king's enemies with as little damage as possible to oneself or one's aeroplane.

On 9 November, his leave up, James ferried a Bristol F.2b (C4819) to France, a twenty-five minute flight from Lympne in Kent to the supply depot at Marquise. After lunch, he flew an RE8 (5040) to Serny. Serny was only a short distance from Estrée Blanche and James was back in the 56 Squadron Mess only two and a half hours after leaving England.

A publicity photograph of Teddie O'Neill.

Ch.13: Cambrai: A Change of Scene

At the beginning of November 1918 the personnel of 56 Squadron had changed considerably. In October, before James had left on leave, twelve new pilots had been posted in, with an additional four arriving during his time in England. Of the pilots who had flown out from London Colney in April 1917, still with the squadron when James had arrived in August, only Hoidge now remained. Leonard Barlow and Gerald Maxwell had been posted to Home Establishment at the end of their tours, and Arthur Rhys Davids and Robert Sloley had both been killed during October. The stalwarts were still there of course – 'Beery' Bowman, Richard Maybery and Hoidge – but there were many new faces in the Mess. The greatest change was perhaps that of Major Blomfield having been replaced as commanding officer by Major Rainsford Balcombe-Brown, who had arrived to ease himself into his new command on 26 October.[1] Replacing the popular and charismatic 'Dickie' Blomfield, who had laid the foundations of the squadron's spirit and morale, and whose personality and driving force had moulded the squadron's sense of unity and its traditions, was an unenviable task. Although an expert pilot, Balcombe-Brown was inclined to be a little supercilious in his manner and could be quite scathing in his opinions – freely expressed – of a pilot's ability, tendencies that lost him both the liking and respect of many of the squadron's pilots. Even so, he commanded the squadron through perhaps its hardest period of duty and was its only commanding officer to be killed in action.

The squadron had been inactive for the first seven days of November, low clouds, drizzle and rain stopping all war flying, and it was not until 8 November that any patrols were flown. Keith Muspratt, now leading B Flight after the loss of Rhys Davids, took the Flight across the Lines over Passchèndaele and attacked a formation of six black and white Albatri over Moorslede. During the fighting, Maxwell Coote was hit in the radiator, force-landing south of Neuve Eglise, and Felix Cobbold, who had been with the squadron for only fourteen days, was wounded, shot down and taken prisoner.[2] A patrol that same morning had lost Phillip Chambers Cowan, another new pilot who had been with the squadron for only eleven days.[3] The month was not starting well for the squadron.

On entering the Mess on his return, James caused a minor sensation: he was wearing his elegant silk copy of the Rumpler pilot's cap. It was the squadron's first view of his new headgear and it rapidly acquired the sobriquet of 'Mac's 'un 'at.'

The next day James travelled by road to 1AD at St.Omer and flew SE5a B37 back to Estrée Blanche. However, Balcome-Brown had already earmarked another SE5a for James' use, SE5a B35, which had been brought from the depot on 5 November by Eric Turnbull, who assured James that it was probably just as good as his cherished B4863. This machine was a Martinsyde-built SE5a and James found it to be very fast.

Rainsford Balcombe-Brown and Richard Blomfield standing outside the 56 Squadron office in late October 1917 on Blomfield handing over command of the squadron to Balcombe Brown. The famous sign on the office door, reads 'Officer Commanding. Enter without knocking.' This instruction had been instituted by Blomfield early in the Squadron's life, when he had said. 'This is not a lady's boudoir, you don't have to knock'.

Rumour had been circulating for some time that the squadron was to move and speculation was rife – Keith Muspratt wrote home: 'We move in a day or two, whither I know not, but there are many exciting rumours' – and these finally resolved into definite orders. The squadron was to leave 9th Wing on 12 November to reinforce the strength of 13th Wing. Its new base was at Laviéville, an aerodrome with excellent facilities just north of the Amiens to Albert road, only a short distance from the latter town.

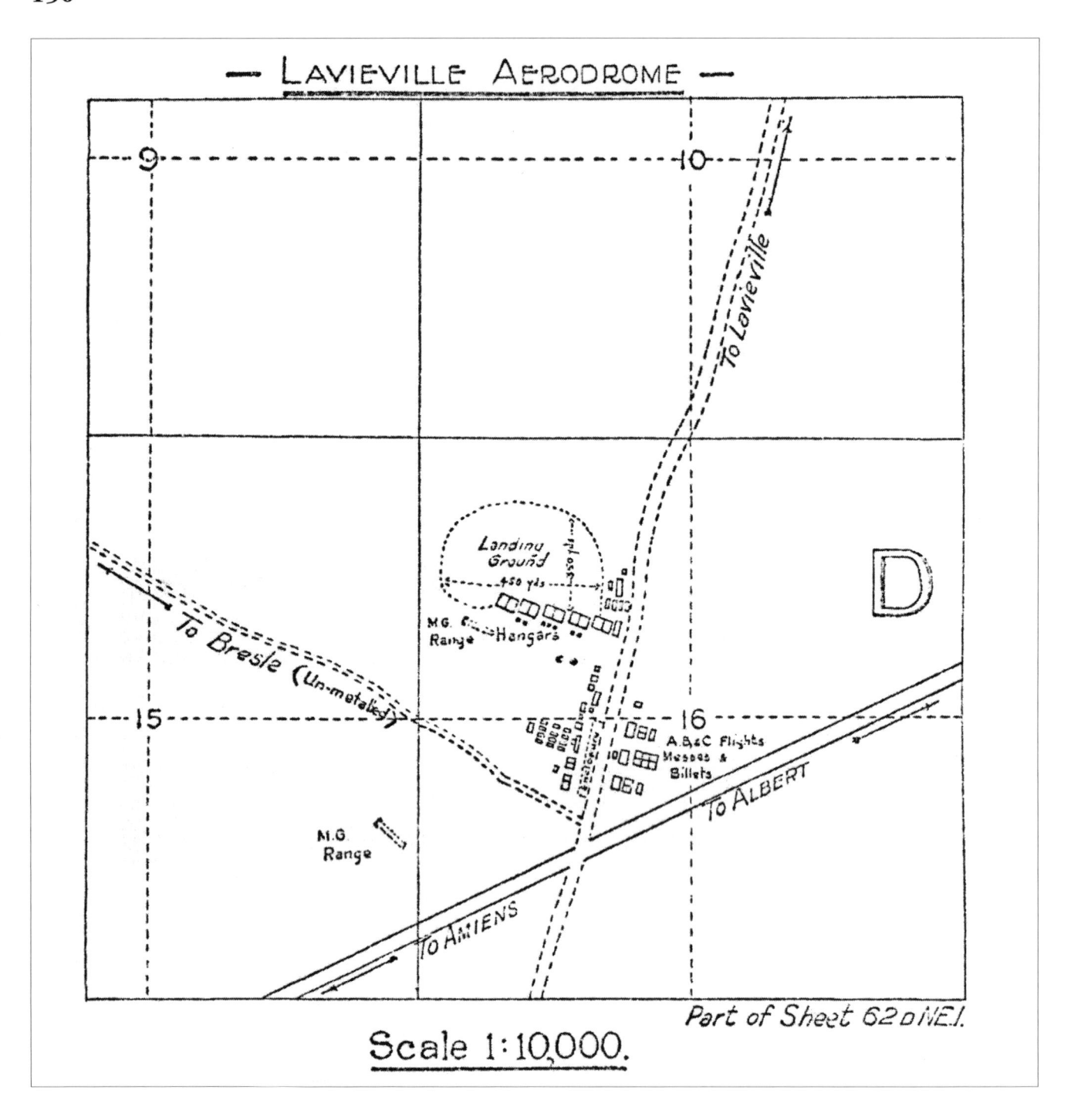

November 11 was spent in packing up the squadron's stores and with the transport leaving for Laviéville. Just after noon the following day, the first six SEs, led by Hoidge, left Estrée Blanche for the new aerodrome. Hoidge had engine trouble and returned to Estrée Blanche after ten minutes, and Eric Turnbull led the remainder of the Flight to 84 Squadron's aerodrome at Le Hameau, an interim stopover where lunch was to be had and inquiries made as to the suitability of weather – the day was very misty – for the flight further south. The remainder of the squadron having finally arrived and having had lunch – that must have severely strained the resources of 84 Squadron's Mess – they flew on to Laviéville, all arriving by 3.00PM.

The layout of the landing field at the new base was a little tricky and the landing approach had to made with some care: one pilot, Burdette Harmon, hit a shed in landing, extensively damaging the SE5a which had to be returned to 2AD for repair.[4]

The accommodation at Laviéville was a vast improvement over that at Estrée Blanche. The aeroplanes were housed in permanent iron hangars; the officers and men in Nissen huts. Although it was hard to leave the comfort of the Mess at Estrée Blanche, with Hoidge's magnificent fireplace, the cold weather and with the worst of the winter yet to come, these last were a welcome change from the tents at the old aerodrome.

*

The squadron had been added to the strength of 13th Wing in preparation for the planned offensive at Cambrai. The bloody battles of Ypres had finally dragged to a halt and a successful offensive, however small, was needed to offset the failures of the year. There were no resources to carry out a full scale offensive – these had been squandered in the mud of Passchèndaele – and the objective of the Cambrai offensive was for a purely local success. It was planned to take Bourlon village, the wood and, importantly, Bourlon Ridge, from which the British observation posts would have a superb view of the German back areas during the coming winter months. The opening of the offensive was planned for 20 November and the part to be played by the squadrons of the RFC was considerable, a total of 289 aeroplanes being deployed.

The officers and men of 56 Squadron knew little of these plans. There were a thousand and one things to do in settling into their new quarters. The weather was generally fine, but each day opened with a heavy ground mist and on the first day at the new base only four flights were possible. These were led by James, to practise formation flying, but even these were abandoned after only ten minutes because of the mist.

The bad weather, heavy mist, low clouds, wind and rain, persisted, and it was not until 15 November that the squadron was able to make its first flights from Laviéville for the purpose of learning the countryside. Landmarks had to be learnt, the position of the aerodromes in the area, plus the general topography of the country and position of the Front Line, all of which were new to the majority of the pilots in the squadron. In addition a great deal of formation flying was practised.

James was familiar with the country, having flown over it while with 29 Squadron, and while leading his Flight in practise and familiarisation flights he also took the opportunity to practise fighting with a new pilot, William Fielding-Johnson, an old acquaintance from his days in 5 Squadron.[5]

The next morning, although there were heavy clouds the weather seemed promising to stay fine all day and Balcombe-Brown flew to Baizieux to inspect the pond there for the purpose of using it for firing practise in the afternoon. After lunch, James led the entire squadron in a formation flight lasting half an hour, after which guns were tested at Baizieux. These test flights were not without hazard: Alexander Dodds crashed on landing from one such, and although he was unhurt his SE5a was badly damaged and had to be returned to 2AD for repair. The extensive testing of engines and guns by the whole squadron continued throughout the entire day. The opening of the offensive at Cambrai was rapidly approaching, the weather forecast was good, and it was essential that the

James in the cockpit of his SE5a wearing his 'Un 'At.

squadron was ready to recommence operations.

Balcombe-Brown took off alone on the morning of 18 November: a five-minute flight to test the weather. Although it was dull, with low clouds, Balcombe-Brown decided that it was good enough for a Line Patrol to be flown and James took B Flight off the ground five minutes after the CO had landed.

James led his newly constituted Flight – Fielding-Johnson, Barry Truscott, Harry Slingsby,[6] Harold Walkerdine,[7] and the

William Spurrett Fielding-Johnson. Fielding-Johnson took command of C Flight on Bowman being posted to 41 Squadron in February 1918. He was credited with six victories before being posted to HE on 29 April 1918.

only remaining member of his original Flight, Maxwell Coote – from 'Albert, up the road to Bapaume', then over the trenches north of Havrincourt, where he turned the six SEs south. The weather was dull, with clouds at 2,000ft, but visibility was good enough to ascertain the layout of the front-line trenches, the object of the patrol. While flying south along the line of trenches, James saw a DFW two-seater, still to the east, but coming west. His orders were that no SE should cross the front lines, but this was too good an opportunity to miss. James went down, got behind the enemy machine, and fired a good burst from both guns. The engine of the DFW stopped, the gunner collapsed inside his cockpit, and the DFW went down in a steep glide. The enemy pilot still had his machine under control and attempted a downwind landing, but badly misjudged his speed, crashing heavily into a trench in a shower of chalky earth four miles behind his own lines at Bellicourt.[8]

James rejoined his Flight – he had gone down to 1,000ft in pursuit of the DFW – and led them home. They were north of St Quentin and were heavily archied on their way back to the lines. James, unfamiliar with the country this far south, had to land at Estrées-en-Chaussée, the home of 35 Squadron, to find their position before returning to Laviéville.

James was pleased that his Flight had scored the first victory from the new base, but soon after landing it was tempered by the squadron's first casualty at Laviéville. John Waters had taken off on a practise flight. After forty-five minutes, the SE was seen to spin, engine full on, and break into pieces at 1,000ft. Waters was killed.[9]

Richard Maybery flew the next patrol, but apart from forced landings by Eric Turnbull and Burdette Harmon at the advanced landing ground that had been set up at Bapaume, this was uneventful.

The next day, 19 November, Reginald Theodore Carlos Hoidge left for Home Establishment. He had joined the squadron at London Colney on 5 January 1917 and was the last to leave of the original pilots who had flown to France in the April of that year. Long overdue to be posted home, Hoidge had refused an earlier transfer because of his great admiration of Blomfield, but with Blomfield's promotion and transfer Hoidge finally accepted his posting. Richard Maybery was given command of C Flight.

The day was spent in more practise flying and tests. The squadron's pilots knew that the offensive was due to be beginning the following morning and last minute adjustments were made to their aeroplanes and guns.

On 20 November the Cambrai offensive opened just as dawn was breaking. Weather conditions for the supportive role to be played by the RFC were poor, with cloud and mist to within 200ft of the ground, in places actually reaching ground level. The two SE5a squadrons of 13th Wing – 56 and 84 – had been ordered to fly Distant Offensive Patrols during the morning, but the weather conditions obviously made these impossible.[10]

At 5.30AM at Laviéville, twenty miles behind the trenches, the reverberation of the guns was clearly felt. At 7.00AM, as the pilots stood on the aerodrome waiting for fresh orders, it was threatening to rain.

Impatient to play their part in the offensive, James and Bowman took their Flights off the ground at 7.20AM. James took his Flight across the Lines at 2,000ft above a gap in the clouds and patrolled between Quéant and Graincourt, before going down to 300ft and flying along the Bapaume to Cambrai road towards Havrincourt. Arriving over Harvincourt Wood, they could plainly see the smoke and gun flashes of the fierce ground fighting, and coming down to 200ft they saw that the British tanks had successfully broken through the German defences of the Hindenburg Line.

James led the patrol along the Lines for a time, but although the air was crowded with British machines there was no sign of any enemy aircraft. After a while, finding the cloud was now down to within a hundred feet of the ground and seeing that there was no threat from enemy aircraft, James turned for home. The Flight having lost touch with each other in the

Fielding-Johnson in SE5a B37 'U'.

appalling conditions, James was now accompanied only by Coote, and as they flew west the weather became so impossible that they were forced to land at the advanced landing ground at Bapaume.[11]

The clouds having lifted a little, James and Coote took off again at 12.25 and flew back along the Bapaume to Albert road, in some places being forced down to ten feet by the thick mist. Five minutes before reaching Laviéville Coote's oil tank burst, but both landed safely.

Bowman's Flight had fared little better. Gardiner had force-landed near La Bellevue due to lack of petrol, and Ronald Townsend had been hit in the engine by ground fire and forced to land near Equancourt. Townsend was unhurt but his machine was badly damaged and the Lewis gun was stolen before the SE could be recovered and sent to 2AD for repair.

Maybery's patrol had taken off to attack a balloon, but had returned 'immediately' because of the weather.

The impossible weather conditions persisted the next day, with rain and drizzle the entire day and there was no flying. The following day, 22 November, was better, but still overcast, and Balcombe-Brown made two short flights to test conditions. On the first, at 11.30AM, he found dense fog down to ground level between Albert and Bapaume, and returned after twenty minutes. He took off again at 12.25PM. He found that although the fog persisted, conditions were much better nearer the trenches. Despite this Balcombe-Brown considered that the weather was still too poor to send out a patrol.[12]

The morning of 23 November was still overcast. Balcombe-Brown took off at 10.00AM to again test the weather. Over Bapaume, he found conditions were already beginning to clear and were improving rapidly On his return, he ordered that Deep Offensive Patrols should be flown as long as conditions continued to improve.

At 10.40AM, James took off with Fielding-Johnson and Coote. Flying at only 3,000ft because of the low cloud, James took his two companions across the Lines just to the south of Bourlon Wood and attacked four Albatros scouts over Cambrai. James opened fire at a red-nosed Albatros with a yellow fuselage, a green tail, and with a large letter K on its top wing. After a short burst from James' guns, the enemy pilot spun down a little before zooming back up. After a period of skirmishing, the enemy scouts retreated to the east and James took Fielding-Johnson and Coote back towards Bourlon Wood, where the ground fighting was intense, the wood itself surrounded by British troops.

There were a great number of enemy aeroplanes over the area of the wood, all concentrated under 3,000ft. James saw a Rumpler coming west over Proville and fought it down from 3,000 to 1,000ft, before leaving it 'apparently OK'. While diving away the Rumpler observer had fired a cluster of white lights, a signal that James had seen before and which he took to mean '*Jadgstaffel* to the rescue'. However, no enemy scouts

Harold John 'Jackie' Walkerdine. 'A fine little kid and so full of life he can hardly keep still for a moment.'

appeared and James and Fielding-Johnson went to the aid of a Bristol Fighter that they saw fighting two Albatros V-Strutters over Marcoing. The pilot of the Bristol fighter saw them coming and attempted to draw his nearest attacker under the SEs. Its companion, at the same height as James, was practically standing on its tail in an attempt to gain height and get above him, but James zoomed, got a little above the enemy scout, turned quickly, and got behind it. A short burst from his Vickers must have hit the enemy pilot and the Albatros went down in a vertical dive, the pilot's cap – an ordinary service type – falling out. The V-Stutter went down, and hit the ground, engine full on, with a 'fearful whack', about a mile east of Noyelles.[13]

James now reformed with Fielding-Johnson and they flew back to Bourlon Wood, where they attacked a large formation of Albatros scouts. James overshot his opponent, the enemy pilot looking round, completely confused, but by the time James had turned to renew his attack the enemy pilot was back in the middle of his formation and James turned away.

There were now additional Albatri above them and James again noticed the green-tailed Albatros with the large K on its top wing. After 'revving round for a while' and watching Richard Maybery attacking a large AEG bomber, James and Fielding-Johnson returned, having had 'a morning's fine fun'.

The squadron had had a morning of varied success. Harmon had sent a two-seater down out of control to land upside down just south of the Arras to Cambrai road and James claimed the Albatros that had crashed by Rumilly. All the SEs from the regular Flights had returned safely to Laviéville – with the exception of Gardiner, who had landed at Bapaume with engine trouble – but Balcombe-Brown, who had taken off at 11.30AM, had tackled an enemy two-seater, turned the wrong way at the crucial moment and the gunner had put an accurate burst through a longeron and the SE's petrol tank. Balcombe-Brown was drenched in petrol and nearly blinded. Fearful that the flames of his exhausts, that were very near the petrol tank, would ignite the escaping petrol, he switched off his engine and dived to almost ground level before switching on his emergency petrol tank, restarting his engine and landing at Lechelle. He later returned to Laviéville, ruefully remarking that it was harder to tackle a well handled enemy two-seater than it looked.[14]

All the Flights went out again in the afternoon, but James failed to take off because of a faulty oil tank. Coote took command of the patrol and led it to the area of Bourlon Wood, where they attacked a formation of Albatri. Coote fired at one of the enemy scouts, which spun away into the clouds, but Balcombe-Brown refused to allow it as a victory, considering it indecisive and lacking confirmation. Bowman claimed the only positive result of the afternoon's fighting, shooting down a brown-coloured Albatros that crashed just north west of Cambrai.[15]

The squadron relaxed that evening with a trip to Amiens, only a twenty-minute car ride from the aerodrome. Here they adjourned to Charlie's Bar where they 'consumed large quantities of oysters'. Amiens was a large town, with a great number of fine shops, not far from Paris or the Channel ports, and almost anything could be bought there. After shopping for various essentials, the pilots enjoyed an excellent dinner at Godbert's famous restaurant before returning to Laviéville by 10.00PM.

For the next two days there were high, westerly winds, low clouds and rain, that again curtailed operations, and James spent the time in short test flights to adjust the rigging of SE5a B35. On the morning of 26 November, the weather had improved a little, being generally fine, but still with patches of cloud and a very high wind.

James took off at 9.20AM with Fielding-Johnson, Walkerdine, and Truscott as escort to a formation of DH4s of 49 Squadron that were bombing the railhead at Rieux, just to the east of Cambrai. The SEs crossed the Lines over Bourlon

Alexander Dodds' SE5a B4890 on the aerodrome of *Jasta* 5 after his capture on 29 November 1917.

but failed to find the bombers, seeing only a group of five Albatri over Cambrai and a trio of two-seaters over Lesdans. All these enemy machines cleared to the east before they could be attacked. The Flight then returned with the exception of Barry Truscott who drifted south, landing at the French aerodrome at Roye to have a faulty carburettor rectified.

During the morning both Maybery and Bowman also took out an escort patrol to escort the DH4s, but neither patrol found the bombers and saw no action, returning to report that enemy air activity over Cambrai was 'very slight'.

Just after 2.00PM, the entire squadron force of twelve machines, under the overall command of Bowman, took off on a combined escort patrol. The weather had deteriorated badly, visibility was very poor, and the DH4s were again not found, so Bowman washed out the squadron formation in order that the Flights could work independently.(16)

James led Truscott, Walkerdine, and Fielding-Johnson to Bourlon, still the scene of heavy fighting on the ground. They dived through the clouds, coming out at 2,000ft, and fired at the enemy infantry in trenches near the village.(17)

The weather again clamped down on 27 November, wind and heavy rain stopping all flying. Local conditions were a little better the next morning, but still not good enough for patrols to be flown. A great deal of local flights, testing engines and guns, was the only flying by the squadron during the day.

James, however, flew a Special Mission, patrolling the Bapaume/Bourlon area at 6,000ft. Although he saw several enemy aircraft, they were some way east of the Lines and he returned after eighty minutes.

Dawn was fine on 29 November: the weather had finally relented and the squadron saw a great deal of action during the day.

At 7.00AM, James took off with Fielding-Johnson, Walkerdine, and Slingsby. Half an hour later they crossed the Lines at 12,000ft, just to the south of St.Quentin, flying north with the sun behind them. After only a few minutes, James saw a DFW at 11,000ft, coming south-west over Bellicourt. He dived, followed by the other SEs, got behind the enemy machine and opened fire. The pilot of the DFW manoeuvred very well, giving his gunner the chance of a good shot at the SE, but after a long burst from both guns the DFW broke up in the air 'the wreckage of the wings fluttering down like so many pieces of small paper, while the fuselage with its heavy engine, went twirling down like a misdirected arrow'. James was unsure exactly where the main wreckage of the DFW finally hit the ground, but judged it must have been a little to the south east of Bellicourt.(18)

James zoomed and looked round for his companions. Slingsby had earlier returned with engine trouble and only Fielding-Johnson and Walkerdine had followed James in his dive on the DFW. James saw that Fielding-Johnson was in some kind of trouble – his stabilising fin had broken in the dive, turning him upside down. After seeing Fielding-Johnson safely back to the Lines, James and Walkerdine flew

Ltn. Hans Schlömer (left) and Fritz Oppenhorst standing by Dodd's SE5a.

to Cambrai, where they attacked eight Albatri that were about to attack Maybery and A Flight. Maybery had seen that there were actually two formations of Albatri, seven machines in each, and he took his Flight down to join forces with James and Walkerdine, but the enemy scouts scattered before they could get into the action.[19]

Maybery then climbed for some extra height: he had seen another formation of Albatri working round to get to the west of the SEs. These dived on the SEs from out of the morning sun. Maybery turned underneath the attack and a general fight began. Both the SEs and Albatri lost a great deal of height during the fighting and Maybery saw that another formation of Albatri, above the action, were about to dive into the fighting. The odds would be too much. Maybery fired a red light for the SEs to break off the combat and reform but they were all fighting so intensely that no one saw his signal. In the event, it was the enemy pilots who finally broke off the action and SEs were able to return to Laviéville.

Eric Turnbull had shot down an Albatros out of control during the fight and although Maybery made no claim for another, which he had sent down in a vertical dive, Balcombe-Brown considered that it had been out of control.[20] On the debit side, Alex Dodds, a promising pilot, had been attacked and forced down by *Ltn.* Fritz Schubert of *Jasta* 6. Dodds landed on *Jasta* 5's aerodrome at Boistrancourt and was taken prisoner.[21]

At noon, eleven SEs took off from Laviéville to fly Deep Offensive patrols. James led Truscott and Walkerdine above the clouds to Arras, but the ground being obscured by low cloud he took them lower and patrolled along the Front Line. As they approached Bourlon they saw several Albatri 'playing in the clouds', but James ignored these and led the SEs north. As the SEs came up to Arras, James saw three DFWs flying over the river Sensée, coming west from Douai. These then turned north over Vitry and as they arrived over Fresnoy, James led Walkerdine and Truscott down to attack them.

James attacked the leader of the trio, but after firing a short burst he had stoppages in both guns. He rectified these and chased after the DFW, noticing as he did so that Walkerdine was tackling one of the other DFWs 'in great style'. Catching up with the DFW, James saw that it was now down to 300ft, its engine stopped, gliding down towards Rouvroy. James closed to within a hundred feet and fired another short burst from both guns. The DFW did a 'terrific' zoom, its top wings folded back, meeting over the fuselage, and all four wings broke off. The fuselage went down and hit the ground, the engine tearing away from the fuselage and rolling several yards from the wreckage.[22]

Turning away from the crash, James realised that he was now very low and over a mile into enemy-held territory. He opened up his throttle to climb away, but his engine merely spluttered. A hurried glance at his pressure gauge showed him that it was reading almost zero. Holding up the nose of his SE with one hand, James furiously pumped his pressure pump with the other. With the SE only a few feet from the ground, the Hispano suddenly started with a heart-warming roar. James climbed a little in an attempt to ascertain his position, but he was too low to locate any landmarks so he flew west by the sun. Passing only a few feet above a German gun position, he took his bearings from the direction in which the gun barrels were pointing and eventually found the British trenches, full of waving troops. He then saw Walkerdine and Truscott a little to the west, joined them and brought them home. This near escape at having to land in enemy territory badly shook James, far more than any actual fighting. Several of his fellow pilots later remarked that it was the only time they had ever seen him shocked out of his habitual calm.

Both DFWs were later confirmed by British AA batteries: James' had crashed near Rouvroy, Walkerdine's at Neuvireuil.

Having shot down two enemy two-seaters in the morning James decided that he would follow his luck, taking off alone after lunch and patrolling to the south of Lens, where he drove off a two-seater working in the area. He saw no other enemy machines and after pinpointing the position of the DFW brought down near Rouvroy, he returned.

The weather continued fine all day on 30 November, although there were low clouds at 2,000ft. James took his Flight out at 9.55AM, crossing the front lines fifteen minutes later and patrolling from Gouzéaucourt to Bourlon, flying at 2,000ft below the clouds. At this height Archie was both heavy and accurate but as the Flight approached Bourlon it slackened, as there were enemy scouts in the area. James led the Flight to attack several of these and although they gained no decisive result they had the satisfaction of driving them away from the Front Line, keeping them well to the east. At 11.15, a pair of LVGs were seen coming west over Fontaine. James immediately dived, secured a good position under the leader, and fired a burst from both guns. The engine of the LVG jerked to a stop and water began to pour from its radiator. The enemy pilot glided down to the west and James let him go, knowing that he would now have to land in allied territory. During the attack the enemy gunner had put an accurate burst of fire into B35, holing the radiator, and James was forced to land near the LVG, which had come down south east of Havrincourt. The SE had almost finished its run when its wheels ran into a small shell hole, tipping it up onto its nose. James clambered out, pulled down the SE's tail and ran to where the LVG had landed. The crew had attempted to set fire to their machine, but had been prevented by the infantry, and the LVG, apart from a few bullet holes, was intact. When James arrived he found that the pilot was badly hurt and having a tourniquet applied to his arm, but the observer was unharmed. James inspected the LVG, that appeared to be brand new, then telegrammed to Laviéville for a breakdown party to be sent with new propeller and a radiator for his SE, and to salvage what they could from the LVG.[23]

While he was waiting for the breakdown party to arrive, James had lunch with a colonel at the nearby Headquarters of 59 Division. The fighting on the ground was particularly fluid, there had been reports that the enemy infantry had broken into the British lines, and the colonel was anxious to know if James had observed anything from the air. James explained that he had been too busy to pay much attention to the ground fighting, other than that the enemy was raining gas shells into Bourlon Wood. After lunch, as James and the Colonel were leaving his dugout, they heard gunfire from above. Looking up, they saw a Pfalz attacking a balloon, which burst into flames. Both occupants took to their parachutes; James, noticing that one came down much quicker than the other, concluded that he was much fatter than his companion.

Kicking his heels while waiting for the breakdown party to arrive, James could see that there were a great many enemy machines now operating over the area, that the fighting was heavy, and the British pilots were hard pressed. He decided to make his way to the advanced landing ground at Bapaume, borrow a machine, and get back into the fighting. He tried to borrow a car at the artillery headquarters, but they refused, so he set off to walk the six miles to the railhead near Vélu, where he hoped to be able to catch a train to Bapaume. Hampered by his heavy, thigh length sheepskin-lined flying boots – known popularly as 'fug boots' – he struggled through mud, slush, and 'all manner of things', startled at one point on his journey by the roar of its engine as an enemy two-seater passed overhead at 3,000ft. This unmolested intrusion into allied air space fuelled James' anger: 'By Jove! I was fed up to be sitting on the ground and seeing that insolent Hun come over getting just what information he wanted.' After watching the enemy machine fly back over its own lines, James trudged on, finally arriving at Vélu where he boarded a train for Bapaume. During the journey, James discussed the ground fighting with some Canadian engineers, who kindly gave him some tea – doubly welcome after his trek. The Canadians were not optimistic that the German counter attacks could be stopped, as they had been ordered to dismantle as much of the railway line – which they had built – as quickly as possible.

After about an hour, as the train was passing the advanced landing ground at Bapaume, James jumped off and made his way to the aerodrome. It was now 6.00PM, far too late to follow his original intention of borrowing a machine, and hearing that a tender was just about to leave for Albert he cadged a lift. James arrived back at Laviéville having had a 'very exciting day's work'.

During the day's fighting the squadron had claimed six victories. Bowman was credited with a two-seater, an Albatros scout out of control, plus a Pfalz destroyed. During the afternoon, Maybery had destroyed two Albatros scouts and Maurice Mealing,[24] a new pilot, had claimed an Albatros out of control.

To offset these successes, George Cawson's[25] SE had broken up in mid-air under fire from the gunner of a two-seater he was attacking and Ronald Townsend had also been shot down and killed.[26]

November had been a bad month for the squadron. Despite the weather curtailing war flying for twenty-four days during the month, including the move to Laviéville, with the squadron

The Happy Warrior. A less formal view of James in his SE5a.

flying operations on only six days, it had suffered a total of six casualties: four pilots killed – one in an accident – and two taken prisoner: proportionally the highest casualty rate of any month since its arrival in France. Although these pilots had all been relatively inexperienced, the squadron could ill afford their loss.

Ch.14: A Remarkable December

The rudder of LVG C.V 9458/17, shot down by James on 30 November, was later mounted on the wall of the ante-room at Baizieux. In this photograph of the ante-room it can be seen at the top right. The officers are L.to R.: Balcombe-Brown, seated; Maurice Mealing; William Fielding-Johnson; unknown; unknown; David Galley.

During the German counter offensive on the last day of November the air fighting had been heavy and fiercely contested, but this came to almost a complete halt on the first day of December. Visibility was bad, with low cloud and mist that kept most of the machines of the *Luftstreikräfte* on the ground and only the British troops had the support of low flying aeroplanes during the fierce ground fighting of the day.

James and Maybery took their Flights out in the morning, but visibility was so limited that both washed out the patrols and returned.

As the weather showed no signs of improving, flying was cancelled for the remainder of the day and James set off in a tender with Corporal Tom Rogers, his Scots mechanic 'who hailed fra Glasgae', to salvage his SE at Havrincourt.[1] The roads were very congested, they had difficulty in getting near the SE, so they left the tender at Trescault and walked the last half mile. The breakdown party had not taken a replacement radiator – James' telegram message requesting one had been unclear – but had fitted a new propeller and filled the SE with petrol and oil. After running the engine for a while to thoroughly warm it, James stuffed two bars of soap – a time-honoured remedy – into the large hole in the radiator made by the gunner's explosive bullet, and Rogers filled the radiator with fresh water. With water pouring out of the damaged radiator, James took off, anxious to get the SE – and himself – away from the enemy shells that were bursting nearby in 'generous quantities', finally landing at Bapaume without a remaining drop of water in the radiator.

After a new radiator had been fitted, James flew back to Laviéville, landing just before 4.00PM. The breakdown party sent out to the LVG had now returned and had made out their report. After attending to the SE, they had attempted to salvage the LVG, but the difficulties in doing so were considerable. It lay beyond the old Hindenburg Line, in a twelve-foot-wide trench, impossible to move without more men and heavy moving equipment. The decision was made to dismantle it, but the work was continually interrupted by heavy shelling that necessitated stopping work to take cover. A near miss caused the wings to collapse, and told that there was a likelihood of German troops overrunning the area it was decided to burn the rest of the machine. The party then returned to James' SE, standing by in order to burn it if there were any danger that it would fall into enemy hands, but at 3.00AM the next morning they were told that the British line was holding firm and that

During the last four days of December 1917 the individual Flight markings of the Squadron's SE5as were changed: B Flight aeroplanes were changed to numbers – 1 to 6 inclusive, James' B4891 being numbered 6. The letters of C Flight moved to the end of the alphabet, V to Z inclusive, taking over the letters formerly used on spare aeroplanes. The letters of A Flight remained unchanged. A little later, the spinner from the LVG was fitted to B4891 and painted red. James estimated that this added three miles an hour to the speed of the SE5a, which could now reach 120mph at 10,000 feet. This photograph of B4891 was taken at Baizieux in March 1918.

the danger had passed.

James was understandably annoyed that they had burnt his LVG,[2] but slightly mollified in that they had brought back the propeller, its spinner, the rudder (marked C.V 9458), the fabric from the wings, with its black crosses – ' which always made very good screens in the Mess' – a Very pistol and cartridges, plus several other odds and ends, although not the observer's gun, which had been 'liberated' by the colonel.[3] Pleased to have these souvenirs[4] of his victory, James nevertheless vowed that if he could help it, he would never again land alongside a downed enemy machine if it meant walking six miles through thick mud in his fug boots.

Although the wind was extremely strong the next day, all the Flights – thirteen SEs in all – left the ground at 9.55AM. Several formations of enemy aircraft were seen, but these dived east before they could be attacked, the SEs keeping well to the west of the Lines because of the strong winds. James was the only member of his Flight to return safely to Laviéville. The wind caused both Walkerdine and Slingsby to crash on landing, and Fielding-Johnson had force-landed at Barastre with engine trouble. The other Flights had faired little better: two pilots – Harmon and Truscott – had also crashed on landing back at Laviéville. The unproductive morning had cost the squadron four aeroplanes and one pilot, Burdette Harmon having been injured in his crash and taken to hospital.

The winds were even stronger the following day, 3 December, and no patrols were flown until the afternoon, when enemy aircraft were reported to be working over the Lines. Maybery took out four SEs, but they were unable to reach the Lines before dark.[5]

During the day, Slingsby fetched a new SE5a from 2AD. This was B4891, one of the third production batch of SE5as built by the Royal Aircraft Factory at Farnborough, powered by a Peugeot-built Hispano-Suiza and incorporating several recent modifications: the elevators had a narrower chord and the undercarriage was the of new, strengthened type.[6] James exercised a flight commander's prerogative and took over B4891 for himself, giving his Martinsyde-built B35 to Barry Truscott, the youngest member of his Flight. Truscott was delighted with the arrangement: B35 was a very good machine and he knew that James, as always, had lavished a great deal of care and attention on it.

James and his mechanics at once set to work on his new machine: tuning the engine, testing guns and Constantinesco gear and having to have all his 'special gadgets' fitted. By 4 December he was 'again ready for the Great War'.

Visibility was 'fair' on 4 December and all three Flights – ten SEs – took off at 7.20AM on Deep Offensive Patrols, James leading a new pilot, Edward Galley,(7) Harold Walkerdine, and Truscott. Walkerdine turned back with an overheating engine, but borrowed another SE and set off again to rejoin the patrol.(8)

The clouds were heavy over German-held territory and the only enemy machines sighted were towards the end of the patrol time when the clouds had cleared a little. The Flight saw no action and returned.

James took his Flight out again at 2.00PM. The SEs crossed the Lines at 13,000ft over Masnieres and flew north. At 3.10PM James led them down to attack five V-Strutters over Bourlon. James latched onto the tail of one of the enemy scouts and drove it down, but was forced to leave it as he was attacked from behind by another. James out-manoeuvred this new opponent, driving it down to 7,000ft, but the enemy pilot was extremely skilful, continually half-rolling to avoid his fire. James finally left this Albatros diving east, 'apparently OK'.

Maybery's Flight now arrived and the remaining Albatri were all driven east. James later attacked a two-seater at 12,000ft over Gonnelieu, driving it down to 6,000ft over Bois de Vaucelles, but he eventually left it as some enemy scouts were coming down from the north to attack him.

Visibility was exceptionally good on 5 December and James took off alone just after 11.00AM to look for any Rumplers that he reasoned would be taking advantage of the good weather. On the way to the Lines he took the opportunity to test the performance of B4891, climbing to 19,000ft, an altitude necessary in any case to be able to intercept the high-flying German reconnaissance machines. The SE performed to his satisfaction and an hour after taking off he saw a Rumpler flying west from Bourlon. Turning to put the sun between himself and the Rumpler, James then turned north to cut off its retreat, biding his time until the enemy machine – that was at his own height – was well west of the Front Lines, deep into allied territory, before attacking it over Boursies. After a short burst, the Rumpler went down in a vertical dive, breaking to pieces at 16,000ft over Hermies. The time was 12.40PM.(9) James landed back at Laviéville, had lunch, then prepared to take out his Flight 'for the afternoon sports', taking off at 1.40PM with Galley, Fielding-Johnson and Truscott.

James' little force was soon depleted: Fielding-Johnson's magneto continually cut out and he could not keep up with the rest of the patrol. David Galley's SE had been hit in the propeller by Archie. The whole machine began to vibrate alarmingly, and Galley switched off his engine and glided to the advanced landing ground at Bapaume. Although a piece of shell had gone through his flying coat and tunic just above the elbow, and had come out at the shoulder without breaking his skin, other than the propeller nothing vital had been hit and Galley flew back to Laviéville, throttled down to lessen the vibration.

James, now only with Truscott, attacked a two-seater over

Edward Galley.

Bantouzelle. Truscott lost James in the dive and when two additional two-seaters appeared, plus an Albatros scout, James was forced to break off his attack on the two-seater to tackle the enemy scout. The enemy pilot manoeuvred very well and seeing that several more enemy scouts were hurrying to join the fight, James broke away and returned, landing at 4.00PM.

That evening James received a telegram from Lt.Col. Playfair, Commanding officer of 13th Wing.(10) 'Congratulations on your show this morning.'

At 9.45 the next morning, James took out the same three pilots. Immediately after crossing the Lines, Fielding-Johnson and Truscott were forced to turn back with engine trouble. James and David Galley flew on and at 10.20 spotted a Rumpler taking photographs over Vendelles. James and

The Opposition: The colourful Albatros D.IIIs and D.Vs of *Jasta* 5 on their aerodrome at Boistrancourt.

Galley went down to attack this machine, but during the dive Galley's radiator blinds broke, chewing up his propeller. James, however, despatched the Rumpler in his now almost workman-like manner. After a short burst from his guns a great deal of material fell out of the enemy machine and it went down out of control, the observer hanging over the side of the fuselage. At 8,000ft the right hand wings of the Rumpler broke off and the wreckage fell in the British Lines at Holnon Wood, a little to the north-west of St Quentin.[11]

James then saw an LVG, coming north from over St Quentin, but by the time he caught up with it, it was too high to engage and as his radiator was boiling he returned to Laviéville for a well-earned lunch.

After lunch, James took out Fielding-Johnson, Galley, Truscott, Franklin and Mealing, with Bowman and Maybery working in collaboration with the patrol. The eight SEs crossed the Lines at 14,000ft over Masnières and flew to the Cambrai area, where James saw a formation of six Albatri flying west over Fontaine-Notre-Dame. He took the SEs to the east of the enemy scouts, giving them time to each pick an opponent before turning and attacking the enemy scouts from behind.

James closed to within thirty yards of the rearmost Albatros and fired a short burst from both guns. The blue-tailed Albatros slowly turned over onto its side before going down in a vertical dive, petrol streaming along its fuselage. James had time to see one of the Albatri, attacked by Mealing, going down, smoke pouring from its engine, before he was attacked by the remaining Albatri, that he now realised were the pilots he had fought on 23 November: all had red noses, yellow fuselages and each sported a different coloured tail: red, black and white striped, and 'dear old Greentail'. These Albatri were from *Jasta* 5 and were not averse to mixing things with the SEs. 'By Jove! They were a tough lot. We continued scrapping with them for half an hour, and they would not go down, although we were above them most of the time.'

However, as in most engagements between evenly matched fighter formations, no positive results were claimed after the initial attack, and both sides having expended their ammunition they broke off the action and returned to their respective aerodromes. Although James had hit another of the Albatri in the engine and it had been seen to dive out of the fight, only the Albatros with the blue tail was credited to him as out of control.

Back at Laviéville, over tea and toast, the fight was discussed and it was agreed by all who had taken part that the pilots of the Albatri had all been at the game for some time.

In the evening, James received another congratulatory telegram, this one from Trenchard. 'Well done. You are splendid. Your work lately has been of the finest.'

There was a great deal of cloud on 7 December. James took B Flight off the ground on a Deep Offensive Patrol at 8.15AM, crossing the Lines over Gouzeaucourt. At 3,000ft, the cloud

Another view of The Opposition: The colourful Albatros D.IIIs and D.Vs of *Jasta* 5 on their aerodrome at Boistrancourt.

ceiling was very low, the SEs were heavily archied, and Galley's machine was hit in the rudder. Because of the unfavourable conditions, James decided to cut the scheduled DOP to a Close Offensive Patrol and took the Flight towards Bois-de-Vancelle where he had noticed an enemy observation balloon. However, the balloon crew were wide awake and by the time the SEs arrived the balloon had been hauled down.

Three quarters of an hour after taking off, James saw an enemy two-seater observing over Bourlon Wood. As he approached the enemy machine he saw that it was a type he had not seen before, and that it had a biplane tail.[12] James dived and fired at long range, succeeding in driving the two-seater down to 300ft east of the wood, too low over enemy territory for James to follow. Twenty-five minutes later, continuing his patrol over the 3rd Army Corps area, James saw an RE8 being attacked by two Albatros scouts. James and the Flight flew to the assistance of the British two-seater. The enemy pilots saw them coming and turned towards the SEs, but being out climbed by them escaped into the cloud cover. Several other formations of enemy scouts were later seen, but these also took advantage of the low cloud to evade the SEs. James then took the Flight home, landing at 10.05AM to report that enemy anti-aircraft fire had been heavy, continuous, and accurate throughout the patrol, with special mention of a battery on the south-west corner of Bourlon Wood. Balcombe-Brown commented on the bottom of James' combat report, 'No decisive engagements but very good work done'.

Bad weather for the next two days prevented any war flying and it was not until the afternoon of 10 December that patrols were able to be flown. After lunch, ten SEs left the ground – five pairs of fighting partners: James and Galley; Bowman and Franklin,[13] Maybery and Truscott; Jarvis[14] and Blenkiron;[15] Mealing and McPherson.[16]

At 3.10, James, Galley, Maybery, and Truscott attacked six Albatri over Bellicourt. James got onto the tail of one Albatros, but had stoppages in both guns and the enemy scout dived away. None of the other pilots gained a decisive result – Maybery had returned with engine trouble – and James reformed the patrol. Ten minutes later he saw Bowman's formation fighting with seven V-Strutters over Bantouzelle. James kept his Flight above the fight to act as top cover, attacking a pair of Albatri that were about to dive on Bowman. During the fighting, Bowman saw an additional five enemy scouts were coming from the south east and as these had the added advantage of height he fired a recall signal and led his Flight back across the Lines.

James and Galley had broken off the fight with the two Albatri and flew towards Havrincourt where they both attacked

Louis Jarvis in the cockpit of an Avro 504. The travelling cinema shows were a welcome distraction on the Western front. Westerns were very popular – and amusing – and Chaplin's Little Tramp was well known, hence the well-executed marking on the fuselage of this Avro.

a two-seater. After James' attack, the enemy machine zoomed, then went down with steam pouring from its radiator. Galley's attack was frustrated by his Lewis gun refusing to cock. Both James and Galley were then chased away from the two-seater by the arrival of several enemy scouts.

All the SEs were back at Laviéville by 3.50PM. Franklin was credited with a two-seater out of control; Mealing with the destruction of a balloon.

Low clouds and mist all day prevented all war flying on 11 December, but conditions had improved a little the next day and the squadron flew patrols in the morning and early afternoon. James led seven SEs off the ground at 9.30AM with orders to fly a Deep Offensive patrol, but conditions were so bad – two pilots lost the patrol in a snowstorm – that even though James cut the sortie to a Line Patrol, he was forced to abandon even this: the clouds were down to 2,000ft, visibility was very poor owing to the thick mist, and he brought the SEs home after an hour, hoping the conditions would improve later in the day.

Ten SEs took off after lunch. It was intended that James would lead one Flight of five, Bowman another, but Bowman failed to get off the ground until fifteen minutes later and never succeeded in finding his Flight.

James led the nine SEs over the Lines at Gonnelieu, chasing away an Albatros scout that was firing into the British trenches. Flying north to Moeuvres, they attacked numerous groups of Albatri but these evaded their attacks by making use of the extensive cloud cover. James then took his force to the south and they attacked several Pfalz D.IIIs that were ground strafing British trenches in the vicinity of Villers-Guislain. The Flight broke up these attacks, dispersing the Pfalz, but gained no positive victories. James then saw a British observation balloon going down in flames and he climbed into the clouds in an attempt to find the culprit.[17] He failed to find the enemy scout responsible and had now lost sight of the Flight. However, he found them again and led them towards Hermies, where he saw a DFW coming back from the British lines, flying at 4,000ft just under the cloud cover. James knew that if he took the SEs down to attack immediately, the enemy pilot would simply climb into the cloud cover and escape, so he took them up through the clouds, waited until they were all in the clear air, signalled for them to stay there, cutting off the DFW's retreat, then dived to attack it, thinking as he did so: 'Now the Hun was for it, whichever way he went'. But the crew of the DFW were highly experienced; they had no intention of falling into James' trap. Full of confidence, they stayed down to fight him. Their confidence was fully justified. They fought James for fully five minutes, but he simply could not gain a favourable attacking position. 'EA put up a most determined and skillful fight and I was not able to use his blind spots for a single second. Moreover, the enemy gunner was shooting very accurately and making splendid deflection, so that when I got down to 500ft I left the EA who went north over Bourlon Wood.' James realised that he had met his match in this particular two-seater crew. 'The Hun was too good for me and shot me about a lot. Had I persisted he certainly would have got me for there was not a trick he did not know.'

James had now irretrievably lost the Flight and he flew south to attack another two-seater that was considerably west of the trenches in the vicinity of Vendhuille. However, as he was approaching it he saw two V-Strutters attacking a balloon just to the south of Metz-en-Couture. James abandoned his intention of attacking the two-seater and flew west to attack the Albatri. He got up to their height over Trescault, but he had forgotten that he had now been out for two and a quarter hours and when almost within range his main petrol tank ran dry. James quickly switched to his emergency tank, but it was almost a minute before his engine restarted and he lost a great deal of height. The Albatri took the opportunity to clear east, but James at least had the satisfaction of knowing that he had frustrated their attempts to destroy the balloon.

During the day, James received another Telegram from Trenchard. 'Many congratulations of getting a DSO. You throughly (sic) deserve it.'

The inclement weather grounded the squadron for the next two days, but the morning of 15 December was fine and Maybery took out a patrol at 7.45AM, saw a good deal of fighting with eight Albatri and shot one down out of control over Bourlon Wood, with Blenkiron claiming another that went spinning down, alternately fast and slow.

James took off alone at 10.15. Climbing steadily, he reached 18,000ft and saw a two-seater over Gouzeaucourt flying towards the Front Line. There was a strong westerly wind blowing and James, anxious to bring the enemy machine down behind the British Lines, knew that an immediate attack would result in the fight being blown to the east. He consequently held his hand and climbed still higher – to 19,800ft – into the morning sun, waiting for the two-seater to come nearer, but as it approached the trenches it turned north and it was obvious that the enemy pilot had no intention of flying any deeper into allied territory. Seeing this, James dived to attack it over Metz, but completely misjudged both his own speed in the dive and that of the two-seater, and after firing only a few shots was forced to turn away to avoid a collision. While he was turning to renew his attack, the enemy pilot dived away to the east. After chasing him for some distance, mindful of the strong wind, James reluctantly let him go, turned to the west and climbed back to 16,000ft.

As he got back to the Front Lines, James saw that the whole sky seemed alive with enemy two-seaters. He selected one, a Rumpler, and attacked it just north of Gonnelieu. This time he made no mistake. After thirty rounds from both guns, the Rumpler half spun to the right, went into a spiral dive for 5,000ft, then dived vertically before hitting the ground half a mile east of Bois-de-Vaucelles. 'Nothing was left of it.'

Although the squadron flew no patrols on 16 December, a great deal of test-flying and 'practising fighting' was done. Balcombe-Browne took up James' SE5a, B4891 to test for himself the effect of the new, narrow-chord elevators He reported that they were most successful, that the SE turned much quicker and could dive without having to adjust the wheel.

Impossible weather conditions of thick cloud, mist and heavy falls of snow grounded the squadron for the next two days. The morning of 19 December was better but still misty and Balcombe-Browne took off to test the weather conditions. He found that the mist had cleared above the clouds, and that patrols would be possible later in the morning.

James took off alone at 9.55AM – the Duty column in the Squadron Record Book recording, 'Chasing EA'. Twenty minutes after takeoff, getting his height over Velu, James saw a pair of Gothas and three two-seaters flying east of Havrincourt Wood at 10,000ft. He immediately gave chase, but was unable to catch them. British AA batteries then pointed out to him a two-seater over Pontruet. James got into a good attacking position and fired several short bursts into the enemy machine, one from directly underneath, and it went steeply down with its left wing low. James watched it fall from 13,000 to 5,000ft, when it then flattened out and flew east. James last saw it,

Maurice Mealing.

about 4,000ft over Morcourt, still going down.

James then flew north and half an hour later drove away another two-seater that was working over Anneux at 17,000ft.

Although James made no claim for the two-seater last seen over Morcourt, Balcombe-Brown commented on the bottom of his combat report: 'If a machine was last seen by AA to crash at 10.40 just N.E of St Quentin, it would be Capt McCudden's, otherwise it is indecisive.' As this enemy machine was not included in the official list of James' victories, it appears that confirmation was not given.

Ten SEs – A and B Flights, led by James and Richard Maybery – took off from Laviéville at 12.15. James and Maybery had agreed to co-operate on this patrol and the ten SEs crossed the Front Lines together: Maybery taking his force over at Marcoing; James taking B Flight a little further north, over Noyelles-s-Escaut.

At 1.00PM Maybery led his Flight down to attack a large formation of Albatri, that immediately split into two sections, one going east, the other north east. The larger of these formations was flying at 5,000ft, just east of Bourlon Wood, and Maybery dived to attack them from 12,000ft.

Meanwhile, to prevent them from joining in the fighting below, James had attacked another formation of six V-Strutters flying slightly higher, and had a long, hard fight with a

Barclay McPherson. McPherson's nickname was 'Ole Bill' which he had painted under the cockpit of his SE5a.

brown-coloured Pfalz and the old opponent, 'Greentail'. These cooperated with 'with great skill', but by firing at them each in turn, James managed to keep them both below the remainder of his Flight, which were fighting other enemy scouts above him. At 2.10PM, having been out for over two hours, James broke off the action, reformed his Flight and returned to Laviéville.

Making out their combat reports, everyone compared notes. In the first fight, Blenkiron reported sending an Albatros down with black smoke pouring from under the pilot's seat, later knocking six inches off another's tail – although not stating quite how he did this. Eric Turnbull had fired at an Albatros that had been fighting James, and had seen it go down steeply until flattening out and flying east.

Richard Maybery was the only pilot who had not returned and it was realised he had not been seen since the initial attack on the first formation of Albatri, when Turnbull thought he had seen him following down a burning Albatros.

Night fell and Richard Maybery was reported as missing. This was a bad blow for the squadron. Maybery was one of its very best pilots and was extremely popular with all ranks in the squadron. His death was all the more tragic because he was due to be posted home to England within the next few weeks. Although he had been on leave in October, Maybery fought with such intensity and concentration that he was again feeling, and looking, tired.[18]

Bad weather again stopped all operational flying on the 20 December and although a small amount of test-flying was carried out the next day, no patrols were flown. James had adjusted the ignition timing on the engine of B4891 by 10%, and a short flight of twenty-five minutes showed that the Hispano-Suiza was now giving an additional 75 revs per minute.

The morning of 22 December was cloudy. Blenkiron took off at 9.50AM to ascertain the height of the clouds over the Front. He returned after twenty-five minutes to report that the clouds were gradually clearing. At 11.00AM. James took off alone on a Special Mission.

Fifty-five minutes after leaving Laviéville, James sighted a pair of DFWs crossing the Lines over Maissemy. James was at 17,000ft, the DFWs a thousand feet below him, passing over Holnon Wood. James went down and attacked the first, closing to a hundred yards before opening fire, stopping its engine and killing or wounding the gunner. The DFW glided west under partial control and seeing that it would eventually have to land in the British Lines, James left it and attacked its companion. The enemy crew had seen James attack their partner and put up a stiff resistance, not allowing him to get into a favourable position or to get any closer than two hundred yards. James fought this DFW as far as St.Quentin without being able to obtain a result, and seeing that the first DFW was now gliding to the east, intending to land behind its own lines, he turned back and fired a short burst from fifty yards range. The DFW went down in a spiral glide and crashed half a mile behind the British Front Line trenches to the south west of St Quentin. The time was 12.05.[19]

During the fighting James' engine cowling had blown off and his windscreen was covered in blood. He thought at first that his nose was bleeding, but then realised that the blood was on the outside of his windscreen. Landing back at Laviéville, and walking round his machine, he found it covered in blood from one of the DFWs.

After lunch, James again took off alone. He attacked a two-

McPherson in 'Ole Bill.'

seater east of Bapaume, but his carburettor was giving trouble, the enemy machine had the advantage of height, and he failed to gain a decision.

The morning of 23 December started quietly. No patrols were flown until the afternoon, but it was to be a red letter day for James. He took off alone at 10.55, flew to his favourite hunting ground west of St.Quentin, and almost immediately saw a trio of enemy two-seaters, west of the British trenches at 15,000ft over Vendelles. The enemy machines were above James, he could not get enough height to make a decisive attack, and he had to be content in driving them to the east, but a little later he saw an LVG coming west, crossing the Front Lines at 17,000ft just to the north of St.Quentin. James caught up with this machine over Étreillers. The enemy pilot turned south, but James got into a good attacking position and fired a burst from both guns. The LVG's engine stopped, water poured out of its radiator, and it dived east towards La Fère. The enemy gunner was standing up in his cockpit, waving his right arm in an apparent token of surrender. Seeing this, James tried to head the LVG west but although it turned a little it still continued to glide, increasing in speed towards the south-east and its own Lines. James could not allow this. He closed the distance and fired another short burst. The LVG went down in a steep dive and crashed between the canal and road at Anguilcourt at 11.25AM.[20]

James regained his height, turned north and twenty-five minutes later saw a high-flying Rumpler, just south of Péronne. James climbed for twenty minutes, reaching 18,200ft, and finally attacked this Rumpler over Beauvois. The Rumpler crew were experienced and fought 'extraordinarily well', fighting James down to 8,000ft over Roupy, but after a burst from both guns at very close range, both the Rumpler's right wings broke off and it crashed in the British Lines near Contescourt. The time was 12.20.[21]

Sgt. Major Cox,[22] who was in the locality of St.Quentin with a salvage party to collect various items from the DFW that James had shot down the previous day, saw this Rumpler crash. Guessing James was the culprit, he salvaged what remained of it.

James then flew north again and attacked a pair of LVGs over Gouzeaucourt at 16,000ft. These crews co-operated very well, using their front guns as well as their rear, giving James a 'fairly warm time'. His petrol was now running low, so after forcing them east of the Lines, James left them and returned.

After lunch, feeling 'very pleased with things' James led his Flight off the ground at 1.55. On the way to the Lines, James spotted a Rumpler coming west over Metz-en-Couture. The enemy pilot saw the SEs and dived east, but he had left it too late. James caught up with him, fired a long burst from both guns, and the Rumpler went down in a steep right-hand spiral

Vzfw. Georg Strasser. Strasser joined *Jasta* 17 in November 1916, flying with the *Jasta* until December 1917, when he was wounded. He was credited with seven victories, two of them balloons on the 10th and 12th of December.

to crash in the British Lines near Gouzeaucourt.[23]

James had gone down to 6,000ft in fighting this Rumpler so he climbed back to his patrol and led them north, crossing the Lines at 13,000ft over Masnières. A group of Albatri – 'our friends with the varied coloured tails' – were seen over Bourlon Wood, but these had a height advantage over the SEs and James led his formation south, climbing hard for twenty minutes to get above the enemy scouts, finally attacking them at 13,000ft over Fontaine. The Albatri were led by 'Greentail', who tried his usual tactic of flying east on being attacked, climbing for a little extra height, then turning back into the fight, hoping to pick an easy victim. James had seen this stratagem before. When the German pilot came back, James was waiting for him and the enemy pilot made off east.

Although the German pilots were slightly lower than the SEs and at a disadvantage, they stayed to fight, standing on their tails and shooting up at the SEs above them. The fight went on for some time, with no decisive result for either side – although Galley was hit in the oil tank and forced to land at the Advanced Landing Ground at Bapaume – and as the fighting got lower and lower over the wood, down to 8,000ft, the enemy pilots broke off the action and dived away to the east.

James fired a recall signal and reformed the Flight over Flesquières. British anti-aircraft fire over Trescault pointed out an LVG coming west over the village and James went down to attack it. Twenty rounds put the LVG up on one wingtip, the enemy gunner holding onto a centre section strut and leaning into the pilot's cockpit. The LVG stalled, then spun, before falling 'just like a leaf', taking three minutes to crash, before finally hitting a light gauge train in a vertical dive, knocking some trucks off the line, a few hundred yards west of Metz-en-Couture.[24]

James followed the yellow-fuselaged LVG down and circled for a while, watching British Tommies running from all directions to look at the remains of the LVG, before he flew back to Laviéville, 'feeling very satisfied, having totally destroyed four enemy two-seaters that day'.

On landing James was met by Balcombe-Brown, who told him that three enemy two-seaters had been reported as having been shot down in the British Lines by an SE5 and asked him if he were the culprit. James admitted that he was, but added there was a fourth.

This was the first time that a pilot of the RFC had totally destroyed four enemy aeroplanes in one day; the weekly RFC communiqué – irreverently known as 'Comic Cuts' – duly reported the feat and James received telegrams of congratulations from Trenchard and several other senior officers of the RFC. That evening the squadron's pilots went into Amiens for a celebratory dinner.

Although the weather was now bitterly cold, with the prevailing wind coming from the east, James would go up alone whenever he could, waiting at heights varying from 17,000 to 20,000ft. He knew that the German reconnaissance machines would be working over the Front Lines and British back areas, taking advantage of the good visibility. Many of the German machines, especially the high-flying Rumplers, came over the Lines at 18,000ft, confident in the knowledge that no British fighter was capable of reaching that height to intercept them, but James and his mechanics had tuned the engine of B4891 so well – and with the addition of what James described as 'so many little things done to it'– that he had no difficulty reaching 20,000ft whenever he wanted, giving the German two-seater crews 'quite a shock' when they were attacked from above.[25]

Snow and mist stopped all flying on 24 December. On 25 December – the fourth Christmas Day of the war – the snow and cloud persisted and only a small amount of test flying was done in the vicinity of the aerodrome, with the exception of James, who took off alone at 11.50. He flew to the Albert, Bapaume, Metz sector, but the weather was 'unfavourable'. He saw no enemy aircraft and he returned in 45 minutes.

The Squadron celebrated Christmas Day in the time-honoured fashion. The squadron's cooks had made a special effort over the Christmas dinner menu and the band played a concert in the evening. Although there was a certain amount of

Richard Maybery. The SE5a is almost certainly B506 (A) the aeroplane in which he was killed on 19 December 1917.

celebration, James commented that it was a quiet Christmas: 'Bowman our star turn in the Mess was in England on leave, having a thorough good time.'[26]

Boxing day was fine, with high cumuli, but only James did any war flying. Taking off alone at 3.00PM. he was out for an hour and fifteen minutes, but saw only a two-seater east of Lens at 3.45 and seven Albatri ten minutes later. He made no attacks on these, and came back to report that the clouds were heavy and building over most of the front of 3rd Army.

James took ten SEs off the ground at 8.45 on the morning of 27 December, but weather conditions were so bad that he washed out the patrol after only fifteen minutes.[27]

The morning of 28 December was a beautifully clear, crisp winter's morning: intensely cold, the glass showing 20 degrees of frost, but with excellent visibility. James liked nothing better than these conditions, which favoured his fighting methods. With the clear visibility and with a strong, north-easterly wind blowing in their favour, he knew that high-flying German reconnaissance aircraft would be out on photo-reconnaissance missions. He left Laviéville at 10.15 and climbed steadily for half an hour, reaching 17,000ft as he approached the Front Lines.

Almost at once James saw a Rumpler, slightly lower, coming from the direction of Bourlon Wood. Wasting no time, he got into a good position, closed the range to 75 yards and fired a short burst from both guns. The Rumpler went down in a right hand spiral, its right hand wings broke away from the fuselage after it had fallen a thousand feet and the wreckage fell in the British Lines, to the north of Velu Wood. The time was 11.15.[28]

Fifteen minutes James later saw another Rumpler, this one coming north over Haplincourt. He quickly secured his favourite attacking position and a burst from both guns sent the enemy machine down in flames, taking two minutes to crash – in a smother of flames – near Flers, twenty miles behind the British Lines.[29]

James had not followed the Rumpler down, staying at 17,000ft. He knew there would be more two-seaters in the area and he had no intention of wasting time in having to climb back to a worthwhile height in order to be able to make an effective attack. His reasoning was sound: British AA shell bursts alerted him to a LVG flying at 16,000ft over Havrincourt. James quickly overhauled the LVG, so fast in fact that the British gunners were still firing as he got within range. Throwing his customary caution to the winds, James flew through the bursts and fired a long burst at extreme range. He had not had time to secure a good position in the LVG's blind spot and he reasoned that this would force the enemy pilot to dive, making it difficult for his gunner to return fire. The tactic was successful. The LVG dived steeply away – James following, estimated that its speed was in the region of 200mph – and as it reached 9,000ft, James opened fire again, this time from only a hundred yards. Flames came out of the fuselage of the LVG and it broke up in mid-air over Havrincourt Wood, the wreckage falling in the British Lines.[30]

'Captain McCudden after a Hun.' Fellow pilot Henry 'Hank' Burden, a talented water colourist, painted this impression of James in action.

James climbed back to 18,000ft and attacked another LVG over Lagnicourt, again pointed out to him by British AA fire. The enemy pilot saw the SE coming and attempted to escape by diving away to the east, but James caught him up just east of the Front Lines and fired a good burst from his Lewis gun at a hundred yards. A small flicker of flame came out of the fuselage of the LVG, but went out almost at once. The enemy pilot dived steeply, kicking his rudder from side to side, skidding wildly in an attempt to throw James off his aim. Steam and boiling water were pouring from the LVG's radiator, which was mounted on the top wing, and James could plainly see the unfortunate observer frantically waving to his pilot as he leaned over the left-hand side of the cockpit in an attempt to evade the boiling water. James had scant sympathy, later observing: 'I hope the water froze over him solid and gave him frost bite'.

His petrol now being nearly exhausted, James turned away from the LVG and returned to Laviéville, landing at 12.35. He had destroyed three enemy two-seaters and badly damaged another. Although James considered that the last LVG, which he had last seen gliding down over Marquion, was under control and made no claim, Balcombe-Brown considered that it might well have crashed, but insisted that confirmation was needed from AA batteries before it could be confirmed as a positive victory.

In the afternoon, James and Balcombe-Brown journeyed to Flers to view the remains of the Rumpler. Arriving at the site of the crash they found only a charred mass of wreckage. James reflected again on the result of his work. 'It was a nasty sight and it brought home to me more than ever the sterner aspect of aerial fighting.'

The successes of the day brought James another telegram from Trenchard. 'Well done again. I wish I could have seen you to have said what I think.'

The next morning, James took out his Flight on a Deep Offensive Patrol, leaving the ground at 9.00AM. The Flight crossed the Lines east of Gouzeaucourt forty-five minutes later and spotted three enemy two-seaters flying west. James led the Flight down to attack these. The pilot of the LVG selected by James proved a wily customer. James fought him down from 13,500ft to ground level, where the enemy pilot switched off his engine, making as if to land in the British Lines. However, starting his engine again to clear a trench, he changed his mind and made a run for it, turning north east towards Havrincourt, flying only ten feet above the ground. Reaching the village, the enemy pilot turned east. Seeing that the LVG would soon cross into its own territory, James dived after it and fired another burst from close range. The LVG spun into the ground in the British Lines, only a hundred yards from the LVG that James had shot down on 23 November. James circled the crash, watching British troops helping the pilot and observer from their wrecked machine.[31]

James climbed to rejoin his Flight. Galley, McPherson, and Blenkiron had all suffered gun stoppages and the other two LVGs had escaped. Flying towards Bois-en-Vancelles, the Flight attempted to attack four Albatros V-Strutters, but these refused to fight, diving away east. Several enemy two-seaters were then seen, patrolling east of Vancelles canal, but these were at 3,000ft, too low to engage, and the Flight returned to Laviéville.

Within forty minutes of returning from this patrol, James took off alone. Visibility was good and he climbed to 18,000ft. Half an hour after take off he attacked an LVG that was crossing the Lines over Lagnicourt. Closing to within a hundred yards, James hit the LVG in the radiator. The enemy pilot dived very steeply, and was now both very low and too far east of the Lines for James to follow and attack again.[32]

It was nearly two hours, almost at the end of his patrol time, before James saw another LVG, over Gouzeaucourt at 15,000ft. The enemy gunner saw James diving to attack them and his

A Hannover CL.II. These two-seaters, known to the pilots of the RFC as 'Hannoveranas' entered service with the German *Schlachtstaffeln* towards the end of 1917, James reporting the first to be seen by 56 Squadron on 6 December. These Hannovers had plywood fuselages, were immensely strong, and able to absorb a great deal of battle damage. The C.IIIa, the most common variant, differed only slightly from the C.II, shown here.

pilot put the LVG into a left hand turn, the gunner firing at James from long range in the hope of driving him off. The strong wind was pushing the enemy machine to the west and James allowed the enemy pilot to continue to circle, knowing that he would eventually have to straighten out to reach the German Lines. As the enemy pilot finally made his dash for safety, James dived and began firing, continuing to do so until the LVG began to break up, then burst into flames, the right-hand wings breaking away from its fuselage and the remainder of the wreckage falling in the British Lines north west of Épéhy.[33]

The time was now 1.55PM: James had been out for two hours and twenty-five minutes, at the very limit of the SE's endurance, and he returned to Laviéville well pleased with his morning's work. 'I had a generous dinner, after which we listened to the gramophone for half an hour, and life again seemed full of cheer.'

That afternoon, James and Balcombe-Brown walked to the nearby village of Heilly to see some infantry officers they knew. It was a beautiful winter's afternoon, with snow underfoot and a brilliant blue sky above. They arrived back at Laviéville at 5.00PM, having walked eight miles in thick snow, and consumed 'immense quantities of toast and jam (not Tickler's)'.[34] The squadron's band played at dinner – music ranging from Poete and Paysan to Dixieland – and afterwards there was dancing in the ante-room and more music. James thought that the squadron's band, which he dignified by the appellation of 'orchestra', was wonderful, considering that it was a great boost to the morale of the squadron.

There was a thick mist next day, 30 December, and no war flying was done. On the last day of the year, only three flights were made: David Galley brought his SE back from Bapaume, where he had force-landed after being hit in the oil tank by one of 'Greentail's' Flight on 23 December, and Eric Turnbull flew two practise flights. During the day a correspondent from the Havas, a French news agency, visited the squadron. He stayed a considerable time, talking to Balcombe-Brown and the rest of the pilots. The remarkable run of victories credited to James was naturally one of the topics of conversation, and the reporter came away with a first-class story. This visit would have repercussions in the new year.

December had not been a good month for 56 Squadron as a whole. Seventeen enemy machines had been brought down, and one balloon, for the loss of four pilots: Richard Maybery in action and three pilots injured in flying accidents. Fourteen of the enemy aircraft credited had been brought down by James. In fact, during December 1917, James *was* 56 Squadron, the squadron's victory lists showing his name for no less than ten consecutive entries. By the end of 1917 James' official score stood at thirty-seven, of which only three relied on his own, unsupported, evidence, the remainder having been confirmed by other sources. This was a remarkable achievement. There can be little doubt that by the end of 1917 James was one of the most efficient destroyers of German aeroplanes that had yet been seen in the skies above France.

Ch.15: 1918: For Valour

Trevor Durrant with friend.

By the end of 1917 the concept of the earlier fighter pilots that air fighting was a sport – albeit a dangerous one – had largely disappeared. The war as a whole had taken a tremendous toll on the traditional British officer class. From the end of 1916, as the need for more officers became more prevalent, greater opportunities for commissions were given to new entrants into the army, and able men already serving were promoted from the ranks. Many of these newly commissioned officers joined the RFC at the commencement of their service; others after having served either as NCOs or subalterns in Front-Line regiments, and with their arrival at the fighter squadrons of the RFC the last vestiges of this 'sporting' concept was finally dispelled. It was recognised that the war was a hard, hazardous duty; that it needed to be skilfully and professionally fought, with carefully thought out tactics and methods. During 1917, brilliant flight commanders – of whom James was only one – began to emerge in the RFC: flight commanders who realised the necessity of a concerted plan of action, to fight as a unit, co-operating with other Flights and squadrons.

*

The New Year started slowly for 56 Squadron. Man-made differentials of time have no impact on nature and there was no change in the weather conditions that had kept the squadron on the ground during the last days of 1917. The first day of 1918 was misty, with low clouds. No patrols were flown, but three pilots took off on solo missions: David Galley, Alfred Blenkiron and James.

James had a double incentive to be flying. He knew that the squadron's victory score now stood at 249, that his own Flight's share of the total was 99, and he was keen to score both the squadron's 250th victory and his Flight's 100th. Despite the sub-zero temperature, James stayed up for two hours. The first possibility, a brown-coloured two-seater over Bourlon Wood, escaped by diving steeply behind its own Lines; the second, a Rumpler attacked over the eastern outskirts of St Quentin after a careful stalk of thirty minutes, was frustrated by his Lewis gun freezing at the critical moment and the ammunition belt of the Vickers breaking, made brittle by the intense cold. James landed at Estrée-en-Chausee for petrol before returning to Laviéville.

Whether it was on New Year's Day when the London newspapers arrived at the squadron or soon after, when they did arrive they were immediately the cause of acute embarrassment to James. They were full of stories of a fair-haired, slight, shy and delicate looking youngster, who spoke delightfully about his comrades, but also praised the courage of his adversaries, and who had scored thirty-seven victories, seven of them in two days. An article in Daily Chronicle, headed 'Young Lionheart of the Air' began: 'Over the snow-bound still ground of France, high in the icy sky, beardless boys of Britain have again been proving that they belong to the breed of the unafraid', then went on to extol the exploits of a 'steel nerved British lad, a tireless wonder'.

The Daily Mail, which had been campaigning relentlessly for more details of British pilots – not only their deeds, but their names – ran an article on 3 January by its feature writer Frederic William Wiles: 'Our Unknown Heroes – Germany's Better Way'. Wiles demanded to know why 'an Englishman whose hobby is bringing down sky Huns in braces and trios between luncheon and tea, and could already claim a bag of 30 enemy aircraft, should have to wait to be killed before a grateful nation can ever learn his name'. This last was a direct reference to Albert Ball, who had been awarded a posthumous Victoria Cross. Wiles went on to point out that the German Air Service was the most popular and fêted branch of the Kaiser's war machine, purely because the propaganda minded

Philip Fletcher Fullard.

Alan John Lance Scott.

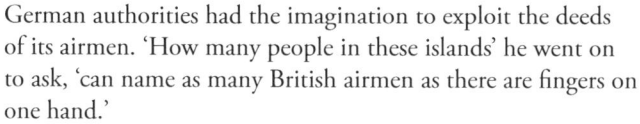

German authorities had the imagination to exploit the deeds of its airmen. 'How many people in these islands' he went on to ask, 'can name as many British airmen as there are fingers on one hand.'

Next came an article: 'Tell Us His Name'. After recounting the fact that a squadron (sic) had been reported as having brought down 99 German aircraft – this was an allusion to the score of 56 Squadron's B Flight – it ended: 'We have fighters better than Immelmann or Boelcke or Richthofen, and need we hide their light under a bushel?'

For the British public, to read of the exploits of its leading airmen, fighting in the clean air high above the squalor of the trenches, would obviously be a relief from the grim news of the fighting on the ground, with its seemingly never ending lists of casualties. It was argued that news of their fighting men who were continually beating the enemy would be a great boost to public morale. Lord Rothermere, the newly-appointed Air Minister, was a newspaper man and he was able to put the case forcibly to high command.

*

In France, the 56 Squadron pilots were unaware of these events; the war continued its relentless pace, broken only by inclement weather. On 2 January, although there were snow clouds at 400ft, James took off with a new pilot, Trevor Durrant, to give him some instruction in fighting.

The third of the month dawned fine and clear and nine SEs left the ground at 10.00AM – Turnbull leading A Flight as a top cover for James, leading B Flight. Fielding-Johnson and Truscott dropped out with engine trouble before the formation reached the Front Lines, but the remaining seven SEs crossed the Lines over St.Quentin and turned north. Flying north east of Bellicourt, James spotted a Rumpler, a little to the north, crossing the Lines over Vendhuile. James chased, caught up with it, and after 'some manoeuvring' got into a good position and opened fire: a short burst from seventy yards range. The Rumpler went down, partially under control, and James zoomed away, regaining his height. He had no intention of following the Rumpler down as he was well east of the front lines and a lucky shot in the engine of his SE could have brought him down in enemy territory. As James looked down to see if he could ascertain the fate of the Rumpler, his attention was diverted by seeing a lone SE fighting six

Baizieux Aerodrome.

V-Strutters over Vendhuile, five miles over the enemy lines. James immediately dived to the aid of this SE but was too late to prevent it being shot down, although the pilot made a reasonably good landing just behind the German front-line trenches. As James flew low over the SE he saw that it was marked with a large letter E on the top wing and realised that the pilot was one of his own Flight, Robert Stewart. To his relief, James saw that Stewart was being helped into a trench by German troops and that night he wrote to Stewart's parents, assuring them of their son's safety.[1]

None of the other SEs had gained any positive result and all were back at Laviéville just before noon.

On 27 December, Brigadier-General Higgins commanding 3rd Brigade had recommended James for a Bar to his DSO and during the day James learnt that this had now been approved.[2]

James took off alone the next day on his usual official duty of 'Chasing Huns', or as he put it in his autobiography 'looking for trouble'. Reaching the Lines, he saw a machine below him, just south of Bellicourt, and as he went down to attack it he saw it was one of the new Hannover CL.IIs, easily distinguishable by its biplane tail. James fired a good deal of rounds into the enemy machine, at close range, but it simply dived away from his fire, completely unperturbed. James, confident of his aim, was of the opinion that it was armoured.[3]

The Hannover CL.II was deceptively small for a two-seater and pilots often confused them with an enemy scout until they closed the range: 'when up pops the enemy gunner from inside his office, and makes rude noises at them with a thing that he pokes at them and spits flames and smoke and little bits of metal which hurt like anything if they hit them'. James had seen several of these machines since he had first encountered one in the previous December, and often saw them in their role of escorting the DFWs and LVGs of the *Flieger Abteilungen*.

The weather on 5 January was dull, misty and overcast the whole day. In the afternoon, James took off again with Trevor Durrant to 'practise fighting', commenting that Durrant was 'very good'.[4]

The first duty on the morning of 6 January was an escort for the DH4s of 49 Squadron on photographic duty. Two enemy machines were seen but only one DH4, and the escort passed without incident.

James took off alone at 11.25AM. He saw six Fokker Triplanes to the west of Cambrai – the first he had seen since the epic fight with Voss the previous September – but the adverse wind was strong, plus the odds were too great, and he returned, landing at 1.49PM.

For the next two days there was haze in the morning, with falls of snow in the afternoon, and there was no war flying.

On 7 January the Daily Mail announced that owing to its tireless efforts 'two of our crack fliers can now be named' and the paper carried large photographs of James and Philip Fullard[5] with the caption: 'Our Wonderful Airmen – Names at Last.' The half column devoted to James had all the elements of a natural, human interest story, telling of his military ancestors, his rise through the ranks, and his two flying brothers. It ended with a brief quote from his mother. 'He tells us hardly anything in his letters about what he has done, sometimes he just puts a line – "brought down two more Huns today" – but nothing more.' On 5 January, after the stories carried in the papers two days before, James had written to his father: 'You have no doubt seen all the bosh in the papers about me, and I want you to promise me not to send the papers any particulars about me, or photos, as that makes one frightfully unpopular with one's comrades.' But the letter had arrived a day too late.

Amelia could hardly be blamed for being extremely proud of her son's achievements – what mother would not be – and her modest account could hardly have added to James' embarrassment, but his reaction was unreasonable, even extreme. With his sensitivity, perhaps overly so in respect of the reaction of his comrades, he wrote an angry letter to his mother, telling her in no uncertain terms that in no circumstances were the family ever again to discuss his work

An official sketch plan of Baizieux aerodrome in 1917. Little had changed when 56 Squadron was based here in January 1918. On the other side of the road from the hangars and landing field, a brick house held the orderly room. Behind the house were the squadron's workshops; clustered around the house were the officers' Mess and quarters and the living quarters of the NCOs. Other ranks were housed in a brick barn, not shown on the sketch. The sketch carries the note: 'Aerodrome has decided slope down from centre to sheds.'

with the newspapers. James was very close to his mother, but he compartmentalised his service life and his personal, family life: each was private, entirely divorced from the other. This reaction was a repeat of the episode of his MC left in the kitchen drawer, and, as then, later resulted in a heartfelt apology to his mother.

*

The morning of 9 January was fine and clear. At 10.15AM, ten SEs – five pairs of fighting partners – left the ground on a DOP. James led his Flight across the Lines at 14,000ft over Flesquières, but it was forty five minutes before he saw any enemy machines: a pair of two-seaters over Bourlon Wood. James attacked the first, a Hannover, closing to within fifty yards, but his Aldis sight was useless, moisture having frozen over the lens, and he was forced to sight by tracer. The Hannover went down in a spiral with petrol or water streaming from it – James was unsure which – and he last saw it at five hundred feet, gliding down under control to the north of Raillencourt.

Fifteen minutes later the Flight saw an Albatros V-Strutter over Ribécourt. They drove this away, leaving it diving east. James then went down to attack an LVG flying over Graincourt at 9,000ft. After a short burst from both guns, the engine of the enemy machine stopped and it went down to the west in a flat spiral glide. James got under its tail and opened fire again, but his Vickers had a No.4 stoppage and he had expended his Lewis gun drum. The LVG continued to glide steeply, finally hitting the ground downwind at great speed.[6]

The bottom of James' combat report on these actions carried two comments by Balcombe-Brown. Of the first combat, with the Hannover – that Balcombe-Brown describes as a 'new type V Strutter two-seater' – he was of the opinion that this was an uncertain victory as no one had seen what finally happened to it. On the question of the LVG, owing to the speed with which it had hit the ground, with a strong wind behind it, Balcombe-Brown considered it to have been a positive victory. This was a double source of satisfaction for James, as he meant that it was the both the hundredth victory for his own Flight and the squadron's 250th.

Dinner that evening was another celebratory event – although as James observed, not as riotous as on the occasion of the squadron's 200th victory – and he received a telegram of congratulation from the new GOC of the RFC, Colonel John Salmond, on his Flight being the first in the RFC to have downed a hundred enemy aircraft.[7]

Strong winds, rain and cloud washed out all flying for the

Douglas Woodman. KIA 11 March 1918.

next two days, and although some test flying was done on 12 January only James did any war flying, taking off at 10.15AM. The clouds were low, at 5,000ft, and he patrolled close to the front lines, hoping to surprise any enemy two-seaters that might be working over the British trenches. He knew that the area of the canal between Masnières and Vendhuille, a distance of seven or eight miles, was a particularly favoured area of their activity, even in bad weather. After a while he saw two LVGs coming towards the canal from the direction of Vaucelles Wood, so he climbed above the clouds, flew east for a time, then came down, finding himself between them, both over Bantouzelle at 3,000ft. James got behind the rearmost and fired a good burst into it. The enemy pilot took no notice and flew on. James now came under attack from the other LVG but on turning to face it and returning its fire, it dived east. James was now very low; German anti-aircraft fire began to come up, including flaming onions, with their unpleasant 'sizzling', so he turned west towards the British Front Line.

James stayed up for over two hours, but saw nothing else within reasonable distance that was worth attacking. As he put it, the more he flew the more 'diplomatic' he was in what he attacked, and he flew back to Laviéville for lunch.

Conditions were much better on 13 January, although the visibility was 'indifferent' and there was a strong west wind. Although eleven SEs took off at 9.25 on a DOP, James was first in the air, taking off alone at 8.40. Fifty-five minutes later he saw an LVG flying north over Bellenglise at 8,000ft. James was up sun from the enemy machine and he glided down, secured a favourable attacking position to within fifty yards without being seen and fired his customary short burst from both guns. Pieces of wood flew off the fuselage of the LVG and it went down in a right hand spiral, gradually steepening, until it finally crashed just east of Le Haucourt at 9.40.[8]

James then flew north. Three Albatros V-Strutters were to the east of him, but he preferred to fight them nearer the British lines and he turned west, the Albatri following. Nearing the front lines, James turned to attack them, but they were 'off like a shot, and away, miles east of the Lines in no time'.

Ten minutes later James saw two DFWs being shelled by British Archie north east of Ronssoy. These were at 5,000ft, below James, and he at once went down, got into position behind the nearest and fired a long burst from both guns. The DFW immediately went down, pouring smoke and water, and crashed just to the north of Vendhuile.[9] James had time to make only a hurried note of the map reference of the crash[10] as he was being attacked by the remaining DFW. James fought this enemy crew for five minutes, but the pilot knew every trick in the book and flew very skillfully. As the fight finally drifted well east of the Lines, James, by now quite low, broke off the action and flew west.

No sooner had he recrossed the Front Lines than British Archie pointed out a pair of LVGs flying west over Éphéy. At 9,000ft these were slightly above James, and as he climbed to their level pieces of shell from a nearby burst from British Archie hit the SE. Undeterred, James flew on. The LVGs were circling over the British Lines, apparently unperturbed by a lone SE5 approaching them. As James came nearer they drew closer together in order to bring their rear guns to bear, but held their fire, waiting until he was in effective range.

James attacked the first from four hundred yards, firing two hundred rounds of Vickers. The LVG stalled, went into a vertical dive, its left hand wings fell off, and it burst into flames, falling in the British Lines just east of Lempire at 10.05AM.[11] The remaining LVG, anxious not to follow the fate of its companion, quickly dived away to the east and James let it go, wanting to conserve his height.

Twenty-five minutes later James saw a DFW crossing the British Lines between Gonnelieu and Gouzeaucourt. James turned west, hoping that the enemy crew would follow him further into British territory, which they did, the enemy machine being so close behind him that James could see the observer looking over his fuselage at him. James was so interested in noting the details of this DFW that he momentarily forgot its front gun, until the enemy pilot opened fire. Brought back to reality, James dived away with the DFW in hot pursuit. 'By Jove! It must have looked comic.'

However, James soon pulled himself together, did a climbing turn and got behind the DFW, which immediately turned east towards its own lines. James pursued it, all the way back to the Front Lines and beyond, but the crew of the DFW were very

Two views of Lester Williams' SE5a B610 in German hands. Williams was shot down and taken prisoner on January 28 1918 by *Ltn*. Schuppau and *Ltn*. Schandva of *Fl.Abt.(A)* 233. In the top view Schuppau and Schandva pose with the wreckage of B610.

experienced, knew how to handle their machine in self defence, and frustrated his every attack. His petrol now running low, James finally left them: 'and so they got home to dinner, and they deserved to'.

During one of the previous days of inactivity, James had had the spinner of the LVG that he had shot down on 30 November fitted to the nose of B4891 and painted a bright red. On his landing back at Laviéville, all his Flight were anxious to know if it had brought him any luck. Having shot down three enemy two-seaters in twenty minutes, James was convinced it had.

The apparent ease with which James had been destroying enemy two-seaters had come to the attention of the CO of 11th Wing, Lt.Colonel A.J.L. Scott,[12] who had requested that James visit the squadrons in his Wing to lecture the pilots on his fighting technique, and after lunch James took off to report to 11th Wing, at Bailleul. Based at Bailleul, flying Nieuports, was 1 Squadron, and as James knew many of its pilots he stayed with them for the next few days, using Bailleul as a base, flying the short distance each day to St-Marie-Cappel to lecture at 19, 20, 57, and 60 Squadrons (flying Spads, Bristol Fighters, DH4s, and SE5as respectively) before returning to Laviéville on 18 January.

The squadron had flown no patrols while James had been

Kenneth William Junor with his SE5a *Bubbly Kid.II.*

away, the weather having been extremely bad, with low clouds, strong winds and rain for the whole five days. On the morning of James' return, Bowman had taken out a strong patrol of ten SEs, but visibility was poor, the clouds were at 4,000ft, getting progressively lower, and he washed out the patrol after an hour and a half.

The weather had improved a little the next morning. Although it was still overcast, visibility was 'fair', and at 10.00AM thirteen SEs – three Flights – took off, under the overall command of James. As the formation reached the front lines, James saw that the clouds were higher over enemy territory and he washed out the patrol in order that the Flights could work independently.

C and A Flights saw a little indecisive action, but Eric Fetch[13] was wounded in the leg by Archie and forced to land at Bapaume, the advanced landing ground.

James and B Flight had a fight with 'Greentail' and his *Jasta*. James fired a good burst from below into the now familiar Albatros, but without result. He was then forced to break off the action by engine trouble and returned, landing at Bapaume. Finding Fetch's machine there – Fetch had been taken to hospital – James flew it back to Laviéville.

At 9.30 on the morning of 20 January another full squadron patrol took off, this time led by Bowman. After an indecisive engagement with a pair of two-seaters and five Fokker Triplanes, Bowman fired a signal, washing out the squadron patrol, and the Flights went their separate ways.

James took his Flight over Cambrai, patrolling over the area 'to annoy the occupants of the numerous Hun aerodromes which were in the vicinity of that town' but he then saw an LVG at 9,000ft over Bourlon Wood. James quickly got into position behind the enemy machine and fired a long burst into it from a hundred yards range. The LVG went down in a spiral for 4,000ft, emitting a great deal of smoke, before either its tail or one wing broke off, the remainder of it going down vertically to crash between Raillencourt and Cambrai, where it burst into flames. The time was approximately 10.30AM.[14]

An hour later, James attacked another LVG, this one flying north-east over Vaucelles at 6,000ft. James closed to within a hundred yards and fired three hundred rounds into the enemy machine, but his Aldis sight had fogged up owing to the warmer air at lower level and his shooting was inaccurate. In spite of this, the LVG went down very steeply, north east of Crevecoeur-s-Escaut at 3,000ft, water pouring from its centre section, but under control. James knew that his failure to destroy this LVG was entirely his own fault in not having had a normal ring and bead sight fitted in the event that anything should make his Aldis sight unusable.

As he turned away from the LVG James had distinctly felt a bullet hit his SE and apprehensively wondered if it had hit anything vital, as he was eight miles east of the lines and at only 2,000ft. All seemed to be in order but the German gunners, seeing James following the LVG far into their territory and knowing he would have to return, decided to have every gun they had ready for him when he did. Flying west, and being so low, he was literally bombarded, not only with conventional Archie, but from field guns, black and white *Minenwerfers*, flaming onions, and both rifle and machine gun fire. He was extremely thankful to finally cross the lines and return to Laviéville.

That afternoon, James and Balcombe-Brown visited a battery of anti-aircraft guns that co-operated with the squadron. These were commanded by a Major Rogers, whose second in command was a Captain Dixon. James found that Dixon knew every type of German machine operating over the sector and was told that his men could always recognise James' SE in the air during his stalking expeditions, often running up to him and reporting, 'Here's Captain McCudden'. Considering that the only difference between B4891 and other SEs was its smaller elevators, James thought them remarkably keen and was further impressed to learn that they knew at a glance the height at which any machine was flying.

James had recently realised that some high-flying Rumplers were every bit as fast at height as B4891 and had a better climb.[15] Making enquiries he had found that these latest versions of the Rumpler, the C.VII, had been re-engined with an extremely high-compression 240hp Maybach engine, had been stripped of the pilot's gun, ammunition and all other unnecessary equipment, and fitted with a specialised camera for use at extremely high altitudes, anything between 20,000 and 24,000ft.[16] In an attempt to catch these Rumplers, James was having the squadron's new workshops at nearby Baizieux fit a set of high compression pistons to a new engine earmarked for B4891.[17] The newly-pistoned engine performed well on the test bench, giving revolutions well in excess of the standard engine fitted to the squadron's aeroplanes, and James set about making further modifications to B4891. He had the exhaust pipes cut down by several feet in length – as he had to B4863 – and had the head fairing behind the cockpit removed. Flying for long periods at extreme heights, where the temperature could be as low as minus 30 degrees centigrade, James had often experienced severe agony as he came down and his blood circulation returned to normal. As a final alteration to B4891 he had a hole cut in the bulkhead of the engine and a simple shutter fitted with the object of providing some warmth in his cockpit from the engine.

On 21 January the squadron spent the entire day moving to a new aerodrome at Baizieux. The reason for this move is not known, Baizieux being only a field away from Laviéville, a short flight of five minutes, but the facilities were better at Baizieux, the landing ground less tricky, and these had possibly influenced the decision to move.

Although weather conditions were unfavourable on 22 January, ten SEs – B and C Flights – left the ground at 12.55, James flying SE5a B35 as a replacement machine for B4891, still having its engine improved at Baizieux. The Flight saw no action and James landed at Bapaume to collect B4891, leaving B35 to be later flown back to Baizieux by Lester Williams.[18]

There was no war flying on 23 January. Flying B35 back from Bapaume the previous day, Williams had been forced to land at Laviéville due to lack of oil pressure, and James, never one to stand on rank, walked over to Laviéville to fly it back to Baizieux.

James took off in B4891 on the morning of 24 January to test the weather conditions. He found that the clouds were scattered from 500 to 6,000ft and that visibility was bad. Consequently, no normal patrols were flown but both Bowman and James flew Special Missions during the day. Bowman took off at 2.10 but flew for only five minutes before returning, reporting that the mist was very thick.

James, however, who had taken off earlier at 1.45PM, found conditions were satisfactory. A DFW over Monchy-le-Preux was pointed out to him by British Archie. James went down and opened fire at two hundred yards, holding down his triggers while closing to within thirty yards. His shots evidently hit the enemy pilot as he could see the observer leaning into the front cockpit, attempting to take over control. James fired again and the DFW went down, alternatively diving and stalling, possibly because the observer was still trying to regain control.

James' letter home to his father on 30 January 1918 with his 'excuses' for not answering before.

At 4,000ft over Vitry the DFW finally went into a spin, and James last saw it at 2,000ft before losing sight of it in the ground mist.[19]

After firing at a balloon over Rumilly, forcing the crew to pull it down, James abandoned the attack due to a stoppage in his Lewis gun. The visibility now worsening, he returned to Baizieux.

The DFW was James' 43rd victory and his sixth since the beginning of 1918. He was the only member of the squadron to have scored in over a month, the last being Richard Maybery, who had shot down an Albatros scout in his last fight on 19 December.

On the morning of 25 January a thick mist over the aerodrome made flying impossible, but after lunch the mist had cleared and the day became fine. Ten SEs left the ground at 1.20PM on a DOP. The other pilots in the squadron were at last to see a change in their run of bad luck.

Bowman and C Flight were the first in action, attacking a formation of five enemy LVGs over Havrincourt. Bowman either killed or wounded the observer in one before sending another down to crash north west of Rumilly. Blenkiron, Mealing and Douglas Woodman[20] also each claimed a victory. Only one of the enemy formation had escaped.

James had led his Flight across the lines over Graincourt, taking them down to attack a DFW over Flésquières. All the Flight made good shooting at this machine, and after a final burst from Trevor Durrant it went down out of control to the

The wreckage of LVG.C.V 9775/17 being examined by RFC and army personnel. This LVG, from *Boghol* 7, crewed by *Ltn.* Werner von Kuczkowski and *Vzfw.* Erich Szafranek, was shot down by James on 2 February 1918 for his 47th official victory. Kuczkowski and Szafranek were both killed. The wreckage of the LVG was given the British captured aircraft number G.130.

south of Cambrai.

Ten minutes later the Flight had an indecisive fight with 'Greentail's' formation over Proville. Throughout the fight, Fielding-Johnson acted as bait for 'Greentail' in the hope that James could jump the enemy flight commander, but 'Greentail' was too experienced a pilot and refused to take the bait. As the fight drifted further east over the enemy lines, the Albatri getting lower and lower, the ever-cautious James broke off the action, reformed the Flight, and flew south. 'Greentail's' formation flew parallel with them as far as St.Quentin, where James attacked a Rumpler flying east of the town at 17,000ft.

After two hundred rounds from various ranges, the Rumpler went down over Urvillers, completely out of control.[21] Going down to attack the Rumpler, James had out-dived his Flight. He was now alone, and seeing Greentail's formation coming down on him, he dived away to the west.

Thirty-five minutes later James attacked a Hannover flying escort to an LVG. His attack had no apparent effect, but he had the satisfaction of driving both enemy machines to the east of Marquion before returning.

Although all the Flight had shot well at the DFW, James judged that Durrant had put in both the best shooting and had fired the final burst, and considered the victory should be credited to him. Balcombe-Brown at first refused to credit James with the Rumpler out of control over Urvillers, considering that further confirmation was needed from the ground as to whether or not it had crashed. However, information later came in from 5th Army infantry at Itancourt, confirming that the Rumpler had crashed and giving the map reference.

Bad weather for the next two days washed out all flying, but on the 28 January the day was fine and bright. The high compression engine had now been installed in B4891 and James took off at 9.05AM, eager to test the result. His hopes were fully realised. Opening up his throttle, he at once felt the extra power of the re-pistoned engine and he climbed to 10,000ft in nine minutes. James landed at 10.45, finding before he did so that the SE could reach 135mph at ground level. This improved rate of climb, vitally important in combat, was a considerable improvement. In official tests, the later production SE5as, powered by the Wolsey Viper engine, took nearly eleven minutes to reach 10,000ft, and it is reasonable to suppose that with a full war load they would take twelve minutes to reach this height. By his expertise and perseverance

James had improved the performance of B4891 by twenty-five per cent over the standard SE5a, a remarkable achievement, especially as it had been achieved with only the resources of a service squadron, with no official sanction or assistance, other than the set of high-compression pistons. James had alone taken the responsibility for the modifications to B4891 and it had proved an unqualified success.[22]

In addition to the higher performance of James' aeroplane, there were of course other factors that came into play. He was now a superb pilot, at one with his aeroplane, which answered instantly to the slightest movement of his hands and feet. He was also an extremely accurate pilot, an important element in wringing the last ounce of performance from his machine. Careless or slip-shod flying could in a moment lose valuable height, height painstakingly gained. At five feet seven, James was also below average height and his slim, lightweight build, all played their part in gaining an extra few hundred feet of altitude. Perhaps the most important element of all in his success was his exceptional speed in situation awareness, quickness of reaction and co-ordination of brain and body, that enabled him to evaluate a situation and immediately respond to it.[23]

Half an hour after landing from this test, James took off again eager to try conclusions with any Rumpler he could find. He found one at 19,000ft over Bellevue but although his new engine did everything he asked of it, serious gun trouble lost him an almost certain victory.

Ten SEs of B and C Flights took off at 1.20PM but only B Flight saw any action, attacking four Albatri over Bourlon Wood. The fighting was inconclusive, but when the Flight returned to Baizieux it was found that Lester Williams was missing. He had last been seen fighting with the Albatri and it was assumed that he had been shot down by one of them, but in fact he been shot down by the crew of a two-seater he had attacked and been taken prisoner. Although the morning's combat had shown no positive results, James had realised during the fighting that his machine was now a good deal superior to anything the enemy had in the air.

The next morning was fine, although hazy. Bowman took out C Flight at 11.00AM and attacked a formation of five Albatri over Beaurevoir. All the members of the Flight each engaged an enemy scout, but these all spun away and escaped east. Only the Albatros attacked by Kenneth Junor[24] was not seen to flatten out and Bowman considered it to have been out of control and awarded it as a victory.

James and David Galley were also out. Galley was forced to land by an overheating engine caused by a broken water connection, but James attacked a Hannover over Noyelles. The enemy pilot dived away, but flattened out at 6,000ft and made off east.

Conditions were still hazy on 30 January and no squadron patrols were to be flown until the afternoon, but James took off alone on a Special Mission at 9.45AM. Forty minutes later he attacked a Hannover at 12,000ft over Bullecourt, closing to a hundred yards and firing both guns, but the enemy pilot dived

Eugene Ronald Macdonald.

away, under control. A little later James attacked three Albatros scouts south of Vendhuille. He fought these for some time – evidence of his confidence in both his ability and the superior performance of B4891 – but was unable to gain a decision, and with the Albatri losing height, which he was reluctant to do, he broke off the action and flew towards Cambrai. Arriving over the town at 18,000ft he saw four enemy scouts climbing for their height over Anneux. When these had reached 14,000ft, James dived on them from his height advantage, a long curving dive that put him into position behind and below an Albatros. James opened fire from fifty yards – a short burst from both guns. Pieces of wood fell off the fuselage of the enemy scout, which turned to the left before going down vertically, smoke pouring from it, completely out of control.

James then turned his attention to another of the enemy scouts, a Pfalz D.III. After a short burst – again from both guns – the Pfalz spiralled down, then stalled, sideslipped for a moment, then continued to fall in a spiral dive. James last saw

Cyril Parry. Parry was a great admirer of James, an admiration he never lost. By the 1960s he had become a highly successful civil engineer. Behind his desk, the wall of his office carried a large studio portrait of James.

it over Fontaine at 6,000ft, still out of control. James next fired at another Albatros, that spun away from his fire. Another then got onto his tail and opened fire 'for all he knew', but James quickly reversed the position, got behind the Albatros and fired with a good burst from both guns until they suddenly stopped: the Lewis gun had finished its drum and the belt of the Vickers had broken. James had decided that the pilots of the remaining Albatros and Pfalz were 'very dud' and although he now had no guns he continued fighting them, 'feeling awfully brave'. At one juncture he nearly ran into the tail of the Pfalz, so close he could have 'thrown a bad egg if I could possibly have got one at that moment'. He chased these two enemy scouts as far as Cambrai, where he finally left them.

James regained his height and twenty-five minutes later, having replaced his Lewis gun drum, he attacked a Rumpler over Graincourt at 18,000ft. After James' initial attack the Rumpler began to go down and James followed, opening fire again from fifty yards until he had expended his Lewis gun ammunition. The belt of his Vickers gun having broken, leaving him no means of continuing the attack, James broke away. He had now been out over two hours and he returned to Baizieux.

James was certain that the first Albatros and Pfalz from the fight over Anneux had crashed, and after landing he telephoned the invaluable Dixon for confirmation. Dixon had witnessed the fight and confirmed that both had crashed.[25]

In the afternoon, B and C Flights flew a patrol, taking off after lunch. At 2.05PM, Bowman attacked an Albatros over Seranvillers, but was forced to leave it as he saw his Flight in combat with four Albatros V-Strutters over Wambaix. Bowman hurried to join the fight, arriving just in time to see Kenneth Junor shoot an Albatros down in flames.[26]

James and B Flight had seen the Albatri attack Bowman's Flight and had joined in the fight. One of the enemy scouts was 'Greentail' and James attacked him, firing a quick burst before zooming away. Fielding-Johnson dived to attack 'Greentail' after James, but lost air pressure in the dive and with no engine had to dive for 8,000ft, followed by 'Greentail'. Fortunately another SE saw Fielding-Johnson's predicament and attacked 'Greentail' forcing the enemy pilot to break away, enabling Fielding-Johnson to restart his engine and get clear.

The penultimate day of January had been a good day for the squadron. Three victories had been won, with no casualties. Sixteen victories had been claimed during the month and although eight of these had been awarded to James, five had gone to new pilots of promise.

Thick fog on the last day of January made flying impossible. Even James was unable to fly and he took the opportunity to answer the last letter he had had from his father. His excuse for not answering sooner is amusing. In the past fourteen days he had flown ten patrols and Special Missions; brought down five enemy aeroplanes; lectured other squadrons on his fighting methods; supervised the fitting of the high compression pistons to the engine of his SE5a; and had flown a number of test flights.

My Dear Dad,

Very many thanks for your welcome letter received about a fortnight ago. I have no other excuse for not answering before other than sheer laziness. Saw Jack this afternoon.[27] He is well. The weather at present is cold and bright, but visibility is poor, so the Hun is not very active.

My Hun total is now 45.[28]

Many thanks for the 1914 ribbon. I have quite a colour scheme now. I do not expect to be home much before March.

I am very content out here, and feel I am doing more out

A Bristol F.2b Fighter. This photograph was taken by James of Bristol Fighter A7163 of 22 Squadron in the autumn of 1917, when the squadron was sharing the aerodrome at Estrée Blanche with 56 Squadron.

here than I should be at home. No more news at present so must close trusting this finds you well as it leaves me at present.

Yours affec'ly
Jim

*

During the first two months of 1918, 56 Squadron still had over a third of its available pilots under training and full advantage would be taken of the bad weather in February to bring the squadron up to full operational strength.

On the first day of the month, thick fog blanketed the aerodrome and no flying was possible. The next day James took off alone at 10.25AM to test the weather conditions in order to ascertain if any patrols could be flown. Ten minutes after taking off he was in the vicinity of Havrincourt Wood at 10,000ft when he saw an LVG. James had not been expecting to see any enemy observation machines up, the weather being so poor, and the crew of the LVG, evidently having seen him, were flying east to the safety of their own lines. James opened up his new engine and overhauled the LVG – 'just as though he were going backwards' – estimating his speed was at least 20mph faster. The enemy pilot tried hard to evade James' fire but a burst from both guns sent the LVG down, first in a vertical dive, then passing over the vertical onto its back, shooting the enemy gunner out of his cockpit. The LVG eventually hit the ground in the British lines, a mile east of Velu.[(29)]

James was pleased by this unexpected victory. 'So now, having ascertained that the weather was good enough for patrol, I flew home to my aerodrome, where I landed just twenty minutes after starting out, having destroyed an enemy machine from a height of 11,000 feet, twenty miles away from my aerodrome. Gee! What a world.'

Thirty-five minutes later, James took off again. He found a high-flying Rumpler, but although he stalked it for some time it had too much of a height advantage and was too far over its own lines to catch.

Both Bowman and James flew Special Missions on the morning of 3 February, James taking off five minutes after Bowman had returned. Bowman had sent a two-seater down in a steep left hand spiral, but lost sight of it in the mist nearer the ground.

James attacked three Hannoveranas over Marquion. As usual his opponent soaked up his fire, although steam was pouring from its damaged radiator as it dived away, under control.

James took his Flight out after lunch, but the visibility was poor and they saw no enemy aircraft. This was the last regular patrol the squadron would fly until 16 February, the weather becoming even colder and conditions generally being unsuitable for any war flying. Bowman flew a Special Mission on 5 February, but saw only four Albatross V-Strutters that climbed away into the clouds before he could get within range.

James flew an engine test in the early afternoon, a short flight of ten minutes, but took off after lunch to fly another – a 'test flight' that lasted an hour and fifty minutes. He patrolled between Ypres, Lens, Arras, and the Scarpe, but saw no enemy machines.

SE5as of C Flight taking off from Baizieux in winter conditions.

Another two hour 'test' the next day, this time flying B35 and patrolling between Arras, Havrincourt and St. Quentin, was again unproductive. Although the visibility was fair, no enemy machines appeared to be working.

The weather was so bad during the next two days that even test flights were impossible. There were a number of horses available for riding at Baizieux and several pilots took the opportunity to ride in the surrounding countryside. Bowman was a particularly fine horseman, and two of the new pilots, Eugene Macdonald[30] and Cyril Parry,[31] were keen riders. Macdonald took on the task of teaching Trevor Durrant to ride and Parry persuaded James to try his skill. James, perfectly at home with man-made methods of conveyance, was less happy with the motion of a horse, laughingly remarking to Parry that he felt sure the up and down motion was caused by the animal missing on one of its cylinders.

On 9 February, Geoffrey 'Beery' Bowman was promoted to Major and given command of 41 Squadron. It was a sad day for the squadron. Bowman had served an unprecedented nine months with the squadron and was its last link with its early days in France.

On 16 February the squadron returned to operations. The day was fine, with good visibility, and at 9.35AM a large patrol of twelve SEs took off – B Flight led by James; C Flight, led by Fielding-Johnson, the new flight commander. The duty was an OP in conjunction with a patrol of Bristol Fighters from 11 Squadron that were flying a reconnaissance in the Le Cateau area. Giving the Bristols time to climb to their height, James led his patrol across the Lines at 16,000ft over Bantouzelle, with C Flight slightly below them. There were a great number of enemy scouts in the air, but these made no attempt to attack the SEs and flew off to the north and east.

Ten minutes after crossing the lines, circling Caudry while waiting for the Bristol Fighters, James saw a Rumpler climbing for height over the town. It was too good an opportunity to let pass. James dived, secured an advantageous position and fired a long burst from both guns. The Rumpler dived vertically and all four wings broke away from the fuselage that fell south west of Caudry, the wings following more slowly, falling over a wide area of the countryside.[32]

Ten minutes later, south of Bois de Vaucelles, James caught a DFW and shot it down in flames to fall at Le Catelet.[33] Turning away from the falling DFW James attacked an LVG, sending it down with water pouring from its radiator, but as he watched it go down he was startled to hear bullets hitting his SE. and looking up he saw 'Greentail' high above him. The enemy pilot had tried a long-range shot, but seeing he was observed, flew off east.

James fired a green light to reform the Flight. He had been hit in one of his elevators by 'Greentail's' fire, putting it out of action, and his Aldis sight and windscreen were both covered in ice due to a leak in his radiator. However, on crossing the lines over Hargicourt, these troubles did not prevent him from attacking a Rumpler. After a long burst from both guns, it went down in a steep dive to the south east, pouring smoke, and was last seen by Fielding-Johnson to go into a right hand spiral dive, apparently out of control.[34]

Making out his combat report after landing, James was delighted with Fielding-Johnstons' confirmation of the last Rumpler as it brought his number of victories to fifty, making him the first British pilot to achieve the half century. Balcombe-Brown, however, refused to allow the claim on Fielding-Johnson's confirmation alone. James was extremely annoyed at this, stamped round to the B Flight sheds, found David Galley's SE5a, B59 – Galley being on leave – had it fuelled and armed and took off again, only fifteen minutes after landing from the patrol.

By the time James sighted a possible victim forty-five minutes later, his anger had subsided and he stalked a Rumpler with all of his usual methodical calm. Realising that Galley's SE did not have the performance of B4891, he let the Rumpler get well to the west, climbing to its height while keeping between it and its own lines to cut off its retreat. The Rumpler pilot saw him, realised the threat and turned east, hoping to outdistance the SE, but James caught up with him over Lagnicourt. A short burst from both guns sent the Rumpler down in a vertical dive, until it broke up in mid-air, the wreckage falling in the British Lines near Lagnicourt.[35] No doubt mentally challenging Balcombe-Brown to refuse to allow *that*, James returned to Baizieux. Balcombe-Brown endorsed his combat report for this action, stating: 'This is the 50th enemy machine accounted for by Captain McCudden.' However, in the evening the AA batteries telephoned to confirm that the disputed Rumpler had been seen to crash, making this last Rumpler James' 51st victory.

Anxious to make up the time lost during the days of bad weather, and no doubt keen to break his own record – gained twice – of four enemy machines shot down in one day, James took off again after lunch, leaving the ground at 2.35, but he saw no enemy aeroplanes near enough to attack and returned after an hour and a half.

The weather continued fine on 17 February and James took off on a Special Mission at 9.50AM. There was a great deal of enemy activity east of Arras and James spotted what he thought were a pair of LVGs at 14,000ft over Guémappe, although closer inspection showed that they were an LVG escorted by an Hannover CL. On seeing the SE approaching, the Hannover pilot deserted his charge and made off, leaving James free to tackle the LVG without hindrance. James fired his usual burst from both guns and the enemy machine went down in a side-slipping dive to disappear into the ground mist.[36]

James now found that his Vickers gun refused to fire, something having broken in the mechanism, and he landed back at Baizieux to have it repaired, taking off again a quarter of an hour later. At 12.10PM he saw a Rumpler over Bourlon Wood. The enemy machine was at 17,500ft, five hundred feet above him, and James stalked it for the next thirty-five minutes, attempting to get up to its height, finally attacking it at 21,000ft when it was again over Bourlon. In his first attack, the belt of his Vickers gun broke due to the intense cold at that height and his Lewis stopped for the same reason. James managed to get his Lewis to fire reasonably well and chased after the Rumpler that was going down fairly steeply, but at 11,000ft over Raillencourt it flattened out, obviously under control.[37]

Artist Leonard Bridgman's dramatic depiction of the death of *Uffz.* Julius Kaiser on 18 February 1918.

James now felt very ill, which he attributed to the intense cold and the rapidity with which he had descended after the Rumpler, so he turned away. Reaching a lower level, being able to breath more oxygen, his heart rate increased, forcing his blood, made sluggish by the cold, around his body more quickly and he felt both faint and exhausted: When he landed back at Baizieux, the blood returning to his veins was agony: 'My word, I did feel ill'.

The rest of the day was successful for the squadron as a whole. Junor shot down an Albatros in flames east of Moeuvres; and in a patrol after lunch Fielding Johnson claimed an Albatros out of control near Fresnoy Wood. Maurice Mealing shot down another in the same fight, the enemy scout hitting the ground near Brancourt-le-Grand.

The weather on 18 February was still favourable, and the first patrol of the day was to bring a great deal of satisfaction amongst the longer-serving members of the squadron.

Taking off at 8.50AM. James led his flight across the lines over Moeuvres. There were few enemy machines in the air, but at 9.40AM James spotted a formation of four Albatros D.Vs flying north over Vitry-en-Artois. With the sun behind them,

Leonard Barlow's funeral in England. March 1918.

he led his Flight down. The surprise was complete. The first intimation the enemy pilots had that they were under attack was James' fire smashing into their leader's machine. The Albatros flew straight on for a brief moment, then burst into flames, turning over onto its side and going down, the enemy pilot falling from his blazing Albatros after a few hundred feet. James had a close view of the Albatros as it went down: it had the letter K and an inverted V on the top wing, and a green tail. It was 'Greentail', the squadron's old adversary. Momentarily reflecting that Maybery had been avenged, James flew on to the next Albatros, this one sporting a blue tail, and shot it down to crash between Beaumont and Quiery-le-Motte, just east of the railway and a bare two and a half miles from the wreckage of 'Greentail', which had hit the ground just to the north of Vitry-en-Artois.[38]

After shooting down the blue-tailed Albatros, James left the patrol. His radiator had boiled dry and he landed at Boiry St.Martin, the home of 12 Squadron, to refill his radiator.

The rest of the Flight had fought the remaining Albatri, but these had spun down and no further decisive results were gained.

Landing back at Baizieux, everyone was jubilant that, as they thought, 'Greentail' had at last been brought down. James reflected that whoever he was the enemy pilot had been 'a very fine fellow' whose fighting qualities he had greatly admired, and hoped that he was dead before he had fallen from his blazing aeroplane. 'He was a German, but he was also a brave man.'

That afternoon, James took off on a Special Mission. He soon spotted what he hoped would be his fifty-fifth victory, a LVG doing a shoot over the Canal de Escaut, between Rumily and Bantouzelle, but as soon as he attacked the LVG, which was at only 3,000ft, dived very steeply to within five hundred feet of the ground. James had no wish to follow it down so low over enemy territory and left it, at least having had the satisfaction of having spoilt its shoot.

James was first in the air the next morning, taking off alone from Baizieux at 9.35AM. The weather was good, if a little hazy. James attacked a pair of Hannovers over Rumily but these co-operated well, he failed to gain a decision and had to be content with driving them east.

From the Squadron Record Book it appears that James had now been excused his duties as a Flight Commander and he took off at 3.35PM, again alone. As he approached the lines he saw four Albatross V-Strutters flying to the east of Havrincourt. The enemy scouts were above him and coming down to attack. James, fully confident that in B4891 he could outrun any Albatros, turned west, thinking: 'You can chase me as far as Albert if you like, but you'll have great difficulty in getting home.' The German flight commander finally realising James' intentions, fired a parting burst from long range before turning his Flight eastwards again. Seeing this, James turned in pursuit, got within range and opened fire. But the enemy pilots had seen him coming and turned to meet his attack. After circling

William Sholto Douglas, Commanding Officer of 84 Squadron.

in the middle of the enemy scouts for some time James finally spun down, followed by the Albatri, but as he recalled: 'I was now an adept at running away when the occasion arose, so I soon outwitted them, and left them to fly back behind their own Lines, at a height of 2,000ft, under the fire of one of our best AA sections, for whilst they pursued me I led them over one of our sections north of Havrincourt Wood.'

The weather on 20 February was too bad for any patrols to go out and the day was taken up with fighting practise and test flights whenever the intermittent rain eased and the clouds had lifted a little.

James took off at 9.10AM on the morning of 21 February to test the weather conditions. Although the clouds were at 10,000ft he found that visibility was good, and he returned to take out his Flight at 9.45. Taking off, Junor flew into James' slipstream and crashed into the firing butts, but the remainder of the Flight carried on, attacking an LVG south of Vitry that evaded them and dived safely away. However, there was little enemy activity and the Flight returned at 11.55AM.

After lunch, James took off alone. He flew towards Arras and Lens, and soon saw a DFW at 9,000ft over Acheville, spotting for its artillery. James wasted no time. He dived, got into his favoured position, and from seventy yards fired just four shots from each of his guns. The DFW, hit in the petrol tank, immediately burst into flames, turned over onto its back and went down to crash on the railway line, just south of Méricourt.[39]

During the day James was shocked to learn of the death of Leonard Barlow, who had been killed in a flying accident at Martlesham Heath on 5 February. During their service together in 56 Squadron, James and Barlow had become close friends, and knowing that Keith Muspratt – another ex-member of his Flight – was also testing at Martlesham Heath James wrote for news of Barlow's death, also taking the opportunity to bring Muspratt up to date with the squadron's news, a strangely stilted, almost formal letter, very unlike his usual breezy style.

> On leaving 56 Squadron in March 1918, James took, or had taken, a number of photographs.

James with the NCOs and men of his Flight. Back row, sixth from the left, is Corp. Ernest Etherington. Front row. L to R.: Corp. E.A. Downing; Corp. Albert Card (James' engine mechanic); Technical Sgt Major. Peter J. Clark; James; Sgt. G.E. Vousden; Sgt. V.L. Reeves; Corp. Tom Rogers (James' engine mechanic); Sgt. G. 'Dobby' Dobriskey. All others unknown.

56 Squadron.
21-2-18
Dear Muspratt,

I hope you are well. I am writing to ask you if you would send me details of the accident to poor Barlow. I was so sorry to read of it.

The Sqdn are still doing well. B Flight, of course, is still well ahead. The Hun totals are as follows. 'B' 121. 'C' 85. 'A' 78.

Had the good fortune to get my 54th on the 18th inst.

Kindly remember me to Carr, Cronyn, and anyone else whom I know at Martlesham.

Trusting you will write soon and every good wish for the future.

Yours sincerely,
J.B. McCudden
PS. Bowman now has his majority and a DSO and is commanding No.41.

Less than six weeks after Leonard Barlow's death, Muspratt was also killed in a flying accident at Martlesham Heath.[40]

Low clouds, wind and rain stopped all war flying for the next two days; the only flying being practise fights with the Camels of 3 Squadron, based at nearby Warloy. The weather cleared a little on 24 February, sufficiently to allow a good deal of test flying, both of aeroplanes and guns, and the delivery of new aeroplanes from 2ASD.

After flying two engine tests in B4891, and testing a new machine, SE5a B121, James took off alone in the afternoon, leaving the ground at 3.10 to look for an enemy two-seater that had been reported ranging for enemy artillery. Fifteen minutes after taking off James saw it to the east of Bourlon Wood, too far off to attack before it flew back into its own territory. James waited for some time, but the enemy machine did not appear again. James returned. There was little enemy activity and he was feeling unwell with a heavy cold.

During the day, Brigadier-General Higgins had made a recommendation for James to be awarded a Victoria Cross. Heading the recommendation: 'For the very greatest gallantry, exceptional perseverance, keenness, and a very high devotion to duty', Higgins went on, listing James' achievements while with 56 Squadron, his aerial victories, the sheer number of patrols flown and his success as a Flight Commander, ending the recommendation with: 'I consider that he is, by the record that he has made, by his fearlessness, by the great service which he has rendered to his Country, deserving of the very highest honour.'

The weather clamped down again the next day, with low cloud, wind and rain, and there was no flying of any description. James spent the day in bed, nursing his cold, and was visited by Lt.Col. Playfair, who told him that he was to go

The ground crew of B Flight in front of B4891 '6'.

home in the very near future, giving him an express order that he was not to fly again before he did so. James was extremely annoyed at this unwelcome news. Although he had now been in France for seven months he still felt fresh, that he was at the height of his game and he was anxious to increase his score of victories to equal that of Manfred von Richthofen, whose last victory, his 63rd, had been in November 1917.[41]

Despite Playfair's injunction, James was determined to fly as much as possible before his posting to Home Establishment and he was delighted when the morning of 26 February dawned bright and clear. In spite of his cold, and having to successfully argue his case with Playfair over the telephone – James was too much of a professional soldier to ignore a direct order – he left the ground alone at 9.55AM.

James throat was extremely sore and he felt very ill but he pressed on, crossed the front lines at 15,000ft and attacked an LVG over Gonnelieu. The enemy pilot fought superbly, half rolling and Immelmann-turning the heavy two-seater – that was marked with a large letter '6' on the top wing, in a similar manner to B4891 – before finally getting away and diving east.

While James had been fighting the LVG three Albatros scouts had attempted to attack him, but had been prevented from doing so by three SE5as of 84 Squadron. James now climbed into the fight, but the Albatri dived east and made good their escape.

James then climbed to the north and at 11.20AM attacked a Rumpler crossing the front lines over Oppy at 17,000ft. He got to within 200 yards and continued firing until the Rumpler first burst into flames, then fell in pieces, the wreckage falling east of Oppy. This action had lasted only a minute.[42]

James then flew south and attacked a DFW and its Hannover escort over Chérisy. The DFW at once dived away towards its own lines, but the Hannover crew stayed to fight. James had fought Hannovers before, but although he had sent several down damaged he had never managed to destroy one. So now, although feeling feverish and light-headed, he made up his mind to shoot this down this Hannover 'or be shot down in the attempt'. He got into a good position, opened fire at 200 yards, and continued firing until the enemy machine broke up in mid air, the pieces falling near Chérisy. The enemy observer had fallen out of the enemy machine, falling into the British lines, but James knew that he must have been dead, as he had fired over 300 rounds into the Hannover at very close range.[43]

James then flew north, climbing for height. Half an hour after despatching the Hannover, he attacked two Rumplers at 18,000ft over Fresnoy. He attacked one of these, but switched his attentions to the other as it flew across his front, opening fire with both guns at three hundred yards until ammunition was finished. Pieces of the Rumpler fell off but it made its escape, back over its own lines.

Reaction now set in. James felt extremely ill. He flew back to Baizieux, feeling 'so ill that I thought I was dying'. On landing, he managed to get unaided out of his SE, but was ready to drop, and staggered into the Mess. However, after he had rested, had a hot drink and got warm, he felt a lot better and was able to make out his combat report, detailing his morning's work. Later, sitting in the Mess, thinking over the events of the morning, he was called to the telephone. The Wing Adjutant was on the line: the infantry at Bullécourt had found a dead German observer, assumed his machine was also down behind

1st A.M.F. Clarke (left) and Sgt. V.L. Reeves with B4891.

the British lines, but could find no sign of it. James apologised, explaining that the observer of the Hannover had fallen out of his machine but that the westerly wind had blown the wreckage just behind the German lines.

Reflecting later on the combats of the morning, James decided that the LVG marked with the large '6' on its top wing, and which had given him such a good fight, was a decoy, engaging his attention so that the three Albatros scouts could attack him. These had been frustrated in their plan by being attacked by the three SE5as from 84 Squadron, and the next morning James flew to Flez, 84 Squadron's base, to thank the pilots concerned. Anthony McCudden was serving in the squadron and was doing very well, having scored six victories since joining it the previous December, but James was quietly advised by the squadron's commanding officer, Sholto Douglas, that Anthony was very reckless. James once again impressed upon his younger brother the need for more caution. After lunching with the squadron, James returned to Baizieux to find that he had been invited to dinner that evening by the staff of 3rd Army Musketry School. He had known the chief instructor there for some time and was aware how interested he was in the work of both himself and the squadron in general. At dinner he met St. Rex Arnold, the well-known artist, who while James was preoccupied made a 'wonderful' caricature of him. James left the school with the sure knowledge that the men knew just how much they owed to the work done by the RFC; that everyday the corps was doing its very best to help the 'Poor Bloody Infantry'.

James took off alone at 2.10PM. on the last day of February. He flew for ninety minutes, patrolling at 17,000ft from Arras to Havrincourt, but although he saw several enemy machines they were too far off to attack.

On 1 March, James took off on a Special Mission at 10.15AM. It was to be his last flight with 56 Squadron: at least on this tour of duty. Although he found a pair of enemy two-seaters doing a shoot over the British lines, he failed to gain a decisive result and returned at 11.55AM.

Low clouds, high winds and snow stopped all flying on 2 March. In the evening the entire squadron – with the exception of Balcombe–Brown, who was on leave – journeyed to Amiens for a farewell dinner in honour of James. A room had been booked at Gobelins, and representatives of all the squadrons of 3rd Brigade were there. Fifty officers sat down to dinner, James sitting alongside Colonel du Tailles, the commandant of Amiens, who after thanking James for what he had achieved then made an impassioned speech, in which with typical French fervour the soul of the immortal Charles Guynemer cried out for vengeance, grateful for every *Boche* that James had brought down. James made what he hoped was a suitable reply, followed by more speeches by members of the various squadrons attending.

After dinner, infantry and artillery officers came in from an adjoining room and insisted on shaking hands with James. Colonel du Tailles then left to the strains of the *Marseillaise* played by the squadron's band. The evening finally ended with the entire company first toasting James, before singing *The King*.

James with B4891.

That night, in bed, James thought over all he had achieved with the squadron, regretting more than ever having to leave the life that was everything to him. Like many pilots, his squadron was his surrogate family and he unashamedly cried at the thought of having to leave it. However, as always, he rationalised his situation: 'I suppose life is full of disappointments, though I must say I've had my share of the good luck also.'

The next evening, James dined at Brigade Headquarters as the guest of Higgins – 'a very pleasant evening', and the following day, 4 March, was invited to tea with General Sir Julian Byng,[44] the commander of Third Army, who on behalf of his army thanked James for his work. To James, the erstwhile teenage air mechanic, who had arrived in France nearly four years ago, with the attainment of NCO rank perhaps his ultimate goal, to be now a highly-decorated captain, the most successful pilot in the RFC, now being personally thanked by a General for his work, must have seemed little short of surreal.

That evening the squadron gave James a personal farewell dinner, an event perhaps closer to his heart than the official event at Gobelins. All present – including many old members of the squadron – wished him the very best of good luck in the future. At the end of the evening James was presented with a silver model of his SE5a, B4891, a token of the squadron's regard and appreciation, for which all ranks had subscribed. James thanked them all, 'as well as my feelings would allow, and then said goodbye'.

The following morning, at 6.00AM, James left Baizieux – or as he put it, 'the dear old Somme country' – in a Crossley tender, driven by 1AM Swift, arriving at Boulogne three hours later in time to catch the morning boat, as always the good ship *Victoria*. Docking at Folkestone at mid-day, James was in London by the afternoon.[45]

*

James had been very happy in 56 Squadron. It was the first squadron in which, as an ex-ranker, he had been totally accepted. The resentment felt by some people – both officers and men – of his progress in the RFC, that had dogged him throughout his commissioned service life, had largely disappeared after his first month with 56 Squadron. There were still one or two people who begrudged him his success, but these kept silent in the face of his obvious talent and devotion to duty that far exceeded their own.[46]

It would be difficult to overestimate James' worth and value to 56 Squadron; his personal contribution to the achievements of the squadron was considerable. Since his taking over command of B Flight in August 1917, the Flight had been credited with 77 victories, with James' own share of the total being 52. This impressive total – over two fifths of the entire squadron score – had been achieved with the loss of only four pilots from his Flight, an indication of the excellence of James' as a patrol leader. His strategy had been simple: the greatest number of victories for the least number of casualties, and his whole approach had been coloured by this concept.

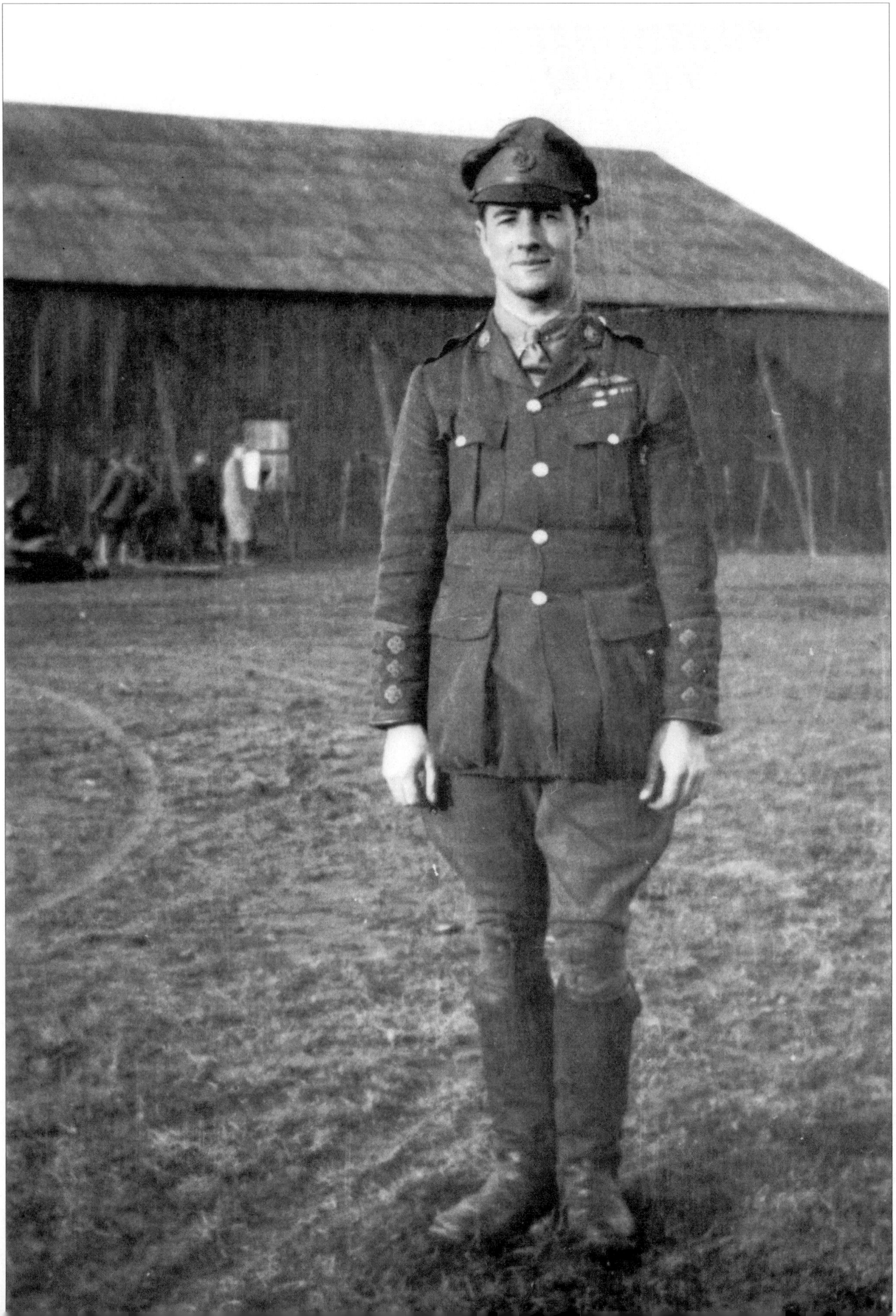

Cyril Marconi Crowe. Crowe was James' replacement as B Flight Commander. Crowe also took over B4891, but crashed in a forced landing at Martinsart. SE5a B4891 was badly damaged and struck off squadron strength. This was a sad end for the most successful SE5a in the RFC. Crowe escaped with bruises.

James stands proudly by the red spinner of B4891.

Facing Page: The Final Farewell. James by the sheds at Baizieux. March 1918.

The silver model of SE5a B4891 presented to James by the officers and men of 56 Squadron when he left for Home Establishment in March 1918.

Ch.16: Ayr and Turnberry: Teaching the Young Idea

The successor to the Sopwith Camel, the Sopwith 7F Snipe.

James was now on leave, but after spending the rest of the day with his family he went the next morning to the Air Ministry to ascertain if there were any details of his next posting. He was told that he was to report on 10 April to the No.1 School of Aerial Fighting at Ayr on the west coast of Scotland, where he was to be a fighting instructor.

James was never happy away from flying for any length of time and hearing through the RFC grapevine that several new types of scouts were being flown at Suttons Farm in Essex, he went there on 10 March and flew the latest product of the Sopwith factory, a Sopwith Snipe: a fifteen-minute flight, climbing to 4,000ft. Unusually, he made no note of the serial number of the Snipe and made no comment on its performance in his logbook, merely the bald statement 'Testing machine'.[1]

It was another eleven days before James flew again: a fifteen-minute 'joyride' in a Sopwith Dolphin[2] from Hounslow on 21 March, his longest period without flying since April 1916 when he had been awarded his RAeC Certificate.

Like many of his contemporaries, while on leave James spent much of his time at the RFC Club in Bruton Street; the company was congenial and he could catch up on all the latest service news. Coming down to breakfast the next morning after returning from Hounslow, he was told by another member that his brother Anthony was missing. James at once wrote to Sholto Douglas, his brother's commanding officer, asking for any further news.

Dear Maj,
I hope you are well. I have just heard from Stubbs about my brother and hope he may be alright. Rather hard luck. I wish you would let me know as soon as possible any news received concerning him.
I suppose you are at present fighting like the devil. I only wish I were out there. I am staying here until April 5th when I go up to Ayr (the Fighting School).
I hope your squadron is doing well. Child is doing the heavy over here, with a string of medals that damn near blind one.
Well sir, I must close now thanking you in anticipation of a line.

James' brusque 'rather hard luck' in referring to his brother may appear to be unfeeling, almost callous, but with no positive details of the fate of Anthony there was little else he could say to Douglas. For people in the fourth year of the war, civilian and service personnel alike, casualties were an accepted part of life in the times in which they lived: grief for the loss of close friends, even one's brother, was no less deeply felt for being privately mourned.[3&4]

The reference to James Child[5] 'doing the heavy' with his display of decorations – he had just been awarded the MC for his work in 84 Squadron – is amusing, given James' own not inconsiderable row of ribbons, even more so in view of the imminent award of his Victoria Cross, gazetted on Friday, 29 March, the details being given on 2 April.[6]

A Sopwith Dolphin, the RFC's first four-gun, single-seat fighter.

Victoria Cross
London Gazette 2nd April 1918

His Majesty the KING has been graciously pleased to approve the award of the Victoria Cross to the undermentioned officer:-

2nd Lieutenant (T./Capt.) James Byford McCudden, DSO., MC., MM., General List and Royal Flying Corps.

For most conspicuous bravery, exceptional perseverance, keenness, and very high devotion to duty.

Captain McCudden has at the present time accounted for 54 enemy aeroplanes. Of these 42 have been definitely destroyed, 19 of them on our side of the lines. Only 12 out of the 54 have been driven down out of control.

On two occasions he has totally destroyed four enemy two-seater aeroplanes on the same day, and on the last occasion all four machines were destroyed in the space of 1 hour and 30 minutes.

While in his present squadron he has participated in 78 offensive patrols, and in nearly every case has been the leader. On at least 30 other occasions, whilst with the same squadron, he has crossed the lines alone, either in pursuit or in quest of enemy aeroplanes.

The following incidents are examples of the work he has done recently:

On the 23rd December, 1917, when leading his patrol, eight enemy aeroplanes were attacked between 2.30PM and 3.50PM. Of these, two were shot down by Captain McCudden in our lines. On the morning of the same day he left the ground at 10.50 and encountered four enemy aeroplanes; of these he shot two down.

On 30th January, 1918, he singlehanded attacked five enemy scouts, as a result of which two were destroyed. On this occasion he only returned home when the enemy scouts had been driven far east; his Lewis gun ammunition was all finished and the belt of his Vickers gun had broken.

As a patrol leader he has at all times shown the utmost gallantry and skill, not only in the manner in which he has attacked and destroyed the enemy, but in the way he has during several aerial fights protected the newer members of his flight, thus keeping down their casualties to a minimum.

This officer is considered, by the record which he has made, by his fearlessness, and by the very great service which he has rendered to his country, deserving of the very highest honour.

In its issue of 4 April, 1918, *Flight* added:
1. The military medal was awarded to this officer (when a Flight Sergeant in the RFC) for consistent gallantry, courage and dash during the month of September 1916, in attacking and destroying an enemy machine, and forcing two others to land. He also twice crossed the enemy's lines at a very low altitude in attacks on hostile balloons under heavy fire.
2. The Military Cross was awarded for conspicuous bravery in action on February 15th 1917, on which occasion this officer followed a hostile machine down to a height of 300ft, and drove it to the ground.

James Martin Child.

3. Captain McCudden earned the bar to his Military Cross for conspicuous gallantry, dash and skill during the period of August 15th – September 28th 1917, when he took part in many offensive patrols (over 30 of which he led) and destroyed five enemy machines, driving three others down out of control.
4. The Distinguished Service Order was bestowed on this officer for conspicuous gallantry on November 29th–30th 1917, when he attacked and brought down an enemy two-seater within our lines, both occupants being taken prisoner. He also encountered an enemy machine during very bad weather conditions at 2,000ft and fought it down to a height of 100ft., when it was destroyed. Captain McCudden came down to within a few feet of the ground, and finally crossed the lines at a very low altitude. Subsequent to the award of the bar to the Military Cross to this officer he had been responsible for the destruction of seven enemy machines, two of which fell in our lines.
5. For his skill and gallantry on November 23rd, 1917, Captain McCudden was awarded a bar to the Distinguished Service Order. On which occasion he destroyed four enemy machines by his fearlessness and clever manoeuvring, three of which fell in our lines. He also dove his patrol against six enemy machines, driving them off.

On the initial gazetting of the award on 29 March, congratulations began to pour in, many from senior officers. One of the first was a handwritten letter from Major-General Trenchard, now Chief of the Air Staff.

Major General Hugh Trenchard, now chief of the Air Staff, wrote to James on March 30 1918 congratulating him on the award of his Victoria Cross.

Air Ministry. Hotel Cecil.
30.3.1918.
Dear McCudden,
   I was delighted to see that the King has awarded you the V.C.
   I am glad not only because (word crossed out) you have got what you have so well deserved but because of all the others in your old squadron and in the whole Flying Corps who get the reflected credit and are encouraged
   I hope your career will be as successful in the future as it has been up to now.
                                                    Yours, v.sincerely
                                                    H Trenchard

The popular press had a field day. In describing the details of James' successful combats it gave its imagination full play.
   He gave his engine her head, got within shot, pouring in pailfuls of Lewis gun ammunition, and used it all up. He let go on his Vickers and brought down two enemy machines in whistling somersaults of wreckage.[7]

Officers of 56 Squadron being presented to his Majesty King George V in the afternoon of March 29, 1918. It was during this visit that the King took the opportunity to tell the squadron that he had recently approved the award of the Victoria Cross to James.

These latest flights of fancy were a constant source of embarrassment to James. He wrote to a friend:

I see the papers are making a fuss again about the ordinary things one does. Why? That's our work. Why fuss about it? I'm so tired of all this limelight business. If only one could be left alone a bit more, and not so much of the hero about it.[8]

It must be said that there is a certain amount of disingenuousness in James' annoyance with the press. On Saturday, 13 July 1918, the *Daily Mail* carried an article, written by James, entitled "Voss's Last Fight", which he had sent to the paper with a covering letter:

'The enclosed is a description of the last aerial fight of Lieutenant Voss, who had shot down 46 allied machines up to the time of his death. It is a true description of a fight in which I may say my patrol was involved.'[9]

The publicity and the award of the VC also brought other unwelcome events. The diarist of the *London Evening News* wrote:

When I saw McCudden last he looked utterly miserable. He was being lionised at a smart West End house. An old lady was cross-examining him about the decorations on his tunic, asking him what each ribbon meant and how he had got it.

To offset these trials, the publicity brought James several new and influential friends who literally opened many doors for him. One of the friendships he made at the RFC Club was with Captain Harley Alec-Tweedie, who was at that time instructing at the School of Special Flying at Gosport.[10] Harley Alec-Tweedie's mother, Mrs. Ethel Alec-Tweedie, a woman of forceful personality, with energy to match, was an author, biographer, historian, journalist, photographer, and talented illustrator. An inveterate traveller, she had been widowed when her two sons were very young but this did nothing to curb her enthusiasm for travel and she was reputed to have visited nearly every country in the world. Leslie, her youngest son, had been killed while serving in the RFC in 1916, and throughout the war she was a driving force behind many charities, including those providing for servicemen. Her flat in Whitehall court was the meeting place of many important and influential people, and was also invariably crowded with friends of her sons.[11]

Harley Alec-Tweedie took James along to one of his mother's soirées and introduced him. Mrs. Alex-Tweedie was immediately struck by James' sincerity and openness.[12] Talking with James, she realised that his life had been one of remarkable achievement and she persuaded him that he should write of it. Later, he diffidently showed her his old red-covered exercise book diary, asking her advice as to whether it could be the basis of a book. She was impressed by the straightforward factual style of his writing, and assured him that a book was well

Ethel Brilliana Alec-Tweedie.

within his capabilities, but James was startled to hear that more than fifty times that amount of words would be needed.

James also met C.G.Grey, the outspoken, often controversial editor of *The Aeroplane*, whose office was only a short distance from the RFC Club. Grey immediately saw the potential of a book by James, not only as a record of his success as a fighter pilot, but as a unique record of the early days of the RFC, and volunteered to read the manuscript, help with any editing that might be needed, and ensure it was published.

James also heard from Maurice Baring, now at the Air Ministry with Trenchard, who told him that William Orpen would like him to sit for his portrait. Orpen had been lunching at the Ritz with Baring, the subject of James' award of the VC was touched upon, and Baring told Orpen that James was in London, reminding him that James was the young pilot whose name he had not known but whom he had beaten at table tennis during his visit to 56 Squadron in the summer of 1917. Orpen said that he would very much like James to sit for his portrait. 'Well, write and ask him', Baring said. Orpen demurred, objecting that he did not know James well enough. 'Right', Baring said, 'I'll write to him'.[13]

A sitting was arranged. Orpen later recalled: 'One morning I heard a cheery voice below and someone came bounding upstairs, and before I saw him he shouted: "Hello Orps – have you a ping-pong table here?" He was the little unknown boy at the 56th Squadron with whom I used to play ping-pong with only a few months before. Now he was the great hero, Major McCudden, V.C., D.S.O., etc., and well he wore his honours, and, like all great people, sat like a lamb.'[14]

As the press coverage continued, James was claimed as a native son by various counties. To the London newspapers he was a Londoner; to the various Surrey weeklies he was a Surrey man, because of his family home in Kingston. To the Irish papers he was of Irish birth. His actual birthplace in Kent became the subject of furious claims and counter claims by the neighbouring boroughs of Chatham and Gillingham. After the gazetting of James' V.C., Chatham had begun to make plans for a suitable presentation. When the Mayor of Gillingham heard of these plans he wrote with some asperity to the local newspaper, the Rochester and Gillingham News , demanding that the paper state that James had been born in the barracks of the Royal Engineers at Gillingham and was therefore a Gillingham man. The editor of the paper accurately pointed out that due to a subsequent adjustment of the local county boundaries, the register recorded that James had been born in Chatham. The Mayor responded with a copy of James' birth certificate, written proof that the Female Hospital of Brompton Barracks was in Gillingham.

This undignified wrangle went on for some time until James himself intervened. Writing from Scotland on 29 April, he tactfully pointed out to the Chatham Borough Council that although he was highly appreciative of the interest shown in him by the residents of Chatham, and having many friends in the borough, he must point out that he had been born in Gillingham, had lived for nine years at 22 Belmont Road in the town, until his parents had moved to Chatham, and that he must consider himself a native of Gillingham.

The issue having been resolved, on 4 June 1918, Gillingham Borough Council unanimously voted to bestow on James its highest honour, as an Honorary Freeman of the Borough. In addition it opened a subscription list for a suitable monetary award to be made to him. James wrote to the borough, thanking them for the honour, expressing his appreciation, but asking that any money subscribed be invested in War Bonds to assist the war effort.

*

One of the far-reaching changes, brought about by the heavy casualties suffered by the RFC in late 1917 and early 1918, was the realisation of the need for dedicated facilities to improve the training of pilots.[15] Training time was increased from fifteen hours to at least fifty hours, with the final stages devoted to instruction in combat techniques at specialised schools of aerial fighting, staffed by experienced pilots who had served at least one tour of duty in France. In late February, early March 1918, one of these schools, No.1 School of Aerial Fighting, was set up at Ayr on the west coast of Scotland, and its commanding officer Lieutenant-Colonel Lionel Rees, VC, took up command on 7 March 1918.[16]

Although situated on relatively flat land – the actual

aerodrome at Ayr was on the peacetime race course – it was hardly an ideal location for a training establishment. The mountains of the Southern Uplands, only a few miles to the south, and the sea, with its frequent, thick mists, were both recipes for disaster if any inexperienced pupil became lost or disorientated while flying. However, its remote location made it suitable for both air-to-ground and air-to-air gunnery, and the nearby railway line made it easily accessible for the arrival of large numbers of pupils.

*

On 10 April James travelled up to Ayr – presumably by train as no flight is recorded in his logbook – to report for duty at the school. He was interviewed by Lionel Rees, who outlined his various duties. Pupils would first be tested to ensure their basic flying skills were adequate. They were then to be taken up in a two-seater with a fighting instructor at the controls for a mock aerial combat against another machine, the instructor explaining fully the reasons for each manoeuvre. The next stage was for the pupil to fly in mock combat against his instructor. These stages, and others, were to be repeated until the instructor was satisfied that the pupil had mastered the fundamentals of combat techniques in both attack and defence. Instructors would also act as flight commanders, flying with a number of pupils to teach them the basics of formation flying and the manoeuvres they would be expected to carry out, in formation, when with their squadrons on active service.

During their training pupils would fly machines fully-armed with live ammunition, firing at both moving and stationary ground targets, and their gunnery skills in the air would be honed by firing at flag targets, marked with the crude outline of an aeroplane, towed behind another machine. Finally, to ascertain and improve their gunnery skills still further, advanced pupils armed with cine camera guns would fly in mock combat against both their fellow pupils and their instructors.

James made his first flights at Ayr the next day, flying a Bristol M.1C[17] – his first flight in the type – for thirty minutes and an SE5a for ten minutes, both being test flights. The following day he flew an Albatros D.I, commenting in his logbook, 'a nice old machine'.[18] James finished the day with brief flights in a Sopwith Camel and a Avro 504.

The morning of 14 April was taken up with a recreational flight in an Avro 504, James piloting a fellow instructor, Captain Taylor, for lunch at Sundrum Castle, five miles from Ayr.[19]

James flew a Bristol M.1C (C4955) in the afternoon, a short flight of thirty minutes to test the weather conditions, which he found to be hazy and unsuitable for any instructional work, and he finished the day's flying by testing SE5a (B660) for twenty minutes, climbing to 4,000ft.

James carried out a good deal of flying on 15 April. He tested an Avro 504J (A9786),[20] had a practice flight in the Albatros D.I, then practised fighting in SE5a B660[21] with Cyril Foggin.[22] This was followed by a twenty-minute practise dogfight – unfortunately his log book does not state with

The Orpen portrait of James.

whom – with James flying a Bristol M.1C (C4955).[23]

In the afternoon he tested the same Bristol monoplane, recording that he reached 10,000ft in seven minutes and 12,000ft in nine. James finished his day as a passenger in a Bristol Fighter flown by Captain J.H.T. Letts, 'taking photographs'.[24]

That evening in the Mess, James was delighted to see a familiar face: Gerald Constable Maxwell, his old comrade from his first days in 56 Squadron when Gerald had commanded A Flight. Gerald Maxwell had been instructing at Ayr – he was in command of C Flight at the school – since the previous November, had been on a short leave in London and had caught the morning train back to Ayr.

The next morning, James took off in Bristol M.1C C 4955 to test its climb, reaching 22,000ft – the highest he had ever flown – in 35 minutes with the pitot tube showing 70 mph, a further demonstration of the excellence of the little Bristol monoplane.

James' next flight of the day was a light-hearted practise combat with Gerald Maxwell: Gerald in an SE5a and James in a Bristol Fighter. Unfortunately neither of their logbooks

Officers of the No.1 School of Aerial Fighting at Ayr, April 1918. Front row. L to R. G.C. Maxwell.MC; W.D. South; S.W. Taylor. MC; K.H. Marshall; L.W.B. Rees.VC. MC.(commanding officer) J.W.Woodhouse.DSO.MC; F. Paterson; James McCudden. VC.DSO.MC.MM.CdeG; F.M. Thomas. Second row. R.J. Sladden.DCM; A.D.C. Browne; J.D. Atkinson; J.R. Bost; L.A. Foers. MC; H.D. Edwards; J.D. Rollo.CdeG; J.M. Burd.MC; I M Harris. Third row. R.M. Makepeace.MC; E.L. Zink; J.R.G. Rowden; R.W. Farquhar; H.W. Elliott; D. Sutherland; H.L. McNaughton; R.W. Weatherby; H.B. Redler.MC. Fourth row. D.H. de Burgh; W.A.G. Young; F.M. Howard; H Jones; A. Armstrong. The number of decorations won by the majority of the pilots in this group is indicative of the combat experience of the instructors at Ayr.

records the outcome, but it must have been well worth seeing. Later in the day, James flew a Spad for the first time, commenting 'nice machine', and finished the day's flying by testing an Avro 504.

The next three days were taken up with routine testing and practice flights: an Avro 504, with an air mechanic in the rear cockpit; a Camel; a Bristol fighter – again with an air mechanic as a passenger – and two Bristol M.1Cs: C4960, and C4955. This last was to become James' personal aeroplane at Ayr and his favourite Bristol.

Ayr was a happy station. In addition to the daily instruction of pupils there was also good deal of social life that entailed flights to and from various locations for lunches and dinners, and James did a great deal of local cross county flying on these visits.

On 23 April, James travelled down to London for a short leave. While in town he visited Orpen for another sitting, visited various friends, and caught up on all the latest service gossip and rumours at what was now the RAF Club.[25]

On the 28th, the penultimate day of his leave, James travelled down to Joyce Green aerodrome to renew contacts with old friends. One was sadly missing: Harold Barnwell, the Vickers test pilot who had taken such an interest in James when he had been stationed at Joyce Green in 1916, had been tragically killed in August 1917 while flying the prototype Vickers FB.26.

While at Joyce Green, James met Arthur Gould Lee, who was instructing there on Sopwith Camels. Gould Lee had served in 46 Squadron from May 1917 until January 1918, first flying Sopwith Pups, then Sopwith Camels. He had flown through – and survived – the Cambrai battles in November 1917, when 46 Squadron had been used in low-level ground strafing, suffering many casualties as a result. Gould Lee and James reminisced over the Cambrai battles, James agreeing wholeheartedly with Gould Lee's opinion that experienced fighter pilots were wasted in such hazardous work.[26]

While at Joyce Green, the Vickers test pilot, now J.P. Chataway, showed James the latest development of the Vickers FB.26 Vampire[27] and allowed James to fly it: first for five minutes at five hundred feet in circuits and bumps around the aerodrome, then for ten minutes, testing its climb to 2,000ft.

While James was at Joyce Green the Vickers Company made him the generous offer of an indefinite loan, for his personal use, of the second prototype Vickers FB.16D, A8963. James had flown the first prototype – named affectionately 'Pot Belly' by Harold Barnwell – in July 1917 and was delighted with his new acquisition, a delight that was to be tempered over the next few days.[28]

On the afternoon of 1 May, his leave over, James left Joyce Green in the FB.16D to return to Ayr. It was to be the most frustrating flight of his life. The weather in the south of England was good and he planned to refuel at Hooton Park on the south bank of the Mersey at Liverpool, but as he flew north-west the clouds began to thicken. To add to his concern over the worsening weather, his engine began to periodically cut out and he had to force-land in a field outside Coxteth, a village to the east of Liverpool. An examination of the engine revealed that the carburettor float was sticking. This was easily remedied but it was now late and the weather was closing in, so James spent the night in the Vickers, flying on the next morning to Hooton, a short flight of only ten minutes. After refuelling, James took off again to ascertain the weather conditions. Finding they were too bad to continue with reasonable safety, he stayed the night at Hooton – presumably in more comfortable accommodation.

The next morning the weather had improved and he set off again, but soon after crossing into Scotland the weather had deteriorated to such an extent that he was again forced to land, this time at the village of Closeburn, ten miles north-west of Dumfries, still over fifty miles south-east of his destination.

Conscious of the Southern Uplands to the south of Ayr, James waited until the weather was a little clearer, then took off again, successfully making the twenty-minute flight to Ayr at the safe height of 5,000ft. Even though the FB.16D was reputedly one of the fastest aeroplanes in the world – at times he had been flying at more than 150mph – it had taken James three days to reach Ayr from Joyce Green, a flight that should have taken only three hours.[29]

Over the next five days James carried out his usual instructional duties, flying his Bristol M.1C (C4955), an SE5a, and an Avro 504, not flying his Vickers again until the afternoon of 8 May, when he tested it in a thirty-minute flight from Ayr to Mauchline and back. Since his return flight of three days before, the engine of the Vickers had been thoroughly overhauled, James had improved its handling characteristics by adjusting the incidence of the tailplane, and had rectified its annoying habit of leaking oil onto the trouser legs of its pilot by fitting a breather to discharge it harmlessly elsewhere.

James flew another test in the Vickers the following morning and on 10 May flew it twice: first in a fifteen-minute practise combat flight, then flying from Ayr to Turnberry and back, testing its rate of climb, reaching 10,000ft in seven and a half minutes and to 15,000ft in thirteen and a half minutes.

James' last flight of the day was in an Avro 504J (D27),

James, his attention elsewhere other than on the cameraman.

a flight that was have an embarrassing result. One of the instructors at Ayr was James Latta,[30] whose home was at Failford House, only six miles from Ayr. After their day's instructing duties, Latta invited James to meet his family and they both flew to Failford House in the Avro, landing in a field at the front of the house.

Mary, Latta's vivacious young sister, was thrilled to be introduced to James, doubly impressed by his standing as Britain's top-scoring fighter pilot and his impressive row of decoration ribbons, and she pleaded with him to take her for a flight in the Avro. Although joy rides for civilians was supposedly against the rules, Lionel Rees generally turned a blind eye to any infringements, many of the instructors at Ayr

The Bristol M.1C. The Bristols were a great favourite of the instructors at Ayr and Turnberry who used them as personal aeroplanes. This view of C5017 shows the clean lines of the little fighter.

took visiting friends and family members for short joyrides, and Mary Latta finally persuaded a far from reluctant James to take her up.[31]

Having installed Mary in the Avro, James took off and climbed to 2,000ft. In the front cockpit, Mary was thoroughly at home in the air, enjoying herself immensely, and was excitedly pointing out local landmarks to James when after a few preliminary splutters the engine of the Avro stopped dead. They had come too far to be able to return to Failford and James immediately checked the terrain below for a suitable landing field. Mary was unaware of any problem, thinking the comparative silence of the glide all part of the flight, and seemed quite unperturbed, even when James shouted above the slipstream to tell her that they would have to make a forced landing.

James selected a suitable field, judged his approach with all his usual skill, and put the Avro gently down in a perfect three-pointer but as it slowly bumped to a standstill James suddenly realised that there was a wide gully, right in its path. He just had time to shout a quick warning to Mary to brace herself, before the Avro lurched into the gully, went down on its nose then turned slowly over onto its back.

James hurriedly scrambled out and extricated Mary from the front cockpit. Luckily neither was hurt, but James was considerably shaken by the thought that Mary could have been injured and was somewhat brusque with a crofter who arrived at the scene, asking if he could help. They had come down at Mauchline, a village some two and a half miles from Failford, and a call to Failford House brought a car to take Mary home. James telephoned Ayr, asking for a tender to pick him up and to bring a guard to place over the Avro.

A Crossley tender duly arrived, driven by a young girl, Ruby Williamson,[32] one of the recruits of the recently formed Women's Royal Air Force, and after leaving a guard over the Avro, they set off to drive back to Ayr.

James was a figure of hero worship to the girls of the WRAF at Ayr, his photograph pasted in many of their albums, and Ruby Williamson was no doubt thrilled with her duty of driving James. If so, she was disappointed. James, no doubt still a little shaken by the near escape Mary Latta had had from serious injury and the possible consequences when Lionel Rees heard of the incident – as he surely would – said almost nothing throughout the ten miles drive back to the aerodrome, only speaking once. It was becoming dark, but Ruby was reluctant to break the silence to ask permission to stop and light the headlamps of the Crossley – its only door was on the passenger side – until James suddenly suggested that it was about time to stop and light up. This done, the journey continued, again in silence, until they arrived back at Ayr and Ruby deposited James outside the officers' mess. As he climbed

Some of the instructors at Ayr had their Bristols painted in individual colour schemes. One example was C4940 which was painted with longitudinal white stripes on the wings and fuselage, three white flashes on each wheel cover, and a white band on its spinner.

out of the Crossley James remembered his manners, turned to Ruby, smiled, and said: 'Goodnight, and please forgive me for being such a boor.'[33]

During the drive, James had thought on how best to explain the breach of discipline to Rees and had decided that the only course of action was to make a clean breast of the whole affair and hope for the best. If he hoped that Rees, in view of his record and standing, would perhaps be a little inhibited at serving out too strict an admonishment to him, James was mistaken. On reporting to Rees' office the next morning, James found that his C.O had no inhibitions in delivering a severe dressing down to a holder of a Victoria Cross. Rees also wore the unobtrusive maroon ribbon of Britain's highest award for gallantry, and his resultant reprimand must have reminded James of that long ago lecture by Sykes at Farnborough in 1913. At its conclusion, Rees then declared the matter closed. Very few at Ayr knew the full story of the episode, but it was common knowledge that James had received a ticking off of rare quality.

On 11 May the No.1 School of Aerial Fighting moved twenty miles south along the coast to the aerodrome at Turnberry, which had been the base of the No.2 Auxiliary School of Air Gunnery since January 1917. The two schools were now amalgamated to become the No.1 School of Aerial Fighting and Gunnery, the courses being expanded in order to train the pilots and gunners of the two-seater fighters, and the crews of the two-seater day bombers.

The school at Turnberry consisted of four Flights: one each of Sopwith Camels, SE5as, Bristol F.2B Fighters, and DH9s. In addition there were the instructors' Bristol M.1Cs, Avro 504Js and Ks, Spads, and several Sopwith Pups. Courses were in two stages. First was an intensive ground gunnery course, then mock combat training in the air. The targets for air-to-ground gunnery were moored out to sea, and each pupil's performance in mock aerial combats was again recorded by camera guns. Various gunnery aids were also improvised, including a moveable mock up of a fuselage armed with a gun, giving pupils the opportunity to fire at small model aeroplanes set up on the firing range. Station dogfights were held twice weekly with pupils versus instructors, the pupils' performance again being assessed by their cine camera gun results.

At Turnberry, the administrative staff, instructors, and pupils were all housed in the splendidly luxurious Turnberry Hotel. Requisitioned from the GSW Railway, the hotel was in an elevated position on the fringe of the famous peacetime golf course, which was on the edge of the cliffs overlooking the

James with his personal favourite, Bristol M.1C. C4955.

sea.(34) The Flight offices and hangars bordered the golf course, but the position of the landing field was far from ideal: flanked by the sea, and with the high wooded hills to the east making landings difficult when the wind was from certain directions.

Turnberry was a happy station with a relaxed atmosphere. Although kept extremely busy, the instructors, free from the stresses of operational flying, could enjoy flying for its own sake. Unlike the instructors of the early war years, who tended to regard their pupils as a nuisance, referring to them as 'Huns', and who had little or no social contact with them, the instructors at Turnberry fully realised the importance of their work, carried out their duties conscientiously, and enjoyed passing on their hard-won expertise to their pupils. On the northern edge of the aerodrome was a farmhouse that served excellent mid-morning snacks, and after a morning's training instructors and pupils would relax there and talk shop.

Social activities were many and varied at the station. Despite the disruption to their daily lives by the daily flying activities – one such was the instructors' habit of flying inverted across the front of the Turnberry Hotel, below its roof level – the residents of Turnberry were friendly, anxious that the RAF should feel at home in their community. One of the instructors and his family were billeted with Mr. L.S. Baikie, the headmaster of the local school at Kirkoswald, who held an open house to the instructors in their off-duty hours. James and others joined in with the Baikie children's games, a favourite being Knights of the Round Table, the pilots armed with various makeshift weapons, with James playing the part of Sir Lancelot. The Balkie's domestic servant was an elderly Scots lady with a broad accent, whom James mercilessly teased, pretending that she was speaking a foreign language which he could not understand and begging her to teach him.

The instructors' Mess at Turnberry was a friendly, cheerful place in which they could thoroughly relax but, except on guest nights, James was seldom seen there in the evenings, retiring after dinner to his room in the hotel to work on his book. None of his fellow instructors knew of his writing, and his absences from the Mess in the social evenings gave many the impression that he was unsociable and rather standoffish.

Many of James' fellow instructors were old friends, but new arrivals, junior instructors, meeting him for the first time, found his rather abrupt manner with them a little disconcerting. With his record of Britain's leading fighter pilot, plus his VC and impressive list of decorations, they tended to be a little wary, unsure of how they should approach him. One such was David Kennedy, a young lieutenant who had been flying Sopwith Camels in 73 Squadron before being shot down. Kennedy had survived unhurt, but was later injured in a flying accident and it was after recovering from this that he was posted to Turnberry. Assigned to James' Flight and reporting to him on arrival, Kennedy was startled when James looked up from his desk and, without any of the usual polite preliminaries, abruptly asked for an explanation as to why he had been shot down. Surprised that his new Flight Commander even knew of his having been shot down, Kennedy explained that while he had been busy attacking an enemy scout he had

James in the cockpit of a Bristol M.1C.

been caught by two others, who had got onto his tail. James quietly but emphatically told him that a properly thinking pilot should never find himself in such a position, adding that if a camera gun of any of his pupils ever showed that Kennedy had been in their sights during combat practise, he was no use to him. Kennedy left James' office feeling slightly depressed: with the confidence of youth – he was only 18½ years old – Kennedy had hitherto thought that he was a pretty good pilot.

In his relationships with his pupils, James was highly motivated to impart to them the skills they would need to survive in France. Of necessity, this entailed having to teach them, in part, by telling them of his own technique and experiences, and he was afraid that this could appear to be boasting, a concern that added to his natural modesty. This was no doubt one reason why at first his pupils found him rather abrupt, but as their courses progressed and they realised the undeniable efficiency of his teaching, with its care and attention to the smallest detail, his constant reiteration of the importance of aerial gunnery, they began to understand him, to know him better as a person, and their respect and admiration for him grew. One pupil later recalled.

McCudden gave a great talk this morning – sort of opened up a bit– and made it very clear that successful pilots are only because they have worked like sin, studied every phase and detail of flying, machines, and the habits and haunts of the Hun. To hear him talk nonchalantly of doing in Germans at 20,000 feet and studying all available material in order that he may know where to go and look for them convinces you that this is surely the greatest game God created. There is nothing like it.[35]

James, less happy with the tedious paperwork, further endeared himself to them when they learnt that he habitually emptied his office trays, unread, into his wastepaper basket.

People other than his pupils had cause to remember James' expertise in the air. Lt.Col. Paul Maltby, on the training staff of the North-Western Area Headquarters in Glasgow, recalled:

I rather fancied myself as an SE.5 pilot and visiting Turnberry one day was ill-advised enough to take on James McCudden in a mock dog fight. We were both flying SEs and it was not long before he was on my tail, and there he remained despite all my efforts to shake him off. He told me afterwards that he was able to anticipate my every manoeuvre by watching the ailerons, elevator and rudder of my machine.[36&37]

On 11 May James ferried C4955 to the new station, returning to Ayr later in the day in a Bristol Fighter flown by John Letts. He then flew back to Turnberry in 'Pot Belly'. One of James' first concerns on the move to Turnberry was finding a reliable man to look after the Vickers, and he finally decided on an Air Mechanic named Tom Somerville.[38] When not in its hangar 'Pot Belly' was parked outside James' office, the centre of attraction to pupils and instructors alike, and Somerville's new job was no sinecure.

"I was excused all parades, which settled it for me, but I was up at the hangars at all hours and sometimes it was no easy job. Whenever any of the new pupils heard about the Vickers they would flock over and try to climb into the cockpit. I was smartly told off for allowing them to do it and Heaven help anyone that McCudden actually caught in the aircraft."[39]

It was about this time that James acquired an English Bulldog, a gift from a female admirer – possibly Teddie O'Neal – and on 11 May, in his last flight of the day, in a Bristol Fighter, John Letts ferried it from Ayr to Turnberry. This bulldog, which James named Bruiser, was a quiet, good natured animal but with all the ferocious appearance of its breed, and James would tease the WRAFs working in the rooms next to his office by allowing Bruiser to wander in and out as he pleased. Bruiser was devoted to James and was somewhat of a one-man dog, but formed an attachment to one of the ground staff, Sergeant Beale,[40] who would look after him when James was absent from Turnberry.

The weather in Scotland in the spring and summer of 1918 was generally fine and warm, and over the next weeks James

Cyril Edgar Foggin. A pre-war photograph, circa 1913.

Albatros D.I 391/16. 'a nice old machine.'

When opened in 1906 the hotel at Turnberry was known as The Station Hotel.

added another thirty-nine hours of flying to his logbook.[41] In the fine evenings, his instructional duties over, James flew alone a great deal for the sheer pleasure of flying, a habit not overly appreciated by his mechanics who had to wait on the aerodrome until he returned. Also, despite – or perhaps because of – the episode with Mary, James and James Latta had become good friends and they often flew to Failford House to visit Latta's family.

During his three months at Turnberry James flew various types of machines: Avros, Bristol Monoplanes, his Vickers, Sopwith Pups, and Camels – on 22 May he commented 'very nice Camel' – and on one occasion an old friend, a DH2, ferrying it from Ayr to Turnberry. One notable flight was on 14 May when he flew a DH9 (C1215) for the first time. True to type, the engine of the de Havilland seized at 4,000ft, but he was within easy gliding distance of the aerodrome and landed without damaging either himself or the machine.

To keep their flying skills up to form, James and the other instructors, armed with camera guns, would often fly mock combats, trying out new tactics and combat manoeuvres, flying against each other in various combinations: Camels against SE5as; Bristol M.1Cs against Camels; Bristol Fighters against SE5as, and similar configurations. These duels were of great interest, watched avidly by the pupils, who no doubt had their favourites. In lighter moments the instructors would occasionally give an aerobatics display at a local fête, or fly mock battles against their fellow instructors in the North Western School in one of its frequent air days at Ayr.

On 1 June, James flew an old foe, an Albatros D.V, in a fifty-minute local test flight. He made no comment in his logbook of his impressions of the German scout, but test flew it again for fifteen minutes the next day. On 3 June, he flew the Albatros again in a twenty-five minute mock combat with another instructor.

James flew his Vickers to London on 10 June, refuelling at Hooton Park and reaching Hendon after a total flying time of 170 minutes – a stark contrast to his flight of three days in May. After a short stay at Hendon – conditions during the flight had been bumpy – he made the short, fifteen-minute flight to Joyce Green to return 'Pot Belly' to the Vickers works.[42]

That night, he visited Mrs. Alec-Tweedie, with the 40,000-word manuscript of *Five Years in the Royal Flying Corps* under his arm. He apologised for his red, sunburnt complexion, explaining that the following wind, which had enabled him to fly the 400 miles from Scotland in three hours – the Vickers had at times reached 140mph – had caught his face.

James' inauguration ceremony as an Honorary Freeman of Gillingham had been set for 13 June – three days away – and with his dislike of any such publicity he was no doubt relieved that during the day the Air Ministry had ordered him to fly a Sopwith Snipe to France the next day.[43]

On 11 June, James took off from Hendon in the Snipe and flew to Lympne in Kent. While the Snipe was being refuelled he took the opportunity to send a telegram to the Gillingham

Pupils and Staff of the No.1 School of Aerial Fighting and Gunnery at Turnberry. This view vividly illustrates the size of the training establishment.

Town Clerk, explaining that he had been ordered to France and that a letter would follow. He then made the hour and a half flight to Doullens, where he handed over the Snipe for testing by the pilots of No.1 Aeroplane Supply Depot.

From Doullens to Valheureux, where 56 Squadron had been based since late March, was a short road trip. That evening James was back in the 56 Squadron Mess, surrounded by old friends, arriving at the squadron just in time to accompany the pilots to 84 Squadron who were giving a dinner to celebrate their squadron's 200th victory.

One of the old faces at Valheureux was that of Gerald Constable Maxwell, who had arrived at the squadron two days before on a refresher course. Maxwell, keen to get back into operational flying, had been frustrated since his arrival by bad weather, but the morning of 12 June was fine and Gerald and James took off together at 10.00AM. They patrolled from Montdidier to La Bassée but saw only one enemy aeroplane, too far off to engage, and returned after nearly two hours in the air. Maxwell entered in his diary: 'Did a show with McCudden in the morning. Went up to 18,500ft for two hours. Felt very ill in consequence.'

Later in the day James travelled to Doullens, where collected the Snipe, flew it to report to RAF Headquarters at Hesdin, then flew it back to Doullens. Leaving the Snipe there he returned to Valheureux, determined to make the most of his opportunity of being back in France.

To the delight of James and Gerald Maxwell, the morning of 13 June was again fine and warm and they both took off at 6.05AM, James flying William Irwin's Viper-powered SE5a (B179) which he had flown for a short test-flight before taking off, commenting that it was a 'very nice machine'.

This time it seemed as if their luck was in. Maxwell's diary reads: 'Did a topping show in morning. Self and McCudden attacked four different two-seaters which we filled with lead but did not get down.'

James did not take the failure to down these two-seaters as philosophically as Maxwell. On the evidence of the accuracy of his shooting with a camera gun while instructing at Turnberry, he knew that his marksmanship was as good as ever. Back at Valheureux, testing the guns of Irwin's SE at the firing butts confirmed his suspicions – they were hopelessly misaligned. James was both furious and disappointed that one of the fundamental rules of his teaching while in the squadron had been so soon forgotten. Eugene Macdonald remembered that he was 'hopping mad' and angrily tore into Irwin for not having his guns properly sighted, pointing out that not only did his own life depend on his guns being accurate but, more importantly, the lives of his comrades.

Later in the day, James collected the Snipe from Doullens, flew it first to Calais, then across the channel to Lympne, and finally to Joyce Green.

At mid-day he visited C.G. Grey in London to discuss a point in his book – which he thought a great joke, calling it the 'Bolo Book.' Grey was surprised that James was not his usual spick and span, well-turned out self, being dirty and oil splattered. James apologised, explaining that the Snipe had spat oil at him all the way back from France. It was only further questioning by Grey that elicited the information that earlier that morning he had been fighting enemy two-seaters in France.

James photographed this Avro 504 at Turnberry, possibly because of the association of the large number '56' it carried on its fuselage.

In the evening James caught the night train back to Turnberry. There was no opportunity to rest, and very next day he flew a Bristol M1.C (C5007) to Renfrew, outside Glasgow, returning the next day to Turnberry. Returning to his instructional duties, for the next two days he flew his favourite Bristol monoplane in three practise fights with pupils.[44]

James had never forgotten his own desire to fly when still an air mechanic, and on 19 June he took up Sergeant Joe Poletti for a five-minute flight in an Avro 504. Poletti was an old comrade – they had shared a billet together while at Auchel with 3 Squadron in 1915. James, perhaps on a rare occasion of showing off, flew a few basic aerobatics, finishing the flight in a spin, delaying recovery until the Avro was very close to the ground. Poletti later recalled. 'I don't mind admitting that I had the wind up. I thought it was curtains for both of us. When we landed McCudden asked me how I'd enjoyed it. I said "swell" – but I didn't mean it.'[45]

During his last eight days at Turnberry James flew twice to visit the Latta family at Failford House, staying the night on 24 June and returning for his last visit the next day to say his final goodbyes to the family.

At the end of his time at Turnberry, before leaving Scotland, the question of James' next posting had been in question. James, of course, like all successful pilots, was keen to return to active duty and squadron life, and was anticipating being given command of a squadron, a posting commensurate with his record and length of service. However, as Britain's most successful fighter pilot, the hierarchy of the RAF was anxious that he should not again fly on active duty in France. He was now a highly publicised, popular hero, and knowing the depth of the recent public mourning in Germany that April on the death of the seemingly invincible Manfred von Richthofen, they no doubt feared the adverse repercussions on morale, both in the RAF and the general public, if James were to be killed on operations.

In January, while still in France with 56 Squadron, James had visited RFC headquarters, possibly at the instigation of Jack Scott, to argue the case for a specialist squadron to be formed with the express task of destroying the German reconnaissance machines in order to deny to German intelligence their vital information. In spite of the obvious value of this proposal his suggestion met with only lukewarm interest. It was rather condescendingly explained to this admittedly successful, but still junior officer, that bigger plans were on hand regarding the air war: the bombing of the German capital and industrial heart of Germany, for instance. On James protesting that as yet there were no machines able to fly to Berlin and back, it was pointed out to him that machines were available capable of flying the

Arthur Gould Lee. MC.

James with Vickers FB.16D ('Pot Belly').

raids – one way. On his return to 56 Squadron he expressed his disgust of these plans in no uncertain terms, both at the lack of interest in the solution of an immediate problem and what he saw as strategic and tactical nonsense.

Aware of these views, the Air Ministry now prevaricated by deciding that James should be given command of 91 Squadron, which had been formed in September 1917 and was now building up to strength at Tangmere. The squadron was earmarked to go to France equipped with the Sopwith Dolphin, and the Ministry's reasoning was possibly that command of a squadron of Dolphins, with their excellent performance at height, would appeal to James, that he would relish the prospect of being in command of a squadron that he could train in his technique and ideas.[46] They may well have been right, but when James learnt that 91 squadron was not expected to be ready for active service in France for several months he was furious, seeing the posting precisely for what it was, a ploy to keep him from operational flying. He made his case so forcibly for an immediate command in France that the authorities rescinded their decision and gave him command of 60 Squadron, to take effect on 9 July.[47&48]

On 30 June, James was in London. He journeyed down to Joyce Green during the day, collected 'Pot Belly' from the Vickers people and flew it to Northolt to visit friends. He then flew on to Farnborough to see 'Jackie' Noakes, his old friend from their days together in 29 Squadron, who was now flying as a test pilot in the experimental section at Farnborough. Noakes found James little changed, if possible even more of a perfectionist, and they had a long talk about the conduct of the air war. James insisted that the destruction of the high flying enemy two-seaters, with their valuable information, was of paramount importance, that the destruction of an enemy fighter – tit for tat – achieved nothing of value to the overall war effort. He told Noakes that he had come to the conclusion that after getting into a favourable attacking position against a

Failford House, the family home of James Latta.

James Latta at Ayr.

James – holding his faithful Box Brownie – with Gerald Constable Maxwell and Edmund Leonard Zink.

two-seater, it should be destroyed in the initial burst. If this was not successful then the attack should be abandoned, as nothing could be gained by any further attempt to out-manoeuvre an enemy machine that had a superior performance at height – here he was no doubt thinking of the *Rubild* Rumplers.

While at Farnborough, James took the opportunity to inspect the SE5a C1126, which had been allocated for him to fly to France when taking up command of 60 Squadron on 9 July.[49] James discussed with a Mr. G. Harris, the aerodrome foreman at Farnborough, the possibility of rigging the SE5a in such a way as to improve its performance at height. They decided that the fitting of two pairs of non-standard incidence wires would increase the amount of 'washout' to the wingtips of the SE, which would result in a slight, but significant, improvement in its performance at all heights, give a small addition to its ceiling height, and also reduce the tendency to

James with a Bristol at Turnberry, showing the relative smallness of the type.

The Flights at the No.1 School of Aerial Fighting and Gunnery at Turnberry 1918

Gerald Constable Maxwell's SE5a Flight.

Above: The Sopwith Camel Flight, with a lone Sopwith Pup first in the line.
Below: Another of the Camel Flights with the Flights instructor's Bristol M.1C. C5016.

stall at the extent of its ceiling. With his mechanic and pilot's eye, James carried out an overall inspection of C1126 and was impressed with its excellence, telling Grey that it was one of the finest pieces of work he had ever seen, which coming from such a perfectionist as James was praise indeed. Leaving Farnborough, James flew back to Hounslow, leaving the Vickers there.

On 3 July, James flew his beloved 'Pot Belly' for the last time, to return it to the Vickers Company at Joyce Green. It was a fine evening, with exceptional visibility, and taking off from Hounslow he first flew south to Kingston, where he threw a few loops over his home. He then climbed to 17,000ft and flew a leisurely course to Joyce Green. Far below, to his left, lay the vast spread of the entire city of London, the patchwork of myriad roofs, its parks and lakes, the Thames piercing its heart; to his right, the casual beauty of the green fields of Kent; further still the coast of the Channel, then the distant fields of France: James was taking his last, valedictory view of England.

Left: James with Bruiser.

Below: A group of fighting instructors at Turnberry. L to R. Philip. E.M. Le Gallais. E.D. 'Spider' Atkinson. Gerald Constable Maxwell. S.W. Taylor and John Leacroft. This photograph was taken in August 1918, after James' death, but includes three of his fellow instructors when he was at Turnberry: Atkinson, Constable Maxwell and Taylor.

A full parade at Turnberry. Gerald Constable Maxwell can easily be distinguished by his beret, just left of centre. James is the first man in the row behind Constable Maxwell. To James' right; the last man in the row is Lt.Col. Rees.

After a fifty-minute flight, he landed at Joyce Green and handed over 'Pot Belly' to the Vickers Company. Its was both his last flight in the rotund little Vickers, and the final flight recorded in his logbook, with the notation. 'Good visibility. Leaving machine.'

James sent this informal portrait to a friend in April 1918, six days after the award of his VC had been gazetted.

Above: About to set off on patrol with Gerald Constable Maxwell. James at Valheureux in June 1918.
Below: The 56 Squadron Mess at Valheureux in 1918.

James proudly poses at Valheureux with the ribbon of his two month old Victoria Cross underneath his wings.

William Roy Irwin. Although Irwin was to be given command of B Flight in 56 Squadron in July 1918, a post he held for over two months before being wounded, in June he incurred the anger of James for neglecting to correctly align and sight his guns, in the eyes of James, a cardinal sin.

Ch.17: The Last Flight

James gave this portrait to Mrs Alec-Tweedie on the morning of 9 July when he left for France.

Henry John Burden.

Tuesday 9 July. James was in London in the morning, probably having stayed the previous night at the RFC Club. At 10.30 he called at Whitehall Court to say goodbye to Mrs. Alec-Tweedie. She had been aware of his earlier tussle with the Air Ministry for a posting to an operational squadron and had asked him then why he was so anxious to get back to France, pointing out that he had already done so much, that he deserved a real rest from the fighting. James had explained that he had only brought down fifty-seven enemy aircraft, plus perhaps another twenty or thirty that had not been officially awarded, and that he must get back to outstrip Manfred von Richthofen's record.[1]

That morning, he assured her that he did not intend to take any unnecessary risks, that he would fight at his own pace, with no 'dashing stunts', and would do nothing foolish like his brother Anthony. Saying goodbye, James then excused himself, saying that he had lots still to do before he left for France but that he would be back in three months and promising her a letter from France the next day.

James' next stop was to say goodbye to his sister Mary, who was working in an annex of the War Office in the National Liberal Club at No.1 Whitehall Place, a short step from Whitehall Court.[2] Busy in the office, Mary was told she had a visitor. She looked up to see James at the door. Because of the newspaper publicity he was by now well-known, recognisable to the general public, and his arrival caused quite a stir amongst the young, mainly female staff. James explained to Mary that he was returning the France that morning, and had called to both say goodbye and to give her his medals for safe keeping, feeling that she was the best person to look after them.

Mary placed the case containing the medals on her desk and left with James to say goodbye in private. They walked

The aerodrome at Auxi-le Chateau.

together to the corner of Whitehall Place and Whitehall, where James hailed a taxi. It was a beautiful sunny day. They said their goodbyes; James hugged her, then stepped back and gave her a smart salute before getting into his taxi. Mary watched it until it was lost to sight in the London traffic.

Back at her desk, Mary opened the case, and proudly showed James' medals to her colleagues: his VC, DSO, MC, MM and *Croix de Guerre*, plus his campaign stars. The head of the office, a colonel, joining the admirers, pointed to his own medal ribbons, commenting 'I would give all these for that one,' his finger on James' Victoria Cross.[3]

*

James arrived at Hounslow sometime after midday. His SE5a C1126 was ready. After he had made a final, walk-round inspection, finding everything to his satisfaction, he climbed into the cockpit, made a few last minute checks, and took off for France.[4]

*

On the aerodrome of Auxi-le-Chateau, the home of 8 and 52 Squadrons,[5] the afternoon had been pleasantly warm and work for the day was coming to a close. A few airmen, still with one or two duties, looked up at the sound of an approaching aeroplane. Their own squadrons' aeroplanes had been bedded down for the night and the arrival of a visiting aeroplane was not unusual, but seeing it was an SE5a, they paused in their activities to watch its landing. Both their own pilots and those who visited often complained that landing at Auxi-Le-Chateau could be tricky, the aerodrome's narrowness being exacerbated by the woods on two sides of the field, and the airmen watched with interest as the pilot of the little scout made his approach, finally touching down in a neat, precise landing, bursts of power bringing it to a stop in front of the tents.

Two of the airmen, Corporals W.H. Burdett[6] of 8 Squadron and L.E. Vallins[7] of 52 Squadron, were standing by the tents and the pilot of the SE beckoned to them. They went over. The pilot asked them where he was. He then asked if they knew the position of Boffles aerodrome. They told him that it was to the north-east, only three or four miles away, just over the rising ground. He thanked them and asked them to help him turn. This done, he acknowledged their help with a wave to stand clear, glanced at the windsock, taxied past the officers' Mess to the other end of the airfield and turned into the wind. Burdett watched the SE5a take off, and was turning away when he saw it suddenly half roll and nosedive into the wood behind the hangars.

Several people immediately ran into the wood. The first to reach the scene of the crash was W. Howard,[8] a corporal in the Royal Army Medical Corps, serving with 8 Squadron, and another RAMC orderly, on detachment from 6 Squadron. Close behind them was Corporal Peter Fulton,[9] a clerk, also

James' grave at Wavans. 1918.

on detachment from 6 Squadron. They found the pilot lying under the wreckage, unconscious, bleeding profusely from his mouth and nose, but still alive. Howard saw that the pilot was a Major, and that his tunic carried the ribbon of a VC and other decorations, but it was not until he removed the pilot's helmet that Burdett, who had now arrived with several other men, recognised the pilot as James, having served with him in 3 Squadron in 1915.

No time was wasted. James was quickly placed on a stretcher, taken out of the wood, placed in a tender, and rushed across the aerodrome to No.21 Casualty Clearing Station.

At the CCS it was found that James had sustained a fracture at the base of his skull and to his lower jaw, both severe. In addition, the bones of his right forearm – the radius and ulna – were both fractured, as was the second rib on his right side.

James died at 8.00PM without regaining consciousness.

*

Later that evening, at Valheureux, the pilots of 56 Squadron were stunned by the news that James had been killed while flying out to take command of 60 Squadron. The next afternoon, all the pilots, with the sole exception of the duty officer, travelled to Wavans, close by the aerodrome at Auxi-le-Chateau, where James was to be buried.[10] All the pilots of 60 Squadron also attended, along with pilots of other squadrons. The sole senior officer present was Major-General John Salmond.[11]

The ceremony, conducted by the Reverend C.W.Riddiford, angered many of those attending. Henry Burden,[12] a Canadian pilot with 56 Squadron, commented: 'It was poorly arranged and rushed through.' Paul Winslow, an American pilot who had only been with the squadron for ten days and knew of James only by repute, was more forthright in his diary entry for the day.[13]

'The ceremony made my blood boil – all in Latin, mumbled so that even if one knew the language, he couldn't have heard it. Nothing human in it at all and far from impressive. Richthofen – an enemy – had a far better funeral, and if anyone deserved a real memorial it was McCudden.'[14]

That night, Mary, coming home from work, turning into Burton Road, Kingston, saw that the curtains were drawn at all the windows of No.37: 'I knew it was Jimmy.'

*

The cemetery at Wavans today.

It is fitting that this account of James McCudden's brief but triumphant life should be concluded in his own words, written in late June while he was in Scotland.[15]

I will carry my readers as far as the month of April, so as to complete my five years with the Royal Flying Corps. In March I had leave, and at the end of March my brother was reported missing. Now he is buried near Le Câteau, where he was killed, over 30 miles behind the enemy's lines, while engaged in escorting a bombing formation on his S.E.5.

No more words are needed in praise of one of the bravest and most gallant boys who ever died for his country than to refer to the spot where he fell, nobly carrying on that offensive spirit which has ever been the most splendid feature of the Royal Flying Corps.

On April 2nd I was gazetted with the Victoria Cross, and there was not a prouder man living when, on the 6th of April, I went to Buckingham Palace and received at the hands of the King a bar to my M.C., the D.S.O. and bar and the Victoria Cross. I will ever remember how the King thanked me for what I had done.

I am now in England training the young idea, but my heart is in France amongst the gallant boys who are daily dying, and those who are dead, having given themselves to that most wonderful Cause —

For King and Country

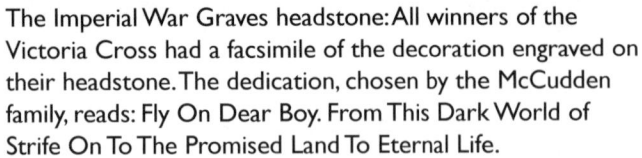

The Imperial War Graves headstone: All winners of the Victoria Cross had a facsimile of the decoration engraved on their headstone. The dedication, chosen by the McCudden family, reads: Fly On Dear Boy. From This Dark World of Strife On To The Promised Land To Eternal Life.

Above Right: A more elaborate cross was later erected over James' grave. In 2008, a French farmer found the original plaque. *Credit Mike O'Connor.*

Right: Paul Stuart Winslow.

Postscript

When peace came in November 1918, with three sons and a husband lost in the war, the McCudden family could have been forgiven for hoping that their personal tragedies had at last ended. It was not to be.

In 1920, McCudden senior was working as a chief clerk at the Air Ministry in London. Still very much the old soldier, 'Little Mac' was popular with his colleagues and thought of as a bit of a character. He was an outgoing, cheerful personality, always happy and proud to talk of his three famous sons and full of his hopes for Maurice, his youngest, sole surviving son. On the evening of Saturday 3 July 1920, as he was leaving for the day, family tradition has it that he stopped at the door of the office and quipped to the staff: 'Man that is born of a woman hath but a short time to live'.

As always, the train from Waterloo was crowded and at Clapham Junction, 'Little Mac', ever the gentleman, got up to offer a young woman passenger his seat. Leaning back against the compartment door, it flew open and he fell onto the tracks in the path of an oncoming train. He was taken to Wandsworth Hospital, but died of his injuries two days later, on Monday 5 July 1920.

Amelia, with only her daughters and one son remaining, could well have retreated into herself, as did so many wives and mothers after their losses in the war, but she was a woman of rare spirit and indomitable courage, courage that was demonstrated in September 1918, barely two months after the death of James, when she had attended a ceremony at Gillingham to receive his illuminated certificate of freedom of the borough from Alderman W H Griffen.[1]

*

During the war many soldiers who had died on the battlefields of France were buried without their remains having being identified.[2] The Reverent David Railton, a British Army Chaplin serving in France, had seen such a grave, its rough cross carrying a pencil-written inscription: 'An Unknown British Soldier'. After the war, Railton suggested that a national monument be established to honour these anonymous soldiers and that a symbolic funeral should be held. Railton's suggestion met with approval from the Dean of Westmister, the British Prime Minister David Lloyd George, and later by King George V, who bowed to overwhelming public opinion. As a symbol of dedication for all the unknown dead, it was decided that a body of an unidentified soldier who had been buried in France should be exhumed and reburied in a dedicated tomb in Westminster Abbey, inscribed as the Tomb of the Unknown Warrior. The body of a soldier was selected and his coffin brought from France on 10 November 1920. The next day, born on a gun carriage of the Royal Artillery, the casket passed through the streets of London to Whitehall, where King George V unveiled the Cenotaph, the symbolic empty tomb of the nation's war dead. The cortège, followed by the King,

Amelia McCudden. Circa 1921.

members of the Royal Family and Ministers of State, then proceeded to the West Nave of Westminster Abbey. Here, with a guard of honour by a hundred winners of the Victoria Cross, it was interred in earth brought from the battlefields of France and Belgium. The grave was then capped with a stone of black Belgian marble.[3]

The idea of a symbolic tomb of an unknown soldier spread to many countries, including the United States of America, and it was decided that a similar burial be carried out on Armistice Day at the Arlington National Cemetery in 1921. Learning of the proposed American ceremony, the British branch of the Pilgrim Fathers' Association suggested that a wreath of flowers, grown in England, should be placed during the ceremony; further that it should be laid by a British mother, representative of all those who had lost sons in the war. Out of over 800 nominations, Amelia McCudden, mother of three sons killed while flying for their county, was unanimously chosen for this honour.

Initially, Amelia was reluctant to accept. The loss of three of her sons, plus the recent death of her husband, had left her devastated: she was in ill health, both physically and to a certain extent, mentally. Hearing of Amelia's hesitation, Sir Thomas Lipton, the prominent entrepreneur and yachtsman, wrote personally to her. Understanding and sympathising with the reasons for her reluctance, he suggested that she should

William McCudden. 'Little Mac'.

have a companion on the trip, and that he would gladly pay all her personal expenses not covered by the Pilgrim Fathers' Association. The ideal companion for Amelia was, of course, Mary, her eldest daughter, but since the loss of her husband Amelia had relied more and more on Mary to oversee the details and business of her daily life. However, Mary had a young son from her first marriage, had remarried, and was pregnant. It was obviously impossible for Mary to accompany her mother and it was decided that Amelia's youngest daughter, Kathleen, now twenty, should go in her stead.

Leaving for Euston Station, en route to Liverpool, mother and daughter were seen off from Kingston by the Mayor and Mayoress of the borough. At Euston, true to his word, Sir Thomas had had their compartment especially adapted for their journey, filled it with flowers, and came personally to wish them bon voyage. On arrival at Liverpool, they were met by the Mayor and Mayoress of the town, the event being filmed by Pathé Movietone News and covered by the local and national newspapers.

Escorted by the chairman of The Pilgrim Fathers' Association, Lieutenant F.J. Kersley, Amelia and Kathleen embarked from Liverpool for America, Amelia proudly wearing on her coat the medals of her three sons.[4]

Due to her health, the first few days of the voyage were difficult for Amelia, but she found that Sir Thomas had thoughtfully arranged that she should have the best cabin accommodation, any medication she needed, and by the end of the voyage she was feeling much stronger.

The fact that the visit was completely spontaneous on the part of the British public, and arranged entirely by the Pilgrim Father's Association, no official arrangements had been made with the authorities in the United States, but the proposed visit had caught the imagination of the American public and on arrival the party was told that the British wreath was to be one of the three laid on the tomb during the ceremony at Arlington National Cemetery. On the morning of the ceremony, the procession from the apse to the tomb was led by the American President, Warren Harding, and the first Lady, followed by the Vice-President and his wife, then the American Mother and Amelia.

The American public had been so touched by the sympathy and support shown by the British public in arranging the visit, that invitations began to pour in to attend ceremonies and dinners at many American – and Canadian – cities, anxious to show their appreciation. It was impossible to accept all of these, and only those from Washington, Philadelphia, New York, Toronto, Montreal, Boston, Providence and Portland were accepted.[5]

The conclusion of the visits to Toronto and Montreal presented a small difficulty. Although Amelia drank very little in the way of alcohol, she was partial to a small shot of whiskey, first thing in the morning and last thing at night. In Montreal this was perfectly acceptable, but returning to the prohibition America of the twenties was a problem. A solution was found: on the train back into America the whiskey travelled in a teapot.

In the ensuing weeks, Amelia was warmly welcomed in those American cities whose invitations had been accepted.: fêted, dined, given the Freedom of the City, and showered with gifts. The first of these receptions was in Philadelphia, organised by the American War Mothers. Representatives of the American Army, Navy, and the National and State governments were present. The President of the American War Mothers greeted Amelia, taking her hand and saying: 'I want to ask you to pledge with me that so long as you live you will never raise your voice or lift your hand to assist in armed conflict against me. Our boys, yours and mine, are lying there in Flanders together, and it is for us to stand together to determine to do our share to prevent future wars.'⁽⁶⁾

In Washington, in addition to the formal dinner – where Amelia was kissed by General Pershing – she was invited to the White House, where she presented the First Lady with a bouquet of British flowers on behalf of the mothers of Britain.

The final visit of the tour was a farewell dinner given in Portland, Maine, that was attended by many eminent people, both from Maine State and Washington, and during the dinner a telegram was received from President Harding:
The White House, Washington.

Please express to Mrs McCudden, on the occasion of the farewell dinner you are giving her, the assurance of my highest regards and best wishes and a pleasant voyage homewards. Her visit has been the means of binding closer the ties among peoples who have sacrificed together in a great human cause.

Warren G Harding

The strenuous programme arranged by the various American bodies imposed a great physical strain on Amelia, and Kersley commented: 'it was only her pluck and almost superhuman efforts that enabled her to keep going'.

At the conclusion of Amelia's visit, one American newspaper commented:

Mrs Amelia E McCudden, Britain's Gold Star Mother, has come and gone, but the result of her visit to the United States will live on for many years, possibly for ever. It was a visit of sentiment, wholly unofficial, and in no way connected with the Government of that great nation from which she came, but, nevertheless, in many ways it had far greater force than if she had come as the direct representative of King George the Fifth.'

The whole trip had taken two months, wonderful months that Amelia had enjoyed immensely, proud of the many tributes paid both to herself and her three dead sons.

Sadly, Amelia McCudden long outlived her remaining son, Maurice. She died at her home in Surbiton in January 1955, aged 87, survived by her two daughters, Mary and Kathleen.

*

At the end of the war, Maurice Vincent, the sole surviving son of William and Amelia, was just a few days from his seventeenth birthday. He had followed the family tradition by enrolling in the army as a boy, but unlike his three brothers who had all joined the Royal Engineers as Buglers, Maurice had joined the RFC as an apprentice and began his training at the Royal Aircraft Factory at Farnborough on 3 March 1916. Quiet, painstaking and thorough in all he did, Maurice was more like James than Bill or Anthony. Again, like James, he was an efficient and conscientious worker and was well liked by his fellow apprentices, no doubt aware of his antecedents. Unsurprisingly, Maurice was passionately keen on flying and during his two years at Farnborough took every opportunity to fly as a passenger with Jack Noakes, James' old comrade in arms, who gave Maurice his first taste of aerobatics in an FE2d.

After passing out as fitter, Maurice served at several RAF stations during 1918 and 1920, including Northolt and

Maurice Vincent McCudden. *Credit Sue Adams.*

Hounslow, where he flew as a passenger with several old friends of his brothers, all happy to give him a number of hours of unofficial flying instruction.

In April 1918, with the establishment of the Royal Air Force, Brooke-Popham, James' erstwhile commanding officer in 3 Squadron, had been promoted to the new RAF rank of Air Commodore, serving as Controller of Aircraft Production for the remainder of the war at the Air Ministry, and in early 1919 was made Director of Aircraft Research. Brooke-Popham had not forgotten his enthusiastic engine fitter and observer of 1915, and when he learnt that his young brother had qualified as a 2AM fitter, he specifically asked for Maurice to be assigned

Maurice racing at Brooklands in the 1920s. Credit Sue Adams.

to him as his personal fitter during a four day inspection tour of the squadrons in southern England. Maurice flew with James' old CO for over fifteen hours in a Bristol Fighter, visiting twelve airfields during the tour. On one occasion there was an anxious half an hour. Flying between the Isle of Grain and Croydon they were temporarily lost in thick fog over Kent, but Brooke-Popham was a highly experienced pilot and they returned safely.

At the end of hostilities the RAF was reduced to a fraction of its wartime establishment – Trenchard was in fact fighting for its very existence – and Maurice realised that his prospects of a career in the RAF were uncertain to say the least. Trenchard took a personal interest in the remaining McCudden brother, anxious that Maurice should maintain the family's tradition of service, and he offered to nominate Maurice for a cadetship in the newly-established RAF College at Cranwell. The family was worried that the fees would be a problem, but talks with 'Grandpa' Marson, now Trenchard's private secretary, and another old friend of James, assured them that this could be overcome. Unfortunately, these plans came to a abrupt halt when the medical examination showed that an old injury to his skull, the result of a boyhood accident, precluded Maurice from flying duties. To Maurice the RAF meant only one thing, flying, and the medical dashed for ever his hope of becoming a pilot. In view of the current uncertain future of the RAF he reluctantly took the decision to leave the RAF after serving for over four years. On 25 April 1920, Maurice Vincent McCudden, Aircraftman 2nd Class No.24402 took his discharge from the RAF as 'surplus to requirements'.

However, all was not lost. Behind the scenes, friends of his brothers were still taking an interest in Maurice and a place was offered to him at the Royal Aircraft Establishment, which had superseded the old Royal Aircraft Factory at Farnborough. Further engineering training would be required to qualify for the position and Maurice studied at the Regent Street Polytechnic in London, finally taking up the post at Farnborough in June 1923, when he was appointed a test assistant and flight observer.

Maurice's medical category placed no restrictions on his flying as a passenger and over the next eight years he made many test flights in a wide variety of aircraft, some of which were highly secret while others were repetitive and boring – in one example, thirty seven flights in one aeroplane testing its fuel consumption.

Although he was unable to fly any service type of aeroplane, Maurice gained a great deal of experience while flying as a passenger, no doubt again receiving many unofficial flying lessons, and in the 1930s obtained a civil pilots' licence. His one unalloyed joy at Farnborough was the two-seat trainer version of the Armstrong-Whitworth Siskin IIIa. The Siskin IIIa, the RAF's first all-metal fighter, which had entered service in January 1924, had taken five years since its original design as a replacement for the SE5a. The prototype two-seat trainer Siskin J7000 at Farnborough was the closest Maurice would come to flying in an SE5a and he had many flights in the Siskin, thoroughly enjoying the aerobatics, piloted by such famous pilots as Henry Waghorn, winner of the 1929 Schneider Trophy, and George Stainforth, who had set a new world speed record of 407.5mph in the Schneider Trophy Race of September 1931, the first man in the world to fly faster than 400mph. But even the Siskin could not meet Maurice's longing for speed. In 1926 he had been introduced to the sport of motor-cycle racing and became an assistant in the pits at Brooklands to the racing team of J S Worters, an ex-RFC pilot. In 1929 Worters offered Maurice a place in his team and over the next three years Maurice rode machines of all types, both single and sidecar combinations, with a great deal of success. He studied the art of motorcycle racing with the same devotion that James had taken to that of air fighting, and was described by the magazine Motor Cycling as one of Britain's cleverest exponents of track racing.

Maurice made his last flight on May 23 1933 in a Hawker Horsley, bringing his total flying time 778 hours, but in the spring of that year his health began to deteriorate and he began to experience severe abdominal pains, that forced him to give up both flying and racing. He was diagnosed with colitis, admitted to Putney Hospital and died there on 13 December 1934, leaving a widow, Emily, and a small daughter, Patricia. Maurice was buried at Kingston and in a special tribute to the last of the McCudden brothers, the RAF provided a funeral party from 3 Squadron.

What Remains

The McCudden brothers are commemorated on the war memorials of the boroughs of both Sheerness and Brompton in Kent. In Sheerness there is a memorial plaque to the McCudden brothers in the SS Henry and Elizabeth Catholic Church, and their histories and photographs are on display in the Heritage Centre in Rose Street. In Brompton, a small row of houses is named McCudden Row and carries a plaque dedicated to James. In Central Avenue, Sittingbourne, Kent, there is a memorial stone to James McCudden. In Sappers Walk in Gillingham, Kent, the memorial wall of the Royal Engineers includes a bas relief statue of James McCudden and his SE5a The McCudden family grave in Maidstone Road Cemetery in Chatham, Kent, is a four sided commemoration of the whole family.

The Imperial War Museum in London has displays dedicated to James McCudden and the museum of the Royal Engineers in Gillingham has displays of uniforms, medals and artefacts of William, James and Anthony McCudden.

During the 1960s, when the RAF began to take delivery of Vickers VC 10 aircraft, they named each individual aeroplane after a winner of the Victoria Cross with a dedication crest just underneath the cockpit. Inside each VC10 was a small, framed narrative with details of each winner. VC10 XV104 was named after James McCudden VC. The VC10 aircraft were finally retired from service with the RAF in 2013.

Maurice while a Test Assistant and Flight Observer at Farnborough. *Credit Sue Adams.*

In Memoriam

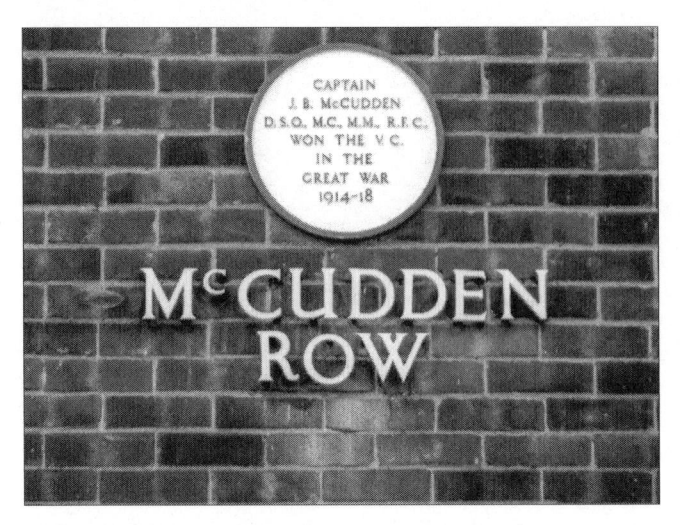

McCudden Row in Brompton.

The memorial stone in Sittingbourne. *Credit K. Wood.*

The family grave in Chatham.

The four sides of the family grave.

Above: William H. McCudden

Above Right: James T.B. McCudden.

Below: William T.J. McCudden & Anthony

Below Right: Arthur Scott Spears & Maurice V. McCudden.

Top Left — William H. McCudden:
Also In Loving Memory of
THEIR FATHER
WILLIAM H. McCUDDEN
LATE WARRANT OFFICER, R.E.
WHO DIED OF INJURIES ACCIDENTALLY
RECEIVED ON THE RAILWAY ON JULY 5TH 1920
AGED 56 YEARS.
R.I.P.

Top Right — James T.B. McCudden:
In Loving Memory
—of—
MAJOR
JAMES T. BYFORD McCUDDEN V.C.
D.S.O. & BAR., M.C. & BAR.,
M.M., CROIX DE GUERRE DE FRANCE
& AMERICAN MEDAL, R.A.F.
ACCIDENTALLY KILLED WHILE FLYING
ON HIS WAY TO DUTY IN FRANCE,
9TH JULY 1918,
AGED 23 YEARS.
R.I.P.

Bottom Left — William T.J. McCudden & Anthony:
Also In Loving Memory of
FLIGHT SERGEANT WILLIAM McCUDDEN R.F.C.
(PILOT INSTRUCTOR),
ACCIDENTALLY KILLED WHILE FLYING AT GOSPORT
1ST MAY 1915,
AGED 24 YEARS.
Also
2ND LIEUT. JOHN ANTHONY McCUDDEN, M.C., D.F.C.
(PILOT)
KILLED IN AERIAL COMBAT
OVER BUSIGNY, NEAR LE CATEAU, FRANCE
18TH MARCH 1918,
AGED 20 YEARS.
R.I.P.

FLY ON DEAR BOYS FROM THIS DARK WORLD OF STRIFE,
ON TO THE LAND OF PROMISE, TO ETERNAL LIFE.
THEY ARE NOT DEAD, SUCH SPIRITS NEVER DIE,
THEY ARE UNQUENCHABLE, THEY ONLY SLEEP.
THE THREE BROTHERS WERE BUGLERS IN THE ROYAL ENGINEERS

Bottom Right — Arthur Scott Spears & Maurice V. McCudden:
Also
ARTHUR SCOTT SPEARS
THEIR BROTHER-IN-LAW,
KILLED BY THE EXPLOSION IN
H.M.S. PRINCESS IRENE
27TH MAY 1915,
AGED 29 YEARS.
R.I.P.
Also
MAURICE VINCENT McCUDDEN
LATE R.A.F.
LAST SON OF MRS. A. McCUDDEN
AND THE LATE W.H. McCUDDEN,
WHO DIED 13TH DECEMBER 1934,

Left & Below: One of the displays in the Imperial War Museum, including two of James McCudden's tunics, his flying helmet, cap, and reputedly the shattered windscreen of SE5a C1126.

Display in the Museum of the Royal Engineers of the medals of the McCudden family who served in the Royal Engineers. At the top are those of William Henry McCudden. Directly below are those of James McCudden. The final row shows the medals of William Thomas McCudden; a photograph of the portrait of James McCudden by William Orpen, and the medals of John Anthony McCudden.

Appendices

Appendix I: The Fatal Crash

Despite James McCudden's status as Britain's leading airman, no official statement as to the cause of his fatal crash was ever made, even if only to refute the rumours that almost immediately began to circulate following the news of his death.[1]

An examination of all that is known about his last flight is hampered by the sparseness of any evidence, some of which is conflicting, but what is certain is that he left England sometime in the early afternoon, probably just after 1PM. The next positive sighting is when he landed at Auxi-le-Chateau at 5.45PM.

It is known that McCudden stopped somewhere en-route to Boffles as he had telephoned Lt.Col. Playfair, commanding 13 Wing, to say that he would arrive at 60 Squadron at about 6.00PM. It has been surmised that this stop was possibly at RAF HQ at Hesdin, but this seems unlikely.[2] Hesdin is only a short distance from Boffles, Auxi-le-Chateau, and the HQ of 13 Wing at Bachimont, making such a stop to telephone his arrival, pointless. However, if McCudden left Hounslow 'shortly after' 1PM[3] and landed at Auxi-le-Chateau nearly five hours later, it follows that he must have stopped somewhere en-route. The distance from Hounslow to Auxi-le-Chateau is just over 171 miles and although it can now never be known at what speed McCudden flew during his last flight, it is not unreasonable to assume that it was at the cruising speed of an SE5a. Given that this was 80mph, he would have estimated before leaving England that the flight to Boffles would take just over two hours. The endurance of an SE5a was two and a half hours, so there is every reason why he would have taken the opportunity to stop en-route to refuel and for a late lunch.[4] The logical place for him to do so would be the large RAF aerodrome at St.Omer, a flight of just under two hours from Hounslow, arriving there sometime between 3.15 and 3.30. From St.Omer to Boffles is only thirty miles, an easy half-hour flight, and if McCudden telephoned Playfair from St.Omer to say that he would arrive at Boffles at 6.pm., this meant that he anticipated leaving St.Omer between 5.15 and 5.30PM. That he did so is evidenced by his arrival at Auxi-le-Chateau at 5.45.

McCudden was no doubt anxious to take command of his squadron as quickly as possible – he certainly would not have taken an undue time over lunch – and a stop at St.Omer of two hours seems excessive, but it is possible that during the flight from Hounslow he had found some minor fault in the handling of C1126. If so, and estimating the time for this to be remedied, he had perhaps thought it necessary to telephone Playfair with a revised time of his arrival at Boffles.

Approaching the aerodrome at Auxi-le-Chateau, McCudden may well have thought that he had arrived at Boffles, which was just under four miles to the N.N.E. Conditions were a little hazy, but as he came lower he would have seen that the aeroplanes on the landing field were Armstrong Whitworth FK8s and RE8s, two-seater reconnaissance aeroplanes. With no SE5as on the field, he would have realised that it could not be Boffles, so decided to land to ascertain his position. Having been told where he was, and that Boffles was only a short flight away, he took off again, crashed and was killed.

For many years the reason for McCudden's fatal crash remained unexplained. An extensive and careful search of the Air Documents at the National Archives in London unearthed only two reports, neither of which state the cause of the accident.[5]

From early in the war, all aeroplanes destroyed or damaged were the subject of an official report on **Army Form W3347. Report on Casualties to Personnel and Machines (when flying).** That of McCudden's crash in not among them. The only official report of the accident is on Army Form 3428. Report on accidental or self inflicted injuries. This form gives the name of the casualty, the extent of his injuries and the cause of his death: in McCudden's case: Aeroplane Crash. Cause: unknown. This last section was signed by C.M. Crowe who took command of 60 Squadron directly after McCudden's death. Attached to this report are copies of the statements made by W H Howard, P S Mulroy and four officers of 52 Squadron who were eyewitnesses of the accident.[6]

Statements of Witnesses in Respect of Accident to Major J B McCudden. VC.,DSO., MC., MM.

Statement by No.134791 Cpl. W. Howard. RAMC.

An SE5a aeroplane landed on this aerodrome at about 5.40PM on Tuesday, 9th July 1918, and after a few minutes took off again. I saw the machine pass over the wood adjoining the aerodrome and immediately afterwards heard a crash. I immediately ran to the spot and was first to reach the machine. It was badly wrecked and I found the pilot unconscious but still breathing. His rank was Major and he wore the V.C. and other decorations. I was afterwards informed that he was Major McCudden. I and other men placed him on a stretcher and took him as quickly as possible to 21 C.C.S.

The machine was numbered C1126.

        Signed. H. Howard. No.134791. Cpl RAMC.
        No.8 Squadron RAF.

Taken down and signed in my presence at No.8 Squadron, RAF, In the Field, this 18th day of July 1918.

        2nd.Lieut. No.60 Squadron, Royal Air Force.

Another statement was made by Peter S. Mulroy.
O.C. No.8 Squadron RAF.
Sir,

With reference to your enquiry regarding SE5 flown by the late Major McCudden, I have the honour to submit report on what I saw of the accident.

The machine arrived on the aerodrome at about 5.40PM on the evening of Tuesday, 9th July, 1918, landed, and in a few minutes took the air again. I noticed that the machine appeared to have some difficulty in clearing the trees on the side of the aerodrome, and being attracted by the sound of the engine looked up and in a matter of seconds heard the crash in the wood.

I immediately ran into the wood and found the machine crashed with Major McCudden under the wreckage; he was bleeding very profusely from the mouth and nose (inserted here in handwriting 'but was alive.' Author). The RMAC Orderly ('identified below' inserted in handwriting. Author) from No.8 Squadron was there just before me, with the RAMC Orderly of No.6 Detached Flight. No time was wasted round the machine and Major McCudden was removed in a tender immediately to No.21 C.C.S. On making enquiries the following morning the C.C.S reported that he had died from injuries received at 8PM on the evening of the 9th instant.

I am unable to give any details as to the cause of the crash as my observation was only a passing one.

Peter S. Mulroy.
Cpl.Clerk.No.18012.'K' Flight, No.6 squadron. RAF
W Howard. Cpl. RAMC.No.134791 No.8 Squadron. RAF
In the Field
16th July 1918

Four officers on the aerodrome at the time of the crash also gave statements.[7]

Lieut. L.H. Fenelon. RAF. No. 52 Squadron stated:

On the 9th July 1918 about 5.45PM I was standing on the aerodrome of 52 Squadron RAF when an SE5 piloted by Major McCudden took off. Machine took off into wind and when at about 100 feet did a vertical turn and flew back across the aerodrome by the side of the wood nearby. The engine appeared to me to be running badly; pilot "rolled" machine which failed to straighten out at 200 feet approx. It crashed nose down into the above mentioned wood.

Lieut. T.H. Barry RGA and RAF. No.52 Squadron stated.

On the evening of the 9th instant I was standing near the Officers' Mess at the southern end of the aerodrome. I saw an SE5 flying from west to east across the aerodrome between 2–300 feet from the ground. The engine was firing irregularly and just after crossing the end of the aerodrome the pilot did a very sharp stalling turn. The nose of the machine dropped and it dived behind the trees. During this dive the noise of the engine ceased.

Lieut. K.V. King RAF. No.52 Squadron stated:

On the 9th inst. at about 5PM I saw the machine (SE5) flying very low over the aerodrome going east towards the wood, on the S.E. side of the aerodrome. He had apparently been "stunting" (rolling). I saw him with nose down and engine off entering the trees. I immediately afterwards heard the sound of the crash. I subsequently visited the scene of the accident and was told the pilot was Major McCudden.

Lieut. E.M. Greenwood. RAF.No.52 Squadron stated;

Last Tuesday evening I was standing by my tent watching an SE5 which was flying over the aerodrome at about 200 feet from the ground, when suddenly the machine did one complete roll to the right and then dived steeply to the ground disappearing from view behind some trees. Ten seconds later, I heard the crash.

Although not called upon as an official witness, Corporal W.H. Burdett later claimed that, along with another mechanic, Corporal L.C. Vallins, he was close by when McCudden landed, who beckoned them over, asked exactly where he was and the direction of Boffles.[8] McCudden then took off, 'put the machine into a nearly vertical climb, seemed to do a half-roll and then nose-dived into the wood behind the hangars. It was usual for scout pilots to perform some little stunt when leaving the aerodrome, and I think that is what he was doing.[9]

One of the various theories as to the cause of the crash was that McCudden was indulging in aerobatics at low height to impress the people on the ground at Auxi-Le-Chateau – Burdett's 'some little stunt' – but this has been dismissed by those who knew McCudden well, pilots and others, as being completely out of character.

Another conclusion that became accepted over the years and which has appeared in print on several occasions, is that McCudden, with a loss of engine power, made the tyro pilot's well known error of attempting to turn back to the aerodrome, lost flying speed, stalled and crashed.[10] No pilot who knew McCudden believed this for one moment, pointing out that not only was McCudden a precise, even neat pilot, but was extremely experienced, having flown many different types of machine and with a vast amount of flying hours.[11]

Hearing of McCudden's death, another pilot wrote: 'The great McCudden is dead. What a blow. He was on his way out to take over 60 Squadron. They say he did a climbing turn off the ground and crashed. I can't believe it. Not McCudden, surely! He was one of the finest pilots in the Corps. Does this mean that even the best and most careful pilot will occasionally tempt fate? Only to find himself the loser.[12]

Eye witness accounts are notorious for differing from each other, even in essential details, no two people seeing events identically, but one of the salient facts, reported by two of the witnesses, is that the engine of the SE5 was 'running badly' (Fenelon) 'firing irregularly'(Barry). Opinions also differed on what flying attitude the SE5 was in just before it crashed into the wood. Fenlon stated a 'vertical turn, followed by a roll'.

Barry stated that the pilot did a 'very sharp stalling turn'. King considered that McCudden had apparently been 'stunting' (rolling) which implies that he had not seen either the 'stunt' or the roll. Greenwood stated that the machine 'did a complete roll to the right'.

Many years later, others who saw the accident said that McCudden did not execute a complete roll, or attempt to do so, but with the passage of time memories become fallible, even distorted.[13] But all accounts, both contemporary and later, agree that the trouble began when the SE5 was low, in a vertical turn, and had insufficient flying speed to clear the trees of the wood.

In the March 1934 issue of the aviation magazine *Popular Flying*, a reader appealed for any witnesses of McCudden's crash. This brought a response, printed in the June issue, from L.C. Vallins. Vallins claimed to be 'the last person in this world that Major McCudden ever spoke to'. He wrote:

"At the time I was a corporal in No.52 Squadron RFC and stationed at a small village named Auxi-le-Chateau. I was on my way across the aerodrome to fetch my dinner when Major McCudden landed in an SE5 and beckoned to me. I went over to see what he required and he wished to know what aerodrome it was and the Squadron stationed there, also the direction in which another aerodrome was, the name of which I forget.

"He thanked me and taxied to the other end of the drome and took off. He did a very steep bank, and when coming out of same his undercarriage caught in the tops of some trees and down he crashed into the woods".[14]

The September 1936 issue of the magazine carried another letter from a purported eyewitness. For some reason, he did not wish his name to be published, but stated that he was an old member of No.8 Squadron, standing on the aerodrome at the time.

"Our aerodrome was not very large, and while it presented no particular difficulty to our fellows in landing their 'Big Acks' (Armstrong Whitworths) it was, according to many scout pilots who flew in from time to time, much more difficult for smaller and faster machines. When, therefore, one day an SE5 was brought down very cleverly, Young (a fellow pilot who was standing beside me) and I both remarked together, 'Some pilot that. What a wonderful landing.'

"As the pilot made no move to get out of his machine, but kept the prop ticking over, we concluded that he really wanted to ask a question, so we walked over and asked if we could help him. We spoke with some respect, because in a similar occasion not long before, after addressing a pilot as 'Old Cock', he turned out to be an inspecting officer, and I was not a little embarrassed when he took off his flying coat to see yards of gold braid. But to return to the SE pilot.

"He asked for the direction of the squadron which I learned later he was flying out to command. We told him, so, after taxiing out into position, he took off again.

"He could not have been any higher than seventy feet when it became obvious that he was in trouble. I said to Young, 'Good God! What's happened to his engine? Young said, quite casually, 'Oh, he's only throttled back'. At that moment the machine was turned back over the aerodrome, and for a second or two I thought Young was right, as the engine appeared to pick up again.

"But alas! It was only for a moment. Again McCudden turned, now back towards the aerodrome, but he could not get down and flew straight into the small wood on the far side. There was a horrible crash. Those nearest rushed to the scene and, while we agreed there could only be one end to such a crash, we waited, hoping against hope that we might be wrong.

"Presently we leaned that the pilot was not dead, but that his case was practically hopeless. He died shortly afterwards. It was then, for the first time, I learned that the pilot I had spoken to only two minutes previously was none other than the famous 'Jimmy' McCudden."

Beneath this letter the magazine printed a photograph of the aerodrome at Auxi-le-Chateau. This was captioned:

Aix(*sic*)Le-Chateau Aerodrome, where Major McCudden, V.C. was killed. Major McCudden took off in the direction N.N.E, reading the top of the photograph as north. After turning, he flew over the three lorries by the side of the road where he turned again, his engine failing as he did so. He crashed into the wood just beyond the right-hand hangar of the three in line.

These details of McCudden's flight, directly after he had taken off, are obviously based on the account of the anonymous eye witness, but are questionable on several points.

Firstly: McCudden had been told that Boffles lay to the North North East. If, as stated, he took off towards the N.N.East, he would have already been heading in the direction of Boffles, which is under four miles from Auxi-le-Chateau – a flight of only a few minutes – and with only a modest amount of height he would have been able to see the aerodrome at Boffles, even allowing for the slightly hazy conditions. There was no reason why he would turn twice after takeoff, as stated, and fly back over the aerodrome. Secondly: the reference by the witness to McCudden crashing into the small wood on the far side of the aerodrome. The woods on that side of the aerodrome are extensive, as can readily be seen from the photograph. Finally, no mention is made of either Burdett or Vallins. The whole of the statement by the anonymous witness suggests that it was influenced by knowledge of the official version of the reason for the crash, that McCudden had attempted to turn back to the aerodrome with a failing engine.

In fact, the caption to the photograph in 1936 issue of Popular Flying that gives the top of the photograph as north, is incorrect. The late Mike O'Connor, researcher and author, in the Arras edition of his series of books, Airfields and Airmen, published the same photograph of the aerodrome at Auxi-le-Chateau, but gave that it is looking south, not north.[15]

From the accounts of the eyewitnesses that gave evidence in the days following the crash, the following sequence of events best fits the salient points. After landing, McCudden taxied to the northern end of the aerodrome, turned into the wind by the side of the road containing the lorries, and took off to the south. This meant that he would have to turn again to set course north-north-east for Boffles, and as soon as he was airborne he turned north, a steep turn in his usual manner, opening the throttle for the necessary power as he approached the wood. With the resultant choking of his engine, he lost flying speed, stalled and crashed into the trees just behind the last hangar of the three.

This scenario is supported by the testimony of Barry and King.

"I was standing near the officers' mess at the southern end of the aerodrome. I saw an SE5 flying from west to east across the aerodrome." (Barry)

"I saw the machine (SE5) flying very low over the aerodrome, going East towards the wood on the S.E. side of the aerodrome." (King) King obviously saw the SE just before McCudden began to bank to the N.N.E.

The proximity of the trees would have presented no problem to McCudden. It is well known that he had a penchant for taking off in a steep climbing turn. This had been remarked on when he was flying DH2s in 29 Squadron, SE5as in 56 Squadron, and while he was at Ayr and Turnberry.[16] The witness statements tend to support that McCudden was taking off from Auxi-Le-Chateau in just such a manner: that he put the SE5a into a 'sharp stalling turn' (Barry) into a 'vertical turn' (Fenelon); 'nearly vertical climb' (Burdett) and the three witnesses who reported that the SE was rolling, King, Greenwood and Burdett – ' seemed to do a half roll', obviously saw the SE5a at the end of its vertical bank, just before it lost flying speed.

As McCudden began a steep banking turn, ample power would have been an absolute necessity. The steeper the turn, the higher must be the airspeed to provide the extra wing lift necessary to keep the vertical upward force equal to the pull of gravity, otherwise the aeroplane will stall. Up to a bank of 60 degrees the stalling speed increases steadily, but from 60 to 80 degrees the stalling speed rises very rapidly. An aeroplane that normally stalls at 45mph, will stall at 65mph in a 60 degree bank, but at 80 degrees bank the stalling speed rises to 110mph. It is therefore evident how important it is, when making a steep turn, to have plenty of power in hand. In a steep, climbing turn, full and, importantly, immediate power, is an absolute necessity. If this is not available, then a crash is inevitable. From available evidence it seems that this is precisely what happened at Auxi-Le-Chateau on the evening of 9 July 1918. McCudden took off in his usual manner. At the beginning of his turning climb, he opened his throttle for the required power. The engine failed to respond, lost power, and the SE5a stalled and crashed. The question remains, what caused this loss of engine power when McCudden opened his throttle?

In 1973, while engaged in extensive research into the history of 56 Squadron, one of the many ex-members of the squadron traced and interviewed was Hubert Charles, the squadron's engineering officer.[17] During conversation, the subject of McCudden and his fatal crash came up. Charles was unaware that the cause of the crash was a subject of controversy and when told, he said: 'Oh, I can tell you about that'.

In July 1918, Charles was an accident investigative officer. On the evening of 9 July he was at 2ASD and received a personal telephone call from Trenchard, asking him to go to Auxi-le-Chateau and look into the possible reasons for McCudden's crash. Charles went straight to Auxi-le-Chateau and on examining the wreckage of C1126 was amazed to see that the type of air filter that had been fitted was the same type that he had personally modified during the first troubles experienced by 56 Squadron with the 1170 Hispano-Suiza engine in 1917. In the interview, Charles had previously explained to the interviewer the troubles, potentially dangerous, experienced by 56 Squadron with the carburettors and air filters of the early SE5 and the latter SE5a in 1917. That an air filter of a faulty design, superseded over a year previously, had been fitted to a production SE5a in 1918, built by the Royal Aircraft Factory at Farnborough seems incredible, but Charles was quite firm on this point.[18] Although he declined to state positively that this was the cause of engine failure at the crucial moment as McCudden took off, he confirmed that the effect of this type of air filter, if partially filled with petrol, would be to choke the engine if the throttle were opened by a pilot in need of an immediate increase in power. As has been seen, some of the witnesses to the crash gave evidence that the engine of C1126 was not running perfectly just before the crash, and this would tend to confirm the supposition that the engine choked when called upon to give more power during a steep climbing turn after take off. When the interviewer put to Charles the suggestion that it was strange that, as an accident investigation officer, looking into the cause of the death of one of Britain's most successful airmen, and with direct and personal access to both Trenchard and his successor, Salmond, his findings to them had not resulted in an official explanation of the crash, he gave a somewhat vague and guarded reply.

Given the evidence, on record, of poor quality control and inspection procedures at the Royal Aircraft Factory, which were experienced by those squadrons operating with the SE5a in France, plus that of Charles, it is difficult not to escape the conclusion that there was an official cover up of the reason for McCudden's fatal crash.

One further, ironical point. In those last few moments before the crash, McCudden had the presence of mind to both switch off the engine ignition and unfasten his seat belt. On impact he was thrown out of his cockpit and was found lying by one of the wings of the wreckage. The reason his elder brother Bill did not survive his fatal crash in 1915 was because he had been strapped into his cockpit and not thrown clear, as was his passenger, who escaped injury. James McCudden was always conscious of this and is known to have advised that before a crash the safety seat belt should be unfastened. Bill McCudden had died because he was strapped in; James McCudden, perhaps because he wasn't. It was a strange twist of fate.

Appendix II: James McCudden: The Leading All-Round Airman of the War

The air war of 1914–1918 saw the emergence of many outstanding airmen. At the time of writing, Manfred von Richthofen is generally considered to be the leading airman of all the nations involved in the conflict; a position held almost by default, mainly on the basis of his eighty aerial victories.[1] However, victory scores are subject to many varying factors, and while an airman's personal score of enemy aeroplanes brought down is no doubt significant, it is far from being of prime importance and is only one aspect of a pilot's overall worth.[2] On the criteria of who was the finest all-round airman of the war, the accolade must surely go to James Thomas Byford McCudden.

During the four years of his service, firstly as a 1AM with 3 Squadron in France in 1914 to his final rise through the ranks to that of a highly decorated commissioned officer with 57 aerial victories to his credit, McCudden had served with an unswerving devotion and keenness in all the various duties he was called upon to undertake. His expertise in engines, and the technicalities of all types of aircraft while serving in 3 Squadron, earned him the implicit trust of both his own pilot and his Flight Commander: in the words of his commanding officer in 3 Squadron, Major-General John Salmond, 'he was at that time one of the best engine fitters we had. His attention to detail and his capacity marked him out for early promotion.' While an unofficial observer/gunner in 3 Squadron, McCudden's youthful keenness – he was still only twenty years of age, the most junior of the NCO aircrew of the squadron – and both his coolness under fire and shooting ability, were such that the new commanding officer of the squadron, Ludlow-Hewitt, at the height of the Fokker menace, chose him whenever possible as his observer. Sent home to England for pilot training, McCudden was found to have a natural, above average ability, and at the completion of his training was selected as an flying instructor, instructing over ninety pupils before his first posting to operational flying in France.

McCudden then flew as a pilot in a two-seater squadron for nearly a month before being posted to 29 Squadron, flying DH2 scouts. After seven months with 29 Squadron, surviving many combats against the vastly superior Albatros scouts, with their higher performance and double the fire power of the DH2, McCudden was credited with five victories,[3] and was posted to Home Establishment to lecture pilots at the training squadrons in fighting techniques, personally demonstrating combat manoeuvres. During this time – a period of five months – he also tested many types of aircraft and flew sorties against the Gothas during their raids on England. Posted back to France, first as a refresher course with 66 Squadron, then to 56 Squadron, in the next seven months he formulated and developed his ideas on the tactics of leading a Flight: tactics that would ensure the maximum damage to the enemy without loss; tactics that resulted in the loss of only four pilots to enemy action in the course of over seventy patrols; tactics that he taught and impressed upon his pilots, some of whom, benefiting from his teaching, themselves later became successful Flight Commanders.[4] In addition to these duties as a Flight Commander, he thought back to the original *raison d'être* of the fighter aeroplane, that of preventing the enemy reconnaissance and artillery-spotting aeroplanes from carrying out their all important duties. To McCudden, this was more important, and certainly more productive to the war effort than the destruction of enemy scouts in a tit-for-tat, dogfight type of operation. Consequently, in addition to his patrols as a Flight Commander, he flew alone on sixty Special Missions – over a hundred hours of combat flying time – and destroyed forty enemy two-seaters in twenty-two weeks of active operational flying. Many of these combats were carried out under extremely difficult physical and mental conditions, flying at heights of anything between 16 and 21,000ft against fast, two-seater enemy reconnaissance machines – some of which, at height, were superior in performance to his SE5a and flown by well-trained and experienced crews. Quite apart from his overall achievements, this record alone would place him as the finest fighter pilot of the war.[5]

Returning to Home Establishment after his service with 56 Squadron McCudden was posted as a fighting instructor to the No.1 School of Aerial Fighting at Ayr, later at Turnberry. While at the school, McCudden both lectured and instructed many embryo fighter pilots on the finer points of aerial combat and gunnery, personally flying both with and against them in practise and mock combat fights. As always, McCudden was conscientious, painstaking and thorough in everything he did, and he took his teaching duties in Scotland extremely seriously. As an instructor, he was acknowledged as being one of the finest at the school.

To put McCudden's superlative record still further into perspective it must be remembered that not only was he still a young man, but that he achieved his success in a Britain in which social class was still a dominant feature, which barred many from advancement in both civilian and military life. In an autocracy, rather than a meritocracy, James McCudden's progression through the ranks in eight years, from a boy bugler in the Royal Engineers in 1910 to that of Major, with his country's highest decoration for bravery, was a remarkable achievement.

Given his overall record, there can be no doubt that James McCudden, VC, DSO+, MC+, MM, Croix de Guerre was the finest all-round airman of the First World War.[6]

Appendix III: Publicity for British Pilots

With the emergence of the first successful fighter pilots, both Germany and France exploited their prowess for propaganda purposes, both with the civilian population and their fighting forces. In Germany, first Oswald Boelcke and Max Immelmann were national heroes, followed by Manfred von Richthofen. In France, Georges Guynemer, René Fonck and others were household names. The German and French high commands regularly reported news of their pilots' victories, news eagerly taken up by the newspapers.

The only successful pilots known to the general public in England were Albert Ball and the Canadian, William Bishop, both through the citations for their Victoria Cross awards. The British newspapers were unable to keep up to date with similar citations, detailing the gallantry awards to other pilots, as these were sometimes not gazetted until up to six months after the promulgation of the award. As an example, the citation giving the details of McCudden's remarkable record in December 1917, which earned him a bar to his DSO, was not published until July 1918, nine days after his death.

During the summer of 1917, the British press had become increasingly clamorous in their demands for details of successful British pilots, arguing that the British people had the right to know of the deeds of their own airmen: that they were equal in bravery and achievement to those of the German and French. Under pressure, the War Office asked for the views of Haig, GOC of the British forces in France. Writing back to the Chief of the Imperial General staff in September, Haig was adamant against any change in the official policy, adding that as GOC of the RFC, Trenchard was fully in agreement with him; was also adverse to any publication of the work done by individual pilots of the Corps. Such publicity would, he said, be both unwise and unfair to other branches of the army; that it would be likely to cause jealousy, both within the RFC and the army as a whole; and that the RFC itself would reject such a policy, being proud of its anonymity, shared with those of their compatriots in the other branches of the army. Finally – and here it seems was the crux of the objections – he stated that, regardless of the system adopted by other countries, the publicity would be against the best traditions of the British Army. Most officers of the RFC paid lip service to the official policy and few cared one way or the other, knowing only too well the embarrassment that could be caused by the naming of individuals by colourful stories in the press. They were in general both amused by the excessive adulation of the French airmen and skeptical of the publicity methods used by some of the Commonwealth countries, particularly Canada. In view of the fact that he would have needed official permission to do so, the visit of the Havas correspondent to 56 Squadron and other squadrons in December 1917, was perhaps a little disingenuous of the British High Command; a way of changing policy without loss of face. It must surely have known the result of such a visit. On 1 January 1918, the British papers were full of stories of the exploits of the fighter pilots – although still unnamed – of the RFC. On 7th January 1918, restrictions were finally lifted and the *Daily Mail* named James McCudden and Philip Fullard as two of the leading British fighter pilots, detailing their successes in highly colourful terms.

Rumpler Rubild 8322/17. When fitted with a Messter strip camera, the Rumpler C.IV with 260 hp Mercedes D.IVa was originally known as the Rumpler C.VI, but the designation was later changed to Rumpler Rubild to emphasize its long-range photo reconnaissance role. Performance of this model was similar to the standard C.IV using the same engine, but the Rubild was often lightened by eliminating equipment to improve its ceiling and speed at altitude.

Appendix IV: Aerial Victories – An Evaluation

Although of little importance in the overall picture of the war, the question of the number of aerial victories awarded to individual fighter pilots of the combatants has become a subject of academic interest to many of those interested in the air fighting of 1914–1918.

The RFC/RAF casualty reports of men and machines in the First World War, held at the National Archive at Kew in London, are to all intents and purposes complete, which enables the historian to give a reasonably accurate assessment of the victory claims by the pilots of the *Luftstreitkräfte*.[1]

With the vast majority of aerial combats fought behind the German trenches and back areas, these German claims are, in the main, accurate, as the evidence, the wreckage, was on the ground. However, from the records at Kew it is apparent that some German pilots could possibly have larger victory scores than were awarded to them. The records show that many allied pilots escaped from a combat – either wounded or otherwise – and successfully returned to their own lines, either crash landing behind them or in some cases returning to their own aerodromes in badly damaged machines that had to be written off as not repairable. In addition, if wounded, the pilot was struck off strength.

The *Jasta* pilots fought a defensive war, rarely crossing into allied territory – combat reports of allied pilots are full of incidents of an enemy pilot, often in an advantageous position, breaking off the action as soon as they had crossed the trenches – and consequently these allied casualties, to either men or machines, were not claimed as victories by the German fighter pilots as they had no means of knowing the outcome of the combats in which they had been involved. If they claimed at all it was merely for a victory as being *Jenseits* (other side).

Unfortunately, an equivalent, complete record of German aircrew killed, wounded, and/or the losses of aircraft, destroyed, damaged or merely forced to land after combat, has not yet been found – they were destroyed, either in the allied bombing of the second world war or by the *Luftwaffe*, who had orders to destroy them in the closing stages of that conflict, or both. Consequently, the validity of the claims by allied pilots for German machines sent down out of control is impossible to evaluate. No doubt, in many instances, the enemy pilot was merely spinning away out of trouble – a common tactic used by both sides – but in others the pilot was either wounded, his machine damaged and genuinely out of control, or both.[2]
If the German equivalent of the British casualty lists in both men and, importantly, machines, were available, there is no doubt that out of control claims by allied pilots could also be evaluated correctly; either confirmed or not. While the German records are incomplete, this is simply not possible.

Categories of Aerial Victories

The question of what constitutes an aerial victory has long been a controversial subject amongst those historians who study the air fighting of the First World War. The RFC and RAF recognised two broad categories: Destroyed, and Out of Control – at one time, aeroplanes Driven Down or Forced to Land, was an additional category, but this seems to have been discontinued later in the war and was not included in a pilot's official tally.

Of particular controversy has been the subject of claims for aeroplanes send down out of control, a type of victory recognised by the British. It has been correctly pointed out that, when out flown or outfought, spinning away out of a fight was a frequent method used by pilots – German and British – to break off a fight; a legitimate evasive manoeuvre. But with the vast majority of the air fighting taking place behind the German lines – sometimes as much as twenty or thirty miles – no British pilot would follow an enemy aeroplane down merely to confirm whether or not it crashed. Such an action would leave him low down over enemy territory, easy prey to any enemy fighters above him, and with having to fight against the prevailing wind – in France nearly always from west to east – to regain the safety of his own lines.

The question has been raised by those air historians who study the activities of the *Luftstreitkräfte*, that many out of control victories claimed and awarded to the pilots of the RFC/RAF were simply the enemy pilot spinning down out of trouble, and an out of control victory claimed by British pilots is now regarded by some historians of the German *Jagdstaffeln*, as a doubtful victory, or even as a legitimate victory at all.

This may well be so, but it raises the question as to what actually constitutes a victory. An aeroplane seen to crash, break up in mid-air, or go down in flames is, of course, a positive victory, more so than one seen to go down out of control, whose ultimate fate was not seen, However, regardless of whether the aeroplane in question was genuinely out of control and ultimately crashed, or whether the pilot – either wounded or unwounded – was able to regain control and crash land somewhere, or even return to his aerodrome, is surely irrelevant. An enemy pilot outfought and forced to withdraw, by whatever means, is still a victory.[3] The question of out of control victories claimed by British pilots could be resolved if the German records were available, not only of pilots who were wounded in action, but more importantly, of losses and replacements of aircraft that crashed, were then repaired, or struck off the strength of the unit concerned.[4]

Individual Victory Scores

To take the number of a pilot's victories and compare it with another in order to evaluate their relative successes as fighter pilots is fraught with difficulties, almost impossible. There are too many variables, chief amongst which is the period of the war in which they fought. The most crucial time in the life of a fighter pilot was undoubtedly his first month or six weeks of combat. If he could survive this period, become completely orientated in the air and absorb the basis skills of his trade, he stood a good chance of surviving his first tour of operational flying – usually six months – and becoming an efficient and experienced fighter pilot. The embryo RFC fighter pilot in the period of late 1916 to the June of 1917 would have been flying a DH2 or an FE8, both obsolescent pusher designs, vastly outclassed by the German Halberstadt and first Albatros types. If he were a little luckier he would be flying a Nieuport 17 or a Sopwith Pup, both nearer in comparison to the performance of the German scouts, but still with only half their firepower.

Conversely, the emerging German fighter pilots of the same period had a vastly superior aeroplane in which to learn their trade and survive that important initial period of combat. They could out-gun or out-run any contemporary British fighter, and the hordes of two-seater BE and FE types were relatively easy targets. This is not to belittle the undoubted achievements of the first fighter pilots of the German Army Air Service. They did their job of destroying the eyes of the enemy extremely well. It was not their fault, or to their discredit, that the equipment that they were given to do that job was vastly superior to that of their opponents.

The embryo fighter pilots of the RFC during the period in question, those who later became high scorers, but scored their initial victories while flying DH2s during their first period of duty in France, illustrates the point. To take just three: James McCudden, five; Geoffrey Bowman, two; Henry Woollett, one. These pilots' later scores were 57, 32, and 35 respectively. Flying the DH2 against technically superior opponents they were content to merely survive.

It is also significant that those pilots of the RFC who flew their first tour a little later, flying Nieuports and Sopwith Pups, did better in their initial tours of duty, as did those pilots who came slightly earlier, when the DH2, FE8 and the early Nieuports were outperforming the Fokker E and Pfalz E types.

Manfred von Richthofen and his contemporaries were highly successful fighter pilots because, quite apart from any other considerations, they were fortunate to begin their careers when the fighter aeroplanes of the *Luftstreitkräfte* were overwhelmingly superior to their opponents.

In the past it was fashionable to decry Richthofen's success, pointing out that the majority of his victories were two-seaters. This is not a valid argument. Richthofen's job was to destroy these. If he was fortunate that they were, in the main, and especially in his first 50 victories, vastly inferior in performance and firepower to his Albatros or Halberstadt, that was hardly his fault. It has been argued that of McCudden's 57 victories, 44 were also two-seaters. But again, that was also McCudden's job, even his *raison d'etre*, and the fast, well-armed LVGs, Rumplers, and DFWs of late 1917 and early 1918, with their experienced and well-trained crews, were far more dangerous opponents – even for an SE5a – than were the British BE and FE types of the earlier period for an Albatros.[5]

It does Richthofen and his fellow pilots more credit to look beyond today's myth and hype of their invincibility. Richthofen was undoubtedly a charismatic leader. He was also a great fighter pilot, but he was not a natural, as was the mercurial Werner Voss, whom many German pilots of the time considered their finest.

The facts are, that if a fighter pilot – of either side – were lucky enough to fly his initial tour of operational flying with the advantage of an aeroplane of superior performance and fire power to that of his opponents, then, with luck, he could look forward to surviving that initial period and gain some success. Richthofen and his exact contemporaries in the autumn of 1916 and the early months of 1917 were just that lucky. By the time the pendulum of technical superiority made its next swing in favour of the British pilots, with the introduction of the SE5, the Sopwith Camel and the Bristol Fighter, Richthofen and his contemporaries were highly experienced and were able to deal with the new allied fighters.

Rumpler Rubild Mb 8186/17 flown by pilot *Ltn*. Oskar Seitz. When fitted with the high-altitude 245hp Maybach Mb.IVa engine, the aircraft was designated the Rubild Mb. The Maybach gave the Rubild Mb even better ceiling and speed at altitude than the Mercedes-powered Rubild. Seitz was instrumental in designing the custom observer's gun mounting that combined a captured Lewis machine gun with the standard Parabellum for additional firepower to defend against Allied fighters.

Appendix V: The Aerial Victories of James McCudden

With 57 officially credited victories, James McCudden stands fourth on the list of British Commonwealth pilots. Many successful pilots who kept a personal tally of their victories, included those which were not officially credited to them – perhaps for lack of confirmation from witnesses – but which they felt were valid. This compilation of McCudden's victories, from

Additional details of McCudden's victories can be found in the main text. *denotes victories not officially credited

No.	Date	Claim	Time	Location	Details	Confirmed By
29 Squadron						
1916						
1	6/9/16	Albatros Two-seater	1.00PM	Gheluwe	Crashed by Menin Road White in colour	Agent
2*	15/9/1916	Two-seater	1.30PM	Messines	DD, Brown in colour,	FTL
3*	16/9/16	Albatros C type	6.30PM	E of Polygon Wood Q1 Sht 28	DD FTL	
	Note: In a citation of 1/10/16 for the award of a Military Medal, McCudden was credited with one enemy machine destroyed and					
4*	21/10/16	Small Rumpler biplane	2.25PM	Armentières	DD	
5*	9/11/16	Two-seater	2.00PM approx.	Gommécourt	DD	
6*	10/11/16	Albatros C type	Early afternoon	Miraumont	DD	
1917						
7*	23/1/17	Albatros D type	10.00AM	Monchy-le-Preux	DDD	
8*	23/1/17	Aviatik	Early afternoon	Adinfer Wood	DDD	
9	26/1/17	Two-seater	10.05AM	Ficheux	Crashed	McCudden
10	2/2/17	Two-seater	2.45PM	Adinfer Wood	Crashed	
11	6/2/17	Albatros C.III	2.00PM	NE corner of Adinfer Wood		AA
12	15/2/17	Roland C.II	12.00AM	E of Monchy	Crashed	Patrol and AA
66 Squadron						
13*	16/7/17	Albatros D type	Evening	E of Ypres	DD*	Entered in logbook
56 Squadron						
14	21/7/17	Albatros D type	7.45-8.00PM	Polygon Wood	OOC, Silver grey	A Rhys Davids
66 Squadron						
15*	22/7/17	Two-seater	4.30PM	Quesnoy	DD	
16*	26/7/17	Albatros D type	8.15PM	Gheluwe	DDD	G L P Henderson
56 Squadron						
17	18/8/17	Albatros D type	7.30AM	E of Houthem	OOC	L Barlow
18	19/8/17	Albatros D type	5.25PM	Gheluvelt	OOC	Patrol
19	20/8/17	Albatros D type	6.50PM	SE of Polygon Wood	In flames	Patrol
20	20/8/17	Albatros D type	7.00PM approx.	Polygon Wood	OOC	Patrol/H Johnston
21*	21/8/17	Albatros D Type	7.45AM	Gheluve	DD	
22*	22/8/17	DFW	6.45–7.20PM	Ypres area	DDD	
23*	4/9/17	Albatros D type	3.00PM	E of Houthulst Forest	DD	
24*	5/9/17	DFW	10.30–10.40AM	Quesnoy	DD	
25*	11/9/17	Albatros D Type	6.15AM	Passchèndaele	DD	
26	14/9/17	Albatros D Type	6.00PM	Roulers	DD	
27*	19/9/17	DFW	11.30AM	Quesnoy	DDD	
28	19/9/17	Rumpler	12.20AM	Radinghem	Crashed	10 Sqdn. and AA
29	21/9/17	Two-seater	1.00PM	Gheluwe	DDD	
30	23/9/17	DFW	6.00PM	Houhem	Crashed	
31*	25/9/17	Type not given			DD	Logbook entry
32	27/9/17	Rumpler C.V	4.00PM	SE of Langémarcke	Flames	British lines
33	28/9/17	Albatros D Type	8.00AM	Houthulst Forest	Broke up in midair	Patrol
34	1/10/17	Rumpler	2.50PM	Herlies	DDD	
35	14/10/17	Albatros D type	10.45AM	Passendale	DD	
36	17/10/17	LVG C.V	11.30AM approx.	Vlamertinghe	Broke up in air	British lines

his combat reports and other sources, has been compiled with the same criteria. Included are those machines which were driven down (DD) or driven down damaged (DDD) by McCudden on the basis that such victories, although not officially credited, are still valid.[1] The final total is very near the estimate given by McCudden to Mrs. Alec-Tweedie in July 1918.
1. Although later discontinued, these categories of victories were so classified in the early RFC communiqués and many squadron victory lists.

Remarks

1st Anzac Corps

two others forced to land.

Crashed. Destroyed by artillery

McCudden included this Albatros in his list of victories he was asked to submit to RFC HQ at the end of December 1917.

Possibly from *Jasta* 14
All red with yellow stripes
Vzfw. Josef Oehler, *Jasta* 24. Killed

Credited in Squadron list

Obflg. Kurt Schönfelder, wounded, *Jasta* 7
Oblt. Ernst Weigand *Jasta* 10, Lightly wounded

Ltn.d.R Bauer seriously wounded, *Uffz*. Allkofer Lightly injured, *Fl.Abt.* (A) 292

Ltn. Gustav Rudolph, *Uffz*. Rudolph Franke, *Fl.Abt.*6

Uffz.Hans Gossler, *Uffz*. Bruno Wiedemann. Gossler fell in British lines, Wiedemann in German lines, *Schutzstaffel* 27b, G.73
Ltn. Herbert Pastor, *Jasta* 29
Possibly from *Fl.Abt.* 5 who reported an observer *Ltn*. Frauenstein slightly wounded on Oct 1

Oblt. Ernst Hädrich & *Flg*. Heinrich Horstmann, *Fl.Abt.* 8, G.81

No.	Date	Claim	Time	Location	Details	Confirmed By
37	21/10/17	Rumpler C.IV 8431/16	1.00PM approx.	Mazingarbe	Crashed	British lines
38	18/11/17	DFW C.V	9.40AM	Bellicourt	Crashed	Patrol and AA
39	23/11/17	Albatros D type	12.00PM	Between Noyelles W & Rumilly	Crashed	Fielding-Johnson
40	29/11/17	DFW.C.V	7.30AM	S.E. of Bellicourt	Broke up in air	Patrol
41	29/11/17	DFW C.V	1.00PM	Rouvroy	Broke up in air	Patrol and AA
42	30 /11/17	LVG C.V 9458/17	11.15PM	Havrincourt	Broke up in air	British lines
43	5/12/17	Rumpler C.VII	12.40PM	Hermies	Broke up in air	British lines
44	6/12/17	Rumpler	10.20AM	Holnon Wood/Francilly	Broke up in air	British lines
45	6/12/17	Albatros D type	3.00PM	Fontaine	OOC	Patrol
46*	7/12/17	Hannover	9.00AM	E of Bourlon Wood	DD	
47*	10/12/17	Two-seater	3.45PM	Havrincourt	DDD	
48	15/12/17	Rumpler	11.05AM	Bois-de-Vaucelles	Crashed	McCudden
49*	19/12/17	Two-seater	10.40AM	N E of St Quentin	DDD	
50	22/12/17	DFW C.V	12.05PM	S W St Quentin	crashed	British lines
51	23/12/17	LVG	11.25AM	Anguilcourt	Crashed	McCudden
52	23/12/17	Rumpler C.VII	12.20PM	Contescourt	Broke up in air	British lines
53	23/12/17	Rumpler	2.40PM	Gouzeaucourt	Crashed	British lines
54	23/12/17	LVG C.V 9446/17	3.30PM	Metz-en-Couture	Crashed	British lines
55	28/12/17	Rumpler	11.15PM	Vélu Wood	Broke up in air	British lines
56	28/12/17	Rumpler	11.30AM	Flers	Flames/crashed	British lines
57	28/12/17	LVG C.V	11.55AM	Havrincourt Wood	Broke up in air	British lines
58	28/12/17	LVG	12.15/12.30PM	Marquion	DDD	
59	29/12/17	LVG	9.55AM	Havrincourt	Crashed	British lines
60*	29/12/17	LVG	12.00PM	Haucourt/Lagnicourt	DDD	
61	29/12/17	LVG	1.50PM	N E Épéhy	Broke up in air	British lines
62*	3/1/18	Rumpler	10.30–11.00AM	Vendhuille	DDD	
63*	9/1/18	Hannover	11.05AM	N of Raillencourt	DDD	
64	9/1/18	LVG	11.30AM	Graincourt	Crashed	E Turnbull and patrol
65	13/1/18	LVG	9.40AM	E of Le Haucourt	Crashed	5th Army AA
66	13/1/18	DFW	9.50AM	N of Vendhuille	Crashed	5th Army AA
67	13/1/18	LVG	10.05AM	Lempire	Broke up in air/flames	5th Arny AA
68	20/1/18	LVG	10.30AM	Between Raillencourt & Cambrai	Broke up in air	3rd Army AA
69	20/1/18	LVG	11.30AM	NE Crevecouer-s-Escaut	DDD	
70	24/1/18	DFW	2.00PM	Monchy-le-Preux	OOC	McCudden
71	25/1/18	Rumpler	2.40PM	Urvillers	Crashed	5th Army infantry
72	30/1/18	Albatros D.V 4565/17	11.15AM	Anneux	OOC/Smoking	AA
73	30/1/18	Pfalz D.III	11.15AM	Anneux	OOC	AA
74	2/2/18	LVG C.V 9775/17	10.40AM	E of Vélu	Crashed	British lines
75*	3/2/18	Hannover	9.40AM approx.	Marquion	DDD	
76	16/2/18	Rumpler	10.40AM	SW Caudry	Broke up in air	Patrol and AA
77	16/2/18	DFW	10.50AM	NE Le Catelet	Flames/broke up in air	Patrol
78*	16/2/18	LVG	11.00AM approx	Le Catelet area	DDD	K. Junor & McC.
79	16/2/18	Rumpler	11.10AM	Hargicourt	OOC	AA
80	16/2/18	Rumpler	12.30PM	Lagnicourt	Broke up in air	British lines

One source gives this machine from Schutzstaffel 29 as being a DFW but the G report gives it as a Mercedes-powered Rumpler.

No.	Date	Claim	Time	Location	Details	Confirmed By
81	17/2/18	LVG	10.25AM	Guémappe	OOC	
82	17/2/18	Rumpler	12.10PM	Raillencourt	DD	
83	18/2/18	Albatros D.V 4448/17	9.40AM	Vitry	In flames	
84	18/2/18	Albatros	9.40AM	Quiery-le-Motte	Crashed	
85	21/2/18	DFW	1.47PM	SE of Méricourt	Flames/crashed	
86	26/2/18	Rumpler	11.20AM	Oppy	Flames/broke up in air	AA
87	26/2/18	Hannover C.II 9389/17	11.30AM	Chérisy	Broke up in air	AA
88	26/2/18	Rumpler	12.00AM	NW of Douai Beaumont	DDD	

Remarks
Ltn. Hans Laito & *Uffz.* Richard Hiltweis, *Fl.Abt.* 5, G.84
*Ltn.*Ernst & *Ltn.d.Res.* Schwarzer, *Fl.Abt.* (A) 259
Vzfw. Karl Bey, *Jasta* 5

Ltn.d.Res. Kurt Dittrich & *Ltn.d.Res.* Manfred Hoettger, *Fl.Abt.*(A) 202
*Ltn.d.Res.*Georg Dietrich & *Ltn.* Dietrich Schenk, *Fl.Abt.*(A) 268
Vzfw. Flohrig & *Gef.* Eckerle, Schutzstaffel 19, G.94
Ltn.d.Res. Alfred Berking & *Uffz.* Max Bröll, *Fl.Abt.* 33. Wreckage given two G Numbers, G.95 & G.96
Ltn. Martin Becker & *Uffz.* Karl Pohlisch, *Fl.Abt.* 225
Possibly from *Jasta* 5

Uffz. Biesenbach & *Uffz.* Anton Bode, *Schutzstaffel* 5, G.104
Ltn.d.Res Friedrich Drückhammer, *Vzfw.* Zehe, *Fl.Abt* 40
Ltn. Hugo Richter & *Ltn.* Emil Tibussek, *Fl.Abt.* 23, G.107
From *Bogohl* 7, Crew taken POW, G.106
Vzfw. Kurt Boje & *Vzfw.* Friedrich Niemann, *Schutzstaffel* 12, G.108
*Ltn.*Klaus Doering & *Ltn.* Hans Dubislaw, *Fl.Abt* 32, G.111
Ltn. Hans Mittag & *Uffz.* Oskar Güntert, *Fl.Abt.* (A) 40, G.112
Ltn. Walter Bergmann & *Flg.* Albert Weinrich, *Fl.Abt* (A) 210, G.113

Vzfw. Kurt Gerschel FW & *Uffz.* Lehnert. Unhurt. POW. *Schutzstaffel* 10, G.118
Possibly *Ltn.* Metzger wd. *Fl.Abt.*(A) 233
Ltn.d.Res. Walter Dern & *Ltn.d.Res.* Georg Müller, *Fl.Abt.* 33, G.119

Possibly *Vzfw* Wilhelm Döfler (P) *Schutzstaffel* 25b, wd. Suffered contusions to head during forced landing G3D Sht. 57B
Pilot Notler (rank unkw), *Ltn.d.Res* Max Pappenheimer, *Fl.Abt.* (A) 264s
Ltn.d.Res Max Ritterman & *Uffz.* Bruns, *Bogohl* 7
Ltn. Gerhard Besser & *Vzfw.* Hans Rautenberg, *Bogohl.* 7, G.124
Uffz. Gustav Mosch & *Ltn.* Friedrich Bracksiek, *Fl.Abt.(A)* 202

Ltn.de.Res. Georg Palloks (pilot), fatally wd. Observer unknown. *Fl.Abt.* (A) 240
Ltn.d.Res. Hermann Büscher & *Ltn.* Schramm, *Fl.Abt* (A) 225s
Vzfw. Adam Barth, *Jasta.*10

Ltn. Werner von Kuczkowski & *Vzfw.* Erich Szafranek, *Boghol* 7, G.130

Ltn.d.Res. Ernst Karlowa & *Uffz.* Albert Fröhlich, *Fl.Abt.* (A) 202
Uffz. Max Hänicke & *Ltn.* Fritz Düsterdieck, *Fl.Abt.* (A) 269

Possibly *Uffz.* Leipner. s.wd., *Ltn.d.Res.* von Frantzius lt.wd, *Fl.Abt.* (A) 202
Vzfw. Lorenz Zeuch & *Gefr.* Heinrich Lechleiter, *Schutzstaffel* 29b, G.137

Possibly *Ltn.*Otto Jablonski & *Vzfw.*Josef Klauke, *Fl.Abt.*(A) 263

Uffz. Julius Kaiser, *Jasta* 35b
Uffz. Joachim von Stein, *Jasta* 35b
Vzfw. Erich Klingenberg & *Ltn.* Karl Heger, *Fl.Abt.* (A) 235
Vzfw. Otto Kresse & *Ltn.* Rudolph Binting, *Fl.Abt.* 7
Uffz. Max Schwaier & *Ltn.* Walter Jäger, *Fl.Abt.*(A)293b

Appendix VI: James McCudden in the Eyes of His Contemporaries

Tryggve Gran, RFC/RAF
Nicknamed 'The Happy Warrior' due to his positive mood, he was the centre of the party when he was among friends. Nobody could feel down when McCudden was around.[1]

James Gascoyne, 2AM, 3 Squadron RFC
He was always a very keen fellow. What I remember most about him was that he had the most wonderful eyesight. With a revolver or rifle he could always find the target. We used to go on the ranges, firing, mostly for revolver practice, but now and again with rifles. And I think that this wonderful eyesight of his was one of the factors that added his success as a fighter pilot. Later on, when we got to France, he could always spot a German aircraft a long time before anyone else in the air.[2]

Sholto Douglas
Writing of Ball as a fighter pilot in 1916 and the emergence of McCudden as a fighter pilot in the same year.
The other outstandingly successful fighter pilot who was to appear at this time, and second only to Ball, was James McCudden. I came to know him very well, and to admire him greatly both as a man and as a pilot. McCudden was a year older than Albert Ball and his life had a very different background; and he adopted his own initiative tactics that were entirely different from those practised by the impetuous Ball. McCudden was a thoughtful tactician, and he was the originator of the formation fighter tactics which later became the rule, with the flight sticking together and never allowing itself to be broken up.
In September 1917, Douglas was commanding 84 Squadron and when the squadron was posted to Estrée Blanche he renewed his acquaintance with McCudden, now a flight commander in 56 Squadron.
By that summer Albert Ball was dead and Edward Mannock was only just emerging. McCudden was our foremost fighter pilot. He had been hard at it since the beginning of the war, and when he asked for a posting to 56 Squadron they were only too happy to have him. His arrival in the middle of August is recorded in the squadron history as "a valuable reinforcement". That speaks as well for the spirit of the men in No.56 Squadron as the later refusal by those of another squadron to have him as their Commanding Officer because he had come from the ranks condemns them for arrogant snobbishness, a state of affairs, which, when I heard about it, made my blood boil.

Of all the men whom I came to know well during the years of the First World War, from Boom Trenchard himself down to the hard-working airmen of my own squadrons, it was Jimmy McCudden who made upon me the strongest impression, and I have always been proud of our friendship. Just over a year younger than I was, McCudden was born in Kent, but there flowed in his veins a mixture of northern and southern Irish and of French blood, and that gave him alertness and enthusiasm and light-heartedness without his having for a moment to resort to flamboyance: qualities that came to be so well appreciated by those of us who knew him well. He also had, greatly to his credit, the best qualities of the young soldier who was proud of being a professional. In appearance McCudden was boyish, with a frank and unaffected manner. But then, so many of them were scarcely more than boys.

After detailing McCudden's career, Douglas goes on: During all this time I had heard a great deal about the progress that Jimmy McCudden was making, and the name that he was acquiring as a fine pilot and a keen fighter; and when I came to know him better I also learnt to appreciate more his views about the future of the rapidly evolving tactics of air fighting. We thought alike about the way in which our work as fighters should be done; and when I found on our arrival at Estrée Blanche that McCudden was there it was an added incentive to me to examine still further the way in which we should conduct this new dimension of fighting in the air.
Douglas was well aware of McCudden's view, that the shooting down of enemy two-seaters was of utmost importance – although at this time, still in the development stage.
But his main interest was in developing his original idea – original enough, that is, for those early days of fighting in the air – about the tactical use of fighters in flights and squadrons; and I shared with him that interest. The Germans were already working along the same lines, as we had discovered earlier in the year, but they were going in for larger formations than we thought either necessary or feasible. He no longer believed in the dog fighting that had been going on almost since the beginning. It had brought to some of the exceptional, lone-wolf pilots the most impressive scores; but McCudden stressed the view that when the new and inexperienced pilots tried to operate on their own they were more often than not picked off and shot down in their early encounters with more experienced German pilots.

Jimmy McCudden insisted that in their fighting the pilots of his flight should stick to him like glue, and that they should never, unless prevented by an accident, become separated from him. McCudden always put the two least experienced in his flight at the back of the formation of five with instructions that if they were attacked from the rear they were to dive for protection underneath the aircraft in front, rather like young chickens rushing to the safety of the cover of the hen. This sound plan soon put a stop to unnecessary casualties among the new boys. It also helped to give them the experience that was so vitally necessary.

From this there evolved the use of the flight as one individual unit. The result was that the leader, in this case Jimmy McCudden himself, shot down most of the Huns while the rest of the flight looked after his tail; and a lot of Huns were shot down in this way with very few casualties. There was some criticism of McCudden in No.56 Squadron on the grounds that he was being selfish and trying to bag all the glory for himself. Such criticism was natural enough for those who were over eager to get into the limelight; but those who had longer and more varied experience at the front realised that McCudden was right. He was a very good pilot, a most accurate shot, and an experienced leader; and I felt that it was up to those who would follow in his footsteps to prove themselves by learning from him.[3]

Wing Commander William Fry, MC
I saw quite a lot of McCudden and we became friends. The first time I met him was at the end of 1915, when he was a sergeant at Farnborough and had just gained his pilot's wings after being an observer in France. The next time was when he was with 29 Squadron at Filescamp farm, Izel-le-Hameau on DH2s as a sergeant pilot and later commissioned, and I was in 60 Squadron which had moved there from Savy Berlette. We met from time to time, right up to his death, mostly at the RFC Club in Bruton Street when our leaves from France or spells at home coincided. The chief reason we became friends was because we were both feeling our way in unfamiliar surroundings. Few RFC pilots understood McCudden's unusual background, which from birth had been entirely military in the days of the old pre-war Regular Army and in the world of NCOs and other ranks. The fact that he did not mix easily was almost entirely due to shyness and lack of confidence and the fact that he was proceeding very warily in an unfamiliar milieu after he became an officer. Service, rigid discipline and correct behaviour were his life, and the average young pilot with his carefree attitude must have seemed a queer sort of bird to him, so it was no wonder that some of them failed to appreciate him. He did not make jokes about service matters, they were much too serious. His demeanor was one of military correctitude; with this he had not a great sense of humour, at any rate for the knock-about fun which passed for humour in the RFC messes.

He was good-looking with a slim and graceful figure and my chief recollection of him is his simple, shining integrity. He was a first class pilot but not one to stunt or throw a machine about for the fun of it. Looking back, I am convinced that McCudden wanted to be friendly and to make friends but was inhibited by his upbringing from making the first approach. There was nothing complicated about him; he was utterly straightforward. No.56 Squadron must have been difficult squadron for him to serve in as a flight commander, for I don't think anyone could deny that there were slightly exclusive overtones. The fact that it was in 56 that he had such a shining success is in itself a great tribute to his character.[4]

2nd Lieutenant J.C.E. Hopkins, RFC/RAF
In 1917 I was training at Dover when he was fighting instructor, I think for the whole wing. He shared a hut with me – a bedroom – at Dover, just for a few nights. I really didn't know him at all well. He was quite patronising in a way, but helpful: he knew I was only a youngster under instruction. We discussed fighting tactics sitting on our beds and talking as we were going to bed. That sort of thing.

He was very abrupt. He had the reputation of having a bit of a chip on his shoulder. Of course, he was in the ranks before the war, he was a regular RFC man and he rose up, and I think this rather got him down. Looking back, I gathered from our conversation that he rather resented us young chaps coming in and posing as pilots. I think he looked upon himself as a professional and we were just ruddy amateurs. And I suppose there was a lot to be said for it.

He was a brilliant pilot. Absolutely outstanding. I had enormous admiration for his flying ability, and I've seen him do the most hair-raising stunts round the aerodrome when he was demonstrating what a Pup could do. His favourite one was to loop directly off the ground when he was taking off and continue looping. On one occasion he looped thirteen times from take-off, just straight off the ground, and when he'd finished he was about five hundred feet high. It was a wonderful piece of flying. And then he used to fly upside down: he'd go up to about a thousand feet, turn the machine upside down, just go round the aerodrome upside down till the engine stopped or something like that – and then he'd go on gliding – and next thing he'd roll it out, get the engine going again and away he'd go. Oh, he was absolutely marvellous, there wasn't a thing he couldn't do with that machine, and we all admired him tremendously.

Hopkins went on to relate the action with the Gothas on 13 June 1917. Only afterwards we heard that he had tackled this Gotha formation before it reached London and he'd dived amongst them and managed to separate some of the machines and help to break up the formation. He then ran out of ammunition but continued to dive in amongst the formation, further dispersing them: a most outstanding and brave deed for any man to do. This was, to a certain extent, hearsay, but it was what we were all talking about on the ground just at that time on the aerodrome.[5]

Sir Gordon Taylor, GC, MC[6]
Late in 1917 a new development took place in the sky over France. It was an action which frankly made me very envious, though fascinated by its efficiency. Disaster had at last overtaken the crews of the high-flying Rumplers which up till now had been virtually immune. This disaster came in the form of a single pilot in a special SE5. James McCudden had started as a mechanic in the Royal Flying corps shortly before the outbreak of war in 1914. He later became an NCO pilot, did well in France, and finally received his commission.

In June of 1917 he had come to 66 Squadron soon after we moved to Estrée Blanche. He was with us for a short time, but very soon realised that he was on the wrong horse.* With his eye on the SE5, he formed a personal liaison with 56 Squadron. McCudden was a transient man who had no tribal bond to keep him in the cockpit behind the single gun and the 80hp Le Rhone, where, not surprisingly, he did not get any Huns. But he was an ambitious, intelligent man and quick to recognize the better fighting potential of the SE5.

A completely different type from Ball, Rhys Davids, and Bishop, McCudden was nevertheless a great pilot. He used his imagination and his intelligence as well and his hands and feet.[7] *Author's note. Taylor was obviously unaware that McCudden was only with 66 Squadron on a month's refresher course.

Air Vice Marshal Major John Oliver Andrews, DSO, MC+
McCudden was in my flight for a short time, in 66. Came out to do a refresher in 66. Pleasant chap; very determined, devoted bloke, out to kill Germans.[8]

Lieutenant Thomas Isbell, RFC
When McCudden came into the mess, his favoured seat was to sit on a table swinging his legs and sitting on his hands. Now, he was a nice and good-looking young fellow, of about twenty-two, twenty-three. And he used to tell us how he'd led his patrol into a bunch of Huns and how many he'd got down. Lots of people might think that he was big-headed. In fact the first time you'd see him, until you knew the man, you probably would think that. But it wasn't that. It was that he was brimming over with self-confidence. The very thing that would strike you from the start, it didn't matter what job he did, was that, when he flew, he flew about three to five hundred feet above his patrol. Now, that may seem odd. It wasn't really, it was a wonderful thing. He would lead his flight into a bunch of Huns and the flight would know perfectly well that they were as safe as could be as long as McCudden was over the top. He would lead them in and, if one of his flight was getting at a disadvantage with Hun, Heaven help that Hun because he'd shoot it down: he had such marvellous shooting power.

I've seen McCudden shoot at targets. We'd all go up and we'd fire at the target, but McCudden would come down and he'd tear the target to shreds. He had such a wonderful, wonderful way of shooting. He only had to fire a matter of twenty rounds and the machine used to fall to pieces. You might fly along and fire two hundred bullets at a machine and the machine would still go floating on and not a bit of damage done apparently. So when McCudden was over his flight, everyone had every confidence that as long as he was there they were safe to go into anything. And what a wonderful fellow he was.[9]

Verschoyle Phillip Cronyn
We were appreciative of McCudden's leadership and as B Flight Commander he was good. In some ways retiring, and perhaps suffering from an inferiority complex because he had come up to a commission through the NCO's ranks, none the less McCudden was a most energetic individual, enthusiastic, hard-working, determined, and a forceful fighter quite unconcerned with his own safety when it came to a dogfight. If this description seems to give the lie to the 'retiring' aspect of his character, it really was only evident in the officers' mess.[10]

Wing Commander James Ira Thomas Jones
I was impressed with the quiet, efficient manner in which he always set about his work. Flying to him meant not only piloting the craft, but looking after the mechanical side. He did his own engine tuning, and it was always in such excellent condition that he was able to get his SE5 to a greater height than anyone else in the squadron. Meticulously careful in all matters, he insisted even upon filling his own ammunition belts and drums. Nothing was ever left to chance by McCudden.

As an observer he recognised the danger to our ground forces of any enemy reconnaissance flights It was true that the Germans did not cross our lines on such work; at least not compared with the visits paid by our craft. This did not deter McCudden. He studied their habits and appears to have set his heart on finding the best method of shooting down these enemy two-seaters, tackling the problem in his usual scientific manner. *After describing McCudden's method of tackling the enemy two-seaters, Jones goes on.* Adopting this stalking type of attack, McCudden was able to score numerous successes, because of his remarkable marksmanship, which he had practised patiently for a long period. So accurate was his aim that he brought a number of planes down by bursts fired at a distance of 200 yards – an extremely difficult task. His final record showed that he had shot down no fewer than eighteen German two-seaters on our side of the lines – an unbeatable record.[11]

Major-General Sir Hugh Montague Trenchard. KCB, DSO
McCudden was like all great pilots, extraordinarily modest and conscientious in all that he did. His skill and daring speak for themselves. Only the finest courage and unsurpassed mastery of the art of flying and fighting in the air could account for such a record of unflagging work and incessant victory. His work was as thorough as it was brilliant and his thoroughness was an important cause of his success. No detail, however small, connected with any branch of his work or with any part of his machine was overlooked. His determination and nerve were tremendous, and there was no finer example of the British pilot.

Major-General John Maitland Salmond, CMG, DSO
McCudden was in No.3 Squadron RFC, which I commanded in August 1914. He was at that time one of the best engine fitters we had, and was trusted implicitly both by his Flight Commander and Lieutenant Conran, whose engine and machine were his particular care. In those days, when engines were very much less reliable than they are today, this meant a very great deal. His attention to detail and his capacity marked him out for early promotion. He was then transferred from No.3 Squadron. I did not meet him again until he was a Captain, and at the height of his victorious career. I am confident that he would agree with me when I say that the secret of his remarkable success lay in the fact that he fought with his head as well as with his great heart.[12]

Gerald Hilton Bowman, DSO, DFC, Belgian *Croix de Guerre*
Young Mac was a great chap, but strict with the boys in his

flight. If they were on the early show the next morning, Mac gave them strict instructions that they were early to bed. Of course, they would wait until he was safely in his tent before coming with us in a tender to the nearest town for a good time. Mac was an outstanding psychological case: a dedicated destroyer, and a shooting genius.(13)

Hubert Noel Charles
McCudden was there for business. He was very, very punctilious, you could have eaten your breakfast off of the floor of his machine. He was a chap who was a very military type in the nice sense. He expected everything frightfully clean, wholesome and punctual, and insisted on it. Well, a person like that has got something which we haven't all got. Especially the punctual part. He was a professional soldier and a shooting genius without even realising it. Had McCudden taken part in what was then the King's prize at Bisley I have very little doubt that he would have put up a very good show. He had this beautiful touch. I remember the first time I ever saw it. We put an empty petrol can with two gallons of water in it down on the aerodrome. Beery Bowman dived down on it – cack-cack-cack-cack – the noise was nobody's business! He never hit the can. McCudden just came round – put-put-put-put. And turned away. He hit it twice – he only fired about four shots. When I said that to Beery he said well, the man's a genius. There's nobody else in the squadron could do what he just did. Of course, at this time, McCudden had the touch buttons I told you about.(14) McCudden had incredible touch and eyesight and he had conscious control over his eustachian tubes after 18,000ft. He could come down from 18,000ft as fast as he liked and just indulge in ordinary conversation. If Beery Bowman came down from 15,000ft, or anything like that, he'd be deaf for a quarter of an hour. McCudden had control over his eustachian tubes, as the Wing Doctor said, like a bird, and not more than one human being in a hundred thousand has got it. So here you've got a chap with amazing eyesight, conscious control over his own eustachian tubes, and the touch of a Bisley artist as far as shooting was concerned. Beery Bowman said that if you gave McCudden a thousand rounds of ammunition he would shoot down as many enemy aircraft as the rest of the squadron would if you gave'em a Leyland truck load. The man was simply a shooting genius.

Another thing. His knowledge of geography was such that he could even spot a small village. He came in one evening and told Marson that he had seen an SE5 crashed at Achiet-le-Grand. Marson said how do you know it was an SE5, how high were you? Nearly 8,000 ft. You recognised it was an SE5 from that height. Oh, yes, it was an SE5 all right. Anyway, Marson said, where the deuce is Achiet-le-Grand? Oh, McCudden said, there's two tiny villages down by the Somme, one of them is Achiet-le-Grand, the other's Achiet-le-Petit. Marson said, you mean that you're as accurate as that in your geography. Oh yes, McCudden said. Anyway, Marson got through to the troops in the area and they said yes, there is an aeroplane crashed and the pilot said that it's a thing called an SE5 and that he's quite alright. And Marson said what squadron is it, and they gave him the squadron – it was 40 or something. Anyway, it wasn't us. McCudden was absolutely right. His extraordinary eyesight coupled with a retentive and active young brain was one of the things he was proud of – he really knew his geography.(15)

Mrs. Alec-Tweedie
Only a boy. A dapper little person, all smiles and simplicity. Just a jolly, healthy-minded boy of twenty-three, who left school at thirteen to become a drummer-boy in the Royal Engineers, where his elder brother was a sergeant. Later that brother went into the Flying Corps as a mechanic, and in 1913 Jimmy, or, as his friends called him, 'Mac' followed him, also as a mechanic, going out to France with the squadron early in the war.

It seems impossible to think he was actually dead in France on Tuesday afternoon (July 9th) he, the boy who had been smiling in my rooms on Tuesday morning as proud as Punch of the Major's Crown he had just fixed to his shoulder. Dead – not from fighting a Hun – for this most experienced flyer and fighter met his death through an accident, only a simple accident. He, the boy covered with ribbons, killed as any novice might have been killed.

He had landed in France. Reported himself at Headquarters and went off again, apparently in the same machine, to join the squadron to which he had just been appointed Major. He had hardly risen from the ground before the spectators noticed something was wrong. The machine swerved, flew low, and behold, caught in some trees, to be followed by a crash. Poor McCudden was dragged out dangerously hurt and insensible, to die that evening at eight o'clock on French soil, the scene of his former glories, but not chasing the enemy as he would have wished, alas! He was buried as a Catholic, and lies not far from so many of his former triumphs – notably in the winter of 1917–18.

Asking him, a few weeks ago, why he was so anxious to get back to France, and was working against all obstacles to do so, he replied. 'Well, you see, I have only brought down fifty-seven Huns – and perhaps twenty or thirty more not properly authenticated – and Richthofen got eighty-one; so I must get back and outstrip his record. It's no good saying the Germans can't fight; they can. I know all about every fight I ever had, and at least five first-class German pilots I can remember.'

And what was the origin of McCudden's success? Hero worship. He adored his elder brother. That brother influenced his life. He told young Mac what was worth doing was worth doing well. Inspired him with the right kind of ambition, the ambition to attain but not at the expense of others, merely by his own thoroughness, and seizing the right opportunity. And so the future VC climbed slowly from bugler-boy to be a great pioneer air fighter. He much regretted his scanty schooling, and said 'I always wish I had the advantage of a public school. After I joined the officers' mess I often felt ill at ease when chaps were talking about things I didn't understand'. And yet his thoroughness was such that every French name and every

Englishman's name in his MS is correctly spelt, and, beyond a few grammatical mistakes, it wants little or no editing. Its is a plain tale plainly told by its own hero, who did not even know he was a hero. And yet McCudden fought well-nigh 200 aerial fights, and twice actually downed four Huns in a day, and got three single-seaters in twenty minutes. He was the son of an old fighter. For his father has had twenty-nine years' service in the Army and, like two of his sons, won medals himself. A fine family record.

McCudden has written a book. I wish I could quote from the MS before me, but the public will have to wait a little for this intensely interesting human document. This book is a wonderful production. He came to me some weeks ago, with an introduction from my son, to ask how many words would be wanted, etc. 'Sixty to eighty thousand was my reply.' He looked aghast – not having the slightest idea how many he had scribbled in pencil, on both sides of the page, in a sort of copy-book. It was hardly an author's manuscript, but the very simplicity of the style of that 1,000 words was its charm, and showed his capacity for doing a thoroughly readable book describing five years in the Royal Flying Corps from the bottom rung to the top pinnacle. Back to Scotland he went to do more, and actually managed to write 40,000 in three weeks, in spite of his daily instructing for fighting pilots. One evening (June 10th) he walked in again, about 10.30PM, looking very red and sunburnt, with the precious new material under his arm. He had left Scotland that afternoon, and had flown 400 miles in two hours and three quarters, had had a bath and some food and explained that the wind, luckily a following one which allowed 140 miles an hour, had caught his face and the sun had scorched it.

'There' he said, 'are 40,000 words more, and written in pencil on one side of the paper only, and I've been its aerial postman,' with a merry laugh. He had wonderful eyes; the dark blue iris seemed to cover the entire pupil, and his long eye-lashes were darker than his fair hair. He was a good-looking boy, but what really impressed one more was his straightforward way, thoroughly, good calm common sense, his honesty of purpose and his youthful joy of life. There was no swank about him. He had simple manners, and spoke in a simple way with true sportsmanlike spirit.

'I'm sure the war will be a long one,' he said. 'I don't intend to take any unnecessary risks with dashing stunts, I mean to kill Huns, but in my own time; I won't bustle or do anything foolish like my brother who was killed sixteen weeks ago.' And yet he was killed in an accident.

My last recollection of him – and that only a few hours before he was killed – was a smiling young man rushing off to his waiting taxi, 'as I've a crowd of little odds and ends to do before I pick up my machine, but I'll be back in three months, and hope my book will be out by then. I'll send you a line from France tomorrow'. This was the third son lost in the Air Force by those splendid Irish parents, and the loss of McCudden VC is not only their loss but a loss to the nation.[16]

Lt.Col. Richard Graham Blomfield, DSO

May 25th 1918
My dear McCudden,
Awfully pleased to get your letter of 3rd March, three days ago. Your remark about the trepidation you had made me smile as have never found that word on your character yet. I showed your letter to the Generals here & it made them sit up when they read your 154mph & 400 miles in 3 hours.[17] It was great, as we are all struggling here to get the U.S.A machines to even do 115 near the ground. The situation is far from bright and the work and worry I have here makes one long for the old days when we were altogether in France. Very sorry to hear about your brother and it must have upset you as you were so fond of him. I am still unattached and don't feel like getting married. I only hope you are the same way but no doubt by the time this reaches you, you will either be engaged or married & although I hate to think of it you may be both. It is grand you getting the VC & your chest must look like the rising sun, but nobody has earned his bits of colour more valiantly than you. Only hope we can get together later on this year. Expect to be Home in July but unfortunately not before.

The best of luck to you and do write me again.

Yours ever,
R.G. Blomfield

Air Chief Marshal Sir Edgar Ludlow-Hewitt, GCB, GBE, CMG, DSO, MC
Although McCudden was a quiet, unassuming, essentially modest person he was nonetheless one of those people who are not easily forgotten. He was far from being the glamorous, fire-eating hero of fiction, and yet there was about him an elusive distinction which somehow arose out of his naturally self-assured and serene disposition. He was a gentleman in the true and real meaning of the word. High principled, tolerant and very generous in his judgements of others he had a natural modesty which I am sure remained untouched by his subsequent fame and success.[18]

Mary Cobley, née McCudden, James' eldest sister
These reflections are exerpted from many letters to the author, and a talk given by Mary in the 1970s to Cross and Cockade International, The First World War Historical Society. The boys, Bill and Jim were full of fun and up to all manner of tricks. Jim was the serious one, but he was inclined to be moody and tearful. He always seemed to be crying. Father came home one day and said to mother. 'What's the matter with Jim today, he's not crying?' But Jim was very organised, liked everything to be just right. He was like me in that respect.

Jim left school at thirteen, long before he should have. Later, when he was in the RFC he felt the loss of education; felt at a loss with his comrades. I think that led to his modesty about his achievements.

Jim was dedicated to flying – all the boys were. Jim thought of nothing else but flying, every spare moment, even later. He was dedicated to his work – lived for it.

He was very modest, hated a fuss. In his letters to me he

never went into details of his fighting. Only said something like, 'Got my thirtieth today.' Very short, no other details. He wrote to me every ten days. (Author's note: Sadly these letters, and those from Mary's mother when she was in America in 1921, have since been lost.) Given his age – 23 – he had wonderful experiences. He often mentioned encounters he had with different fighters. Immelmann – he mentioned him many times – and Voss, and Richthofen. He often said that if he was spared he would like to go to Germany after the war to meet some of the families of the boys he had been fighting and tell them what wonderful sons they had. I think that sympathy for the Germans was because our grandmother was German, from Göttingen.[19] He did everything that was possible to (word obscured) at that time. He didn't want to take life, but he had to, didn't he? It was one or the other, wasn't it?

I think how he went is just how he would have wanted to have gone. He was not a very big fellow. He was slight, but always very dapper and smart. He had a beautiful complexion – almost girlish. He was my favourite brother and I was his favourite sister. He always talked about things with me, things he couldn't talk to mother about. I'm very proud of him – of all my family really.

Casualty card of James McCudden. Only the list of decorations gives a hint of his achievements.

James with Bruiser, a one-man dog.

Appendix VII: McCudden on Air Fighting

McCudden wrote two treatises on the subject of fighting in the air.[1] The first was obviously written when he had returned from his month's refresher course with 66 Squadron in early August 1917. Compared with many other pilots of the time, he was still relativity inexperienced, which makes it highly unlikely that it was written at any official request. By the syntax – quite unlike McCudden's usual style – and the many abbreviations, it gives the impression of being scribbled notes, yet to be edited.

*

I am compiling these notes on Aerial Fighting at the present time. I hope it will be understood that I am merely describing my impressions and views, which are the result of experience and knowledge gained during a brief stay with the RFC in France, and also talks with well known pilots in France.

Aerial fighting and tactics have changed very little during the last six months. The only apparent difference being that many more machines are now employed and also that the individual skill of pilots in manoeuvring and more general knowledge of tactics appertaining to aerial fighting is shown by both our own and enemy pilots.

Roughly 80% of the machines used by the enemy now are scouts, and the majority of the scouts used are the Albatros V Strutter, the Halberstadt and *Walfisch* scouts having on the British part of the line almost disappeared, judging by the reports by experienced scout pilots. Two new types have been seen lately by pilots behind the lines, but very few details are yet to hand.

A rough description of one is. A machine with little or no dihedral, two pairs of struts to each pair of wings, which are of the same length and a long fuselage tapering to a knife edge. Judging from these descriptions these machines must be very like an Halberstadt or Fokker Biplane.

A new type of two seater has appeared in the DFW Aviatik which is used for art obs and reconnaissance. I saw a captured one with a 220 Benz which had a very well streamlined body and had got a good performance. The front gun of this machine would be very difficult to use with any effect because the engine and cowling masks nearly all the forward view of the pilot.

Other two seaters in use by the enemy are the Aviatik, which hardly ever crosses the line, and the large Albatros and Rumplers, the former of which, one lot are used principally for long reconnaissance photos. These usually fly very high and are painted underneath a light blue or light grey, which blend with the blue sky when high and are very difficult to follow with one's eye for any length of time.

In fighting enemy scouts now, they do not always attack us from above as they usually did before, but they fly a little below you and gather speed before zooming up underneath your tail and get in a good burst before losing all this speed. Directly you show fight, they either dive very steeply or fall purposely out of control in a most realistic manner for a few thousand feet before regaining control and climbing again to repeat this tactic. I think they do this because some of the British scouts are superior in climb and manoeuvre, principally the later. Then the Hun is at a disadvantage and as soon as it becomes a fight of this nature he breaks it off and tries to attack again as soon as the circumstances suit his tactics.

For instance, the Sopwith Scout up high keeps its height at say, 16,000ft, better than a V-Strutter while manoeuvring so that unless the EA are in superior numbers when attacking the S.S., they will not stay long enough for the superior manoeuvring climb of the S.S. at this height to make itself apparent.

I had a good instance of this recently when a patrol of S.S. of which I was a member were attacked by several V Strutters from about our own level. Executing a few turns the S.S. got above and started to drive the EA down with the exception of one, who remained above and then dived onto an S.S. who was on a Hun's tail. This EA must have been very alert for as soon as I did a quick turn and got on his tail he was upside down and falling over and over in an extraordinary manner before I fired a shot at him. The Huns always do this when out-manoeuvred and never stay to let the superior manoeuvring of the British machines put them at a disadvantage, unless they are in superior numbers or at an advantage in any other way.

A Hun will stay to manoeuvre against a S.P.A.D. or Nieuport or S.E. but will never manoeuvre against a Sopwith Camel or Scout for long, as these machines turn so very quick. The way some of the Hun scouts fall out of control is really astounding and must be very misleading to some of our newer pilots.

The composition of the hostile formation is very varied at present. You will see them in ones, two, three, four, fives and sixes and often more, and you often see three and two very high up apparently having no interest in life whatever, but no doubt they belong to a patrol or formation lower down. The colours which some of the EA are painted makes them very difficult to discern, even when quite close, and many cunning efforts are made to disguise their markings.

The skill of the enemy scout pilots at present is very varied and one sees some extraordinary good flying by some of them, while on the other hand I have been told by quite trustworthy pilots that they have chased Hun scouts who could only turn one way and have only been prevented from registering on an easy target by a more wily Hun who has appreciated his unfortunate comrade's predicament and has driven our machine off the former's tail.

The height at which EA are met is anything between 2 and 20,000 feet.

It is my opinion that enemy machines are now showing better morale and enterprise than they did at the end of February, and the heavy air fighting now takes place near our lines than ever before. However, at the time of the V-Strutter Albatros it can be easily recognised from a distance when flying in such a way that you get a side view of them, by its having a very tail low appearance and also a large substantial tail fin. Even when flying level it has a tail low appearance. Looking at it from behind it has a very pronounced washout on all wingtips. The length of the machine appears to be unduly long owing to the tail plane extending behind the end of the machine.

Another reason why the Hun scouts always break off an engagement with Pups is because they know that these machines cannot match them in a dive as the S.P.A.D. and SE can. Also they have a greater speed than the Pup.

Very good sport was experienced recently during a fight between S.P.A.Ds, SEs, Camels and Nieuports and about 20 Huns just east of the lines. A formation of FE2ds were about 2,000 feet below the fight and all the Huns that were driven down were caught by the FEs who were able of course to fire in a wide arc above. It was a comic if not surprising sight to see one Rolls FE on the Hun scout's tail, absolutely turning on its wingtip much to the discomfort of the Hun pilot who eventually out dived the FE but certainly could not out manoeuvre it.

The speed of the V-Strutter is very good. I should say at least 115mph at 10,000 feet, and they turn quicker than a S.P.A.D.

Enemy machines when doing Art Obs or photography near the lines now often do so in pairs or with a single scout as escort. This was noticed quite recently. At 4PM I saw three DFW Aviatik east of Armentieres, shelling our lines just south of Armentieres. I engaged them and drove one down, with the aid of another Sopwith which made the other two abandon their shoot. I went to the same place in the evening and saw two of the same type with a scout doing the same shoot. This time however they kept well behind the lines. The next evening however a Hun two-seater which shelled Aire recently was escorted by several scouts and remained over Aire for nearly half an hour at 14,000 feet. I mention these incidentals because I think this is a departure from the usual Hun practice.

I had a good look over a captured V-Strut Albatros and think that its visibility is quite good. It has, however, a large blind spot in front and below which is obscured by the engine, guns and fittings. Otherwise the view forward, upward, sideways and behind is excellent.

The majority of fighting now takes place between 12 and 16,000ft, but just at present the Hun will not prolong a scrap, but spins away as soon as he has had sufficient. The last few days (word obscured) the end of July the Hun has had a very bad time and there are indications that his morale is being rather badly shaken.

The Huns now attack our balloons often, and usually select a day when the clouds are anything between 4 & 8. They come over in twos and threes as a rule and while one is attacking the other one or two companions are protecting the former from attack or drawing away AA to make the task of the Hun attacking the balloon as easy as possible. Following their attack, successful or otherwise, they at once make for the lines as soon as possible and climb into the clouds again.

Apart from attacking balloons, Hun scouts have lately been coming well behind our lines during cloudy or hazy weather and firing on transport, and have come as far back as over heavy batteries. This practice can be somewhat turned to our advantage, if our pilots go up voluntarily and fly in the clouds or near our balloon. This is done quite a lot by some Sqdn pilots who are keen and like a lot of flying because the chance of getting a Hun down in our lines under the above circumstances is great and it is naturally the wish of most pilots to get a Hun down on our side. A V-Strutter Albatros was driven down quite recently in our line while after our balloons.

The Hun usually is more over our lines during N.E. and E. winds than when a W. or S.W. wind is blowing. I think this is because of better visibility with E. winds, but it certainly gives us the advantage while fighting and the Hun drifts over our lines.

At 3.15PM on 31st July while above the clouds over Polygon Wood I saw an Albatros at about 12,000ft diving west. I flew S.W. and intercepted him over Kemmel at 6,000ft. I attacked from above but after doing two half turns lost height badly and got below. I now dived after him into a cloud. I went down hoping to see him in (word obscured) the cloud. I then saw he had climbed up into the cloud and was now just leaving the cloud and was going N. I chased him but was outdistanced and EA eventually got back to his side in cloud. I mention this incident because it shows that Huns always come over our lines during cloudy weather and also that one should never dive past a cloud into which Hun has disappeared over our side of the lines as he is sure to keep his height as much as possible.

In conclusion, I may say that these notes were written with the object of enlightening the future fighting pupils, and not to give more experienced pilots tips, as the average pilot is so conservative but in any case there may be some food for reflection and argument even by our budding star turns.

Also in these notes I have referred several times to myself, and have done this with the intention of adding a little personal experience to those which I have gleaned from others and to make a little interesting reading apart from the perhaps somewhat dry notes contained herein.

*

The second treatise, written in January 1918, was an official request from the Air Ministry. This was later published, heavily edited, in an official pamphlet. What follows is McCudden's submission, written in the same Army Book.[2] Alterations are noted by*.

January 1918
Fighting the S.E.5

Having been requested to write some notes on the above heading, I must ask readers* to consider them as the method of an individual (myself) and not as an effort to lay down anything like hard and fast rules when fighting the SE Scouts.

Enemy scouts are not very often seen above 15,000 during the winter months, the reason being, I suggest, that the V-Strutter which constitutes the bulk of E.A. scouts is a very cold machine in comparison with the SE so that enemy pilots do not go up high during the cold weather, unless for some reason, therefore I usually take my patrol over the lines at anything over 14,000ft. Nine times out of ten I am above E.A. scouts during the whole of the patrol.

In attacking enemy scouts surprise is usually aimed at and the sun and wind direction are a great help.* If you think the E.A. have not seen you try to attack from the E. and when going down give the rear machines of your formation plenty of time to close up so that each member can pick 1 E.A. simultaneously. *Pilots have probably come across a patrol of Albatros scouts of the following colours, red nose, yellow fuselages and each machine having a different coloured tail, namely red, yellow, blue, silver, green, and black and white longitudinal stripes. This formation are (sic) composed of experienced fighters and I am proud to say that on Dec.6th I got my formation of 6 machines E. of these E.A. and gave my pilots time to each select an E.A. and we all attacked together, but we only got two. Have seen this formation of E.A. several times since but it is very hard to surprise them.*

While attacking E.A. scouts one should keep plenty of engine so as to keep above the formation of E.A. the whole time. I find that if SEs attack E.A. from above that they can remain above the whole time, but now I find that as soon as we attack scouts one of them* slinks off out of the scrap and climbs his utmost until he is above the top SE and then he comes back and it just the thought that there is one Hun above you that spoils the situation, so as soon as I see the one Hun going off I climb as well and this usually frustrates his intentions.

I consider it a patrol-leader's work to pay more attention to the main points affecting a fight than to do all the fighting oneself. The main points are 1. arrival of more E.A. who have tactical advantage. ie. Height. 2. Patrol drifting too far E. 3. Patrol getting below bulk of enemy formation. As soon as these any of these points occur it is time to take advantage of the SE's superior speed over E.A. scouts and break off the fight, rally behind leader and climb W. of E.A. until you are above E.A. before attacking again.*

TWO-SEATERS
I have had many more combats with two-seaters than scouts so I hope I am able to give you a few hints.

I think a lot of pilots overestimate the death-dealing qualities of the observer's gun, at the same time one should not become careless because E.A. observers are usually highly trained and can shoot very accurately, especially at quite long range. Therefore, when attacking a two-seater it should be a pilot's main object after surprise to get to close range (100 yds) without letting E.A. gunner shoot at you. This is quite possible because* I shot down 6 two-seaters in succession without E.A. gunners getting a single shot at me although in each case the E.A. had seen me approaching and had good time to make up his mind what to do. The 6 E.A. were not shot down in one fight but were successive combats on different days. Two-seaters keep a very good look out above but pay very little attention under their level, therefore try to surprise them from underneath and climb up under their fuselage and tail plane. The position from which a pilot can damage a two-seater most at the least risk to himself is 100 yds behind it and 50ft below. If, however, you are in this position and the E.A. turns, you will at once come under his fire and your objective is to keep out of his field of fire,* so therefore keep under his tail, so that if he turns right you turn left and vice-versa. To do this manoeuvre successfully, one must have superior speed to do the outside circle which is the inevitable position if one uses E.A. tail as cover to the best advantage whist E.A. is turning. As soon as the E.A. gunner sees he cannot fire at you he will try the other direction. Now, whilst changing from one bank to the other E.A. will be in a good position to fire*. Try a short burst to confuse the pilot. His tendency when alarmed is to dive which is just what you want him to do. No gunner can stand upright in a machine that is doing over 120mph and do accurate shooting because the wind pressure is blowing him flat on the fuselage. In several cases I have seen a two-seater dive so steeply and fast that the gunner is blown flat on the fuselage. When this happens you need not worry about E.A. rear gun. I find that when one is diving on the tail of a two-seater one does not need to allow deflection just shoot straight at him. The chances of fighting a two-seater is greater W. of the line than E. because when a two-seater is attacked W. of the line 9 times out of ten he will first push his nose down and do S-turns, so that after you have had some practice you will be able to sit under his tail as safe as anywhere provided you do not become careless. On the contrary, a two-seater attacked E. of the line only need to keep going round one way and he can do this for any length of time* until another E.A. arrives.

This happened to me recently. I attacked an LVG just over the line and he at once started a left-hand circle and was doing all the shooting. However, I did not worry as the wind was E. and we were drifting W. so I knew that if he wanted to get back he would have to stop turning so at last he got fed up and dived E. and I got him.

In fighting two-seaters W. of the line pilots should think before attacking what the E.A.'s job is so as to let E.A. get as far W. as he wishes to go, so that you will have ample time to down him before he gets E. of the Lines. Most two-seaters will stand a lot of shooting at before giving any evidence of damage.** I find that it is very difficult to shoot the pilot from directly behind because you probably hit the gunner first who collapses in a heap and you go on shooting and you are simply filling the observer with lead and also the huge petrol tank which is usually between the pilot and gunner and the pilot gets off so once you have got the gunner you can afford to close right up and shoot the pilot at your leisure.

**The above measure of attacking a two seater is what I advise, but a good deal of practice is necessary before you are able to keep up with a two-seater without being shot about, at close range.

I have had a lot of combats with two-seaters and have only been hit by their fire very seldom indeed, and then only one or two bullets. The advantages and possibilities of this form of attack should be obvious to anyone who gives the subject thought. Even at 50ft below an E.A. at 100 yds one has to zoom ever so slightly to get one's sight on an E.A. and it is to be remembered that the SE's guns fire at an upward angle to the line of flight.*

In conclusion I wish to point out that although I have achieved good success with this method of attack, I think the Huns will take measures to repel this form of attack in one way or the other and I also contend that a two-seater *well manned* is more than a match for a scout no matter how well handled.

While in 56 Squadron, McCudden wrote the following notes, copies of which were given to all pilots of the squadron.

56 Squadron
Notes On Gun Sighting and Shooting

It is impossible to sight guns so that at all ranges they will shoot where the sights are pointing. So that one takes the greatest range at which it is reasonable to open fire at Huns and one ensures that at all distances up to this maximum range all the ordinary ammunition and a good many tracer will hit where the sights are pointing. This maximum range is 100 yards. The distance is difficult to judge, but it has been found that this is the distance which in fact most pilots describe as '20 yards' or 'point blank' range and begin to wonder if they are going to run into the Hun or not.

An aeroplane is a very difficult target to hit and there is only a small part of it worth hitting – the engine and the pilot – and deflection i.e. aiming well in front, always has to be allowed for, and the further away one is the greater the deflection has to be allowed.

But all the difficulties disappear rapidly the closer you get – experienced pilots who realise what 'getting close' really means, rarely engage Huns without bringing them down. Those who have become really expert nearly always get to within 30 yards, which is closer, in fact, than those who have not tried it think it is possible to get to another machine in the air with safety. When you have got really close, the guns fire where the sights are pointing, the deflection necessary becomes smaller, and you have won more than half the battle by frightening the Hun badly by showing him that you really mean to hit him and not merely make noises at him; then too, the closer you get the safer your own position becomes, for with single-seaters the more difficult it becomes for him to get on your tail, and he variably puts his nose down in finding you so close, thus giving you a stationary target; and with two-seaters you must get very close under his tail or else you cannot avoid his back gunfire when he turns by keeping under his tail on the outside circle.

In most cases where a pilot attacks a Hun and does not bring him down, it is for one of two reasons.
1. He hasn't got to within point blank range before opening fire.
2. He hasn't kept his guns correctly sighted.
The disadvantages of opening fire before reaching point blank range are very great.
1. Your guns will not shoot near where the sights are pointing, and even if they did, the deflection necessary becomes enormous.
2. You warn the EA of your presence before you can hope to hit him, and thus give him time to turn or run away or start manoeuvring to attack you – resulting in an indecisive combat.
3. You waste your small stock of ammunition and may develop a stoppage and have finished your Lewis drum by the time you have got close enough to make your guns into the valuable weapons of attack they can be.
4. If you habitually open fire at a range greater than 100 yards, you will frighten every Hun you meet and you may put a stray bullet or two into his machine, but never bring Huns down. If you reserve your fire for point black range your combat will be in nearly every case decisive.

The method of sighting the guns on an S.E.5 is as follows. Note: No tracer ammunition of any sort must be used because it does not fire consistently straight and accurately.
A 100 yards range is used.
1. Sight the Vickers Gun on the target by means of the barrel reflector.
2. Fire a burst of 7 or 8 rounds of ordinary ammunition at the target. Paint a 4 inch bull over the main point of impact of those shots.
3. Adjust the Aldis and auxiliary sights exactly on this bull.
4. Paint a 4 inch bull 12 inches vertically above the first bull, and without moving the machine adjust the Lewis by means of the barrel reflector and Lewis adjustment on this bull.
5. Fire bursts of 7 or 8 rounds of ordinary ammunition from the Lewis and adjust the Lewis until its mean point of impact is on the upper bull.

The guns are now correctly sighted for shooting at 100 yards. If you are taking a chance shot at any greater range, remember that your shots will fire below where your sights are pointing.

Appendix VIII: Greentail

The identity of the pilot of 'Greentail', the Albatros so often met by the patrols of 56 Squadron after the squadron had moved to Laviéville on 12 November 1918, has long been a subject of speculation amongst researchers into the air war of 1914–1918.

Despite McCudden's belief that he had shot down this Albatros pilot on 18 February 1918, 'Greentail' was obviously a pilot of great experience – in all probability a high scorer – and no German pilot of such standing was reported lost in action on that date.

As has been seen, the green-tailed Albatros that McCudden shot down on 18 February 1918 was flown by Julius Kaiser of *Jasta* 35b. However, at the time of the first sighting of 'Greentail' by the pilots of 56 Squadron on 23 November, *Jasta* 35b was based at Aertrycke with the German Fourth Army and did not move into the area of 56 Squadron's operations until 30 November 1918. The only German *Jagdstaffeln* based in the area on 23 November was *Jasta* 5, based at Neuvilly, and *Jagdgeschwader Nr.*1 (*Jagdstaffeln* Nos. 4,6,10, and 11) which had moved to the area on 22 November, flying its first patrols later that day. However, an examination of the War Diary of *Jagdgeschwader Nr.*1 shows that none of its pilots were in action on the days that 56 Squadron pilots reported combats with 'Greentail'.

From this evidence it would appear that 'Greentail' and his patrol, who were all recognised by the pilots of 56 Squadron as being very experienced pilots, were almost certainly from *Jasta* 5. Unfortunately, no copy of the *Jasta* 5 War Diary has yet been found and photographs of the *Jasta's* aeroplanes during the period in question are scarce, but it is known that *Jasta* 5 carried a large white chevron on the top wings of its aeroplanes and also marked them with a large letter, possibly the pilot's initials. This would point to the possibility that the pilot of the Greentailed Albatros, with the large letter 'K' and the white chevron on its top wing was flown by *Vizefeldwebel* Otto Könnecke of *Jasta* 5.

Könnecke was born in Strasbourg on 20 December 1892. He served in *Fliegerbattalion No.*4 in 1913, where he learnt to fly. In December 1916 he was posted to *Jasta* 25 in Macedonia, where he was credited with three victories and awarded the Bulgarian order of the Soldier's Cross for Bravery 1st Class. On 7 May 1917 Könnecke was posted to *Jasta* 5, in France, scoring his first victory with the *Jasta* on 28 May. A steady, rather than a rapid scorer, Könnecke had been credited with ten victories by the end of 1917, gradually adding to his successes until May 1918, when he was promoted to *Leutnant*. After his promotion, Könnecke steadily increased his victory score, was awarded the Golden Military Merit Cross in May 1918; the Knight's Cross with Swords of the Royal Hohenzollern House Order in July and the *Pour le Merité* in September. Könnecke survived the war with a total of 35 victories, claiming the last – personally and for *Jasta* 5 – only nine days before the end of hostilities. He joined the civil airline Lufthansa in 1926 and the *Luftwaffe* in 1935. He died in January 1956.

Otto Könnecke, along with *Ltn.* Fritz Rumey and *Ltn.* Josef Mai, made up a formidable trio of fighter pilots, all serving with *Jasta* 5, who were collectively credited with 110 victories.

Three formidable air fighters of *Jasta* 5. Various pilots of the *Jasta* made up Greentail's Flight, which was constantly meeting the pilots of 56 Squadron in combat during the winter of 1917/1918. Left to Right: Fritz Rumey (45 Victories), Otto Könnecke (35 victories), and Josef Mai (30 victories). Both Rumey and Könnecke were awarded the *Pour le Mérite* and Mai was nominated for it.

Endnotes

Chapter 1: Family and Childhood
1. They would have a daughter and five sons, four of whom joined the army.
2. In 1885, William's brother, James, was also awarded the Society's Bronze medal for saving two soldiers from drowning in Dover Harbour.
3. Although christened Amelia, and is shown as such in official documents, birth and marriage certificates, etc., Amelia much preferred the French style, Amélie, and used it in her family and private life.
4. It was merely an example of a common practice of the time: that of giving a boy his mother's maiden name as one of his Christian names.
5. Mary Cobley (née McCudden) Letter to Author.
6. In *McCudden VC*, Christopher Cole noted that many later attained senior rank.
7. Griffith Brewer F.R.AeS. An early aviator, Brewer held Ballooning Certificate No.2, and flew in the Gordon Bennett Balloon Races of 1906, 1907, 1908 and 1922. A great friend and admirer of the Wright brothers, Brewer was the first Englishman to fly with Wilbur Wright and gained a USA Aviator's Certificate on a Wright in 1914. Brewer flew de Havilland Moths in 1929 and in 1930 qualified as an Autogiro pilot at the age of 62. He crossed the Atlantic in the Zeppelin *Hindenburg* and later flew in the *Graf Zeppelin*. Brewer died in 1948.

Chapter 2: The New Recruit
1. Geoffrey Bowman, who served with McCudden in 56 Squadron, described him to the author as a 'shooting genius'.
2. This manual is now in the museum of the Royal Engineers at Chatham.
3. Henry Robert Moore Brooke-Popham (RAeC Certificate No. 108 dated 8 July 1911). Brooke-Popham was seconded from the Oxford and Bucks Light Infantry. As a Captain he joined the Air Battalion in March 1912 and was appointed Commanding Officer of 3 Squadron on formation of the Military Wing of the RFC in 1912. In 1914 he was on RFC HQ Staff as Deputy Assistant Quartermaster General; then CO of Third Wing in March 1915. Brooke-Popham held many high staff posts in RFC and RAF before retiring as Air Chief Marshall Sir H R M Brooke-Popham. GCVO, KCB,CMG,DSO, AFC. Brooke-Popham died in 1953.
4. The German Army Air Service adopted this system from the outset.
5. Corporal Frank Ridd (RFC No.26) was the first NCO pilot in the RFC. On 4 June 1912 he passed his test on a Bristol Boxkite and was awarded Royal Aero Club Certificate No.227 dated 4 June 1912, the first certificate to be awarded to an 'other rank.'
6. Staff Sergeant R H V Wilson was the second NCO pilot in the British Army, earning his RAeC Certificate (No.232) on 18 June 1912. On 5 July 1912 he was killed in a flying accident. He was the first NCO pilot of the RFC to be killed.
7. William Victor Strugnell, a former school friend of William and James McCudden, served with the Air Battalion and took his RAeC Certificate No.253 on 24 July 1912. Strugnell went to France at the outbreak of war with 5 Squadron. He was a Sergeant Pilot with 3 Squadron in 1915 and was commissioned as a 2nd Lieutenant in 1915. Strugnell was awarded an MC in 1916 and a bar on 26 July 1917 while serving as a Flight Commander in 54 Squadron. He ended the war with seven victories. Strugnell retired from the RAF in 1946 as a Group Captain and died in January 1973.
8. Alan Geoffrey Fox (RAeC Certificate No.176 dated 30 January 1912). A Royal Engineer, Fox served with the Air Battalion. He was killed on 9 May 1915 while serving in 16 Squadron.
9. Sergeant J Starling was a former Royal Engineer. His RFC number was 2, making him the second man to be transferred into the new corps. He served in France with the Aircraft Park and was commissioned Lieutenant in March 1915. He was twice Mentioned in Despatches and in December 1917 was promoted to Temp. Lt. Colonel.
10. Sergeant Charles Brockbank (RFC No.203) was the sergeant in charge of the maintenance of the aeroplanes at the depot at Farnborough. He served in France as a Flight Sergeant at the Aircraft Park from 16 August 1914 and was commissioned in December 1916. He retired with the rank of Squadron Leader in May 1929.
11. George Habden Raleigh (RAeC Certificate No. 96 dated 16 March 1912). Major Raleigh (Essex Regt.) took command of 4 Squadron in September 1912. He was killed in a flying accident near Dunkirk on 22 January 1915.
12. Thomas Hudson (RFC No.77). A former drill sergeant in the Grenadier guards, Hudson was the first recruiting sergeant of the RFC and was responsible for allocating RFC numbers to the initial members of the corps. He was commissioned in 1917 and retired as a Squadron leader in 1946.
13. Baron Trevenen James (RAeC Certificate No.230 dated 4 June 1912). A Royal Engineer, James was seconded to the RFC and was the pioneer of wireless telegraphy in the RFC. He was ranging for artillery when he was shot down and killed on 15 July 1915 while serving with 6 Squadron.
14. Frederick Hugh Sykes (RAeC Certificate No.95 dated 20 June 1911). In early 1913, Captain Sykes was promoted to major and appointed as Commanding Officer of the Military Wing of the RFC. Sykes rose steadily through the higher ranks of the RFC and RAF and ended the war as a Brigadier-General on the General Staff. C.G. Grey, when editor of Aero, described Sykes as a man who 'has rather more knowledge of the theory of flying machines than most people in the industry itself'.

15. Thomas O'Brien Hubbard (RAeC Certificate No.222 dated 8 June 1912). After serving with 3 Squadron as a Flight Commander, Hubbard was promoted to Major and given command of 11 Squadron. Hubbard (known throughout the Corps as 'Mother' Hubbard) was an extremely popular officer in the RFC, being described as ' a gentle retiring character with an endearing stutter'. When 11 Squadron's little Vickers FB5 Fighter – affectionately known as the 'Gunbus' – was replaced by the much larger and heavier FE2b, Hubbard likened the pilot and gunner's nacelle in the replacement to a Highland shooting lodge, with room to spare for a bored gunner to indulge in such pursuits as Swedish exercises.

16. Captain Geoffrey de Havilland was a pre-war pilot, aeroplane designer and manufacturer. With the success of his second biplane design in 1910 he joined the staff of His Majesty's Balloon Factory in 1911 as designer and test pilot. By 1912 the Balloon Factory had become the Royal Aircraft Factory and de Havilland was working on the designs of the SE and BE types. In June 1914 de Havilland left the Factory to join the Aircraft Manufacturing Company. His first design for the company was the DH1 which was the forerunner of the DH2, that was to equip 24 Squadron, the RFC's first dedicated single-seater fighter squadron. Ronald Campbell Kemp succeeded de Havilland as the RFC's chief test pilot. At the beginning of the 1914–1918 war Kemp joined the RFC. During the war he was chief test pilot for Short Brothers.

17. Lt Eric Lewis Conran (RAeC Certificate No.342 dated 22 October 1912). Conran went to France in 1914 as a pilot with 3 Squadron. He later commanded 29 Squadron. At this time, Conran's Bleriot was Gnome-engined Bleriot X1, No.219, which had been presented to the War Office by the International Correspondence Schools in January 1913.

18. Manufactured in Switzerland, the Moto-Rêve was a quality built motorcycle, in production until the mid 1920s. McCudden's cycle was a circa 1907–1909, 290cc V Twin model. Drive was direct from the engine pulley on the rear wheel, and the driver had to pedal the machine to start it. As it had no clutch the engine had to be stopped every time the cycle was brought to a halt.

19. Lt. Reginald Cholmondeley (RAeC Certificate No. 271 dated 13 August 1912). Cholmondeley was the first officer of the Military wing to make a flight at night. On 16 April 1913 he flew from Larkhill to Upavon and back by moonlight. Cholmondeley went to France in 1914 as a Flight Commander at the Aircraft Park. In March 1915, on the final day of the battle of Neuve Chapelle, Cholmondeley was serving with 3 Squadron. His aeroplane was being loaded with converted French shells for use as bombs when one dropped on its nose and exploded. Cholmondeley and eleven men were killed and four men seriously wounded.

20. S W Pyne (RFC No.574). Pyne joined the RFC on 30 January 1913. He went France with 3 Squadron as a 1st Class Air Mechanic.

21. R Keith (Cuth) Barlow (RFC No.331).

22. John Ramsey (RFC No.3) earned a Queen's South African Medal serving as a corporal with 9 Company Royal Engineers. He later transferred to the Air Battalion. He was promoted to sergeant for saving the airship Nulli Secundas that had broken away from its moorings during a storm on 10 October 1907. Ramsey, after opening the escape valves, found them too slow, so split the nose, using a knife tied onto the end of a long pole. He was promoted to sergeant on 13 May 1912. Ramsey was later (1915) promoted to Temp Captain and QM.

23. Capt. Clement Robert Wedgewood Allen (RAeC Certificate No. 159 dated 4 November 1911). Allen was killed in a flying accident at Netheravon in March 1914.

24. Thomas Henry Charles Hinds (RFC No. 51). Hinds enlisted in September 1910, and later transferred from the Air Battalion to the RFC. From 13 August 1914 in served in France with 2 Squadron. He later became a Disciplinarian Sergeant Major, having evidently outgrown his penchant for reckless driving.

25. *Five Years in the Royal Flying Corps*, James McCudden. London. The Aeroplane & General Publishing Co. Ltd. 1918.

26. Lt. Vivian Hugh Nicolas Wadham (RAeC Certificate No. 243 dated 6 July 1912). Along with his observer, Sgt. Piper, Wadham was KIA on January 17th 1916, while serving as a Capt. with 15 Squadron.

27. Major John Maitland Salmond (RAeC Certificate No. 272 dated 13 August 1912). Salmond served in the RFC and RAF throughout the war. He first commanded 3 Sqd in 1914; then 2nd Wing; 2 Bdge; 5 Bdge; 6 Bdge; and CO Training. In January 1918 he became GOC RFC (later RAF) until January 1919. After a distinguished career in the RAF between the wars, and WW2, Sir John Salmond GCB,CMG,CVO DSO and Bar retired in 1943. He died, aged 86, in 1968.

28. Lt. B.H. Barrington-Kennett, the first adjutant of the RFC, had been seconded from the Grenadier Guards. Barrington-Kennett was determined that the RFC should combine the smartness of the guards with the efficiency of the Royal Engineers, who made up the majority of the personnel of the RFC. He later rejoined his regiment and was KIA in May 1915.

Chapter 3: War

1. At the outbreak of war in 1914 the role of the aeroplane was still seen purely as one of reconnaissance, a natural extension of the cavalry, and opinion remained divided as to whether it was absolutely necessary to arm aeroplanes; indeed, many people still persistently held the view that the aeroplane would have no practical use in war. Although some thought had been given to the potential of the aeroplane as an offensive weapon, the development of fighting aeroplanes had not been pursued with any sense of urgency. Consequently, not one of the 64 aeroplanes that the infant Royal Flying Corps took to France with the British Expeditionary Force on 13 August 1914 was armed for fighting in the air. The aeroplanes that equipped the four squadrons of the RFC in 1914 were a varied collection of two-seater types: Numbers 2 and 4 Squadrons were equipped with the Royal Aircraft Factory designed BE2; 3 Squadron with

Bleriots, Henry Farmans and a single BE8; and 5 Squadron operated Henry Farmans, Avros and two BE8s.

2. *Five Years in the Royal Flying Corps*. James Thomas Byford McCudden. The Aeroplane and General Publishing Co. Ltd. London. 1918. Note. Subsequent small quotes in the text from *Five Years in the Royal Flying Corps* will not be noted. Other quotations will be noted as FYITRFC.

3. This Blériot Parasol, No.616, powered by an 80hp Gnome engine, had been purchased from the Blériot Aéronautique (France) for £1,200. On 7 August 1914 it was flown from Brooklands to Farnborough for service with the RFC and allocated the service number 616. Conran flew it to France on 14 August 1914. It served with 3 Squadron until 16 March 1915, when it was returned to the 1st Aircraft Park. Issued to 5 Squadron on 21 March, it was finally struck off strength on 25 May 1915.

4. Philip Bennett Joubert de la Ferté KCB, CMG, DSO. Joubert attended the Royal Military Academy Woolwich and was commissioned in 1907 in the Royal Artillery. In 1913 he achieved a long-held ambition to fly, taking his RAeC Certificate No.280 dated 3 September 1912. Seconded as a flying officer to the RFC in March 1913, he served first with 2 Squadron before moving to 3 Squadron as a Flight Commander. On 19 August 1914, Joubert flew the first reconnaissance of the war by the RFC. Joubert later commanded 15 and 1 Squadrons, 21st and 14th Wings before becoming Officer Commanding the RAF in Italy in 1918. Joubert had a long and distinguished career in the RAF, finally retiring as an Air Chief Marshal in November 1945. He died in January 1965.

5. H.J. Gardiner (RFC No.386) 1AM. Gardiner enlisted in the RFC on 23 September 1912. In 1914, he was awarded the French Médaille Militaire for gallantry. Gardiner was promoted to Flight Sergeant in June 1916 and in the RAF Muster Roll in 1918 was listed as a Chief Mechanic.

6. George Frederick Pretyman was awarded his RAeC (No.341) on 22 October 1912. In December1916, Pretyman was promoted CO of 1 Squadron and later commanded 13th Wing. Wing Commander Pretyman DSO. MBE. retired from the RAF in November 1929.

7. Arthur Claude Robins. As a corporal, Robins learnt to fly at Netheravon and was awarded his RAeC Certificate No.793 on 21 May 1914. Robins left the RAF in 1919. He later worked for the de Havilland Company in Canada. Robins died in Swindon in the late 1950s.

8. Robert Reginald Skene. Awarded RAeC Certificate No.568 on 21 July 1913. Before enlisting in the RFC, Skene was the company pilot for the Martin-Handasyde Company and was reputedly the first Englishman to loop the loop.

9. Reginald David George Gorrie Macrostie MBE. Macrostie was later (October 1917) commissioned in the Royal Dublin Fusiliers. He transferred to the RAF at the end of WW1. He retired as a Squadron Leader in April 1948.

10. With the benefit of hindsight, McCudden later added: 'I have experienced that feeling since, and I realise that war is the most fiendish and cruel slaughter that it is possible to conceive.'

11. Guy L. Cruickshank DSO, MC. Cruickshank leant to fly in France and was awarded his certificate from the Aero Club de France (No. 1520). While a Flight Commander in 70 Squadron, Cruickshank was shot down and killed in action on 15 September 1916.

Chapter 4: France

1. G.S. Chapman (RFC No. 728) was a direct entry into the RFC on 2 June 1913. At the time he drove McCudden and others to Amiens he was serving with 4 Squadron.

2. D. Abraham (RFC No. 736). Abraham was a direct entry into the RFC on 10 June 1913. Abraham was a rigger on Conran's machine. Flying with Conran in September 1914 he unsuccessfully bombed a German observation balloon. Abraham was promoted to Flight Sergeant on 1 September 1917. He was listed as Chief Mechanic (Carpenter) in the 1918 RAF Muster Roll.

3. *Flêchettes*. From the French for small arrow or dart. These were a steel projectile, about five inches long and three-eighths of an inch in diameter with a vaned tail to stabilise its flight. A canister holding about 250 *flêchettes* was carried under the fuselage of the machines and they were released by pulling a wire. Primarily designed to be thrown onto horse lines and enemy troops, they were found to be ineffective. However, *flêchettes* are still in use today in various, more lethal forms.

4. In FYITRFC, McCudden states that the machines of 3 Squadron left about midday on 17 August. This is an error.

5. Evelyn Walter Copeland Perry (RAeC Certificate No.130 dated 12 September 1911). Herbert Edward Parfitt (RFC No.724). As a 2AM Parfitt flew to France on 13 August 1913. Perry and Parfitt were the first RFC casualties on active service in France.

6. The transport vehicles of the RFC squadrons in the early months of the war were a conglomeration of private and service cars, plus the commercial vehicles of shops and stores. One, painted bright scarlet, belonged to HP Sauce – The World's Appetizer.

7. David Samuel Jillings (RFC No.9). Jillings had transferred from the Grenadier Guards to the RFC on 21 January 1913. He was recommended for a Victoria Cross for the action of 22 August, but as an observer he was not considered to be acting on his own initiative. The award was refused on these grounds and he was awarded an MC, gazetted in January 1915 after he had been commissioned. Jillings retired from the RAF as a Squadron leader in October 1926. He served again in the Second World War and finally retired in 1946.

8. *The War in the Air*. Raleigh and Jones. Vol. 1, page 304. Oxford. The Clarendon Press 1922. In FYITRFC, McCudden states 3 Squadron had orders to leave Maubeuge at 8AM on the morning of 25 August and that he left with Joubert at 1.15PM. The official history, *The War in The Air,* states that the retreat of the RFC began on 24 August, but that 3 Squadron had left for Le Cateau in the early morning of 23 August. In 1918, while writing FYITRFC, McCudden appears to have been

two days out in his recollection of the retreat of 1914. This is understandable given the almost constant daily moves of the squadrons and the hectic workload of the officers and men, working under great strain for twelve days and nights. Also, he was writing while in Scotland, long after the event, and from various remarks made was not writing from his diary.

9. Walter George Webb (RFC No.191). As a Royal Engineer, Webb served with the No.1 Balloon Company before being posted to the RFC on 6 July 1912. Webb was posted to 3 Squadron in November 1913 as a 1AM. Webb leant to fly in 1915 (RAeC Certificate No.1330 dated 11 June 1915). As a Flight Sergeant in 45 Squadron, Webb was killed in action on 26 January 1917 while flying Sopwith One and a Half Strutter A1074.

10. Hubert Dunsterville Harvey-Kelly took his RAeC Certificate No.501 on 30 May 1913. A pilot with 2 Squadron on the outbreak of war, H-K, as he was known, was reputed to be the first pilot of the RFC to land in France on 13 August 1914. An extremely popular pilot – described by one of his contemporaries as 'the funniest man I have ever known' – H-K's unorthodox approach to military service possibly delayed his promotion to the command of a squadron, but early in 1915 he was given command of 3 Squadron. Later, while in command of 19 Squadron, Harvey-Kelly was wounded, shot down and taken POW on 29 April 1917, possibly a claim by *Leutnant* Kurt Wolff of *Jasta* 11. Harvey-Kelly died of his wounds a few days later.

11. Edward Jones Street (RFC No.224) transferred to the RFC from the Coldstream Guards. He was awarded his RAeC Certificate No.439 as a Sergeant Pilot on 18 March 1913. Street served with 2 Squadron in France from 12 August 1914. He was awarded the French *Médaille Militaire* for gallantry between 21–30 August 1914. Street was commissioned in July 1916.

12. Lionel Evelyn Oswald Charlton CB, CMG, DSO, served in the Second Boer War (1899–1902) with the Lancashire Fusiliers. Charlton learnt to fly in 1913 (RAeC Certificate No.609 dated 29 August 1913) and flew to France in 1914 as a Flight Commander with 3 Squadron. He later commanded 8 Squadron. Charlton retired from the RAF in 1928 with the rank of Air Commodore. He died in April 1958.

13. As James and Charlton took off from the south of Le Câteau, German forces were entering the town from the north

14. The official site for this move, given in WITA is Touquin, which is less than a mile from Pézarches.

15. Lt. Victor Somerset E. Lindop was awarded his RAeC certificate No.754 on 24 March 1913. Lindop failed to return from a reconnaissance on 7 September. His BE8 No.479 came down near Signy and was burnt. Lindop, the first casualty of 3 Squadron due to enemy action and the first RFC pilot to be taken prisoner, was later interned in Holland.

16. The sacking of villages by the retreating Germans forces was common, causing observers some disgust at the treatment of the civilian population. Philip Joubert later wrote. 'What we saw during the advance confirmed our impressions from the air as to the unspeakableness of the Hun in his methods of dealing with the civilian population. I saw half a dozen villages on fire during the first days of the battle, twenty miles west of Mons, where by no possible means could there have been any armed resistance to the passage of the Huns. It was simply frightfulness on the part of the Uhlans, and what we saw later on the ground at Pezarches, Coulommiers, and La Fère was a clear indication of willful and unnecessary destruction of private property.'

17. Lt. Dermot Lang Allen flew to France with 3 Squadron at the outbreak of war. He had been awarded his RAeC Certificate No.318 on 15 October 1912.

18. Reginald Cholmondley was another pioneer aviator. He learnt to fly in 1912 and was awarded RAeC Certificate No. 271 on 13 August 1912. At the time he delivered the Bristol Scout to 3 Squadron he was attached to the Aircraft Park, but on 16 April 1913, while a member of 3 Squadron, he had flown a Maurice Farman by moonlight from Larkhill to the Central Flying School at Upavon and back again, the first pilot of the RFC to fly at night.

19. Anthony Loftus Bryan was another pioneer pilot who learnt to fly in France, his Certificate No. 1355Fr dated 27 March 1905.

20. Frederick George Dunn (RAeC Certificate No.728 dated 23 January 1914).

21. Reginald Hugh Carr had been chief mechanic for pioneer aviator Grahame-White. Carr leant to fly in 1913, taking his RAeC Certificate No. 504 on 2 June 1913. Claude Grahame-White was perhaps the best known of Britain's pre-war aviators. He learnt to fly in France in 1909, one of the first Englishmen to learn to fly, his Aviator's Certificate numbered 6. In 1911 Grahame-White opened a flying school at Hendon, London and his flying displays there attracted vast crowds. Hendon later became an RAF aerodrome and at the present time is the site of the RAF Museum.

22. Evans. No details known.

23. The SE2 was a product of the Royal Aircraft Factory at Farnborough. In its original form it was first handed over to the Military Wing on 17 January 1914 and flown by the pilots of 5 and 3 Squadrons, who reported favourably on its performance. In April it was flown back to Farnborough for extensive modifications and in this final form it was issued to 3 Squadron. In his book *Aeroplanes of the Royal Flying Corps (Military Wing)*, J.M. Bruce states that the squadron received the SE2 on 27 October, while it was at Moyenneville – the location given by McCudden in *Five Years in The Royal Flying Corps* – but on 27 October, 3 Squadron was at St.Omer.

24. Along with its later development, the Type LA, these Moranes were extremely tricky machines to fly. One pilot later recalled that the Morane could not be left to its own devices for a single moment; it demanded continual attention. The elevator was extremely sensitive; the least movement of it would stand the machine on its nose or tail. Lateral control in the Type L was by wing warping and the aileron control of the Type LA was little better. In addition, the rudder was too small, which

made it difficult to turn the machine quickly. Despite these faults, the Moranes were well-built, sturdy aeroplanes, were liked by those pilots who had mastered their idiosyncrasies, and did sterling service in the early days of the RFC in France.

Chapter 5: First War Flights

1. McCudden was not yet quite as expert in French as he thought. In 'ce' he put the accent under the 'e' instead of the 'c'.
2. This was a reference to HMS *Formidable*, sunk off Portland Bill in the English Channel on 1 January 1915 with the loss of 547 men from her complement of 780.
3. O.T.V. Bowyer (RFC No.582). Bowyer was accidentally killed by the bomb explosion at Gonneham aerodrome on 12 March 1915. Bowyer was buried at Chocques MilitaryCemetery.
4. F.G. Dunn (RFC No. 1372). Dunn had leant to fly as a civilian and was awarded his RAeC Certificate No.728 on 23 January 1913. Dunn was posted to 3 Squadron in France on 3 October 1914. He was commissioned as a 2nd Lieutenant on 27 April 1915 and promoted to Captain on 1 December 1915.
5. *Five Years In the Royal Flying Corps*. McCudden described these shells as being filled with shrapnel, which burst in the shape of a fan, and considered them more dangerous than the high explosive shells the Germans would later use.
6. William Claude Kennedy Birch (RAeC Certificate No.375 dated 17 December 1912).
7. Dermot Roberts Hanlon (RAeC Certificate No.311 dated 1 October 1912).
8. D. Corbett-Wilson was another English pilot who learnt to fly in France: certificate No. 722 Fr. dated 18 January 1912. Corbett-Wilson was later shot down and killed by anti-aircraft fire over Fournes on 10 May 1915.
9. No initial is given in RYITRFC, but this was possibly Harold Blackburn (RAeC Certificate No.79 dated 9 May 1911).
10. Again, no initial is given in FYITRFC, but this was possibly Digby Crunden Cleaver (RAeC Certificate No.1666 dated 28 August 1915).
11. William Henry Burns (RFC No.100). Described as a giant of a man, nicknamed 'Tiny', Burns went to France with 3 Squadron on 13 August 1914. As a Flight Sergeant, Burns was fatally wounded by shrapnel on 26 September 1915 while acting as a ground signaller.
12. Sergeant John Groves Patrick Beazley Angell (RFC No.297).
13. Recorded casualties were: Killed: Capt. Cholmondeley; Joseph Lester Costigan (RFC No.194) W. Barker (RFC No. 534) O.T.V. Bowyer (RFC No.582) G. Cook (RFC No.589) A.T.J. Morgan (RFC No.872) A.H.C. Cuff (RFC No.1192). Wounded: S. Bird (RFC No.1171).
14. FYITRFC.
15. The cause of the accident was never fully discovered. In the squadron it was surmised that while loading the bombs a safety wire had been accidentally pulled. The official history, *The War in the Air* (Vol. 2 Page 97), although not certain of the cause states that the bombs, which it describes as 'makeshift', had no safety device other than a lead shearing pin and that one of the bombs, inadvertently dropped on its nose, had exploded.
16. Conran eventually recovered from his wounds and he and McCudden were to serve together again when Conran was given command of 29 Squadron on 23 May 1916. After serving in Egypt, Conran retired from the RAF in 1921.
17 In Mid-April 1915, Bill McCudden had been posted to 13 Squadron at Fort Grange, Gosport. By this time Bill was a very experienced pilot, with over 200 hours of flying time, and he was instructing while the squadron was working up to strength in preparation for leaving for France. On 1 May, after posting a typically light-hearted letter to his mother, Bill learnt that he had been granted weekend leave and he intended to motorcycle home that evening with his good friend Sergeant R.C. Newman after carrying out his last instructional flight of the day. This was in Blériot 2854, an elderly machine, but which had been recently overhauled at Brooklands. Immediately after Bill had taken off at 6.30PM it was obvious that something was wrong. The engine of the Blériot was running badly and sounded choked. At 150ft the machine banked to the left, side-slipped and crashed on a polo field. Not wearing his safety harness, Bill was thrown forward and killed instantly, but his passenger, Lt. Norman Reed, an American, was thrown clear by the impact and survived with only minor injuries. An investigation into the cause of the accident revealed that, unknown to Bill, the petrol flow lever had been wrongly set, which gave an excessive supply of petrol to the carburettor, causing the engine to choke and loose power. Realising this, Bill had attempted to turn back to the aerodrome, had lost flying speed, stalled, and crashed. The circumstances of the accident and its initial cause are remarkably similar to the later death of his younger brother.
18. In FYITRFC, James wrote of his feelings at the time in an almost a matter-of- fact manner: 'This was a bad blow for me, as I had always looked up to him so much and I felt his loss very keenly indeed. However, I suppose it had to be.' Writing over three years of war later, during which his younger brother and many friends had been killed, James had perhaps become somewhat inured to death.
19. Donald Swain Lewis (RAeC Certificate No.216 dated 14 May 1912). Lewis was an early advocate and pioneer of wireless telegraphy and its use in machines operating with artillery. Lewis was killed in action by anti-aircraft fire over Wytschaete on 9 April 1916 while serving with 1 Squadron.
20. Reginald Arthur Saunders (RAeC Certificate No.1182, dated 16 April 1915). Saunders was later wounded in action on 14 March 1916 while serving with 1 Squadron. He later died of his wounds.
21. FYITRFC.
22. No initials are given in FYITRFC, but this was possibly Wilfred Watts, (RAeC Certificate No.633 dated 17 September 1913) the only Watts listed to have gained his certificate early enough to have flown in 3 Squadron at this date.
23. H.R.M. Brooke-Popham. Brooke-Popham had joined the

RFC from the Air Battalion and was the first commanding officer of 3 Squadron when it was formed on 13 May 1912. At the outbreak of war he went to France as a member of Sir David Henderson's Headquarters staff. For further details see The New Recruit, Note 3.

24. On the evening of July 25, 1915, Capt. Lanoe Hawker of 6 Squadron, flying a Bristol Scout, armed with a Lewis gun mounted at an angle to miss the propeller, destroyed an enemy two-seater in flames. Hawker was awarded a Victoria Cross, the first to be awarded for a combat in the air between opposing aeroplanes.

25. Kurt Wintgens was awarded the *Pour Le Mérite* on 1 July 1916 after his eighth victory, the fourth German pilot to win the award. He was killed in action on 25 September 1916. Wintgens was credited with 19 victories.

26. Max Immelmann, a Saxon, was perhaps the most renowned of the early Fokker E.III pilots. After scoring 15 victories, he was killed in action on 18 June 1916.

27. Ibid.

28. Harold Richard Johnson (RAeC Certificate No.703, dated 11 December 1913).

29. William Henry Roberts (RFC No.332). Roberts later trained as a pilot (RAeC Certificate No. 4670 dated 16 May 1917).

30. Francis Thomas Courtney (RAeC Certificate No.874 dated 20 August 1914).

31. George Thornton (RFC No 364).

32. George Lockhart P. Henderson (RAeC Certificate No.1134, dated 31 March 1915).

33. Allan Victor Hobbs (RAeC No.1155, dated 2 April 1915).

34. Charles Edward G. Tudor-Jones. Tudor-Jones was buried in Raismes Cemetery.

35. Edgar Ramsey Ludlow-Hewitt (RAeC Certificate No.887, dated 19 August 1914). Ludlow-Hewitt want to France as a Captain with 1 Squadron in March 1915. He was as given command of 3 Squadron on 2 November 1915. In 1916 he commanded 3rd Wing and in 1918 was GOC 10th Brigade. Ludlow-Hewitt had a distinguished career in the RAF, retiring in November 1945 as Air Chief Marshal Sir Edgar Ludlow-Hewitt GCB, GBE, CMG, DSO, MC. He died in August 1973.

36. Rupert Henry Steinbach Mealing (RAeC Certificate No.809, dated 6 June 1914).

37. This was possibly Morane 5095 from 3 Squadron, which had landed behind the German lines on 22 October, when the pilot had become lost in heavy cloud.

38. Tone Paul Hippolyte Bayetto (RAeC certificate No.488 dated 22 May 1913). He later served in both 24 and 66 Squadrons. Bayetto was a popular officer in the RFC, not least because his father, being head chef at one of London's leading hotels, was always happy to give any of his son's RFC friends a good meal, gratis.

39. Letter (copy) in author's collection.

40. Wilfred Victor Ellison (RFC No.814). Ellison was nicknamed 'Fonso' because of his resemblance to King Alphonso of Spain. Ellison had transferred from the Royal Horse Guards to the RFC in February 1913 and went to France with RFC HQ on 12 August 1914. Ellison was second in command of 3 Squadron's portable wireless plant, housed in two horse-drawn carts. Ellison was promoted to sergeant in October 1915 and awarded the Croix de Guerre in February 1916. In early 1917, Ellison was a gunner in 34 Squadron. Ellison was still serving as a Warrant Officer in the RAF in February 1931.

41. FYITRFC

42. Ibid

43. Ibid

44. Robert John Lillywhite (RAeC Certificate No.720 dated 1 January 1914).

45. William Spurrett Fielding-Johnson. A Captain in the Leicestershire Yeomanry, Fielding-Johnson was awarded a Military Cross while serving with his regiment in France. He transferred to the RFC in 1915, joining 3 Squadron as an observer on 16 October. Fielding-Johnson later trained as a pilot and served again with James McCudden in 56 Squadron, where he scored six victories. Fielding-Johnson served as an air gunner in WW2, baling out over Holland later in the war. In WW2 he added a DFC to his MC. He retired as a Wing Commander and died in 1953.

Chapter 6: Fledgling Instructor

1. The Henry Farman F.20 was perhaps the best known of the Henry Farman series of designs. The first F.20 to be taken on charge by the RFC was on 18 March 1913, and by the outbreak of war several were on the strength of both 3 and 5 Squadrons, with others serving as trainers at the flying schools.

2. William Boyle Power (RAeC Certificate No.838 dated 1 July 1914). Another of the early NCO pilots of the RFC, Power leant to fly at the Central Flying school at Upavon while still a 1AM. He was commissioned a 2nd Lieutenant in May 1916, but was killed in a flying accident at Farnborough on 17 July 1916.

3. The Avro 504A was the training variant on the Avro 504. A later variant, the Avro 504K was standardised as the sole training aeroplane of the RFC and RAF and was still in use as such in the 1930s.

4. As far as is known, this is the last letter McCudden wrote to Addie. McCudden's letters to Addie are held by the Imperial War Museum, London.

5. In FYITRFC McCudden states that this was his first solo, but his flying log book gives this as being on the 16 April. In *McCudden VC*, Cole speculates that this discrepancy may be due to the speed with which McCudden wrote his autobiography in 1918, with no opportunity to check the manuscript against his logbook This is a possible explanation, but it is hardly likely that McCudden would be mistaken over the date and location, or above all, the name of the instructor who had sent him off on his first solo. It seems possible that the solo flight on 30 March was an unofficial solo, not entered into his logbook as such.

6. Ibid.

7. Maurice Walker Piercey (RAeC Certificate No.1842 dated 7 October 1915). Piercey was a direct entrant into the RFC on 22 November 1913. In 1916, Piercey served in 24 Squadron under the command of Lanoe Hawker VC, flying DH2s. Piercey was promoted to Flt. Sgt. (First Class pilot) in November 1916 and commissioned as a 2nd Lieutenant on 27 March 1917.

8. James Thomas Byford McCudden (RFC No. 892) RAeC Certificate No.2745 dated 16 April 1916.

9. No initials are given in FYITRFC and no early details have been found.

10. Geoffrey Hilton Bowman (RAeC Certificate No.2969 dated 7 June 1916). Bowman was commissioned in the Royal Warwickshire Regiment, transferring to the RFC in March 1916. Bowman joined 29 Squadron on 7 July and scored two victories with the squadron. After serving in Home Establishment, Bowman was posted to 56 Squadron on 11 May 1917 as C Flight Commander. A formidable air fighter, he served ten months in 56 Squadron, and was credited with 22 victories. In February 1918 he was promoted to major and given command of 41 Squadron, where he scored another eight victories, bringing his total to 32. After the war, Bowman served in Russia, and continued to serve in the RAF until he retired in 1934. At the outbreak of WW2 in 1939, Bowman was recalled to the RAF and served in various capacities until he was retired in December 1941. Wing Commander Geoffrey Hilton Bowman, DSO, DFC, Belgian *Croix de Guerre*, died on 25 March 1970.

11. Airco DH1. A two-seat pusher biplane designed by Geoffrey de Havilland for the Aircraft Manufacturing Company (Airco) the DH1 was the first of the series of aircraft which were to bear his name.

12. BE2d. A product of the Royal Aircraft Factory, the BE2 series equipped the RFC squadrons from the very first days of the war. Two-seat, reconnaissance aeroplanes – except for the unsuccessful BE12 – the BE2 series was replaced in France by the RE8, another product of the Factory.

13. Geoffrey de Havilland's next design for Airco, the DH2, was a single-seater pusher, conceived purely as a fighter aeroplane. The first production DH2s went to France in January 1916 and were added piecemeal to Nos. 5,11 and 18 Squadrons. In February 1916, 24 Squadron arrived in France, the first dedicated single-seater fighter squadron of the RFC, fully equipped with the DH2.

14. Designed by the Royal Aircraft Factory, The FE2d was a sturdy, two-seat pusher fighter/reconnaissance aeroplane, armed with two guns for the observer/gunner, seated in the front of the nacelle, with a fixed gun for the pilot. Along with the DH2, the FE2b, and its later variant the FE2d, was to play no small part in combating the menace of the Fokker monoplanes, but in their turn were to be outclassed by the new Albatros fighters which came into service with the German Army Air Force at the end of 1916.

15. Frank Wilkes Goddard (RFC No.329). Goddard was seconded to the RFC from the Wiltshire Regt in August 1912 and posted to 3 Squadron. Later posted to 5 Squadron as a 1AM, he went to France with the squadron on 14 August 1914.

16. George John Malcolm (RAeC Certificate No.678 dated 5 November 1913). On the evening of 9 July, Major Malcolm and 2Lt. G.E. Chancellor travelled to the depot at St.Omer to take delivery of FE2d A20 and fly it back to 20 Squadron. Malcolm took off over the wood bordering the aerodrome, but at a height of fifty feet the engine failed. The FE crashed into the trees and burst into flames. Both Malcolm and 18-year old Chancellor were killed. They were buried the next morning at St.Omer.

17. E H Lascelles. Lascelles was wounded in action by anti-aircraft fire on 2 August.

18. Stringer: see note 21.

19. Reginald Stuart Maxwell (RAeC Certificate No. 1375, dated 30 June 1915). Maxwell first flew FE2bs with 25 Squadron before being posted to 20 Squadron. In December 1916 he was promoted to Major, commanding 18 Squadron. In January 1917, Maxwell was awarded an MC. In 1918, in his second tour in France, Maxwell commanded 54 Squadron, equipped with the Sopwith Camel. Maxwell was credited with four victories flying FE2s and five flying Sopwith Camels. In 1919 he was awarded a DFC. Maxwell stayed in the RAF after the war and served in Iraq and Mesopotamia.

20. George Allan Exley (RAeC Certificate No.3566 dated 17 September 1916). Exley enlisted as a motorcyclist with the Royal Engineers in October 1915 and was commissioned into the Kings Own Yorkshire Light Infantry in August 1915 before being seconded to the RFC. Exley was killed in a flying accident on 14 January 1917 while flying as a pilot in 29 Squadron.

21. This was Capt. Guy Neville Teale (RAeC Certificate No.1283 dated 5 May 1915) and Corporal James W. Stringer, killed in FE2d A18. Stringer served in the Royal Navy for ten years before being invalided out. He joined the RFC in Oct 1915. As a gunner, Stringer was credited with one aerial victory. Two other FEs also crashed: Capt. R. Blatherwick and 2AM A. Stanley, both injured in FE2d A16, and 2Lt. D. Davies and Corporal W. Moore, both injured in FE2d A11. Moore was severely injured and died in hospital in England the following September.

22. Cecil Clarence Statt. Oxford and Buckinghamshire Light Infantry.

23. Herbert James Hamilton. Hamilton was commissioned in the Duke of Cornwall's Light Infantry in August 1915, transferring to the RFC in February 1916. He later trained as a pilot and served as a Captain in 1 and 29 Squadrons, scoring six victories. Hamilton was killed in a flying accident in England in June 1918.

24. In his combat report Maxwell commented that his own FE was: 'much faster than the other FE, which had no opportunity for firing at the hostile machine, being left behind.'

25. FYITRFC

26. There is some confusion here. In *Five Years in the Royal Flying Corps*, McCudden writes that this photo reconnaissance was flown with Lt. Lascelles and that the weather was so bad that the reconnaissance had to be abandoned. He then writes that he flew with Exley in the afternoon on a reconnaissance to the Menin area, which was uneventful apart from some anti-aircraft fire. But his logbook is quite clear on the flights flown on this day. This is further evidence that McCudden did not have his early logbook with him when he was writing his autobiography in 1918.
27. George Farmer (RFC No. 940).
28. Most probably H.S. Hughes (RFC No.1092).
29. Major W.H.C. Mansfield. Commissioned in the King's Shropshire Light Infantry, Mansfield transferred to the RFC in January 1914 and learnt to fly at the CFS. He flew to France with 2 Squadron in August 1914. Mansfield took command of 20 Squadron on 13 July 1916. At the end of the war Mansfield was a Major (temporary Lt.Col.). He resigned his commission in 1919.

Chapter 7: Scout Pilot

1. Letter from Geoffrey Bowman. Author's collection.
2. Jack Noakes (RAeC Certificate No. 1092 dated 20 February 1915). During the war, Noakes was commissioned in the field. He stayed in the RAF after the war serving in the 1920s and 30s. At the first RAF pageant in 1920 – later known as the RAF Display – Flt.Lt. Jack 'Oojie' Noakes amazed the crowd with his 'crazy flying', a term he originated. Noakes retired from the RAF with the rank of Air Commodore.
3. Cyril Telford Latch (RAeC Certificate No.1969 dated 22 October 1915).
4. McCudden, unlike many of his contemporaries, gave considerable thought to both the strategy and tactics of the air war. Writing in 1918, reflecting on this somewhat shambolic raid, he concluded that there was something radically wrong with the German Army Air Service at this time, pointing out that some twenty or thirty British machines were flying eight miles over German held territory, at heights ranging from eight to fourteen thousand feet, yet not a single enemy machine had attempted to interfere with them. Both he and the lone FE were flying over Lille at thirteen thousand feet, worried only by occasional Archie, yet in 1915 the raid could not have been carried out under the same conditions and in 1917 would have been resolutely attacked by the new German *Jagdstaffeln*.
5. William Arthur Grattan-Bellew (RAeC Certificate No.1039 dated 17 January 1915).
6. Cyril Hamilton Blyth Readman. (RAeC Certificate No.3688 dated 30 June 1916).
7. Diary, James McCudden. Copy, author's collection.
8. FYITRFC.
9. On the Headquarters copy of the combat report of this action, General Trenchard pencilled across the bottom: 'A Lewis gun ought not to be jamming like this – why is it – H.T.' The following day the officer commanding II Brigade answered that the cause was usually due to weak charges.

10. Ibid.
11. In his logbook, McCudden described this machine as an Aviatik 1914 type. He noted that it had no tail fin so it was in all probability an Aviatik C.II, a variant which was briefly at the Front between the Aviatik C.I and C.III.
12 McCudden's diary entry detailing this combat is clearly dated September 16, but both his logbook and combat report, give this combat as having taken place on 15 September, during the morning patrol and before the escort duty in the afternoon. In his logbook entry, the left hand column, giving the dates of the flights, the first notation of the 16th has been crossed through and altered to 'ditto', i.e., the 15th.
13. Norman Brearley (RAeC Certificate No. 2231 dated 20 December 1915). Flying an OP on 9 November 1916, Brearley was shot down and crashed in No-Man's Land. Wounded in his lungs, he lay in a shell hole until dark then crawled through the wire and into the British trenches. After the war Brearley returned to his native Australia, becoming one of the country's leaders in commercial aviation. Brearley was knighted in 1970. Sir Norman Brearley CBE, DSO, MC, AFC, FRAeS died on 9 June 1989.
14. Frederick William Honnet (RAeC Certificate No. 2422 dated 9 February 1916).
15. These were either the Pomeroy or Brock type, although McCudden's remark that he could see his 'tracers' hitting the wings of the Albatros on 16 September, indicates that 29 Squadron were using the Buckingham type at this time.
16. Between the months of September and November 1916, RFC casualties had been high: nearly 400 when the emerging *Jagdstaffeln* had begun to outclass the best fighter aeroplanes the RFC could put into the air. In late 1916 and the early spring of 1917, it was against these, and the obsolete reconnaissance aeroplanes of the RFC, that the embryo German fighter pilots began to score their first aerial victories, gaining valuable experience in the evolving tactics of air fighting.
17. Ivan Curlewis (RAeC Certificate No.2472 dated 19 February 1916).
18. Harold James Payn RAeC Certificate No.2528 dated 31 October 1916). Between the wars, Payn flew as a test pilot, firstly for the Air Ministry, then Supermarine Aviation (Vickers) Ltd., where he was assistant designer and technical adviser to R.J. Mitchell, designer of the Supermarine Spitfire.
19. Sidney Edward Cowan (RAeC Certificate No.1639 dated 23 August 1915). Cowan was awarded a Military Cross in May 1916, followed by two Bars. He was killed on 17 November 1916 in a collision with W.S.F. Saundby. (see Note 31)
20. This was possibly R.J. Robinson (RFC No. 801).
21. There is some confusion here. Although FYITRFC relates that the enemy machine had no gunner on board, in both his combat report and diary entry, McCudden states that although he met with no return fire, he could clearly see the enemy gunner.
22. Geoffrey Terrence Arthur Reginald Hill.
23. This Roland was Bowman's first victory of a total of 32. The balloon was his second.

24. Oswald Frederick Grevalte Ball. Ball was later killed in action while flying with 13 Squadron on 5 April 1917. He was no relation to Captain Albert Ball VC.
25. William Frederick Leach (RFC No.714). As a 1AM, Leach went to France with 3 Squadron on 13 August 1914. Leach served as a Sergeant observer with 9 Squadron in October 1916 and was commissioned on 27 October, so was evidently visiting old friends in 3 Squadron on this occasion. Leach was wounded on 16 August 1917 while serving as an observer with 9 Squadron and died of his wounded two days later. He had been awarded a DSO, gazetted in September 1917.
26. The official report on this 'accident' signed by Grattan-Bellew, states that the windscreen of the DH2 came off and broke the propeller, which cut the tail boom. He was evidently saving McCudden from an accusation of 'pilot error'.
27. Captain Alistair C Bolton. WIA and POW 9 November 1916.
28 On 9 November 1916, on the same patrol as Brearley. (See note 11) 2nd Lieutenant H.A. Hallam was shot down and made POW. Both Brearley and Hallam were in combat with the Albatros scouts of *Jasta* 1.
29. FYITRFC and McCudden's diary entry. Copy in author's collection.
30. The Halberstadt D-Types were very manoeuvrable and well liked by the German pilots of the time. This particular Halberstadt may have been one of the later type, the D.V, powered by the 150hp Benz BZIII engine, but even the Halberstadt D.II and D.III, both with 120hp engines, were much faster than the already obsolescent DH2.
31. William Spenser Fitzherbert Saundby killed in collison with S.E. Cowan on 17 November 1916.
32. This was an Albatros C.V/16, powered by the eight-cylinder 220hp Mercedes Benz Bz.IV engine. With a speed of over a hundred miles an hour, the Albatros C.V was far faster than the DH2.
33. Arthur Gerald Knight (RAeC Certificate No.2063 dated 11 November 1915). After flying with 4 Squadron, Knight was posted to 24 Squadron in June 1916, where he was credited with seven victories and was awarded a DSO and MC. Knight scored an additional victory in 29 Squadron before his death.
34. Manfred von Richthofen was the most successful German fighter pilot of the war, credited with 80 victories. He was shot down and killed on 21 April 1918 by ground fire.
35. FYITRFC
36. Alexander Jennings (RAeC Certificate No.2732 dated 8 April 1916).
37. In FYITRFC McCudden gives this aerodrome as being at Croiselles, a little to the north west of Pronville.
38. In their book *Under the Guns of The Red Baron*, authors Franks, Giblin and McCrery postulate that this Albatros – which was flying black and white streamers from its struts – was flown by Manfred von Richthofen, who claimed McCudden as his fifteenth victory on 27 December 1916. While the time, place and circumstances match those of McCudden's report of the action – even to Richthofen's claim that his victory crashed near Ficheux, close by McCudden's own account that the Albatros pilot left him at Brasseux – in his combat report Richthofen gives his adversary as a 'Vickers two-seater', Vickers being the maker the German pilots mistakenly gave to the RAF manufactured FE2bs and 2ds. It is difficult to see why Richthofen, in a prolonged combat, would mistake the single-seat DH2 for the much larger FE two-seater – by this time he was familiar with the FE type, having already shot down five, plus two DH2s. In addition, before making their initial attacks, the Albatros pilots flew for some time on a parallel course with the DH2 patrol, giving them ample time to observe that they were single-seaters. No FE2 was lost in the area or time during the day. If McCudden was Richthofen's claim for his fifteenth victory – which he reported to have seen to have crashed – then his fifteenth victory claim is invalid.
39. These Model 1914 jackets, essentially identical to the 1902 model service dress jackets issued to ground troops, were worn by officers, NCOs, and other ranks of the RFC. Those worn by the officers, usually privately purchased, were usually of finer material. Cloth 'pips' denoting rank were carried on each collar. However, many officers, seconded from their regiments into the RFC, wore their regimental tunics and badges.
40. Norman Arthur Birks (RAeC Certificate No.3525 dated 12 September 1916). On 5 April 1917, flying one of 29 Squadron's newly issued Nieuports (Nieuport 23 A6791) Birks was wounded in action, shot down and taken prisoner. He was credited to *Vzfw*. Carl Menckoff of *Jasta* 3 for his third victory. Birks died on 16 June 1989 aged 96.
41. The Casualty Report on this incident states that on taking off, the wheels of the DH2 became stuck in the mud of the aerodrome and a gust of wind blew it over. The damage was extensive: Top right and left hand panes smashed; four longerons smashed; front of nacelle smashed; gravity tank damaged. The cause given for the accident is perhaps another instance of the CO's policy of keeping his pilots out of official trouble
42. In 24 Squadron, the Commanding Officer, Major Lanoe Hawker, had secured the Lewis gun on the squadron's DH2s in a fixed position, reasoning that the aeroplane was more effective aimed as a gun. From this and other mentions, it seems that 29 Squadron's DH2s still had the gun mounted on what Hawker had described as 'a wobbly' mounting.
43. In *Five Years In The Royal Flying Corps*, this account of the fight with the Fokker differs to that given by McCudden in his combat report, in which he stated: 'I was then attacked from my left rear by HA No.2 who knocked off a large piece of my propeller.' In his book *McCudden VC*, Coles surmises that an excusable touch of vanity possibly caused McCudden to modify the real version for publication. This may be so, but in his diary entry of the event, written at the time, McCudden wrote that the spent cartridge cases were the cause.
44. Cecil Victor de Burgh Rogers. McCudden described Rogers as 'very young and rash, albeit full of pluck… this youngster was a very gallant fellow'. Rogers was killed in action on 21 April 1917, credited to *Leutnant* Kurt Wolff of *Jasta* 11 for his

18th victory.
45. Norman A. Benge.
46. In FYITRFC he later wrote: 'I honestly declare that I simply missed that Hun because I did not at the time possess that little extra determination that makes one get one's sight on a Hun and makes one's mind decide that one is going to get him or know the reason why, for that Hun was an absolute sitter.'
47. Arthur John Pearson. Pearson fought at the first battle of the Somme with the Machine Gun Corps and was awarded a Military Cross in August 1916 for bringing back his machine gun and a wounded man after five hours pinned down in a shell hole. Pearson transferred to the RFC and after pilot training was posted to 29 Squadron. Pearson was shot down in flames and killed on 9 March 1917. He was Manfred von Richthofen's twenty-fifth victory.
48. In his 1968 biography, *McCudden VC*, Chris Cole rightly calls this a copy-book victory. It was the type of victory McCudden would repeat many times in his later career.
49. In 1918, in FYITRFC, McCudden later wrote: 'Studying the Hun: In fact, this branch of work alone, just studying the habits, work and psychology of the enemy aeroplane crews, constitutes a complete education of great interest.'
50. Leslie Montague Scudmore Essell. Essell served in 29 Squadron from 20 December 1916 until 26 May 1917. No other details.
51. In combat with *Jasta* Boelcke, Lund was wounded and shot down on 25 February 1917. Although only one DH2 was lost during the day, *Leutnant* Werner Voss of the *Jasta* was awarded two DH2s shot down and *Leutnant* König was awarded another.
52. Carter was wounded in the leg on 26 February 1917.
53. Henry 'Duke' Meintjes (RAeC Certificate No. 2385 dated 2 January 1916). A South African, Meintjes had served with 60 Squadron from May 1916 until February 1917. Promoted to C Flight Commander, Meintjes was credited with four victories while with the squadron and won a Military Cross. In April 1917 Meintjes returned to France as a Flight Commander in 56 Squadron and was credited with another four victories before he was wounded on 7 May 1917.
54. John Bowley Quested. Quested flew as an observer with 11 Squadron in 1915. After training as a pilot, he rejoined the squadron to fly FE2bs. On 27 December Quested and his observer, Lt. H.J.M. Dicksee, were shot down just behind the British trenches. Dicksee was wounded, but Quested was unhurt. In July 1917, after a period of instructing in England, Quested was posted to 40 Squadron for the refresher course mentioned here, but was injured in a crash. Quested was credited with eight victories, all with 11 Squadron, and was awarded an MC and a *Croix de Guerre*.
55. Thomson. No details, but by McCudden's mention he was also serving in 11 Squadron at this time.

Chapter 8: Fighting Instructor

1. The Band of Hope was a temperance society of the time.
2. 'Teddie' O'Neill was the stage name of Emma Louise Neale, born on Christmas Day 1898. In 1916 she was one of the famous Gaiety Girls, dancing in the various musical revues and shows in London's West End. George Edwardes, the manager of the Gaiety Theatre, had introduced the first Gaiety Girls in the 1890s: they were described as 'polite and well-behaved young ladies, a symbol of ideal womanhood' and many of them married into the British aristocracy. Among Teddie's contemporaries in the Gaiety Girls were Jessie Matthews, Evelyn Lay and Cecily Courtneidge. Cecily Courtneidge had a brother, Charles, serving in the RFC with 46 Squadron, and it was possibly though this connection that McCudden first met Emma (Teddie). When Christopher Cole's *McCudden VC* was published in 1967, Emma confided in her niece Diana that she had been in love with James McCudden and that they had discussed marriage. 'Teddie' O'Neill finally retired from the stage in 1920. Emma Louise Neal died on 9 September 1969.
3. Albert Ball (RAeC Certificate No. 3375 dated 15 October 1915). Ball was one of the first single-seater scout pilots in the RFC. Flying Nieuports in 11 Squadron, he claimed his first victory on 16 May 1916. By 22 August his score had risen to eleven. He was then transferred to 60 squadron. By the end of September 1916, Ball had scored an additional twenty victories, bringing his total to 31. He was then posted to Home Establishment. In April 1917, Ball returned to active duty in France as a Flight Commander in the newly-formed 56 Squadron. While with the squadron he was credited with another thirteen victories, bringing his total to 44.

Ball was killed on 7 May 1917. The circumstances of his death remain unclear, and are still controversial. Ball was awarded to Lothar von Richthofen, younger brother of Manfred von Richthofen, as his 19th victory, but his claim was for a triplane, whereas Ball was flying an SE5, a biplane. German officers, who immediately went to the scene of Ball's crash and examined the wreckage, stated that there was no evidence of combat damage, either by fire from an aircraft or by anti-aircraft fire, and that Ball had died from the result of the crash, not from gunshot wounds. In June 1918, Ball was awarded a posthumous Victoria Cross.
4. In *Five Years in The Royal Flying Corps*, James wrote: 'It seems to me that in the Flying Corps the very best fellows are always those who are killed. It is so awful when the good fellows one meets in the RFC are killed in some way or the other, that one sits and thinks, "Oh, this damned war and its cursed tragedies." After all, I suppose it is to be, and we cannot alter destiny.'
5. Edward Mannock (RAeC Certificate No.3895 dated 28 November 1916). At this time Mannock was nearly thirty years of age, old for a fighter pilot. In April 1917, his training at Joyce Green completed, Mannock was posted to 40 Squadron, equipped with Nieuport scouts. After a shaky start with 40 Squadron, Mannock was credited with 16 victories before being posted to Home Establishment in January 1918. Mannock returned to France in March 1918 as a Flight Commander in 74 Squadron, commanded by Keith 'Grid' Caldwell. In 74 Squadron, much loved by its pilots, he

established his reputation as one of the finest patrol leaders and flight commanders in the RAF. In June 1918, Mannock was promoted to major and given command of 85 Squadron. Estimates of the number of his victories vary – officially it is 59 enemy aeroplanes destroyed – but empirical evidence points to it being well in excess of 76. On 26 July 1918, Mannock was killed by ground fire, crashing just behind the German lines. He has no known grave. Edward 'Mick' Mannock, MC and Bar, DSO and Bar was posthumously awarded a Victoria Cross, gazetted on 18 July 1919.

6. Raymond H Longman (RAeC Certificate No.7692 16 January 1919).

7. Thomas Mottershead (RFC No.1396). While a Sergeant Pilot in 25 Squadron, Mottershead was awarded a DCM in November 1916 for conspicuous gallantry during a bombing raid. In January 1917, Mottershead was serving in 20 Squadron, flying FE2ds. While on a routine patrol on 7 January, Mottershead and his observer Lt. Gower, were attacked by *Vzfw*. Walter Göttsch of *Jasta* 8. Göttsch's fire hit the petrol tank of the FE and it burst into flames that engulfed Mottershead. While Gower sprayed Mottershead with a fire extinguisher, attempting to put out the flames, Mottershead, despite being in agony from his burns, flew on, selected a suitable landing place, turned into the wind and put the burning FE gently down. On touching down the FE overturned, throwing Gower clear but pinning Mottershead under the engine. With the aid of nearby troops, Gower extricated the burned and injured Mottershead from the blazing wreckage. Mottershead was rushed to hospital, still talking cheerfully to his rescuers, but died of his injuries five days later. For his bravery and fortitude in saving the life of his observer, Mottershead was awarded a posthumous VC in February 1917.

8. Harry Lewis Pateman, KIA with 15 Sqdn on 6 Feb 1917 in BE2e 7144.

9. Ernest N. Haxton (RFC No.649, RAeC Certificate No.3223 dated 15 July 1916). While flying with 11 Squadron, Haxton and his observer were both killed in action on 10 October 1916.

10. Thomas Francis Beere (RFC No.734). Joined RFC 9 June 1913. According to McCudden's letter, Beere was serving in 41 Squadron in October1916. Beere was commissioned as 2Lt. in October 1917. He retired in December 1922.

11. Herbert Selden Long (RAeC Certificate No.1046 dated 25 January 1915). 29 Squadron.

12. Payn. See note 18 Chapter 7.

13. Herman W. von Poellnitz (RAeC Certificate No. 1953 dated 26 October 1915). 24 Squadron.

14. Martin. No details traced.

15. Richard Harold Barnwell (RAeC Certificate No. 278 dated 3 September 1912). Barnwell was tragically killed at Joyce Green on 25 August 1917, flying the prototype Vickers Vampire FB26. Barnwell took the Vampire up to several thousand feet, completed two of three loops, made a low pass, shooting up the airfield, then pulled up in a zoom to 2,000ft.

At the top of the zoom the Vampire went into a right-hand spin, failed to flatten out, and dived straight into the ground. Barnwell was killed instantly. He was 38 years old.

16. One contemporary of James described the Martinsyde G.100 as a flying machine with many pleasing qualities: 'it ambled through the air with rather a gentle burbling sound and seemed to get around the country fairly quickly.'

17. Of all the aeroplanes produced during the First World War, Cecil Lewis, a superb pilot, considered the Sopwith Pup to be by far the prettiest to look at and the sweetest on the controls. He also liked the Bristol Scout, although he commented that it was so small that even an average-sized man had to be eased in with a shoehorn. At well over six feet in height, Lewis found the cockpit very narrow, restricting his movements of the controls, and he managed to crash the Bristol on his first flight on the type. McCudden, at only five feet seven, would have had no such difficulty.

18. In 1916, those squadrons in France flying the BE12 suffered heavy casualties. At the end of September, Major-General Trenchard wrote to the Director of Air Organisation: 'I have come to the conclusion that the BE12 aeroplane is not a fighting machine in any way.' After commenting further on the heavy losses in the squadrons – 'we are losing more of these machines than we can afford in pilots' – he concluded: 'I cannot do anything else but to recommend that no more be sent out to this country.'

19. George Lockhart P Henderson(RAeC Certificate No.1143, dated 31 March 1915). Henderson had served in 3 Squadron in 1915 and had been wounded in action with a Fokker E-Type on 2 December 1915. He later commanded 66 Squadron from June to October 1917.

20. The first production run of a hundred Martinsyde G100s was powered by the 120hp Beardmore engine. In February 1916 the up-rated 160hp Beardmore became available, was adopted as the standard power plant for the type, and the later production runs of the Martinsyde were designated as the G102. However, some of these later machines were still powered by the 120hp engine and McCudden's logbook entry makes it clear that 4001 was one such machine.

21. See France. Note 8.

22. J.R. Skinner (RFC No.2994) 2AM.

23. The DH5 was Geoffrey de Havilland's attempt to design a tractor-type scout that solved the problem of the pilot's view being obstructed by the top wing. This was achieved by a back-staggered top wing, which placed it behind the pilot. The prototype DH5 first flew in the autumn of 1916, but the first production contracts were not awarded until January 1917. Owing to production delays, the first squadron to be equipped with the new fighter, 24 Squadron, did not receive its first DH5s until 1 May 1917. The DH5 was not an unqualified success as a fighter, and was used mainly as a low level ground attack aeroplane. The DH5 flown by McCudden in April, while at Dover, was obviously an early example of the type, but unfortunately – and unusually – his logbook does not give its serial number.

24. One of the great aeroplanes of WW1, the DH4 was first flown in mid-August 1916. A two-seat aeroplane, the DH4 was designed to fulfil the dual roles of fighter-reconnaissance and bombing and the first production contracts were placed in January 1917, 55 Squadron receiving its first DH4s that month. The DH4 was powered by several makes of engine, but it was with the magnificent V-12 Rolls Royce engine, of various marks, that it achieved its greatest success in the role of a high-performance day bomber. McCudden's logbook entry gives the serial number of the DH4 he flew in April 1917 as A2164, making it a DH4 of the first production batch.

25. The prototype of the Sopwith Pup – officially the Sopwith Scout – first flew in February 1916. It allegedly acquired its nickname after its first test flight, when Harry Hawker, the Sopwith Company's test pilot, declared it not only delightful to fly, but the prettiest little aeroplane so far built. Brigadier-General Sir Sefton Brancker, Director of Air Organisation, hurried down to Brooklands to see the little fighter for himself. When he arrived at the racetrack, he found the new scout standing close by a Sopwwith 1½ Strutter, a considerably bigger machine. 'Good God!' exclaimed Brancker. 'Your 1½ Strutter has had a pup.' Armed with a single synchronised Vickers gun, the Pup was first flown operationally in France in September 1916 by the squadrons of the RNAS. 54 Squadron RFC received its first Pups in October 1916, and it was later used by 46 and 66 Squadrons. The Sopwith Pup was considered by the pilots of WW1 to be the perfect flying machine. It had no vices – it was said that it could easily be landed on a tennis court – and it was held in great affection by all who flew it.

26. The series of French-designed Nieuports scouts were used extensively by the RFC. At this time, 65 Reserve Squadron at Wyton had at least eight Beardmore-built Nieuports on charge, all transferred from the RNAS.

27. Reginald Hugh Carr (RAeC Certificate No.504 dated 2 June 1913).

28. In 1918, when higher authority relaxed its views on the views on publicity, and the Daily Mail and other newspapers had run news stories on James McCudden and other prominent pilots, the *Sheerness Guardian* finally ran the story: The cleverness of his 'looping' has never been beaten in Sheppey, and that is saying a lot. We were specifically requested at the time to make no mention as to whom the aviator was, as it was against the principles of members of the RFC to have names publicly announced for any individual work. The article then went on to describe the display as: 'a series of exhibition of evolutions in the air which delighted all who saw them'.

29. John Anthony McCudden transferred from the Royal Engineers to the RFC in May 1916. In March 1917 he was accepted for pilot training and posted to No.8 Reserve Squadron at Netheravon. On 4 April 1917, he made his first solo after three hours and twenty minutes of dual instruction. He was then transferred to No.10 Reserve Squadron at Joyce Green for advanced training. On 26 June he was promoted to sergeant and took the RFC NCO pilot's certificate No.281. In September 1917, Anthony was posted to 25 Squadron, based at Auchel in France, to fly DH4s. Anthony flew with 25 Squadron for two months, flying bombing raids on enemy aerodromes, railway junctions and artillery positions. Anthony was commissioned in December 1917 and on the 30th of the month was posted to 84 Squadron, equipped with the SE5a. On 30 January, Anthony claimed his first victory as a scout plot: an Albatros scout out of control south of Cambrai. Five additional enemy aircraft fell under his guns – two Rumpler C-Types, a Fokker Dr.I, and two Albatros D.V – before he was shot down and killed on 18 March 1918 by *Leutnant* Hans Wolff of *Jasta* 11. On 19 March, Anthony John McCudden, MC, was buried with full military honours at St.Souplet.

30. Unfortunately, McCudden's logbook entries of his flights in various Vickers machines at this time are lacking in some details, but his comment on this flight in FYITRFC, that this machine was very much like the FE8 to fly, indicates that it was the FB26 Vampire, also a pusher design.

31. In FYITRFC McCudden wrote that this was his first crash in 450 hours of flying, either forgetting or discounting his crash in a DH2 after his abortive attempt at a loop while in 29 Squadron.

32. Herbert Parker (RFC No.514). Parker entered the RFC as a recruit in December 1912. He went to France at the outbreak of war with 2 Squadron. He was commissioned as a 2Lt. in January 1918 and retired in January 1938.

33. In the vernacular of the day a 'sociable'machine was one in which pilot and passenger sat side-by-side. The only Vickers that had this seating arrangement was the Vickers FB25, designed as a Zeppelin fighter. The design was not a success, control was said to be poor and during trials at Martlesham Heath it was destroyed in a crash.

34. This was probably Frederick Fox, an RNAS pilot from Grain.

35. James was extremely angry and frustrated that enemy aeroplanes were flying, almost with impunity, over England. He later wrote: 'How insolent these damned *Boches* did look, absolutely lording the sky above England… I simply hated the Hun more than ever.' Sentiments exactly echoed by many pilots who flew in the Battle of Britain in 1940.

36. It is interesting that an account by one of the Gotha pilots, *Leutnant* von Seydkitz-Kurzbach, published just after the raid, mentions that shortly after crossing the English coast on the return flight, his Gotha was persistently attacked in a manner 'showing the practised hand of a Somme pilot' that could only have been either McCudden or Fox.

37. A7352 was later sent to Martlesham Heath were it was tested in late July. Its performance was considerably worse than the 100hp Le Rhône-engined A7351, the first of the production batch, and it was ultimately scrapped.

38. One of the bad points was the inaccessibility of the Hispano engine, which was enclosed in a streamlined cowling under the low-set top wing, making it very difficult to service. McCudden flew the FB16d again on 5 June, recording its climb to 10,000ft in eight and a quarter minutes, with a speed near the ground of 147mph. McCudden was to meet the FB16

later in his career, in a more personal way.

39. Cyril Marconi Crowe (RAeC Certificate No.898 dated 8 September 1914). A pilot of vast experience, Crowe had first served as an observer in 3 Squadron in 1915. After pilot training he was posted to 8 Squadron in December 1915 and flew with the squadron until May 1916, when he was transferred to 16 Squadron, flying with the squadron throughout the Somme battles. In March 1917 he was posted as a Flight Commander to London Colney, where 56 Squadron was working up to strength. In 1918, he commanded both 60 and 85 Squadrons. Crowe was credited with 15 victories in WW1 and was awarded an MC and a DFC. In WW2 he again served in the RAF with the rank of Wing Commander. He died in 1974.

40. Richard Graham Blomfield (RAeC Certificate No. 1538 dated 6 August 1915). An Australian, Blomfield had taken command of 56 Squadron on 6 February 1917. He died in Hampshire on 16 March 1940.

41. 46 Squadron, equipped with Sopwith Pups, flew into Suttons Farm, Essex, on 10 July 1917. It returned to France on 30 August.

42 On receiving warning of the approach of the Gothas, 6th Brigade Horse Guards ordered 56 Squadron into the air to intercept them, not knowing that the squadron had flown back to France two days previously, indicative of the inefficiency of the Home Defence Forces.

43. The method of this second attack differs from that related in FYITRFC and is taken from McCudden's diary entry of the day. Copy in author's collection.

44. One British pilot reported later that he had seen three or four small, dark-coloured scouts escorting the bombers.

45. 2Lt W.G. Salmon was from 63 Training Squadron. He had taken off from Joyce Green in Sopwith Pup A6230. There are no reports of him being seen in action with the Gothas on 7 July, but while attacking one he had been hit across the eyes. He managed to keep control and return to Joyce Green, but collapsed while coming in to land, crashed from 100ft and was killed instantly.

Chapter 9: France Again

1. Philip Edmund Mark Le Gallais. Le Gallais had also been in 29 Squadron in 1916/1917.

2. At this time, McCudden had flown over 463 hours.

3. John Oliver Andrews (RAeC Certificate No.1924 dated 19 October 1915). After serving as an observer with 5 Squadron in June 1915, Andrews trained as a pilot in early 1916 and went to France with 24 Squadron in the February of that year, flying DH2s. He quickly gained a reputation as a talented and aggressive fighter pilot and was made a Flight Commander. While with 24 Squadron, Andrews was credited with seven victories – one of which was *Oberleutnant* Stefan Kirmaier, *Staffelführer* of Jasta 2 – with an additional six enemy aeroplanes driven down. In October 1916 he was awarded an MC, followed by a Bar in December. In early 1917 he joined 66 Squadron, then forming up at Filton with Sopwith Pups, and as a Flight Commander flew with the squadron to France on 3 March. By the end of July he had been credited with another ten victories, including five enemy machines forced to land, bringing his total to 23. In July 1917 he was awarded a DSO. After posts in Home Establishment Andrews returned to France in March 1918 as Flight Commander in 70 Squadron, but on the formation of the RAF on 1 April 1918 he was given command of 209 Squadron, equipped with Sopwith Camels. In December 1918 he commanded 221 Squadron, flying with the White Russian forces in southern Russia. Andrews remained in the RAF between the wars and held many varied posts: he attended two universities, and both the RAF Staff and Imperial Defence Colleges. He was promoted to Squadron Leader in 1924, to Wing Commander in 1932, and Group Captain in 1937. At the outbreak of WW2 he was made an Air Commodore. He retired as an Air Vice Marshal in 1945. John Oliver Andrews, MC and Bar, DSO, KCK, died on 28 May 1989.

4. On their return to Estrée Blanche from Bekesbourne, the pilots of the squadron – possibly inspired by the variegated colour schemes of the German Albatros pilots – had painted their SE5s in highly individual colour schemes. Gerald Maxwell's SE had a red nose; another, named *Conchita*, carried the painting of a Spanish dancer; Edric Broadberry's machine was decorated with a fearsome crocodile; and another, as remarked by McCudden, was striped like a zebra. These markings only lasted a short time before they came to the notice of 9th Wing HQ, which ordered the markings to be removed, immediately.

5. William Victor 'Struggy' Strugnell (RAeC Certificate No.253 dated 24 July 1917). Strugnell, from a Regular Army family, had been at the garrison school at Brompton Barracks with the nine-year old James and his elder brother William. With William, Strugnell was also one of the first NCOs pilots in the RFC – William's RAeC certificate was dated 13 August, twenty days after that of his friend. At the outbreak of war in August 1914, Strugnell went to France with 5 Squadron. In early 1915 he was a Sergeant Pilot in 3 Squadron, but by July 1915 had been commissioned and was flying with 1 Squadron, where he was credited with one victory, an Aviatik C-type out of control, and awarded an MC. Promoted to Flight Commander, he joined 54 Squadron in France early in 1917, where he was credited with a further five victories, and a balloon. For his 'conspicuous bravery and devotion to duty' while with 54 Squadron he was awarded a Bar to his MC in July 1917. Strugnell remained in the RAF after the war, serving in a variety of posts until his retirement as a Group Captain in 1945. He died in January 1977, aged 84.

6 Phillip Bernard Prothero. In 1916, Prothero served with 24 Squadron, flying the squadron's Bristol scout, and was credited with two victories. On 14 May 1917 he was posted as A Flight Commander to 56 Squadron, as a replacement for Albert Ball. While with 56 Squadron, Prothero was credited with an additional six victories. On 26 July 1917, Prothero was shot down and killed by *Vizefeldwebel* Artur Muth of *Jasta* 7.

7. Gerald Joseph Constable Maxwell. At the outbreak of war on 4 August 1914, Gerald Constable Maxwell enlisted in 1st Regiment of the Lovat Scouts, which had been formed by his uncle, Lord Lovat for service during the Boer war. After serving with the Scouts at Gallipoli and Egypt, Constable Maxwell transferred to the RFC in September 1916. On 11 December 1916, a natural pilot, he soloed after only twenty two minutes dual instruction on a Maurice Farman Longhorn. Posted to 56 Squadron on 12 March 1917, he flew to France with the squadron on 7 April as a member of A Flight, commanded by Albert Ball. After Prothero's death, Constable Maxwell became the A Flight Commander. Constable Maxwell was posted to Home Establishment in October 1917, after being credited with 21 victories – all with 56 Squadron. On 10 June 1918, after a period of instructing at the No.1 School of Aerial Fighting at Ayr, Scotland, he was posted to 56 Squadron for a month's refresher course and was credited with a further six victories, bringing his total to 27. Constable Maxwell resigned his commission in 1921 with the rank of Squadron Leader. During the 1930s, he joined the Royal Auxiliary Air Force and at the outbreak of war in 1939 was recalled to the RAF. During the latter stages of the Battle of Britain he was made an acting Wing Commander, as Wing Commander Tactics at Fighter Command, and by 1941 was Station Commander at Ford in Hampshire. Constable Maxwell loved to fly: his logbook for WW1 shows that he flew thirty-seven different types of aeroplanes including several German machines. Between the wars he flew his own Hornet Moth, and during his time at Ford flew many of the types used by the station. He entered the jet age by flying a Gloster Meteor, bridging the generations of aeroplanes from the Maurice Farman of 1916 – which could hover in a stiff breeze – to the 400mph Meteor of 1944. His final total of aeroplanes flown is reputed to have been 168 types. Gerald Joseph Constable Maxwell, MC, DFC, died of a heart attack on 12 December 1959.

8. Arthur Percival Foley Rhys Davids. After completing his last term at Eton in May 1916, Rhys Davids went straight into the RFC, reporting for his initial training on 17 August. Rhys Davids flew to France with 56 Squadron on 7 April 1917, and by October had been credited with 25 victories – one of which was Werner Voss, a renowned German pilot with 48 victories – and had been awarded an MC and Bar and a DSO. Rhys Davids was shot down and killed on 27 October 1917, by *Leutnant* Karl Gallwitz of *Jasta* Boelcke. Rhys Davids has no known grave. He is commemorated on the Flying Services Memorial at Arras.

9. Leonard Monteagle Barlow (RAeC Certificate No.3426 dated 22 August 1916). In October 1913, Barlow won the Mitchell Scholarship to study electrical Engineering at the City and Guilds Technical College. After winning the Salomon's Scholarship Barlow was engaged in research as a senior student, finally graduating in 1916. Another of the original pilots of 56 Squadron, Barlow flew to France with the squadron on 7 April 1917. A skilled and aggressive air fighter, by 1 October he had been credited with 20 victories and had been awarded an MC with two Bars. On 21 October 1917 he was posted to Home Establishment. On 5 February 1918 Barlow was killed while testing Sopwith Dolphin C3779 at Martlesham Heath.

10. Verschoyle Philip Cronyn (RAeC Certificate No. 2007 dated 15 October 1915). A Canadian, Cronyn learnt to fly on flying boats in Toronto in July 1915, but gained his RFC pilot's brevet (821) at the Central Flying School at Upavon on 20 November 1915. His RAeC Certificate was then issued, backdated to 15 October. Cronyn was posted to 56 Squadron on 28 June 1917 and served with the squadron until he was invalided home on 28 September. During 1917, Cronyn's elder brother Richard was also with the RFC in France, serving in 1 Squadron.

11. This was the largest air fight of the war to date. From 5,000 to 17,000ft, Sopwith Camels, SE5s, Sopwith Triplanes from the Naval squadrons, DH5s, FE2s, and Spads were fighting over forty Albatros scouts, with enemy two-seaters working at lower heights.

12. Although McCudden did not claim this Albatros, he included it as his sixth victory in a list of his victories that he was asked to submit in December 1917. This was possibly *Ltn*. Hans Helmigk of *Jasta* 27. Some sources give Helmigk as being injured in an accident on this date, others that he crashed as a result of combat. McCudden also listed the Albatros he forced down on 26 July as his seventh victory. Although an unknown hand has pencilled 'indecisive' on the copy of his combat report at Wing HQ, it was credited to him as being out of control.

13. With hindsight, McCudden believed that this Albatros pilot was possibly Heinrich Gottermann, *Staffelführer* of Jasta 15, who at this time had been credited with ten balloons. Gottermann was credited with 39 victories, including 17 balloons, before he was killed in a flying accident while testing a Fokker Triplane on 30 October 1917.

14. By 24 September 1917, Sopwith A 7311 was at the 18th Wing Fighting School at London Colney. At the end of October 1917 it was at the School of Aerial Fighting at Ayr, where presumably it ended its days.

Chapter 10: 56 Squadron

1. Thomas Bertram Marson. Marson had served in the second Boer War of 1899 as a trooper in The Leicestershire yeomanry. At the outbreak of war in 1914, Marson joined the 3rd County of London Yeomanry and was commissioned as a 2nd Lieutenant. In August 1915, while fighting at Gallipoli, Marson was wounded below the right knee by shrapnel and his leg was later amputated. In November 1916, anxious to return to active duty, he was seconded to the RFC, joining 56 Squadron as its Adjutant/Recording Officer on 16 January 1917. Marson later became private secretary to General Trenchard.

2. In FYITRFC McCudden states that he arrived at Estrée Blanche on the evening of 15 August, but the sequence of events shows that it was on the 14th. However, he signed the officer's reporting book, making him officially a member of the squadron, on the 15 August.

3. Richard Aveline Maybery. Maybery was born at The Priory,

Brecon, Wales. He attended Sandhurst, winning first prize for field engineering, tactics and strategy. In 1913, Maybery was commissioned in the 21st Lancers, joining the regiment in India. As a cavalryman, Maybery fought on the Indian frontier and was wounded at the battle of Shrabkadr. Unable to sit a horse because of his wound, Maybery was seconded to the RFC and leant to fly in Egypt. Maybery was posted to 56 Squadron on 17 June 1917, and while with the squadron was credited with 21 victories and awarded an MC and bar. Maybery was killed on 19 December 1917 by anti-aircraft fire from *K-flakbatterie* 108 commanded by a *Leutnant* Thiel. He was buried close by the batterie, on the road from Haynecourt to Sailly, but was later re-interred in Flesquieres Hill British Cemetery.

4. Robert Hugh Sloley. Sloley was born in South Africa, the only son of Sir Herbert and Lady Charlotte Sloley. Sloley first served in the Royal Artillery before being seconded to the RFC. Sloley was posted to 56 Squadron on 21 July 1917 and was credited with eight victories before being shot down and killed on 1 October 1917 by *Leutnant* Xaver Dannhuber of *Jasta* 26 for his sixth victory.

5. Eric Leslie Lowe Turnbull. Turnbull joined 56 Squadron on 28 May 1917 and served eight months with the squadron, an exceptionally long tour of duty. Turnbull was given command A Flight on 19 December 1917, and posted to Home establishment on 26 January 1917. Although he scored only three victories, Turnbull was acknowledged to be an exceptional flight commander.

6. Keith Knox Muspratt (RAeC Certificate No. 2789 dated 27 April 1916). Muspratt learnt to fly while in his last year at Sherborne School. As soon as he was old enough he enlisted in the RFC and taught at the Central Flying School, where one of his pupils was Arthur Rhys Davids. Muspratt was posted to 56 Squadron on 21 May 1917. While serving with the squadron he was credited with eight victories and was awarded an MC. After leaving the squadron for Home Establishment on 13 November 1917, Muspratt was posted as a test pilot to Martlesham Heath, where he was killed while testing a new type on 16 March 1918.

7. Reginald Theodore Carlos 'Georgie' Hoidge. A Canadian, Hoidge was an architect in civilian life. He served first with the Canadian Royal Garrison Artillery, but transferred to the RFC in 1916. Hoidge was posted to 56 Squadron in January 1917 while it was working up to strength at London Colney, and was one of the original pilots to fly with the squadron to France on 7 April. Hoidge flew with the squadron for six months, was credited with twenty-seven victories and awarded an MC before returning to Home Establishment on 31 October 1917. Hoidge returned to France in the late autumn of 1918 as a flight commander in 1 Squadron, where he added a Fokker D.VII to his victory score. Hoidge died in 1963.

8. Ian Henry David Henderson. Ian Henderson was the only son of Lieutenant-General Sir David Henderson, first GOC of the RFC in France. Ian Henderson transferred to the RFC from his regiment, the Argyll and Sutherland Highlanders.

In 1916 Henderson flew BE12s with 19 squadron, scoring two victories in August that year and an additional victory in November flying a Spad. He was awarded an MC for his work with the squadron. After a period of Home Establishment, Henderson was posted to 56 Squadron in February 1917 as a flight commander, but after an accident was posted to Eastern Group before the squadron left for France. Henderson rejoined 56 Squadron on 25 June 1917 as the B Flight Commander, and was credited with four victories until replaced by James McCudden on 15 August. Henderson was killed in a flying accident at Ayr on 21 June 1918.

9. Maxwell Henry Coote (RAeC Certificate No.6894 dated 17 January 1917). Coote was posted to 56 Squadron on 4 June 1917 and flew with the squadron until 27 November 1917 when he was posted to Home Establishment. He was credited with three victories.

10. This was not a manufacturing error. The cable was a new type that had been tested and found satisfactory.

11. Ernest Etherington was a corporal in B Flight.

12. Nearly a year later, when Gerald Maxwell was again serving with the squadron on a refresher course, he was reminded of this incident. 'Well,' he replied. 'I'm afraid that at that time we just didn't realise Mac's worth.'

13. In a conversation with the author, Colonel Edward David Galley, who served as a Captain with McCudden in 56 Squadron, recalled: 'at Sandhurst we were told that the prefect soldier had two qualities in equal proportions: discipline and initiative. We were further told that this was seldom, if ever, found. Jimmie McCudden was the nearest I have ever seen to that ideal.'

14. *McCudden VC*. Christopher Cole. (page 109) William Kimber & Co. London 1967. Alex Grey was a 2AM in B Flight.

15. Tom Rogers was a corporal mechanic in B Flight.

16. Bert Card was a corporal and is shown in the squadron records as an engine mechanic.

17. Hubert Noel Charles. Charles, a brilliant young engineer, served twice as equipment officer with 56 Squadron: from 6 December 1916 to 1 June 1917; then from 17 June to 5 November 1917, when he was transferred to 9th Wing.

18. Herbert Arnold Johnston. Johnston was posted to 56 Squadron on 9 August 1917 and flew with the squadron until 4 November 1917 when he was posted to Home Establishment. While with the squadron he was credited with two victories.

19. In Leonard Barlow, James had found a kindred spirit. With his pre-war training as an engineer, his technical approach to his duties – he was known in the squadron as the 'gadget king' – echoed that of James, although he was less concerned with tactics and in that respect perhaps the more aggressive air fighter.

20. Harold Montague Rushworth. Rushworth was posted to 56 Squadron on 10 August 1917. On 10 August he was shot down by *Gefreiter* Müller and *Unteroffizier* Elschenbroich of *Schutzstaffel* 11 and taken prisoner.

21. McCudden's views on the SE5a, written in 1918, are worth

quoting fully. 'The SE5 which I was now flying was a most efficient fighting machine, far and away superior to the enemy machines of that period. It had a Vickers gun, shooting forward through the propeller, and a Lewis gun shooting forward over the top plane, parallel to the Vickers, but above the propeller. The pilot could also incline the Lewis gun upwards in such a way that he could shoot vertically upwards at a target that presented itself. As a matter of fact, these guns were rarely used in this manner, as it was quite a work of art to pull this gun down and shoot upwards, and at the same time manage one's machine accurately. The idea of using a Lewis gun on the top plane of an SE was first put forward by the late Captain Ball, who used his top gun with such excellent success in another squadron flying Nieuports. However, the modern machine has nowadays such a climb and reserve of power that it is quite usual for a machine to get some speed first and then do a vertical zoom towards an opponent who is above and get in a burst of fire before losing all its speed and falling down in a stalled condition. Other good points of the SE5 were it's great strength, its diving and zooming powers and its splendid view. Apart from this, it was a most warm, comfortable and easy machine to fly.'

22. William Janson Potts (RAeC Certificate No. 3743 dated 18 October 1916). Potts transferred to the RFC from the Royal Artillery in late 1916 and was posted to 56 Squadron on 7 August 1917. Potts was shot down and killed on 21 September1917 by *Leutnant* Haack and *Leutnant* Klostermann of *Fl.Abt.(A)* 227.

23. Charles Hugh Jeffs. Jeffs transferred to the RFC from the Border Regiment and was posted to 56 Squadron on 18 August 1917. Jeffs was credited with five victories before he was shot down and taken prisoner on 5 October 1917 by *Oberleutnant* Bruno Loerzer of *Jasta* 26.

24. Geoffrey Miles Wilkinson. Wilkinson first joined 56 Squadron on 20 April 1917 but was wounded on 28 May. He rejoined the squadron on 15 August 1917, but was shot down and killed on 10 October 1917 by *Leutnant* Dannhuber of *Jasta* 26.

25. *Vzfw*. Josef Oehler of *Jasta* 24. Killed.

26. FYITRFC states that Arthur Rhys Davids was on this patrol, but he is not shown as being so in the Squadron Record Book, and he did not return from leave until the 22nd of the month.

27. This DFW was from *Fl.Abt.(A)* 210, crewed by *Leutnant* Albert Wolluhn and *Flieger* Otto Koch, who were both killed.

28. *Under Britisk Flag*. Tryggve Gran. Boghandel 1919. Page 164–165. Jens Hermann Tryggve Gran (RAeC Certificate No.5000 dated 2 August 1917). Gran was born in Bergen, Norway in 1888, the son of a wealthy shipyard owner. As a young skiing instructor he was a member of Captain Scott's Artic expedition in 1911 and in 1912 was one of the eleven man party that found the bodies of Scott and his companions. Gran was later awarded the Polar Medal by King George V. In 1914, Gran learnt to fly at the Louis Bleriot school in Paris, predating his RAeC certificate by three years. On 30 July he became the first pilot to fly across the North Sea, leaving from Scotland and landing at Reevtangen, near Stavanger, four hours and ten minutes later: a flight of 289 miles. Worldwide acclaim for this feat was denied to Gran by the news of events in Europe and the Balkans that led to the outbreak of war. In 1916, Gran requested the Norwegian Government that he be attached to the RFC. This was granted, but in view of Norway's neutrality he was ordered to give his name as Teddy Grant, a Canadian. Under this pseudonym, Gran served with the RFC for the remainder of the war, firstly in 39 Home Defence Squadron, then with 44 Squadron. In both squadrons, Gran flew several sorties during the Gotha raids in 1917 and it was probably at this time that he met James McCudden.

On 2 September 1917, Gran was posted to 70 Squadron in France, but was transferred two days later to 101 Squadron – where he flew a Sopwith Pup – as a night fighter pilot, and FE2bs on night bombing raids. On 30 November, Gran was wounded in the leg and invalided to England. For his work in 101 Squadron, Gran was awarded an MC. Recovering from his wound, he served in 78 Squadron and later in Russia. Tryggve Gran died at his home near Oslo in 1980, aged 91.

29. Possibly *Vizefeldwebel* Wilhelm Reiss of *Jasta* 3, who was killed.

Chapter 11: Autumn above the Salient

1. Ernest Leslie Foot (RAeC Certificate No.2257 dated 20 December 1915). Foot, not surprisingly known as 'Feet' was one of the early pilots of the RFC. He served first with 11 Squadron, where he became friends with Albert Ball, and when the scout Flight of 11 Squadron was transferred to 60 Squadron in August 1916 it included both Ball and Foot. Foot was awarded three victories in 11 Squadron and two more in 60 Squadron. On 10 March 1917, Foot was posted to 56 Squadron as a flight commander, but was injured in a car accident the evening before the squadron was to fly to France. In 1923, flying a Bristol M1, Foot was killed in a flying accident while taking part in the Grosvenor Trophy Race.

2. *Flying Corps Headquarters*. Maurice Baring, Page 255, Wm. Blackwood and Sons, Edinburgh and London 1968. Diplomat, wit and man of letters, Maurice Baring was a near perfect example of a polymath. At the age of forty, Baring went to France in 1914 as a member of Sir David Henderson's staff. On General Trenchard succeeding to the command of the RFC from Henderson in August 1915, he inherited Baring as his ADC. Baring became a legend in the RFC for his handling of the bluff, inarticulate Trenchard, who later wrote. 'He was a man I could always trust. He was my mentor and guide.' One of Baring's contemporaries later wrote of him: 'There never was a staff officer in any army, in any nation, in any century, like Major Maurice Baring… The Flying Corps owed much more to this man than they know or think.' Maurice Baring died in Beaufort castle, near Inverness, Scotland, in December 1945.

3. Neither Jeffs not Potts claimed this Albatros, it is not mentioned in their combat reports, and McCudden makes no mention of seeing its attacker.

4. It was about this time that Arthur Rhys Davids, a classical scholar of some repute, insisted that the correct plural of Albatros was Albatri. In a conversation with the author in the 1960s, Bowman recalled: 'We much preferred it to the verbal atrocity of Albatrosses.' The term was later widely used throughout the RFC and RAF and is used in the text from now on.

5. In writing FYITRFC, McCudden related the incident with the DFW as having happened on September 4, but both the Squadron Record Book and the casualty report on SE5a B519 make it clear that it had happened on 5 September.

6. This was possibly *Vizefeldwebel* Alfred Muth of *Jasta* 27, killed in action over Moorslede.

7. A Prussian, born in Bresnau, Silesia, Manfred von Richthofen entered a cadet military academy at the age of eleven, graduating from the senior academy in 1911 with the rank of *Leutnant*. At the outbreak of war in 1914, Richthofen was serving in Russia with his regiment, *Ulanen-Reg. Nr.*1. Richthofen transferred to the *Fliegertruppe* (the German air service) in May 1915, serving first as an observer before training as a pilot. On 1 September 1916, Richthofen joined *Jasta* 2, commanded by Oswald Boelcke, and began his career as a fighter pilot. In January 1917, Richthofen was given command of *Jasta* 11 and later commanded *Jagdgeschwader* I. Manfred von Richthofen was the most successful German fighter pilot of the war, being credited with 80 victories before his death on 21 April 1918, when he was shot down by ground fire.

8. Werner Voss was born in Krefeld in 1897 and enlisted in the local militia at the outbreak of war, serving first in Russia with a Hussar regiment. Voss rose rapidly through the ranks from *gefreiter* to *unteroffizier* in May 1915, winning an Iron Cross 2nd class. Voss transferred to the *Fliegertruppe* in August 1915, serving first as an observer before training as a pilot. Voss was an exceptional pilot and was first assigned as an instructor, but eventually, on 21 November 1916, was posted to *Jasta* 2. After being credited with 28 victories he was posted first to *Jasta* 5, then held temporary command of both *Jagdstaffeln* 29 and 14, before being made *Staffelführer* of *Jasta* 10 in July 1917. Voss had been credited with 48 victories when he was shot down and killed in combat with 56 Squadron RFC on 23 September 1917.

9. Oskar von Boenigk transferred to the German Air Service in December 1915, serving as an observer before training as a pilot. He was posted to *Jasta* 4 in June 1917, claiming seven victories before being given command of *Jasta* 21 in October 1917. Boenigk survived the war with a total of 26 victories. Boenigk served in WW2, was taken prisoner by Russian forces in May 1945, and died in captivity in January 1946.

10. McCudden described the Fokker Triplane: 'This machine has stagger single struts, middle plane shorter than top, and bottom plane shorter than the middle plane, and the chord of the planes decreases from top to bottom plane. The struts are staggered outwards from the machine " Halberstadt" type rudder with no fin. No dihedral. Stationary motor.'

His description of the Pfalz was headed: 'Fokker: This is (sic) a slight dihedral and stagger, very sharply (unreadable) Morane type wings, tail piece and rudder. Bottom plane smaller than top. Am uncertain whether it has V struts or parallel. Am also uncertain whether engine is stationary or rotary.'

Sloley's descriptions of the new types are more detailed. The Pfalz he described as 'a biplane of the "Fokker" type, with Fokker tail and Albatros type planes, sharp and cut away at the wing tips, and grey in colour.' His description of the wings of the Fokker Triplane was similar to that of McCudden's, but he had noted that 'the fuselage was of a large square section, and the rudder large, partly balanced, and without fin, and was coloured yellow and brown.' He later stated that tracer from the Triplane suggested that it had two guns and that both the new types 'appeared quite equal to the Albatros scout in performance at that height, 11,000ft.'

11. Researchers have long believed that only two Fokker Triplanes were at the Front at this date: 102/17 and 103/17, but in a letter to the author in the late 1960s, the late Douglas Whetton wrote: 'A further Triplane came up to *JG*I on September 5th 1917, at least according to the Bodenschatz papers. Oskar Boenigk flew it on a number of sorties, it was a dirty grey/green/brown colour, but the serial number was not noted and I have not been able to check it.' Oskar von Boenigk was posted to *Jasta* 4, a component of *JG*I on 24 June 1917. He later commanded *JG*II and survived the war, claiming a total of 26 victories.

12. Under another name, this game was still being marketed in the 1970s.

13. In FYITRFC McCudden wrote: During the first fortnight in September I had the most rotten luck that I think it is possible for a fighting pilot to experience. I can count up to at least six scouts which I very likely would have shot down in the early part of September alone.

14. Possibly *Obflm*. Kurt Schönfelder of *Jasta* 7, wounded on 11 September.

15. Frederick James Horrell. Horrell joined 56 Squadron on 25 July 1917 and was struck off strength on being taken to hospital on 25 September.

16. 'Shut his engine off and went down in a flat spiral, vibrating most violently. I think I knocked a lump out of him. Last saw him still going down at 4,000ft.' McCudden diary entry 14 September 1917.

17. In all probability, this was *Leutnant* Julius Schmitt of *Jasta* 3.

18. Norman Howard Crow had joined 56 Squadron on 17 August. He credited to *Vizefeldwebel* Carl Menckhoff of *Jasta* 3.

19. The sequence of events in FYITRFC seems to imply that this action took place the previous day, but McCudden's combat report makes it clear that it took place on the 16 September.

20 . This was possibly *Ltn.d.R*. Richard Grüter of *Jasta* 17 who crash-landed but survived. The crash was confirmed by Lt. Soden of 60 Squadron.

21 . This Rumpler, McCudden's eleventh victory, was from *Fl.Abt.(A)* 292, crewed by *Ltn.d.R*. Bauer and *Uffz*. Allkofer,

both severely injured in the crash. This victory was confirmed by pilots of 10 Squadron, who had observed the Rumpler crash.

22. In *McCudden VC*, Cole gives that this 'Sopwith' was a Sopwith Camel, borrowed from 70 Squadron, but at this time 70 Squadron had moved from Estrée Blanche and were based at Poperinghe. McCudden's logbook entry gives only 'Sopwith'. No.66 Squadron may well have received a Camel to familiarise them with the type – they were re-equipped with the type in October – but if this had been a Camel, a type he had not previously flown, McCudden would surely have followed his usual custom and commented on its characteristics in his logbook. Cole gives the date of this flight as the 22 September, but McCudden's logbook gives it as the 21st.

23. *Other Days*. Verschoyle Phillip Cronyn, Hunter Printing London Ltd., Ontario, Canada, 1976.

24. This particular German scout had first been reported by Captain Collett of 70 Squadron on 31 August 1917. Collett made a sketch of this machine for RFC HQ, that showed a double pair of wing struts each side of the fuselage, and he estimated that it was slightly larger than the normal Albatros, which it closely resembled. McCudden and Hoidge both reported on this machine, their descriptions closely matching that given by Collett, but it fits no German scout known to have been in service at this time. The most likely explanation seems to be that it was the experimental Pfalz D-Type.

25. Potts had been shot down by a two-seater crew, *Ltn.* Haack and *Ltn.* Klostermann of *Fl.Abt.(A)* 227.

26. *Ltn.* Gustav Rudolph and *Uffz.* Rudolf Franke of *Fl.Abt.* 6.

27. Harold Alan Hamersley, an Australian, was commissioned in the AIF and fought at Gallipoli in 1915. After transferring to the RFC and training as a pilot, Hamersley was posted to 60 Squadron in early September 1917. Hamersley was credited with thirteen victories while serving with 60 Squadron, and was awarded an MC before being posted to Home Establishment in May 1918. Hamersley had a long and varied career in the RAF both between the wars and in WW2. He died in December 1967.

28. Keith Logan 'Grid' Caldwell. A New Zealander, Caldwell learnt to fly privately in 1915 while in the New Zealand Territorial Infantry. He arrived in England in 1916 and enlisted in the RFC in April. After pilot training, he was posted to France and joined 8 Squadron in late July. Caldwell flew BE2ds with the squadron, scoring one victory, a Roland, until 18 November 1916, when he was posted to 60 Squadron to fly Nieuport scouts. In February 1917, Caldwell was promoted to captain and given command of C Flight. On his posting to HE in October, Caldwell had been credited with eight victories and been awarded an MC. In 1918, Caldwell was given command of 74 Squadron and took it to France in April , adding another 16 victories to bring his total victories to 25 and winning a DFC and Bar, plus the Belgian *Croix de Guerre*. Known as 'Grid' because he referred to all aeroplanes as 'Grids', Caldwell was one of the most popular officers in the RFC and RAF. Returning to New Zealand after the war, Caldwell became a farmer, but retained his enthusiasm for flying, serving in the reserve and as a member of local flying clubs. At the outbreak of WW2, Caldwell served in the RNZAF and in 1945 was Air Officer Commanding at RNZAF HQ in London. Keith Logan 'Grid' Caldwell CBE, MC, DFC and Bar, ED, MID, *Croix de Guerre* (Belgian) died in November 1980, 30 minutes after cranking his car and remarking that it was time he handed in his flying kit. He was 85 years old.

29. Robert Leslie Chidlaw-Roberts (RAeC Certificate No.2527 dated 23 January 1916). Chidlaw-Roberts joined the RFC in May 1915, straight from Sandhurst. He served for six months as an observer with 2 Squadron before training as a pilot. After flying with 18 Squadron for eight months, he was posted to 60 Squadron in August 1917. He served in 60 Squadron until January1918, was credited with nine victories and awarded an MC before being posted to Home Establishment in January 1918. In the summer of 1918, he returned to France and operational flying as a Flight Commander in 40 Squadron, destroying a balloon in September to bring his victory claims to ten. He died in June 1989.

30. Chidlaw-Roberts interview.

31. Keith 'Grid' Caldwell. Letter to author.

32. FYITRFC.

33. Bowman's account of the fight written in the early 1940s.

34. Ibid

35. Ibid

36. Caldwell.

37. Voss was later reburied by the Germans in the Cemetery (*Kameradengrab*) at Langemark.

38. FYITRFC. If anything, McCudden's statement that Voss 'put bullets through all our machines' was understating the case. Hamersley managed to land his badly damaged machine at 29 Squadron's aerodrome at Poperinghe. In the brief flurry of that first encounter, Voss had shot through the left-hand bottom engine bearer; two top planes and the centre section; spars, ribs, rudder and kingpost; the water jacket on the right-hand side of the engine; radiator, propeller, CC gear; generator and oil pipes, and had put numerous holes in the fabric. The SE5a B539 was beyond repair in 60 Squadron's workshops and was returned to No.1AD. Chidlaw-Roberts' machine was also considerably shot about. Cronyn's machine had been badly damaged by Voss. The woodwork of the right-hand upper and lower planes had been shot through; the left-hand longeron was almost cut in two, and the right lower longeron had a bullet hole through it; one of the ribs of the tailplane had been fractured by a bullet, and there were several bullet holes in the wings and fuselage. In addition to the damage caused by Voss, there was considerable damage by Archie. It was also returned to No.1AD for repair. Maybery's machine had also been badly damaged, hit in the upper right-hand longeron, necessitating its return to No.1AD, and Muspratt had force-landed with a bullet in his radiator, sump, and oil pipe.

39. McCudden filed no Combat Report for this action, nor does he mention it in FYITRFC. Presumably he did not consider it worthy of mention or a claim for a possible victory.

40. These enemy scouts were from *Jasta* 10. The first Albatros was flown by *Obltn*. Ernst Weigand, who was killed; *Uffz*. August Werkmeister, the pilot of the Pfalz, was also killed. The pilot of the second Albatros, that crashed by Houthulst Forest, must have escaped with his life as there are no other recorded German losses for the day that fit the time and place. Four days later, Weigand and Werkmeister – who had been with *Jasta* 10 for only two days – were buried alongside each other in the churchyard of St.Joseph's Church.

41. The 'Gothas' were in all probability AEG G.IVs, possibly from a *Staffel* of *Kagohl* IV, which operated a mixed complement of twin- and single-engined aeroplanes.

42. This Rumpler C.V was from *Schusta* 27b, crewed by *Uffz*. Hans Gossler and *Uffz*. Bruno Wiedermann. Gossler fell in the German lines; Weidermann in the British. Both are commemorated on a plaque in the German Military Cemetery at Langemark. The British reported on all enemy machines brought down behind the British lines, each machine being given a G number. This Rumpler was G.73.

43. This was *Ltn*. Herbert Pastor of *Jasta* 29.

44. The Albatros pilot was in all probability *Oblt*. Otto Schmidt, *Staffelführer* of *Jasta* 29, who claimed a 'jenseits' (on the other side) for his 10th victory. Although Schmidt claimed a Sopwith Pup, none were lost on 28 September and time and place fit for his combat with James McCudden.

45 Rhys Davids had wandered off alone after the initial fight with the Albatri and had sent down an Albatros in a vertical dive, twin columns of smoke pouring from its engine.

46. These Albatri were flown by *Ltn*. Kurt Wissemann and Carl Menckhoff of *Jasta* 3. Menckhoff survived a crash-landing, but Wissemann was killed.

Chapter 12: Gains and Losses

1. Arthur William Keen (RAeC Certificate No.2298 dated 17 January 1916). In 1916, Keen had flown with 70 Squadron, flying Sopwith 1½ Strutters, scoring one victory, a Fokker D.III. After being rested, he returned to France as a Flight Commander in 40 Squadron, and was credited with another eleven victories before again returning to England. In June 1918 he returned to France to take command of 40 Squadron after the death in action of its commanding officer, Roderic Dallas, who at the time of his death was credited with 32 victories. Keen was credited with an additional two victories in 1918, bringing his total to 14, before being severely injured and badly burnt in a flying accident on 15 August, dying of his injuries on 12 September.

2. Although McCudden concluded in his combat report that this Rumpler was 'more or less under control' when he last saw it, it was later confirmed as a victory, presumably as having been driven down. An observer from *Fl.Abt*. 5, a *Ltn*. Frauenstein, is given as seriously wounded on Oct 1.

3. Sloley was credited to *Ltn*. Xaver Dannhuber of *Jasta* 26 for his sixth victory of an eventual eleven.

4. This was quite possible. At this time the Germans had begun to armour their *Infanterieflieger* aeroplanes

5. This Albatros was flown by *Ltn*. Max Roemer of *Jasta* 10, who was killed in the crash.

6. Stanley James Gardiner. Gardiner had been posted to 56 Squadron on 17 August 1917.

7. Gilbert. See later note.

8. Rhys Davids reported seeing two Fokker Triplanes, that he described as having 'no dihedral, large extensions, Nieuport tail, Fokker rudder and Martinsyde-shaped wings, engine possibly rotary. Climb appeared good.' From German records of Fokker Triplanes taken on charge by the *Jagdstaffeln*, it would appear that, after the loss of Fokker Triplanes F1.102/17 and 103/17, no more Fokker Triplanes were at the Front until about the middle of October, when *Jasta* 11 received six, but from these combat reports of 56 Squadron, and other squadrons, it is possible that there were additional Fokker Triplanes at the Front from the beginning of October 1917 and possibly at the end of September.

9. David Jordon Reason had been posted to 56 Squadron on 10 September.

10. Almost certainly Francis H. Harrison (RFC No.622). Harrison went to France on 14 August as a 1AM in 5 Squadron. Harrison was promoted to Temp. Sgt. Major in August 1917.

11. This was a considerable journey to have undertaken: as the crow flies, a round trip of approximately 80 miles, much of it over roads in appalling condition.

12. Charles Hugh Jeffs had claimed five victories since joining the squadron on 18 August and was a pilot of some promise.

13. *An Onlooker in France 1917–1919*. William Orpen, Williams and Norgate, London, 1921. William Orpen (1878–1931) was a well known portrait artist of the time who went to France in 1917 as an official war artist, making many drawings and paintings of life on the Western Front. During October 1917 Maurice Baring and Orpen visited 56 Squadron several times – Orpen once soundly beating McCudden at ping-pong – and he arranged to paint portraits of 'Georgie' Hoidge and Arthur Rhys Davids. In 1918, back in London, he painted James McCudden. An Irishman, Orpen was born in Dublin in 1878, was knighted in 1918, and died in 1931, aged 53.

14. Arthur Gordon Jones-Williams. After service with Welsh Regiment, Jones-Williams – known to all as 'John-Willie' – transferred to the RFC in August 1916. He joined 29 Squadron in March 1917, becoming a Flight Commander in May. Jones-Williams claimed eight victories while with 29 Squadron and was awarded an MC and Bar. After a period of rest, Jones-Williams returned to France in 1918 as a Flight Commander in 65 Squadron, adding another three victories, to bring his total to eleven. Jones-Williams stayed in the RAF after the war. In April 1929, with Flt. Lt. N.H. Jenkins, he flew the Fairy Long Range Monoplane non-stop from England to India, a distance of 3,950 miles in 50 hours 39 minutes. However, this failed to break the record for a long range flight, which stood at 4,912miles, and in December, Jones-Williams and Jenkins set off again, only to crash in Tunisia. Both pilots were killed.

15. Hugh Vivian Champion de Crespigny (RAeC Certificate

No.1009 dated 26 February 1915). In 1915 Champion de Crespigny first flew in France as a pilot with 11 Squadron, where he was awarded an MC. In early March 1917 de Crespigny was posted to 60 Squadron as a Flight Commander, but there is little record of his time with the squadron.
On 22 March 1917, at nineteen years of age, he was given command of 29 Squadron until 21 July, when he handed over command to Charles Chapman. On 4 October, after the death of Chapman, de Crespigny returned to 29 Squadron and resumed command. In June 1918, he returned to France to take command of 65 Squadron, where in won a DFC. At the end of the war he commanded 65 Wing. Awarded a Permanent Commission in 1919, Champion de Crespigny remained in the RAF after the war. He served in the Second World War, retired in 1945 and died in 1969.

16. Charles Meredith Bouverie Chapman (RAeC Certificate No.1491, dated 31 July 1915). Chapman had flown with 24 Squadron in 1916, scoring three victories and was awarded an MC. In 1917 he joined 29 Squadron as a Flight Commander, was promoted to Major in July and took command. While serving with 29 Squadron, Chapman claimed another four victories, bringing his total to seven. On 1 October, German night bombers attacked 29 Squadron's aerodrome at Poperinghe. Amongst the fourteen casualties was Chapman, who was fatally injured.

17. This was incorrect. Karl Emil Schäfer of *Jasta* 28, credited with 30 victories, had been shot down and killed on the evening of 5 June 1917 by a FE2b crew of 20 Squadron: Lts. H.L. Satchell and T.A. Lewis. Rhys Davids made no victory claim on 5 June.

18. This was possibly flown by *Oblt*. Rudolf Berthold, *Staffelführer* of *Jasta* 18, who was wounded during the day, a bullet smashing his right upper arm.

19. James Nelson Cunningham was a Canadian from Moose Jaw, Saskatchewan. He was 24 years old.

20. He had been shot down and killed by *Ltn.d.R*. Hans Hoyer of *Jasta* 36. Born in Scarborough, Reginald Preston-Cobb had joined the RFC in 1917 and had been posted to 56 Squadron on 27 September. He was nineteen years of age. He has no known grave.

21. McCudden's combat report states 80mph, but this was obviously a typing error by the squadron clerk. McCudden's logbook entry states it as being 40mph.

22. Geoffrey Bowman. Logbook entry.

23. This LVG was from *Fl.Abt*. 8. The pilot was *Flg*. Heinrich Horstmann, the observer *Obltn*. Ernst Hädrich. Horstmann and Hädrich are both buried in The Huts British Military Cemetery.

24. McCudden later had a cigarette box made from the LVG's propeller.

25. An Australian, from Lyndoch, South Australia, John Driffield Gilbert had travelled to England in 1915 to enlist. He was shot down by *Ltn*. Ernst Udet of *Jasta* 37 for his 14th victory.

26. Geoffrey Belville Shone died of his wounds on No.27 Ambulance Train in the early hours of the next morning. He was the third victory of *Vzfw*. Willi Kampe of *Jasta* 37.

27. This Rumpler C.IV No.8431/16 was from *Fl.Abt*. 5, crewed by *Ltn*. Hans Laitko and *Uffz*. Richard Hiltwein. The wreckage was designated G.84.

28. Arthur Rhys Davids had been shot down and killed during a morning patrol on 27 October, the fifth victory of *Ltn*. Karl Gallwitz of *Jasta* 2.

29. The culprit was Harry Slingsby. On 31 October, after a fight with a number of Albatri, Richard Maybery had forcelanded B4863 at 1 Squadron's aerodrome at Bailleul. On 2 November Slingsby travelled to Bailleul to fly the SE back to Estrée Blanche. Taking off in the gathering darkness, he hit a house, smashing off all four wings and undercarriage, and severely twisting the fuselage, completely demolishing B4863. McCudden had little sympathy, remarking rather caustically: 'the only thing that was undamaged was himself'.

30. Clive Franklyn Collett (RAeC Certificate No.1057 dated 29 January 1915). A New Zealander, Collett joined the RFC in 1914 and was commissioned in March 1915. He served several months in France, but was seriously injured in a flying accident when flying an aeroplane back to England. After recovering, in 1916 he became a test pilot, flying many types of aircraft, and in January 1917 made an experimental parachute jump. In the summer of 1917, Collett was posted as a Flight Commander to 70 Squadron to fly Sopwith Camels and by early September had been credited with eleven victories and awarded an MC and Bar. On 9 September he was wounded and returned to England. Returning to experimental and test flying, Collett was killed on 23 December 1917, while flying a captured Albatros over the Firth of Forth. This was Albatros DVa. D.2129/17 (G.56) flown by *Vzfw*. Ernst Clausnitzer of *Jasta* 4 that had been forced down intact on 16 July 1917 by Lt. Langsland of 23 Squadron.

31. This was possibly G.56. See above note on Collett.

Chapter 13: Cambrai. A Change of Scene

1. Rainsford Balcombe-Brown (RAeC Certificate No.1258 dated 12 May 1915). A New Zealander, Balcombe-Brown had taken his RAeC ticket at the British Flying School at Le Crotoy in France. He was awarded an MC, gazetted on 26 July 1916, for destroying a balloon while flying a unfamiliar type of aeroplane. Balcombe-Brown was shot down and killed on 2 May 1918 by *Obltn*. Erich Löwenhardt, *Staffelführer* of *Jasta* 10. He was buried in Carnoy Military Cemetery.

2. Felix Rudolf Chevallier Cobbold was shot down by *Ltn*. Fritz Loerzer of *Jasta* 26.

3. Phillip Chambers Cowan was an Irishman, born in Dublin, who transferred from the 8th Manchester Regt. to the RFC in 1916. He was claimed by *Ltn*. Hans von Habler of *Jasta* 36. Cowan's younger brother, Sydney Edward Cowan MC and Bar, had been killed on 17 November 1916 while serving with 29 Squadron.

4. This was the second aeroplane Harmon had wrecked in ten days. On 2 November, he had crashed when his engine had

failed to pick up after a dive. The SE was a total wreck and was returned to 2AD. Harmon was admitted to hospital with broken teeth and a cut mouth.

5. See note 44, First War Flights.

6. Harry Slingsby (RAeC Certificate No.1818 dated 4 October 1915). Slingsby was posted to 56 Squadron on 20 October 1917. He was taken ill on 15 December, admitted to hospital on 27 December and finally struck off strength on 29 December.

7. Harold John Walkerdine, a native of Derbyshire, joined the RFC in March 1916. He was commissioned in June 1916, trained as a pilot in August 1917, and was posted to 56 Squadron on 2 November. Eighteen years old, 'Jackie' Walkerdine was a very popular pilot in the squadron and was credited with seven victories before being wounded in action on 11 April 1918. Walkerdine was seriously injured in a flying accident in October 1918, but survived the war and died on 18 June 1966. The author is the proud possessor of Walkerdine's copy of *Five Years in The Royal Flying Corps*.

8. This DFW C.V was from *Fl.Abt.(A)* 259. *Ltn.* Ernst and *Ltn.d.R.* Schwarzer were both wounded.

9. John Patrick Waters was from Hampshire, the son of Brigadier General W.H. Waters and Mrs. Waters. He was eighteen years of age.

10. The other squadrons of the Army (Fighter) Wing, those flying Sopwith Camels, Pups, and DH5s, had been ordered to fly low-level bombing and ground-strafing missions on the enemy aerodromes, and the front-line and support trenches. These were dangerous duties in normal weather conditions, but conditions on the first morning of the offensive contributed to their casualty rate of 33%.

11. The other members of the patrol, Slingsby and Fielding-Johnson, also failed to return directly to Laviéville. Slingsby landed two miles from the aerodrome due to lack of petrol and Fielding-Johnson had been forced to land at 3 Squadron's aerodrome at Warloy by engine failure.

12. When weather conditions were poor it was left to the judgement of individual squadron commanders whether or not to send out patrols. Balcombe-Brown evidently considered the lives and experience of pilots such as McCudden, Bowman, and Maybery, too important to needlessly squander in the hazardous work of ground-strafing, where an experienced and valuable flight commander could be shot down by a lucky enemy machine gunner as easily as the most inexperienced member of the Flight.

13. This was *Vzfw.* Karl Bey of *Jasta* 5, who was killed.

14. This two-seater crew was possibly from *Fl.Abt.* 23: *Ltn.* Wussow and *Uffz.* Kammell, who claimed a 'Sopwith' west of Crevecoeur-s-Escaut.

15. This was possibly either *Ltn.* Karl August Schönebeck, who force landed at Epinoy, or *Ltn.* Hans Wolff, who overturned in a forced landing at Avesnes-le-Sec. Both these pilots were from *Jasta* 11, a component of *Jagdgeschwader Nr.*1, which had arrived in the area on 22 November.

16. This was 49 Squadron's first bombing attempt on the Western Front and inexperience may have contributed to their failure to meet their escorts.

17. The details of this action were detailed in a special report, which was submitted to Wing by Balcombe-Brown. The first of its kind to be sent by the squadron, it was titled: Report of Attack on Enemy Infantry.

18. This DFW was from *Fl.Abt.* 202, crewed by *Ltn.d.R.* Kurt Dittrich and *Ltn.d.R.* Manfred Hoettger.

19. These Albatros scouts were from *Jagdstaffeln* 5 and 6.

20. One of these Albatri was from *Jasta* 5. *OffzSt.* Josef Mai crash-landed Albatros D.V 2082/17 at 10.20 (German time).

21. Alexander Dodds had joined 56 Squadron on 6 October. Dodds was *Ltn.* Schubert's 5th and last victory.

22. DFW from *Fl.Abt(A)* 268 crewed *by Ltn.d.R.* Georg Dietrich and *Ltn.* Deitrich Schenk, both killed.

23. This LVG C.V, No.9458/17 (G.94), was from *Schutzstaffel* 19. The badly wounded pilot, *Vzfw.* Flohrig, died on his way to hospital, but the observer, *Gefr.* Eckerle was unhurt.

24. Maurice Edmund Mealing was born in High Wycombe, Buckinghamshire. He enlisted in the King's Shropshire Light Infantry, where he was promoted to corporal. In May 1916, Mealing transferred to the RFC, was commissioned, and served as an observer in 15 Squadron. After training as a pilot, he was posted to 56 Squadron on 18 October but was taken to hospital five days later. He rejoined 56 Squadron on 17 November. His victory on 30 November was the first of fourteen. Mealing was shot down on 24 March 1918, claimed by a crew of a two-seater he had been fighting: *Ltn.* Treeder and *Uffz.* Zetter of *Fl.Abt.* 245. Mealing was seen by another pilot to be waving, standing alongside his crashed SE5a, but he was later reported as killed, shot by advancing German troops. He was awarded an MC, gazetted in May 1918.

25. George Adrian Cawson first enlisted at the age of fifteen and a half with the Hawke Battalion, Royal Naval Division. While later serving with the Artists Rifles (London Regiment) he transferred to the RFC and was posted to 56 Squadron on 11 October. Cawson was shot down by *Vzfw.* Voigt and *Vzfw.* Kruse of *Schusta* 12. He was nineteen years old.

26. At twenty-eight years old, Ronald Travis Townsend was one of the oldest pilots in the squadron. Commissioned in 1910, at the outbreak of war he was serving as a captain in the Gordon Highlanders. Townsend had trained as an accountant in civilian life and in 1915 he was working in the financial department of the Canadian Pay and Record office. Unhappy with this post he transferred to the RFC in April 1917, trained as a pilot and was posted to 56 Squadron on 18 October. Townsend was shot down and killed by *Vzfw.* Josef Mai of *Jasta* 5 for his 5th victory. Townsend was married, with two daughters.

Chapter 14: A Remarkable December

1. In FYITRFC McCudden states that he and Rogers left at 'about 7.00AM', but the Squadron Record book clearly shows that he did not return from his aborted patrol in the morning until 8.00AM.

2. His annoyance was later exacerbated by the fact that

the German counterattack never reached anywhere near Havrincourt and the remains of the brand new LVG.
3. Balcombe-Brown was ordered by Wing to submit a full report on the aborted attempt to salvage the LVG.
4. The spinner of the LVG was later fitted to McCudden's SE, increasing its speed by 3mph; the rudder was hung in the Mess and remained with the squadron for the remainder of the war.
5. On 3 December, Brigadier-General J.F.A. Higgins, commanding III Brigade, filled out an Army Form W.3121 recommending McCudden for another decoration. After detailing McCudden's victories in the last two days of November, he summarised: 'Since being awarded a bar to his Military Cross, this officer has destroyed seven enemy machines, two of which crashed our side of the lines. In all he has accounted for 22(sic) enemy machines. His pluck and determination have been a fine example to his Squadron.'
6. SE5a B4880 was the first production SE5a to be fitted with elevators of reduced chord. Tested at 1AD on 12 December 1917, it was found to be considerably lighter on the controls, recovery from a dive was much quicker, and it flattened out easier on landing. In the summer of 1917, with the first 200hp SE5as being received, the heavier engine, together with the slightly higher landing speed, had imposed an increase on the load carried by the original steel undercarriage. This had led to failures of the undercarriage, with damage ranging from broken propellers to near write-offs. Major Blomfield had brought this weakness to the attention of 9th Wing, with the request that something should be done. Consequently, a new undercarriage was designed: the front legs were two narrow inverted 'vees' of ash, faired together to give the appearance of a single, tapered strut. The rear legs were also of ash, and the whole undercarriage had been moved forward two inches to improve the balance. Officially, this new undercarriage was the 'three strut undercarriage', but it was generally known as 'the wooden undercarriage'.
7. Edward David George Galley. Galley had served as an observer in 22 Squadron in 1916 before being wounded on 24 March 1917. After training as a pilot, he was posted to 56 Squadron on 26 November 1917. He was promoted to the command of B Flight on 9 April 1918 and was posted to HE on 16 May 1918.
8. A fellow pilot described Harold 'Jackie' Walkerdine as 'a fine little kid and so full of life he can hardly keep still for a moment'.
9. This Rumpler C.VII, a series of the type new to McCudden, was from *Fl.Abt.* 33 crewed by *Ltn.* Alfred Berking and *Uffz.* Max Bröll. Pieces of the Rumpler were still falling twenty minutes later and the disparate parts were given two G. Nos: G.95 and G.96.
10. Patrick Henry Lyon Playfair (RAeC Certificate No.283 dated 3 September 1912). Playfair transferred from the Royal Field Artillery to the RFC in 1912. He served first in 2 Squadron, but flew to France in 1914 with 4 Squadron. He flew as a flight commander in 11 Squadron before commanding 8 Squadron. Playfair served in the RAF throughout his life. He died in 1974.
11. In FYITRFC this enemy two-seater is given as a DFW, a lapse of memory on McCudden's part when writing his autobiography, his combat report stating that it was a Rumpler. This machine was from *Fl.Abt.* 225, flown by *Ltn.* Martin Becker and *Uffz.* Karl Pohlisch. Both were killed.
12. This was a Hannover – probably a CL.II – which had just entered service with the *Luftstreitkräfte*. These aeroplanes were small for a two-seater and in the coming months were often mistaken for Albatros scouts. Over the next three months, James would become familiar with the type – known to RFC pilots as Hannoveranas.
13. Leslie Nansen Franklin served twice with 56 Squadron. Joining first on 28 October 1917, he was admitted to hospital on 13 March 1918 but rejoined the squadron on 30 May 1918. Franklin was shot down and killed on 14 July 1918 by the crew of a two-seater, *Ltn.* Enke and *Vzfw.* Leopold, unit unknown.
14. Louis William Jarvis. Jarvis, a Londoner, had served in the army at Gallipoli in 1915 before returning to England and transferring to the RFC. After pilot training he was posted to 56 Squadron on 14 October 1917. He was credited with seven victories before returning to HE on 24 May 1918. Jarvis later served in 1 and 29 Squadrons.
15. Alfred Victor Blenkiron (RAeC Certificate No.4842 dated 3 June 1917). Blenkiron served in the Somerset Light infantry before transferring to the RFC in 1916. He flew from March to August 1916 as an observer in 22 Squadron; then a few days with 23 Squadron before joining 25 Squadron in December 1916. Blenkiron was credited with two victories with 25 Squadron. He was wounded on 29 January 1917 in an action for which he was awarded an MC. After pilot training he joined 56 Squadron on 3 December 1917. He was credited with two victories with the squadron. He later flew with 15 Squadron and was credited with another victory, bringing his total to five.
16. Barclay McPherson (RAeC Certificate No. 5176 dated 3 September 1917). McPherson was posted to 56 Squadron on 19 November 1917. On 1 April 1918, he was shot down and taken prisoner by *Hptm.* Wilhelm Reinhard of *Jasta* 6 for his eleventh victory.
17. *Vzfw.* Georg Strasser of *Jasta* 17 who claimed a balloon at Villers Faucan.
18. Richard Maybery's great friend, Geoffrey Bowman, who had left on leave on 15 December, four days before Maybery's loss, recalled in 1968: 'Richard was tired and I asked him to take my leave. I was still fresh, didn't need it, and was only going to Paris anyway. He wouldn't hear of it and I never saw him again.' Although the squadron's pilots believed that Maybery had been shot down by the German pilot known to them as 'Greentail', he had in fact been shot down by a *K-Flackbatterie*, commanded by a *Ltn.* Thiel, and was buried close by the guns, south of the village of Haynecourt, by the side of the road to Sailly. Maybery was later reburied in Flesquières Hill Cemetery.
19. This DFW was from *Schutzstaffel* 5. The pilot, *Uffz.*

Biesenbach was taken prisoner but the gunner, *Uffz.* Anton Bode, was dead. The DFW was designated G.104.

20. This LVG was from *Fl.Abt.* 40 crewed by *Ltn.d.R.* Friedrich Drückhammer and *Vzfw.* Zehe.

21. This Rumpler C.VII, No.8003/17(Works No. 3020) was from *Fl.Abt.* 23, crewed by *Ltn.* Hugo Richter and *Ltn.* Emil Tibussek, both killed. The wreckage was designated G.107.

22. Sgt. Major B.G.Cox (RFC No.259). Cox transferred to the RFC from the 16th Lancers in July 1912 and was posted to 3 Squadron. Cox went to France on 14 August 1914 as a sergeant in 5 Squadron.

23. This Rumpler (G.106) was from *Bogohl* 7. Although the crew were taken prisoner, there is no mention of their capture in the German casualty lists, showing again how incomplete they are.

24. This LVG.C.V, No.9446/17, was from *Schutzstaffel* 12, crewed by *Vzfw.* Kurt Boje (pilot) and *Vzfw.* Friedrich Niemann (gunner). Both were killed.

25. In winter, with a full war load, the ceiling of the average SE5a was 17,000ft.

26. In fact, 'Beery' Bowman was actually in Paris, having a 'thorough good time.'

27. During the day, Brigadier Higgins forwarded to Wing his recommendation for the award to McCudden of a Bar to his DSO.

28. This Rumpler was from *Fl.Abt.* 32. *Ltn.* Klaus Doering and *Ltn.* Hans Dubislaw, both killed. G.111.

29. Rumpler from *Fl.Abt.(A)* 40. *Ltn.* Hans Mittag and *Uffz.* Osker Güntert, both killed. G.112.

30. LVG C.V from *Fl.Abt.(A)* 210. *Ltn.* Walter Bergmann and *Flg.* Albert Weinrich, both killed. G.113.

31. This LVG was from *Schutzstaffel* 10. The pilot, *Vzfw.* Kurt Gerschel, was mortally wounded, but the gunner, *Uffz.* Lehnert, was unhurt and taken prisoner. G.118.

32. This was possibly an LVG from *Fl.Abt.(A)* 233. The unit had a *Ltn.* Metzger seriously wounded in an airfight.

33. LVG from *Fl.Abt.* 33. The crew, *Ltn.d.R.* Walter Dern and *Ltn.d.Res.* Georg Müller, were both killed. G.119.

34. This was a reference to the ubiquitous tins of Tickler's Plum and Apple jam, that were issued in vast quantities to the British troops in France. In 1914 Thomas Tickler, a grocer from Grimsby, had won the contract to supply the BEF with tins of jam, which, when empty, were put to all manner of use, even improvised into home-made bombs. After the war, Tickler's became a household name and only ceased trading in 1970.

Chapter 15: 1918: For Valour

1. Robert John Glenn Stewart had been in the squadron for a month and a day, having been posted in on 2 December 1918. He was the 14th aerial victory of *Ltn.* Ludwig Hanstein of *Jasta* 35b.

2. Brigadier-General John Frederick A. Higgins (RAeC Certificate No.264 dated 30 July 1912). Higgins, known as 'Josh', had transferred to the RFC from the Royal Artillery. In 1913 he was commanding officer of 5 Squadron, taking the squadron to France at the outbreak of war in 1914. After commanding 4th Wing in England, Higgins was given command of 3rd Wing in June 1915. At the end of January 1916, as a Brigadier-General, he took command of III Brigade, a post he held during the battles of the Somme, Messines, Ypres and Cambrai, and still held in February 1918. A popular commanding officer, Higgins was affectionately known throughout both the RFC and RAF as 'All Bum and Eyeglass'.

3. These Hannovers had plywood-covered fuselages and were capable of absorbing an immense amount of punishment.

4. Trevor Durrant was born in Woking, Kent. He joined the RFC on 5 August 1916 and served as an observer with 55 Squadron from November 1916 to June 1917. On 4 May 1917, with his pilot, he was credited with a single victory. After training as a pilot, Durrant was posted to 56 Squadron on 7 December 1917. McCudden's assessment of Durrant's potential was fully justified. He was credited with his first victory on 25 January 1918, adding another three by the beginning of May. May was his most successful month, adding another six to his total – three on 3 May alone. He scored his last victory on 13 May, bringing his overall total to eleven. On 16 May, Durrant was promoted to Captain and took command of B Flight, but was killed that same day in a fight with Fokker Triplanes of *Jasta* 6. He was awarded to *Ltn.d.R.* Hans Kirschstein of the Jasta for his thirteenth victory. One of his fellow pilots later wrote of Durrant: 'Trevor Durrant has held a place in my memory for the last fifty years as the finest Englishman I ever knew.'

5. Philip Fletcher Fullard was born in Hatfield, Hertfordshire in June 1897. In 1916 he was serving with the Royal Fusiliers, but learnt to fly at his own expense and transferred to the RFC. His flying abilities were such that he was made a flying instructor in December 1916. In May 1917 he was posted to 1 Squadron in France, flying Nieuport scouts. Fullard flew with the squadron until 15 November, was credited with forty victories, and was awarded an MC and Bar, and a DSO, before breaking a leg while playing football on 17 November, and invalided home. Fullard remained in the RAF after the war, and was one of a select party of pilots who visited the USA to give flying exhibitions in 1919. Fullard served in the Second World War, becoming an Air Commodore and Air Officer Commanding 246 Group. Fullard was made a CBE, awarded an AFC, and finally retired from the RAF at the end of the war. Philip Fullard died on 24 April 1984.

6. This 'LVG' was possibly a misidentification for an Halberstadt CL.II. On 9 January, *Schutzstaffel* 25b, which was equipped with the type, had a pilot, *Vzfw.* Wilhelm Dörfler, taken to hospital after suffering contusions to his forehead after a forced landing.

7. In January 1918, John Maitland Salmond had succeeded Trenchard as GOC of the RFC in France.

8. Map reference 62B.h31B. This LVG was from *Fl.Abt.(A)* 264. After crash landing, the pilot, named Notler – rank unknown – found his observer, *Ltn.d.R.* Max Pappenheimer dead in his cockpit. Source: Letter from the CO of *Fl.Abt.(A)* 264 to

Pappenheimer's parents.

9. This DFW was from *Bogohl* 7. The observer, *Ltn*. Max Rittermann, was killed. The pilot, *Uffz*. Hans Bruns, was seriously wounded and died of his wounds seven days later.

10. Map reference.57B.S27a.

11. According to German records, this LVG, also from *Bogohl* 7, crashed at Gouzeaucourt, killing both the crew, *Vzfw*. Hans Rautenberg and *Ltn*. Gerhard Besser. Map ref. 62B.F16b. This LVG was designated G.124.

12. Alan John Lance Scott (RAeC Certificate No. 975 dated 20 December 1914). Scott was a New Zealander who transferred to the RFC from the Sussex Yeomanry. A crash during pilot training, breaking both his legs, meant that he could only walk with the aid of two sticks and had always to be helped into his cockpit. He first flew Sopwith 1½ Strutters as a Flight Commander with 43 Squadron, before being given command of 60 Squadron in March 1917. A determined air fighter, Scott scored five victories with 60 squadron and was awarded an MC before he was wounded on 10 July 1917 and invalided home. During the Battle of Ypres in July 1917, and the Battle of Cambrai in November, he commanded 11th Wing. In 1918 he was made commandant of the Central Flying School, staying in the post until the end of the war and being awarded an AFC. Scott fell ill during the flu epidemic after the war and died in January 1922, aged 38.

13. Eric Herbert Monckton Fetch (RAeC Certificate No.3768 dated 1 November 1916). Fetch had joined the squadron on 30 November 1917. He never returned to the squadron.

14. This was an LVG from *Fl.Abt.(A)* 202. *Uffz*. Gustav Mosch and *Ltn*. Friedrich Bracksiek, both killed.

15. McCudden had realised how vitally important it was to be able to reach and destroy the high-flying German reconnaissance machines, with their vital information, and his success in this was a unique achievement of incalculable worth. Geoffrey Bowman once remarked to the author, with tongue only slightly in his cheek 'The Hun didn't know what the hell was going in our back areas around Cambrai. Every time they sent a two-seater over, young Mac knocked it down.'

16. These Rumplers were known as *Rubild* and although their engines were a lower horsepower rating than the 260hp of the normal Rumpler C.VIIs, the power fall-off at these extreme altitudes was much lower, where the power ratio was seen to advantage. Although McCudden shot down a total of sixteen Rumplers a study of his combat reports makes it very unlikely that any were *Rubild* Rumplers, as these were attacked at heights considerably lower than the 20,000ft at which these machines habitually operated.

17. It is not known from where he had acquired these, but they were the pistons being used in the latest versions of the Wolsley-manufactured Hispano-Suiza engine.

18. Lester Janson Williams had joined the squadron on 14 December 1917. He was shot down and taken prisoner on 28 January 1918 by a two-seater crew, *Ltn*. Schuppau and *Ltn*. Schandva of *Fl.Abt.(A)* 233.

19. Bowman, who signed James' combat report, was of the opinion that the DFW had very probably crashed. This was possibly a DFW from *Fl.Abt.(A)* 240, who reported an observer, *Ltn.d.R.* Georg Palloks, fatally wounded over Wancourt. The squadron's Victory Lists now showed McCudden's name for no less than sixteen consecutive victories.

20. Douglas Woodman was twenty years old. He was posted to 56 Squadron on 13 November 1917 and served until 11 March 1918 when he was shot down and killed by *Vzfw*. Edgar Scholtz of *Jasta* 11 for his second victory.

21. This Rumpler was from *Fl.Abt.(A)* 225 crewed by *Ltn*. Schramm and *Ltn.d.R.* Hermann Büscher. Both were wounded, Büscher fatally.

22. It would be thought that higher authority would have taken some note of these improvements and taken steps to have them incorporated into the production aircraft coming from both the Royal Aircraft Factory and its subcontracted factories. Since its early days in France, the SE5 and SE5a had undergone numerous improvements, carried out by the squadrons in the field; the engineering officers of the squadrons conferring and sharing the various ways they had individually found to iron out faults, some minor, some more vital. These had been advised to the Royal Aircraft Factory, who had largely ignored them, taking the draconian attitude: 'We make them; you fly them.'

23. The office of Charles Grey, editor of the *The Aeroplane*, was close by the RFC club and many pilots of the day visited him there. Grey had devised a test to gauge their quickness of situation awareness, vital in a pilot. He would lay out a set of dominoes, face down on his table, and time how long it took a pilot to turn them over and arrange them in order. He found that the average pilot would take anything from 55 to 65 seconds, but McCudden always finished in a minute, and at one time in less than 55 seconds.

24. Kenneth William Junor was a Canadian from Toronto. He arrived in England in March 1916 with the Canadian 11th Machine Gun Company and four months later was in France. Junor transferred to the RFC in 1917, trained as a pilot and was posted to 56 Squadron on 15 December 1917. Junor served four months with the squadron, scoring eight victories, and had been awarded an MC before being shot down and killed on 23 April 1918 by *Ltn*. Egon Koepsch of *Jasta* 4 for his second victory.

25. The German casualty lists give *Ltn*. Adam Barth of *Jasta* 10, flying Albatros D.V 4565/17, as having been shot down and killed over Anneux, but the Pfalz pilot must have escaped without injury as there are no German reports of any other loss at that time and in that area.

26. This was *Obltn*. Bruno Justinus, acting commanding officer of *Jasta* 35b while *Ltn*. Hanstein, the *Staffelführer*, was on leave.

27. John Anthony, his younger brother, serving with 84 Squadron.

28. At this time, actually forty-six.

29. LVG C.V 9775/17 from *Bogohl* 7 crewed by *Ltn*. Werner von Kuckzowski and *Vzfw*. Erich Szafranek. G.130.

30. Eugene Ronald Macdonald, a Scot from Ayr, had joined

the squadron on 19 January. He remembered that on his arrival nobody seemed to take any notice of him, and he was left to his own devices, the other pilots being busy with their own affairs. But later he was shown the models of enemy aeroplanes that had been made and painted to McCudden's instructions and was given advice by him on the best way to tackle them. ERM, as he was known, flew with the squadron until 18 July 1918, and although he was credited with no official victories, was a valuable member of the squadron. Fifty years later, when Cyril Parry was arranging the 56 Squadron 1968 reunion dinner, he confided to the author. 'One person I'd really like to see again is little E.R. Macdonald. He was a quiet little chap, but when you looked round he was always there – in the thick of it.'

31. Cyril Parry, a Welshman, was typical of the new officers who were bringing a more professional outlook to the business of fighting in the air. He had joined the Royal Welch Fusiliers as a band boy in 1907 and by 1917 was an NCO weapons instructor. Watching with increasing frustration each draft of men he had trained leaving for France, he transferred to the RFC, reporting to the Central Flying School in October 1917. Parry was posted to 56 Squadron on 3 January 1918. As a great admirer of McCudden, and with a similar professional approach, under McCudden's teaching Parry developed into a fine patrol leader and was given command of A Flight on 18 May 1918. While with 56 Squadron, Parry was credited with four victories and awarded a DFC for leading his patrols with 'exceptional skill and gallantry'. On 1 July, 1918 Parry was posted as a flight commander to 60 Squadron, but was badly injured in a flying accident on 29 July, and spent the remainder of the war in hospital. After the war, Parry became a highly successful civil engineer. After a long illness, Cyril Parry died on 22 April 1975 at his home in Welwyn, Hertfordshire.

32. Rumpler from *Fl.Abt.(A)* 202, crewed by *Ltn.d.R.* Ernst Karlowa and *Uffz.* Albert Fröhlich.

33. This DFW was from *Fl.Abt.(A)* 269, crewed by *Uffz.* Max Hänicke and *Ltn.* Fritz Düsterdieck, both killed.

34. This Rumpler was later confirmed by AA batteries to have burst into flames at 5,000ft and hit the ground near Gouy. Although this is obviously a definite victory, there are no fatal casualties given in the German lists that match. However, one possibility is a crew from *Fl.Abt.(A)* 202: *Uffz.* Leipner, pilot, seriously wounded, and *Ltn.d.R.* von Frantzius, observer, slightly wounded. No location is given in the German casualty lists, but *Fl.Abt.(A)* 202, based at Guise, was operating with the German 18 *Armee* that had been supporting the activities of 2 *Armee* since the beginning of February.

35. Rumpler from *Schusta* 29b. The pilot, *Vzfw.* Lorenz Zeuch, and the observer, *Gefr.* Heinrich Lechleiter, were both killed. G.137.

36. British AA reported that this LVG was definitely out of control, but they did not see it crash due to the mist. Balcombe-Brown considered it would have crashed and awarded it to McCudden as his 52nd victory. The German casualty lists give no fatal casualties, or wounding in the area, so this crew evidently escaped with their lives.

37. McCudden later reported that this Rumpler had an exceptionally fine climb and that, in addition to the heights at which it flew, makes it highly likely that it was a *Rubild* Rumpler.

38. These two Albatros scouts were from *Jasta* 35b. The first pilot shot down by McCudden was *Uffz.* Julius Kaiser. The blue tailed Albatros was flown by *Uffz.* Joachim von Stein, who although hit in the shoulder managed to crash-land the Albatros and was taken to field Hospital No.204. Source: The *Jasta* 35b war diary, that exactly matches all the cirumstances of the action as reported by the pilots of 56 Squadron. However, Kaiser was not 'Greentail' the pilot so often fought by 56 Squadron. See Appendix 5.

39. This victory was confirmed by three separate AA batteries of 1st Army, and was from *Fl.Abt.(A)* 235. The crew, *Vzfw.* Erich Klingenberg and *Ltn.* Karl Heger, were both killed.

40. B Flight, 56 Squadron, was tragically unlucky in the number of its pilots lost in flying accidents: Barlow, Muspratt, Henderson, and last of all, James McCudden.

41. The Richthofen brothers, Manfred and Lothar, had left operational flying in December 1917, later attending the conferences at the signing of the Brest-Litovsk Treaty. Manfred von Richthofen was not to resume scoring until 12 March 1918.

42. From *Fl.Abt.* 7. The crew, *Vzfw.* Otto Kresse and *Ltn.* Rudolph Binting, were both killed.

43. *Uffz.* Max Schwaier, the pilot, and the observer, *Ltn.* Walter Jäger of *Fl.Abt.* 293, were both killed. This was McCudden's 57th and last victory.

44. Julian Byng had joined the Army in 1883, serving with the 10th Hussars both in the Sudan and the 2nd Boer War. After commanding a cavalry division at the First Battle of Ypres in 1915, he went to Gallipoli to command 9th Corps. In May 1916 he was back in France, commanding the Canadian Corps at the battle of the Somme, and, in April 1917, his most famous victory, Vimy Ridge. In June 1917 Byng was given command of Third Army, commanding it during the battles of Cambrai, the Second Battle of the Somme and the Battle of Amiens. After the war Byng was raised to the peerage as Baron Byng of Vimy. Byng later became Governor-General of Canada, and in 1928 commissioner of the Metropolitan Police. Before his death in 1935, Byng had been promoted to Field Marshal and made a viscount.

45. McCudden's replacement as B Flight Commander was Cyril Marconi Crowe, the original commander of the Flight when 56 Squadron had flown to France in April 1917. Crowe took over McCudden's machine, B4891, but returning from a patrol on 21 March, he ran out of petrol, crash-landed badly, and B4891, perhaps the most successful SE5a in the RFC, was sent to the repair park at 2ASD and reduced to scrap.

46. One such was Maxwell Henry Coote, who served under McCudden in B Flight. Interviewed by the author in the late 1960s, he expressed the opinion: 'Of course, the trouble with McCudden was that he just wasn't officer material'. Unaware that there was a problem with McCudden – other than

that suffered by the German Air Service – and conscious of McCudden's achievements, the author wondered what precisely, in Coote's opinion, constituted 'officer material'.

Chapter 16: Ayr & Turnberry: Teaching the Young Idea

1. In the spring of 1917, the Air Board had drawn up specifications for twelve future types of aeroplanes. Specification Type A.1(a) set out the requirements for single-seat fighters: a speed of 135mph at 15,000ft; an average rate of climb of 1,000ft a minute above 10,000ft; a ceiling of at least 25,000ft. Endurance should be for three hours, and the armament three machine guns with 1,000 rounds of ammunition – although the third gun, pivoted to fire upwards, was optional. The Sopwith Company had either not received this specification or decided to ignore it, and their new fighter – named the Snipe – was a development of the successful Sopwith Camel, even to the extent that it initially used the same power unit. However, W.O. Bentley had designed the B.R.2 engine, which tested in October 1917 gave 234hp, fulfilling Bentley's expectations. One of the six prototype Snipes, B9963, was fitted with the new engine and was tested at Farnborough in late November 1917. This Snipe went through various modifications and after a series of tests at Martlesham Heath, ending in late February 1918, it was flown to France for operational evaluation on 13 March. It was considered by one pilot as vastly superior to any scout at the front, being manoeuvrable and easy to land, but it appears that it was not appreciably better in performance than the Sopwith Camel – J.M. Bruce would later describe it as 'the mediocre Snipe' comparing it unfavourably with its stable companion, the earlier Sopwith Dolphin. Despite this, the Sopwith 7.F.1 Snipe, became the standard fighter for the RAF in the last year of the war, equipping 43, 208 and 78 Squadrons, and 4 Squadron AFC. Post-war it was the RAF's standard single-seat fighter, equipping eleven squadrons until declared obsolete in 1928.

2. The Sopwith Dolphin entered service in November 1917, when 19 Squadron received the first of the type, and the squadron was full equipped by January 1918. 23 and 79 Squadrons also flew the type in France, and it was used by 78 and 141 Squadron in Home Defence. The Dolphin was an unconventional aeroplane. To improve the pilot's view, its wings were negative (back) staggered, with the pilot's head in a somewhat exposed and, in the event of overturning in a force landing, hazardous position. Although it had had many of the technical faults of its day, the Dolphin was an excellent fighter aeroplane, well liked by the pilots who flew it, and their reports of its handling qualities and performance, especially at height, were highly complimentary. The late Jack M. Bruce, the foremost expert on the aeroplanes of the RFC and RAF, considered that the Dolphin was the best operational fighter of its period, superior to the SE5a with the same power-plant.

3. Major Douglas had written to Amelia McCudden on 19 March.

84 Squadron
R.F.C. B.E.F.
19.3.1918
Dear Mrs. McCudden,
I am sorry to say your son went missing yesterday. I am afraid I can give you no definite news or even a conjecture as to his fate. He went out yesterday with fourteen of our machines on an important patrol about twenty miles over the lines. We ran into a big formation of German scouts and a mixed fight ensued. Everyone was so busy scrapping that they cannot say what happened to your son. All we know is that he did not return. We can only hope for the best – which is quite likely – that a lucky shot hit his engine or radiator. In that case he stood no chance of getting back to our lines, and would have to land and be taken prisoner. His engine may have failed too. One cannot say. I sincerely hope you will get definite news of his safety very soon.
I was exceedingly sorry to lose your son, as he was quite one of my best pilots, and I am sure that given a little luck he would have emulated the success of his elder brother.
He was extraordinarily brave – too brave if anything; he often took risks that ninety-nine per cent of humanity would refuse to take. I most sincerely regret the loss of an exceedingly gallant pilot, and I hope he will turn up all right in due course. Your son had shot down seven Huns since being with this squadron.

I am, yours sincerely,
W.S. Douglas (Major).

4. On 18 March, Anthony McCudden had been shot down while flying escort duty for the DH4s of 5 Naval Squadron that were bombing Busigny aerodrome. German fighters numbering nearly fifty machines came up to meet the attack and casualties amongst the escorting fighters were heavy: 54 Squadron lost two pilots killed and three taken prisoner. In addition to Anthony McCudden, 84 Squadron lost another pilot, killed. The German *Jagdstaffeln* involved in the fighting were from *Jagdgeschwader* 1 commanded by Manfred von Richthofen – who claimed a pilot from 54 Squadron for his 66th victory. Anthony McCudden was shot down by *Ltn*. Hans Joachim Wolff of *Jasta* 11 for his first victory of an eventual ten. Anthony McCudden came down near the German aerodrome at Escaufort and was buried the following day, with full military honours, at St.Souplet.

5. James Martin Child (RAeC Certificate No. 2377 dated 31 January 1916). Child transferred to the RFC from the Manchester Regiment in 1916. He served first as an observer with 8 Squadron, one of his pilots being Sholto Douglas. After pilot training Child flew Spads with 19 Squadron, scoring three victories and being Mentioned in Despatches before posted to HE for a rest. In the autumn of 1917 he returned to France as a Flight Commander with 84 Squadron, was credited with another five victories by the end of November and awarded an MC. Child was also awarded the Order of Leopold and the *Croix de Guerre*. He returned to England as an instructor in

February 1918 and was later posted to Canada, where he was killed in August 1918.

6. In late March 1918, King George V was visiting his forces in France, including the squadrons of the RFC. In the afternoon of 29 March, His Majesty inspected officers and men of 56 Squadron and took the opportunity to inform the squadron that he had recently approved the award of a VC to McCudden.

7. *The Illustrated Sunday Chronicle*, quoted by Cole in *McCudden VC*. On 20 March, the *Evening Standard* had carried a similar article headed: "Flying Hero. Brilliant Record of a Boy from Eton. Victor over Voss." This gave full details of Arthur Rhys Davids, his days at Eton, and his record in 56 Squadron, related to the reporter by one of his sisters.

8. Ibid.

9. This article was not published until after McCudden's death.

10. Squadron Leader Harley Alec-Tweedie was killed in a flying accident in Transjordon in 1921.

11. Mrs. Ethel Brillana Alec-Tweedie died in April 1940, aged 78.

12. She later wrote: 'Only a boy. A dapper little person, all smiles and simplicity.'

13. *An Onlooker In France, 1917–1919*. Sir William Orpen, Williams and Norgate, London, 1921.

14. The portrait – not thought to be one of Orpen's best works – was not finished until after McCudden's death. It shows a McCudden very unlike his many photographic portraits: a thinner faced, rather severe person, but with a forthright, steady gaze.

15. When James and his contemporaries had trained in 1916, the requirements before a pilot was sent to France to fly on active service was rudimentary to say the least, in that they must have spent at least fifteen hours in the air, to have been 'encouraged' in so-called 'trick' flying and given every opportunity to practise fighting manoeuvres. No formal instruction was given to meet these requirements and many pilots arrived at their squadron without even having flown the type of aeroplane with which it was equipped and in which they would have to fight.

16. Lionel Wilmot Brabazon Rees (RAeC Certificate No.392 dated 7 January 1913). Rees was commissioned in the Royal Garrison Gunners in December 1903. On leave from West Africa in the summer of 1914 when war was declared, Rees immediately volunteered for the RFC and was posted to the Central Flying School to train as a service pilot. In July 1915, Rees went to France as a Flight Commander with 11 Squadron, and won an MC with the squadron before being posted to the CFS in November as an instructor. In February 1916, Rees was given command of 32 Squadron, equipped with the DH2, and took the squadron to France the following May. On 1 July 1916, the first day of the battle of the Somme, Rees flew an action that was to result in the award of a VC. Attacking ten German bombers single-handed, Rees was badly wounded in the leg, and on returning had to be helped from his cockpit. The wound was more serious than at first thought and after a long period of convalescence, ending in March 1917, Rees could walk only with the aid of two canes. With the entry of America in the War in April 1917, Rees went to America with the Balfour Military Mission. Back in England, on 1 March 1918, he was given command of the No.1 School of Aerial Fighting at Ayr, remaining in command until the end of the war. Rees was an exceptional pilot and far from a desk commander. Flying accidents were relatively rare at Ayr, but during the first week of his new command two student pilots in C Flight, that was equipped with the fiery Sopwith Camel, were killed, followed by another the following day. Two Americans were also killed, one an instructor with over 300 hours of flying time. This resulted in the Camel being regarded as a jinx aeroplane. To restore morale and renew confidence in the Camel, Rees gave a performance of startling brilliance in one. Never going above 500 feet he 'fought the treetops', spinning the Camel repeatedly and never recovering above fifty feet. Rees retired from the RAF in 1931 as a Group Captain, but returned to serve in WW2 as a Wing Commander. Lionel Wilmot Brazabon Rees VC, OBE, MC, AFC, died in Nassau on 28 September 1955 from leukaemia. He was buried with full military honours in the RAF Cemetery.

17. This excellent little fighter had been designed by Frank Barnwell in the early summer of 1916, the first prototype flying in July. Its speed for the time was amazing, a phenomenal 132mph. In 1916, at a time when the little Bristol could have gained air supremacy for the hard-pressed RFC, long before the appearance of the SE5 or the Sopwith Camel, rumours of its performance had reached the RFC Messes. It was eagerly awaited by pilots who were fighting and dying in inferior aeroplanes, but stupidity and prejudice in high quarters condemned it and it never entered active squadron service in France. There were a number of Bristol M.1 Monoplanes at Ayr and the little monoplanes became the personal mounts of some of the instructors. One of these was Gerald Constable Maxwell, who first flew one on 3 April, 1918, judging it 'very nice'. The following day he flew it again in mock combats, with fellow instructors flying an SE5 and a Camel. After this flight he noted in his diary, 'monoplane is the nicest machine I have ever flown'. The next day Constable Maxwell flew an SE5a in a mock combat against a fellow instructor, Cyril Foggin, flying his personal Bristol. 'Self on SE and he (Foggie) on monoplane. I could not do anything against him as the mono out zooms an SE every time.' The implications of this casual statement by Constable Maxwell are staggering. An aeroplane that could have been in front-line service with the squadrons in France in the autumn of 1916, the era of the DH2 and FE8, both obsolescent pusher designs, was still, over eighteen months later, capable of out-flying the latest equipment of the fighter squadrons then in France.

18. This Albatros D.I, 391/16, was flown by *Ltn*. Karl Büttner of *Jasta* 2 when he was shot down by Captain G.A. Parker and Lt. H.E. Harvey of 8 Squadron on 16 November 1916. Büttner's personal marking, 'Bü' was still visible on the fuselage of the Albatros, only partially obscured by an added band

carrying a British roundel.

19. In 1917, Sundrum Castle, the oldest inhabited castle in Scotland, was owned by an Ernest Coats, a director of the firm of Paisley, thread manufacturers. Captain Taylor was possibly a personal friend of Coats, who would have been only too happy to meet Britain's foremost fighter pilot.

20. Built by S.E. Saunders Ltd. of East Cowes, Isle of Wight.

21. Built by Vickers Ltd. at Weybridge.

22. Cyril Edgar Foggin (RAeC Certificate No. 349 dated 29 October 1912). Foggin was one of the earliest pioneer pilots in England. The year he earned his RAeClub certificate he bought his own machine, a Blackburn monoplane. Foggin flew in France with 1 Squadron, progressing through the ranks from airman to sergeant until commissioned as a 2nd Lieutenant. On 27 April 1916, Foggin was wounded in his left eye while attacking a hostile two-seater and wore a patch over the eye for the rest of his short life. In 1918, Foggin was commanding 41 Squadron when he was killed on 30 July in a motor car accident.

23. Built by The Bristol and Colonial Aeroplane Co. Ltd. Bristol.

24. John Herbert Towne Letts (RAeC Certicficate No.2618 dated 24 March 1916). Letts was commissioned in the Lincolnshire Regiment, but transferred to the RFC in May 1916. After a short time with 27 Squadron, Letts flew with 48 Squadron in France as a Flight Commander before being shot down, slightly wounded, on 11 May 1917 after scoring his fourth victory. His wound did not keep him from active duty and the next day he claimed two Albatros scouts. Letts continued to score steadily with 48 Squadron, winning an MC and bringing his total victories to thirteen before he was posted to HE in September 1917. In March 1918, Letts was posted as an instructor to the No.1 School of Aerial Fighting at Ayr. In October 1918 Letts was posted to 64 Squadron in France as a Flight Commander. On 11 October, after visiting friends at 32 Squadron at La Bellevue, Letts took off in SE5a C6484 but was killed before gaining height in a similar accident to that which had killed James McCudden the previous July.

25. The RFC/RAF Club in Bruton Street finally closed in December 1921 and moved to new premises in Piccadilly.

26. Arthur Stanley Gould Lee transferred to the RFC from his regiment, the Sherwood Foresters. In May 1917 he was posted to 46 Squadron in France and served with the squadron until January 1918, credited with seven victories and awarded an MC. In a period of eight days during the Battle of Cambrai, Gould Lee was shot down three times while carrying out low level strafing operations, each time being reported as missing. Gould Lee remained in the RAF after the war, held many important and diplomatic posts in the 1930s, and served in the Second World War, finally retiring in 1946 as an Air Vice-Marshal. After his retirement he became an author, writing biographies, fiction and two highly acclaimed books of his experiences as a pilot in WW1: *No Parachute*, and *Open Cockpit*. A friendly, approachable man, always happy to talk – and inform – of his experiences in both world wars, in 1972 Gould Lee became President of the Cross and Cockade Society, Great Britain, The Society Of World War One Aero Historians, a post he held until his death in 1975.

27. This would have been one of the three built, reclassified after modifications as the FB.26a.

28. It is highly probable that the Vickers Company had previously written to James, making him this offer, and that he went to Joyce Green with the express purpose of collecting '*Pot Belly*'.

29. McCudden later described this eventful flight in a letter to Richard Blomfield, his old CO, who was in America with the British Aviation Mission. Blomfield wrote back from Washington: I showed your letter to several generals here, and it made them sit up when they read of your 154mph. It was great, as we are all struggling here to get the USA machines to even do 115 near the ground.

30. James Douglas Latta (RAeC Certificate No.2067 dated 16 November 1915.) After a brief time as a pilot in 5 Squadron, flying two-seaters, Latta was posted as a scout pilot to 1 Squadron in February 1916. In June 1916 he was credited with three victories – one aeroplane and two balloons – and awarded an MC before being posted to 66 Squadron in October as a Flight Commander, flying Sopwith Pups. Before being wounded on 8 June 1917, Latta was credited with two more victories while with 66 Squadron. Latta remained in the United Kingdom for the remainder of the war in various training posts.

31. That James Latta himself did not take his sister for her joyride is typical of the reluctance of some of the instructors at Ayr to take close relatives for flights, preferring that a fellow instructor should do so. Gerald Maxwell, visited by his mother, his two brothers and his sister, was agreeable to take up his sister, but resolutely refused to pilot his mother for a flight, saying that it 'wouldn't feel right' but was quite happy to entrust her to Cyril Foggin.

32. Ruby Whyte Williamson, Service No.3790. Ruby Williamson joined the WRAF in 1917 and served until 1919.

33. Cole, recounting this incident in *McCudden VC*, attributes McCudden's silence to his being unused to seeing women in uniform, that he was unsure how to address them, and that he was tongue-tied with embarrassment. Cole may well have been correct in this assumption, but it seems at odds with what is known of James McCudden. He was popular with the opposite sex, had had several girl friends, including the very attractive Teddie O'Neal, and was certainly not shy in female company.

34. The Turnbery Hotel is still there today, a luxury 5 star resort, offering the 'ultimate golf experience on the world's original golf resort'.

35. Bogart Rogers, a pupil at No.1 School of Aerial Fighting, Ayr. Quoted in *Aces Falling*, Peter Hart, Widenefeld & Nicolson, London, 2007.

36. *McCudden VC*. Christopher Cole, William Kimber, London, 1967.

37. This technique of watching for the movement of an opponent's control surfaces was common amongst the successful pilots of WW1. In 1941, while station commander

at Ford, Gerald Constable Maxwell used the same technique to disconcert a young pilot with similar illusions regarding his flying abilities.
38. No details found.
39. Ibid.
40. E.W. Beale, RFC No.1310, was a direct entry into the RFC in July 1914. He was promoted to Sergeant in July 1917, a rank he held until the end of the war. In 1920–21 he served as a Flight Sergeant with 30 Squadron in Mesopotamia. After McCudden's death, Bruiser lived with the family at Kingston, but unfortunately attacked a young girl. Reluctant to have him destroyed, the family gave him to a friend of McCudden. Apparently, Bruiser lived happily on a farm in Ireland until his death.
41. At the end of his time at Turnberry, McCudden had flown a total of 867 hours 10 minutes.
42. It is probable that McCudden had already been informed that his duties at Turnberry were coming to an end; that he would soon be promoted to Major and given command of a squadron in France.
43. Unfortunately McCudden's logbook does not give the serial number of this Snipe, but it was most probably the first Snipe (E.6137) of the production order of 400 built by Boulton & Paul Ltd of Norwich.
44. Although McCudden's logbook shows this as a 'Bristol Mono' he incorrectly entered the serial number as 5955 – which was an Avro 504 – instead of 4955.
45. Ibid.
46. The value of McCudden's destruction of the German reconnaissance machines had already been realised by RAF Headquarters in France. On 15 April, Brigadier-General Higgins had asked Balcombe-Brown to submit names of pilots who could be sent up singly to shoot down the German artillery and reconnaissance machines, 'as McCudden used to do'.
47. One of the earliest fighter squadrons of the RFC, 60 Squadron had a proud record. It had flown in France since May 1916, but after heavy casualties in the Battles of the Somme it had been withdrawn from operations on 3 August 1917. After retraining as a single-seater fighter squadron, it recommenced operations on 23 August, flying Nieuport scouts and Morane Type Ns, and over the next few months, with such pilots as Albert Ball and 'Duke' Meintjes, it began to build its reputation as one of the finest fighter squadrons in the RFC. During 1917 the squadron had amongst its ranks such pilots as Keith 'Grid' Caldwell, Willie Mays Fry, and Robert Chidlaw-Roberts. By the time of McCudden being given command, 60 Squadron was one of the most successful fighter squadrons in the RAF. For further reading on 60 Squadron, see *No.60 Squadron, RFC/RAF*, Alex Revell, Aviation Elite Units Series, 41, Osprey Publishing, 2011.
48. For many years it was believed that 85 Squadron had first been considered as McCudden's command, but that he had been rejected by the pilots of the squadron. The squadron had flown out to France under the command of William Bishop, a Canadian, who had been credited with 47 victories and awarded a Victoria Cross while serving with 60 Squadron in 1917. Bishop had been given command of 85 Squadron in May 1918, but that June was being posted to Canadian Headquarters to assist in the formation of the Canadian Air Force. As was prevalent in 1918, 85 Squadron's pilots were the usual mixed complement of British, Colonial, and American pilots. One of the latter, John McGavock Grider, kept a diary, that was later edited by his friend and fellow member of the squadron, Elliot White Springs, and published in America in 1926, entitled *Diary of an Unknown Aviator*. The diary entry for 23 June, records: 'The general came over and had tea with us and asked us who we wanted for C.O. He wanted to send us McCudden but we don't want him. He gets Huns for himself but doesn't give anybody else a chance at them. The rest of the squadron objected because he was once a Tommy and his father was a sergeant major in the old army. I couldn't see that that was anything against him. But these English have great ideas of caste.' Apart from the fact that it is highly unlikely that a General would ask any group of junior officers for their choice of a squadron commander, the allegation of McCudden not giving other pilots a chance of victories is completely unfounded. Although admittedly, by the very nature of things, a Flight Commander would have first chance of any victory in an initial attack, both McCudden's record as a patrol leader in 56 Squadron, and his reputation throughout the RFC and RAF at this time, completely refutes this view. Additionally, members of his flight such as Barlow, Rhys Davids, Muspratt, and others, scored persistently during his tenure. As to the question of his 'lowly' origins, McCudden came from a distinguished army family, whereas Mick Mannock, ultimately given command of 85 Squadron, was the son of an undistinguished corporal with a rather unsavoury character. An ironic twist. It must be said that *Diary of an Unknown Aviator* is a blend of highly coloured fact and fiction, which never lets fact get in the way of a good story. A case in point is a highly detailed account of seeing McCudden one evening in Murray's night club in London, holding court to a number of girls and causing a near riot by officers flocking to his table to congratulate him on his Victoria Cross. The entry is dated 13 May. McCudden's logbook places him firmly as flying at Turnberry, both previous to, on, and subsequent to that date.
49. SE5a C1126 was one of the production batch, C1051–1150, built at the Royal Aircraft factory at Farnborough.

Chapter 17: The Last Flight

1. Manfred von Richthofen had been killed on 21 April 1918. He had been credited with 80 victories.
2. The fact that he visited Mary suggests that he had not stayed the night at Kingston, where he would have seen her earlier that morning, but had previously said goodbye to his family, possibly the previous evening. Although he made light of them, these partings were always painful. Writing to Teddie, telling her that he was going back to France, he had said. 'Look in on my mater and my sisters. You know a fellow can't say all

he feels, and I always want to cry inwardly when I leave them, because they look such a lot of things. Cheer them up when you can and put a good face on things.'

3. Conversations and correspondence with Mrs. Mary Cobley. In 1918, Mary had already been touched by personal tragedy. Her husband, Arthur Scott Spears, a Chatham shipwright, had been amongst a party of 76 dockyard workers aboard HMS *Princess Irene*, a steamship that had been requisitioned by the Royal Navy and converted into a mine layer. During the morning of 27 May 1915, the *Princess Irene* was anchored off Port Victoria, Isle of Grain, being loaded with 500 mines, when she suddenly blew up, killing 379 men, including Arthur, leaving Mary a widow at twenty-two years of age and three months pregnant.

4. In *McCudden VC* Coles says that McCudden collected this SE5a at Hounslow. Cole gives no reference source for this and an extensive search has failed to reveal any further evidence confirming that C1126 was collected by McCudden at Hounslow. However, the consensus of informed opinion is that it was ferried to RAF Hounslow for service equipment – such as the Lewis and Vickers guns – to be installed there.

5. No.8 Squadron, flying Armstrong Whitworth FK8s, had been based at Auxi-le-Chateau since 12 April 1918. No.52 Squadron, equipped with the RE8, had joined them on 30 June.

6. W.H. Burdett. RFC No.4054. Another Burdett, G.C. Burdett, possibly a brother of W.H. Burdett, had also served with McCudden in 3 Squadron in 1915.

7. L.E. Vallins. RFC No.5448.

8. W.H. Howard. Corporal in the RAMC (Service No. 134791). Howard was attached to 8 Squadron as a medical orderly.

9. Peter S. Fulton. Corporal (Service No.18012). Fulton was a clerk in 'K' Flight of 6 Squadron, on detachment to 8 Squadron.

10. James McCudden is buried in the British Military Cemetery at Wavans (No.8/1). Wavans was a small cemetery used by No.21 CCS and contains only 44 graves, one of which is a German. Twelve airmen are buried here, ten probably from accidents on the airfield at Auxi-le-Chateau, but strangely for such a small cemetery, it contains two of the greatest fighter pilots of the war. Two rows back from McCudden's grave is that of Robert Alexander Little DSC and Bar, DSO and Bar. Little, an Australian, was credited with 47 victories before his death on the night of 27 May 1918.

11. Major-General John Salmond GOC the RAF in France. In his biography of Salmond, *Swifter than Eagles*, John Laffin states that Salmond was in London on 9 July when he was told of McCudden's death. If this is correct it means that Salmond must have flown to France to attend the funeral of his former air mechanic in 3 Squadron. This would be entirely in keeping with this great commander and kindly man, who had always taken a great interest in McCudden's career and promoted it on several occasions.

12. Henry John Burden. A native of Ontario, Burden had joined 56 Squadron in February 1918. During his service with the squadron he was credited with 16 victories and awarded a DSO and a DFC. Returning to Canada after the war, Burden was active in flying for many years until his death on 28 March 1968.

13. Paul Stuart Winslow had been posted to 56 Squadron on 29 June 1918, transferring to the United States Air Service on 12 September 1918.

14. Winslow's reference to Richthofen is ironic. Richthofen had been buried by the British with full military honours: a cortege, a full platoon of infantry, and a firing party fired three volleys over his grave, followed by the Last Post. Even today, the name of James McCudden brings a blank stare from the man in the street in England, while that of von Richthofen – the Red Baron – evokes immediate recognition. Perhaps if James McCudden had belonged to the officer class by birth, rather than by merit, more care and thought would have been given to his funeral, making it worthy of his dedication and devotion to duty.

15. *Five Years In The Royal Flying Corps*.

Appendix I: The Fatal Crash

1. One rumour, current at the time, was that McCudden had stopped somewhere before landing at Auxi-le-Chateau, had lunched with friends and had a drink too many, which had impaired his judgement in taking off again. Apart from the fact that the accident happened long after any lunch party would have been over, McCudden's landing at Auxi-le-Chateau was seen to be precise, showing perfect judgment, plus it was well known that he was a near teetotaller.

2. *McCudden VC*, Christopher Cole.

3. Ibid.

4. A report in *Flight* reported that he had 'landed at a depot to refuel'.

5. There are many reports of injuries to officers and men, ranging from fatalities to toes cut off while digging latrines, and other minor injuries, but nothing on the death of Britian's foremost airman.

6. The statement by Howard, witnessed by the officer from 60 Squadron, is unsigned by either. The statement by Mulroy and Howard is signed by both men.

7. None of the copies of these officers' statements is signed by them.

8. See Note 7. The Last Day.

9. Ibid. Burdett also stated that in his opinion, the engine of the SE5a was running perfectly, which at that moment, while taxing away, it no doubt was.

10. When the suggestion was put to him that McCudden had attempted to turn back, Cyril Parry, a no-nonsense Welshman who had flown with McCudden in 56 Squadron, snorted with derision before forcibly exclaiming: 'bloody nonsense, by people who didn't know the man'.

11. McCudden's total flying time was 868 hours 15 minutes, plus the time of his flight to Auxi-le Chateau. Of these, 270 hours and 15 minutes were flying various SE5as.

12. *Tiger Squadron*, Wing Commander Ira 'Taffy' Jones, DSO, MC, DFC, MM, W.H. Allen, London, 1954.

13. As an example of this, an Australian pilot serving with 52 Squadron at the time of the crash, recalling the event many years later, confirmed that McCudden had not been stunting, but stated that the crash was due to him taking off during a violent storm, conditions not mentioned by any other witness. Another witness claimed that McCudden made a 'bumpy landing' – directly contradicting Young's testimony – and that after landing McCudden got out of his cockpit and was surrounded by officers and men before taking off again.

14. Vallins makes no mention of Burdett being with him. See The Last Flight.

15. *Airfields and Airmen: Arras*. Mike O'Connor, Pen & Sword Military, An imprint of Pen & Sword Books Ltd., South Yorkshire, 2004. Mike O'Connor was an ex-Concorde pilot of vast experience. During research for the series he flew over the sites of the aerodromes and cemeteries of WW1 and would have been absolutely correct in his compass reading. Mike O'Connor died in 2012, but had confirmed to the author that the caption in *Popular Flying* was incorrect.

16. Two of the many witnesses to this were Edward Mannock and William MacLanachan when McCudden had visited them at 40 squadron in October 1917. It was nearly dark when the visit was over and McCudden had climbed hurriedly into his SE5a, let the mechanics suck in the engine, gave the self starter one or two turns and took off. MacLanachan recalled: 'the SE5 had no sooner left the ground than McCudden turned her round on an almost vertical bank, waved to us and flew off.'

* 40 squadron were having a considerable amount of engine troubles with their newly-issued SE5as and MacLanachan ruefully remarked: 'He's got faith in his engine. With ours such a take off with a cold engine would have been suicidal.' Mannock had laughed. 'Yes – absolutely confident. He's a good fellow, young Mac, one of the best.'

* *Fighter Pilot*. ' McScotch ' Newnes, London, 1935.

17. Hubert Noel Charles was the Engineering Officer (Equipment Officer) with 56 Squadron from 6 December 1916 to 5 November 1917. Charles, an exceptional engineer, with an honours degree in engineering before he was twenty years old, had come to the attention of General Salmond for his work on engine tuning, in particular on Salmond's own aeroplane. In 1916, Salmond had been told by Trenchard to keep a look out for an engineering officer of more than usual ability – especially in being able to think for himself – to be posted to 56 Squadron, which was to be equipped with a new fighter, the SE5. Trenchard quite rightly foresaw that there would be problems with the first SE5s, problems that would need a first class engineer to sort out and in December 1916, Charles' work on Salmond's engine brought him to London Colney, where 56 Squadron was forming up.

The performance of the original thirteen SE5s flown by the squadron was extremely poor, and Charles was responsible for their improvement. The aeroplanes had many minor faults that were relatively simple to correct, but there were serious problems with the Zenith 58 DC carburettors and the inadequate draining of petrol from the air filters if anything other than normal flying was carried out. Once in France, the metering and altitude control systems of the carburettors were redesigned by Charles. The bodies of the carburettors were set up on faceplates in the squadron's workshop lorries and working from Charles' drawings the squadron's mechanics machined them to incorporate his modifications. Working day and night, all the carburettors were converted and tested on the test bench. When the first six were found to be satisfactory, each was fitted to the engine of an SE5 and test flown to ascertain that each engine was now capable of throttling down satisfactorily at all altitudes. Within three weeks the effective ceiling of the squadron's SE5s had been improved by 5,000ft.

It had also been found that it was necessary to modify the air intake drains. If too much petrol had got into the air intake, when the throttle was opened the engine would cut out. Any aerobatics however moderate – even steep turns – were dangerous if the air intake did not drain quickly. Charles and Hoidge made empirical experiments with the intakes, filling them with petrol, then tilting them in their hands into all positions, until they rapidly drained of petrol. After each intake had been modified and fitted to the engine of an SE5, Hoidge then flew it, carrying out right- and left-hand spins, one after the other, to test their modifications.

During the evening celebrations for the 56 Squadron's 200th victory on 30 September 1917, Charles was told by Maurice Baring that Trenchard had selected him to be on his personal staff, with the remit to investigate troubles with aircraft over the entire Front, and in November 1917 Charles was posted to RFC HQ, at Chateau St.Andre, Hesdin, as a Special Aeroplane Troubles Officer, serving first under Trenchard, then Salmond. His remit was to investigate any reported lack of performance, staying with any squadron until a remedy had been found; deal with any structural failures, and fires in the air due to mechanical malfunctions, and to investigate any unexplained flying accidents. Charles served in this capacity for the last twelve months of the war and was twice Mentioned in Despatches.

The work that Charles had carried out on their carburettors had come to the attention of the manufacturers, Zenith, who were impressed with his modifications, carried out in the field with only basic equipment, modifications on which they could improve only slightly in their own test laboratories using sophisticated scientific equipment. After the war, the managing director personally contacted Charles with the offer of employment with the company, a lucrative offer which Charles was happy to accept.

In 1930 Charles was chief engineer of the MG Motor Company and was responsible for the design of all MG racing cars between 1930 and 1938. He later became chief engineer with Dowty Rotol Airscrews, until joining the Austin Motor company in 1941. Hubert Charles died in 1982, aged 88.

18. That the inspection and quality control at the Royal Aircraft Factory at Farnborough and at the sub-contractors

building the SE5a left much to be desired is clear from many documents in the National Archives. In 1917 and into 1918, the commanding officers of the squadrons flying the SE5 and SE5a brought to the attention of the RAF at Farnborough many of the defects – some minor, others more major – which their respective engineering officers had rectified in the squadrons, rectifications often passed on to their counterparts experiencing similar or identical problems. Charles recalled that the Factory's responses to these reports were often Draconian to say the least: on the order of 'we build 'em; you fly 'em'. One such report, which illustrates the lack of quality control at the Factory, was submitted in December 1917 by Major Balcombe-Brown, the commanding officer of 56 Squadron, to Colonel Bettington, commanding 2ASD.

No.56 Squadron
Royal Flying Corps
13th December
Dear Colonel,

Just a note telling you about the defects on SE5 No.B.4880, which Capt. Maybery flew away from 2 A.S.D. the afternoon that I was over to see you. Of course Capt. Maybery should really not have flown the machine away considering the state it was in, and the weather on that day, but I was very anxious to get the machine here so off he went.
1. Rev. counter was not working, because the shaft of the rev. drive gear box was broken off in the cam shaft cover. However, the engine sounded alright and I told Maybery it was revving quite enough for him to go.
2. Radiator thermometer was broken, therefore the temperature of the water was not registering at all.
3. Petrol pressure valve was not properly split-pinned. That was fixed up temporarily by one of your mechanics.
4. Oil breather was broken off.
5. On arrival here, the top of the float chamber of the carburettor was nearly off, owing to it not being sufficiently tightened up. We usually lock ours with a piece of wire.
I do not mean this to be a sort of grouse, because really I was wrong in allowing Maybery to fly off with the machine in that condition, but as it was an RAF-built machine I wanted that one particularly, and as regards the actual flying to the aerodrome in the bad weather, I knew Maybery was equal to that.

You also asked about the system we sometimes adopt for increasing the oil capacity on some machines that use a very large quantity of oil. Here is an extract of my report.
The pump which drains the crankcase is of a larger capacity than that which feeds the oil system of the engine – consequently any oil which may be in the crankcase is forced into the tank, which may or may not be already full.
If insufficient room is left in the oil tank when filling, to accommodate the oil left in the machine, the possible duration of the flight is reduced – the oil capacity not being sufficient.
The oil capacity has been increased on some engines which use a large quantity of oil, by connecting the crankcase to the delivery pipe of the crankcase draining pump, thus making the crankcase a part of the oil tank, and allowing of the tank being completely filled.
If this were done on all engines, greater oil capacity could be obtained on all machines and the bursting of tanks would be avoided.

Yours sincerely
R. Balcombe-Brown

Balcombe-Brown was noted for his somewhat caustic, sarcastic manner, in this case subtly toned down when addressing a superior officer, but the main thrust of his complaint is clear, especially in the fundamental problem of the oil capacity, a problem solved by Charles and his mechanics in 56 Squadron in early 1917.

There may well have been more such accidents, due to faulty inspection procedures or insufficient maintenance. On 11 October 1918 a Captain John Letts, who had served with McCudden at Turnberry and Ayr, was killed in a remarkably similar accident. The official report of the death of Letts recorded that in taking off he 'rolled the machine and nose dived into the ground: machine caught fire and was destroyed'. Letts was flying SE5a C6484, built by Wolseley Motors Ltd. Lett's father was later told that while Letts was gaining height over the aerodrome, (he) 'fell when only 200 or 300 feet up and was killed'. A friend was told that Lett's engine had stalled after takeoff and that he tried to turn back and side slipped into the ground. Perhaps Letts was taking off in a steep bank, in a similar way in which he may have seen McCudden take off at Ayr or Turnberry.

It is interesting that in the Wolseley Instruction manual: Wolseley 'Viper' Aero Engines, Hispano-Suiza W.4.A* Type, the type of carburettor shown is the 58 D.C. Type 'Zenith' carburettor. In his 1973: *Some Historical Notes on the SE5*, in the section devoted to SE5 (A) Viper, Charles wrote:

'As a matter of interest the 58D.C. carburettor shown on Page 46 of the Wolseley W.4.A* handbook depicts the type of carburettor perfected by us for the '1170'. The great majority of Vipers actually in use were in fact fitted with the 55.D.C. double venturi carburettor which entirely superseded the older D.C. 58 D.C. model.'

In view of the information in the Wolseley manual, the possibility arises that a few of the older 58 D.C. model carburettors which had not been modified to the specifications set down by Charles while in 56 Squadron were possibly fitted to some of the first Viper-engined SE5as.

Appendix II: McCudden as Finest Airman

1. In the 1960s no less a person than Air Vice Marshal 'Johnnie' Johnson, a highly successful and decorated fighter pilot of the Second World War, ranked Richthofen as the greatest fighter pilot of the 1914–1918 war, seemingly on the criteria alone of Richthofen's eighty victories.
2. See Appendix III.
3. Also, on 27 December 1916, out-flying Manfred von

Richthofen, who erroneously claimed McCudden as his fifteenth victory.

4. There were many fine flight commanders in the RFC/RAF, but McCudden was one of the first to lead his Flight in this way and his example and teaching in this respect inspired many flight commanders. One such was Edward Mannock, who in his turn taught others. The worth of McCudden's teaching and influence in the whole concept of tactically leading a Flight is incalculable.

5. McCudden himself admitted that a well-flown two-seater was more than a match for an SE5a. Although Manfred von Richthofen also shot down forty-six two-seaters during his six and a half months of active, operational flying, sixteen of these were various BE2 variants, no match for his Albatros with its vastly superior manoeuvrability and double the fire power. Of the thirteen FE2 types he shot down, all were of the FE2b variant, considered easy meat by the German fighter pilots, and only one FE2d, the higher-powered, more formidable opponent.

Of the remaining seventeen two-seaters – three were Sopwith 1½ Strutters, eight were RE8s, one an FK8 – only five could be considered a dangerous opponent, the excellent Bristol F2b. This is in no way an attempt to disparage von Richthofen's undoubted abilities as a fighter pilot: he was successfully doing his job, the destruction of enemy two-seaters, and it was hardly his fault that his opponents were flying vastly inferior aeroplanes, but merely to put his successes against enemy two-seaters, and those of McCudden, into objective perspective.

6. After the war McCudden was also posthumously awarded the Aero Club of America Medal of Honour.

Appendix IV: Aerial Victories

1. At the end of each day's operations, all squadrons of the RFC/RAF made out Casualty Reports on Army Form W.3347: Royal Flying Corps. REPORT ON Casualties to Personnel and Machines (When Flying).

2. Apart from the fact that an experienced pilot could tell if an aeroplane going down was genuinely out of control or just spinning away to evade further attack – and many commanding officers of squadron took a pilot's experience into account when evaluating this type of claim – not all out-of-control claims were for aircraft last seen spinning away out of a fight. Many were considered to be out of control and claimed as such because either damage to the machine or wounding of the pilot caused it to go down in such a way that was indicative that the machine was no longer under control, in a manner which was aberrant to normal flying.

3. To use a sporting analogy, a boxer who wins on points or by causing his opponent to retire hurt, rather than by a knockout, is no less the victor.

4. The esoteric, widely dispersed information contained in the few existing *Jasta* war diaries, the reminiscences, private diaries, and letters home of German airmen, is full of such instances.

5. McCudden himself admitted that a well-flown enemy two-seater of the period was more than a match for an SE5a.

Appendix VI: McCudden in the Eyes of his Contemporaries

1. *Under British Flag*, Tryggve Gran, Gyldedalsken Boghandel, Norway, 1919. *Author's Note: Some paraphrasing has been undertaken for clarity and brevity.*

2. J.V. Gascoyne (RFC No.719) went to France with 3 Squadron on 4 August 1914.

3. *Years of Combat*, Sholto Douglas, Marshal of the Royal Air Force, Lord Douglas of Kirtleside, Collins, London, 1963.

4. *Air of Battle*, Wing Commander William Fry, MC, William Kimber, London, 1974. William Mayes Fry – 'Willie' as he was known throughout the RFC – was one of that select hierarchy, the first fighter pilots of the RFC. At the outbreak of war in 1914, Fry enlisted as a private in the London Rifle Brigade and went to France in November 1914. On Christmas Eve 1914, he participated in the now famous Christmas Truce, an event that he recalled many times throughout his life. In the spring of 1915, questions were asked in the House of Commons regarding the number of under-age soldiers in serving in France. Fry had gone to France when he was nine days short of his eighteenth birthday and as a result was sent back to England.

Fry then applied for a commission in the Somerset Light Infantry, was accepted and sent to Trinity College, Oxford for officer training. Having served in the trenches in the winter of 1914, Fry was anxious not to 'go back into the mud again,' so he volunteered, and was accepted, for transfer to the Royal Flying Corps, undertaking his pilot instruction at Castle Bromwich in May 1916. Fry took his RAeC Certificate, No. 3003, on 24 May 1916, and was posted to 12 Squadron in France on 30 June. After four months, flying bombing and reconnaissance duties in BE2s with 12 Squadron, Fry was posted in September to St. Omer for a ten day course for training as a scout pilot, and on 1 October was posted to 60 Squadron.

Fry served in 60 Squadron until mid-February 1917, flying as a member of C Flight, with such redoubtable pilots as 'Duke' Meintjes, and Keith 'Grid' Caldwell. When finally posted to Home Establishment on 19 February, Fry had been flying continuously in France for eight months. After a month in England, Fry was anxious to return to France and wrote to his old comrade 'Duke' Meintjes, who was now serving in France as a flight commander with the newly formed 56 Squadron, asking for a posting to the squadron. Meintjes was only too keen to have Fry in his Flight, and Fry was posted to 56 Squadron, but on his arrival in France he was met by a tender from 60 Squadron: the squadron commander, Major Scott, anxious not to lose such a valuable and experienced pilot, had had the posting to 56 Squadron rescinded. Fry served another two months in 60 Squadron, flying as deputy leader of C Flight, carrying out 118 operational flights in 170 hours of war flying, but at the end of June he had a personal disagreement with Scott and was posted to Home Establishment. During his two tours with 60 Squadron, Fry had been credited with five victories, and on 11 May, in support of British troops attacking near Rouex, he had led his Flight in two consecutive patrols, attacking the German trenches from 300ft. For these actions Fry was awarded an MC. After a period instructing at the School of Special Flying at Gosport, Fry applied again for a posting to France and was assigned as a flight commander with 23 Squadron, flying Spads, where he scored an additional four victories. One of these, on 6 January 1918, was Ltn. Walter von Bülow-Bothkamp, Staffel Führer of Jasta B, a German ace with 28 victories. After four months with the squadron, following a crash landing, Fry was sent to hospital, first in France, then in England. Having recovered, Fry once again asked for an active service posting, and on 25 April joined 79 Squadron, equipped with Sopwith Dolphins, as a flight commander. He scored one more victory with the squadron – a Fokker Triplane destroyed over Bray – but his stay was brief. He crashed landed on the edge of the aerodrome and, although uninjured, was examined by the Wing doctor and sent to hospital on 29 May. This was the end of Fry's operational flying in France. Since July 1916 he had served in four operational squadrons; flown 637 flying hours in 381 offensive patrols; had been credited with eleven victories and awarded an MC.

Fry was in hospital for nearly two months suffering from Flying Sickness D – flying exhaustion – but after discharge he was posted to No.3 Fighting School. Fry was en route for the Middle East when the war ended, and he remained there until the end of 1919, when he was posted to RAF HQ in Cologne, serving with 29 and 79 Squadrons. After being offered only a short term commission in the RAF, Fry left the service at the end of 1919 to study Forestry at Brazenose College, Oxford. However, the pull of service life was too strong, and in July 1921 Fry was back in the RAF. He served for the next thirteen years in England and the middle East, with five squadrons, until retiring in 1934. Fry returned to active service at the outbreak of the Second World War in 1939 and served in various posts, including periods in France and Belgium in 1945 – for which he was Mentioned in Despatches – finally retiring with the rank of Wing Commander on 15 July 1945. He had served over twenty five years in the RFC/RAF. William Mayes Fry died on 4 August 1992, three months ten days short of his ninety-sixth birthday.

5. IWM Sound Archive.
6. Patrick Gordon Taylor was an Australian, born in Mosman, Sydney. Rejected for service with the Australian Flying Corps at the outbreak of war, Taylor went to Britain and was commissioned in the RFC, joining 66 Squadron in May 1917. He served with the squadron for nearly eight months and was awarded an MC. Taylor returned to Australia after the war and had a distinguished career in civil aviation during the inter-war years. During an airmail flight from Australia to New Zealand in 1935, as second pilot and navigator to Charles Kingsford Smith, engine failure of the starboard engine necessitated that fuel and cargo had to be jettisoned. Gordon Taylor made six journeys out onto the wing in efforts to drain the oil from the faulty engine and transfer it to the overheating port engine. Taylor was successful; aeroplane and crew landed safely at Mascot, nine hours later. For his efforts in saving the aircraft, Taylor was awarded the Empire Gallantry medal, which was later superseded by the George Cross. During the Second World War Taylor served as a ferry pilot with the ATA. Taylor was knighted in 1954 and died in Honolulu, Hawaii, in December 1966.
7. *Sopwith Scout 7307*, Sir Gordon Taylor, Cassell, London, 1968.
8. John Oliver Andrews was seconded to the RFC from his regiment, the Royal Scottish Regiment, in 1914. In June 1915 he flew as an observer with 5 Squadron before training as a pilot in October 1915. As one of the original pilots of 24 Squadron, he flew to France with the squadron on February 7 1916, flying DH2s. Andrews quickly became a successful fighter pilot, was promoted to Flight Commander and awarded an MC and Bar. Andrews left 24 Squadron in November 1916. He had been credited with seven confirmed victories, with an additional six machines driven down. After a brief period in England, Andrews returned to France in April 1917 as a Flight Commander in 66 Squadron. He was awarded another five victories while flying with 66 Squadron. Later in the war Andrews commanded 209 Squadron. At the end of the war, Andrews' total victories, including those forced to land or forced down, was twenty four, and he had been awarded a DSO.

In 1919, Andrews commanded 221 Squadron in Russia, supporting the counter-revolutionary Russian White Army. He remained in the RAF, serving in various theatres in the inter-war years, and by 1939 was an Air Commodore. Andrews served throughout WW2, finally retiring from the RAF with the rank of Air Vice Marshal in April 1945. John Oliver Andrews DSO, MC and Bar, Companion of the Most Honourable Order of the Bath, died on 29 May 1989.
9. Thomas Isbell flew with 41 Squadron. He was wounded, shot down, and taken POW on 21 March 1918.
10. *Other Days*, Verschoyle Phillip Cronyn, Private printing, 1976.
11. *An Air Fighter's Scrapbook*, Wing Commander Ira Jones, DSO, MC, DFC, MM, Penguin Books, Middlesex England, 1942.
12. Tributes by Trenchard and Salmond were included in FYITRFC, both writing before McCudden's death. Ranks are given as at that time.
13. Letter to author.
14. The rather clumsy method of firing both guns by a cycle-type brake handle on the control column of the SE5a was considered by McCudden to be detrimental to accurate shooting. The slight movement of the control column in pulling on the handle had the effect of throwing the whole aeroplane, and hence the sight, off target. McCudden wanted a touch button arrangement of twin triggers on the control column, requiring no more than three ounces of pressure to fire the guns. The top of a control column from a Sopwith Camel was obtained, which was of a round, spade-like shape, with twin triggers. By skillful modification and adjustments by Charles, McCudden was given his three ounce pressure triggers. In November 1917, 59 spade grips were dispatched to France

for use on SE5a. The grip was later made a standard fitting on the type.
15. Interview with H.N. Charles. Author 1973.
16. "McCudden, The Airman VC", Mrs. Alec-Tweddie. Article in the August 1918 edition of *The English Review*.
17. At this time Blomfield was in Washington D.C. with the British Aviation Mission.
18. Quoted in *McCudden VC*, Christopher Cole, 1967, Kimber & Co., London.
19. Actually, their paternal great grandfather, Frederick Noding, born circa 1786 in Göttingen, a university city in Lower Saxony. It appears that Noding and several of his family had settled in England sometime in the early 1800s, or possibly even earlier. Frederick served as a Royal Marine aboard HMS *Defence* at the battle of Trafaglar, his marine service record giving his nationality as British. After leaving the Marines, Frederick married an Elizabeth Farley, from Beeding in Kent. One of their four daughters, Frances, married Thomas William Byford, James McCudden's maternal grandfather. I am greatly indebted to Lynne Cowley for this and other information on the McCudden family.

Appendix VII: McCudden on Air Fighting.

1. Both were written in an *Army Book 136*, later in the possession of his sister Mary.
2. The second treatise of January 1918 is given here as it was written in *Army Book 136* and is probably McCudden's first draft. In its published form the pamphlet differs in some respects to this draft. Small changes have been ignored, but for the interest of historians, larger additions, deletions and substitution of paragraphs have been noted. Some of these may have been made by McCudden himself, others – such as the deletion of his fight with the multi-coloured Albatros scouts – were obviously those made by the Air Ministry.
* pilots.
* When intelligently used. (added)
* to * deleted.
* more likely than not their leader, flies off out of the fight and climbs his utmost until he is above the top SE and then he comes back and it is just the thought that there is one above you that divides your attention and nullifies your advantage in height. (Substituted and added)
* When any of the above circumstances occurs I fire a red light, which is a signal to my patrol to break off the fight and fellow me, and we find that this is very effective. I think it is bad policy to stay and fight when E.A. are above you because an Albatros scout turns quicker that the SE and the Hun certainly puts up a more skilful and determined fight when he is at an advantage than otherwise.(added)
* in December (added)
* If however, you are in this position and E.A. turns, you will at once come under his fire, and your object is to keep out of his field of fire as much as possible; therefore, keep in a direct line behind his fuselage, so that if he turns to the right you turn to the left and vice versa. (Substituted)
* at you if you are not quick enough. (added)
* and he can then do all the shooting whilst you can do practically none. Whilst turning like this, help for the E.A. is practically certain to arrive in the form of E.A. scouts . (added)
* This happened to me recently, I attacked an LVG just over the line and he at once started a left-hand circle and was doing all the shooting. However, I did not worry as the wind was E. and we were drifting W. so I knew that if he wanted to get back he would have to stop turning so at last he got fed up and dived E. and I got him. (deleted)
** These two paragraphs are transposed.
* As a final tip, one should be very alert when firing at an E.A. at close range, so that when E.A falls to pieces, as they often do after being fired at a lot, one does not fly through the wreckage. I narrowly missed flying through a pair of E.A.'s wings recently. (added)
* in which the pilot and observer co-operate well (substituted)

Glossary

British Terms and Abbreviations

C.O.P.	Close Offensive Patrol
D.O.P.	Deep Offensive Patrol
1ASD.	No.1 Aeroplane Depot
2ASD.	No.2 Aeroplane Depot

German Terms and Abbreviations

Bombengeschwader	*Bogohl*	Bombing unit
Feldflieger Abteilung	*Fl.Abt.*	Field Aviation Unit
Feldflieger Abteiling(A)	*Fl.Abt.(A)*	Field aviation unit for co-operation with artillery
Flugabwehrkanonen	*Flak*	Anti-aircraft battery
Jagdstaffel	*Jasta*	Fighter unit
Jagdgeschwader	*JG*	Grouping of four Jagdstaffeln
Jastaführer		Fighter unit CO
Kette		Flight
Schlachstaffel	*Schlasta*	Support unit for ground troops
Schutzstaffel	*Schusta*	Support unit for Fleiger Abteilung

German Ranks and British Equivalent

Feldwebel	*Fw.*	Sergeant
Flieger	*Flg.*	Private
Gefreiter	*Gfr.*	Lance corporal
Hauptmann	*Hptm.*	Captain
Oberleutnant	*Oblt.*	Lieutenant
Leutnant	*Ltn.*	2nd Lieutenant
Leutnant der Reserve	*Ltn.d.R.*	2nd lieutenant of Reserve
Oberst	*Obst.*	Colonel
Oberflugmeister	*Obflgmstr.*	Chief Petty officer
Offizierstellvertreter	*OffzSt.*	Warrant officer
Rittmeister	*Ritt.*	Captain (of cavalry)
Vizefeldwebel	*Vzfw.*	Sergeant Major

Other Abbreviations

Wd.	Wounded
lt.wd	Lightly wounded
s.wd	Seriously wounded
F.wd	Fatally wounded

Select Bibliography

Baring, M. *Flying Corps Headquarters 1914–1918*. G. Bell & Sons, London, 1920.
Robertson, B. *British Military Aircraft Serials*. Ian Allen, London, 1969
Bruce, J. *The Aeroplanes of the Royal Flying Corps (Military Wing)*. Putnam, London, 1982.
Cole C. *McCudden VC*. Kimber, London, 1967.
Cronyn, V. *Other Days*. Privately Published, 1976.
Douglas, S. Y*ears of Combat*. Collins, London, 1963.
Duiven, R. Abbott, D-S. *Schlachtflieger!* Schiffer Military History. Atglen, PA, USA, 2006.
Franks, N. Bailey, N. Duiven, R. *The Jasta Pilots*. Grub St., London, 1996.
Franks, N. Bailey, N. Duiven, R. *The Jasta War Chronology*. Grub St., London, 1998.
Franks, N. Bailey, N. Duiven, R. *Casualties of the German Air Service*. Grub St., London, 1999.
Fry, W.M. *Air of Battle*. Kimber, London, 1974.
Gray, P. & Thetford, O. *German Aircraft of the First World War*. Putnam, London, 1962.
Henshaw, T. *The Sky Their Battlefield*. Grub St. London, 1995.
Hobson, C. *Airmen Died in the Great War, 1914–1918*. J.B. Hayward & Son, Suffolk, 1995.
Imrie, A. *Pictorial History of the German Army Air Service*. Ian Allen, London, 1971.
Jefford, C. *RAF Squadrons*. Airlife Publishing Ltd.. Shrewsbury. 1988.
Jones. I. *Tiger Squadron*. W.H.Allan, London, 1954.
Jones, H. & Raleigh, W. *The War in the Air*, Vols. 1–VI Oxford University Press, London, 1921–1937.
MacLanachan, W. (M'Scotch) *Fighter Pilot*. Newnes. London. 1936.
McCudden J. *Five Years in the Royal Flying Corps*. The Aeroplane & General Publishing Co., London, 1918.
McInnes, L. Webb, J.A. *Contemptible Little Flying Corps*. The London Stamp Exchange, Ltd., 1991.
O'Connor, M. *Airfields & Airmen: Arras*. Pen & Sword Military, Yorkshire, 2002.
Penrose, H. *British Aviation: The Great War and Armistice*. Putnam, London, 1969.
Revell, A. *The Vivid Air*. Kimber, London, 1978.
Revell, A. *Brief Glory*. Kimber, London, 1984.
Revell, A. *High in the Empty Blue*. Flying Machines Press, Mountain View, USA, 1996.
Taylor, Sir S. *Sopwith Scout 7309*. Cassell, London, 1968.
Various authors: *The Royal Aircraft Factory FE2b/d*. RAF Museum/*Cross & Cockade International*, 2009.

Index

Note: Numbers in italics denote an illustration.
McCudden flew many types of aircraft; only those of particular note are listed, by their initial appearance.

A

Abbott, Dan S.: 291
Abraham, D.: 24, 27, 30, 257
Achiet-le-Grand: 71, 247
Achiet-le-Petit: 247
Adams, S.: 6
Adinfer Wood: 71, 76, 78, 79, 240
Aerodromes
    Abbeville: 30, 61, 63, 64
    Abeele: 60, 67, 68, 70, 75, 85
    Acheville: 187
    Amiens: 24, 30, 75, 150, 154, 168, 190
    Annequin: 33
    Auchel: 39, 102, 209
    Auxi-le-Chateau: 219, 220, 232, 234, 235
    Ayr: 194, 199, 201, 202, 206, 235
    Bailleul: 56, 104, 109, 110, 113, 127, 128, 129, 134, 144, 145, 146, 177
    Baizieux: 151, *174*, 179, 182, 184, 185, 186, 189, 190, 191
    Boffles: 219, 232, 233, 234, 235
    Busigny: 280
    Estrée Blanche: 97–99, 101–109, 111–113, 115, 120, 122, 124, 125, 127, 129, 135, 136, 139, 140–151, 183, 244, 245
    Filescamp Farm: 69
    Izel-le-Hameau: 69, 70, 72, 73, 75, 76, 79, 244
    Joyce Green: 83, 85, 89, 90, 91, 93, 96, 97, 147, 200, 210, 215
    La Bellevue: 153
    La Lovie: 98
    Laviéville: 150–154, 156, 157, 159, 160, 161, 162, 164, 165, 166, 168, 169, 170, 171, 172, 174, 176, 177, 178, 179
    Le Crotoy: 39
    Lozinghem: 40, 124
    Poperinghe: 98
    Rochford: 106
    Roye: 155
    St.Omer: 30, 60, 125
    Valheureux: 208, 216, 217, 220
    Warloy: 188
Aeroplane Depots
    No.1: 120, 129, 149, 208
    No.2: 83, 150, 151, 153, 160, 188
Aertrycke: 254
Aire: 40, 139, 141, 143
Aizlewood: 92
Albermarle Fort: 11
Albert: 71, 150, 152, 153, 157, 168
Alec-Tweedie, E.: 197, 198, 207, 218, 247, 280, 281
Alec-Tweedie, H.: 197, 280
Alec-Tweedie, L.: 197
Alexandria: 8
Alhambra Theatre: 82
Allen, C.R.W.: 20, 21, 24, 258
Allen, D.L.: 29, 258
Allkofer: 241, 271
Amiens. See under Aerodromes
Andrews, J.: 98, 246, 267, 288
Angell, J.G.P.B.: 38, 258
Anguilcourt: 167, 242
Annay: 104
Anneux: 165, 181, 242, 277
Armentières: 40, 62, 67, 68, 102, 112, 115, 118, 130, 131, 146, 240
Arnold, R.: 190
Arras: 69, 70, 71, 75, 76, 79, 98, 100, 135, 147, 154, 156, 183–185, 187, 190
Ascq: 112
Ashford: 67, 86
Atkinson, E.D.: *214*
Auchel: 103
Auchy: 129
Audenarde: 58, 119
Avensnes-le Compte: 125
Avensnes-le-Sec: 275
Ayr: 83

B

Bachimont: 232
Baikie, L.S.: 204
Bailey, F.W.: 291
Baker, L.: 6
Balcombe-Brown, R.: *149*, 151, 153–156, 159, 163, 165, 168, 170, 171, 175, 178, 180, 185, 190, 274
Ball, A.: *80*, 91, 94, 118, 141, 172, 237, 244, 246, 264
Ball, O.F.G.: 71, 72, 263
Bantouzelle: 161, 163, 176, 184, 186
Bapaume: 71, 72, 152, 153, 154, 155, 157, 159, 161, 167, 168, 171, 178, 179
Barastre: 160
Baring, M.: 118, 135, 141, 143, 198, 291
Barker, W.: 259
Barlow, L.M.: 101, *106*, 107, 111, 112, 118, 124, 125, 130–132, 135, 136, 141, 145, 146, 149, 185, 187, 188, 240, 268
Barlow, R.K.: (Cuth) 20, 21, 23, 256
Barming: 90, 94
Barnwell, H.: 85, 90, 94, 200, 201, 265

Barrington-Kennett, B.H.: 22, 256
Barry, T.H.: 233, 234, 235
Barth, A.: 243, 277
Basingstoke: 54
Basseux: 75
Bauer, R.: 241, 271
Bavay: 112
Bayetto, T.P.H.: *46*, 49, 260
BE.12: 86
Beale, E.W.: 206, 282
Beaumont: 186, 242
Beaurevoir: 181
Beauvois: 167
Becelaere: 119, 126, 133, 139, 144
Becker, M.: 243, 275
Beere, T.F.: 85, 265
Bekesbourne: 93–95
Bellenglise: 176
Bellevue: 181
Bellewarde Lake: 64
Bellicourt: 152, 155, 163, 173, 174, 240, 242
Benge, A.N.: 76, 77, 264
Bentley, W.O.: 279
Bergmann, W.: 243, 276
Berking, A.: 243, 275
Berlaimont: 24, 25
Berles-au-Bois: 78
Berthold, R.274
Besser, G.243, 277
Béthune: 31, 35, 36, 40, 57, 75, 76, 125, 139, 146
Bettington, C.A.: 285
Bey, K.: 243, 274
Biesenbach: 243, 276
Binting, R.: 243, 278
Birch, W.C.K.: 37, 259
Bird, S.: 258
Birks, N.A.: 76, 78, 263
Bishop W.A.: 237, 246
Bixschoote: 62, 102, 115, 120, 121, 126, 132, 133, 144
Blackburn, H.: 37, 259
Blainville: 78
Blankerberghe: 65
Blatherwick, R.: 261
Blenkiron, A.V.: 165, 166, 170, 172, 179, 275
Bleriot X1 No.389: 23
Blomfield, R.G.: 94, 95, 98, 107, 119, 139, 141, 146, 147, 149, 152, 248, 267
Bock, G.: 6
Bode, A.: 243, 275
Bodenschatz, K.: 271
Boelcke, O.: 173, 237
Boenigk, O, von: 122, 271
Boesinghe: 61, 62
Boiry St.Martin: 186
Bois de Biez: 40, 43, 55, 57, 139

Bois de Vaucelles: 161, 163, 165, 170, 184, 242
Boistrancourt: 156, 163
Boje, K.: 243, 276
Bolton, A.C.: 73, 263
Bombengeschwader (*Bogohl*)
   7: 180, 243, 276, 277
Boulogne: 79, 107, 191
Bourlon: 151, 155, 156, 157, 161, 185
Bourlon Ridge: 151
Bourlon Wood: 151, 153, 154, 155, 157, 163, 164, 165, 168, 169, 172, 175, 178, 181, 185, 188, 242
Boursies: 161
Bowman, G.H.: 6, 23, 53, 60, 67, 68, 68, 69, 94, 107, *110*, 113, 118, *121*, 122, 126–129, 131, 132, 134, 135, 137, 140, 141, 143, 144, 145, 149, 152, 153, 154, 155, 157, 161, 163, 169, 178, 179, 181, 182, 183, 184, 188, 239, 246, 247, 255, 261
Bowyer, O.T.V.: 35, 259
Bracksiek, F.: 243, 277
Brancker, Sir, S.: 266
Brancourt-le-Grand: 18
Brandenburg, E.: 89, 91, 9
Brearley, N.: 63, 73, 26
Brecon: 268
Brewer, G.: 11, 256
Bridgman, L.96
Brigades
   II: 60, 62, 116
   III: 69, 116, 190
   V: 135
Bristol Scout: 29
Broadberry, E.: 267
Brockbank, C.J.: 16, 254
Bröll, M.: 243, 275
Brompton: 227
Brompton Barracks: 9
Brooke-Popham, H.R.M.: 14, *20*, 21, *23*, 36, 40, 225, 256, 259
Bruay: 103
Bruce, J.: 249, 279, 291
Bruges: 64
Bruiser, bulldog: 206, 214
Bruns, H.: 243, 277
Brussels: 58
Bryan, A.L.: 30, 258
Bullécourt: 98, 181, 189
Bülow-Bothkamp, W. von: 288
Burden, H.J.: 170, 218, 220, 283
Burdett, G.C.: 283
Burdett, W.H.: 219, 233–235, 283
Burns, W.H.: 37, 42, 258
Büscher, H.: 243, 277
Bush: 84
Büttner, K.: 280
Byford, Amelia: 9

Byford, Thomas: 9
Byng, Sir Julian: 191, 278

C

Cadford: 84
Caestre: 139, 143
Calais: 31, 64, 75, 95, 125, 146, 208
Caldwell, K.L.: (Grid): 133, 272
Cambrai: 119, 151–155, 156, 162, 174, 178, 180–182, 200, 242
Canal de Escaut: 186
Canterbury: 87
Card, B.: 107, 188, 269
Carency: 124
Carleton, B.: 82
Carloy: 8
Carman: 84
Carnoy, Military Cemetery: 274
Carr, R.H.: 31, 89, 148, 188, 258, 266
Carter, L.L.: 78, 79, 264
Cassel: 40, 61
Casualty Clearing Station No.21: 220, 233
Caudron: 3
Caudry: 184, 242
Cawson, G.: 157, 275
Central Flying School: 53, 89
Chantilly: 26
Chapman, C.M.B.: 143, 274
Chapman, G.S.: 25, 257
Charles, H.N.: 6, 108, *116*, 235, 246, 269, 284, 285
Charlie's Bar: 154
Charlton, E.O.: 26, 27, 30, 257
Chataway, J.P.: 200
Chatham: 9, 87, 92, 198, 227
Chérisy: 189, 242
Chidlaw-Roberts, R.: 133, 272
Child, J.M.: 194, 196, 279, 280
Cholmondeley, R.: 20, *20*, 24, 30, 32, 35, 37, 38, 256, 259
Clairmarais: 55, 56, 61
Clark, N.: 6
Clarke, F.: 190
Clausnitzer, E.: 147, 274
Cleaver, D.C.: 37, 259
Clerk, P.J.: 188, 233
Closeburn: 102
Coats, E.: 282
Cobbold, F.: 149, 274
Cobley, Mrs. M. (née McCudden): 6, 248, 256
Cole, C.: 6, 256, 291
Collett, C.: 123, 145, 148, 274
Comines: 58, 126, 129, 132, 146
Compiègne: 26
Conran, E.L.: *17*, *20*, 21, 23, *28* 29–31, 35, 37, 38, 39, 60, 62, 256, 259
Constable Maxwell, G.J.: 101, *105*, 107, 109, 110, 111, 113, 115, 118, 125, 127, 128, 129, 131, 132, 135–137, 140, 143, 144, 146, 149, 199, 208, 212, *214, 215*, 216, 268
Contescourt: 167, 242
Cook, G.259
Cooper, J.: 6
Coote, M.H.: 107, 109, 111, 112, *114*, 121, 149, 152–154, 269, 278
Corbett-Wilson, D.: 37, 39, 259
Cortemarck: 98, 102, 144, 146
Costigan, J.L.: 259
Coucou: 63
Coulommiers: 28, 29
Courtney, F.T.: 42, 260
Courtneidge, Cecily: 264
Courtneidge, Charles: 264
Courtrai: 58
Cowan, P.C.: 149, 274
Cowan, S.E.: 66, 74, 262
Cowley, L.: 6
Cox, B.G.: 167, 276
Coxteth: 201
Creeth: 146
Crespigny, H.V.C de.: 143, 273
Crevecoeur-s-Escaut: 178, 242
Crocodile, troopship: 8
Croiselles: 263
Cronyn, V.P.: 101, *106*, 107, 108, 109, 110, 112, 113, 118, 131, 132, 148, 188, 246, 268, 291
Crow, N.: *129*, 129, 271
Crowe, C.M.: 6, 4, 94, *110*, *193*, 232, 267, 278
Croydon: 86, 87, 106
Cruickshank, G.L.: 24, 257
Cuff, A.H.C.: 259
Cunningham, E.: 100
Cunningham, J.N.: 144, 274
Curlewis, I.: 65, 66, 70, 73, 262
Curteis: 76

D

Dallas, R.: 273
Dadizele: 58, 108
Daily Chronicle: 172
Daily Mail: 174, 197, 237
Dannhuber, X.: 144, 269, 270, 273
Dartford: 83
Davies: 100
Deal: 87, 91
Dee, Steamer: 23, 24
Dern, W.: 243, 276
DH1: 54
DH2: 54
DH4: 88
DH5: 88
Dietrich, G.: 243, 275
Dittrich, K.: 243, 275

Dixmude: 55, 98, 101
Dobriskey, G.: 188
Dodds, A.: 151, 155, 156, 275
Doering, K.: 243, 276
Dolland, Honora.: 8
Don: 38, 50, 146
Dörfler, W.: 243, 276
Douai: 43, 45, 49, 78, 98, 156, 242
Douglas, S.: 187, 190, 194, 244, 279, 291
Doullens: 208
Dover: 90, 95, 106
Downing, E.A.: 188
Drückhammer, F.: 243, 276
Dubislaw, H.: 243, 276
Duiven, R.: 291
Dungeness: 87
Dunkirk: 64, 90, 95, 98, 100
Dunn, F.G.: 30, 35, 258
Durrant, T.: 172, 173, 174, 179, 180, 184, 276
Düsterdieck, F.: 243, 278

E
Eastchurch: 11
Eckerle: 243, 275
Edwards, G.33
Ellis: 54
Ellison, W.V.: 48, 260
Elschenbroich, W.: 269
Enke: 275
Épéhy: 171, 176, 242
Equancourt: 153
Ernst, *initials unkown*: 241, 274
Escadrille de chasse NS.12: 41
Escaufort: 279
Essell, L.: 78, 264
Estaires: 130, 131, 139
Estreés-en-Chaussée: 24, 152, 172
Etherington, E.: 107, 188, 269
Étreillers: 167
Evans, Capt.: 31
Exley, G.H.: 56, 57, 58, 261

F
Failford: 202
Failford House: 201, 202, 207, 209, *211*
Farman, Maurice: S7, 13
Farmer, G.: 59, 262
Farnborough: 15, 52, 54, 67, 160, 203, 210, 212, 214
Farnborough Royal Aircraft Factory: 226
Farnborough. Royal Engineers Balloon School: 13
FE2d: 55
Felixstowe: 95
Fenelon, L.H.: 233, 235
Ferdinand, F.: 22
Fère-en-Tardenois: 29, 30

Fetch, E.H.M.: 178, 277
Festubert: 31
Ficheux: 76, 77, 240
Fielding-Johnson, W.S.: 49, 50, 151–155, 159–162, 173, 180, 182, 184, 185, 242, 260, 274
Flers: 169, 170, 242
Flésquières: 168, 175, 179
Flieger Abteilung
5: 241
6: 241
7: 243, 278
8: 241
23: 243, 276
32: 243, 276
33: 243, 275, 276
40: 243
48: 41
62: 41
202: 275
225: 243, 275, 277
245: 275
293: 279
Flieger Abteilung (A)
40: 243, 276
202: 243, 278
210: 243, 276
225: 243
233: 177, 243, 277
235: 243, 278
240: 243, 277
259: 241, 275
263: 243
264s: 243, 276
268: 243, 275
269: 243, 278
292: 241
293b: 243, 278
Flohrig: 243, 275
Foggin, C.: 199, *206*, 281
Fokker, A: 41, 125
Fokker M5K: 41
Fontaine: 157, 182, 242
Fontaine-Notre-Dame: 162
Folkestone: 67, 89, 107, 191
Fonck, R.: 237
Foot, E.L.: 118, 270
Formidable HMS: 34
Fort Grange: 53, 6
Fosse 8, 48
Foulness Point: 91
Fournes: 37, 39
Fox, A.G.: 15, *20*, 255
Fox, F.: 266
Francilly: 242
Franke, R.: 241, 272

Franklin, L.N.: 161, 163, 164, 275
Frank's Farm: 83
Franks, N.: 291
Frantzius, von: 243, 278
Frauenstein: 241, 273
Frelinghien: 129
French, Sir John: 28
Fresnoy: 156, 189
Fresnoy Wood: 185
Freuge: 57
Frezenberg: 135
Fröhlich, A.: 243, 278
Fromelles: 62
Fry, W.M.: 6, 87, 244, 287, 291
Fullard, P.F.: 173, 174, 237, 276
Fulton, P.: 219, 283

G

Galley, E.D.G.: 6, 159, *161*, 161–164, 168, 170–172, 181, 185, 275
Gallwitz, K.: 148, 268, 274
Gannon, R.: 6
Gardiner, H.J.: 23, 257
Gardiner, S.J.: 141, 144, 153, 154, 273
Garros, R.: 41
Gascoyne, J.: 244, 287
Gayer, P.E.100
George V.: 197, 223
Gerschel, K.: 243, 276
Gheluve: 108, 112, 240
Gheluvelt: 62, 111, 240
Gheluwe: 65, 103, 131, 132, 240
Gilbert, J.: 141, 144, 146, 273, 274
Gillingham: 89, 198, 207, 227
Givenchy: 146
Glew: 54
Gobelins, restaurant: 190, 191
Godbert's, restrauant: 154
Goddard, F.W.: 55, 261
Goodwin Sands: 87
Gommécourt: 69, 70, 72, 73, 74, 79, 240
Gonneham: 31, 33, 34–36, 39
Gonnelieu: 161, 164, 165, 176, 189
Gorre: 31
Gosport: 39
Gossler, H.: 241, 273
Gotterman, H.: 268
Göttingen: 249
Göttsch, W.: 265
Gouzeaucourt: 157, 162, 165, 167, 168, 170, 176, 242
Gower, W.E.: 264
Graincourt: 152, 175, 179, 182, 242
Gran, T.: 115, *116*, 122, 143, 244, 287
Grant. See Gran.
Grattan-Bellew, W.A.: 62, 66, 72, 73, 74, 76, 77, 79, 83, 262

Gravesend: 90
Gray, A.J.: 107
Gray, B.: 6
Gray, P.: 291
Grech, J.: 6
Greentail: 162, 166, 168, 171, 178, 180, 182, 184, 186, 253, 275, 278
Greenwood, E.M.: 233, 234
Grey, C.G.: 198, 208, 214, 256
Grider, J. McG.: 283
Griffen, W.H.: 223
Grüter, R.271
Guémappe: 185, 242
Guise: 279
Güntert, O.: 243, 276
Guymemer, G.: 190, 237

H

Haack, *initials unknown*: 270, 272
Habler, H.: 274
Hädrich, E.: 241, 274
Hagen, K.E.: 6
Haig, D.: 93, 94, 237
Haines: 124
Hänicke, M.: 243, 278
Hallam, H.A.: 70, 73
Hamersley, H.A.: 133, 272
Hamilton, H.J.: 57, 58, 261
Hanlon, D.R.: 37, 259
Hanstein, L.: 277
Haplincourt: 169
Harding, W.G., President: 224, 225
Hargnicourt: 242
Harmon, B.: 150, 152, 154, 160
Harris, G.: 212
Harris, R.: 6
Harrison, F.H.: 142, 273
Hart, P.: 6
Harvey, H.: 280
Harvey-Kelly, H.D.: 26, 35, 38, 40, 258
Harwich: 95
Hatton, I.: 6
Haubourdin: 50, 146
Haucourt: 242
Havas, news agency: 171
Havilland, G, 'de: 19, 256, 261
Havrincourt: 151, 152, 157, 159, 163, 165, 169, 170, 184, 186, 190, 241, 242
Havrincourt Wood: 169, 183, 187, 242, 275
Hawker, L.: 260
Haxton 85, 265
Haynecourt: 269, 275
Hayward, W.C.: 33
Hazebrouck: 40, 139, 141, 143
Heber: 41

Hébuterne: 79
Heger, K.: 243, 278
Heilly: 171
Heimingen, J.: 6
Helmigk, H.: 268
Henderson, Sir D.: 28
Henderson, G.L.P.: 43, 86, 98, 100, 102, 107, *113*, 240, 259, 265
Henderson, I.H.D.: 269
Hendon: 148, 207
Henshaw, T.: 6, 291
Herlies: 139, 240
Hermies: 161, 164, 242
Herne Bay: 87, 106
Hesdin: 79, 23
Heu, J.: 41
Higgins, J.F.A.: 174, 188, 191, 275, 276, 277
Hill, G.T.R.: 68, 75, 76, 77, 262
Hiltwein, R.: 241, 274
Hindenberg Line: 159
Hinds, T.: 20, 256
Hinges: 31
Hobbs, A.V.: 42, 43, 45, 260
Hobson, C.: 291
Hoettger, M.: 243, 275
Hoidge, R.T.C.: 107, 112, 113, 115, 118, *121*, 125–128, 132, 137, 139, 141, 143, 144 149–152, 269
Hollenzollern Redoubt: 48
Holman: 84
Holnon Wood: 162, 166
Honnett, F.W.: 64, 65, 262
Hooge: 129, 145
Hooglede: 129
Hooton Park: 201, 207
Hopkins, J.C.F.: 245
Horrell, F.J.: 128, 271
Horstmann, E.H.: 274
Horstmann, H.: 241
Hounslow: 88, 194, 214, 219, 232
Houthem: 62, 109, 118, 130, 131, 133, 146, 240
Houthulst: 126, 146
Houthulst Forest: 61, 101, 111–113, 121, 126, 128, 129, 135, 136, 240
Howard, W.H.: 219, 220, 232, 233, 283
Hoyer, H.: 274
Hubbard, T.O'B.: 19, 256
Hudson, T.: 18, 255
Hughes, D.: 6
Hughes, H.S.: 58, 261
Hughes: 84
Humbercamp: 73, 77
Hunt: 84
Hythe: 82, 88

I

Immelmann, M.: 39, 41, 43, 45, 46, 173, 237, 249, 260
Imrie, A.: 291
Irwin, W.R.: 208
Isbell, I.S.: 246, 288
Isle of Sheppey: 11, 86, 92
Itancourt: 180

J

Jablonski, O.: 243
Jagdgeschwader
  *Jagdgeschwader Nr.*I: 121, 254, 274
Jagdstaffeln
  1: 70
  2 (later *Jasta* Boelcke): 74, 75, 148, 264, 268, 280, 288
  3: 128, 270, 273
  4: 122, 147, 253, 271, 274, 277
  5: 155, 156, *162*, 162, *163*, 242, 243, 254, 275
  6: 156, 253, 275, 276
  7: 241, 271
  8: 265
  10: 121, 128, 241, 243, 253, 271, 273, 274, 277
  11: 253, 266, 271, 274, 277, 279
  14: 241
  15: 268
  17: 168, 271, 275
  18: 109, 274
  23: 147
  24: 241, 270
  25: 254
  26: 143, 144, 269, 270, 274
  27: 268, 271
  29: 241, 271, 273
  35b: 243, 253, 277, 278
  36: 274
Jäger, W.: 243, 278
James, B.T.: 14, 19, *23*, 52, 254
Jarrett, P.: 6
Jarvis, L.W.: 164, 275
Jefford, C.: 291
Jeffs, C.H.: 111, 115, 118, *119*, 121, 128, 137, *140*, 143, 270
Jennings, A.: 75, 263
Jillings, D.S.: 25, 256
Joffe: 28, 50
Johnson, H.R.: 42, 49, 50, 260
Johnson, J.: 286
Johnston, H.A.: 108, 109, 111, 112, 117, 121, 137, 240
Jones, H.A.: 257, 291
Jones, J.I.T.: 246, 288, 289
Jones-Williams, A.G.: 143, 273
Joubert de la Ferté, P.: 23, 25, 26, 27, 28, 29, 30, 257, 258
Joyce Green: 85, 87, 91, 92, 95, 106, 200, 201, 214
Juilly: 26, 28
Junor, K.W.: *178*, 181, 182, 187, 242, 277
Justinus, B.: 277

K
Kaiser, J.: 185, 243, 253, 278
Kammell, *initials unknown*: 274
Kampe, W.
Kampfgeschwader (*Kagohl*)
　　3: 89, 91, 95
Karlowa, E.: 243, 278
Keane, D.: 82
Keen, A.W.: 139
Kemmel: 251
Kemmel Hill: 68
Kemp, R.: 19, 256
Kennedy, D.: 204
Kersley, F.J.: 224, 225
Keudell, H. von: 70
Kidd, A.: 29
Kiegan: 135
Kimm, D.W.D.: 10
King, K.V.: 233, 234, 235
King's Lynn: 88
Kingston: 198
Kipling, R.: 48
Kirkoswald: 204
Kirmaier, S.: 267
Kirschstein, H.: 276
Klauke, J.: 243
Klingenberg, E.: 243, 278
Klostermann, *initials unknown*: 270, 272
Kluck von: 28
Knight, A.G.: 74, 263
Koch, O.: 270
Koepsch, E.: 277
König, E.: 264
Konnecke, O.: 253
Kresse, O.: 243, 278
Kruse: 275
Kuczkzowski, W. von: 180, 243, 277
Kurzbach, S. von: 266

L
La Bassée: 33, 35, 39, 42, 45, 49, 50, 51, 68, 129, 135, 146, 208
Le Cateau: 24, 25, 184, 221
Le Catelet: 184, 242
La Fère: 26, 167
Laffin, J.: 283
Lagnicourt: 170, 185, 242
Laitko, H.: 241, 274
Lane, S.: 147
Langémarke: 101, 109, 110, 115, 132, 136, 240
Langhin-au-Werppes: 38
Larkhill: 14, 20
Lascelles, E.H.: 55, 58, 261
Latta, J.D.: 102, 207, *211*, 211, 281
Latta, M.: 201, 202, 207
Latch, C.T.: 60, 61, 62, 262
Lay, E.: 263
Leach, W.F.: 73, 263
Leacroft, J.: *214*
Lechelle: 154
Lechleiter, H.: 243, 278
Ledeghem: 144
Lee, G.A.: 201, *210*, 281
Leffrinckhoucke: 100
Le Gallais, P.E.M.: 98, 106, 214, 267
Le Hameau: 150
Le Harcourt: 176
Lehnert: 243, 276
Leipner: 243, 278
Lempire: 176, 242
Lens: 39, 42, 49, 98, 100, 104, 130, 135, 147, 157, 169, 183, 187
Leopold: 275
Lesdans: 155
Lethridge: 84
Letts, J.H.T.: 199, 206, 281
Lewis, C.A.: 265
Lewis, D.S.: 39, 259
Lewis, T.A.: 274
Leysdown: 11
Liettres: 139
Lille: 55, 62, 67, 119
Lillers: 36, 40, 50, 125
Lillywhite, R.J.: 49, 260
Lindop, V.S.E.: 28, 29, 258
Linselles: 69
Lipton, Sir T.: 223, 224
Little, R.A.: 284
Liverpool: 201
Lloyd George, D.: 223
Loerzer, B.: *140*, 143, 170
Loerzer, F.: 274
London Colney: 112, 149, 152
Long, H.S.: 265
Longman, R.: 84, 265
Loos: 42
Lorraine, V.: 82
Löwenhardt, E.: 274
Lozinghem: 39, 50
Ludlow-Hewitt, E.R.: 43, 45, 47, 49, 236, 248, 260
Luebbe, H.: 41
Lund, R.J.S.: 78, 79, 264
Lympne: 88, 148, 207, 208

M
Macdonald, E.R.: 6, *181*, 184, 208, 277, 278
Macedonia: 254
MacLanachan, W.: 291
Macrostie, R.: 23, 24, 257

Mai, J.: 253, 275
Maidstone: 83, 86, 90, 91
Maidstone Road Cemetery: 227
Maissemy: 166
Malcolm, G.J.: 55, 261
Maltby, P.: 205
Mannock, E. 'Mick': *80*, 84, 85, 244, 264, 265
Mansfield, W.: 59, 262
Marcoing: 154, 165
Marden: 67
Marquion: 170, 180, 183, 242
Marquise: 148
Marson, T.B.: 107, *110*, 122, 146, 226, 247, 268
Martin: 84, 265
Martinsart: 193
Martinsyde G.100: 86
Martlesham Heath: 89, 148, 187, 188
Mary, Princess: 15
Mary, Queen: 15
Masnières: 161, 162, 168, 175
Mason, W.W.100
Mason's Yard: 107
Matthews, J.: 264
Maubeuge: 24, 25
Mauchline: 201, 202
Maurice, Interpreter: 24
Maxwell, R.S.: 55, 56, 57, 58, 261
Maybery, R.A.: 107, 111, 113, 118, *121*, 129, 134, 136, 137, 140, 144, 149, 152, 153, 154, 155, 156, 157, 159, 160, 161, 162, 163, 165, 166, *169*, 171, 179, 185, 268
Mazingarbe: 146, 240
McCudden, Amelia, Mother: 8, 9, 80, 81, 223, 224, 225, 256, 279
McCudden, Aurora, Grandmother: 8
McCudden, C.J.: *8*
McCudden, E.: 227
McCudden, Henry, Great Grandfather: 8
McCudden, James, Grandfather: 8
McCudden, James, Uncle: 8
McCudden, James, Thomas, Byford,
   Personality as boy: 10
   Enters Garrison School, Brompton Barracks: 10
   Leaves school: 10
   Enlists in Royal Engineers: 11
   Posted to Gibraltar: 12
   Transfers to RFC: 13, 15
   Accident with Farman and Caudron aeroplanes: 17
   Arrives in France: 24
   First wound: 24
   First war flight: 35
   Promoted to corporal: 31
   Promoted to sergeant: 39
   News of Bill's death: 39
   First aerial combat: 43
   Awarded *Croix de Guerre*: 50
   Leaves 3 Sqdn for pilot training: 51
   Awarded RAeC Certificate: 53
   Posted to Central Flying School: 53
   Awarded Pilot 2nd class Certificate: 53
   Awarded Pilot 1st Class Certificate: 54
   Posted to 20 Sqdn: 55
   Posted to 29 Sqdn: 59
   1st victory: 62
   Awarded Military Medal: 67
   Promoted to 2nd Lieutenant: 75
   Awarded Military Cross: 79
   Posted to 56 Squadron: 107
   Awarded Bar to MC.141
   Awarded DSO: 164
   Awarded Bar to DSO: 174
   Recommended for Victoria Cross: 188
   Victoria Cross gazetted: 194
   Made Honorary Freeman of Gillingham: 223
   Last Flight: 218
   Death: 220
   Grave: 220, 221, 222
McCudden, John, Anthony, 'Jack', Brother: 8, 9, 12, *37*, 80, 89, 124, *128*, 182, 190, 194, 218, 221, *229, 231*, 266, 279
McCudden, J.V.: 8
McCudden, Kathleen, Anne, Sister: 6, *8*, 9, 40, 80, 224, 225
McCudden, Mary, Amelia, Sister: *8*, 9, 10, 12, 51, 80, 81, 218, 219, 220, 224, 225, 226, 248
McCudden, Maurice, Vincent, Brother: *8*, 9, 80, 223, 225, 226, 227, *229*
McCudden, P.: 227
McCudden, William, T. Henry, Father: *8*, 8, 10, 37, 80, 89, 127, 182, 223, 224, 229
McCudden, William, Thomas, James, Brother: 8, 9, 10, 13, 14, *19*, 23, *24*, 29, 34, 39, 225, *229, 231*, 235, 259
McEvoy: 29
McInnes, L.: 291
McPherson, B.: 163, *166, 167*, 170, 275
Meakin, 'Addie': 21, 30, 32, 34, 36, 38, 39, 41, 42, 52
Mealing, M.: 157, 159, 161, 163, 164, *165*, 179, 185, 275
Mealing, R.H.S.: 43, *45*, 50, 51, 260
Meintjes, H.: 79, 80, 82, 94, 264
Melun: 27
Melville: 139
Menin: 55, 63, 65, 66, 102, 104, 108, 109, 111, 115, 126, 127, 128, 129, 131, 132, 136, 144, 145, 146, 240
Menckhoff, C.: 263, 271, 273
Menin Ridge Road, Battle of: 131
Mercatel: 74, 78
Méricourt: 187
Merville: 40
Messines: 62, 63, 240
Metz: 165, 168
Metz-en-Couture: 164, 167, 168, 242
Metzger, 243, 276
Milton, W.: 100

Miraumont: 73, 74, 240
Mitchell, R.J.: 262
Mittag, H.: 243, 276
Moeuvres: 164, 185
Monchy: 75, 76, 77, 79, 240
Monchy-au-Bois: 77, 78, 130
Monchy-le-Preux: 76, 179, 240, 242
Mons: 27
Montdidier: 208
Mont Kemmel: 104
Montreuil: 29
Moorslede: 109, 115, 139, 140, 149
Morbceque: 132
Morcourt: 165
Morgan, A.T.J.: 259
Morris, G.: 6
Mosch, G.: 243, 277
Mottershead, T.: 85, 265
Moyenneville: 30
Müller, *initials unknown:* 269
Müller, G.: 243, 276
Mulroy, P.S.: 232, 233
Muspratt, K.K.: 107–109, 111–113, *115*, 118, 120, 123, 134, 141, 144–146, 149, 187, 188, 269
Muth, A.: 267, 271

N
Nanteuil: 29
Neal, D.: 6
Neal, E.L. Stage name: *'O'Neill. "Teddie":* 81, 84, 147, 206, 264
Neal, G.: 6
Netheravon: 20
Neuve Chapelle: 37
Neuve Eglise: 149
Neuvilly: 254
Neuvireuil: 157
Niemann, F.: 243, 276
Nieuport: 65, 101
No.1 School of Aerial Fighting: 83, 194, 198, 200, 203, 236
No.1 School of Aerial Fighting, Officers at: *200*
No.1 School of Aerial Fighting and Gunnery: 203, 204, 236
No.2 School of Auxiliary Gunnery: 203
Noakes, J.: 60, 61, 68, 70–73, 76, 210, 225, 262
Noding, F.: 289
Notler: 243, 276
Notre Dame de Lorette: 124
Noyelles: 154, 181, 242
Noyelles-s-Escaut: 165

O
O'Connor, M.: 234, 291
Oehler, J.: 241, 270
O'Neill, 'Teddie.' 84, *148*, 206: (See also Neal)
Oppenhorst, F.: 156

Oppy: 189, 242
Orabi, Ahmed: 8
Orfordness: 83
Orpen, W.: 143, 198, 200, 231, 273
Ostend: 65, 95

P
Pallocks, G.: 243, 277
Pappenheimer, M.: 243, 276
Parfitt, H.E.: 24, 257
Paris: 27, 28, 32, 154
Parker, H.: 91, 266, 280
Parry, C.: 6, *182*, 184, 278
Passchèndaele: 62, 126, 149, 151, 240
Passendale: 240
Pastor, H.: 241, 273
Pateman: 85, 265
Payn, H.J.: 65, 74, 75, 262, 265
Pearson, A.J.: 77, 78, 264
Pegg, S.R.: 100, 141
Pégoud, A.: 21
Pengelly, C.: 6
Penrose, H.: 291
Péronne: 167
Perry, E.W.C.: 24, 258
Pershing, General, J.J.: 225
Pézarches: 27, 28
Piercey, M.W.: 53, 55, 261
Pinney: 37
Pitt, F.H.: 100
Playfair, P.H.L.: 161, 188, 189, 232, 276
Ploegsteert: 62, 109
Ploegsteert Wood: 64
Plum Farm: 135
Poelcapelle: 64, 111, 119, 121, 122, 132, 133, 136
Poellnitz, H.W. Von: 265
Pohlisch, K.: 243, 275
Poletti, J.: 209
Polygon Wood: 64, 99, 104, 109, 111, 140, 240, 251
Pont-de-Nieppe: 144
Pontruet: 165
Poperinghe: 125, 141, 145
Port Meadow: 18
Port Said: 8
Potts, W.J.: 111, 118, *119*, 125, 132, 270
Power, W.B.: 52, 53, 260
Preston-Cobb, R.: 143, 144
Pretyman, G.F.: 23, 37, 38, 256
Princip, G.: 22
Pronville: 75
Prothero, P.: 101, 267
Proville: 153, 180
Pyne, S.W.: 20, 24, 256

Q
Quéant: 152
Quesnoy: 57, 63, 103, 120, 130, 240
Quested, J.: 79, 98, 106, 264
Quiery-le-Motte: 186

R
Radinghem: 131, 240
Railton, Reverend D.: 223
Raismes: 260
Raleigh, G.H.: 18, *20*, 254
Raleigh, W.: 256, 291
Raillencourt: 175, 178, 185, 242
Ramsey, J.: 20, 256
Ramsgate: 91
Rautenberg, H.: 243, 277
Readman, C.H.B.: 62, 262
Reason, D.: 141, 273
Redhill: 67
Reed: 84
Reed, N.: 259
Rees, L.: 198, 199, 201, 203, *215*, 280, 281
Reeves, V.L.: 188, 190
Reinhard, W.: 275
Reiss, W.: 270
Renfrew.: 209
Revell, A.: 291
Rhys Davids, A.P.F.: 101, *105*, 107, *114, 118,* 118, 121, 123, 126, 128, 129, 132–136, 139–141, 143, 144, 146, 147, 149, 240, 246, 268
Ribécourt: 175
Richter, H.: 243, 276
Richthofen, M. von: 74, 121, 123, *127*, 135, 141, 143, 173, 189, 209, 218, 220, 236, 237, 239, 249, 271
Ridd, Frank: 15, 23, 255
Riddel, 54
Riddiford, Reverend C.W.: 220
Rieux: 154
Rittermann, M.: 243, 277
Robecq: 57
Roberts, E.P.: 42
Roberts, W.H.: 260
Robertson, B.: 291
Robey, G.: 82
Robins, A.C.: 23, 29, 257
Robinson, R.J.: 67, 262
Rochester: 106
Rochford: 106
Roemer, M.: 273
Rogers, B.: 281
Rogers, C.V. de Burgh: 76, 263
Rogers, T.: 107, 110, 159, 188, 269
Rollincourt: 78
Rolls, G.H.: 100
Ronssoy: 176

Rossini, P.P.: 100
Rothermere, Lord: 173
Roubaix: 55
Roulers: 55, 58, 108, 109, 112, 115, 126–129, 131, 132, 144, 240
Roupy: 167
Rouvroy: 156, 157, 242
Royal Aircraft Factory
Royal Engineers
Air Battalion: 18
Balloon School. No.1 Company: 13, 14
No.2 (Aeroplane) Company: 13, 14
No.24 Field Company: 8
Royal Aircraft Park: 52
Royal Flying Corps, Formation: 14
Rudolph, G.: 241, 272
Ruebens, P.: 33
Rumey, F.: 253
Rumilly: 154, 179, 186, 212
Rushworth, H.: 110, 269

S
St.Denis Westrem: 92
St.Eloi: 61, 63
St.Jean: 142
St Juliaan: 141, 142, 143, 146
St.Julien: 113
Ste-Marie-Cappel: 146, 177
St.Omer: 30, 31, 54, 55, 67, 68, 108, 123, 129, 139, 149, 232
St.Pieter: 140
St.Pol: 76
St.Quentin: 24, 26, 152, 155, 162, 165, 166, 167, 172, 173, 180, 184, 242
St.Souplet: 279
Sailly: 275
Salisbury: 54
Salisbury Plain: 19
Salmon, W.G.: 33, 267
Salmond, J.M.: 21, 23, 29, 33, 34, 37, 38, 39, 175, 220, 236, 246, 256, 276
Salomé: 42, 49
Samson, C.R.: 36
Satchell, H.L.: 274
Saundby, W.S.F.: 74, 263
Saunders, J.: 6
Saunders, R.A.: 40, 43, 44, 45, 46, 259
Savoy. Hotel: 106
Savy Berlette: 245
Schafer, K.: 143
Schäfer, K.E.: 274
Schandva: 177, 277
Schenk, D.: 243, 275
Schlömer, H.: 156
Schmidt, O.: 273
Schmitt, J.: 128, 171

Schneider, F.: 41
Scholtz, E.: 277
Schönebeck, K.A.: 274
Schönfelder, K.: 241, 271
Schönfelder, P.: 240
School of Military Engineering, Gillingham: 9
Schramm: 243, 277
Schubert, F.: 156, 275
Schuppau: 177, 277
Schutzstaffel (*Schusta*)
    5: 243, 275
    10: 276
    12: 243, 276
    19: 243, 275
    25b: 243, 276
    27b: 241
    29b: 243, 278
Schwaier, M.: 243, 278
Schwarzer: 241, 274
Scott, A.J.L.: 173, 177, 277
SE2: 31
SE5: 94
Sellwood, B.: 6
Senlis: 26, 28
Sensée: 77, 156
Sernavillers: 182
Serches: 30
Serny: 148
Serris: 17
Shabkdar, Battle of: 118
Sheerness: 10, 33, 87, 89, 91, 227
Sheernes Garrison School: 11
Shiffingham: 84
Shoeburyness: 91, 92
Shone, G.: 274
Shorncliffe: 89
Sittingbourne: 227
Skene, R.R.: 23, 257
Skinner, J.R.: 87, 265
Slingsby, H.: 151, 160, 274, 274
Sloane: 53
Sloley, R.H.: 107, 109, 111–113, 118, 120–122, 128, 129, 131, 139, 140, 149, 155, 269
Smith, A.: 6
Smith, H.: 100
Smith-Dorrien, H.L.: 29
Soden, F.O.: 271
Soissons: 30
Somerville, T.: 206
Southend: 93, 95, 96, 106
Souchez: 39, 124
Southhampton: 54
Spears, A.S.: 229, 283
Squadrons RFC/RAF
    No.1: 14, 58, 109, 113, 177

No.1 Reserve Squadron: 53
No.2: 14
No.3: 14, 19, *20*, 21, 23, 25, 26, 30, 36, 37, 38, 39, 41, 42, 43, *50*, 50, 60, 73, 87, 151, 188, 209, 220, 227, 236
No.4: *19*
No.5: 30, 55, 58
No.6: 58, 61, 220
No.7: 58
No.8: 219, 234
No.9 Reserve Squadron: 88
No.10: 240
No.10 Reserve Squadron: 83, 89
No.11: 40, 70, 72, 77, 184
No.12: 72, 186
No.13: 72
No.15: 256, 275
No.19: 98, 109, 177
No.20: 54, 55, 59, 61, 177
No.23: 98
No.22: 137, 183
No.24: 60, 66
No.25: 54, 124
No.27: 98, 103, 129, 144, 146
No.29: 53, 59, 62, 69, 72, 79, 80, 87, 99, 100, 118, 141, 235, 236, 244
No.32: 78
No.35: 152
No.40: 139, 146
No.41: 53, 152, 184
No.46: 200
No.48: 282
No.49: 91, 154, 174
No.50: 93
No.52: 219, 234
No.54: 100
No.55: 112, 119, 120
No.56: 53, 93, 94, 95, 98, 106, 152, 244, 253
No.57: 177
No.60: 72, 75, 87, 130, 146, 177, 210, 220, 232
No.63 Reserve Squadron: 83
No.63: CFS: 84
No.64: 88
No.65: 273, 274
No.65 Reserve Squadron: 88
No.66: 93, 95, 97, 98, 103, 109, 115, 132, 236, 245, 246, 250
No.70: 98, 112, 143
No.73: 204
No.74: 263
No.84: 150, 152, 187, 189, 190, 194, 208, 244
No.91: 210
No.4 RNAS: 90, 95
No.9 RNAS: 90
SS Henry and Elizabeth Catholic Church: 227
Staden: 128

Stainforth, G.: 226
Stampkot: 135
Stanley, A.: 260
Starling, J.: 16, 23, 155, 254
Statt, C.C.: 57, 261
Steenvoorde: 61
Stein, J. Von: 243, 278
Stewart, R.: 174, 276
Strasbourg: 254
Strasser, G.: *168*, 275
Street, E.J.: 26, 259
Stringer, J.W.: 55, 261
Strugnell, Victor: 15, *23*, 100, 254, 267
Sugden, Dr. J.: 6
Sunday Chronicle: 280
Sundrum Castle: 199, 281
Suttons Farm: 194
Swift, 191
Sykes, F.H.: 19, 27, 203, 254
Szafranek, E.: 180, 243, 277

T
Tailles du. Col.190
Tattersall: 84
Taylor, A.: 6
Taylor, Sir, P.G.: 245, 288, 291
Taylor, S.W.: 199, *214*
Taylor, T.: 100
Teale, G.N.: 261
Tel-el-Kebir, Battle of: 8
Tewfik, Pasha: 8
Thetford, O.: 291
Thiel: 269, 275, 276
Thielt: 55
Thiepval: 70
Thomas, J.D.: 100
Thomson: 79, 82, 264
Thornton, G.: 42, 259
Tibussek, E.: 243, 276
Tilbury: 96
Tourcoing: 55
Townsend, R.D.: 153, 157, 275
Treeder: 275
Treizennes: 140, 141
Trenchard, H.: 93, 95, 99, 118, 135, 137, 138, 162, 164, 168, 170, 196, 226, 235, 237, 244, 246
Trescault: 159, 164, 168
Truscott, B.: 151, 154, 155, 156, 157, 160, 161, 162, 163, 173
Tudor-Jones, E.C.G.: 42, 43, 45, 260
Turnberry: 201, 203, 204, 206, 207, 208, 209, 235
Turnberry Hotel: 203, 204, *207*
Turnbull, E.L.L.: 6, 107, *111*, 113, 118, 125, 144, 149, 152, 156, 166, 171, 173, 242, 269
Turner, K.K.: 67

U
Udet, E.: 274
Urvillers: 180, 242

V
Valenciennes: 41, 43, 44
Valheureux: 208, 216, 220
Vallins, L.E.: 219, 223, 234, 284
Vandersteen, W.: 6
Vaucelles: 178
Vaucelles Wood: 176
Vaulx-Vraucourt: 72, 73
Vélu: 157, 165, 168, 183, 242
Vendelles: 161, 167
Vendhuille: 164, 173, 174, 175, 176, 181, 242
Vendin-le-Vieil: 43
Verdun: 125
Vickers ES1. (Bullet): 148
Vickers FB5: 40
Vickers FB9: 83
FB.12: 90, 94
FB16a: 94
FB 16d: 90
FB 26: 90
VC10: 227
VC10, XV: 104, 227
Victoria, Princess: 15, 107
Victoria, Steamship: 106, 191
Villers-Bretonneux: 24
Villers Faucan: 275
Villers-Guislain: 164
Vimy Ridge: 124, 125
Violanes: 35, 51
Viper, HMS: 8
Vitry: 78, 156, 179, 187
Vitry-en-Artois: 185, 186
Vlamertinghe: 66, 145, 240
Voigt: 275
Von Tirpitz Farm: 142
Voss, W.: 121, 122 125, *127*, 135, 138, 143, 174, 197, 239, 249, 264, 271, 272
Vousden, G.E.: 188

W
Wadham, V.H.N.: *20*, 21, 30, 256
Waghorn, H.: 226
Walkerdine, H.J.: 151, *154*, 154, 155, 156, 157, 160, 161, 274
Walters, H.T.: 100
Wambaix: 182
Wancourt: 278
Ware, R.: *16*
Warneton: 103, 132
Waters, J.P.: 152, 274
Waters, W.H.: 274
Waters, Mrs W.H.: 274

Watts, W.W.: 40, 52, 258
Wavans: 220, 221
Webb, J.: 52
Webb, W.G.: 25, 35, 39, 53, 258
Weigand, E.: 128, 241, 273
Weiltje: 142
Weinrich, A.: 243, 276
Weinschenk, A.: 109
Werkmeister, A.: 273
Wervicq: 58, 108, 130, 131, 144
West Malling: 90
Westroosebeke: 137, 144
Whetton, D.: 271
White, G.H.: 29
Whitehall Court: 197, 218
Whitehall Place: 218, 219
White Springs, E.: 283
Wiedermann, B.: 241, 273
Wiles, F.W.: 172
Wilkinson, G.M.: 111, 115, 129, 132, 144, 270
Williams, L.J.: 177, 179, 181, 277
Williamson, R.W.: 202, 281
Wilson, R.H.V.: 15, 254
Wingles Tower: 125.147
Wings
   1st: 36, 42
   6th: 83, 90, 97
   7th: 88
   9th: 115, 116, 150
   11th: 60, 177
   13th: 151, 152, 161, 232
Winslow, P, S.: 220, 222, 283

Wintgens, K.: 41, 260
Wissmann, K.: 273
Wolff, H.J.: 266, 274, 279
Wolff, K.: 135, 258
Wolluhn, A.: 270
Wolsey, Sir Garnet.: 8
Wood, K.: 6
Woodiwis, I.N.: 38, 39
Woodman, D.: 175, 179, 277
Woollett, H.: 239
Woolwich: 92
Worters, J.S.: 226
Wussow, *initials unknown*: 274
Wyton: 88
Wytschaete: 108, 145

Y

Young, *initials unknown*: 234
Ypres: 55, 57, 58, 60, 62, 64, 66, 68, 99, 100, 102, 113, 116, 118, 125, 127, 131, 132, 136, 142, 143, 144, 145, 146, 147, 151, 183, 240
Ypres-Comines Canal: 118

Z

Zandvoorde: 108, 111, 128, 143
Zeebrugge: 65
Zehe: 243, 276
Zetter, *initials unknown*: 275
Zeuch, L.: 243, 278
Zillebeke Lake: 128
Zink, E.L.: 212
Zonnebecke: 108, 109, 110, 113, 126, 132, 140, 144

Printed in Great Britain
by Amazon